THE
PUBLIC GENERAL ACTS
AND GENERAL SYNOD MEASURES
1983

[IN THREE PARTS]

PART I
(Chapters 1–35)

with
Lists of the Public General Acts
Local Acts and an Index

LONDON
HER MAJESTY'S STATIONERY OFFICE
1984
£127·00 net

ISBN 0 11 840234 X

THIS PUBLICATION

relates to

the Public General Acts

and General Synod Measures

which received the Royal Assent in 1983

in which year ended the THIRTY-FIRST

and began the THIRTY-SECOND year

of the Reign of HER MAJESTY

QUEEN ELIZABETH THE SECOND

That year comprised

the end of the Fourth Session of the

Forty-Eighth Parliament

and

the beginning of the First Session

of the Forty-Ninth Parliament

of the United Kingdom of Great Britain

and Northern Ireland

Produced in England by W. J. SHARP
Controller and Chief Executive of Her Majesty's Stationery Office
and Queen's Printer of Acts of Parliament

CONTENTS

PART I

PART II

PART III

TABLE I

Alphabetical List of the Public General Acts of 1983

	Part	Page
Agricultural Holdings (Amendment) (Scotland) Act (c. 46) ...	II	1055
Agricultural Marketing Act (c. 3)	I	203
Appropriation Act (c. 27)	I	605
Appropriation (No. 2) Act (c. 48)	II	1145
British Fishing Boats Act (c. 8)	I	249
British Nationality (Falkland Islands) Act (c. 6)	I	221
British Shipbuilders Act (c. 15)	I	305
British Shipbuilders (Borrowing Powers) Act (c. 58)	II	1413
Car Tax Act (c. 53)	II	1185
Civil Aviation (Eurocontrol) Act (c. 11)	I	273
Coal Industry Act (c. 60)	II	1417
Companies (Beneficial Interests) Act (c. 50)	II	1175
Consolidated Fund Act (c. 1)	I	1
Consolidated Fund (No. 2) Act (c. 5)	I	220
Consolidated Fund (No. 3) Act (c. 57)	II	1412
Conwy Tunnel (Supplementary Powers) Act (c. 7)	I	227
Copyright (Amendment) Act (c. 42)	II	1033
Coroners' Juries Act (c. 31)	I	775
County Courts (Penalties for Contempt) Act (c. 45)	II	1054
Currency Act (c. 9)	I	256
Dentists Act (c. 38)	II	825
Diseases of Fish Act (c. 30)	I	759
Divorce Jurisdiction, Court Fees and Legal Aid (Scotland) Act (c. 12)	I	280
Education (Fees and Awards) Act (c. 40)	II	925
Energy Act (c. 25)	I	569
Finance Act (c. 28)	I	663
Finance (No. 2) Act (c. 49)	II	1159

TABLE II

Chronological List of the Public General Acts of 1983

Chapter		Part	Page
1	Consolidated Fund Act	I	1
*2	Representation of the People Act	I	3
3	Agricultural Marketing Act	I	203
4	Pig Industry Levy Act	I	214
5	Consolidated Fund (No. 2) Act	I	220
6	British Nationality (Falkland Islands) Act	I	221
7	Conwy Tunnel (Supplementary Powers) Act	I	227
8	British Fishing Boats Act	I	249
9	Currency Act	I	256
10	Transport Act	I	263
11	Civil Aviation (Eurocontrol) Act	I	273
12	Divorce Jurisdiction Court Fees and Legal Aid (Scotland) Act	I	280
13	Merchant Shipping Act	I	289
14	International Transport Cinventions Act	I	298
15	British Shipbuilders Act	I	305
16	Level Crossings Act	I	311
17	Plant Varieties Act	I	314
18	Nuclear Material (Offences) Act	I	320
*19	Matrimonial Homes Act	I	327
*20	Mental Health Act	I	343
*21	Pilotage Act	I	485
22	Ports (Reduction of Debt) Act	I	535
23	Water Act	I	537
24	Licensing (Occasional Permissions) Act	I	561
25	Energy Act	I	569
26	Pet Animals Act 1951 (Amendment) Act	I	603
27	Appropriation Act	I	605
28	Finance Act	I	663
29	Miscellaneous Financial Provisions Act	I	743
30	Diseases of Fish Act	I	759

*Consolidation Act.

*Consolidation Act.

TABLE III

Alphabetical List of the Local and Personal Acts of 1983

	Chapter
Ashridge (Bonar Law Memorial) Trust Act	vii
Associated British Ports Act	viii
British Railways (Liverpool Street Station) Act	iv
British Waterways Act	ii
Commons Registration (Glamorgan) Act	ix
Greater London Council (General Powers) Act	iii
Greater London Council (Money) Act	xv
Hampshire Act	v
King's College London Act	xii
Lloyds Bowmaker Act	xiii
London Transport (Liverpool Street) Act	xi
Milford Haven Conservancy Act	xix
Parkeston Quay Act	vi
Pwllheli Harbour Act	xiv
Severn–Trent Water Authority Act	xvi
Staffordshire Act	xviii
Standard Chartered Merchant Bank Act	xvii
Tor Bay Harbour (Torquay Marina &c.) Act	x
Ullapool Pier (Works) Order Confirmation Act	i

TABLE IV

Chronological List of the General Synod Measures of 1983

Measures passed by the General Synod of the Church of England which received the Royal Assent during the year 1983

		Part	*Page*
No. 1	Pastoral Measure	II	1421
No. 2	Church of England (Miscellaneous Provisions) Measure.	II	1535

THE PUBLIC GENERAL ACTS OF 1983

Consolidated Fund Act 1983

1983 CHAPTER 1

An Act to apply certain sums out of the Consolidated Fund to the service of the years ending on 31st March 1983 and 1984. [8th February 1983]

Most Gracious Sovereign,

WE, Your Majesty's most dutiful and loyal subjects, the Commons of the United Kingdom in Parliament assembled, towards making good the supply which we have cheerfully granted to Your Majesty in this Session of Parliament, have resolved to grant unto Your Majesty the sums hereinafter mentioned; and do therefore most humbly beseech Your Majesty that it may be enacted, and be it enacted by the Queen's most Excellent Majesty, by and with the advice and consent of the Lords Spiritual and Temporal, and Commons, in this present Parliament assembled, and by the authority of the same, as follows:—

Issue out of the Consolidated Fund for the year ending 31st March 1983.

1. The Treasury may issue out of the Consolidated Fund of the United Kingdom and apply towards making good the supply granted to Her Majesty for the service of the year ending on 31st March 1983 the sum of £1,509,761,000.

Issue out of the Consolidated Fund for the year ending 31st March 1984.

2. The Treasury may issue out of the Consolidated Fund of the United Kingdom and apply towards making good the supply granted to Her Majesty for the service of the year ending on 31st March 1984 the sum of £35,955,985,500.

Short title.

3. This Act may be cited as the Consolidated Fund Act 1983.

Representation of the People Act 1983

1983 CHAPTER 2

An Act to consolidate the Representation of the People Acts of 1949, 1969, 1977, 1978 and 1980, the Electoral Registers Acts of 1949 and 1953, the Elections (Welsh Forms) Act 1964, Part III of the Local Government Act 1972, sections 6 to 10 of the Local Government (Scotland) Act 1973, the Representation of the People (Armed Forces) Act 1976, the Returning Officers (Scotland) Act 1977, section 3 of the Representation of the People Act 1981, section 62 of and Schedule 2 to the Mental Health (Amendment) Act 1982, and connected provisions; and to repeal as obsolete the Representation of the People Act 1979 and other enactments related to the Representation of the People Acts. [8th February 1983]

BE IT ENACTED by the Queen's most Excellent Majesty, by and with the advice and consent of the Lords Spiritual and Temporal, and Commons, in this present Parliament assembled, and by the authority of the same, as follows:—

PART I

PARLIAMENTARY AND LOCAL GOVERNMENT FRANCHISE AND ITS EXERCISE

Parliamentary and local government franchise

Parliamentary electors.

1.—(1) A person entitled to vote as an elector at a parliamentary election in any constituency is one who—

(*a*) is resident there on the qualifying date (subject to subsection (2) below in relation to Northern Ireland); and

(*b*) on that date and on the date of the poll—

(i) is not subject to any legal incapacity to vote (age apart); and

(ii) is either a Commonwealth citizen or a citizen of the Republic of Ireland;

and

(*c*) is of voting age (that is, 18 years or over) on the date of the poll.

(2) A person is not entitled to vote as an elector at a parliamentary election in any constituency in Northern Ireland unless he was resident in Northern Ireland during the whole of the period of three months ending on the qualifying date for that election.

(3) A person is not entitled to vote as an elector in any constituency unless registered there in the register of parliamentary electors to be used at the election.

(4) A person is not entitled to vote as an elector—

(*a*) more than once in the same constituency at any parliamentary election;

(*b*) in more than one constituency at a general election.

Local government electors.

2.—(1) A person entitled to vote as an elector at a local government election in any electoral area is one who—

(*a*) is resident there on the qualifying date; and

(*b*) on that date and on the date of the poll—

(i) is not subject to any legal incapacity to vote (age apart); and

(ii) is either a Commonwealth citizen or a citizen of the Republic of Ireland;

and

(*c*) is of voting age (that is, 18 years or over) on the date of the poll.

PART I

(2) A person is not entitled to vote as an elector in any electoral area unless registered there in the register of local government electors to be used at the election.

(3) A person is not entitled to vote as an elector—

(*a*) more than once in the same electoral area at any local government election; and

(*b*) in more than one electoral area at an ordinary election for any local government area which is not a single electoral area.

Disfranchisement of offenders in prison etc.

3.—(1) A convicted person during the time that he is detained in a penal institution in pursuance of his sentence is legally incapable of voting at any parliamentary or local government election.

(2) For this purpose—

(*a*) " convicted person " means any person found guilty of an offence (whether under the law of the United Kingdom or not), including a person found guilty by a court-martial under the Army Act 1955, the Air Force Act 1955 or the Naval Discipline Act 1957 or on a summary trial under section 49 of the Naval Discipline Act 1957, or by a Standing Civilian Court established under the Armed Forces Act 1976, but not including a person dealt with by committal or other summary process for contempt of court; and

1955 c. 18.
1955 c. 19.
1957 c. 53.
1976 c. 52.

(*b*) " penal institution " means an institution to which the Prison Act 1952, the Prisons (Scotland) Act 1952 or the Prison Act (Northern Ireland) 1953 applies; and

1952 c. 52.
1952 c. 61.
1953 c. 18 (N.I.).

(*c*) a person detained for default in complying with his sentence shall not be treated as detained in pursuance of the sentence, whether or not the sentence provided for detention in the event of default, but a person detained by virtue of a conditional pardon in respect of an offence shall be treated as detained in pursuance of his sentence for the offence.

(3) It is immaterial for the purposes of this section whether a conviction or sentence was before or after the passing of this Act.

Qualifying date.

4.—(1) In England and Wales and Scotland, 10th October in any year is the qualifying date for a parliamentary or local government election at which the date fixed for the poll falls within the period of twelve months beginning with 16th February in the next following year.

PART I

(2) In Northern Ireland, 15th September in any year is the qualifying date for such a parliamentary election as is mentioned above, subject to the Secretary of State's power under section 13(2) below.

Residence.

5.—(1) For the purposes of sections 1 and 2 above any question as to a person's residence on the qualifying date for an election—

(*a*) shall be determined in accordance with the general principles formerly applied in determining questions as to a person's residence on a particular day of the qualifying period within the meaning of the Representation of the People Act 1918; and

1918, (7 and 8 Geo. 5.) c. 64.

(*b*) in particular regard shall be had to the purpose and other circumstances, as well as to the fact, of his presence at or absence from the address in question.

(2) Without prejudice to those general principles, a person's residence in a dwelling house shall not be deemed for the purposes of sections 1 and 2 to have been interrupted—

(*a*) by reason of that person's absence in the performance of any duty arising from or incidental to any office, service or employment held or undertaken by him, if he intends to resume actual residence within six months of giving it up and will not be prevented by the performance of that duty; or

(*b*) by reason of permission being given by letting or otherwise for its occupation furnished by some other person—

(i) if the permission is given in the expectation that throughout the period for which it is given the person giving it or his wife or her husband will be absent in the performance of any such duty as is mentioned above; or

(ii) if the first mentioned person intends to resume actual residence within nine weeks of giving it up and will not be prevented by the permission given as mentioned above.

(3) A person who is detained at any place in legal custody shall not by reason thereof be treated for the purposes of sections 1 and 2 as resident there.

Residence: merchant seamen.

6. At any time when a merchant seaman is not resident in the United Kingdom and would have been resident there but for the nature of his occupation, he shall be entitled to be treated for the purposes of sections 1 and 2 above as resident—

(*a*) at any place at which he would have been resident but for the nature of his occupation; or

PART I

(*b*) at any hostel or club providing accommodation for merchant seamen at which he commonly stays in the course of his occupation.

For this purpose " merchant seaman " means any person not having a service qualification whose employment or the greater part of it is carried out on board seagoing ships, and includes any such person while temporarily without employment.

Residence: detained and voluntary mental patients.

7.—(1) A person who is detained at any place by virtue of any enactment relating to persons suffering from mental disorder shall not by reason thereof be treated for the purposes of sections 1 and 2 above as resident there.

(2) In the following provisions of this section—

" assistance " does not include assistance necessitated by blindness or other physical incapacity ;

" mental hospital " means any establishment maintained wholly or mainly for the reception and treatment of persons suffering from any form of mental disorder ;

" patient's declaration " means a declaration made under this section by a voluntary mental patient ;

" voluntary mental patient " means a person who is a patient in a mental hospital but is not liable to be detained there by virtue of any enactment.

(3) A person who on the qualifying date is a voluntary mental patient shall not be entitled to be registered as mentioned in section 12(1) or (2) below except in pursuance of a declaration made with reference to that date in accordance with subsection (4) below.

This subsection is without prejudice to the registration of a voluntary mental patient by virtue of his residence at an address other than the mental hospital in which he is a patient in any case in which he would be entitled to be so registered apart from this subsection and the following subsections of this section.

(4) A voluntary mental patient may make a declaration under this subsection if he is able to do so without assistance ; and a patient's declaration—

(*a*) shall be made with a view to registration in the register of electors for a particular year and with reference to the qualifying date for that register,

(*b*) shall be made during the 12 months ending with the qualifying date by reference to which it is made but shall not have effect if after it is made and before that date the declarant ceases to be a voluntary mental patient or cancels the declaration,

PART I

(*c*) may be made by a declarant notwithstanding the fact that by reason of his age he is not yet entitled to vote,

(*d*) shall state that it was made by the declarant without assistance, and shall state—

(i) the date of the declaration,

(ii) that on that date and, unless it is the qualifying date, on the qualifying date next following the declarant is or will be a voluntary mental patient,

(iii) the address of the mental hospital in which the declarant is a voluntary mental patient,

(iv) the address where the declarant would be resident in the United Kingdom if he were not a voluntary mental patient or, if he cannot give any such address, an address (other than a mental hospital) at which he has resided in the United Kingdom,

(v) that on the date of the declaration the declarant is a Commonwealth citizen or a citizen of the Republic of Ireland, and

(vi) whether the declarant had on the date of the declaration attained the age of 18 years and, if he had not, the date of his birth,

and a patient's declaration shall be attested in the prescribed manner.

(5) If a person—

(*a*) makes a patient's declaration declaring to more than one address, or

(*b*) makes more than one patient's declaration bearing the same date and declaring to different addresses,

the declaration or declarations shall be void.

(6) A patient's declaration may at any time be cancelled by the declarant and (subject to subsection (5) above) a patient's declaration bearing a later date shall, without any express cancellation, cancel a declaration bearing an earlier date if it is made with reference to the same qualifying date.

(7) A voluntary mental patient whose patient's declaration is made with reference to the qualifying date for any register shall be treated in relation to that register—

(*a*) as resident on the qualifying date at the address specified in the declaration pursuant to paragraph (*d*)(iv) of subsection (4) above;

(*b*) in the case of registration in Northern Ireland, as resident in Northern Ireland during the whole of the period of 3 months ending on the qualifying date; and (*c*) in any case, until the contrary is proved, as being a Commonwealth citizen or a citizen of the Republic of Ireland of the age appearing from the declaration and as not being subject to any legal incapacity except as so appearing.

(8) Where a patient's declaration appearing to be properly made out and attested is transmitted to the registration officer in the proper manner, the declarant shall, until the contrary is proved, be treated for the purposes of registration as having been from the date of the declaration or such later date, if any, as appears from it, and as continuing to be, qualified to be registered as an elector.

(9) No patient's declaration shall be specially made by a person for the purpose of local government elections, and any patient's declaration made for the purpose of parliamentary elections shall have effect also for the purpose of local government elections; but—

(*a*) a patient's declaration may be made for the purpose of local government elections only by a person who is a peer subject to a legal incapacity to vote at parliamentary elections; and

(*b*) where so made, shall be marked to show that it is available for local government elections only, but shall in all other respects be the same as any other patient's declaration.

Registration of parliamentary and local government electors

Registration officers.

8.—(1) For the registration of electors there shall be electoral registration officers (in this Act referred to as "registration officers").

(2) In England and Wales—

(*a*) the council of every district and London borough shall appoint an officer of the council to be registration officer for any constituency or part of a constituency coterminous with or situated in the district or borough, and

(*b*) the Common Council shall appoint an officer to be registration officer for the part of the constituency containing the City and the Inner Temple and the Middle Temple.

(3) In Scotland, the council of every region and islands area shall appoint an officer of the council for their area or for any adjoining region or islands area, or an officer appointed by any combination of such councils, to be registration officer for any constituency or part of a constituency which is situated within that region or islands area.

PART I

(4) In Northern Ireland, the Chief Electoral Officer for Northern Ireland is the registration officer for each constituency.

Registers of electors.

9.—(1) It is every registration officer's duty to prepare and publish in each year—

(*a*) a register of parliamentary electors for each constituency or part of a constituency in the area for which he acts; and

(*b*) a register of local government electors for the local government areas or parts of local government areas included in the area for which he acts.

(2) The registers of parliamentary electors and of local government electors shall so far as practicable be combined, the names of persons registered only as local government electors being marked to indicate that fact.

(3) A registration officer's general duty to prepare and publish registers of electors in conformity with this Act includes the duty to take reasonable steps to obtain information required by him for that purpose (without prejudice to any specific requirement of this Act or regulations under it).

Preparation of registers.

10. With a view to the preparation of registers, the registration officer shall—

(*a*) have a house to house or other sufficient inquiry made as to the persons entitled to be registered (excluding persons entitled to be registered in pursuance of a service declaration);

(*b*) have prepared and published electors lists showing the persons appearing to him to be entitled to be registered together with their qualifying addresses;

(*c*) determine all claims for registration duly made by any person, and all objections to any person's registration duly made by another person appearing from the electors lists to be himself entitled to be registered including claims and objections asking for the omission, insertion or alteration of a date as that on which a person will become of voting age and entitled to be treated as an elector.

Correction of registers.

11.—(1) Where a register of electors as published does not carry out the registration officer's intention—

(*a*) to include the name of any person shown in the electors lists as a person entitled to be registered, or (*b*) to give or not to give in a person's entry a date as that on which he will attain voting age, or as to the date to be given, or

(*c*) to give effect to a decision on a claim or objection made with respect to the electors lists,

then (subject to the decision on any appeal from a decision on a claim or objection) the registration officer on becoming aware of the fact shall make the necessary correction in the register.

(2) Where—

(*a*) paragraph (a) of subsection (1) above does not apply, but

(*b*) the registration officer is satisfied by such evidence as he may require that any person whose name is not included in a register of electors as published is entitled to be registered in that register,

the registration officer shall make the necessary correction in the register.

(3) An alteration made in a register of electors under subsection (1) or subsection (2) above on or after the date on which notice of an election is given shall not have effect for the purposes of that election.

(4) No alteration shall be made in a register of electors as published otherwise than under—

(*a*) subsection (1) or subsection (2); or

(*b*) the provisions of sections 56 to 58 below relating to appeals.

Right to be registered.

12.—(1) A person who may be entitled to vote as an elector at parliamentary elections for which any register is to be used is entitled to be registered in that register, subject to—

(*a*) section 7(3) above, as to a person who on the qualifying date is a voluntary mental patient, and subsections (3) and (4) below as to one who on the qualifying date has a service qualification ; and

(*b*) any enactment imposing a disqualification for registration as a parliamentary elector.

(2) A person who may be entitled to vote as an elector at local government elections for which any register is to be used is entitled to be registered in that register, subject to—

(*a*) section 7(3) above, as to a person who on the qualifying date is a voluntary mental patient, and subsections (3) and (4) below as to one who on the qualifying date has a service qualification ; and

PART I

(*b*) any enactment imposing a disqualification for registration as a local government elector.

(3) A person who on the qualifying date has a service qualification is not entitled to be registered as mentioned in subsection (1) or subsection (2) above except in pursuance of an appropriate service declaration; and in this subsection and in subsection (4) below "appropriate service declaration" means—

(*a*) in the case of a person who on the qualifying date is a member of the forces or the wife or husband of such a member, a service declaration made in accordance with section 15 below and in force on that date; and

(*b*) in any other case, a service declaration made in accordance with that section with reference to that date.

(4) Subsection (3) above does not apply to a person who on the qualifying date is the wife or husband of a member of the forces if on that date—

(*a*) that person has no other service qualification;

(*b*) that person is resident in the United Kingdom; and

(*c*) no appropriate service declaration is in force in respect of that person.

(5) A person otherwise qualified is entitled to be registered in a register of parliamentary electors or a register of local government electors if he will attain voting age before the end of the twelve months following the day by which the register is required to be published; but, if he will not be of voting age on the first day of those twelve months—

(*a*) his entry in the register shall give the date on which he will attain that age; and

(*b*) until the date given in the entry he shall not by virtue of the entry be treated as an elector for any purposes other than purposes of an election at which the day fixed for the poll is that or a later date.

Publication of registers.

13.—(1) Registers of parliamentary and local government electors or, in Northern Ireland, of parliamentary electors, shall be—

(*a*) prepared and published once a year, and

(*b*) published not later than 15th February,

and registers published in any year shall be used for elections at which the date fixed for the poll falls within the period of twelve months beginning with 16th February in that year.

(2) The Secretary of State has power to make regulations altering the interval in Northern Ireland between the qualifying date and the date of publication of the registers of parliamentary

PART I

electors by changing either date, and any such regulations may make such consequential provisions (including the modification of any enactment contained in this or any other Act) as may appear to the Secretary of State to be necessary.

(3) If any part of a register is not published within the time required by this section, then until the day following that on which it is published the corresponding part of the previous register shall continue in use.

(4) Where any part of the register used at an election is a part continued in force by subsection (3) above, the Representation of the People Acts (including this Act) shall have effect in relation to the election and the area to which that part relates as if the qualifying date by reference to which that part was prepared were the qualifying date for the election.

Service qualifications and declarations for registration

Service qualification.

14.—(1) A person has a service qualification for the purposes of this Act who—

(*a*) is a member of the forces,

(*b*) (not being such a member) is employed in the service of the Crown in a post outside the United Kingdom of any prescribed class or description,

(*c*) is employed by the British Council in a post outside the United Kingdom,

(*d*) is the wife or husband of a member of the forces,

(*e*) is the wife or husband of a person mentioned in paragraph (*b*) or paragraph (*c*) above and is residing outside the United Kingdom to be with her husband or, as the case may be, his wife,

and where a person leaves the United Kingdom to take up employment or residence as mentioned above or returns to the United Kingdom at the end of such employment or residence, the employment or residence shall be deemed to begin from the time of leaving or to continue until the time of returning, as the case may be.

(2) For the purposes of section 1(2) above a person ceasing to have a service qualification shall be treated as if he were resident in Northern Ireland for the period during which he had a service qualification.

Service declaration.

15.—(1) A service declaration shall be made only—

(*a*) by a person who has a service qualification, or

(*b*) subject to any prescribed conditions, by a person about to leave the United Kingdom in such circumstances as to acquire a service qualification,

PART I

and a service declaration may be made by such a person notwithstanding the fact that by reason of his age he is not yet entitled to vote.

(2) A service declaration made by a member of the forces or the wife or husband of such a member shall, if not cancelled, continue in force so long as the declarant has a service qualification, except in so far as regulations provide that the declaration shall cease to be in force on a change in the circumstances giving the service qualification.

(3) A service declaration made by any other person shall be made with a view to registration in the register of electors—

(*a*) for a particular year; and

(*b*) with reference to the qualifying date for that register.

(4) A service declaration made with reference to any qualifying date shall be made during the twelve months ending with that date, but shall not have effect if after it is made and before that date—

(*a*) the declarant ceases to have a service qualification; or

(*b*) the declarant cancels the declaration; or

(*c*) in so far as regulations so provide, there is a change in the circumstances giving the service qualification.

(5) No service declaration shall be specially made by a person for the purpose of local government elections, and any service declaration made for the purpose of parliamentary elections shall have effect also for the purpose of local government elections; but—

(*a*) a service declaration may be made for the purpose of local government elections only by a person who is as a peer subject to a legal incapacity to vote at parliamentary elections; and

(*b*) where so made, shall be marked to show that it is available for local government elections only, but shall in all other respects be the same as other service declarations.

(6) If a person—

(*a*) makes a service declaration declaring to more than one address, or

(*b*) makes more than one service declaration bearing the same date and declaring to different addresses,

the declaration or declarations shall be void.

(7) A service declaration may at any time be cancelled by the declarant and (subject to subsection (6) above) a service declaration bearing a later date shall without any express cancellation

cancel a declaration bearing an earlier date if, in the case of a service declaration made otherwise than by a member of the forces or the wife or husband of such a member, it is made with reference to the same qualifying date.

Contents of service declaration.

16. A service declaration shall state—

(*a*) the date of the declaration,

(*b*) where the declarant is a member of the forces or the wife or husband of such a member, that on that date the declarant is, or but for the circumstances entitling him to make the declaration would have been, residing in the United Kingdom,

(*c*) in the case of any other declarant, that on that date and, unless it is a qualifying date, on the qualifying date next following he is or will be, or but for those circumstances would have been, residing in the United Kingdom,

(*d*) the address where the declarant is or, as the case may be, will be or would have been residing in the United Kingdom or, if he cannot give any such address, an address at which he has resided in the United Kingdom,

(*e*) that on the date of the declaration the declarant is a Commonwealth citizen or a citizen of the Republic of Ireland,

(*f*) whether the declarant had on the date of the declaration attained the age of 18 years, and, if he had not, the date of his birth, and

(*g*) such particulars (if any) as may be prescribed of the declarant's identity and service qualifications,

and (except where the declarant is a member of the forces or the wife or husband of such a member) shall be attested in the prescribed manner.

Effect of service declaration.

17.—(1) A member of the forces or the wife or husband of such a member whose service declaration is in force on the qualifying date shall be treated for the purposes of registration, and any other person whose service declaration is made with reference to the qualifying date for any register shall be so treated in relation to that register—

(*a*) as resident on the qualifying date at the address specified in the declaration;

(*b*) in the case of registration in Northern Ireland, as resident in Northern Ireland during the whole of the period of three months ending on the qualifying date; and

PART I

(*c*) in any case, until the contrary is proved, as being a Commonwealth citizen or a citizen of the Republic of Ireland of the age appearing from the declaration and as not being subject to any legal incapacity except as so appearing.

(2) Where a service declaration appearing to be properly made out and (where required) attested is transmitted to the registration officer in the proper manner, the declarant shall, until the contrary is proved, be treated for the purposes of registration as having had from the date of the declaration or such later date, if any, as appears from it, and as continuing to have, a service qualification.

Place and manner of voting at parliamentary elections

Polling districts and places at parliamentary elections.

18.—(1) Every constituency shall be divided into polling districts and subject to the provisions of this section there shall be a polling place designated for each polling district.

(2) In England and Wales it is the duty of the council of each district or London borough to divide their area into polling districts for the purpose of parliamentary elections for so much of any constituency as is situated in their area, and to designate the polling places for those polling districts, and to keep the polling districts and polling places under review, in accordance with the following rules—

(*a*) the council shall exercise the powers conferred by this section with a view to giving all electors in so much of the constituency as falls within their area such reasonable facilities for voting as are practicable in the circumstances ;

(*b*) in the case of a county constituency, each parish or community shall in the absence of special circumstances be a separate polling district or districts ;

(*c*) the polling place for any polling district shall be an area in that district, except where special circumstances make it desirable to designate an area wholly or partly outside the polling district, and shall be small enough to indicate to electors in different parts of the polling district how they will be able to reach the polling station ;

(*d*) a polling place need not be designated for any polling district, if the size and other circumstances of the district are such that the situation of the polling stations does not materially affect the convenience of the electors or any body of them.

(3) In Scotland it is the returning officer's duty to make the division into polling districts and to designate the polling places, and to keep the polling districts and polling places under review in accordance with the following rules—

(*a*) the returning officer shall exercise the powers conferred by this section with a view to giving all electors in the constituency such reasonable facilities for voting as are practicable in the circumstances ;

(*b*) each electoral area established for the purpose of local government elections which is within the constituency, and that part within the constituency of any such area which is partly within the constituency and partly within another constituency, shall, in the absence of special circumstances, be a separate polling district or districts ;

(*c*) the polling place for any polling district shall be an area in that district, except where special circumstances make it desirable to designate an area wholly or partly outside the polling district, and shall be small enough to indicate to electors in different parts of the polling district how they will be able to reach the polling station ;

(*d*) a polling place need not be designated for any polling district, if the size and other circumstances of the district are such that the situation of the polling stations does not materially affect the convenience of the electors or any body of them.

(4) In the case of a polling district for which no polling place is designated the polling district shall be taken to be the polling place for the purposes of this Act.

(5) If any interested authority or not less than 30 electors in a constituency make a representation to the Secretary of State that the powers conferred by this section have not been exercised so as to meet the reasonable requirements of the electors in the constituency or any body of those electors, the Secretary of State shall consider the representation and may, if he thinks fit—

(*a*) direct the council (or in Scotland, the returning officer) by whom the powers are exercisable, to make any alterations which the Secretary of State thinks necessary in the circumstances, and

(*b*) if the council or returning officer fails to make those alterations within a month after the direction is given, himself make the alterations,

and any alterations made by the Secretary of State under this subsection shall have effect as if they had been made by the council or returning officer.

PART I

In this subsection the expression "interested authority", in relation to any constituency, means—

(i) as respects England, the council or where there is no such council the parish meeting of a parish which is wholly or partly situated within the constituency;

(ii) as respects Wales, the council of a community which is so situated;

(iii) as respects Scotland, the council of any region, islands area or district within whose area the constituency is wholly or partly situated.

(6) On the exercise of any power given by this section, the council or returning officer—

(*a*) shall publish in the constituency a notice showing the boundaries of any polling districts or polling places constituted as a result of the exercise of the power; and

(*b*) unless the power was exercised by the Secretary of State, shall also send him a report giving the same information.

(7) Subsections (2) to (6) above do not apply to Northern Ireland, and in Northern Ireland the polling districts and polling places are those for the time being established under the law relating to the election of members to serve in the Northern Ireland Assembly.

(8) Regulations—

(*a*) may provide for adapting the register in force for the time being to any alteration of polling districts, and

(*b*) may make special provisions for cases where any alteration of polling districts is made between the publication of any electors lists and the coming into force of the register prepared from those lists,

but except in cases for which provision is made by regulations an alteration of polling districts shall not be effective until the coming into force of the first register prepared from electors lists published after the alteration is made.

(9) An election shall not be questioned by reason of—

(*a*) any non-compliance with the provisions of this section; or

(*b*) any informality relative to polling districts or polling places.

Voting at parliamentary elections.

19.—(1) A person voting as an elector at a parliamentary election shall do so in person at the polling station allotted to him under the parliamentary elections rules except in so far as this section makes exceptions for— PART I

(*a*) those registered as service voters;

(*b*) those unable or likely to be unable to go in person to the polling station for one of the following reasons—

(i) the general nature of the occupation, service or employment of the person in question;

(ii) that person's service as a member of any of Her Majesty's reserve or auxiliary forces;

(iii) the particular circumstances of that person's employment on the date of the poll either as a constable or, for a purpose connected with the election, by the returning officer;

(iv) at a general election, the candidature in some other constituency of that person or that person's wife or husband;

(v) at a general election, the fact that that person is acting as returning officer for some other constituency;

(vi) at a general election, the particular circumstances of that person's employment on the date of the poll by the returning officer for some other constituency for a purpose connected with the election in that constituency;

(*c*) those unable or likely to be unable, by reason either of blindness or any other physical incapacity or of religious observance, to go in person to the polling station or, if able to go, to vote unaided;

(*d*) those unable or likely to be unable to go in person from their qualifying address to the polling station without making a journey by air or sea;

(*e*) those no longer residing at their qualifying address;

(*f*) those registered by virtue of a patient's declaration under section 7 above;

(*g*) those who have a service qualification depending on marriage to, and residence outside the United Kingdom to be with, a person having a service qualification; and

(*h*) those unable or likely to be unable to go in person to the polling station by reason of the general nature of the occupation, service or employment of, and their resulting absence from their qualifying address to be with, their husband or wife.

(2) A person registered as a service voter may vote by proxy unless he is entitled in pursuance of an application made under subsection (4) below to vote by post.

PART I

(3) A person not registered as a service voter if unable or likely to be unable to go in person to the polling station by reason either—

(*a*) of the general nature of his occupation, service or employment, or

(*b*) of his service as a member of any of Her Majesty's reserve or auxiliary forces,

may vote by proxy if he applies to be treated as an absent voter and is likely to be at sea or out of the United Kingdom on the date of the poll.

(4) A person mentioned in paragraphs (*a*) to (*f*) of subsection (1) above may vote by post if he applies to be treated as an absent voter and provides an address in the United Kingdom to which a ballot paper is to be sent for the purpose, but—

(*a*) a person shall not be entitled to vote by post if he is not registered as a service voter and there is in force an appointment of a proxy to vote for him; and

(*b*) a person shall not be entitled to vote by post on the ground that he no longer resides at his qualifying address if at the time of his application he resides at an address in the same area; and

(*c*) a person registered as a service voter shall not be entitled to vote by post on any ground other than his being so registered.

For the purposes of this subsection an address shall not be treated as in the same area as a qualifying address unless it would be so treated under section 22(3) below for the purposes of that section.

(5) A person who is not registered as a service voter but who either—

(*a*) has made a service declaration in respect of a qualification depending on marriage as described in subsection (1) above, or

(*b*) is as a married person unable or likely to be unable to go to the poll by reason of absence in the circumstances there described,

has the like right to vote by proxy and, in the case dealt with by paragraph (*b*) above, the like right to vote by post as a person unable or likely to be unable to go to the poll by reason of the general nature of his occupation, service or employment.

(6) A person, whether registered as a service voter or not—

(*a*) may vote in person as an elector notwithstanding any appointment of a proxy to vote for him, if he applies for a ballot paper for the purpose before a ballot paper has been issued for him to vote by proxy; but

(*b*) shall not be entitled to vote in person as an elector—

(i) where he may vote by proxy by virtue of an appointment for the time being in force and he does not so apply; or

(ii) where he has applied to be treated as an absent voter and is entitled in pursuance of the application to vote by post.

(7) A person not registered as a service voter may vote at any polling station in the constituency if he is entitled to vote in person but unable or likely to be unable to go to the polling station allotted to him by reason of the particular circumstances of his employment on the date of the poll either—

(*a*) as a constable; or

(*b*) by the returning officer, for a purpose connected with the election.

(8) Nothing in this section confers a right to vote on a person not having the right apart from this section.

Absent voters at parliamentary elections.

20.—(1) An application to be treated as an absent voter at parliamentary elections shall be made to the registration officer and shall be allowed by him if he is satisfied that the applicant is, or will if registered be, entitled under section 19 above to vote as an absent voter.

(2) The application shall be for a particular election only, unless it is based on—

(*a*) the general nature of the applicant's occupation, service or employment; or

(*b*) the applicant's physical incapacity; or

(*c*) the necessity of a journey by sea or air to go from the applicant's qualifying address to his polling station; or

(*d*) the ground that the applicant no longer resides at his qualifying address.

(3) An application based on one of the grounds mentioned in subsection (2) above shall be for an indefinite period but where such an application is allowed the applicant shall cease to be entitled to be treated as an absent voter in pursuance of it if—

(*a*) he applies to the registration officer to be no longer so treated; or

(*b*) he ceases to be registered at the same qualifying address or becomes so registered as a service voter; or

PART I

(*c*) the registration officer gives notice that he has reason to believe there has been a material change of circumstances, and the prescribed period elapses after the giving of the notice.

(4) This section applies to an application based on the grounds related to the applicant's marriage referred to in paragraphs (*g*) and (*h*) of section 19(1) as it applies to an application based on the general nature of the applicant's occupation, service or employment.

(5) The registration officer shall keep a record of absent voters and of the addresses provided by them as the addresses to which their ballot papers are to be sent.

Proxies at parliamentary elections.

21.—(1) A person is not entitled to have more than one person at a time appointed as a proxy to vote for him at a parliamentary election.

(2) A person is not capable of being appointed to vote or of voting as proxy at a parliamentary election unless—

(*a*) he is not subject (age apart) to any legal incapacity to vote at a parliamentary election as an elector, and

(*b*) he is either a Commonwealth citizen or a citizen of the Republic of Ireland,

and a person is not entitled to vote as proxy at the same election in any constituency on behalf of more than two electors of whom that person is not the husband, wife, parent, grandparent, brother, sister, child or grandchild.

(3) A person otherwise qualified is capable of voting as proxy at a parliamentary election at which he is of voting age on the date of the poll, and of being appointed proxy for that purpose before he is of voting age.

(4) Subject to the foregoing provisions of this section a person is capable of being appointed proxy to vote at a parliamentary election and may vote in pursuance of the appointment.

(5) The appointment shall be made by the registration officer by means of a proxy paper issued by him on the elector's application, and it is the registration officer's duty to issue a proxy paper in pursuance of any application duly made to him, if he is satisfied—

(*a*) that the applicant is or will be registered for elections to which the application relates and entitled in respect of that registration to have a proxy appointed; and

(*b*) that the proxy is capable of being and willing to be appointed.

(6) The appointment may be cancelled by the elector by giving notice to the registration officer and shall cease to be in force on the issue of a proxy paper appointing a different person to vote for him, whether in respect of the same registration or elsewhere, but, subject to that, shall remain in force—

(*a*) in the case of an appointment for a person registered as a service voter, for all elections for which he remains registered as a service voter at the same qualifying address ; and

(*b*) in the case of an appointment for a person not registered as a service voter, for all elections at which he is entitled to vote by proxy in pursuance of the same application to be treated as an absent voter.

(7) Stamp duty is not chargeable on any instrument appointing a proxy under this section.

(8) The registration officer shall keep a record of electors for whom proxies have been appointed and of the names and addresses of the persons appointed.

Voting as proxy at parliamentary elections.

22.—(1) A person voting as proxy for an elector at a parliamentary election shall do so in person at the elector's polling station, except in so far as this section entitles the proxy to vote by post.

(2) A proxy may exercise the right to vote as such at a parliamentary election by post if—

(*a*) he applies so to do and provides an address in the United Kingdom to which a ballot paper is to be sent for the purpose ; and

(*b*) either—

(i) he is entitled to vote by post as an absent voter at the election ; or

(ii) that address is not in the same area as the elector's qualifying address.

(3) For the purposes of this section, an address shall not be treated as in the same area as a qualifying address unless—

(*a*) both addresses are in the same electoral division of Greater London, or

(*b*) both addresses are in the same electoral division of a county in England and, if either address is in a parish, both are in the same parish, or

(*c*) both addresses are in the same electoral division of a county in Wales and in the same community, or

(*d*) both addresses are in the same electoral division in Scotland, or

PART I

(*e*) both addresses are in the same ward in Northern Ireland.

(4) A proxy is not entitled to exercise the right to vote as such in person at any election for which his application to exercise that right by post is allowed.

(5) Any such application shall be made to the registration officer and shall be allowed by him in any case where he is satisfied—

(*a*) that the elector is or will be registered as such for elections to which the application relates ; and

(*b*) that there is in force an appointment of the applicant as his proxy to vote in respect of that registration ; and

(*c*) that the conditions entitling the applicant to vote by post are fulfilled.

(6) Where any such application is based on the applicant's right to vote by post as an elector, then—

(*a*) if that right extends only to a particular election, the application shall also extend only to that election ;

(*b*) in any other case, the application shall be for an indefinite period but, where it is allowed, the applicant shall cease to be entitled to vote by post in pursuance of that right if—

(i) he ceases to have the right to vote by post as an elector, or has that right only by virtue of a new application ; or

(ii) he ceases to be proxy for the elector, or is so only by virtue of a new appointment.

(7) Where any such application is based on the situation of the address to which the ballot paper is to be sent, it shall be for an indefinite period but, if it is allowed, the applicant shall cease to be entitled to vote by post in pursuance of it if—

(*a*) he applies for a ballot paper not to be sent to that address ; or

(*b*) he ceases to be proxy for the elector, or is so only by virtue of a new appointment.

(8) The registration officer shall keep a record of the persons whose applications to vote by post as proxy are for the time being allowed and of the addresses provided by them as the addresses to which their ballot papers are to be sent.

Conduct of parliamentary elections

Rules for parliamentary elections.

23.—(1) The proceedings at a parliamentary election shall be conducted in accordance with the parliamentary elections rules in Schedule 1 to this Act.

(2) It is the returning officer's general duty at a parliamentary election to do all such acts and things as may be necessary for effectually conducting the election in the manner provided by those parliamentary elections rules.

(3) No parliamentary election shall be declared invalid by reason of any act or omission by the returning officer or any other person in breach of his official duty in connection with the election or otherwise of the parliamentary elections rules if it appears to the tribunal having cognizance of the question that—

(*a*) the election was so conducted as to be substantially in accordance with the law as to elections; and

(*b*) the act or omission did not affect its result.

Returning officers: England and Wales.

24.—(1) In England and Wales, the returning officer for a parliamentary election is—

(*a*) in the case of a county constituency which is coterminous with or wholly contained in a county, the sheriff of the county;

(*b*) in the case of a borough constituency which is coterminous with or wholly contained in a district, the chairman of the district council;

(*c*) in the case of any other constituency wholly outside Greater London, such sheriff or chairman of a district council as may be designated in an order by the Secretary of State made by statutory instrument;

(*d*) in the case of a constituency which is coterminous with or wholly contained in a London borough, the mayor of the borough;

(*e*) in the case of a constituency wholly or partly in Greater London which is situated partly in one London borough and partly in a district or any other London borough, the mayor of such London borough or the chairman of such district council as may be designated in an order by the Secretary of State made by statutory instrument.

The City, the Inner Temple and the Middle Temple shall be treated for the purposes of this section as if together they formed a London borough.

(2) A parliamentary election is not liable to be questioned by reason of a defect in the title, or want of title, of the person presiding at or conducting the election, if that person was then in actual possession of, or acting in, the office giving the right to preside at or conduct the election.

PART I

Returning officers: Scotland.

25.—(1) In Scotland, the returning officer for a parliamentary election is—

(*a*) in the case of a constituency wholly situated in one region or islands area, the person under section 41 below who is, or who may discharge the functions of, the returning officer at elections of councillors for the regional or islands council;

(*b*) in the case of a constituency situated in more than one region or islands area, such person mentioned above as the Secretary of State may by order direct.

(2) The council of a region or of an islands area shall place at the disposal of the returning officer for a constituency wholly or partly situated in that region or islands area, for the purpose of assisting the returning officer in the discharge of any functions conferred on him in relation to a parliamentary election in that constituency, the services of officers employed by the council.

(3) The council of a district shall, if so requested by the returning officer for a constituency wholly or partly situated in that district, place at the returning officer's disposal, for the purpose of assisting him as mentioned in subsection (2) above, the services of officers employed by the council.

Returning officer: Northern Ireland.

26. In Northern Ireland, the Chief Electoral Officer for Northern Ireland is the returning officer for each constituency.

Returning officers generally.

27.—(1) It is for the returning officer as such to execute the writ for a parliamentary election, and the office of returning officer is a distinct office from that by virtue of which he becomes returning officer.

(2) Where a person takes any office by virtue of which he becomes returning officer, he (and not the outgoing holder of the office) shall complete the execution of any writ for a parliamentary election previously issued and not yet returned.

(3) A person is not subject to any incapacity to vote at a parliamentary election by reason of being or acting as returning officer at that election.

Discharge of returning officer's functions in England and Wales.

28.—(1) In England and Wales the duties of the returning officer for a parliamentary election (except those mentioned in subsection (2) below) shall be discharged, as acting returning officer—

(*a*) in the case of a constituency for which the chairman of a district council or the mayor of a London borough is returning officer by virtue of section 24(1) above, by the registration officer appointed by that council; PART I

(b) in the case of any other constituency, by such registration officer as may be designated in an order made by the Secretary of State.

(2) The duties excepted from subsection (1) above are—

(a) any duty imposed on a returning officer under rule 3 of the parliamentary elections rules; and

(b) any duty so imposed under rule 50 of those rules which the person (if any) who for the time being holds the office of returning officer reserves to himself and undertakes to perform in person.

(3) The returning officer shall give to the acting returning officer written notice of any duties which he reserves to himself under paragraph (b) of subsection (2) above, and that paragraph shall, in the case of any election, apply to the duties (if any) of which the notice is so given not later than the day following that on which the writ is received, and to no others.

(4) In the discharge of the duties imposed by subsection (1) an acting returning officer has all the powers, obligations, rights and liabilities of the returning officer under this Act, and this Act has effect accordingly.

(5) An acting returning officer has power to appoint deputies to discharge all or any of those duties, but the appointment requires the Secretary of State's approval where the deputy's powers extend—

(a) to matters other than the receipt of nomination papers and connected matters; or

(b) to the taking or deciding of objections to nomination papers.

(6) Section 25 of the Sheriffs Act 1887 (death of sheriff) does not authorise the under-sheriff to discharge the duties of returning officer, and upon a sheriff's death the acting returning officer shall discharge all the sheriff's duties as returning officer until another sheriff is appointed and has made the declaration of office. 1887 c. 55.

Payments by and to returning officer.

29.—(1) No consideration shall be given by or to a returning officer for the making out, receipt, delivery or return of the writ for a parliamentary election or, subject to the following provisions of this section, otherwise in connection with its execution.

(2) Nothing in subsection (1) above shall be taken as applying to any inclusive salary payable to a returning officer in

PART I

respect of the office by virtue of which he becomes returning officer.

(3) The Treasury shall by statutory instrument prescribe a scale of maximum charges in respect of services rendered and expenses incurred by a returning officer for the purposes of or in connection with parliamentary elections, and may revise the scale as and when they think fit.

(4) A returning officer shall be entitled to his reasonable charges, not exceeding the sums specified in that scale, in respect of services and expenses of the several kinds so specified which have been properly rendered or incurred by him for the purposes of or in connection with a parliamentary election.

(5) The amount of any such charges shall be charged on and paid out of the Consolidated Fund on an account being submitted to the Treasury, but the Treasury may if they think fit, before payment, apply for the account to be taxed under the provisions of section 30 below.

(6) Where the superannuation contributions required to be paid by a local authority in respect of any person are increased by any fee paid under this section as part of a returning officer's charges at a parliamentary election, then on an account being submitted to the Treasury a sum equal to the increase shall be charged on and paid out of the Consolidated Fund to the authority.

(7) On the returning officer's request for an advance on account of his charges, the Treasury may, on such terms as they think fit, make such an advance.

(8) The Treasury may make regulations as to the time when and the manner and form in which accounts are to be rendered to them for the purposes of the payment of a returning officer's charges.

Taxation of returning officer's account.

30.—(1) An application for a returning officer's account to be taxed shall be made—

(*a*) where the account relates to an election in a constituency in England or Wales or in Northern Ireland, to the county court,

(*b*) where the account relates to an election in a constituency in Scotland, to the Auditor of the Court of Session,

and in this section the expression " the court " means that court or Auditor.

(2) On any such application the court has jurisdiction to tax the account in such manner and at such time and place as the

court thinks fit, and finally to determine the amount payable to the returning officer. **PART I**

(3) On any such application the returning officer may apply to the court to examine any claim made by any person against him in respect of matters charged in the account; and the court, after notice given to the claimant and after giving him an opportunity to be heard and to tender any evidence, may allow or disallow or reduce the claim objected to with or without costs; and the determination of the court shall be final for all purposes and as against all persons.

(4) Any reference in this section to the county court shall be taken, in relation to Northern Ireland, as a reference to the county court having jurisdiction at the place for the delivery of nomination papers at the election in question.

Place and manner of voting at local government elections

Polling districts and stations at local government elections.

31.—(1) For elections of county councillors (other than councillors of the Greater London Council), the county council may divide an electoral division into polling districts, and may alter any polling district, and for elections of London borough or district councillors the London borough or district council may divide the London borough or district or any ward thereof into polling districts, and may alter any polling district.

(2) In Scotland, for elections of regional or islands councillors the regional or islands council may divide an electoral division into polling districts and may alter any polling district, and for elections of district councillors the district council may divide a ward into polling districts and may alter any polling district; but in the absence of special circumstances those polling districts shall be those which were last designated for the purpose of parliamentary elections under section 18 above.

(3) Any power to constitute polling districts for the purpose of local government elections shall be exercised so that electors from any parliamentary polling district wholly or partly within the electoral area can, in the absence of special circumstances, be allotted to a polling station within the parliamentary polling place for that district unless the parliamentary polling place is outside the electoral area.

(4) Any polling district formed for the purpose of the election of councillors for any ward of a London borough shall, if the ward is wholly included in the electoral area for the election of a councillor of the Greater London Council, be a polling district for the election of a councillor of that Council for that electoral area.

PART I

(5) If the polling districts in an electoral area for the election of a councillor of the Greater London Council or in part of such an area are not determined by subsection (4) above—

(*a*) the council of the London borough which includes that electoral area, or

(*b*) in the case of an electoral area which includes the City, the Inner Temple and the Middle Temple, the City of Westminster,

may divide that area or, as the case may be, that part of that area, into polling districts, and may alter any polling district, and subsection (3) above applies to the power conferred by this subsection.

Voting at local government elections.

32.– (1) All persons voting as electors at a local government election shall do so in person at the polling station allotted to them by the rules under section 36 or section 42 below except in so far as this section makes exceptions for—

(*a*) those registered as service voters;

(*b*) those unable or likely to be unable to go in person to the polling station for one of the following reasons—

(i) the general nature of the occupation, service or employment of the person in question;

(ii) that person's service as a member of Her Majesty's reserve or auxiliary forces;

(iii) the particular circumstances of that person's employment on the date of the poll either as a constable or, for a purpose connected with the election, by the returning officer;

(iv) at an ordinary election, the fact that that person is acting as returning officer at an ordinary election of councillors for some other electoral area;

(v) at an ordinary election, the particular circumstances of that person's employment on the date of the poll by the returning officer at an ordinary election of councillors for some other electoral area for a purpose connected with the election in that area;

(*c*) those unable or likely to be unable, by reason either of blindness or any other physical incapacity or of religious observance, to go in person to the polling station or, if able to go, to vote unaided;

(*d*) those unable or likely to be unable to go in person from their qualifying address to the polling station without making a journey by air or sea;

(*e*) those registered by virtue of a patient's declaration under section 7 above;

PART I

(*f*) those who have a service qualification depending on marriage to, and residence outside the United Kingdom to be with, a person having a service qualification ; and

(*g*) those unable or likely to be unable to go in person to the polling station by reason of the general nature of the occupation, service or employment of, and their resulting absence from their qualifying address to be with, their husband or wife.

(2) A person registered as a service voter may at any local government election vote by proxy.

(3) Where—

(*a*) a person is registered at the same qualifying address both as a parliamentary and as a local government elector, and is not so registered as a service voter, and

(*b*) there is in force an appointment of a proxy to vote for him at parliamentary elections in respect of that registration, being an appointment based on the general nature of his occupation, service or employment,

then, in respect of that registration, at local government elections at which postal voting is allowed he shall be treated as an absent voter and may vote by proxy.

(4) Unless treated as an absent voter under subsection (3) above, any of the persons mentioned in paragraphs (*b*) to (*e*) of subsection (1) above who is not registered as a service voter may vote by post at any local government election at which postal voting is allowed, if he applies to be treated as an absent voter and provides an address in the United Kingdom to which a ballot paper is to be sent for the purpose.

(5) A person who is not registered as a service voter but who either—

(*a*) has made a service declaration in respect of a qualification depending on marriage as described in subsection (1), or

(*b*) is as a married person unable or likely to be unable to go to the poll by reason of absence in the circumstances there described,

has the like right to vote by proxy and, in the case dealt with by paragraph (*b*) above, the like right to vote by post as a person unable or likely to be unable to go to the poll by reason of the general nature of his occupation, service or employment.

(6) A person, whether registered as a service voter or not—

(*a*) may vote in person as an elector notwithstanding any appointment of a proxy to vote for him, if he applies for a ballot paper for the purpose before a ballot paper has been issued for him to vote by proxy ; but

PART I

(*b*) shall not be entitled to vote in person as an elector—

(i) where he may vote by proxy by virtue of an appointment for the time being in force and he does not so apply ; or

(ii) where he has applied to be treated as an absent voter and is entitled in pursuance of the application to vote by post.

(7) A person not registered as a service voter, if he is entitled to vote in person, but unable or likely to be unable to go in person to the polling station allotted to him by reason of the particular circumstances of his employment on the date of the poll either as a constable or, for a purpose connected with the election by the returning officer, may vote at any polling station of the electoral area.

(8) Postal voting shall be allowed at all local government elections, except, in England and Wales, elections of parish or community councillors.

(9) Nothing in this section shall be taken as conferring a right to vote on a person not having the right apart from this section.

Absent voters at local government elections.

33.—(1) An application to be treated as an absent voter at local government elections shall be made to the registration officer and shall be allowed by him if he is satisfied that the applicant is, or will if registered be, entitled under section 32 above to vote as an absent voter.

(2) The application shall be for a particular election only, if it is based on—

(*a*) the applicant's service as a member of any of Her Majesty's reserve or auxiliary forces ; or

(*b*) the fact that the applicant is acting as returning officer in some other electoral area ; or

(*c*) the particular circumstances of the applicant's employment on the date of the poll either as a constable or by a returning officer ;

(*d*) religious observance ; or

(*e*) a patient's declaration under section 7 above.

(3) An application not based on one of the grounds mentioned in subsection (2) above shall be for an indefinite period but, where such an application is allowed, the applicant shall cease to be entitled to be so treated as an absent voter in pursuance of it if—

(*a*) he applies to the registration officer to be no longer so treated ; or

(*b*) he ceases to be registered at the same qualifying address, or becomes so registered as a service voter ; or

PART I

(c) the registration officer gives notice that he has reason to believe that there has been a material change of circumstances, and the prescribed period elapses after the giving of notice.

(4) The registration officer shall keep a record of absent voters and of the addresses provided by them as the addresses to which their ballot papers are to be sent.

Proxies at local government elections.

34.—(1) Except in the case of a service voter who is as a peer subject to a legal incapacity to vote at parliamentary elections, no person shall be specially appointed proxy to vote at local government elections, but any appointment of a person to vote as proxy at parliamentary elections shall have effect also for the purpose of local government elections.

(2) Subject to subsection (3) below, in the case of a service voter who is as a peer subject to a legal incapacity to vote at parliamentary elections, any person shall be capable of being appointed proxy to vote at local government elections for him and may vote in pursuance of the appointment, but not more than one person at a time shall be appointed on behalf of any service voter.

(3) A person—

(a) is not capable of being appointed under subsection (2) above to vote, or of voting, as proxy at a local government election unless he is not subject (age apart) to any legal incapacity to vote at the election as an elector and is either a Commonwealth citizen or a citizen of the Republic of Ireland;

(b) otherwise qualified is capable of voting as proxy at a local government election at which he is of voting age on the date of the poll, and of being appointed proxy for that purpose before he is of voting age.

(4) A person voting as proxy at a local government election may do so by post if—

(a) he applies to vote as proxy by post and provides an address in the United Kingdom to which a ballot paper is to be sent for the purpose, and

(b) he is entitled to vote by post as an absent voter at the election,

but a person voting as proxy at a local government election, unless entitled to do so by post, shall do so in person at the elector's polling station.

(5) The registration officer shall keep a record of electors for whom proxies have been appointed and of the names and addresses of the persons appointed.

PART I

(6) Subsections (5) to (7) of section 21 and subsections (4), (5), (6) and (8) of section 22 above apply for the purposes of local government elections as they apply for the purposes of parliamentary elections.

Conduct of local government elections in England and Wales

Returning officers: local elections in England and Wales.

35.—(1) In England and Wales every county council shall appoint an officer of the council to be the returning officer for elections of councillors of the county and every district council shall appoint an officer of the council to be the returning officer for the elections of councillors of the district and an officer of the council to be the returning officer for elections of councillors of parishes or communities within the district.

(2) The returning officer at an election of a councillor of the Greater London Council shall be the proper officer of the borough which constitutes or includes the electoral area for which the election is held or, in the case of the electoral area which includes the City, the Inner Temple and the Middle Temple, the proper officer of the City of Westminster.

(3) The returning officer at an election of London borough councillors shall be the proper officer of the borough.

(4) The returning officer at any election mentioned in subsections (1) to (3) above may by writing under his hand appoint one or more persons to discharge all or any of his functions.

(5) A local government election in England and Wales is not liable to be questioned by reason of a defect in the title, or want of title, of the person presiding at or conducting the election, if that person was then in actual possession of, or acting in, the office giving the right to preside at or conduct the election.

Local elections in England and Wales.

36.—(1) Elections of councillors for local government areas in England and Wales shall be conducted in accordance with rules made by the Secretary of State.

(2) Rules made under this section shall apply the parliamentary elections rules in Schedule 1 to this Act, subject to such adaptations, alterations and exceptions as seem appropriate to the Secretary of State.

(3) When the following ordinary elections fall to be held in the same year—

(*a*) the ordinary election of district councillors for any district ward, and

(*b*) the ordinary election of parish or community councillors for any parish or community, or any parish or community ward, which is coterminous with or situated in that district ward, the polls at those elections shall be taken together and one-half of the cost of taking the combined polls shall be treated as attributable to the holding of each election.

PART I

(4) All expenditure properly incurred by a returning officer in relation to the holding of an election of a councillor for a principal area (that is, a county, Greater London, a district or a London borough) shall, in so far as it does not, in cases where there is a scale fixed for the purposes of this section by the council for that area, exceed that scale, be paid by that council.

(5) All expenditure properly incurred by a returning officer in relation to the holding of an election of a parish or community councillor shall, in so far as it does not, in cases where there is a scale fixed for the purposes of this section by the council of the district in which the parish or the community is situated, exceed that scale, be paid by the district council, but any expenditure so incurred shall be chargeable only on the parish or community for which the election is held.

(6) Before a poll is taken at an election of a councillor for any local government area in England and Wales the council of that area or, in the case of an election of a parish or community councillor, the council who appointed the returning officer shall, at the request of the returning officer or of any person acting as returning officer, advance to him such reasonable sum in respect of his expenses at the election as he may require.

(7) Rules made under this section shall be—

(*a*) made by statutory instrument;

(*b*) subject to annulment in pursuance of a resolution of either House of Parliament.

Ordinary day of local elections in England and Wales.

37. In every year the ordinary day of election of councillors is the same for all local government areas in England and Wales and is—

(*a*) the first Thursday in May;

(*b*) such other day as may be fixed by the Secretary of State by order made not later than 1st February in the year preceding the first year in which the order is to take effect.

The power to make an order under this section is exercisable by statutory instrument.

Nominations and candidate's death in local election in England and Wales.

38.—(1) At local government elections in England and Wales—

(*a*) the nomination paper shall give for each person subscribing it his electoral number (that is, his number as an elector for the electoral area); and

PART I

(*b*) a telegram (or any similar means of communication) consenting to a nomination shall be admissible instead of the candidate's written consent.

(2) If at a contested local government election in England and Wales proof is given to the returning officer's satisfaction before the result of the election is declared that one of the persons named or to be named as a candidate in the ballot papers has died, then the returning officer—

(*a*) shall countermand the poll, or

(*b*) if polling has begun, shall direct that the poll be abandoned,

and the provisions of section 39(5) below shall apply.

Local elections void etc. in England and Wales.

39.—(1) If in England and Wales at an election of a councillor for a local government area—

(*a*) the poll is countermanded or abandoned for any reason, or

(*b*) no person is or remains, or an insufficient number of persons are or remain, validly nominated to fill the vacancy or vacancies in respect of which the election is held,

the returning officer (or, in the case of an election of a councillor of the Greater London Council, the proper officer of the Council) shall order an election to fill any vacancy which remains unfilled to be held on a day appointed by him.

That day shall be within the period of 42 days (computed according to section 40 below) beginning with the day fixed as the day of election for the first-mentioned election.

1972 c. 70.

(2) If for any other reason an election to an office under the Local Government Act 1972, other than that of chairman of a parish or community council or parish meeting or parish or community councillor, is not held on the appointed day or within the appointed time, or fails either wholly or in part or becomes void, the High Court may order an election to be held on a day appointed by the court.

(3) The High Court may order that the costs incurred by any person in connection with proceedings under subsection (2) above shall be paid by the local authority concerned.

(4) In a case not falling within subsection (1) above—

(*a*) if any difficulty arises with respect to an election of parish or community councillors or of an individual parish or community councillor, or to the first meeting of a parish or community council after an ordinary election of parish or community councillors, or (*b*) if a parish or community council is not properly constituted because an election is not held or is defective or for any other reason, PART I

the district council—

(i) may by order make any appointment or do anything which appears to them necessary or expedient for the proper holding of such an election or meeting and properly constituting the council, and

(ii) may, if it appears to them necessary, direct the holding of an election or meeting and fix the date for it.

(5) Where an election is ordered to be held under this section—

(*a*) rules under section 36 above relating to the notice to be given of an election and the manner in which an election is to be conducted apply in relation to the election so ordered to be held as they applied or would have applied in relation to the election which has not been duly held or has failed or become void;

(*b*) no fresh nomination is necessary in the case of a candidate who remains validly nominated for that election.

(6) An order made—

(*a*) under this section may include such modifications of the provisions of—

(i) this Part of this Act (and the rules under section 36), and

(ii) the Local Government Act 1972, 1972 c. 70.

as appear to the High Court, or, as the case may be, the district council, necessary or expedient for carrying the order into effect;

(*b*) by a district council under subsection (4) above with respect to an election of parish or community councillors may modify the provisions of—

(i) this Act (and the rules with respect to such elections under section 36); and

(ii) any other enactment relating to such elections.

(7) In the case of a common parish council under which are grouped, by virtue of section 11(5) of the Local Government Act 1972 (grouping of parishes), parishes situated in different districts, references in subsections (4) and (6) above to the district council shall be construed as references to the council of the district in which there is the greater number of local government electors for the parishes in the group.

(8) Two copies of every order made by a district council under this section shall be sent to the Secretary of State.

PART I

(9) If a municipal election in a London borough is not held on the appointed day or within the appointed time or becomes void, the municipal corporation shall not thereby be dissolved or be disabled from acting.

Timing as to local elections in England and Wales.

40.—(1) When the day on which anything is required to be done by section 37 or section 39 above is a Sunday, day of the Christmas break, of the Easter break or of a bank holiday break or a day appointed for public thanksgiving or mourning, the requirement shall be deemed to relate to the first day thereafter which is not one of the days specified above.

In this subsection—

" bank holiday break " means any bank holiday not included in the Christmas break or the Easter break and the period beginning with the last week day before that bank holiday and ending with the next week day which is not a bank holiday ;

" Christmas break " means the period beginning with the last day before Christmas Day and ending with the first week day after Christmas Day which is not a bank holiday ;

" Easter break " means the period beginning with the Thursday before and ending with the Tuesday after Easter day.

(2) Where under subsection (1) above the day of election is postponed, the day to which it is postponed shall be treated for the purposes of this Act and the Local Government Act 1972 as the day of election.

1972 c. 70.

(3) In computing any period of time for the purpose of any rules under section 36 above or for the purposes of section 39 any day specified in subsection (1) shall be disregarded ; but where between the giving of a notice of election and the completion of the poll a day is declared to be a bank holiday or day of public thanksgiving or mourning, the foregoing provison, so far as it relates to any such rules, shall not operate to invalidate any act which would have been valid apart from that provision.

This subsection, so far as it relates to any such rules, has effect subject to the provisions of those rules.

Conduct of local government elections in Scotland

Returning officers: local elections in Scotland.

41.—(1) Every local authority in Scotland shall appoint an officer of the authority to be the returning officer for each election of councillors for the authority, and if the person so appointed dies, resigns or is for any other reason unable to act, the authority may appoint another person to be returning officer at that election. PART I

(2) A returning officer in Scotland appointed under this Act may by writing under his hand appoint one or more persons to discharge all or any of his functions.

(3) A local government election in Scotland is not liable to be questioned by reason of a defect in the title, or want of title, of the person presiding at or conducting the election, if that person was then in actual possession of, or acting in, the office giving the right to preside at or conduct the election.

42.—(1) Elections of councillors for local government areas in Scotland shall be conducted in accordance with rules made by the Secretary of State. Local elections in Scotland.

(2) Rules made under this section shall apply the parliamentary elections rules in Schedule 1 to this Act subject to such adaptations, alterations and exceptions as seem appropriate to the Secretary of State.

(3) Without prejudice to the generality of subsection (2) above, rules made under this section shall prescribe that the nomination paper of a candidate for election as a councillor for a local government area in Scotland shall contain a statement declaring that the candidate—

(*a*) consents to be nominated as a candidate ;

(*b*) if elected, will accept office as a councillor and will faithfully perform the duties of the office ;

(*c*) has attained the age of 21 years and is a Commonwealth citizen or citizen of the Republic of Ireland and not subject to any legal incapacity, and

(*d*) is not subject to any of the disqualifications for office set out in section 31 of the Local Government (Scotland) Act 1973 (disqualifications for office as local authority member). 1973 c. 65.

(4) The statement mentioned in subsection (3) above shall also contain particulars of the candidate's qualification for office under paragraphs (*a*) to (*d*) of section 29(1) of that Act of 1973 (qualifications for office as local authority member), in such form as may be prescribed by rules made under this section.

(5) All expenditure properly incurred by a returning officer in relation to the holding of an election of a councillor to a local authority shall be paid by the council of that authority, but only (in cases where there is a scale fixed for the purposes of this section by that council) in so far as it does not exceed that scale.

PART I

(6) Before a poll is taken at an election for a councillor for a local government area in Scotland, the council for that area shall, at the request of the returning officer or of any person acting as returning officer, advance to him such reasonable sum in respect of his expenses at the election as he may require.

(7) Rules made under this section shall be—

(*a*) made by statutory instrument;

(*b*) subject to annulment in pursuance of a resolution of either House of Parliament.

Day of ordinary local elections in Scotland, and other timing provisions.

43.—(1) In every year in which ordinary elections of councillors for local government areas in Scotland are held, the day of election is the first Thursday in May.

(2) Where—

(*a*) the day or the last day on which anything is required or permitted to be done by any rules under section 42 above, or

(*b*) the day on which anything is required to be done under subsection (1) above, or section 44(2) or section 45(1) below,

is a Sunday, Christmas Day, New Year's Day, Good Friday, bank holiday, or a public holiday, or a day appointed for public thanksgiving or mourning, the requirement or permission shall be deemed to relate to the first day thereafter which is not one of the days before mentioned, but, save as aforesaid or as otherwise expressly provided in this Act or by the Local Government (Scotland) Act 1973, in reckoning a number of days for the purposes of this Act, the days before specified shall not be excluded.

1973 c. 65.

(3) Where an election is postponed under subsection (2) above, the day on which the election is held shall be treated as the day of election for all purposes of this Act or that Act of 1973 relating to that election.

(4) Where a day is declared to be a bank holiday or day of public thanksgiving or mourning, nothing in subsection (3) above affects the validity of any act done in relation to an election before or on the date of the declaration.

Candidate's death in local election in Scotland.

44.—(1) If at a contested election of a councillor for a local authority in Scotland proof is given to the returning officer's satisfaction before the result of the election is declared that one of the persons named or to be named as a candidate in the ballot papers has died, then the returning officer—

(*a*) shall countermand the poll, or

PART I

(*b*) if polling has begun, shall direct that the poll be abandoned.

(2) The returning officer for the election which by reason of such countermanding or abandonment has not been duly held or has failed—

(*a*) shall order an election to be held as soon as practicable after that, on a date to be fixed by him ; and

(*b*) shall remain the returning officer for that election.

(3) At any such election, no fresh nomination is necessary in the case of a candidate who remained validly nominated for the election in respect of which the poll was countermanded or abandoned.

Non-election of local authority etc. in Scotland.

45.—(1) If in Scotland—

(*a*) for any reason a local authority or members of a local authority are not elected in accordance with the provisions of this Act and the Local Government (Scotland) Act 1973, and the case is not otherwise provided for, or

1973 c. 65.

(*b*) there is for any reason no legally constituted local authority for any area, or

(*c*) the number of members of a local authority then in office is less than the quorum ascertained in accordance with the provisions of Schedule 7 to that Act of 1973 (meetings and proceedings of local authorities),

the Secretary of State may direct the holding of an election for filling such vacancies as exist, and the election shall be held as soon as practicable after that, on a date to be fixed by him.

(2) The Secretary of State may in that direction—

(*a*) make such provision as appears to him expedient for authorising any person to act in place of a local authority pending the election of members of the authority by an election under subsection (1) above ; and

(*b*) make such incidental, consequential, transitional or supplemental provision as appears to him to be necessary or proper.

Supplemental provisions as to local government elections

Further provision as to local election voting.

46.—(1) At a local government election for any electoral area no person shall as an elector and no person shall as proxy for any one elector—

(*a*) give more than one vote for any one candidate ; or

(*b*) give more votes in all than the total number of councillors to be elected for the electoral area.

PART I

(2) No person is subject to any incapacity to vote at a local government election by reason of his being or acting as returning officer at that election.

Loan of equipment for local elections.

47.—(1) Any ballot boxes, fittings and compartments provided for parliamentary elections out of moneys provided by Parliament, may, on request, be lent to the returning officer at a local government election on such terms and conditions as the Treasury may determine.

(2) Any ballot boxes, fittings and compartments provided by or belonging to—

1972 c. 70. (*a*) a local authority within the meaning of the Local Government Act 1972, or

1973 c. 65. (*b*) a local authority within the meaning of the Local Government (Scotland) Act 1973,

as the case may be, shall, on request, and if not required for immediate use by that authority, be lent to the returning officer at an election held under those Acts on such terms and conditions as may be agreed.

Validity of local elections, and legal costs.

48.—(1) No local government election shall be declared invalid by reason of any act or omission of the returning officer or any other person in breach of his official duty in connection with the election or otherwise of rules under section 36 or section 42 above if it appears to the tribunal having cognizance of the question that—

(*a*) the election was so conducted as to be substantially in accordance with the law as to elections ; and

(*b*) the act or omission did not affect its result.

(2) A local government election, unless questioned by an election petition within the period fixed by law for those proceedings, shall be deemed to have been to all intents a good and valid election.

(3) The council which is required to pay the expenses properly incurred by a returning officer in relation to any local government election may treat those expenses as including all costs properly incurred by the returning officer in connection with or in contemplation of any legal proceedings arising out of the election (including any criminal proceedings against the returning officer), whether or not the proceedings are in fact instituted.

(4) In Scotland the election of a member of a local authority shall not be affected by reason only of any nullity or irregularity in the election of any other member of the authority.

Supplemental provisions as to parliamentary and local government elections

Effect of registers.

49.—(1) The register of parliamentary electors shall for the purposes of this Part of this Act be conclusive on the following questions—

(*a*) whether or not a person registered in it was on the qualifying date resident at the address shown;

(*b*) whether or not that address is in any constituency or any particular part of a constituency;

(*c*) whether or not a person registered as an elector in a constituency in Northern Ireland was during the whole of the period of three months ending on the qualifying date resident in Northern Ireland;

(*d*) whether or not a person registered in it is registered as a service voter.

(2) The register of local government electors shall for the purposes of this Part be conclusive on the following questions—

(*a*) whether or not a person registered in it was on the qualifying date resident at the address shown;

(*b*) whether or not that address is in any local government area or any particular part of a local government area;

(*c*) whether or not a person registered in it is registered as a service voter.

(3) The relevant special lists prepared under this Act for a parliamentary or local government election shall, for the purposes of this Part, be conclusive on the following questions—

(*a*) whether or not a person's right to vote at the election is exercisable by post;

(*b*) whether or not there is in force an appointment of a proxy to vote for any person and (if so) who is appointed.

(4) Any entry in the register of parliamentary or local government electors, if it gives a date as that on which the person named will attain voting age, shall for any purpose of this Part relating to him as elector be conclusive that until the date given in the entry he is not of voting age nor entitled to be treated as an elector except for the purposes of an election at which the day fixed for the poll is that or a later date.

(5) A person registered as a parliamentary or local government elector, or entered in the list of proxies, shall not be excluded from voting on the ground—

(*a*) that he is not a Commonwealth citizen or citizen of the Republic of Ireland, or

PART I

(*b*) that he is not of voting age, or

(*c*) that he is otherwise subject to any legal incapacity to vote,

or that on the qualifying date or the date of his appointment, as the case may be—

(i) he was not a Commonwealth citizen or citizen of the Republic of Ireland, or

(ii) he was otherwise subject to any legal incapacity to vote,

but this provision shall not prevent the rejection of the vote on a scrutiny or affect his liability to any penalty for voting.

Effect of misdescription.

50. No misnomer or inaccurate description of any person or place named—

(*a*) in the register of parliamentary electors, or

(*b*) in the register of local government electors, or

(*c*) in any list, record, proxy paper, nomination paper, ballot paper, notice or other document required for the purposes of this Part of this Act, and the parliamentary elections rules,

affects the full operation of the document with respect to that person or place in any case where the description of the person or place is such as to be commonly understood.

Corrupt and illegal practices lists.

51.—(1) The registration officer shall in each year make out a corrupt and illegal practices list containing—

(*a*) the names and descriptions of the persons who, though otherwise qualified to be registered in the register of parliamentary electors for each constituency or part of a constituency for which he acts, are not so qualified by reason of having been convicted or reported guilty of a corrupt or illegal practice ; and

(*b*) a statement of the offence of which each person has been found guilty.

(2) The proper officer of the authority of each local government area shall in each year make out a corrupt and illegal practices list containing—

(*a*) the names and descriptions of the persons, who, though otherwise qualified to be registered in the register of local government electors for the area for which he acts, are not so qualified by reason of having been convicted or reported guilty of a corrupt or illegal practice ; and

(*b*) a statement of the offence of which each person has been found guilty.

PART I

Discharge of registration duties.

52.—(1) A registration officer shall comply with any general or special directions which may be given by the Secretary of State with respect to the arrangements to be made by the registration officer for carrying out his registration duties.

(2) Any of the duties and powers of a registration officer may be performed and exercised by any deputy for the time being approved by the Secretary of State or, in Scotland, by the council which appointed the registration officer, and the provisions of this Act apply to any such deputy so far as respects any duties or powers to be performed or exercised by him as they apply to the registration officer.

(3) In England and Wales, any acts authorised or required to be done by or with respect to the registration officer may, in the event of his incapacity to act or of a vacancy, be done by the proper officer of the council by whom the registration officer was appointed.

(4) In England and Wales, a district council or a London borough council may assign officers to assist the proper officer of the council in acting on the requisition of a registration officer or otherwise carrying out any of his duties in relation to the registration of electors and the conduct of parliamentary elections upon such terms as may be agreed between the council and the person carrying out the duties.

(5) In Scotland, the council of a region or islands area may assign officers to assist the registration officer in carrying out any of his duties in relation to the registration of electors upon such terms as may be agreed between the council and the person carrying out the duties.

Power to make regulations as to registration etc.

53.—(1) Provision may be made by regulations—

(*a*) with respect to the form of the register of electors and of the electors lists or any special lists or records required by this Act in connection with the register or with any election;

(*b*) with respect to the procedure to be followed in the preparation of the register, the electors lists and any such special lists or records as mentioned above, and with respect to the time, place and manner of their publication; and

(*c*) generally with respect to any matters incidental to the provisions of this Act so far as those provisions relate to the registration of electors or to voting by post or proxy.

(2) Those incidental matters include the time and manner of preparation and publication and form of, and the making and

PART I

determination of claims or objections with respect to, the corrupt and illegal practices lists.

(3) Without prejudice to the generality of subsections (1) and (2) above, regulations made with respect to the matters mentioned in those subsections may contain any such provisions as are mentioned in Schedule 2 to this Act.

Payment of expenses of registration.

54.—(1) Any expenses properly incurred by a registration officer in the performance of his registration duties (in this Act referred to as " registration expenses ") shall (except in Northern Ireland) be paid by the local authority by whom the registration officer was appointed.

(2) The registration expenses of the Chief Electoral Officer for Northern Ireland shall be paid out of moneys provided by Parliament.

(3) Any fees or other sums received by the registration officer in respect of his registration duties, other than sums paid to him in respect of his registration expenses—

(*a*) shall be accounted for by him and paid to the local authority by whom he was appointed ;

(*b*) in the case of the Chief Electoral Officer for Northern Ireland, shall be accounted for by him to the Secretary of State and paid into the Consolidated Fund.

(4) On the request of a registration officer for an advance on account of registration expenses—

(*a*) the local authority by whom the registration officer was appointed may, if they think fit, make such an advance to him of such an amount and subject to such conditions as they may approve ; or

(*b*) in the case of the Chief Electoral Officer for Northern Ireland, the Secretary of State may, if he thinks fit, make such an advance to him of such an amount and subject to such conditions as the Secretary of State may approve.

(5) Any registration expenses or contributions to them paid by the Common Council shall be paid out of the general rate and any sums paid to the Common Council under this section shall be placed to the credit of that rate.

Ascertainment of amount of registration expenses.

55.—(1) The registration expenses payable to a registration officer—

(*a*) include all proper and reasonable charges for his own personal remuneration for performing his registration duties and for the remuneration and expenses of any staff provided by a local authority to enable him to perform them ; but

(*b*) do not include any sum on account of the use of premises, furniture or equipment provided by a local authority in excess of the amount by which that authority's expenditure has been actually and directly increased by the use of those premises or of that furniture or equipment in connection with registration.

(2) The Secretary of State may frame a scale of registration expenses applicable to all or any class or classes of those expenses, and may alter the scale as and when he thinks fit, and any expenses incurred by a registration officer of a class to which the scale is applicable—

(*a*) shall be taken to be properly incurred if they do not exceed the maximum amount determined by or in accordance with the scale ; and

(*b*) shall be taken not to have been properly incurred so far as they do exceed that amount, unless the sanction (whether previous or not) of the Secretary of State and of the local authority is specially given for the excess.

(3) Nothing in paragraph (*a*) of subsection (2) above shall be construed as entitling a registration officer to receive payments in excess of the expenses actually incurred by him, except his proper and reasonable charges for his own personal remuneration.

(4) If any question arises whether any expenses incurred by a registration officer of a class to which no scale framed under this section is applicable have been properly incurred or not, that question shall be referred to the Secretary of State, and his decision on the question shall be final.

(5) This section does not apply to Northern Ireland.

Registration appeals: England and Wales.

56.—(1) An appeal lies to the county court—

(*a*) from any decision under this Act of the registration officer on any claim for registration or objection to a person's registration made to and considered by him,

(*b*) from any decision under this Act of the registration officer disallowing a person's application to be treated as an absent voter or to vote by post as proxy, in any case where the application is not made for a particular election only,

(*c*) from any decision under this Act of the registration officer to place or not to place against any name in the register a mark indicating that the person registered is, or is not, registered as a service voter,

PART I

(*d*) from any decision under this Act of the registration officer to make or not to make an alteration in a register as published,

but an appeal does not lie where the person desiring to appeal has not availed himself of a prescribed right to be heard by or make representations to the registration officer on the matter which is the subject of the appeal, or has not given the prescribed notice of appeal within the prescribed time.

(2) No appeal lies from the decision of the Court of Appeal on appeal from a decision of the county court under this section.

(3) An appeal to the county court or Court of Appeal by virtue of this section which is pending when notice of an election is given shall not prejudice the operation as respects the election of the decision appealed against, and anything done in pursuance of the decision shall be as good as if no such appeal had been brought and shall not be affected by the decision of the appeal.

(4) Notice shall be sent to the registration officer in manner provided by rules of court of the decision of the county court or of the Court of Appeal on any appeal by virtue of this section, and the registration officer shall make such alterations in the electors lists or register as may be required to give effect to the decision.

(5) The registration officer shall undertake such duties in connection with appeals brought by virtue of this section as may be prescribed and shall on any such appeal be deemed to be a party to the proceedings, and the registration expenses payable to a registration officer shall include any expenses properly incurred by him by virtue of this subsection.

(6) This section applies in relation to decisions on claims and objections with respect to any corrupt and illegal practices list as it applies in relation to the decisions mentioned in subsection (1) above but as if a reference to that list were included in the reference to the electors list and with any other prescribed modifications.

Registration appeals: Scotland.

57.—(1) Section 56 above applies to Scotland subject to the following modifications—

(*a*) subsection (2) shall be omitted ;

(*b*) an appeal lies on any point of law from any decision of the sheriff under this section to the court of three judges constituted under subsection (2) below ; and

(*c*) for any reference to the Court of Appeal there shall be substituted a reference to that court of three judges.

(2) The court for hearing appeals under paragraph (*b*) of subsection (1) above shall consist of three judges of the Court of Session who shall be appointed by the Court of Session by act of sederunt and of whom one judge shall be appointed from each division of the Inner House and one from the Lords Ordinary in the Outer House; and the Principal Clerk of Session shall be the clerk of the court.

PART I

(3) The Court of Session may by act of sederunt fill any vacancy in the court of three judges, and regulate its sittings and forms of process so as to carry out the provisions of this Act; and acts of sederunt under this section may be made, and the court of three judges may sit, either during the sitting of the Court of Session or in vacation or recess.

Registration appeals: Northern Ireland.

58. Section 56 above, except subsections (2) and (4), applies to Northern Ireland, and—

(*a*) any decision of a county court upon a point of law under section 56(1) shall be appealable in the same way and subject to the same provisions as a corresponding decision under the law relating to the registration of electors for elections of members to sit in the Northern Ireland Assembly and the reference in subsection (3) of that section to the Court of Appeal shall be construed accordingly; and

(*b*) any power to make rules of court with respect to appeals under that law applies to appeals under this section.

Supplemental provisions as to members of forces and service voters.

59.—(1) In this Part of this Act, the expression " member of the forces "—

(*a*) means a person serving on full pay as a member of any of the naval, military or air forces of the Crown raised in the United Kingdom; but

(*b*) does not include a person serving only as a member of a reserve or auxiliary force except in so far as regulations provide that it shall include persons so serving during a period of emergency.

(2) Where a person—

(*a*) is not a member of the forces as defined by subsection (1) above, but

(*b*) is, in the performance of his duty as a member of any of Her Majesty's reserve or auxiliary forces, absent on the qualifying date from an address at which he has been residing,

any question arising under section 5(2) above whether his residence at that address has been interrupted on that date by

PART I

his absence in the performance of that duty shall be determined as if the performance of it did not prevent his resuming actual residence at any time after that date.

(3) Arrangements shall be made by the appropriate government department for securing that (so far as circumstances permit) every person having a service qualification by virtue of paragraph (*a*) or (*b*) of section 14(1) above shall—

(*a*) have an effective opportunity of exercising from time to time as occasion may require the rights conferred on him by this Act in relation to the making and cancellation of service declarations and of appointments of a proxy, and in relation to voting by post; and

(*b*) receive such instructions as to the effect of this Act and any regulations made under it, and such other assistance, as may be reasonably sufficient in connection with the exercise by him and any wife of his or, as the case may be, by her and any husband of hers, of any rights conferred on them as mentioned above.

In this subsection " the appropriate government department " means, in relation to members of the forces, the Ministry of Defence, and in relation to any other person means the government department under which he is employed in the employment giving the service qualification.

(4) In relation to persons having a service qualification by virtue of paragraph (*c*) of section 14(1), the British Council shall be under a corresponding obligation to that imposed by subsection (3) above on the appropriate government department.

Offences

Personation.

60.—(1) A person shall be guilty of a corrupt practice if he commits, or aids, abets, counsels or procures the commission of, the offence of personation.

(2) A person shall be deemed to be guilty of personation at a parliamentary or local government election if he—

(*a*) votes in person or by post as some other person, whether as an elector or as proxy, and whether that other person is living or dead or is a fictitious person; or

(*b*) votes in person or by post as proxy—

(i) for a person whom he knows or has reasonable grounds for supposing to be dead or to be a fictitious person; or

(ii) when he knows or has reasonable grounds for supposing that his appointment as proxy is no longer in force.

(3) For the purposes of this section, a person who has applied for a ballot paper for the purpose of voting in person or who has marked, whether validly or not, and returned a ballot paper issued for the purpose of voting by post, shall be deemed to have voted.

Other voting offences.

61.—(1) A person shall be guilty of an offence if—

(*a*) he votes in person or by post, whether as an elector or as proxy, or applies to be treated as an absent voter or to vote by post as proxy, at a parliamentary or local government election, knowing that he is subject to a legal incapacity to vote ; or

(*b*) he applies for the appointment of a proxy to vote for him at parliamentary or local government elections, knowing that he or the person to be appointed is subject to a legal incapacity to vote ; or

(*c*) he votes, whether in person or by post, or applies to vote by post, as proxy for some other person at a parliamentary or local government election, knowing that that person is subject to a legal incapacity to vote.

For the purposes of this subsection references to a person being subject to a legal incapacity to vote do not, in relation to things done before polling day at the election or first election at or for which they are done, include his being below voting age if he will be of voting age on that day.

(2) A person shall be guilty of an offence if—

(*a*) he votes as elector otherwise than by proxy either—

(i) more than once in the same constituency at any parliamentary election, or more than once in the same electoral area at any local government election ; or

(ii) in more than one constituency at a general election, or in more than one electoral area at an ordinary election of councillors for a local government area which is not a single electoral area ; or

(iii) in any constituency at a general election, or in any electoral area at such an ordinary election as mentioned above, when there is in force an appointment of a person to vote as his proxy at the election in some other constituency or electoral area ; or

(*b*) he votes as elector in person at a parliamentary or local government election at which he is entitled to vote by post ; or

(*c*) he votes as elector in person at a parliamentary or local government election, knowing that a person appointed to vote as his proxy at the election either has already voted in person at the election or is entitled to vote by post at the election ; or

(*d*) not being a service voter, he applies for a person to be appointed as his proxy to vote for him at parliamentary elections without applying for the cancellation of a previous appointment of a third person then in force or without withdrawing a pending application for such an appointment.

(3) A person shall be guilty of an offence if—

(*a*) he votes as proxy for the same elector either—

(i) more than once in the same constitutency at any parliamentary election, or more than once in the same electoral area at any local government election ; or

(ii) in more than one constituency at a general election, or in more than one electoral area at an ordinary election of councillors for a local government area which is not a single electoral area ; or

(*b*) he votes in person as proxy for an elector at a parliamentary or local government election at which he is entitled to vote by post as proxy for that elector ; or

(*c*) he votes in person as proxy for an elector registered as a service voter at a parliamentary or local government election knowing that the elector is entitled to vote by post at the election ; or

(*d*) he votes in person as proxy for an elector at a parliamentary or local government election knowing that the elector has already voted in person at the election.

(4) A person shall also be guilty of an offence if he votes at a parliamentary election in any constituency as proxy for more than two persons of whom he is not the husband, wife, parent, grandparent, brother, sister, child or grandchild.

(5) A person shall also be guilty of an offence if he knowingly induces or procures some other person to do an act which is, or but for that other person's want of knowledge would be, an offence by that other person under the foregoing subsections of this section.

(6) For the purposes of this section a person who has applied for a ballot paper for the purpose of voting in person, or who has marked, whether validly or not, and returned a ballot paper issued for the purpose of voting by post, shall be deemed to have voted, but for the purpose of determining whether an application for a ballot paper constitutes an offence under subsection (4) above, a previous application made in circumstances

which entitle the applicant only to mark a tendered ballot paper shall, if he does not exercise that right, be disregarded.

(7) An offence under this section shall be an illegal practice, but—

(*a*) the court before whom a person is convicted of any such offence may, if they think it just in the special circumstances of the case, mitigate or entirely remit any incapacity imposed by virtue of section 173 below; and

(*b*) a candidate shall not be liable, nor shall his election be avoided, for an illegal practice under this section of any agent of his other than an offence under subsection (5) above.

Offences as to declarations.

62.—(1) A person who—

(*a*) makes a patient's declaration or a service declaration—

(i) when he is not authorised so to do by section 7(4) or section 15(1) above, as the case may be, or

(ii) except as permitted by this Act, when he knows that he is subject to a legal incapacity to vote, or

(iii) when he knows that it contains a statement which is false, or

(*b*) attests a patient's declaration or a service declaration, as the case may be, when he knows—

(i) that he is not authorised to do so, or

(ii) that it contains a false statement as to any particulars required by paragraph (*d*) of section 7(4), or by regulations under section 15, as the case may be,

shall be liable—

except in Northern Ireland, on summary conviction to imprisonment for a term not exceeding 6 months or to a fine not exceeding level 4 on the standard scale or to both;

in Northern Ireland, on summary conviction to imprisonment for a term not exceeding 3 months or to a fine not exceeding £50 or to both, or on conviction on indictment to imprisonment for a term not exceeding 6 months or to a fine not exceeding £100 or to both.

(2) Where the declaration is available only for local government elections the reference in subsection (1) above to a legal incapacity to vote refers to a legal incapacity to vote at local government elections.

PART I

Breach of official duty in parliamentary elections.

63.—(1) If a person to whom this section applies, or who is for the time being under a duty to discharge as deputy or otherwise any of the functions of such a person, is, without reasonable cause, guilty of any act or omission in breach of his official duty, then, subject to subsection (4) below, he shall be liable on summary conviction to a fine not exceeding level 3 on the standard scale, or, in Northern Ireland, a fine not exceeding £100.

(2) No person to whom this section applies shall be liable for breach of his official duty to any penalty at common law or under any enactment other than—

(*a*) section 65 below,

(*b*) section 66 below, or

(*c*) section 99(1) below,

nor shall any action for damages lie in respect of the breach by such a person of his official duty.

(3) Those to whom this section applies are—

(*a*) the Clerk of the Crown (or, in Northern Ireland, the Clerk of the Crown for Northern Ireland),

(*b*) any sheriff clerk, registration officer, returning officer, presiding officer, or clerk or assistant employed by such an officer, in connection with his official duties, and

(*c*) any postmaster,

and the expression " official duty " shall for the purposes of this section be construed accordingly, but shall not include duties imposed otherwise than by the law relating to parliamentary elections or the registration of parliamentary electors.

(4) Nothing in this section imposes liability to summary prosecution on a returning officer for a parliamentary election in Scotland or on a person under a duty to discharge the functions of such a returning officer.

Breach of official duty in local elections.

64.—(1) If a person to whom this section applies, or who is for the time being under a duty to discharge as deputy or otherwise any of the functions of such a person, is, without reasonable cause, guilty of any act or omission in breach of his official duty, he shall be liable on summary conviction to a fine not exceeding level 3 on the standard scale.

(2) No person to whom this section applies shall be liable for breach of his official duty to any penalty at common law, nor shall any action for damages lie in respect of the breach by such a person of his official duty.

(3) Those to whom this section applies are—

(*a*) any registration officer or person whose duty it is to prepare a corrupt and illegal practices list under section

51(2) above or clerk or assistant employed by him in connection with his official duties, PART I

(*b*) any person whose duty it is to act as returning officer at or to take part in the conduct of a local government election or to be responsible after a local government election for the used ballot papers and other documents (including returns and declarations as to expenses),

and the expression " official duty " shall for the purposes of this section be construed accordingly but shall not include duties imposed otherwise than by the law relating to local government elections or the registration of local government electors.

Tampering with nomination papers, ballot papers etc.

65.—(1) A person shall be guilty of an offence, if, at a parliamentary or local government election, he—

(*a*) fraudulently defaces or fraudulently destroys any nomination paper ; or

(*b*) fraudulently defaces or fraudulently destroys any ballot paper, or the official mark on any ballot paper, or any declaration of identity or official envelope used in connection with voting by post ; or

(*c*) without due authority supplies any ballot paper to any person ; or

(*d*) fraudulently puts into any ballot box any paper other than the ballot paper which he is authorised by law to put in ; or

(*e*) fraudulently takes out of the polling station any ballot paper ; or

(*f*) without due authority destroys, takes, opens or otherwise interferes with any ballot box or packet of ballot papers then in use for the purposes of the election ; or

(*g*) fraudulently or without due authority, as the case may be, attempts to do any of the foregoing acts.

(2) In Scotland, a person shall be guilty of an offence if—

(*a*) at a parliamentary or local government election, he forges any nomination paper, delivers to the returning officer any nomination paper knowing it to be forged, or forges or counterfeits any ballot paper or the official mark on any ballot paper ; or

(*b*) at a local government election, he signs any nomination paper as candidate or in any other capacity certifies the truth of any statement contained in it, knowing such statement to be false ; or

(*c*) he fraudulently or without due authority, as the case may be, attempts to do any of the foregoing acts.

PART I

(3) A person guilty of an offence under this section at a parliamentary election shall be liable—

(*a*) if he is a returning officer, a presiding officer or clerk in attendance at a polling station, or a clerk in attendance at the proceedings in connection with the issue or receipt of postal ballot papers, to imprisonment for a term not exceeding 2 years;

(*b*) if he is any other person, to imprisonment for a term not exceeding 6 months.

(4) If, at a local government election in England and Wales, a person is guilty of any offence specified in paragraph (*a*) of subsection (1) above, or of any attempt to commit such offence, he shall be liable on summary conviction to imprisonment for a term not exceeding 6 months or to a fine not exceeding level 2 on the standard scale or to both.

(5) A person guilty of an offence under this section at a local government election (other than an offence punishable under subsection (4) above) shall—

(*a*) if he is a returning officer, a presiding officer or clerk appointed to assist in taking the poll or counting the votes or a clerk appointed to assist at the proceedings in connection with the issue or receipt of postal ballot papers, be liable, on conviction on indictment, to imprisonment for a term not exceeding 2 years;

(*b*) if he is any other person, be liable—

(i) on summary conviction to a fine not exceeding the statutory maximum or to imprisonment for a term not exceeding 6 months or to both;

(ii) on conviction on indictment to a fine or to imprisonment for a term not exceeding 6 months or to both.

Requirement of secrecy.

66.—(1) The following persons—

(*a*) every returning officer and every presiding officer or clerk attending at a polling station,

(*b*) every candidate or election agent or polling agent so attending,

shall maintain and aid in maintaining the secrecy of voting and shall not, except for some purpose authorised by law, communicate to any person before the poll is closed any information as to—

(i) the name of any elector or proxy for an elector who has or has not applied for a ballot paper or voted at a polling station;

(ii) the number on the register of electors of any elector who, or whose proxy, has or has not applied for a ballot paper or voted at a polling station; or

(iii) the official mark.

(2) Every person attending at the counting of the votes shall maintain and aid in maintaining the secrecy of voting and shall not—

(*a*) ascertain or attempt to ascertain at the counting of the votes the number on the back of any ballot paper;

(*b*) communicate any information obtained at the counting of the votes as to the candidate for whom any vote is given on any particular ballot paper.

(3) No person shall—

(*a*) interfere with or attempt to interfere with a voter when recording his vote;

(*b*) otherwise obtain or attempt to obtain in a polling station information as to the candidate for whom a voter in that station is about to vote or has voted;

(*c*) communicate at any time to any person any information obtained in a polling station as to the candidate for whom a voter in that station is about to vote or has voted, or as to the number on the back of the ballot paper given to a voter at that station;

(*d*) directly or indirectly induce a voter to display his ballot paper after he has marked it so as to make known to any person the name of the candidate for whom he has or has not voted.

(4) Every person attending the proceedings in connection with the issue or the receipt of ballot papers for persons voting by post shall maintain and aid in maintaining the secrecy of the voting and shall not—

(*a*) except for some purpose authorised by law, communicate, before the poll is closed, to any person any information obtained at those proceedings as to the official mark; or

(*b*) except for some purpose authorised by law, communicate to any person at any time any information obtained at those proceedings as to the number on the back of the ballot paper sent to any person; or

(*c*) except for some purpose authorised by law, attempt to ascertain at the proceedings in connection with the receipt of ballot papers the number on the back of any ballot paper; or

(*d*) attempt to ascertain at the proceedings in connection with the receipt of the ballot papers the candidate for whom any vote is given in any particular ballot paper or communicate any information with respect thereto obtained at those proceedings.

PART I

(5) No person having undertaken to assist a blind voter to vote shall communicate at any time to any person any information as to the candidate for whom that voter intends to vote or has voted, or as to the number on the back of the ballot paper given for the use of that voter.

(6) If a person acts in contravention of this section he shall be liable on summary conviction to imprisonment for a term not exceeding 6 months.

PART II

THE ELECTION CAMPAIGN

The election agent

Appointment of election agent.

67.—(1) Not later than the latest time for the delivery of notices of withdrawals for an election, a person shall be named by or on behalf of each candidate as the candidate's election agent, and the name and address of the candidate's election agent shall be declared in writing by the candidate or some other person on his behalf to the appropriate officer not later than that time.

(2) A candidate may name himself as election agent, and upon doing so shall, so far as circumstances admit, be subject to the provisions of this Act both as a candidate and as an election agent, and, except where the context otherwise requires, any reference in this Act to an election agent shall be construed to refer to the candidate acting in his capacity of election agent.

(3) One election agent only shall be appointed for each candidate, but the appointment, whether the election agent appointed be the candidate himself or not, may be revoked.

(4) If whether before, during or after the election the appointment of an election agent is revoked or an election agent dies, another election agent shall be appointed forthwith and his name and address declared in writing to the appropriate officer.

(5) The declaration as a candidate's election agent of a person other than the candidate shall be of no effect under this section unless it is made and signed by that person or is accompanied by a written declaration of acceptance signed by him.

(6) Upon the name and address of an election agent being declared to the appropriate officer, the appropriate officer shall forthwith give public notice of that name and address.

(7) In this Part of this Act the expression " appropriate officer " means—

(*a*) in relation to a parliamentary election, the returning officer ;

(b) in relation to a local government election, the proper officer of the authority for which the election is held.

PART II

Nomination of sub-agent at parliamentary elections.

68.—(1) In the case of a parliamentary election for a county constituency an election agent for a candidate may appoint to act in any part of the constituency one, but not more than one, deputy election agent (in this Act referred to as a sub-agent).

(2) As regards matters in a part of the constituency for which there is a sub-agent the election agent may act by the sub-agent and—

(a) anything done for the purposes of this Act by or to the sub-agent in his part of the constituency shall be deemed to be done by or to the election agent; and

(b) any act or default of a sub-agent which, if he were the election agent, would be an illegal practice or other offence against this Act shall be an illegal practice and offence against this Act committed by the sub-agent, and the sub-agent shall be liable to punishment accordingly; and

(c) the candidate shall suffer the like incapacity as if that act or default had been the election agent's act or default.

(3) One clear day before the day of the poll the election agent shall declare in writing the name and address of every sub-agent to the appropriate officer, and the appropriate officer shall forthwith give public notice of the name and address of every sub-agent so declared.

(4) The appointment of a sub-agent—

(a) shall not be vacated by the election agent who appointed him ceasing to be election agent, but

(b) may be revoked by whoever is for the time being the candidate's election agent,

and in the event of the revocation of the appointment or of the death of a sub-agent another sub-agent may be appointed, and his name and address shall be forthwith declared in writing to the appropriate officer, who shall forthwith give public notice of the name and address so declared.

(5) The declaration to be made to the appropriate officer, and the notice to be given by him, under subsection (3) or subsection (4) above shall specify the part of the constituency within which any sub-agent is appointed to act.

Office of election agent and sub-agent.

69.—(1) Every election agent and every sub-agent shall have an office to which all claims, notices, writs, summonses and documents may be sent, and the address of the office shall be—

(a) declared to the appropriate officer at the same time as the appointment of the agent; and

PART II

(*b*) stated in the public notice of the name of the agent.

(2) The office—

(*a*) of the election agent for a parliamentary election shall be within the constituency or an adjoining constituency or in a London borough or district which is partly comprised in or adjoins the constituency, and that of a sub-agent shall be in the area within which he is appointed to act; and

(*b*) of an election agent for a local government election shall be within the local government area or in the constituency or one of the constituencies in which the area is comprised or in a London borough or district which adjoins it.

(3) Any claim, notice, writ, summons or document delivered at the office of the election agent or sub-agent and addressed to him, shall be deemed to have been served on him and every election agent or sub-agent may in respect of any matter connected with the election in which he is acting be sued in any court having jurisdiction at the place where his office is situated.

Effect of default in election agent's appointment.

70.—(1) If no person's name and address is given as required by section 67 above as the election agent of a candidate who remains validly nominated at the latest time for delivery of notices of withdrawals, the candidate shall be deemed at that time to have named himself as election agent and to have revoked any appointment of another person as his election agent.

(2) If—

(*a*) the person whose name and address have been so given as those of the candidate's election agent (not being the candidate himself) dies, and

(*b*) a new appointment is not made on the day of the death or on the following day,

the candidate shall be deemed to have appointed himself as from the time of death.

(3) If the appointment of a candidate's election agent is revoked without a new appointment being made, the candidate himself shall be deemed to have been appointed (or re-appointed) election agent.

(4) Where a candidate is by virtue of this section to be treated as his own election agent, he shall be deemed to have his office—

(*a*) at his address as given in the statement as to persons nominated; or

(*b*) if that address is outside the permitted area for the office, at the qualifying address of the person (or first person) named in that statement as his proposer.

PART II

(5) Where in a local government election in Scotland a candidate is by virtue of this section to be treated as his own election agent, he shall be deemed to have his office—

(*a*) at his address as given in his nomination paper or papers, or

(*b*) if that address is outside the permitted area for the office, at the address of the person named as the proposer of the candidate in the nomination paper first delivered in which the address of the proposer is in the local government area.

(6) The appropriate officer on being satisfied that a candidate is by virtue of this section to be treated as his own election agent, shall forthwith proceed to publish the like notice as if the name and address of the candidate and the address of his office had been duly given to him under sections 67 and 69 above.

Elections where election agent not required.

71. A candidate—

(*a*) at an election in England of parish councillors, or in Wales of community councillors, or

(*b*) at any election under the local government Act which is not a local government election,

need not have an election agent, and accordingly the foregoing provisions of this Part of this Act do not apply to those elections.

Election expenses

Making of contracts through election agent.

72.—(1) The election agent of a candidate shall appoint every polling agent, clerk and messenger employed for payment on behalf of the candidate at an election, and hire every committee room hired on behalf of the candidate.

(2) A contract by which any election expenses are incurred shall not be enforceable against a candidate at the election unless made by the candidate himself or by his election agent, but this subsection does not relieve the candidate from the consequences of any corrupt or illegal practice having been committed by his agent.

(3) The references in this section to an election agent shall, in relation to a parliamentary election where sub-agents are allowed, be taken as references to the election agent acting by himself or a sub-agent.

Payment of expenses through election agent.

73.—(1) Except as permitted by section 74 below, or in pursuance of section 78 or section 79 below, no payment and no advance or deposit shall be made—

(*a*) by a candidate, or

(*b*) by any agent on behalf of a candidate, or

PART II

(*c*) by any other person,

at any time in respect of election expenses otherwise than by or through the candidate's election agent.

(2) Every payment made by an election agent in respect of any election expenses shall, except where less than £2, be vouched for by a bill stating the particulars and by a receipt.

(3) The references in the foregoing provisions of this section to an election agent shall, in relation to a parliamentary election where sub-agents are allowed, be taken as references to the election agent acting by himself or a sub-agent.

(4) All money provided by any person other than the candidate for any election expenses, whether as gift, loan, advance or deposit, shall be paid to the candidate or his election agent and not otherwise.

(5) The foregoing provisions of this section shall not be deemed to apply to any sum disbursed by any person out of his own money for any small expense legally incurred by him if the sum is not repaid to him.

(6) A person who makes any payment, advance or deposit in contravention of subsection (1) above, or pays in contravention of subsection (4) above any money so provided as mentioned above, shall be guilty of an illegal practice.

Candidate's personal expenses, and petty expenses.

74.—(1) The candidate at an election may pay any personal expenses incurred by him on account of or in connection with or incidental to the election, but the amount which a candidate at a parliamentary election may pay shall not exceed £100, and any further personal expenses so incurred by him shall be paid by his election agent.

(2) The candidate shall send to his election agent within the time limited by this Act for sending in claims a written statement of the amount of personal expenses paid as mentioned above by the candidate.

(3) Any person may, if so authorised in writing by the candidate's election agent, pay any necessary expenses for stationery, postage, telegrams (or any similar means of communication) and other petty expenses, to a total amount not exceeding that named in the authority, but any excess above the total amount so named shall be paid by the election agent.

(4) A statement of the particulars of payments made by any person so authorised shall be sent to the election agent within the time limited by this Act for sending in claims, and shall be vouched for by a bill containing that person's receipt.

PART II

Prohibition of expenses not authorised by election agent.

75.—(1) No expenses shall, with a view to promoting or procuring the election of a candidate at an election, be incurred by any person other than the candidate, his election agent and persons authorised in writing by the election agent on account—

(*a*) of holding public meetings or organising any public display; or

(*b*) of issuing advertisements, circulars or publications; or

(*c*) of otherwise presenting to the electors the candidate or his views or the extent or nature of his backing or disparaging another candidate,

but paragraph (*c*) of this subsection shall not—

(i) restrict the publication of any matter relating to the election in a newspaper or other periodical or in a broadcast made by the British Broadcasting Corporation or the Independent Broadcasting Authority; or

(ii) apply to any expenses not exceeding in the aggregate the sum of 50p which may be incurred by an individual and are not incurred in pursuance of a plan suggested by or concerted with others, or to expenses incurred by any person in travelling or in living away from home or similar personal expenses.

(2) Where a person incurs any expenses required by this section to be authorised by the election agent—

(*a*) that person shall within 14 days after the date of publication of the result of the election send to the appropriate officer a return of the amount of those expenses, stating the election at which and the candidate in whose support they were incurred, and

(*b*) the return shall be accompanied by a declaration made by that person (or in the case of an association or body of persons, by a director, general manager, secretary or other similar officer of the association or body) verifying the return and giving particulars of the matters for which the expenses were incurred,

but this subsection does not apply to any person engaged or employed for payment or promise of payment by the candidate or his election agent.

(3) The return and declaration under the foregoing provisions of this section shall be in the prescribed form, and the authority received from the election agent shall be annexed to and deemed to form part of the return.

(4) A copy of every return and declaration made under subsection (2) above in relation to a parliamentary election in England, Wales or Northern Ireland shall be sent to the Clerk of the Crown within 14 days after the date of publication of the result

PART II

of the election by the person making the return or declaration, and rule 57 of the parliamentary elections rules applies to any documents sent to the Clerk of the Crown under this subsection.

In this subsection references to the Clerk of the Crown in relation to an election in Northern Ireland are references to the Clerk of the Crown for Northern Ireland.

(5) If a person—

(*a*) incurs, or aids, abets, counsels or procures any other person to incur, any expenses in contravention of this section, or

(*b*) knowingly makes the declaration required by subsection (2) falsely,

he shall be guilty of a corrupt practice; and if a person fails to send any declaration or return or a copy of it as required by this section he shall be guilty of an illegal practice, but—

(i) the court before whom a person is convicted under this subsection may, if they think it just in the special circumstances of the case, mitigate or entirely remit any incapacity imposed by virtue of section 173 below; and

(ii) a candidate shall not be liable, nor shall his election be avoided, for a corrupt or illegal practice under this subsection committed by an agent without his consent or connivance.

(6) Where any act or omission of an association or body of persons, corporate or unincorporate, is an offence declared to be a corrupt or illegal practice by this section, any person who at the time of the act or omission was a director, general manager, secretary or other similar officer of the association or body, or was purporting to act in any such capacity, shall be deemed to be guilty of that offence, unless he proves—

(*a*) that the act or omission took place without his consent or connivance; and

(*b*) that he exercised all such diligence to prevent the commission of the offence as he ought to have exercised having regard to the nature of his functions in that capacity and to all the circumstances.

Limitation of election expenses.

76.—(1) No sum shall be paid and no expense shall be incurred by a candidate at an election or his election agent, whether before, during or after an election, on account of or in respect of the conduct or management of the election, in excess of the maximum amount specified in this section, and a candidate or election agent knowingly acting in contravention of this subsection shall be guilty of an illegal practice.

(2) That maximum amount is— PART II

(*a*) for a candidate at a parliamentary election—

(i) in a county constituency, £2,700 together with an additional 3.1p for every entry in the register of electors to be used at the election (as first published); and

(ii) in a borough constituency, £2,700 together with an additional 2.3p for every entry in the register of electors to be used at the election (as first published);

(*b*) for a candidate at a local government election—

(i) at an election to the Greater London Council, £500 together with an additional 3p for every entry in the register of electors to be used at the election (as first published);

(ii) at any other local government election, £120 together with an additional 2.4p for every entry in the register of electors to be used at the election (as first published).

(3) The Secretary of State may by order vary a maximum amount of candidates' election expenses specified in subsection (2) above where in his opinion there has been a change in the value of money since the last occasion on which that amount was varied by such an order, and the variation shall be such as in his opinion is justified by that change.

An order under this subsection shall not be made unless a draft of the order has been laid before, and approved by resolution of, each House of Parliament; and the power to make the order is exercisable by statutory instrument.

(4) If the register to be used at the election is not published before the day of publication of the notice of election then for any reference in subsection (2) above to an entry in that register there shall be substituted a reference to an entry in the electors lists for that register as first published which gives the name of a person appearing from those lists to be entitled to be registered.

(5) The maximum amount mentioned above for a candidate at a parliamentary election is not required to cover the candidate's personal expenses.

(6) Where at an election a poll is countermanded or abandoned by reasons of a candidate's death, the maximum amount of election expenses shall, for any of the other candidates who then remain validly nominated, be twice or, if there has been a previous increase under this subsection, three times what it would have been but for any increase under this subsection; but the maximum amount shall not be affected for any candidate by the change in the timing of the election or of any step in the proceedings at the election.

PART II

Expenses limit for joint candidates at local election.

77.—(1) Where there are two or more joint candidates at a local government election the maximum amount mentioned in section 76 above shall, for each of those joint candidates, be reduced by a quarter or, if there are more than two joint candidates, by one-third.

(2) Where two or more candidates appoint the same election agent, or by themselves or any agent or agents—

(*a*) employ or use the services of the same clerks or messengers at the election, or

(*b*) hire or use the same committee rooms for the election, or

(*c*) publish a joint address, circular or notice at the election,

those candidates shall for the purposes of this section be deemed to be joint candidates ; but—

(i) the employment and use of the same clerk, messenger or committee room, if accidental or casual, or of a trivial and unimportant character, shall not be deemed of itself to constitute persons joint candidates ;

(ii) nothing in this subsection shall prevent candidates from ceasing to be joint candidates.

(3) Where—

(*a*) any excess of expenses above the maximum allowed for one of two or more joint candidates has arisen owing to his having ceased to be a joint candidate, or to his having become a joint candidate after having begun to conduct his election as a separate candidate,

(*b*) the change was made in good faith,

(*c*) the excess is not more than under the circumstances is reasonable, and

(*d*) the total election expenses of the candidate do not exceed the maximum amount allowed for a separate candidate,

the excess shall be deemed to have arisen from a reasonable cause for the purposes of section 167 below.

Time for sending in and paying claims.

78.—(1) Every claim against a candidate or his election agent in respect of election expenses which is not sent in to the election agent within 14 days after the day on which the result of the election is declared shall be barred and not paid.

(2) All election expenses shall be paid within 28 days after that day.

(3) An election agent who pays a claim in contravention of subsection (1) or makes a payment in contravention of subsection (2) above shall be guilty of an illegal practice ; but where the election court reports that it has been proved to the court by the candidate that any payment was made by an election agent without the sanction or connivance of the candidate—

(*a*) the candidate's election shall not be void, nor

(*b*) shall he be subject to any incapacity under this Act by reason only of that payment having been made in contravention of this section.

(4) The claimant or the candidate or his election agent may apply to the High Court or to a county court for leave to pay a claim for any election expenses, although sent in after that period of 14 days or although sent in to the candidate and not to the election agent, and the court on cause shown to their satisfaction may by order grant the leave.

In relation to an application in respect of expenses for a local government election in Scotland the reference in this subsection to the High Court shall be omitted.

(5) Any sum specified in the order of leave may be paid by the candidate or his election agent and when paid in pursuance of the leave shall not be deemed to be in contravention of subsection (2) above.

(6) Except in Scotland, the jurisdiction vested by subsection (4) above in the High Court in matters relating to parliamentary elections shall, subject to rules of court, be exercised by—

(*a*) one of the judges for the time being on the rota for the trial of parliamentary election petitions,

(*b*) in Northern Ireland, one of the judges of the High Court or the Court of Appeal for the time being selected under section 108 of the Judicature (Northern Ireland) Act 1978, 1978 c. 23.

sitting either in court or at chambers, or by a master of the Supreme Court in manner directed by and subject to an appeal to those judges.

(7) The jurisdiction vested by subsection (4) in a county court may, except in Northern Ireland, be exercised otherwise than in open court and, in Northern Ireland, shall be exercised in such manner as may be provided by rules of court.

An appeal lies to the High Court from any order of a county court made by virtue of subsection (4).

Disputed claims.

79.—(1) If the election agent disputes any claim sent in to him within the period of 14 days mentioned in section 78 above or refuses or fails to pay the claim within the period of 28 days so mentioned, the claim shall be deemed to be a disputed claim.

(2) The claimant may, if he thinks fit, bring an action for a disputed claim in any competent court, and any sum paid by the candidate or his agent in pursuance of the judgment or order of the court shall not be deemed to be in contravention of section 73(1) above or of section 78(2).

PART II

(3) If the defendant in the action admits his liability but disputes the amount of the claim, that amount shall, unless the court on the plaintiff's application otherwise directs, be forthwith referred for taxation—

(*a*) to a Circuit judge nominated under subsection (1)(*a*) of section 68 of the Supreme Court Act 1981, or

1981 c. 54.

(*b*) to the master, registrar or other proper officer of the court,

and the amount found due on the taxation shall be the amount to be recovered in the action in respect of the claim.

(4) Subsections (4) to (7) of section 78 apply in relation to a disputed claim as they apply in relation to a claim for election expenses sent in after that period of 14 days.

Election agent's claim.

80. So far as circumstances admit, this Act applies to an election agent's claim for his remuneration and to its payment in like manner as if he were any other creditor, and if any difference arises about the amount of the claim, the claim shall be a disputed claim within the meaning of this Act and be dealt with accordingly.

Return as to election expenses.

81.—(1) Within 35 days after the day on which the result of the election is declared, the election agent of every candidate at the election shall transmit to the appropriate officer a true return in the form set out in Schedule 3 to this Act, or to the like effect, containing as respects that candidate a statement of all payments made by the election agent together with all the bills and receipts.

(2) The return shall deal under a separate heading or sub-heading with any expenses included in it—

(*a*) as respects which a return is required to be made under section 75(2) above; or

(*b*) which are on account of the remuneration or expenses of speakers at public meetings.

(3) The return shall also contain as respects that candidate—

(*a*) a statement of the amount of personal expenses, if any, paid by the candidate;

(*b*) a statement of all disputed claims of which the election agent is aware;

(*c*) a statement of all the unpaid claims, if any, of which the election agent is aware, in respect of which application has been or is about to be made to the High Court or county court;

(*d*) a statement of all money, securities and equivalent of money received by the election agent from the candidate or any other person for the purposes of election expenses incurred or to be incurred, with a statement of the name of every person from whom they may have been received.

(4) Where the candidate is his own election agent, a statement of all money, securities and equivalent of money paid by the candidate shall be substituted in the return as to election expenses for the statement of money, securities and equivalent of money received by the election agent from the candidate.

(5) Where after the date at which the return as to election expenses is transmitted, leave is given by the court under section 78(4) above for any claim to be paid, the candidate or his election agent shall, within seven days after its payment, transmit to the appropriate officer a return of the sums paid in pursuance of the leave, accompanied by a copy of the order of the court giving the leave, and in default he shall be deemed to have failed to comply with the requirements of this section without such authorised excuse as is mentioned in section 86 below.

Declarations as to election expenses.

82.—(1) The return transmitted under section 81(1) above shall be accompanied by a declaration made by the election agent in the form in Schedule 3 to this Act.

(2) At the same time that the election agent transmits that return, or within seven days afterwards, the candidate shall transmit or cause to be transmitted to the appropriate officer a declaration made by him in the form in that Schedule.

(3) Where the candidate is out of the United Kingdom when the return is so transmitted—

(*a*) the declaration required by subsection (2) above may be made by him within 14 days after his return to the United Kingdom, and

(*b*) in that case, the declaration shall be forthwith transmitted to the appropriate officer,

but the delay authorised by this provision in making the declaration shall not exonerate the election agent from complying with the provisions of this Act relating to the return and declaration as to election expenses.

(4) An election agent's or a candidate's declaration as to election expenses under this section may be made either before a justice of the peace or before any person who is—

(*a*) in England and Wales, the chairman or proper officer of the Greater London Council, a county council or a district council, or the mayor or proper officer of a London borough;

(*b*) in Scotland, the proper officer of a regional, islands or district council;

(*c*) in Northern Ireland, the clerk of a district council.

PART II

(5) Where the candidate is his own election agent, the declaration by an election agent as to election expenses need not be made and the declaration by the candidate as to election expenses shall be modified as specified in the form in Schedule 3.

(6) If a candidate or election agent knowingly makes the declaration required by this section falsely, he shall be guilty of a corrupt practice.

Where no return and declarations needed at parliamentary elections.

83. Notwithstanding anything in sections 81 and 82 above, no return or declaration as to election expenses shall be required in the case of a person—

(*a*) who is a candidate at a parliamentary election, but is so only because he has been declared by others to be a candidate; and

(*b*) who has not consented to the declaration or taken any part as a candidate in the election.

Penalty for failure as respects return or declarations.

84. Subject to the provisions of section 86 below, if a candidate or election agent fails to comply with the requirements of section 81 or section 82 above he shall be guilty of an illegal practice.

Penalty for sitting or voting where no return and declarations transmitted.

85.—(1) If, in the case of any candidate, the return and declarations as to election expenses are not transmitted before the expiry of the time limited for the purpose, that candidate shall not, after the expiry of that time, sit or vote in the House of Commons as member for the constituency for which the election was held until—

(*a*) either that return and those declarations have been transmitted, or

(*b*) the date of the allowance of an authorised excuse for the failure to transmit that return and those declarations,

and if he sits or votes in contravention of this subsection he shall forfeit £100 for every day on which he so sits or votes.

(2) In the application of subsection (1) above to a candidate at a local government election—

(*a*) the reference to sitting or voting in the House of Commons for the constituency for which the election was held shall be taken as a reference to sitting or voting in the council for the local government area for which the election was held; and

(*b*) £50 shall be substituted for £100 and, instead of civil proceedings for a penalty, summary proceedings may be instituted under the Magistrates' Courts Act 1980, or, in Scotland, in the sheriff court, and the person charged

1980 c. 43.

shall be liable on conviction to a fine not exceeding the amount of the penalty which would be recoverable in civil proceedings.

(3) A proceeding for an offence under this section shall be commenced within one year after the offence was committed and the time so limited by this section shall, in the case of any proceeding under the Magistrates' Courts Act 1980, be substituted for any limitation of time contained in that Act. 1980 c. 43.

(4) For the purposes of subsection (3) above—

(*a*) where the service or execution of the writ or other process on or against the alleged offender is prevented by the absconding or concealment or act of the alleged offender, the issue of a writ or other process shall be deemed to be a commencement of a proceeding; but,

(*b*) where paragraph (*a*) does not apply, the service or execution of the writ or other process on or against the alleged offender, and not its issue, shall be deemed to be the commencement of the proceeding.

(5) Subsections (3) and (4) above do not apply in Scotland.

Authorised excuses for failures as to return and declarations.

86.—(1) A candidate or his election agent may apply for relief under this section to—

(*a*) the High Court, except in relation to a local government election in Scotland;

(*b*) an election court; or

(*c*) a county court.

(2) Relief under this section may be granted—

(*a*) to a candidate, in respect of any failure to transmit the return and declarations as to election expenses, or any part of them, or in respect of any error or false statement in them; or

(*b*) to an election agent, in respect of the failure to transmit the return and declarations which he was required to transmit, or any part of them, or in respect of any error or false statement in them.

(3) The application for relief may be made on the ground that the failure, error or false statement arose—

(*a*) by reason of the applicant's illness; or

(*b*) where the applicant is the candidate, by reason of the absence, death, illness or misconduct of his election agent or sub-agent or of any clerk or officer of such agent; or

(*c*) where the applicant is the election agent, by reason of the death or illness of any prior election agent of the

PART II

candidate, or of the absence, death, illness or misconduct of any sub-agent, clerk or officer of any election agent of the candidate; or

(*d*) by reason of inadvertence or any reasonable cause of a like nature,

and not by reason of any want of good faith on the applicant's part.

(4) The court may—

(*a*) after such notice of the application in the constituency or local government area, as the case may be, as it considers fit, and

(*b*) on production of such evidence of the grounds stated in the application and of the good faith of the application, and otherwise, as it considers fit,

make such order for allowing an authorised excuse for the failure, error or false statement as it considers just.

(5) Where it is proved to the court by the candidate—

(*a*) that any act or omission of the election agent in relation to the return and declarations was without the sanction or connivance of the candidate, and

(*b*) that the candidate took all reasonable means for preventing the act or omission,

the court shall relieve the candidate from the consequences of the act or omission of his election agent.

(6) An order under subsection (4) above may make the allowance conditional on the making of the return and declaration in a modified form or within an extended time, and upon the compliance with such other terms as to the court seem best calculated for carrying into effect the objects of this Part of this Act.

(7) An order under subsection (4) shall relieve the applicant for the order from any liability or consequences under this Act in respect of the matter excused by the order.

(8) The date of the order, or if conditions and terms are to be complied with, the date at which the applicant fully complies with them, is referred to in this Act as the date of the allowance of the excuse.

(9) Except in Scotland, the jurisdiction vested by the foregoing provisions of this section in the High Court in matters relating to parliamentary elections shall, subject to rules of court, be exercised by—

(*a*) one of the judges for the time being on the rota for the trial of parliamentary election petitions,

(*b*) in Northern Ireland, one of the judges of the High Court or the Court of Appeal for the time being selected under section 108 of the Judicature (Northern Ireland) Act 1978, 1978 c. 23.

sitting either in court or at chambers, but shall not be exercisable by a master.

(10) The jurisdiction vested by this section in a county court may, except in Northern Ireland, be exercised otherwise than in open court and, in Northern Ireland, shall be exercised in such manner as may be provided by rules of court.

(11) An appeal lies to the High Court from any order of a county court made by virtue of this section.

Court's power to require information from election agent or sub-agent.

87.—(1) Where on an application under section 86 above it appears to the court that any person who is or has been an election agent or sub-agent has refused or failed to make such return, or to supply such particulars, as will enable the candidate and his election agent respectively to comply with the provisions of this Act as to the return or declarations as to election expenses, the court, before making an order under that section, shall order that person to attend before the court.

(2) The court shall on the attendance of that person, unless he shows cause to the contrary, order him—

(*a*) to make the return and declaration, or

(*b*) to deliver a statement of the particulars required to be contained in the return,

as the court considers just, within such time, to such person and in such manner as it may direct, or may order him to be examined with respect to the particulars.

(3) If a person fails to comply with any order of the court under this section, the court may order him to pay a fine not exceeding £500.

Publication of time and place for inspection of returns and declarations.

88. At a parliamentary election—

(*a*) the returning officer shall, within 10 days after the end of the time allowed for transmitting to him returns as to election expenses, publish in not less than two newspapers circulating in the constituency for which the election was held, and shall send to each of the election agents, a notice of the time and place at which the returns and declarations (including the accompanying documents) can be inspected ; but

(*b*) if any return or declaration has not been received by the returning officer before the notice is despatched for publication, the notice shall so state, and a like notice about that return or declaration, if afterwards received, shall within 10 days after the receipt be published in like manner and sent to each of the election agents other than the agent who is in default or is agent for the candidate in default.

PART II

Inspection of returns and declarations.

89.—(1) Any returns or declarations (including the accompanying documents) sent to the appropriate officer under section 75, section 81 or section 82 above—

(*a*) shall be kept at the appropriate officer's office or some convenient place appointed by him, and

(*b*) shall at all reasonable times during the two years next after they are received by him be open to inspection by any person on payment of the prescribed fee,

and the appropriate officer shall on demand and at the prescribed fee provide copies of them or any part of them.

(2) After the expiry of those two years the appropriate officer—

(*a*) may cause those returns and declarations (including the accompanying documents) to be destroyed, or

(*b*) if the candidate or his election agent so require, shall return them to the candidate.

(3) Any returns or declarations sent under section 75 shall be returned not to the candidate (if he or his election agent so require) but to the person sending them, if he so requires.

Election expenses at elections where election agent not required.

90.—(1) In relation to an election of parish councillors in England or of community councillors in Wales—

(*a*) section 76(1) above has effect as if for the references to an election agent there were substituted references to any agent of the candidate;

(*b*) sections 72 to 75 and 78 to 89 above do not apply, and instead the provisions of Schedule 4 to this Act have effect but the form of declaration as to election expenses shall be that prescribed by rules under section 36 above relating to the election of parish or, as the case may be, community councillors, or a form to the like effect.

(2) At an election under the local government Act which is not a local government election, sections 72 to 89 do not apply, and if a candidate at that election or any person on behalf of a candidate at that election knowingly pays any sum or incurs any expense, whether before, during or after that election, on account of or in respect of the conduct or management of the election he shall be guilty of an illegal practice.

Publicity at parliamentary elections

Candidate's right to send election address post free.

91.—(1) A candidate at a parliamentary election is, subject to Post Office regulations, entitled to send free of any charge for postage to each elector one postal communication containing matter relating to the election only and not exceeding 2 ounces in weight.

(2) He is also, subject as mentioned above, entitled to send free of any charge for postage to each person entered in the list of proxies for the election one such communication as mentioned above for each appointment in respect of which that person is so entered.

(3) A person shall not be deemed to be a candidate for the purposes of this section unless he is shown as standing nominated in the statement of persons nominated, but until the publication of that statement any person who declares himself to be a candidate shall be entitled to exercise the right of free postage conferred by this section if he gives such security as may be required by the Post Office for the payment of postage should he not be shown as standing nominated as mentioned above.

(4) For the purposes of this section, "elector" means a person—

(*a*) who is registered as a parliamentary elector in the constituency in the register to be used at the election, or

(*b*) who, pending the publication of that register, appears in the electors lists for that register (as corrected by the registration officer) to be entitled to be so registered,

and accordingly includes a person shown in the register or electors lists as below voting age if it appears from that register or those lists that he will be of voting age on the day fixed for the poll, but not otherwise.

Broadcasting from outside United Kingdom.

92.—(1) No person shall, with intent to influence persons to give or refrain from giving their votes at a parliamentary or local government election, use, or aid, abet, counsel or procure the use of, any television or other wireless transmitting station outside the United Kingdom for the transmission of any matter having reference to the election otherwise than in pursuance of—

(*a*) arrangements made with the British Broadcasting Corporation for it to be received and re-transmitted by that Corporation; or

(*b*) arrangements made with the Independent Broadcasting Authority or a programme contractor (within the meaning of the Broadcasting Act 1981) for it to be received by the Authority or contractor and re-transmitted by the Authority.

1981 c. 68.

(2) An offence under this section shall be an illegal practice, but the court before whom a person is convicted of an offence under this section may, if they think it just in the special circumstances of the case, mitigate or entirely remit any incapacity imposed by virtue of section 173 below.

(3) Where any act or ommission of an association or body of persons, corporate or unincorporate, is an illegal practice under

PART II

this section, any person who at the time of the act or omission was a director, general manager, secretary or other similar officer of the association or body, or was purporting to act in any such capacity, shall be deemed to be guilty of the illegal practice, unless he proves—

(*a*) that the act or omission took place without his consent or connivance; and

(*b*) that he exercised all such diligence to prevent the commission of the illegal practice as he ought to have exercised having regard to the nature of his functions in that capacity and to all the circumstances.

Broadcasting during elections.

93.—(1) In relation to a parliamentary or local government election—

(*a*) pending such an election it shall not be lawful for any item about the constituency or electoral area to be broadcast from a television or other wireless transmitting station in the United Kingdom if any of the persons who are for the time being candidates at the election takes part in the item and the broadcast is not made with his consent; and

(*b*) where an item about a constituency or electoral area is so broadcast pending such an election there, then if the broadcast either is made before the latest time for delivery of nomination papers, or is made after that time but without the consent of any candidate remaining validly nominated, any person taking part in the item for the purpose of promoting or procuring his election shall be guilty of an illegal practice, unless the broadcast is so made without his consent.

(2) For the purposes of subsection (1) above—

(*a*) a parliamentary election shall be deemed to be pending during the period ending with the close of the poll and beginning—

(i) at a general election, with the date of the dissolution of Parliament or any earlier time at which Her Majesty's intention to dissolve Parliament is announced; or

(ii) at a by-election, with the date of the issue of the writ for the election or any earlier date on which a certificate of the vacancy is notified in the London Gazette in accordance with the Recess Elections Act 1975; and

1975 c. 66.

(*b*) a local government election shall be deemed to be pending during the period ending with the close of the poll and beginning—

(i) at an ordinary election, 5 weeks before the day

fixed as the day of election in accordance with section 37 above or, in Scotland, section 43 above; or

(ii) at an election to fill a casual vacancy, with the date of publication of notice of the election.

Imitation poll cards.

94. No person shall for the purpose of promoting or procuring the election of any candidate at a parliamentary election issue any poll card or document so closely resembling an official poll card as to be calculated to deceive, and subsections (2) and (3) of section 92 above apply as if an offence under this section were an offence under that section.

Election meetings

Schools and rooms for parliamentary election meetings.

95.—(1) Subject to the provisions of this section, a candidate at a parliamentary election is entitled for the purpose of holding public meetings in furtherance of his candidature to the use at reasonable times between the receipt of the writ and the date of the poll of—

(*a*) a suitable room in the premises of a school to which this section applies;

(*b*) any meeting room to which this section applies.

(2) This section applies—

(*a*) in England and Wales, to county schools and voluntary schools of which the premises are situated in the constituency or an adjoining constituency, and

(*b*) in Scotland, to any school of which the premises are so situated, not being an independent school within the meaning of the Education (Scotland) Act 1980, 1980 c. 44.

but a candidate is not entitled under this section to the use of a room in school premises outside the constituency if there is a suitable room in other premises in the constituency which are reasonably accessible from the same parts of the constituency as those outside and are premises of a school to which this section applies.

(3) This section applies to meeting rooms situated in the constituency, the expense of maintaining which is payable wholly or mainly out of public funds or out of any rate, or by a body whose expenses are so payable.

(4) Where a room is used for a meeting in pursuance of the rights conferred by this section, the person by whom or on whose behalf the meeting is convened—

(*a*) may be required to pay for the use of the room a charge not exceeding the amount of any actual and necessary expenses incurred in preparing, warming, lighting and cleaning the room and providing attendance for the

PART II

meeting and restoring the room to its usual condition after the meeting; and

(*b*) shall defray any damage done to the room or the premises in which it is situated, or to the furniture, fittings or apparatus in the room or premises.

(5) A candidate is not entitled to exercise the rights conferred by this section except on reasonable notice; and this section does not authorise any interference with the hours during which a room in school premises is used for educational purposes, or any interference with the use of a meeting room either for the purposes of the person maintaining it or under a prior agreement for its letting for any purpose.

(6) The provisions of Schedule 5 to this Act have effect with respect to the rights conferred by this section and the arrangements to be made for their exercise.

(7) For the purposes of this section (except those of paragraph (*b*) of subsection (4) above), the premises of a school shall not be taken to include any private dwelling house, and in this section—

(*a*) the expression " meeting room " means any room which it is the practice to let for public meetings; and

(*b*) the expression " room " includes a hall, gallery or gymnasium.

(8) This section does not apply to Northern Ireland.

Schools and rooms for local election meetings.

96.—(1) Subject to the provisions of this section, a candidate at a local government election is entitled for the purpose of holding public meetings in furtherance of his candidature to the use free of charge at reasonable times between the notice of election and the day preceding the day of election of—

(*a*) in England and Wales, a suitable room in the premises of a county or voluntary school situated in the electoral area for which he is a candidate, or, in a parish or community, as the case may be, in part comprised in that electoral area;

1980 c. 44.

(*b*) in Scotland, a suitable room in the premises of any school (not being an independent school within the meaning of the Education (Scotland) Act 1980) situated in the electoral area for which he is a candidate (or, if there is no such school in the area, in any such school in an adjacent electoral area) or any suitable room the expense of maintaining which is payable by the council of an islands area or district.

(2) Where a room is used for a meeting in pursuance of the rights conferred by this section, the person by whom or on whose behalf the meeting is convened shall defray any expense

incurred by the persons having control over the room or any damage done to the school premises or to the furniture, fittings or apparatus in them. PART II

(3) A candidate is not entitled to exercise rights conferred by this section except on reasonable notice; and this section does not authorise the use of any room used as part of a private dwelling house or any interference with the hours during which the school premises are used for educational purposes.

(4) Any question arising under this section as to what is reasonable or suitable shall be determined in England or Wales by the Secretary of State, and in Scotland, where the question arises in relation to a room in the premises of a school, by the persons having control of the school and, in the case of a room maintained by a council, by that council.

Disturbances at election meetings.

97.—(1) A person who at a lawful public meeting to which this section applies acts, or incites others to act, in a disorderly manner for the purpose of preventing the transaction of the business for which the meeting was called together shall be guilty of an illegal practice.

(2) This section applies to—

(*a*) a political meeting held in any constituency between the date of the issue of a writ for the return of a member of Parliament for the constituency and the date at which a return to the writ is made;

(*b*) a meeting held with reference to a local government election in the electoral area for that election on, or within three weeks before, the day of election.

(3) If a constable reasonably suspects any person of committing an offence under subsection (1) above, he may if requested so to do by the chairman of the meeting require that person to declare to him immediately his name and address and, if that person refuses or fails so to declare his name and address or gives a false name and address, he shall be liable on summary conviction to a fine not exceeding level 1 on the standard scale, and—

(*a*) if he refuses or fails so to declare his name and address or

(*b*) if the constable reasonably suspects him of giving a false name and address,

the constable may without warrant arrest him.

This subsection does not apply in Northern Ireland.

Premises not affected for rates.

98. The use of any premises for the holding of public meetings in furtherance of any person's candidature at a parliamentary or local government election does not render any person liable to be rated or to pay any rate for the premises.

PART II

Agency by election officials and canvassing by police officers

Officials not to act for candidates.

99.—(1) If—

(*a*) any returning officer at a parliamentary or local government election, or

(*b*) any officer or clerk appointed under the parliamentary elections rules, or the rules under section 36 or section 42 above, as the case may be, or

(*c*) any partner or clerk of any such person,

acts as a candidate's agent in the conduct or management of the election, he shall be guilty of an offence, but nothing in this subsection prevents a candidate from acting as his own election agent.

(2) An offence under subsection (1) in relation to an election in Scotland shall not be tried on indictment but shall be punishable on summary conviction by a fine not exceeding level 4 on the standard scale.

Illegal canvassing by police officers.

100.—(1) No member of a police force shall by word, message, writing or in any other manner, endeavour to persuade any person to give, or dissuade any person from giving, his vote, whether as an elector or as proxy—

(*a*) at any parliamentary election for a constituency, or

(*b*) at any local government election for any electoral area,

wholly or partly within the police area.

(2) A person acting in contravention of subsection (1) above shall be liable on summary conviction to a fine not exceeding level 3 on the standard scale, or, in Northern Ireland, to a fine not exceeding £100, but nothing in that subsection shall subject a member of a police force to any penalty for anything done in the discharge of his duty as a member of the force.

(3) In this section references to a member of a police force and to a police area are to be taken in relation to Northern Ireland as references to a member of the Royal Ulster Constabulary and to Northern Ireland.

Conveyance of voters to and from poll

No hiring of vehicles to convey voters.

101.—(1) A person shall not let, lend, or employ any public vehicle for the purpose of the conveyance of electors or their proxies to or from the poll at an election, and if he does so knowing that the public vehicle is intended to be used for that purpose he shall be guilty of an illegal hiring.

(2) A person shall not hire, borrow or use for the purpose of the conveyance of electors or their proxies to or from the poll at an election any public vehicle the owner of which he knows to be prohibited by subsection (1) above from letting, lending or employing for that purpose, and if he does so he shall be guilty of an illegal hiring.

(3) In this section " public vehicle " means any public stage or hackney carriage or any carriage kept or used for the purpose of letting out for hiring. PART II

102. If any payment or contract for payment is knowingly made, either before, during or after an election, for the purpose of promoting or procuring the election of a candidate on account of the conveyance of electors or their proxies to or from the poll, whether for the hire of carriages, or for railway fares, or otherwise—

No payments for conveyance of voters.

(*a*) the person making the payment or contract, and

(*b*) if he knew it to be in contravention of this Act, any person receiving the payment or being a party to the contract,

shall be guilty of an illegal practice.

103.—(1) Nothing in sections 101 and 102 above prevents a carriage being let, hired, employed or used by an elector or his proxy or several electors or their proxies at their joint cost, for the purpose of being conveyed to or from the poll.

Provisions supplemental to ss. 101 and 102.

(2) No person shall be liable to pay any duty or to take out a licence for any carriage by reason only of the carriage being used without payment or promise of payment for the conveyance of electors or their proxies to or from the poll.

104. In sections 101 to 103 above—

" Carriage " in ss. 101 to 103.

(*a*) " carriage " includes for the purposes of those sections—

(i) any mechanically propelled vehicle intended or adapted for use on roads, and

(ii) any vehicle drawn by such a vehicle,

and any such vehicle as so described shall be deemed to be a public vehicle for the purposes of section 101 if used as such ; and

(*b*) the provisions of those sections, except section 103(2), apply in relation to horses or other animals as they apply in relation to carriages, and any reference in section 101 to a public vehicle includes a reference to horses or other animals kept or used for drawing such vehicles.

105.—(1) Where the nature of a county constituency is such that any electors or proxies for electors resident there are unable at a parliamentary election for that constituency to reach their polling place without crossing the sea or a branch or arm of the sea, nothing in this Act prevents the provision of means for conveying those electors or proxies by sea to their polling place.

Access to polling place by sea.

(2) The amount of any payment for such means of conveyance as are mentioned in subsection (1) above may be in addition to the maximum amount of expenses allowed by this Act.

PART II

(3) No restriction on the expenses to be incurred by a returning officer shall prevent a returning officer employing special steamers or boats for the purposes of a parliamentary election in any constituency in Scotland having a polling place or polling places so situated as not to be accessible except by sea, but the expenses so incurred shall be included in the returning officer's account, and shall be subject to taxation.

Other illegal practices, payments, employments or hirings

False statements as to candidates.

106.—(1) A person who, or any director of any body or association corporate which—

(*a*) before or during an election,

(*b*) for the purpose of affecting the return of any candidate at the election,

makes or publishes any false statement of fact in relation to the candidate's personal character or conduct shall be guilty of an illegal practice, unless he can show that he had reasonable grounds for believing, and did believe, the statement to be true.

(2) A candidate shall not be liable nor shall his election be avoided for any illegal practice under subsection (1) above committed by his agent other than his election agent unless—

(*a*) it can be shown that the candidate or his election agent has authorised or consented to the committing of the illegal practice by the other agent or has paid for the circulation of the false statement constituting the illegal practice; or

(*b*) an election court find and report that the election of the candidate was procured or materially assisted in consequence of the making or publishing of such false statements.

(3) A person making or publishing any false statement of fact as mentioned above may be restrained by interim or perpetual injunction by the High Court or the county court from any repetition of that false statement or of a false statement of a similar character in relation to the candidate and, for the purpose of granting an interim injunction, prima facie proof of the falsity of the statement shall be sufficient.

(4) The foregoing provisions of this section do not apply to or in relation to an election of councillors in Scotland.

(5) Any person who, before or during an election, knowingly publishes a false statement of a candidate's withdrawal at the election for the purpose of promoting or procuring the election of another candidate shall be guilty of an illegal practice.

PART II

(6) A candidate shall not be liable, nor shall his election be avoided, for any illegal practice under subsection (5) above committed by his agent other than his election agent.

(7) In the application of this section to an election where a candidate is not required to have an election agent, references to an election agent shall be omitted and the reference in subsection (6) above to an illegal practice committed by an agent of the candidate shall be taken as a reference to an illegal practice committed without the candidate's knowledge and consent.

(8) Except in Scotland, the jurisdiction vested by subsection (3) above in the High Court in matters relating to parliamentary elections shall, subject to rules of court, be exercised by—

(*a*) one of the judges for the time being on the rota for the trial of parliamentary election petitions,

(*b*) in Northern Ireland, one of the judges of the High Court or the Court of Appeal for the time being selected under section 108 of the Judicature (Northern Ireland) Act 1978, 1978 c. 23.

sitting either in court or at chambers, or by a master of the Supreme Court in manner directed by and subject to an appeal to those judges.

(9) The jurisdiction vested by subsection (3) in a county court may, except in Northern Ireland, be exercised otherwise than in open court, and, in Northern Ireland, shall be exercised in accordance with rules of court.

An appeal lies to the High Court from any order of a county court made by virtue of subsection (3).

Corrupt withdrawal from candidature.

107. Any person who corruptly induces or procures any other person to withdraw from being a candidate at an election, in consideration of any payment or promise of payment, and any person withdrawing in pursuance of the inducement or procurement, shall be guilty of an illegal payment.

Premises not to be used as committee rooms.

108.—(1) If a person—

(*a*) hires or uses any premises to which this section applies, or any part of them, for a committee room for the purpose of promoting or procuring the election of a candidate, or

(*b*) lets any premises to which this section applies or any part of them knowing that it was intended to use them or that part as a committee room,

he shall be guilty of an illegal hiring.

PART II

(2) Where the election is an election under the local government Act, the reference in subsection (1) above to letting any premises or part of premises includes a reference to permitting the use of any premises or part of premises.

(3) This section applies to any premises—

(*a*) which are licensed for the sale of any intoxicating liquor for consumption on or off the premises or on which refreshment of any kind (whether food or drink) is ordinarily sold for consumption on the premises, or

(*b*) where any intoxicating liquor is supplied to members of a club, society or association, other than a permanent political club,

but this section does not apply to the hiring, using, letting or permitting the use of any part of premises which is ordinarily let for the purpose of—

(i) chambers, or offices, or

(ii) the holding of public meetings or of arbitrations,

if that part has a separate entrance and no direct communication with any part of the premises on which any intoxicating liquor or refreshment is sold or supplied as mentioned above.

(4) This section also applies—

(*a*) in England and Wales, to the premises of all schools maintained or assisted by a local education authority and all other schools in respect of which grants are made out of moneys provided by Parliament to the person or body of persons responsible for the management of the school;

1980 c. 44.

(*b*) in Scotland, to the premises of all schools other than independent schools within the meaning of the Education (Scotland) Act 1980; and

S.I. 1972/1263 (N.I. 12).

(*c*) in Northern Ireland, to the premises of all schools other than independent schools within the meaning of the Education and Libraries (Northern Ireland) Order 1972.

For the purposes of this section, the premises of a school shall be taken to include any dwelling house which forms part of the school and is occupied by a person employed for the purposes of the school.

Payments for exhibition of election notices.

109.—(1) No payment or contract for payment shall for the purpose of promoting or procuring the election of a candidate at an election be made to an elector or his proxy on account of the exhibition of, or the use of any house, land, building or premises for the exhibition of, any address, bill or notice, unless—

(*a*) it is the ordinary business of the elector or proxy as an advertising agent to exhibit for payment bills and advertisements; and

(b) the payment or contract is made in the ordinary course of that business.

(2) If any payment or contract for payment is knowingly made in contravention of this section either before, during or after an election—

(a) the person making the payment or contract, and

(b) if he knew it to be in contravention of this Act, any person receiving the payment or being a party to the contract,

shall be guilty of an illegal practice.

Printer's name and address on election publications.

110.—(1) A person shall not—

(a) print or publish, or cause to be printed or published, any bill, placard or poster having reference to an election or any printed document distributed for the purpose of promoting or procuring the election of a candidate, or

(b) post or cause to be posted any such bill, placard or poster as mentioned above, or

(c) distribute or cause to be distributed any printed document for that purpose,

unless the bill, placard, poster or document bears upon its face the name and address of the printer and publisher.

(2) For the purposes of this section, any process for multiplying copies of a document, other than copying it by hand, shall be deemed to be printing and the expression " printer " shall be construed accordingly.

(3) A candidate or election agent acting in contravention of this section shall be guilty of an illegal practice, and any other person so acting shall on summary conviction be liable to a fine not exceeding level 3 on the standard scale, or, in Northern Ireland, to a fine not exceeding £100.

In relation to an election where candidates are not required to have election agents the reference to an election agent shall be omitted and the reference to any person other than the candidate shall be construed accordingly.

Prohibition of paid canvassers.

111. If a person is, either before, during or after an election, engaged or employed for payment or promise of payment as a canvasser for the purpose of promoting or procuring a candidate's election—

(a) the person so engaging or employing him, and

(b) the person so engaged or employed,

shall be guilty of illegal employment.

PART II

Providing money for illegal purposes.

112. Where a person knowingly provides money—

(*a*) for any payment which is contrary to the provisions of this Act, or

(*b*) for any expenses incurred in excess of the maximum amount allowed by this Act, or

(*c*) for replacing any money expended in any such payment or expenses,

except where the payment or the incurring of the expenses may have been previously allowed in pursuance of section 167 below to be an exception, that person shall be guilty of an illegal payment.

Bribery, treating and undue influence

Bribery.

113.—(1) A person shall be guilty of a corrupt practice if he is guilty of bribery.

(2) A person shall be guilty of bribery if he, directly or indirectly, by himself or by any other person on his behalf—

(*a*) gives any money or procures any office to or for any voter or to or for any other person on behalf of any voter or to or for any other person in order to induce any voter to vote or refrain from voting, or

(*b*) corruptly does any such act as mentioned above on account of any voter having voted or refrained from voting, or

(*c*) makes any such gift or procurement as mentioned above to or for any person in order to induce that person to procure, or endeavour to procure, the return of any person at an election or the vote of any voter,

or if upon or in consequence of any such gift or procurement as mentioned above he procures or engages, promises or endeavours to procure the return of any person at an election or the vote of any voter.

For the purposes of this subsection—

(i) references to giving money include references to giving, lending, agreeing to give or lend, offering, promising, or promising to procure or endeavour to procure any money or valuable consideration ; and

(ii) references to procuring any office include references to giving, procuring, agreeing to give or procure, offering, promising, or promising to procure or to endeavour to procure any office, place or employment.

(3) A person shall be guilty of bribery if he advances or pays or causes to be paid any money to or for the use of any other

person with the intent that that money or any part of it shall be expended in bribery at any election or knowingly pays or causes to be paid any money to any person in discharge or repayment of any money wholly or in part expended in bribery at any election.

(4) The foregoing provisions of this section shall not extend or be construed to extend to any money paid or agreed to be paid for or on account of any legal expenses incurred in good faith at or concerning an election.

(5) A voter shall be guilty of bribery if before or during an election he directly or indirectly by himself or by any other person on his behalf receives, agrees, or contracts for any money, gift, loan or valuable consideration, office, place or employment for himself or for any other person for voting or agreeing to vote or for refraining or agreeing to refrain from voting.

(6) A person shall be guilty of bribery if after an election he directly or indirectly by himself or by any other person on his behalf receives any money or valuable consideration on account of any person having voted or refrained from voting or having induced any other person to vote or refrain from voting.

(7) In this section the expression " voter " includes any person who has or claims to have a right to vote.

Treating.

114.—(1) A person shall be guilty of a corrupt practice if he is guilty of treating.

(2) A person shall be guilty of treating if he corruptly, by himself or by any other person, either before, during or after an election, directly or indirectly gives or provides, or pays wholly or in part the expense of giving or providing, any meat, drink, entertainment or provision to or for any person—

(*a*) for the purpose of corruptly influencing that person or any other person to vote or refrain from voting; or

(*b*) on account of that person or any other person having voted or refrained from voting, or being about to vote or refrain from voting.

(3) Every elector or his proxy who corruptly accepts or takes any such meat, drink, entertainment or provision shall also be guilty of treating.

Undue influence.

115.—(1) A person shall be guilty of a corrupt practice if he is guilty of undue influence.

(2) A person shall be guilty of undue influence—

(*a*) if he, directly or indirectly, by himself or by any other person on his behalf, makes use of or threatens to make

PART II

use of any force, violence or restraint, or inflicts or threatens to inflict, by himself or by any other person, any temporal or spiritual injury, damage, harm or loss upon or against any person in order to induce or compel that person to vote or refrain from voting, or on account of that person having voted or refrained from voting; or

(*b*) if, by abduction, duress or any fraudulent device or contrivance, he impedes or prevents the free exercise of the franchise of an elector or proxy for an elector, or so compels, induces or prevails upon an elector or proxy for an elector either to vote or to refrain from voting.

Supplemental

Rights of creditors.

116. The provisions of this Part of this Act prohibiting—

(*a*) payments and contracts for payments,

(*b*) the payment or incurring of election expenses in excess of the maximum amount allowed by this Act; or

(*c*) the incurring of expenses not authorised by the election agent,

do not affect the right of any creditor, who, when the contract was made or the expense was incurred, was ignorant of that contract or expense being in contravention of this Act.

Savings as to parliamentary elections.

117.—(1) Where a person has been declared by others to be a candidate at a parliamentary election without his consent, nothing in this Part of this Act shall be construed to impose any liability on that person, unless he has afterwards given his assent to the declaration or has been nominated.

(2) Nothing in this Part makes it illegal for an employer to permit parliamentary electors or their proxies to absent themselves from his employment for a reasonable time for the purpose of voting at the poll at a parliamentary election without having any deduction from their salaries or wages on account of their absence, if the permission—

(*a*) is (so far as practicable without injury to the employer's business) given equally to all persons alike who are at the time in his employment, and

(*b*) is not given with a view to inducing any person to record his vote for any particular candidate at the election, and

(*c*) is not refused to any person for the purpose of preventing him from recording his vote for any particular candidate at the election, but this subsection shall not be construed as making illegal any act which would not be illegal apart from this subsection.

PART II

Interpretation of Part II.

118. In this part of this Act, unless the context otherwise requires—

"appropriate officer" has the meaning given by section 67(7) above;

"candidate"—

(*a*) in relation to a parliamentary election, means a person who is elected to serve in Parliament at the election or a person who is nominated as a candidate at the election, or is declared by himself or by others to be a candidate on or after the day of the issue of the writ for the election, or after the dissolution or vacancy in consequence of which the writ was issued;

(*b*) in relation to an election under the local government Act, means a person elected or having been nominated or having declared himself a candidate for election, to the office to be filled at the election;

"committee room" does not include any house or room occupied by a candidate as a dwelling, by reason only of the candidate transacting business there with his agents in relation to the election, and no room or building shall be deemed to be a committee room by reason only of the candidate or any agent of the candidate addressing in it electors, committee members or others;

"date of the allowance of an authorised excuse" has the meaning given by section 86(8) above, or paragraph 7 of Schedule 4 to this Act, as the case may be;

"declaration as to election expenses" means a declaration made under section 82 above, or, as the case may be, paragraph 3 of Schedule 4 to this Act;

"disputed claim" has the meaning given by section 79(1) above as extended by section 80 above;

"election expenses" in relation to an election means expenses incurred, whether before, during or after the election, on account of or in respect of the conduct or management of the election;

"money" and "pecuniary reward" shall (except in sections 113 and 114 above) be deemed to include—

(*a*) any office, place or employment, and

(*b*) any valuable security or other equivalent of money, and

(*c*) any valuable consideration,

and expressions referring to money shall be construed accordingly;

PART II

"payment" includes any pecuniary or other reward;

"personal expenses" as used with respect to the expenditure of any candidate in relation to any election includes the reasonable travelling expenses of the candidate, and the reasonable expenses of his living at hotels or elsewhere for the purposes of and in relation to the election;

"return as to election expenses" means a return (including the bills and receipts to be transmitted with it) to be made under section 81(1) above, or, as the case may be, paragraph 3 of Schedule 4 to this Act.

Computation of time for purposes of Part II.

119.—(1) Where the day or last day on which anything is required or permitted to be done by or in pursuance of this Part of this Act is any of the days mentioned in subsection (2) below—

(*a*) the requirement or permission shall be deemed to relate to the first day thereafter which is not one of those days; and

(*b*) in computing any period of not more than 7 days for the purposes of this Part any of the days so mentioned shall be disregarded.

(2) The days referred to in subsection (1) above are—

(*a*) a Sunday;

(*b*) a day of the Christmas break, of the Easter break, or of a bank holiday break; and

(*c*) a day appointed for public thanksgiving or mourning.

(3) In this section—

1971 c. 80.

"bank holiday break" means any bank holiday under the Banking and Financial Dealings Act 1971 (in England and Wales, in Scotland or in Northern Ireland, as the case may be) which is not included in the Christmas break or the Easter break and the period beginning with the last weekday before that bank holiday and ending with the next weekday which is not a bank holiday under that Act,

"Christmas break" means the period beginning with the last weekday before Christmas Day and ending with the first weekday after Christmas Day which is not a bank holiday,

"Easter break" means the period beginning with the Thursday before and ending with the Tuesday after Easter Day,

but so much of this subsection as includes in a bank holiday break a period before and after a bank holiday does not apply in Scotland or Northern Ireland to a bank holiday which is not also a bank holiday in England and Wales, except in Scotland New Year's Day.

Part III

Legal Proceedings

Questioning of a parliamentary election

120.—(1) No parliamentary election and no return to Parliament shall be questioned except by a petition complaining of an undue election or undue return (" a parliamentary election petition ") presented in accordance with this Part of this Act. Method of questioning parliamentary election.

(2) A petition complaining of no return shall be deemed to be a parliamentary election petition and the High Court—

(*a*) may make such order on the petition as they think expedient for compelling a return to be made ; or

(*b*) may allow the petition to be heard by an election court as provided with respect to ordinary election petitions.

121.—(1) A parliamentary election petition may be presented by one or more of the following persons— Presentation and service of parliamentary election petition.

(*a*) a person who voted as an elector at the election or who had a right so to vote ; or

(*b*) a person claiming to have had a right to be elected or returned at the election ; or

(*c*) a person alleging himself to have been a candidate at the election.

(2) The member whose election or return is complained of is hereinafter referred to as the respondent, but if the petition complains of the conduct of a returning officer, the returning officer shall for the purposes of this Part of this Act be deemed to be a respondent.

(3) The petition shall be in the prescribed form, state the prescribed matters and be signed by the petitioner, or all the petitioners if more than one, and shall be presented to the High Court, or to the Court of Session, or to the High Court of Northern Ireland, depending on whether the constituency to which it relates is in England and Wales, or Scotland or Northern Ireland.

(4) The petition shall be presented by delivering it to the prescribed officer or otherwise dealing with it in the prescribed manner ; and the prescribed officer shall send a copy of it to the returning officer of the constituency to which the petition relates, who shall forthwith publish it in that constituency.

(5) The petition shall be served as nearly as may be in the manner in which a writ or summons is served or in such other manner as may be prescribed.

PART III

Time for presentation or amendment of parliamentary election petition.

122.—(1) Subject to the provisions of this section, a parliamentary election petition shall be presented within 21 days after the return has been made to the Clerk of the Crown, or to the Clerk of the Crown for Northern Ireland, as the case may be, of the member to whose election the petition relates.

(2) If the petition questions the election or return upon an allegation of corrupt practices and specifically alleges a payment of money or other reward to have been made by the member or on his account or with his privity since the time of that return in pursuance or in furtherance of the alleged corrupt practice, it may be presented within 28 days after the date of the payment.

(3) A petition questioning the election or return upon an allegation of an illegal practice may, so far as respects that illegal practice, be presented—

(*a*) within 21 days after the day specified in subsection (4) below ; or

(*b*) if specifically alleging a payment of money or some other act to have been made or done since the day so specified by the member to whose election the petition relates or an agent of his, or with the privity of that member or his election agent, in pursuance or in furtherance of the alleged illegal practice, within 28 days after the date of the payment or other act.

(4) The day referred to in subsection (3) above is the tenth day after the end of the time allowed for transmitting to the returning officer returns as to election expenses at the election or, if later—

(*a*) that on which the returning officer receives the return and declarations as to election expenses by that member and his election agent ; or

(*b*) where the return and declarations are received on different days, the last of those days ; or

(*c*) where there is an authorised excuse for failing to make the return and declarations, the date of the allowance of the excuse, or if there was a failure as regards two or more of them, and the excuse was allowed at different times, the date of the allowance of the last excuse.

(5) An election petition presented within the time limited by subsection (1) or subsection (2) above may, for the purpose of questioning the election or return upon an allegation of an illegal practice, be amended with the leave of the High Court within the time within which a petition questioning the election upon the allegation of that illegal practice could be presented under subsection (3).

(6) Subsections (3), (4) and (5) above apply—

(*a*) notwithstanding that the act constituting the alleged

illegal practice amounted to a corrupt practice; and

(*b*) to a corrupt practice under section 75 above, as if it were an illegal practice.

(7) For the purposes of this section, an allegation that an election is avoided under section 164 below shall be deemed to be an allegation of corrupt practices, notwithstanding that the offences alleged are or include offences other than corrupt practices.

(8) Except in Scotland, the jurisdiction vested by subsection (5) in the High Court shall, subject to rules of court, be exercised—

(*a*) by one of the judges for the time being on the rota for the trial of parliamentary election petitions,

(*b*) in Northern Ireland, by one of the judges of the High Court or the Court of Appeal for the time being selected under section 108 of the Judicature (Northern Ireland) Act 1978, 1978 c. 23.

sitting either in court or at chambers, or by a master of the Supreme Court in manner directed by and subject to an appeal to those judges.

Constitution of election court and place of trial.

123.—(1) A parliamentary election petition shall be tried by—

(*a*) two judges on the rota for the trial of parliamentary election petitions, and the judges for the time being on that rota shall, unless they otherwise agree, try the election petitions standing for trial according to their seniority,

(*b*) in Northern Ireland, the two judges of the High Court or the Court of Appeal for the time being selected under section 108 of the Judicature (Northern Ireland) Act 1978,

and the judges presiding at the trial of a parliamentary election petition are hereinafter referred to as the election court.

(2) The election court has, subject to the provisions of this Act, the same powers, jurisdiction and authority as a judge of the High Court (or, in Scotland, a judge of the Court of Session presiding at the trial of a civil cause without a jury) and shall be a court of record.

(3) The place of trial shall be within the constituency for which the election was held, but—

(*a*) the High Court may, on being satisfied that special circumstances exist rendering it desirable that the petition should be tried elsewhere, appoint some other convenient place for the trial; and

PART III

(*b*) if that constituency is wholly or partly in Greater London, the petition may be heard at such place within Greater London as the High Court may appoint.

(4) The election court may adjourn the trial from one place to another within the constituency.

Judges' expenses and reception: England and Wales and Northern Ireland.

124. In relation to the trial of a parliamentary election petition—

(*a*) in England and Wales and Northern Ireland, the travelling and other expenses of the judges and all expenses properly incurred in receiving the judges and providing them with necessary accommodation and with a proper court shall be defrayed by the Treasury out of moneys provided by Parliament;

(*b*) in Northern Ireland, the judges shall be received—

(i) if the petition relates to a county constituency, by the sheriff; and

(ii) if the petition relates to a borough constituency, by the sheriff of the county or county borough which includes the constituency or the greater part of the constituency, or by a person named by that sheriff.

Judges' expenses and reception: Scotland.

125. In relation to the trial of a parliamentary election petition in Scotland—

(*a*) the judges shall be received at the place where they are about to try a parliamentary election petition in the same manner and by the same authorities, as far as circumstances admit, as a judge of the High Court of Justiciary is received at a circuit town, and shall be attended by such officer or officers as shall be necessary;

(*b*) the travelling and other expenses of the judges, and of the officer or officers in attendance on them, and all expenses properly incurred in providing the judges with a proper court shall be defrayed by the Treasury out of moneys provided by Parliament.

Attendance of House of Commons shorthand writer.

126.—(1) The shorthand writer of the House of Commons or his deputy shall attend the trial and shall be sworn by one of the judges of the election court faithfully and truly to take down the evidence given at the trial and from time to time as occasion requires to transcribe that evidence or cause it to be transcribed.

(2) The shorthand writer shall take down the evidence and from time to time transcribe it or cause it to be transcribed

and a copy of the evidence shall accompany the certificate given by the election court to the Speaker.

(3) In Scotland and Northern Ireland the expenses of the shorthand writer shall be deemed to be part of the expenses incurred in receiving the judges.

Questioning of a local election

Method of questioning local election.

127. An election under the local government Act may be questioned on the ground that the person whose election is questioned—

(*a*) was at the time of the election disqualified, or

(*b*) was not duly elected,

or on the ground that the election was avoided by corrupt or illegal practices or on the grounds provided by section 164 or section 165 below, and shall not be questioned on any of those grounds except by an election petition.

Presentation of petition questioning local election.

128.—(1) A petition questioning an election under the local government Act may be presented either by four or more persons who voted as electors at the election or had a right so to vote, or by a person alleging himself to have been a candidate at the election.

(2) A person whose election is questioned by the petition, and any returning officer of whose conduct the petition complains, may be made a respondent to the petition.

(3) The petition shall be in the prescribed form signed by the petitioner and shall be presented in the prescribed manner—

(*a*) in England and Wales, to the High Court;

(*b*) in Scotland, to the sheriff principal of the sheriffdom in which the election took place or, where the election was in respect of a local authority whose area is situated within more than one sheriffdom, to the sheriffs principal of the sheriffdoms in which the area of the authority is situated.

(4) In England and Wales the prescribed officer shall send a copy of the petition to the proper officer of the authority for which the election was held, who shall forthwith publish it in the area of that authority.

Time for presentation or amendment of petition questioning local election.

129.—(1) Subject to the provisions of this section, a petition questioning an election under the local government Act shall be presented within 21 days after the day on which the election was held.

PART III

(2) If the petition complains of the election—

(*a*) on the ground of a corrupt practice, and

(*b*) specifically alleges that a payment of money or other reward has been made or promised since the election by a candidate elected at the election, or on his account or with his privity, in pursuance or furtherance of that corrupt practice,

it may be presented at any time within 28 days after the date of the alleged payment or promise, whether or not any other petition against that person has been previously presented or tried.

(3) If the petition complains of the election—

(*a*) on the ground of an illegal practice, and

(*b*) specifically alleges a payment of money or other act made or done since the election by the candidate elected at the election, or by an agent of the candidate or with the privity of the candidate or his election agent, in pursuance or in furtherance of that illegal practice,

it may be presented at any time within 28 days after the date of that payment or act, whether or not any other petition against that person has been previously presented or tried.

(4) If the petition complains of an election where election expenses are allowed on the ground of an illegal practice, it may be presented at any time within 14 days after the day specified in subsection (5) below.

(5) The day referred to in subsection (4) above is—

(*a*) that on which the appropriate officer receives the return and declarations as to election expenses by that candidate and his election agent; or

(*b*) where the return and declarations are received on different days, the last of those days; or

(*c*) where there is an authorised excuse for failing to make the return and declarations, the date of the allowance of the excuse, or if there was a failure as regards two or more of them and the excuse was allowed at different times, the date of the allowance of the last excuse.

(6) An election petition presented within the time limited by subsection (1) or subsection (2) above may for the purpose of complaining of the election upon an allegation of an illegal practice, be amended with the leave of the High Court within the time within which a petition complaining of the election on the ground of that illegal practice could, under this section, be presented.

PART III

In the application of this subsection to an election of councillors in Scotland, the reference in this subsection to subsection (2) above shall be omitted and for the reference to the High Court there shall be substituted a reference to the election court or the sheriff.

(7) Subsections (3), (4), (5) and (6) above apply—

(*a*) notwithstanding that the act constituting the alleged illegal practice amounted to a corrupt practice; and

(*b*) to a corrupt practice under section 75 above as if it were an illegal practice.

(8) For the purposes of this section, an allegation that an election is avoided under section 164 below shall be deemed to be an allegation of corrupt practices, notwithstanding that the offences alleged are or include offences other than corrupt practices.

(9) In relation to an election where candidates are not required to have election agents there shall be omitted—

(*a*) the references in subsection (3) and paragraph (*a*) of subsection (5) above to an election agent; and

(*b*) paragraphs (*b*) and (*c*) of subsection (5).

Election court for local election in England and Wales, and place of trial.

130.—(1) A petition questioning an election in England and Wales under the local government Act shall be tried by an election court consisting of a barrister qualified and appointed as provided by this section.

(2) A barrister shall not be qualified to constitute an election court—

(*a*) if he is of less than 15 years standing, or

(*b*) if the court is for the trial of an election petition relating to any local government area—

(i) in which he resides; or

(ii) which is included in a circuit on which he practises as a barrister.

(3) The judges for the time being on the rota for the trial of parliamentary election petitions, or any two of those judges—

(*a*) may annually appoint as many barristers, not exceeding five, as they may think necessary as commissioners for the trial of petitions questioning elections in England and Wales under the local government Act; and

(*b*) shall from time to time assign the petitions to be tried by each commissioner.

(4) If the commissioner to whom the trial of a petition is assigned dies, or declines to act or becomes incapable of acting, those judges or two of them may assign the trial to be conducted or continued by any other of the commissioners appointed under this section.

PART III

(5) The election court has for the purposes of the trial the same powers and privileges as a judge on the trial of a parliamentary election petition.

(6) The place of trial shall be within the area of the authority for which the election was held, except that the High Court may, on being satisfied that special circumstances exist rendering it desirable that the petition should be tried elsewhere, appoint some other convenient place for the trial.

(7) The election court may in its discretion adjourn the trial from one place to another within the local government area or place where it is held.

Accommodation of and attendance on court.

131.—(1) The proper officer of the authority for which the election was held shall provide suitable accommodation for holding the election court constituted under section 130 above and any expenses incurred by him for the purposes of this section and section 132 below shall be paid by that authority.

(2) The election court so constituted may employ officers and clerks as prescribed, and all constables and bailiffs shall give their assistance to the court in the execution of its duties.

(3) A shorthand writer (whose expenses, according to a prescribed scale, shall be treated as part of the expenses incurred in receiving the election court) shall attend the trial before that court, and—

(*a*) shall be sworn by the court faithfully and truly to take down the evidence given at the trial, and

(*b*) shall take down such evidence at length,

and a transcript of the notes of the evidence taken down by him shall, if the election court so directs, accompany the court's certificate.

Remuneration and allowances.

132.—(1) The remuneration and allowances to be paid to the commissioner for his services in respect of that trial and to any officers, clerks or shorthand writers employed under section 131 above in relation to that trial shall be fixed by a scale made and varied by the judges on the rota for the trial of parliamentary election petitions, with the Treasury's approval.

(2) The remuneration and allowances shall be paid in the first instance by the Treasury and shall be repaid to the Treasury on their certificate by the authority for which the election was held.

Repayments under ss. 131 and 132.

133.—(1) The election court constituted under section 130 above may in its discretion order that—

(*a*) the expenses referred to in section 131 above, incurred by the proper officer of the authority for receiving the court, or

PART III

(b) the remuneration and allowances referred to in section 132 above,

shall be repaid, wholly or in part, to the proper officer of the authority or to the Treasury, as the case may be—

(i) when, in the opinion of the election court, the petition is frivolous and vexatious, by the petitioner;

(ii) when, in the opinion of the election court, the respondent has been personally guilty of corrupt practices at the election, by that respondent.

(2) The order so made for the repayment of any sum by a petitioner or respondent may be enforced as an order for payment of costs, but a deposit made or a security given under this Part of this Act shall not be applied for any such repayment until all costs and expenses payable by the petitioner or respondent to any party to the petition have been satisfied.

Election court for local election in Scotland and place of trial.

134.—(1) An election petition questioning an election of councillors in Scotland, and all proceedings incidental to and consequent on it, except as otherwise provided, shall be tried—

(a) by the sheriff principal of the sheriffdom within which the challenged election took place; or

(b) where the election was in respect of a local authority whose area is situated within more than one sheriffdom, by the sheriffs principal of the sheriffdoms in which the area of the authority is situated; and where in such a case the sheriffs principal are unable to reach a unanimous decision, they shall state a case for the Court of Session and the Court may pronounce any deliverance which it would have been competent for the sheriffs principal to make.

(2) The election court has for the purposes of the trial the same powers and privileges as a judge on the trial of a parliamentary election petition, except that any fine or order of commital unless imposed or made by the Court of Session in consequence of a case stated under subsection (1) above may, on summary application by the person aggrieved, be discharged or varied by the Court of Session, or in vacation by the judge acting as vacation judge on such terms, if any, as the Court of Session or judge may think fit.

(3) The place of trial shall be such place within the sheriffdom or sheriffdoms in which the area of the local authority is situated as the election court may determine.

(4) The election court may in its discretion adjourn the trial from one place to another within that sheriffdom or those sheriffdoms.

PART III

(5) The travelling and other expenses of the sheriff principal incurred by him in the execution of his duties under this Part of this Act shall be paid by the authority for which the election was held, but the election court may order repayment of those expenses to that authority by the parties to the petition or any of them, in such proportion as shall to the court seem proper.

(6) A shorthand writer shall attend at the trial of the petition, and shall be sworn by the election court faithfully and truly to take down the evidence given at the trial, and he shall take down the evidence at length.

Consequences of local election declared void.

135.—(1) Where on a petition questioning an election under the local government Act—

(*a*) the election of any person has been declared void, and

(*b*) no other person has been declared elected in his place,

a new election shall be held to fill the vacancy in the same manner as on a casual vacancy.

(2) For the purposes of that election any duties to be performed by any officer shall, if he has been declared not elected, be performed by a deputy or other person who might have acted for him if he had been incapacitated by illness.

(3) This section does not apply to Scotland

Procedure on all election petitions

Security for costs.

136.—(1) At the time of presenting an election petition or within three days afterwards the petitioner shall give security for all costs which may become payable by him to any witness summoned on his behalf or to any respondent.

(2) The security shall be—

(*a*) in the case of a parliamentary election petition, £1000; and

(*b*) in the case of a petition questioning an election under the local government Act, such amount not exceeding £500 as the High Court, or a judge of the High Court, on summons, directs,

and shall be given in the prescribed manner by recognisance entered into by any number of sureties not exceeding four or by a deposit of money, or partly in one way and partly in the other; but in Scotland—

(i) the amount mentioned in paragraph (*b*) above shall be such amount not exceeding £500 as the election court or the sheriff directs; and

(ii) the persons finding caution for that amount may exceed four.

(3) Within the prescribed time, not exceeding five days after the presentation of the petition, the petitioner shall serve on the respondent a notice of the presentation of the petition, and of the nature of the proposed security, and a copy of the petition.

(4) Within a further prescribed time, not exceeding five days after service of the notice, the respondent may object in writing to any recognisance on the ground that any surety is insufficient or is dead or cannot be found or ascertained for want of a sufficient description in the recognisance, or that a person named in the recognisance has not duly acknowledged the recognisance.

(5) In the case of an election under the local government Act—

(*a*) in subsection (3) above, the service shall be in the prescribed manner;

(*b*) in that subsection and subsection (4) above, the periods mentioned shall be five days and not as prescribed.

(6) An objection to a recognisance shall be decided in the prescribed manner.

(7) If the objection is allowed, the petitioner may within a further prescribed time not exceeding five days, remove it by a deposit in the prescribed manner of such sum of money as will, in the opinion of the court or officer having cognisance of the matter, make the security sufficient.

(8) If no security is given as required by this section or any objection is allowed and not removed as mentioned above, no further proceedings shall be had on the petition.

Petition at issue.

137. The petition shall be at issue—

(*a*) on the expiry of the time limited for objections; or

(*b*) if an objection is made, on that objection being disallowed or removed, whichever happens last.

List of petitions.

138.—(1) The prescribed officer shall—

(*a*) as soon as may be, make out a list of all election petitions at issue presented to the court of which he is officer, placing them in the order in which they were presented, and

(*b*) keep at his office a copy of the list, open to inspection in the prescribed manner,

and the petitions questioning elections under the local government Act shall be in a separate list, a copy of which shall be sent to each of the judges for the time being on the rota for the trial of parliamentary election petitions.

PART III

(2) The petitions shall, so far as convenient, be tried in the order in which they stand in the list.

(3) In the case of a petition questioning an election under the local government Act, two or more candidates may be made respondents to the same petition, and their cases may be tried at the same time, but for the purposes of this Part of this Act the petition shall be deemed to be a separate petition against each respondent.

(4) Where more petitions than one are presented relating to the same election or to elections under the local government Act held at the same time for more than one electoral area in the same local government area, all those petitions shall be bracketed together in the election list and shall be dealt with as one petition, standing, unless the High Court otherwise direct, in the election list in the place where the last of them would have stood if it had been the only petition presented.

(5) Subsections (1), (2) and (4) above do not apply in relation to petitions questioning an election of councillors in Scotland but where two or more of those petitions are presented relating to the same election they shall be tried together.

Trial of petition.

139.—(1) An election petition shall be tried in open court, without a jury, and notice of the time and place of trial shall be given in the prescribed manner, not less than, in the case of a parliamentary election petition, 14 days and in any other case, seven days, before the day of trial.

(2) The election court may in its discretion adjourn the trial from time to time, but the trial shall, so far as is practicable consistently with the interests of justice in respect of the trial, be continued from day to day on every lawful day until its conclusion.

(3) The trial of a parliamentary election petition shall be proceeded with notwithstanding the acceptance by the respondent of an office vacating his seat in Parliament and notwithstanding the prorogation of Parliament; and the trial of a petition questioning an election under the local government Act shall be proceeded with notwithstanding that the respondent has ceased to hold the office his election to which is questioned by the petition.

(4) On the trial of a petition, unless the court otherwise directs, any charge of a corrupt practice may be gone into, and evidence in relation to it received, before any proof has been given of agency on behalf of any candidate in respect of the corrupt practice.

In relation to an election in England and Wales under the local government Act, this subsection applies as if corrupt practices included illegal practices.

(5) On the trial of a petition complaining of an undue election and claiming the seat or office for some person, the respondent may give evidence to prove that that person was not duly elected, in the same manner as if he had presented a petition against the election of that person.

(6) If the petition relates to an election conducted under the parliamentary elections rules or the rules under section 36 or section 42 above and it appears that there is an equality of votes between any candidates at the election, and that the addition of a vote would entitle any of those candidates to be declared elected then—

(*a*) any decision under the provisions as to equality of votes in the parliamentary elections rules or the rules under section 36 or section 42, as the case may be, shall in so far as it determines the question between those candidates, be effective also for the purposes of the petition ; and

(*b*) in so far as that question is not determined by such a decision, the court shall decide between them by lot and proceed as if the one on whom the lot then falls had received an additional vote.

Witnesses.

140.—(1) Witnesses shall be summoned and sworn in the same manner as nearly as circumstances admit as in an action tried in the High Court, but this subsection does not apply to Scotland in relation to an election of councillors.

(2) On the trial a member of the election court may, by order signed by him, require any person who appears to him to have been concerned in the election to attend as a witness, and any person refusing to obey the order shall be guilty of contempt of court.

(3) The election court may examine any person so required to attend or who is in court although he is not called and examined by any party to the petition.

(4) A witness may, after his examination by the court, be cross-examined by or on behalf of the petitioner and respondent, or either of them.

(5) The Director of Public Prosecutions shall obey any direction given him by the election court with respect to the summoning and examination of any witness to give evidence at the trial.

PART III

(6) The Director of Public Prosecutions shall without any direction from the court cause any person appearing to him to be able to give material evidence as to the subject of the trial to attend the trial and shall, with the leave of the court, examine him as a witness.

(7) Subsections (5) and (6) above do not apply to Scotland, and in Scotland one of the deputes of the Lord Advocate or the procurator-fiscal of the district shall attend the trial of the petition as part of his official duty and shall give all necessary assistance to the court with respect to the citation of witnesses and the recovery of documents.

Duty to answer relevant questions.

141.—(1) A person called as a witness respecting an election before any election court shall not be excused from answering any question relating to any offence at or connected with the election—

(*a*) on the ground that the answer to it may incriminate or tend to incriminate—

(i) that person or that person's husband or wife, or

(ii) in Scotland, that person ; or

(*b*) on the ground of privilege.

(2) An answer by a person to a question put by or before any election court shall not, except in the case of any criminal proceeding for perjury in respect of the evidence, be in any proceeding, civil or criminal, admissible in evidence against—

(*a*) that person or that person's husband or wife ; or

(*b*) in Scotland, that person.

(3) A witness who answers truly all questions which he is required by the election court to answer shall be entitled to receive a certificate of indemnity signed by a member of the court stating that the witness has so answered.

(4) The giving or refusal to give a certificate of indemnity to a witness by an election court trying a petition questioning an election under the local government Act shall be final and conclusive.

Certificate of indemnity.

142.—(1) Where a person has received a certificate of indemnity under section 141 above in relation to an election, and any legal proceeding is at any time instituted against him for—

(*a*) any corrupt or illegal practice committed by him previously to the date of the certificate at or in relation to the election, or

(*b*) any illegal payment, employment or hiring so committed, or

(*c*) any offence under section 99(1) or section 110 above or section 149 below, so committed,

PART III

the court having cognizance of the case shall on production of the certificate stay the proceeding, and may in their discretion award to that person such costs as he may have been put to in the proceeding.

(2) Nothing in this section, and sections 140 and 141 above, and section 143 below, shall be deemed to relieve a person receiving a certificate of indemnity from any incapacity under this Act or from any proceedings to enforce that incapacity (other than a criminal prosecution).

Expenses of witnesses.

143.—(1) The reasonable expenses incurred by any person in appearing to give evidence at the trial of an election petition, according to the scale allowed to witnesses on the trial of civil actions, may be allowed to him by a certificate of the election court or of the prescribed officer.

(2) If the witness was called and examined by virtue of section 140(2) above, the expenses referred to in subsection (1) above shall be deemed part of the expenses of providing a court, but otherwise they shall be deemed costs of the petition.

This subsection does not apply to Scotland in relation to an election of councillors.

Conclusion of trial of parliamentary election petition.

144.—(1) At the conclusion of the trial of a parliamentary election petition, the election court shall determine whether the member whose election or return is complained of, or any and what other person, was duly returned or elected or whether the election was void, and the determination so certified shall be final to all intents as to the matters at issue on the petition.

(2) The election court shall forthwith certify in writing the determination to the Speaker.

(3) If the judges constituting the election court—

(*a*) differ as to whether the member whose election or return is complained of was duly elected or returned, they shall certify that difference and the member shall be deemed to be duly elected or returned ;

(*b*) determine that the member was not duly elected or returned but differ as to the rest of the determination, they shall certify that difference and the election shall be deemed to be void.

(4) Where any charge is made in the petition of any corrupt or illegal practice having been committed at the election the court shall, in addition to giving a certificate, and at the same time, make a report to the Speaker as required by sections 158 and 160 below and also stating whether corrupt or illegal practices have, or whether there is reason to believe that corrupt or illegal practices have, extensively prevailed at the election.

PART III

(5) The election court may at the same time make a special report to the Speaker as to matters arising in the course of the trial an account of which in the judgment of the court ought to be submitted to the House of Commons.

(6) Every report sent to the Speaker under this section shall be signed by both judges of the election court and if the judges differ as to the subject of the report, they shall certify that difference and make no report on the subject on which they so differ.

(7) The House of Commons, on being informed by the Speaker of a certificate and any report of an election court, shall order the certificate and report (if any) to be entered in their Journals and shall give the necessary direction—

(*a*) for confirming or altering the return, or

(*b*) for issuing a writ for a new election, or

(*c*) for carrying the determination into execution as the circumstances may require,

and where the court make a special report, the House of Commons may make such order in respect of that report as they think proper.

Conclusion of trial of local election petition.

145.—(1) At the conclusion of the trial of a petition questioning an election under the local government Act, the election court shall determine whether the person whose election is complained of, or any and what other person, was duly elected, or whether the election was void, and the determination so certified shall be final to all intents as to the matters at issue on the petition.

(2) The election court shall forthwith certify in writing the determination to the High Court.

(3) Where a charge is made in the petition of any corrupt or illegal practice having been committed at the election the court shall, in addition to giving a certificate, and at the same time, make a report in writing to the High Court as required by sections 158 and 160 below and also stating whether any corrupt practices have, or whether there is reason to believe that any corrupt practices have, extensively prevailed at the election in the area of the authority for which the election was held or in any electoral area of that authority's area.

(4) The election court may at the same time make a special report to the High Court as to matters arising in the course of the trial an account of which in the judgment of the court ought to be submitted to the High Court.

(5) A copy of any certificate or report made to the High Court shall be sent by the High Court to the Secretary of State.

(6) The High Court shall by the signatures of two or more of its judges certify a copy of the certificate mentioned in subsection (5) above to the proper officer of the authority for which the election was held.

(7) The foregoing provisions of this section, except subsection (1) above, do not apply to Scotland, but where in a petition questioning an election of councillors in Scotland a charge is made of any corrupt or illegal practice having been committed at the election, the court—

(*a*) shall determine the matters mentioned in sections 158 and 160 below; and

(*b*) shall also determine whether any corrupt practices have, or whether there is reason to believe that any corrupt practices have, extensively prevailed at the election and whether illegal practices, payments, employments or hirings committed in reference to the election for the purpose of promoting the election of a candidate at the election have or have not so extensively prevailed that they may be reasonably supposed to have affected the result of the election.

Special case for determination of High Court.

146.—(1) If, on the application of any party to a petition made in the prescribed manner to the High Court, it appears to the High Court that the case raised by the petition can be conveniently stated as a special case, the High Court may direct it to be stated accordingly and the special case shall be heard before the High Court.

(2) In the case of a parliamentary election petition, the High Court shall certify to the Speaker its decision on the special case.

(3) In the case of a petition questioning an election in England and Wales under the local government Act, a statement of the decision on the special case shall be sent by the High Court to the Secretary of State and the High Court shall by the signatures of two or more of its judges also certify that statement to the proper officer of the authority for which the election was held.

(4) If it appears to the election court on the trial of an election petition that any question of law as to the admissibility of evidence or otherwise requires further consideration by the High Court, the election court may postpone the granting of a certificate until the question has been determined by the High Court, and for this purpose may reserve the question by stating a case for the decision of the High Court.

In the application of this subsection to Northern Ireland the references to the High Court are to the Court of Appeal.

PART III

(5) In Scotland the decision of the Court of Session on a special case under subsection (1) above shall be final and in the case of a petition questioning an election of councillors in Scotland, the application under subsection (1) for a direction for the statement of a case for the Court of Session shall be made to the election court.

Withdrawal of petition.

147.—(1) A petitioner shall not withdraw an election petition without the leave of the election court or High Court on special application, made in the prescribed manner and at the prescribed time and place.

In the application of this subsection to a petition questioning an election of councillors in Scotland there shall be omitted the reference to the High Court.

(2) The application shall not be made until the prescribed notice of the intention to make it has been given in the constituency or local government area to which the petition relates.

(3) Where there are more petitioners than one, the application shall not be made except with the consent of all the petitioners.

(4) If a petition is withdrawn the petitioner shall be liable to pay the costs of the respondent.

Evidence required for withdrawal of petition.

148.—(1) Before leave for the withdrawal of an election petition is granted, there shall be produced affidavits—

(*a*) by all the parties to the petition and their solicitors, and

(*b*) if the election was an election at which candidates are required to have election agents, by the election agents of all of those parties who were candidates at the election,

but the High Court may on cause shown dispense with the affidavit of any particular person if it seems to the court on special grounds just so to do.

In the application of this subsection to an election of councillors in Scotland, the reference to the High Court is to an election court, but, if the election was a local government election, the sheriff may act instead of the election court.

(2) Each affidavit shall state that, to the best of the deponent's knowledge and belief—

(*a*) no agreement or terms of any kind whatsoever has or have been made, and

(*b*) no undertaking has been entered into, in relation to the withdrawal of the petition,

but if any lawful agreement has been made with respect to the withdrawal of the petition, the affidavit shall set forth that agreement and shall make the foregoing statement subject to what appears from the affidavit. PART III

(3) The affidavits of the applicant and his solicitor shall further state the ground on which the petition is sought to be withdrawn.

(4) Copies of those affidavits shall be delivered to the Director of Public Prosecutions a reasonable time before the application for the withdrawal is heard, and the court—

(*a*) may hear the Director of Public Prosecutions or his assistant or other representative (appointed with the Attorney General's approval) in opposition to the allowance of the withdrawal of the petition ; and

(*b*) shall have power to receive the evidence on oath of any person or persons whose evidence the Director of Public Prosecutions or his assistant, or other representative, may consider material.

In the application of this subsection to an election of councillors in Scotland the references to the Director of Public Prosecutions include references to the procurator-fiscal.

(5) Where more than one solicitor is concerned for the petitioner or respondent, whether as agent for another solicitor or otherwise, the affidavit shall be made by all such solicitors.

(6) Except in Scotland, the jurisdiction vested by subsection (1) above in the High Court in matters relating to parliamentary elections shall, subject to rules of court, be exercised—

(*a*) by one of the judges for the time being on the rota for the trial of parliamentary election petitions,

(*b*) in Northern Ireland, by one of the judges of the High Court or the Court of Appeal for the time being selected under section 108 of the Judicature (Northern Ireland) Act 1978, 1978 c. 23.

sitting either in court or at chambers, or may be exercised by a master of the Supreme Court in manner directed by and subject to appeal to those judges.

Penalty for corrupt withdrawal and breach of s. 148.

149. If a person makes any agreement or terms, or enters into any undertaking, in relation to the withdrawal of an election petition, and such agreement, terms or undertaking—

(*a*) is or are for the withdrawal of the election petition in consideration of any payment, or in consideration that the seat or office should at any time be vacated, or in consideration of the withdrawal of any other election petition, or

(*b*) is or are (whether lawful or unlawful) not mentioned in

PART III

the affidavits referred to in section 148 above,

he shall be liable—

(i) on conviction on indictment (except in Northern Ireland) to imprisonment for a term not exceeding one year or to a fine or to both ;

(ii) on conviction on indictment in Northern Ireland to imprisonment for a term not exceeding one year or to a fine not exceeding £200 or to both.

Substitution of new petitioner.

150.—(1) On the hearing of the application for leave to withdraw, any person who might have been a petitioner in respect of the election may apply to the court to be substituted as a petitioner, and the court may, if they think fit, substitute him accordingly.

(2) If the proposed withdrawal is in the opinion of the court the result of any agreement, terms or undertaking prohibited by section 149 above or induced by any corrupt bargain or consideration, the court may by order direct—

(*a*) that the security given on behalf of the original petitioner shall remain as security for any costs that may be incurred by the substituted petitioner, and

(*b*) that, to the extent of the sum named in the security, the original petitioner and his sureties shall be liable to pay the costs of the substituted petitioner.

(3) If the court does not so direct, then security to the same amount as would be required in the case of a new petition, and subject to the like conditions, shall be given on behalf of the substituted petitioner before he proceeds with his petition and within the prescribed time after the order of substitution.

(4) Subject to the above provisions, a substituted petitioner shall, as nearly as may be, stand in the same position and be subject to the same liabilities as the original petitioner.

Report on withdrawal.

151.—(1) In every case of the withdrawal—

(*a*) of a parliamentary election petition, the court giving leave for the withdrawal shall make a report to the Speaker as required by subsection (2) below ; and

(*b*) by leave of the election court, of a petition questioning an election in England and Wales under the local government Act, that court shall make a report in writing to the High Court as so required.

(2) The report shall state whether in the court's opinion the withdrawal of the petition was—

(*a*) the result of any agreement, terms or undertaking, or

PART III

(*b*) in consideration of any payment, or in consideration that the seat or office should at any time be vacated or in consideration of the withdrawal of any other election petition or for any other consideration,

and, if so, shall state the circumstances attending the withdrawal.

Abatement of petition.

152.—(1) An election petition shall be abated by the death of a sole petitioner or of the survivor of several petitioners.

(2) The abatement shall not affect the liability of the petitioner or any other person to the payment of costs previously incurred.

(3) On the abatement the prescribed notice of it shall be given in the constituency or local government area to which the petition relates; and within the prescribed time after the notice is given, any person who might have been a petitioner in respect of the election may apply to the election court or High Court in the prescribed manner and in the prescribed time and place to be substituted as a petitioner; and the court may, if it thinks fit, substitute him accordingly.

(4) Security shall be given on behalf of a petitioner so substituted, as in the case of a new petition.

(5) In the application of this section to an election of councillors in Scotland the reference in subsection (3) above to the High Court shall be omitted, and the sheriff may act instead of the election court.

Withdrawal and substitution of respondents before trial.

153.—(1) If before the trial of an election petition a respondent other than a returning officer—

(*a*) gives the prescribed notice that he does not intend to oppose the petition or dies, or

(*b*) where the petition questions a parliamentary election or return, is summoned to Parliament as a peer by a writ issued under the Great Seal of the United Kingdom or the House of Commons have resolved that his seat is vacant, or

(*c*) where the petition questions an election under the local government Act, resigns or otherwise ceases to hold the office to which the petition relates,

notice of any of those matters shall be given in the constituency or local government area to which the petition relates, and, within the prescribed time after the notice is given, any person who might have been a petitioner in respect of the election may apply to a member of the election court or to the High Court to be admitted as a respondent to oppose the petition, and shall be admitted accordingly, except that the number of persons so admitted shall not exceed three.

PART III

(2) The notice to be given under subsection (1) above in any local government area shall be such as may be prescribed.

(3) A respondent who has given the prescribed notice that he does not intend to oppose the petition shall not be allowed to appear or act as a party against the petition in any proceedings on the petition, and if the petition relates to a parliamentary election he shall not sit or vote in the House of Commons until the House of Commons has been informed of the report on the petition.

(4) Where a respondent to a parliamentary election petition has given that notice in the prescribed time and manner, the High Court or either of the judges constituting the election court shall report that fact to the Speaker.

(5) In the application of this section to an election of councillors in Scotland, the reference to the High Court shall be omitted and the sheriff may act instead of the election court.

Costs of petition.

154.—(1) All costs of and incidental to the presentation of an election petition and the proceedings consequent on it, except such as are by this Act otherwise provided for, shall be defrayed by the parties to the petition in such manner and in such proportions as the election court or High Court may determine.

(2) In particular—

(*a*) any costs which in the opinion of the election court or High Court have been caused by vexatious conduct, unfounded allegations or unfounded objections on the part either of the petitioner or of the respondent, and

(*b*) any needless expense incurred or caused on the part of the petitioner or respondent,

may be ordered to be defrayed by the parties by whom it has been incurred or caused whether or not they are on the whole successful.

(3) In the application of this section to Scotland, references to the High Court shall be omitted in relation to an election of councillors.

Neglect or refusal to pay costs.

155.—(1) Subsection (2) below applies if a petitioner neglects or refuses—

(*a*) in the case of a parliamentary election petition, for six months after demand, and

(*b*) in the case of a petition questioning an election under the local government Act, for three months after demand,

to pay to any person summoned as a witness on his behalf or to the respondent any sum certified to be due to that person or the respondent for his costs, and the neglect or refusal is, within one year after the demand, proved to the satisfaction of the High Court, or, in Scotland, the election court.

(2) Where subsection (1) above applies, every person who under this Act entered into a recognisance relating to that petition shall be held to be in default of the recognisance, and—

(a) the prescribed officer shall thereupon certify the recognisance to be forfeited, and

(b) it shall be dealt with as if forfeited by the Crown Court, or, in Northern Ireland, under the Fines Act (Ireland) 1851, as the case may be,

1851 c. 90.

but in Scotland the prescribed officer shall, where otherwise competent under the provisions of this subsection—

(i) certify that the conditions contained in the bond of caution have not been fulfilled ; and

(ii) it shall then be competent for the party or parties interested to register that bond, and do diligence upon it as accords of law.

Further provisions as to costs.

156.—(1) Where upon the trial of an election petition it appears to the election court—

(a) that a corrupt practice has not been proved to have been committed in reference to the election by or with the knowledge and consent of the respondent to the petition, and

(b) that the respondent took all reasonable means to prevent corrupt practices being committed on his behalf,

the court may make one or more orders with respect to the payment either of the whole or such part of the costs of the petition as the court think right as provided by subsection (2) or subsection (5) below.

(2) If it appears to the court that corrupt practices extensively prevailed in reference to the election, the court may order the whole or part of the costs to be paid—

(a) in the case of a parliamentary election, by the constituency for which the election was held ; and

(b) in the case of an election under the local government Act, by the authority for which the election was held.

(3) The Treasury shall—

(a) pay any costs ordered to be paid by a constituency under subsection (2) above, and

(b) obtain repayment of the amount so paid from the authority liable to pay registration expenses for that constituency,

PART III

but that authority shall be entitled to the like contribution, if any, from any other local authority, and any such contribution shall be paid in like manner as if those costs were registration expenses, and the Treasury may recover any advance so made by deduction from any sums payable under Part I of this Act to that authority or in any other manner.

In relation to Northern Ireland the reference to the authority liable to pay registration expenses shall be taken as a reference to the district council for the district in which the constituency is wholly or partly situated and, where more than one council is concerned, those costs shall be paid by them in such proportion as the Secretary of State may direct.

(4) Where under subsection (3) above the Treasury pay any costs ordered to be paid by a constituency which is situated—

(*a*) partly in one district or London borough and partly in another, or

(*b*) partly in a London borough and partly in the City and the Inner Temple and the Middle Temple,

the authority from which the Treasury are to obtain repayment of the amount under this section shall be the authority which appointed the registration officer who is acting returning officer for the constituency, and such contributions shall be made to that authority by any other local authority as the Secretary of State may direct.

(5) If it appears to the court that any person or persons is or are proved, whether by providing money or otherwise, to have been extensively engaged in corrupt practices, or to have encouraged or promoted extensive corrupt practices in reference to the election, the court may, after giving that person or those persons an opportunity of being heard by counsel or solicitor and examining and cross-examining witnesses to show cause why the order should not be made—

(*a*) order the whole or part of the costs to be paid by that person, or those persons or any of them, and

(*b*) order that if the costs cannot be recovered from one or more of those persons they shall be paid by some other of those persons or by either of the parties to the petition.

(6) Where any person appears to the court to have been guilty of a corrupt or illegal practice, the court may, after giving that person an opportunity of making a statement to show why the order should not be made, order the whole or any part of the costs of or incidental to any proceeding before the court in relation to that offence or to that person to be paid by that person to such person or persons as the court may direct.

Part III

Appeals and jurisdiction.

157.—(1) No appeal lies without the special leave of the High Court from the decision of the High Court on any question of law, whether on appeal or otherwise, under the foregoing provisions of this Part of this Act, and if leave to appeal is granted the decision of the Court of Appeal in the case shall be final and conclusive.

(2) Subject to the provisions of this Act and of the rules made under it, the principles, practice and rules on which committees of the House of Commons used to act in dealing with election petitions shall be observed, so far as may be, by the High Court and election court in the case of election petitions, and in particular the principles and rules with regard to—

(*a*) agency,

(*b*) evidence,

(*c*) a scrutiny, and

(*d*) declaring any person elected in place of any other person declared not to have been duly elected,

shall be observed, as far as may be, in the case of a petition questioning an election under the local government Act as in the case of a parliamentary election petition.

(3) The High Court has, subject to the provisions of this Act, the same powers, jurisdiction and authority with respect to an election petition and the proceedings on it as if the petition were an ordinary action within its jurisdiction.

(4) The duties to be performed in relation to parliamentary elections by the prescribed officer under this Part shall be performed by such one or more of the masters of the Supreme Court (Queen's Bench Division) as the Lord Chief Justice may determine.

(5) There shall be awarded to those masters respectively, in addition to their salaries payable apart from this subsection, such remuneration for the performance of their duties in relation to parliamentary elections under this Part as the Lord Chief Justice with the Treasury's consent may determine.

(6) The duties to be performed in relation to elections under the local government Act by the prescribed officer under this Part shall be performed by the prescribed officer of the High Court.

(7) In the application of this section to Scotland, subsections (1) and (4) to (6) above and, in relation to elections of councillors, subsection (3) above, shall be omitted, but the duties to be performed in relation to parliamentary elections by the prescribed officer under this Part shall be performed by the Principal Clerk of Session.

PART III

(8) Subsection (1) above does not apply in Northern Ireland and, in the application of subsections (4) and (5) to Northern Ireland, the references to the Lord Chief Justice are references to the Lord Chief Justice of Northern Ireland and the reference to any master of the Supreme Court (Queen's Bench Division) is a reference to an officer of the Supreme Court of Judicature of Northern Ireland.

Consequences of finding by election court of corrupt or illegal practice

Report as to candidate guilty of a corrupt or illegal practice.

158.—(1) The report of an election court under section 144 or section 145 above shall state whether any corrupt or illegal practice has or has not been proved to have been committed by or with the knowledge and consent of any candidate at the election, and the nature of the corrupt or illegal practice.

(2) For the purposes of sections 159 and 160 below—

(*a*) if it is reported that a corrupt practice other than treating or undue influence was committed with the knowledge and consent of a candidate, he shall be treated as having been reported personally guilty of that corrupt practice, and

(*b*) if it is reported that an illegal practice was committed with the knowledge and consent of a candidate at a parliamentary election, he shall be treated as having been reported personally guilty of that illegal practice.

(3) The report shall also state whether any of the candidates has been guilty by his agents of any corrupt or illegal practice in reference to the election ; but if a candidate is reported guilty by his agents of treating, undue influence or any illegal practice, and the court further reports that the candidate has proved to the court—

(*a*) that no corrupt or illegal practice was committed at the election by the candidate or his election agent and the offences mentioned in the report were committed contrary to the orders and without the sanction or connivance of the candidate or his election agent, and

(*b*) that the candidate and his election agent took all reasonable means for preventing the commission of corrupt and illegal practices at the election, and

(*c*) that the offences mentioned in the report were of a trivial, unimportant and limited character, and

(*d*) that in all other respects the election was free from any corrupt or illegal practice on the part of the candidate and of his agents,

then the candidate shall not be treated for the purposes of section 159 as having been reported guilty by his agents of the offences mentioned in the report.

PART III

In relation to an election where candidates are not required to have election agents, for paragraphs (*a*) and (*b*) above the following paragraphs shall be substituted—

"(*a*) that no corrupt or illegal practice was committed at the election by the candidate or with his knowledge or consent and the offences mentioned in the report were committed without the sanction or connivance of the candidate, and

(*b*) that all reasonable means for preventing the commission of corrupt and illegal practices at the election were taken by and on behalf of the candidate,".

Candidate reported guilty of corrupt or illegal practice.

159.—(1) If a candidate who has been elected is reported by an election court personally guilty or guilty by his agents of any corrupt or illegal practice his election shall be void.

(2) A candidate at a parliamentary election shall also be incapable from the date of the report of being elected to and sitting in the House of Commons for the constituency for which the election was held or any constituency which includes the whole or any part of the area of the first-mentioned constituency as constituted for the purposes of the election—

(*a*) if reported personally guilty of a corrupt practice, for ten years;

(*b*) if reported guilty by his agents of a corrupt practice or personally guilty of an illegal practice, for seven years;

(*c*) if reported guilty by his agents of an illegal practice, during the Parliament for which the election was held.

(3) A candidate at an election under the local government Act shall also be incapable from the date of the report of holding any corporate office in the local government area for which the election was held, or in any local government area which includes the whole or any part of the area of the first-mentioned local government area as constituted for the purposes of the election, or, if the election was in Scotland, of holding any corporate office in Scotland—

(*a*) if reported personally guilty of a corrupt practice, for ten years,

(*b*) if reported guilty by his agents of a corrupt practice, for three years,

(*c*) if reported personally guilty or guilty by his agents of an illegal practice, during the period for which the candidate was elected to serve or for which if elected he might have served,

and if at the date of the report he holds any such corporate office, then the office shall be vacated as from that date.

PART III

In this subsection " corporate office " in England and Wales means the office of chairman, mayor or councillor of a county, London borough, district or parish or community council or of chairman of a parish or community meeting; and in Scotland the office of councillor of any local authority.

(4) The provisions of this section as to the consequences of the report that a candidate was guilty by his agents of a corrupt or illegal practice have effect subject to the express provisions of this Act relating to particular acts which are declared to be corrupt or illegal practices.

Persons reported personally guilty of corrupt or illegal practices.

160.—(1) The report of the election court under section 144 or section 145 above shall state the names of all persons (if any) who have been proved at the trial to have been guilty of any corrupt or illegal practice and whether they have been provided with certificates of indemnity, but in the case of someone—

(*a*) who is not a party to the petition, or

(*b*) who is not a candidate on behalf of whom the seat or office is claimed by the petition,

the election court shall first cause notice to be given to him, and if he appears in pursuance of the notice shall give him an opportunity of being heard by himself and of calling evidence in his defence to show why he should not be so reported.

(2) It is the duty of the Director of Public Prosecutions to obey any directions given to him by the election court with respect to any person to whom such a notice is given.

(3) The report shall be laid before the Attorney General with a view to his instituting or directing a prosecution against such persons as have not received certificates of indemnity, if the evidence should, in his opinion, be sufficient to support a prosecution.

(4) Subject to the provisions of section 174 below, a candidate or other person reported by an election court personally guilty of a corrupt practice shall for five years from the date of the report be incapable—

(*a*) of being registered as an elector or voting at any parliamentary election in the United Kingdom or at any election in Great Britain to any public office, and

(*b*) of being elected to and sitting in the House of Commons, and

(*c*) of holding any public or judicial office,

and, if already elected to the House of Commons or holding such office, shall from that date vacate the seat or office.

PART III

(5) Subject to the provisions of section 174, a candidate or other person reported by an election court personally guilty of an illegal practice shall for five years from the date of the report be incapable of being registered as an elector or voting at any parliamentary election or at any election to a public office held—

(*a*) if the offence was committed in reference to a parliamentary election, for or within the constituency for which it was held or for or within any constituency or local government area wholly or partly within the area of the first-mentioned constituency as constituted for the purposes of the election;

(*b*) if the offence was committed in reference to an election under the local government Act, for or within the local government area for which the election was held or for or within any constituency or local government area wholly or partly within the area of the first-mentioned local government area as constituted for the purposes of the election.

Where the offence was committed in reference to an election of councillors in Scotland, for the reference to an election to a public office there shall be substituted a reference to an election to the office of councillor.

(6) Without prejudice to the generality of the provisions of section 205(2) below, nothing in subsection (4) or subsection (5) above affects matters relating to the Northern Ireland Assembly or local elections or holding office in Northern Ireland.

(7) The provisions of this section as to the consequences of the report that a candidate was guilty by his agents of a corrupt or illegal practice have effect subject to the express provisions of this Act relating to particular acts which are declared to be corrupt or illegal practices.

Director of Public Prosecutions' duty to report corrupt practice

Justice of the Peace.

161. Where a justice of the peace is reported by an election court to have been guilty of any corrupt practice in reference to an election, whether he has obtained a certificate of indemnity or not, it is the duty of the Director of Public Prosecutions to report the case to the Lord Chancellor with such evidence as may have been given of the corrupt practice.

Member of legal and certain other professions.

162. Where a barrister, advocate, solicitor or any person who belongs to any profession the admission to which is regulated by law is reported by an election court to have been guilty of any corrupt practice in reference to an election, whether he has obtained a certificate of indemnity or not—

(*a*) it is the duty of the Director of Public Prosecutions to

PART III

bring the matter before the Inn of Court, High Court or tribunal having power to take cognizance of any misconduct of the person in his profession ; and

(*b*) the Inn of Court, High Court or tribunal may deal with him as if the corrupt practice were misconduct by him in his profession.

Holder of licence or certificate under Licensing Acts.

163.—(1) If it appears to an election court that a person holding a licence or certificate under the Licensing Acts has knowingly permitted any bribery or treating in reference to any election to take place upon his licensed premises—

(*a*) the court shall, after affording him such rights as are conferred on those about to be reported under section 160(1) above, report the fact; and

(*b*) whether that person has obtained a certificate of indemnity or not, it is the duty of the Director of Public Prosecutions to bring the report before the licensing authority from whom, or on whose certificate, that person obtained his licence, and the licensing authority shall cause the report to be entered in the proper register of licences.

(2) The entry of the report in that register shall be taken into consideration by the licensing authority in determining whether they will or will not grant a renewal of the licence or certificate of the person reported and may be a ground, if the authority think fit, for refusing renewal.

Further provision as to avoidance of elections and striking off votes

Avoidance of election for general corruption etc.

164.—(1) Where on an election petition it is shown that corrupt or illegal practices or illegal payments, employments or hirings committed in reference to the election for the purpose of promoting or procuring the election of any person at that election have so extensively prevailed that they may be reasonably supposed to have affected the result—

(*a*) his election, if he has been elected, shall be void, and

(*b*) he shall be incapable of being elected to fill the vacancy or any of the vacancies for which the election was held.

(2) An election shall not be liable to be avoided otherwise than under this section by reason of general corruption, bribery, treating or intimidation.

(3) An election under the local government Act may be questioned on the ground that it is avoided under this section.

Avoidance of election for employing corrupt agent.

165.—(1) If at a parliamentary or local government election a candidate or his election agent personally engages as a canvasser or agent for the conduct or management of the election any person whom he knows or has reasonable grounds for supposing to be subject to an incapacity to vote at the election by reason—

(*a*) of his having been convicted or reported of any corrupt or illegal practice within the meaning of this Act or of the law relating to elections for the Northern Ireland Assembly, or

(*b*) of his having been convicted more than once of an offence under the Public Bodies Corrupt Practices Act 1889, 1889 c. 69.

the candidate shall be incapable of being elected to fill the vacancy or any of the vacancies for which the election is held.

(2) A local government election may be questioned on the ground that the person whose election is questioned was, at the time of the election, by virtue of this section incapable of being elected.

(3) A vote given for a person who, at the time of the election, was by virtue of this section incapable of being elected shall not, by reason of that incapacity, be deemed to be thrown away so as to entitle another candidate to be declared elected, unless given at a poll consequent on the decision of an election court that he was so incapable.

Votes to be struck off for corrupt or illegal practices.

166.—(1) Where, on a parliamentary election petition claiming the seat for any person, a candidate is proved to have been guilty by himself, or by any person on his behalf, of bribery, treating or undue influence in respect of any person who voted at the election there shall, on a scrutiny, be struck off from the number of votes appearing to have been given to the candidate one vote for every person who voted at the election and is proved to have been so bribed, treated or unduly influenced.

(2) If any person who is guilty of a corrupt or illegal practice or of illegal payment, employment or hiring at an election votes at the election, his vote shall be void.

(3) If any person who is subject under any enactment relating to corrupt or illegal practices to an incapacity to vote at a parliamentary election or an election to any public office votes at that election, his vote shall be void.

Power to except innocent act from being illegal practice, payment, employment or hiring

Application for relief.

167.—(1) An application for relief under this section may be made to the High Court or an election court or else, if in

PART III

respect of a payment made in contravention of section 78(1) or (2) above, or of paragraph 1 of Schedule 4 to this Act, to a county court.

(2) If it is shown to the court by such evidence as to the court seems sufficient—

(*a*) that any act or omission of any person would apart from this section by reason of being in contravention of this Act be an illegal practice, payment, employment or hiring,

(*b*) that the act or omission arose from inadvertence or from accidental miscalculation or from some other reasonable cause of a like nature, and in any case did not arise from any want of good faith, and

(*c*) that such notice of the application has been given in the constituency or, as the case may be, the area of the authority for which the election was held, as to the court seems fit,

and under the circumstances it seems to the court to be just that either that or any other person should not be subject to any of the consequences under this Act of the act or omission, the court may make an order allowing the act or omission to be an exception from the provisions of this Act making it an illegal practice, payment, employment or hiring and upon the making of the order no person shall be subject to any of the consequences under this Act of that act or omission.

(3) In relation to an election of councillors in Scotland, the references in subsection (1) to applications to the High Court or a county court shall be omitted.

(4) Except in Scotland, the jurisdiction vested by the above provisions of this section in the High Court in matters relating to parliamentary elections shall, subject to rules of court, be exercised by—

(*a*) one of the judges for the time being on the rota for the trial of parliamentary election petitions,

(*b*) in Northern Ireland, one of the judges of the High Court or the Court of Appeal for the time being
1978 c. 23. selected under section 108 of the Judicature (Northern Ireland) Act 1978,

sitting either in court or at chambers but shall not be exercisable by a master.

(5) The jurisdiction vested by this section in a county court may, except in Northern Ireland, be exercised otherwise than in open court, and, in Northern Ireland, shall be exercised in accordance with rules of court.

An appeal lies to the High Court from any order of a county court made under this section.

Prosecutions for corrupt or illegal practices

Prosecutions for corrupt practices.

168.—(1) A corrupt practice shall be punishable on conviction on indictment or on summary conviction (including conviction under section 171 below by an election court), but a person shall not be prosecuted summarily where there may be occasion to exercise the powers conferred by subsections (1) and (2) of section 174 below.

(2) A person convicted on indictment of a corrupt practice, other than personation or aiding, abetting, counselling or procuring the commission of the offence of personation, shall be liable—

(*a*) except in Northern Ireland, to imprisonment for a term not exceeding one year or to a fine;

(*b*) in Northern Ireland, to imprisonment for a term not exceeding one year or to a fine not exceeding £200.

(3) A person who commits the offence of personation or of aiding, abetting, counselling or procuring the commission of the offence of personation shall be guilty of an offence and if convicted of it on indictment shall be liable to imprisonment for a term not exceeding two years.

(4) A person shall be liable if summarily convicted of a corrupt practice—

(*a*) by a magistrates' court in England and Wales or a court of summary jurisdiction in Scotland, to imprisonment for a term not exceeding 3 months or to a fine not exceeding the statutory maximum or to both;

(*b*) by a court of summary jurisdiction in Northern Ireland, to imprisonment for a term not exceeding 3 months or to a fine not exceeding £100 or to both;

(*c*) by an election court, to imprisonment for a term not exceeding 6 months, or, in England and Wales or in Scotland, to a fine not exceeding the statutory maximum, or in Northern Ireland, to a fine not exceeding £200.

(5) In England and Wales and Northern Ireland a person charged with personation shall not be convicted by a magistrates' court or, save under section 171 below, committed for trial, except on the evidence of not less than two credible witnesses.

(6) In Scotland, a person charged with personation shall not be convicted except on the evidence of not less than two credible witnesses.

PART III

(7) If it appears to the court by which any person holding a licence or certificate under the Licensing Acts is convicted of the offence of bribery or treating that the offence was committed on his licensed premises—

(*a*) the court shall direct the conviction to be entered in the proper register of licences, and

(*b*) the entry shall be taken into consideration by the licensing authority in determining whether they will or will not grant a renewal of the licence or certificate, and may be a ground, if the authority think fit, for refusing its renewal.

Prosecutions for illegal practices.

169. A person guilty of an illegal practice shall on summary conviction (including conviction under section 171 below by an election court) be liable to a fine not exceeding level 3 on the standard scale, or, in Northern Ireland, to a fine not exceeding £100; and on a prosecution for an illegal practice it shall be sufficient to allege that the person charged was guilty of an illegal practice.

Conviction of illegal practice on charge of corrupt practice etc.

170. A person charged with a corrupt practice may, if the circumstances warrant such finding, be found guilty of an illegal practice (which offence shall for that purpose be an indictable offence), and a person charged with an illegal practice may be found guilty of that offence notwithstanding that the act constituting the offence amounted to a corrupt practice.

Election petition offences in England and Wales and Northern Ireland.

171.—(1) The Director of Public Prosecutions shall obey any direction given to him by an election court with respect to the prosecution by him of offenders, and if it appears to him that a person who has not received a certificate of indemnity has been guilty of a corrupt or illegal practice, he shall—

(*a*) without any such direction, prosecute that person for that offence before the election court, or

(*b*) if he thinks it expedient in the interests of justice, prosecute him before any other competent court.

(2) Where a person prosecuted before an election court appears before the court, the court shall proceed to try him summarily unless the court thinks it expedient in the interests of justice that he should be tried before some other court, but in the case of a corrupt practice, the court before proceeding to try him summarily shall give him the option of being tried by a jury.

PART III

(3) The Magistrates' Courts Act 1980 (or, in Northern Ireland, the Magistrates' Courts (Northern Ireland) Order 1981) shall, in principle and so far as practicable, apply to the prosecution of an offence summarily before an election court in like manner as if it were an offence punishable only on summary conviction, and accordingly—

1980 c. 43.
S.I. 1981/1675 (N.I. 26).

(*a*) the attendance of any person may be enforced,

(*b*) the case heard and determined,

(*c*) any summary conviction by such court carried into effect and enforced,

(*d*) the case's costs paid, and

(*e*) the case's record dealt with,

under that Act or Order in like manner as if the court were a magistrates' court for the county or place in which the conviction took place, but no appeal lies against a conviction by an election court.

(4) Where—

(*a*) the person prosecuted does not appear before the court, or

(*b*) the court thinks it expedient in the interests of justice that he should be tried before some other court, or

(*c*) the person prosecuted elects under subsection (2) above to be tried by a jury,

and the court is of opinion that the evidence is sufficient to put that person on trial for the offence, the court shall order that person to be prosecuted either on indictment or before a magistrates' court, as the case may require, for the offence and thereupon shall proceed as directed by subsection (6), (7) or (8) below, but, except where the accused has elected to be tried by a jury, a corrupt practice shall not for the purposes of the following provisions of this section be deemed to be an indictable offence if the election court think that it should be prosecuted summarily.

(5) The court may name the court before whom the person is to be prosecuted and for all purposes preliminary to and of and incidental to the prosecution the offence shall be deemed to have been committed within the jurisdiction of the court so named.

(6) If the accused is present before the court and the offence is an indictable offence, the enactments relating to charges before justices against persons for indictable offences shall in principle and so far as practicable apply and the court shall commit him for trial.

PART III

(7) If the accused is present before the court and the offence is not an indictable offence, the election court—

(*a*) shall order him to be brought before the magistrates' court before whom he is to be prosecuted ; or

1976 c. 63.

(*b*) grant him bail in accordance with the Bail Act 1976 subject to a duty (or, in Northern Ireland, cause him to give bail) to appear before that magistrates' court.

(8) If the accused is not present before the court, the court shall as circumstances require issue a summons for his attendance, or a warrant to apprehend him and bring him before a magistrates' court.

(9) The magistrates' court before whom he attends or is brought shall—

(*a*) if the offence is an indictable offence, on proof only of the summons or warrant and the identity of the accused, commit him for trial ; and

(*b*) if the offence is not an indictable offence, proceed to try the case or, if the magistrates' court is not the court before which he is directed to be prosecuted, order him to be brought before that court,

1980 c. 43.

and sections 18 to 23 and 25 and 26 of the Magistrates' Courts Act 1980 shall (in either case) not apply.

(10) This section does not apply in Scotland.

Election petition offences in Scotland.

172.—(1) If at the trial in Scotland of an election petition the election court grants a warrant for the apprehension, commitment or citation of any person suspected of being guilty of a corrupt or illegal practice, the case shall be reported to the Lord Advocate in order that that person may be brought to trial before the High Court of Justiciary or the sheriff principal according to the nature of the case.

(2) It is the duty of the advocate depute or, in his absence, the procurator-fiscal, if it appears to him that a corrupt or illegal practice has been committed by any person who has not received a certificate of indemnity, to report the case to the Lord Advocate with a view to that person being brought to trial before the proper court, although no warrant may have been issued by the election court.

(3) All prosecutions directed to be tried in the sheriff court shall be tried by the sheriff principal.

(4) Any criminal court in Scotland, before which a prosecution is instituted on indictment for a corrupt practice, may order the accused to pay to the prosecutor the prosecutor's reasonable costs of the prosecution.

PART III

Incapacities on conviction of corrupt or illegal practice.

173. Subject to the provisions of section 174 below, but in addition to any punishment as provided by the above provisions—

(*a*) a person convicted of a corrupt practice on indictment or by an election court shall be subject to the incapacities imposed by section 160(4) above as if at the date of the conviction he had been reported personally guilty of that corrupt practice ; and

(*b*) a person convicted of an illegal practice shall be subject to the incapacities imposed by section 160(5) as if at the date of the conviction he had been reported personally guilty of that illegal practice.

Mitigation and remission of incapacities

Mitigation and remission etc.

174.—(1) Where—

(*a*) any person is subject to any incapacity by virtue of the report of an election court, and

(*b*) he or some other person in respect of whose acts the incapacity was imposed is on a prosecution acquitted of any of the matters in respect of which the incapacity was imposed,

the court may order that the incapacity shall thenceforth cease so far as it is imposed in respect of those matters.

(2) Where any person who is subject to any incapacity as mentioned above is on a prosecution convicted of any such matters as are mentioned above, no further incapacity shall be taken to be imposed by reason of the conviction, and the court shall have the like power (if any) to mitigate or remit for the future the incapacity so far as it is imposed by section 160 above in respect of the matters of which he is convicted, as if the incapacity had been imposed by reason of the conviction.

(3) A court exercising any of the powers conferred by subsections (1) and (2) above shall make an order declaring how far, if at all, the incapacities imposed by virtue of the relevant report remain unaffected by the exercise of that power, and that order shall be conclusive for all purposes.

(4) Where a person convicted of a corrupt or illegal practice is subsequently reported to have been guilty of that practice by an election court, no further incapacity shall be imposed on him under section 160 by reason of the report.

(5) Where any person is subject to any incapacity by virtue of a conviction or of the report of an election court, and any witness who gave evidence against that person upon the proceeding for the conviction or report is convicted of perjury in respect

PART III

of that evidence, the incapacitated person may apply to the High Court, and the court, if satisfied that the conviction or report so far as respects that person was based upon perjury, may order that the incapacity shall thenceforth cease.

(6) Except in Scotland, the jurisdiction vested in the High Court by subsection (5) above in matters relating to parliamentary elections shall, subject to rules of court, be exercised—

(*a*) by one of the judges for the time being on the rota for the trial of parliamentary election petitions,

(*b*) in Northern Ireland, by one of the judges of the High Court or the Court of Appeal for the time being selected under section 108 of the Judicature (Northern Ireland) Act 1978,

1978 c. 23.

either in court or at chambers, or by a master of the Supreme Court in manner directed by and subject to an appeal to those judges.

Illegal payments, employments or hirings

Illegal payments etc.

175.—(1) A person guilty of an offence of illegal payment, employment or hiring shall, on summary conviction, be liable to a fine not exceeding level 3 on the standard scale, or, in Northern Ireland, to a fine not exceeding £100; and on a prosecution for such an offence it shall be sufficient to allege that the person charged was guilty of an illegal payment, employment or hiring as the case may be.

(2) A candidate or election agent who is personally guilty of an offence of illegal payment, employment or hiring shall be guilty of an illegal practice, and if an offence of illegal payment, employment or hiring is committed with the candidate's knowledge and consent at an election where candidates are not required to have election agents, the candidate shall be guilty of an illegal practice.

(3) Any person charged with an offence of illegal payment, employment or hiring may be found guilty of that offence, notwithstanding that the act constituting the offence amounted to a corrupt or illegal practice.

General provisions as to prosecutions

Time limit for prosecutions.

176.—(1) A proceeding against a person in respect of any offence to which this section applies shall be commenced within one year after the offence was committed, and the time so limited by this section shall, in the case of any proceedings under the Magistrates' Courts Act 1980 (or, in Northern Ireland, the Magistrates' Courts (Northern Ireland) Order 1981) for any such

1980 c. 43.
S.I. 1981/1675 (N.I. 26).

offence, whether before an election court or otherwise, be substituted for any limitation of time contained in that Act or Order. PART III

(2) For the purpose of this section, the issue of a summons, warrant or other process (in this subsection collectively "the process") shall be deemed to be a commencement of the proceeding—

(*a*) where the service or execution of the process on or against the alleged offender is prevented by his absconding or concealment or act; but

(*b*) except as mentioned in paragraph (*a*) above, service or execution of the process on or against the alleged offender, and not its issue, shall be deemed to be that commencement.

(3) This section applies to any corrupt or illegal practice, any illegal payment, employment or hiring and any offence under section 99(1), section 110 and section 149 above.

Local election offence punishable summarily.

177. A prosecution for any offence punishable summarily committed in reference to an election under the local government Act—

(*a*) may be instituted before any magistrates' court in the county in which the local government area for which the election was held is situated or which it adjoins; and

(*b*) the offence shall be deemed for all purposes to have been committed within the jurisdiction of that court.

This section does not apply in Scotland.

Prosecution of offences committed outside United Kingdom.

178.—(1) Proceedings under this Act in respect of an offence alleged to have been committed outside the United Kingdom by a Commonwealth citizen or citizen of the Republic of Ireland may be taken before the appropriate court in the United Kingdom having jurisdiction in the place where the person charged is for the time being.

(2) Any period fixed by law as the period within which proceedings may be commenced shall, in the case of any such proceedings as are mentioned in subsection (1) above, be reckoned as from the date on which the person charged first landed in the United Kingdom next after the commission of the offence, and for the purposes of this provision a person entering Northern Ireland by land shall be deemed so to land in the United Kingdom.

PART III

Offences by associations.

179. Where—

(*a*) any corrupt or illegal practice or any illegal payment, employment or hiring, or

(*b*) any offence under section 110 above,

is committed by any association or body of persons, corporate or unincorporate, the members of the association or body who have taken part in the commission of the offence shall be liable to any fine or punishment imposed for that offence by this Act.

Evidence by certificate of holding of elections.

180. On—

(*a*) any prosecution for a corrupt or illegal practice or for any illegal payment, employment or hiring, and

(*b*) any proceedings for a penalty under section 85 above or paragraph 4 of Schedule 4 to this Act,

the certificate of the returning officer at an election—

(i) that the election mentioned in the certificate was duly held, and

(ii) that the person named in the certificate was a candidate at the election,

shall be sufficient evidence of the facts stated in it.

Director of Public Prosecutions.

181.—(1) Where information is given to the Director of Public Prosecutions that any corrupt or illegal practice has occurred in reference to any election, it is his duty to make such inquiries and institute such prosecutions as the circumstances of the case appear to him to require.

(2) The Director by himself or by his assistant or by his representative appointed under subsection (3) below shall attend the trial of every election petition.

(3) The Director may nominate, with the Attorney General's approval, a barrister or solicitor of not less than ten years standing to be his representative for the purposes of this Part of this Act and that representative shall receive such remuneration as the Treasury may approve.

1979 c. 31.

(4) The Director in performing any duty under this Act shall act in accordance with regulations under the Prosecution of Offences Act 1979, and subject to them in accordance with the directions (if any) given to him by the Attorney General; and any assistant or representative of the Director in performing any duty under this Part shall act in accordance with those regulations and directions (if any) and with the directions given to him by the Director.

(5) There shall be allowed to the Director and his assistant or representative for the purposes of this Part (other than his general duties under subsection (1) above) such allowances for expenses as the Treasury may approve.

PART III

(6) The costs incurred in defraying the expenses of the Director incurred for those purposes (including the remuneration of his representative) shall, in the first instance, be paid by the Treasury, and so far as they are not in the case of any prosecution paid by the defendant shall be deemed to be expenses of the election court; but if for any reasonable cause it seems just to the court so to do, the court shall order all or part of those costs to be repaid to the Treasury by the parties to the petition, or such of them as the court may direct.

(7) In the application of this section to Scotland, subsections (2) to (6) shall be omitted.

(8) In the application of this section to Northern Ireland, the reference to the Prosecution of Offences Act 1979 does not apply. 1979 c. 31

Supplemental

Rules of procedure

182.—(1) The authority having for the time being power to make rules of court for the Supreme Court may make rules for the purposes of Part II and this Part of this Act.

(2) In relation to the power conferred by subsection (1) above to make rules—

(*a*) that power shall be exercisable by statutory instrument, and be treated for the purposes of the Statutory Instruments Act 1946 as if conferred on a Minister of the Crown; and 1946 c. 36.

(*b*) a statutory instrument containing rules under subsection (1) shall be subject to annulment in pursuance of a resolution of either House of Parliament.

(3) This section does not apply to Scotland, but the Court of Session has power to make acts of sederunt for the purposes of Part II and this Part.

(4) This section does not apply to Northern Ireland.

Costs.

183.—(1) The rules of the Supreme Court with respect to costs to be allowed in actions, causes and matters in the High Court shall in principle and so far as practicable apply to the costs of petition and other proceedings under Part II or this Part of this Act, and the taxing officer shall not allow any costs higher than would be allowed in any action, cause or matter in the High Court on a common fund basis.

(2) Where any costs or other sums are, under the order of an election court or otherwise under this Part, to be paid by any person, those costs or sums shall be due from that person to the person or persons to whom they are to be paid and, if payable to the Treasury, shall be a debt due to Her Majesty and in either case may be recovered accordingly.

PART III

(3) The above provisions of this section do not apply to Scotland, but those costs shall, subject to any regulations which the Court of Session may make by act of sederunt, be taxed as nearly as possible according to the same principles as expenses between solicitor and client are taxed in a cause in the Court of Session, or, when incurred in relation to an election of councillors, the sheriff court.

Service of notices.

184.—(1) Any summons, notice or document required to be served on any person with reference to any proceeding respecting an election for the purpose of causing him to appear before the High Court, the county court, or any election court, or otherwise or of giving him an opportunity of making a statement, or showing cause, or being heard by himself before any court for any purpose of this Part of this Act may be served—

(*a*) by delivering it to that person, or by leaving it at, or sending it by post by a registered letter or by the recorded delivery service, to his last known place of abode in the constituency or, as the case may be, the area of the authority for which the election was held; or

(*b*) if the proceeding is before any court in such other manner as the court may direct.

(2) In proving service by post under this section it shall be sufficient to prove that the letter was prepaid, properly addressed, and registered or recorded with the Post Office.

Interpretation of Part III.

185. In this Part of this Act, unless the context otherwise requires—

"appropriate officer" has the same meaning as in section 67(7) above;

"candidate" has the same meaning as in Part II of this Act and the saving in section 117(1) above applies in relation to this Part as in relation to Part II;

"costs" includes charges and expenses;

"date of the allowance of an authorised excuse" has the meaning assigned to it by section 86(8) above or paragraph 7 of Schedule 4 to this Act, as the case may be;

"declaration as to election expenses" means a declaration made under section 82 above or, as the case may be, paragraph 3 of Schedule 4 to this Act;

"judicial office" includes the office of justice of the peace;

1964 c. 26.

"Licensing Acts" means the Licensing Act 1964 and the

Acts amending that Act, or the corresponding enactments forming part of the law of Scotland or Northern Ireland; PART III

"money" and "pecuniary reward" shall be deemed to include—

(*a*) any office, place or employment, and

(*b*) any valuable security or other equivalent of money, and

(*c*) any valuable consideration,

and expressions referring to money shall be construed accordingly;

"payment" includes any pecuniary or other reward;

"prescribed" means prescribed by rules of court, or, in Northern Ireland, such rules under section 55 of the Judicature (Northern Ireland) Act 1978; 1978 c. 23.

"public office" means any office—

(*a*) under the Crown, or

(*b*) under the charter of a city or borough, or

(*c*) under the Acts relating to local government or public health or public education,

whether the office is that—

(i) of mayor, provost, chief magistrate, chairman, alderman, councillor, member of a board, commission or other local authority in any local government or other area; or

(ii) of proper officer or other officer under a council, board, commission or other authority; or

(iii) of any other office to which a person is elected or appointed under any such charter or enactment as is mentioned above, including any other municipal or parochial office;

"return as to election expenses" means a return made under section 81 above or, as the case may be, paragraph 3 of Schedule 4 to this Act;

"Speaker" includes Deputy Speaker and, where the office of Speaker is vacant, Clerk of the House of Commons, or any other officer for the time being performing the duties of Clerk of the House of Commons.

Computation of time for purposes of Part III.

186. Section 119 above applies in computing any period of time for the purposes of this Part of this Act as for the purposes of Part II of this Act.

PART IV

SPECIAL PROVISIONS AS TO OTHER LOCAL ELECTIONS

England and Wales, and Scotland

Application of Act to certain local elections.

187.—(1) The following provisions of this Act—

(*a*) in Part I, sections 51(2), 60 and 66,

(*b*) Parts II and III,

(*c*) in this Part, section 189,

so far as they apply to an election in England and Wales of—

(i) district, parish or community councillors, or

(ii) the chairman of a district, parish or community council or a parish meeting,

have effect subject to such adaptations, modifications and exceptions as may be made by rules under section 36 above, but nothing in this subsection affects the operation of section 96 or section 100 above.

(2) Sections 48 (1) and (2) and 64 above have effect as if any reference in them to a local government election included a reference to any other election under the local government Act.

Parts II and III as to local elections in Scotland.

1973 c. 65.

188. Except in the phrase " election to any public office " wherever it is used, references in Parts II and III and section 189 of this Act to elections or to elections under the local government Act do not include references to elections under the Local Government (Scotland) Act 1973 other than elections of councillors.

Voting offences at certain local elections.

189.—(1) If a person—

(*a*) votes, or induces or procures any person to vote, at an election under the local govenrment Act which is not a local government election,

(*b*) knowing that he or that person is prohibited by any enactment from voting at that election,

he shall be guilty of an illegal practice.

(2) A candidate shall not be liable nor shall his election be avoided for any illegal practice under subsection (1) above committed without his knowledge or consent.

Voting offences at election of councillors in Scotland.

190. A person who at an election of councillors in Scotland—

(*a*) fabricates, in whole or in part, or alters, defaces, destroys, abstracts or purloins any ballot paper, or

(*b*) personates any person entitled to vote at the election, or

(*c*) falsely assumes to act in the name or on behalf of any person so entitled to vote, or

PART IV

(*d*) interferes with the delivery or collection of any ballot papers, or

(*e*) delivers any ballot paper under a false pretence of being lawfully authorised to do so,

shall be liable on summary conviction to a penalty not exceeding level 2 on the standard scale, or to imprisonment for any period not exceeding three months and shall be deemed to have committed an illegal practice.

The City

Municipal elections in the City.

191.—(1) For the purposes of—

(*a*) sections 51(2), 60 and 61 in Part I of this Act,

(*b*) the whole of Part II of this Act except sections 96 and 99,

(*c*) the whole of Part III of this Act,

(*d*) section 189 above and sections 192 to 198 below, and

(*e*) the whole of Part V of this Act,

" local government election " and " election under the local government Act " include a municipal election in the City (that is, an election to the office of mayor, alderman, common councilman or sheriff and also the election of any officer elected by the mayor, aldermen and liverymen in common hall),

" corporate office " includes each of those offices,

" local government area " includes the City,

" clerk of the authority " means in relation to the City, the town clerk of the City,

" electoral area " means in relation to a ward election, the ward, and in relation to any other municipal election in the City, the City.

In relation to municipal elections in the City those enactments have effect subject to the modifications mentioned in sections 192 to 196 below.

(2) Schedule 6 to this Act has effect as regards the operation of Part II (ward elections) of the City of London (Various Powers) Act 1957. 1957 c. x.

Corrupt and illegal practices lists.

192. In relation to municipal elections in the City—

(*a*) in section 51(2) above, for " qualified to be registered in the register of local government electors " substitute " qualified to vote at a municipal election in the City "; and

(*b*) the town clerk of the City shall omit from each ward list the names of all persons mentioned in the corrupt and illegal practices list, and that list shall be printed and appended to every copy of each ward list.

PART IV

Personation and other voting offences.

193. In relation to municipal elections in the City—

(*a*) in sections 60 and 61 above " vote " does not include voting otherwise than on a poll ; and

(*b*) in section 61(2), paragraph (*a*)(ii) does not apply.

Broadcasting.

194. In relation to municipal elections in the City—

(*a*) neither section 92 nor section 93 above apply by virtue of section 191 above to municipal elections in the City other than ward elections ; and

(*b*) for the purposes of section 93(1) a ward election shall be deemed to be pending during the period beginning—

(i) in the case of an annual election three weeks before the day fixed for the election, and

(ii) in other cases with the day on which the precept is issued,

and ending in all cases with the day of the poll (or, if no poll is taken, with the day fixed for the election).

Disturbances at meetings.

195. In relation to municipal elections in the City—

(*a*) in section 97 above the reference to the day of election shall be taken as a reference to the day fixed for the election and (where a poll is taken) any day after that up to and including the day of the poll ; but

(*b*) in relation to a meeting held with reference to an election other than an annual election that section does not apply to an offence committed on or before the day on which the precept is issued.

Costs or expenses.

196. In relation to municipal elections in the City, any costs or expenses directed to be paid under section 132 or under section 156(2) above by the authority for which the election was held shall—

(*a*) if incurred in respect of a ward election, be paid out of the general rate ; and

(*b*) in any other case, be paid by the chamberlain of the City out of the City's cash.

Candidate's expenses: ward, and liverymen in common hall, elections.

197.—(1) For a candidate at a ward election in the City the maximum amount of election expenses is £120 together with an additional 2·4p for every elector (taken according to the enumeration of the ward list to be used at the election) ; but the provision made by section 76(6) above for increasing the maximum amount of election expenses in the event of a candidate's death applies to the maximum amount under this subsection.

(2) A candidate at an election by liverymen in common hall need not have an election agent, his maximum amount of election expenses is £900, and section 90 above and Schedule 4 to this Act apply at such an election as they apply to an election of parish councillors, but the form of declaration as to election expenses shall be such as may be prescribed by Act of Common Council.

(3) The Secretary of State may by order vary a maximum amount of the candidate's election expenses specified in subsection (1) or subsection (2) above where in his opinion there has been a change in the value of money since the last occasion on which that amount was varied by such an order, and the variation shall be such as in his opinion is justified by that change.

An order under this subsection shall not be made unless a draft of the order has been laid before, and approved by resolution of, each House of Parliament; and the power to make the order is exercisable by statutory instrument.

Effect of avoidance of election to corporate office.

198. In relation to the City, where a candidate who has been elected to a corporate office is—

(*a*) by a certificate of an election court, or

(*b*) by a decision of the High Court,

declared not to have been duly elected, acts done by him in execution of the office before the time when the certificate or decision is certified to the clerk of the authority for which the election was held shall not be invalidated by reason of that declaration.

PART V

GENERAL AND SUPPLEMENTAL

Supplemental

Translations of statutory forms into Welsh language.

199.—(1) The Secretary of State may by regulations prescribe a translation into the Welsh language of any form required to be used by this Act (whether it is a form set out in a Schedule to this Act or one prescribed by rules or regulations made under this Act); and where such a translation has been so prescribed it may be used, in place of the form, in connection with elections in Wales.

(2) Where in the case of a form so set out or prescribed the requirement as to its use may be satisfied by the use of a form to the like effect or of that form with adaptations, it may be so

PART V

satisfied also in the case of a translation prescribed under this section.

(3) Nothing in this section shall be taken to prejudice the use of any translation in a case where its use is lawful apart from this section.

Public notices, and declarations.

200.—(1) Where the returning officer for a parliamentary election is required or authorised by this Act to give any public notice, he shall do so by advertisements, placards, handbills or such other means as he thinks best calculated to afford information to the voters.

(2) Any person before whom a declaration is authorised to be made under this Act may take the declaration.

Regulations.

201.—(1) Any power conferred by this Act to make regulations shall, except where this Act otherwise provides, be a power exercisable by the Secretary of State by statutory instrument.

(2) A statutory instrument containing regulations so made shall not come into force unless or until it is approved by resolution of each House of Parliament; but this subsection does not apply to—

(*a*) rules made under sections 36 and 42 above;

(*b*) regulations made under section 199 above and section 203(4) below.

Interpretation

General provisions as to interpretation.

202.—(1) In this Act, unless the context otherwise requires—

"Attorney General" includes the Solicitor General in cases where the Attorney General is interested or otherwise unable to act;

"the City" means the City of London;

"Clerk of the Crown" means Clerk of the Crown in Chancery;

"Common Council" means the Common Council of the City;

"dwelling house" includes any part of a house where that part is occupied separately as a dwelling house;

"election" means a parliamentary election or an election under the local government Act.

"election court" means—

(*a*) in relation to a parliamentary election petition, the judges presiding at the trial;

(*b*) in relation to a petition questioning an election

under the local government Act, the court constituted under this Act for the trial of that petition ; PART V

" election petition " means a petition presented in pursuance of Part III of this Act ;

" elector " in relation to an election, means any person whose name is for the time being on the register to be used at that election, but does not include those shown in the register as below voting age on the day fixed for the poll ;

" legal incapacity " includes (in addition to any incapacity by virtue of any subsisting provision of the common law) any disqualification imposed by this Act or any other Act ;

" parliamentary election petition " means an election petition questioning a parliamentary election or return ;

" parliamentary elections rules " means the parliamentary elections rules in Schedule 1 to this Act ;

" person " includes (without prejudice to the provisions of the Interpretation Act 1978) an association corporate or unincorporate ; 1978 c. 30.

" prescribed " except in Part III of this Act means prescribed by regulations ;

" proper officer " means in England and Wales one within the meaning of section 270(3) and (4) of the Local Government Act 1972, and in Scotland one within the meaning of section 214 and paragraph 2(1) of Part I of Schedule 27 to the Local Government (Scotland) Act 1973 ; 1972 c. 70. 1973 c. 65.

" registration duties " includes the duties of a registration officer as such with respect to voting by post or by proxy, with respect to any corrupt and illegal practices list and with respect to the lists of rooms to the use of which candidates are entitled under this Act ;

" service voter " means a person who has made a service declaration and is registered or entitled to be registered in pursuance of it ;

" standard scale " has the meaning given by section 75 of the Criminal Justice Act 1982 ; 1982 c. 48.

" statutory maximum " has the meaning given by section 74 of the Criminal Justice Act 1982 ;

" sub-agent " has the meaning given by section 68(1) above ;

" voter " means a person voting at an election and includes a person voting as proxy and, except in the parliamentary elections rules, and the rules under section 36 and 42 above, a person voting by proxy, and " vote " (whether noun or verb) shall be construed accordingly,

PART V

except that in those rules any reference to an elector voting or an elector's vote shall include a reference to an elector voting by proxy or an elector's vote given by proxy.

(2) For the purposes of the Representation of the People Acts a person shall be deemed not to have attained a given age until the commencement of the relevant anniversary of the day of his birth.

Local government provisions as to England and Wales.

203.—(1) In this Act, unless the context otherwise requires, in relation to England and Wales—

"electoral area" means any electoral division, London borough, ward, district, parish, community or other area for which the election of councillors is held under the local government Act;

"local authority" means a county council, the Greater London Council, a district council, a London borough council or a parish or community council;

1972 c. 70.

"local government Act" means the Local Government Act 1972;

"local government area" means a county, London borough, district, parish or community;

"local government election" means the election of councillors for any electoral area.

(2) Subject to any express provision contained in Part I of this Act, that Part, so far as it has effect for the purpose of parliamentary elections or of elections of councillors of the Greater London Council, applies in relation to the City as if it were a London borough, and as if the Common Council were a London borough council.

For the purposes of this subsection the Inner Temple and the Middle Temple shall be treated as forming part of the City.

(3) The modifications made by subsection (2) above do not affect section 52(4) above.

(4) This Act applies in relation to the Isles of Scilly as if those isles were a county and as if the council of those isles were a county council, except that—

(*a*) paragraph 1(1) of Schedule 2 and any reference to a person acting in pursuance of the requisition of the registration officer shall apply as if the isles were a district and the council were a district council;

(*b*) the provisions of Part I relating to the conduct of local government elections shall have effect in relation to those isles subject to such adaptations as the Secretary of State may by regulations prescribe.

(5) For the purposes of section 265 of the Local Government Act 1972 (application to Isles of Scilly) the provisions of this Act as to rules made by the Secretary of State under section 36 above shall be deemed to be contained in a public general Act relating to local government. PART V 1972 c. 70.

Scotland and Northern Ireland

204.—(1) This section has (in addition to any express application elsewhere in this Act) effect for the general application of this Act to Scotland, and accordingly— General application to Scotland.

" electoral area ", in relation to a local government election, means the electoral division or ward for which the election is held ;

" local authority " means a regional, islands or district council ;

" local government Act " means the Local Government (Scotland) Act 1973 ; 1973 c. 65.

" local government area " means a region, islands area or district ; and

" local government election " means an election of councillors by local government electors for an electoral area.

(2) For a reference to a borough constituency substitute a reference to a burgh constituency.

(3) For a reference to the High Court substitute a reference to the Court of Session and for a reference to the county court or a judge of that court substitute a reference to the sheriff.

(4) The power conferred by section 57 above on the Court of Session to make acts of sederunt for the appointment of judges to hear appeals under that section or to fill any vacancy among the judges so appointed is not required to be exercisable by statutory instrument.

(5) A reference to the Director of Public Prosecutions or the Attorney General refers to the Lord Advocate.

(6) For a reference to a plaintiff or defendant substitute respectively a reference to a pursuer or defender, for a reference to a recognisance substitute a reference to a bond of caution and for a reference to an injunction substitute a reference to an interdict.

(7) Any reference to the report of an election court shall, in relation to an election court trying a petition questioning an election of councillors in Scotland, be construed as a reference to a finding of the court, and the expression " reported of a corrupt or illegal practice " shall be construed accordingly.

PART V

(8) For a reference to the register of licences substitute a reference to the register kept in pursuance of section 20 of the Licensing (Scotland) Act 1976.

1976 c. 66.

1973 c. 65.

(9) Section 231 of the Local Government (Scotland) Act 1973 (application to sheriff in cases of difficulty) applies to the provisions of sections 41 to 45 above as that section applied to those provisions immediately before their repeal and re-enactment by this Act.

1918, (7 & 8 Geo. 5) c. 64.

1881, (44 & 45 Vict.) c. 40.

(10) Notwithstanding the repeal by this Act of sections 19 and 43 of the Representation of the People Act 1918, those sections shall continue to have such effect as they had immediately before that repeal in relation to regulation 16 of section 2 of the Universities Elections Amendment (Scotland) Act 1881.

General application to Northern Ireland.

205.—(1) This section has (in addition to any express application elsewhere in the Act) effect for the general application of this Act to Northern Ireland, and accordingly—

(*a*) a reference either to the Attorney General or the Director of Public Prosecutions refers to the Attorney General for Northern Ireland;

(*b*) subject to subsection (2) below, a reference to any enactment shall be construed as a reference to that enactment as it applies in Northern Ireland.

(2) Nothing in this Act affects the law relating to local government in Northern Ireland.

Operation

Transitional and saving provisions, amendments and repeals.

206. In Schedule 7 to this Act—

(*a*) Part I has effect as to its transitional and saving provisions, and

(*b*) Part II has effect as to its provisions relating to the interpretation of other Acts,

and subject to that Schedule—

(i) the enactments and order specified in Schedule 8 to this Act have effect subject to the amendments consequent on this Act specified in that Schedule; and

(ii) the enactments and orders specified in Schedule 9 to this Act (of which those in Part I are obsolete) are repealed or revoked to the extent specified in the third column of that Schedule.

Citation and commencement.

207.—(1) This Act may be cited as the Representation of the People Act 1983, and is included among the Acts which may be cited as the Representation of the People Acts.

(2) This Act shall come into force on such day as the Secretary of State may by order made by statutory instrument appoint

SCHEDULES

Section 23.

SCHEDULE 1

Parliamentary Elections Rules

Arrangement of rules

SCH. 1

Action to be taken before the poll

23. Notice of poll.
24. Postal ballot papers.
25. Provision of polling stations.
26. Appointment of presiding officers and clerks.
27. Special lists.
28. Issue of official poll cards.
29. Equipment of polling stations.
30. Appointment of polling and counting agents.
31. Declaration of secrecy.

The poll

32. Admission to polling station.
33. Keeping of order in station.
34. Sealing of ballot boxes.
35. Questions to be put to voters.
36. Challenge of voter.
37. Voting procedure.
38. Votes marked by presiding officer.
39. Voting by blind persons.
40. Tendered ballot papers.
41. Spoilt ballot papers.
42. Adjournment of poll in case of riot.
43. Procedure on close of poll.

Counting of votes

44. Attendance at counting of votes.
45. The count.
46. Re-count.
47. Rejected ballot papers.
48. Decisions on ballot papers.
49. Equality of votes.

PART IV

FINAL PROCEEDINGS IN CONTESTED AND UNCONTESTED ELECTIONS

50. Declaration of result.
51. Return to the writ.
52. Record of returns at Crown Office.
53. Return or forfeiture of candidate's deposit.

PART V

DISPOSAL OF DOCUMENTS

54. Sealing up of ballot papers.
55. Delivery of documents to Clerk of the Crown.
56. Orders for production of documents.
57. Retention and public inspection of documents.
58. Disposal of documents in Scotland.
59. Disposal of documents in Northern Ireland.

Part VI

Death of Candidate

Appendix of Forms

Part I

Provisions as to Time

Timetable

1. The proceedings at the election shall be conducted in accordance with the following Table.

Timetable

Proceeding	*Time*	
Issue of writ	In the case of a general election, as soon as practicable after the issue of the proclamation summoning the new Parliament.	In the case of a by-election, as soon as practicable after the issue of the warrant for the writ.
Publication of notice of election.	In the case of a general election or by-election, not later than 4 in the afternoon on the second day after that on which the writ is received.	
Delivery of nomination papers.	In the case of a general election, between the hours of 10 in the morning and 4 in the afternoon on any day after the date of publication of the notice of election, but not later than the sixth day after the date of the proclamation summoning the new Parliament.	In the case of a by-election, the same as in the case of a general election, except that the last day shall be a day fixed by the returning officer and shall be not earlier than the third day after the date of publication of the notice of election nor later than the seventh day after that on which the writ is received.
Delivery of notices of withdrawals of candidature.	Within the time for the delivery of nomination papers at the election.	

SCH. 1

<table>
<tr><th>Proceeding</th><th colspan="2">Time</th></tr>
<tr><td>The making of objections to nomination papers.</td><td colspan="2">In the case of a general election or a by-election, during the hours allowed for delivery of nomination papers on the last day for their delivery and the hour following; but—
(a) no objection may be made in the afternoon of that last day except to a nomination paper delivered within 24 hours of the last time for its delivery, and in the case of a nomination paper so delivered no objection may be so made to the sufficiency or nature of the particulars of the candidate unless made at or immediately after the time of the delivery of the nomination paper; and
(b) the foregoing provisions do not apply to objections made in pursuance of rule 15(2).</td></tr>
<tr><td>Publication of statement of persons nominated.</td><td colspan="2">In the case of a general election or a by-election, at the close of the time for making objections to nomination papers or as soon afterwards as any objections are disposed of.</td></tr>
<tr><td>Polling ... ...</td><td>In the case of a general election, between the hours of 7 in the morning and 10 at night on the tenth day after the last day for delivery of nomination papers.</td><td>In the case of a by-election, between the hours of 7 in the morning and 10 at night on the day fixed by the returning officer, which shall not be earlier than the eighth nor later than the tenth day after the last day for delivery of nomination papers.</td></tr>
</table>

Computation of time

2.—(1) In computing any period of time for the purposes of the Timetable—

(*a*) a Saturday or Sunday,

(*b*) a day of the Christmas break, of the Easter break or of a bank holiday break, or

(*c*) a day appointed for public thanksgiving or mourning,

shall be disregarded, and any such day shall not be treated as a day for the purpose of any proceedings up to the completion of the poll nor shall the returning officer be obliged to proceed with the counting of the votes on such a day.

(2) In this rule " bank holiday " means—

1971 c. 80. (*a*) in relation to a general election, a day which is a bank holiday under the Banking and Financial Dealings Act 1971 in any part of the United Kingdom,

(*b*) in relation to a by-election, a day which is a bank holiday under that Act in that part of the United Kingdom in which the constituency is situated,

but at a general election sub-paragraph (*b*) and not sub-paragraph (*a*) of this paragraph applies in relation to any proceedings—

(i) commenced afresh by reason of a candidate's death ; and

(ii) extending, by reason of riot or open violence, beyond the time laid down by the Timetable.

(3) In this rule— SCH. 1

"bank holiday break" means any bank holiday not included in the Christmas break or the Easter break and the period beginning with the last weekday before that bank holiday and ending with the next weekday which is not a bank holiday,

"Christmas break" means the period beginning with the last weekday before Christmas Day and ending with the first weekday after Christmas Day which is not a bank holiday,

"Easter break" means the period beginning with the Thursday before and ending with the Tuesday after Easter Day,

"weekday" does not include a Saturday,

but so much of this paragraph as includes in a bank holiday break a period before and after a bank holiday does not apply to bank holidays other than New Year's Day which are not bank holidays in England and Wales.

PART II

STAGES COMMON TO CONTESTED AND UNCONTESTED ELECTIONS

ISSUE OF WRIT AND NOTICE OF ELECTION

Issue of writ

3.—(1) Writs for parliamentary elections shall continue to be sealed and issued in accordance with the existing practice of the office of the Clerk of the Crown.

(2) Each writ shall be in the form in the Appendix and shall be directed to the returning officer by the title of his office as returning officer (and not by his name) and conveyed to him.

(3) Her Majesty may by Order in Council—

(*a*) specify the manner in which writs are to be conveyed, whether by post, by an officer appointed by the Lord Chancellor or, as regards Northern Ireland, the Secretary of State, or otherwise, and make different provision for different classes of writs ; and

(*b*) provide for the giving of receipts for writs by persons to whom they are delivered or who may receive them in the course of their conveyance.

(4) Delivery of the writ to a person for the time being authorised by law to act as deputy for the officer who by virtue of his office is returning officer shall be as good as delivery to the returning officer.

SCH. 1

(5) An Order in Council under this rule—

(*a*) may require a returning officer to provide an address to which writs are to be conveyed and any change of that address; and

(*b*) may provide for recording those addresses; and

(*c*) may provide that the delivery of a writ to a person found in and for the time being in charge of a place so recorded as the office of a returning officer shall be as good as delivery to that returning officer.

(6) The person to whom the writ is delivered shall endorse the date of receipt on the writ in the form shown in the Appendix.

(7) A draft of an Order in Council under this rule shall be laid before Parliament, and any such Order may provide for any incidental or supplemental matter.

Conveyance of writ to acting returning officer

4.—(1) For an election in a constituency in England and Wales the writ shall (notwithstanding anything in rule 3 above) be conveyed to the acting returning officer if the returning officer—

(*a*) has so requested by notice in the form prescribed by an Order in Council under rule 3 and received by the Clerk of the Crown one month or more before the issue of the writ; and

(*b*) has not revoked it by a further notice in the form so prescribed and received within such time as is mentioned above.

(2) A notice under this rule has effect in relation to all constituencies—

(*a*) of which the person giving it is returning officer at the time of giving it; or

(*b*) of which he or a successor in office becomes returning officer by virtue of that office.

(3) Where by virtue of this rule writs are conveyed to the acting returning officer paragraph (5) of rule 3 applies in relation to him as it applies in relation to a returning officer.

Notice of election

5.—(1) The returning officer shall publish notice of the election in the form in the Appendix, stating—

(*a*) the place and times at which nomination papers are to be delivered, and

(*b*) the date of the poll in the event of a contest,

and the notice shall state that forms of nomination paper may be obtained at that place and those times.

Sch. 1

(2) The notice of election shall state the date by which—

(a) applications to be treated as an absent voter, and

(b) other applications and notices about postal or proxy voting, must reach the registration officer in order that they may be effective for the election.

(3) In addition the registration officer shall give notice of the date mentioned in paragraph (2) above in the constituency by such means as he thinks best calculated to bring the information to the notice of those concerned.

Nomination

Nomination of candidates

6.—(1) Each candidate shall be nominated by a separate nomination paper, in the form in the Appendix delivered—

(a) by the candidate himself, or

(b) by his proposer or seconder,

to the returning officer at the place fixed for the purpose, but the paper may be so delivered on the candidate's behalf by his election agent if the agent's name and address have been previously given to the returning officer as required by section 67 of this Act or are so given at the time the paper is delivered.

(2) The nomination paper shall state the candidate's—

(a) full names,

(b) home address in full, and

(c) if desired, description,

and the surname shall be placed first in the list of his names.

(3) The description, if any, shall not exceed 6 words in length, and need not refer to his rank, profession or calling so long as, with the candidate's other particulars, it is sufficient to identify him.

Subscription of nomination paper

7.—(1) The nomination paper shall be subscribed by two electors as proposer and seconder, and by eight other electors as assenting to the nomination.

(2) Where a nomination paper bears the signatures of more than the required number of persons as proposing, seconding or assenting to the nomination of a candidate, the signature or signatures (up to the required number) appearing first on the paper in each category shall be taken into account to the exclusion of any others in that category.

(3) The nomination paper shall give the electoral number of each person subscribing it.

SCH. 1

(4) The returning officer—

(*a*) shall supply any elector with a form of nomination paper at the place and during the time for delivery of nomination papers, and

(*b*) shall at any elector's request prepare a nomination paper for signature,

but it is not necessary for a nomination to be on a form supplied by the returning officer.

(5) A person shall not subscribe more than one nomination paper at the same election and, if he does, his signature shall be inoperative on any paper other than the one first delivered, but he shall not be prevented from subscribing a nomination paper by reason only of his having subscribed that of a candidate who has died or withdrawn before delivery of the first mentioned paper.

(6) In this rule—

" elector " means a person—

(*a*) who is registered as a parliamentary elector in the constituency in the register to be used at the election, or

(*b*) who, pending the publication of that register, appears from the electors lists for that register as corrected by the registration officer to be entitled to be so registered,

and accordingly includes a person shown in the register or electors lists as below voting age if it appears from it that he will be of voting age on the day fixed for the poll, but not otherwise ; and

" electoral number " means—

(i) a person's number in that register, or

(ii) pending the publication of the register, his number (if any) in the electors lists for that register.

Consent to nomination

8.—(1) A person shall not be validly nominated unless his consent to nomination—

(*a*) is given in writing on or within one month before the day fixed as the last day for the delivery of nomination papers,

(*b*) is attested by one witness, and

(*c*) is delivered at the place and within the time for the delivery of nomination papers,

subject to paragraph (2) below.

(2) If the returning officer is satisfied that owing to the absence of a person from the United Kingdom it has not been reasonably practicable for his consent in writing to be given as mentioned above, a telegram (or any similar means of communication) consenting to his nomination and purporting to have been sent by him shall be deemed for the purposes of this rule to be consent in writing given

by him on the day on which it purports to have been sent, and attestation of his consent shall not be required. SCH. 1

(3) A candidate's consent given under this rule—

(*a*) shall state the day, month and year of his birth ; and

(*b*) shall state—

(i) that he is aware of the provisions of the House of Commons Disqualification Act 1975 ; and 1975 c. 24.

(ii) that to the best of his knowledge and belief he is not disqualified for membership of the House of Commons.

Deposit

9.—(1) A person shall not be validly nominated unless the sum of £150 is deposited by him or on his behalf with the returning officer at the place and during the time for delivery of nomination papers.

(2) The deposit may be made either—

(*a*) by the deposit of any legal tender, or

(*b*) by means of a banker's draft, or

(*c*) with the returning officer's consent, in any other manner,

but the returning officer may refuse to accept a deposit sought to be made by means of a banker's draft if he does not know that the drawer carries on business as a banker in the United Kingdom.

Place for delivery of nomination papers

10.—(1) The returning officer shall fix the place at which nomination papers are to be delivered to him, and shall attend there during the time for their delivery and for the making of objections to them.

(2) Except in Scotland, the place shall be in—

(*a*) the constituency ; or

(*b*) the registration area which includes the constituency ; or

(*c*) unless the constituency is a borough constituency, in a district adjoining the constituency or registration area.

For the purposes of paragraph (*b*) above "registration area" means—

(i) in England and Wales, the area of two or more constituencies which have the same registration officer ;

(ii) in Northern Ireland, the county borough of Belfast and each county.

(3) In Scotland the place shall be in—

(*a*) the constituency ; or

(*b*) the district or (if more than one) any of the districts in which the constituency is situated ; or

(*c*) any district adjoining the district or districts (as the case may be) in which the constituency is situated.

SCH. 1

Right to attend nomination

11.—(1) Except for the purpose of delivering a nomination paper or of assisting the returning officer, and subject to paragraph (4) below, no person is entitled to attend the proceedings during the time for delivery of nomination papers or for making objections to them unless he is—

(*a*) a person standing nominated as a candidate, or

(*b*) the election agent, proposer or seconder of such a person,

but where a candidate acts as his own election agent he may name one other person who shall be entitled to attend in place of his election agent.

(2) Where a person stands nominated by more than one nomination paper, only the persons subscribing as proposer and seconder—

(*a*) to such one of those papers as he may select, or

(*b*) in default of such a selection, to that one of those papers which is first delivered,

shall be entitled to attend as his proposer and seconder.

(3) The right to attend conferred by this rule includes the right—

(*a*) to inspect, and

(*b*) to object to the validity of,

any nomination paper.

(4) A candidate's wife or husband is entitled to be present at the delivery of the candidate's nomination, and may afterwards, so long as the candidate stands nominated, attend the proceedings referred to in paragraph (1) above, but without any such right as is conferred by paragraph (3) above.

Decisions as to validity of nomination papers

12.—(1) Where a nomination paper and the candidate's consent to it are delivered and a deposit is made in accordance with these rules, the candidate shall be deemed to stand nominated unless and until—

(*a*) the returning officer decides that the nomination paper is invalid ; or

(*b*) proof is given to the returning officer's satisfaction of the candidate's death ; or

(*c*) the candidate withdraws.

(2) The returning officer is entitled to hold a nomination paper invalid only on one of the following grounds—

(*a*) that the particulars of the candidate or the persons subscribing the paper are not as required by law ;

(*b*) that the paper is not subscribed as so required ; and

(*c*) that the candidate is disqualified by the Representation of the People Act 1981.

1981 c. 34.

(3) The returning officer shall give his decision on any objection to a nomination paper as soon as practicable after it is made.

(4) Where he decides that a nomination paper is invalid, he shall endorse and sign on the paper the fact and the reasons for his decision.

(5) The returning officer's decision that a nomination paper is valid shall be final and shall not be questioned in any proceeding whatsoever.

(6) Subject to paragraph (5) above nothing in this rule prevents the validity of a nomination being questioned on an election petition.

Withdrawal of candidates

13.—(1) A candidate may withdraw his candidature by notice of withdrawal—

(*a*) signed by him and attested by one witness, and

(*b*) delivered to the returning officer at the place for delivery of nomination papers.

(2) Where a candidate is outside the United Kingdom, a notice of withdrawal signed by his proposer and accompanied by a written declaration also so signed of the candidate's absence from the United Kingdom shall be of the same effect as a notice of withdrawal signed by the candidate; but where the candidate stands nominated by more than one nomination paper a notice of withdrawal under this paragraph shall be effective if, and only if—

(*a*) it and the accompanying declaration are signed by all the proposers except any who is, and is stated in that declaration to be, outside the United Kingdom; or

(*b*) it is accompanied, in addition to that declaration, by a written statement signed by the candidate that the proposer giving the notice is authorised to do so on the candidate's behalf during his absence from the United Kingdom.

Publication of statement of persons nominated

14.—(1) The returning officer shall prepare and publish a statement showing the persons who have been and stand nominated and any other persons who have been nominated, with the reason why they no longer stand nominated.

(2) The statement shall show the names, addresses and descriptions of the persons nominated as given in their nomination papers, together with the names of the persons subscribing those papers.

(3) The statement shall show the persons standing nominated arranged alphabetically in the order of their surnames, and, if there are two or more of them with the same surname, of their other names.

(4) In the case of a person nominated by more than one nomination paper, the returning officer shall take the particulars required by the foregoing provisions of this rule from such one of the papers as the candidate (or the returning officer in default of the candidate) may select, but if the election is contested a candidate standing

SCH. 1 nominated may require the returning officer to include in the statement the names of the persons subscribing a second and third nomination.

Disqualification by Representation of the People Act 1981

1981 c. 34. 15.—(1) If it appears to the returning officer that any of the persons nominated might be disqualified by the Representation of the People Act 1981 he shall, as soon as practicable after the expiry of the time allowed for the delivery of nomination papers, prepare and publish a draft of the statement required under rule 14 above.

(2) The draft shall be headed " Draft statement of persons nominated " and shall omit the names of the persons subscribing the papers but shall contain a notice stating that any person who wishes to object to the nomination of any candidate on the ground that he is disqualified for nomination under the Representation of the People Act 1981 may do so between the hours of 10 in the morning and 4 in the afternoon on the day and at the place specified in the notice ; and the day so specified shall be the day next after the last day for the delivery of nomination papers.

Adjournment of nomination proceedings in case of riot

16.—(1) Where the proceedings for or in connection with nomination are on any day interrupted or obstructed by riot or open violence—

(*a*) the proceedings shall be abandoned for that day, and

(*b*) if that day is the last day for the delivery of nomination papers, the proceedings shall be continued on the next day as if that were the last day of such delivery,

and that day shall be treated for the purposes of these rules as being the last day for such delivery (subject to any further application of this rule in the event of interruption or obstruction on that day).

(2) Where proceedings are abandoned by virtue of this rule nothing—

(*a*) may be done after they are continued if the time for doing it had passed at the time of the abandonment ;

(*b*) done before the abandonment shall be invalidated by reason of the abandonment.

Method of election

17.—(1) If the statement of persons nominated shows more than one person standing nominated, a poll shall be taken in accordance with Part III of these rules.

(2) If the statement of persons nominated shows only one person standing nominated, that person shall be declared to be elected in accordance with Part IV of these rules.

Part III

Contested Elections

General Provisions

Poll to be taken by ballot

18. The votes at the poll shall be given by ballot, the result shall be ascertained by counting the votes given to each candidate and the candidate to whom the majority of votes have been given shall be declared to have been elected.

The ballot papers

19.—(1) The ballot of every voter shall consist of a ballot paper, and the persons shown in the statement of persons nominated as standing nominated, and no others, shall be entitled to have their names inserted in the ballot paper.

(2) Every ballot paper shall be in the form in the Appendix, and shall be printed in accordance with the directions in that Appendix, and—

(*a*) shall contain the names and other particulars of the candidates as shown in the statement of persons nominated;

(*b*) shall be capable of being folded up;

(*c*) shall have a number printed on the back;

(*d*) shall have attached a counterfoil with the same number printed on the face.

(3) The order of the names in the ballot paper shall be the same as in the statement of persons nominated.

The official mark

20.—(1) Every ballot paper shall be marked with an official mark, which shall perforate the ballot paper.

(2) The official mark shall be kept secret, and an interval of not less than seven years shall intervene between the use of the same official mark at elections for the same constituency.

(3) The official mark used for ballot papers issued for the purpose of voting by post shall not be used at the same election for ballot papers issued for the purpose of voting in person.

Prohibition of disclosure of vote

21. No person who has voted at the election shall, in any legal proceeding to question the election or return, be required to state for whom he voted.

SCH. 1

Use of schools and public rooms

22.—(1) The returning officer may use, free of charge, for the purpose of taking the poll—

(*a*) a room in a school to which this rule applies;

(*b*) a room the expense of maintaining which is payable out of any rate.

This rule applies—

(i) in England and Wales, to a school maintained or assisted by a local education authority or a school in respect of which grants are made out of moneys provided by Parliament to the person or body of persons responsible for the management of the school;

1980 c. 44.

(ii) in Scotland, to a school other than an independent school within the meaning of the Education (Scotland) Act 1980;

(iii) in Northern Ireland, to a school in receipt of a grant out of moneys appropriated by Measure of the Northern Ireland Assembly.

(2) The returning officer shall make good any damage done to, and defray any expense incurred by the persons having control over, any such room as mentioned above by reason of its being used for the purpose of taking the poll.

(3) The use of a room in an unoccupied house for that purpose does not render a person liable to be rated or to pay any rate for the house.

(4) In Northern Ireland this rule does not apply to any school adjoining or adjacent to any church or other place of worship nor to any school connected with a nunnery or other religious establishment.

ACTION TO BE TAKEN BEFORE THE POLL

Notice of poll

23.—(1) The returning officer shall in the statement of persons nominated include a notice of the poll, stating the day on which and hours during which the poll will be taken.

(2) The returning officer shall also give public notice (which may be combined with the statement of persons nominated) of—

(*a*) the situation of each polling station;

(*b*) the description of voters entitled to vote there; and

(*c*) the mode in which voters are to vote.

(3) The returning officer shall as soon as practicable after publication of a notice of poll give to each of the election agents a description in writing of the polling districts.

Postal ballot papers

24. The returning officer shall as soon as practicable send to those entitled to vote by post, at the addresses provided by them for the purpose, a ballot paper and a declaration of identity in the prescribed form, together with an envelope for their return.

Provision of polling stations

25.—(1) The returning officer shall provide a sufficient number of polling stations and, subject to the following provisions of this rule, shall allot the electors to the polling stations in such manner as he thinks most convenient.

(2) One or more polling stations may be provided in the same room.

(3) The polling station allotted to electors from any polling district shall be in the polling place for that district.

(4) In a constituency in Scotland comprising the whole or any part of more districts than one, there shall be at least one polling station in each of those districts.

(5) The returning officer shall provide each polling station with such number of compartments as may be necessary in which the voters can mark their votes screened from observation.

Appointment of presiding officers and clerks

26.—(1) The returning officer shall appoint and pay a presiding officer to attend at each polling station and such clerks as may be necessary for the purposes of the election, but he shall not appoint any person who has been employed by or on behalf of a candidate in or about the election.

(2) The returning officer may, if he thinks fit, preside at a polling station and the provisions of these rules relating to a presiding officer shall apply to a returning officer so presiding with the necessary modifications as to things to be done by the returning officer to the presiding officer or by the presiding officer to the returning officer.

(3) A presiding officer may do, by the clerks appointed to assist him, any act (including the asking of questions) which he is required or authorised by these rules to do at a polling station except order the arrest, exclusion or removal of any person from the polling station.

Special lists

27. The registration officer shall as soon as practicable prepare the following special lists—

(*a*) a list (in these rules referred to as " the absent voters list ") giving the name and number on the register of every person entitled to vote at the election as an absent voter;

SCH. 1

(*b*) a list (in these rules referred to as "the list of proxies") giving—

(i) the names and numbers on the register of the electors for whom proxies have been appointed (omitting any of those electors who are registered as service voters and entitled to vote by post); and

(ii) the names and addresses of the persons appointed;

(*c*) a list of any persons entitled to vote by post as proxy at the election.

Issue of official poll cards

28.—(1) The returning officer shall as soon as practicable send to electors and their proxies an official poll card, but a card need not be sent to any person—

(*a*) as an elector if he is placed on the absent voters list for the election; or

(*b*) as a proxy if his application to vote as such by post is allowed for the election.

(2) An elector's official poll card shall be sent or delivered to his qualifying address, and a proxy's to his address as shown in the list of proxies.

(3) The official poll card shall be in the prescribed form and shall set out—

(*a*) the name of the constituency;

(*b*) the elector's name, qualifying address and number on the register;

(*c*) the date and hours of the poll and the situation of the elector's polling station.

(4) Paragraph (6) of rule 7 above applies for the interpretation of this rule.

Equipment of polling stations

29.—(1) The returning officer shall provide each presiding officer with such number of ballot boxes and ballot papers as in the returning officer's opinion may be necessary.

(2) Every ballot box shall be so constructed that the ballot papers can be put in it, but cannot be withdrawn from it, without the box being unlocked.

(3) The returning officer shall provide each polling station with—

(*a*) materials to enable voters to mark the ballot papers;

(*b*) instruments for stamping on them the official mark;

(*c*) copies of the register of electors or such part of it as contains the names of the electors allotted to the station;

(*d*) the parts of any special lists prepared for the election corresponding to the register of electors or the part of it provided under sub-paragraph (*c*) above.

(4) A notice in the form in the Appendix, giving directions for the guidance of the voters in voting, shall be printed in conspicuous characters and exhibited inside and outside every polling station. SCH. 1

(5) In every compartment of every polling station there shall be exhibited a notice as follows—

(*a*) " The voter may vote for only one candidate " ; or

(*b*) " The voter may vote for not more than one candidate ".

Appointment of polling and counting agents

30.—(1) Each candidate may, before the commencement of the poll, appoint—

(*a*) polling agents to attend at polling stations for the purpose of detecting personation ; and

(*b*) counting agents to attend at the counting of the votes.

(2) The returning officer may limit the number of counting agents, so however that—

(*a*) the number shall be the same in the case of each candidate ; and

(*b*) the number allowed to a candidate shall not (except in special circumstances) be less than the number obtained by dividing the number of clerks employed on the counting by the number of candidates.

(3) Notice in writing of the appointment, stating the names and addresses of the persons appointed, shall be given by the candidate to the returning officer and shall be so given not later than the second day (computed like any period of time in the Timetable) before the day of the poll.

(4) If an agent dies, or becomes incapable of acting, the candidate may appoint another agent in his place, and shall forthwith give to the returning officer notice in writing of the name and address of the agent appointed.

(5) The foregoing provisions of this rule shall be without prejudice to the requirements of section 72(1) of this Act as to the appointment of paid polling agents, and any appointment authorised by this rule may be made and the notice of appointment given to the returning officer by the candidate's election agent, instead of by the candidate.

(6) In the following provisions of these rules references to polling and counting agents shall be taken as references to agents —

(*a*) whose appointments have been duly made and notified ; and

(*b*) where the number of agents is restricted, who are within the permitted number.

(7) Any notice required to be given to a counting agent by the returning officer may be delivered at or sent by post to the address stated in the notice of appointment.

SCH. 1

(8) A candidate may himself do any act or thing which any polling or counting agent of his, if appointed, would have been authorised to do, or may assist his agent in doing any such act or thing.

(9) A candidate's election agent may do or assist in doing anything which a polling or counting agent of his is authorised to do; and anything required or authorised by these rules to be done in the presence of the polling or counting agents may be done in the presence of a candidate's election agent instead of his polling agent or counting agents.

(10) Where by these rules any act or thing is required or authorised to be done in the presence of the polling or counting agents, the non-attendance of any agents or agent at the time and place appointed for the purpose shall not, if the act or thing is otherwise duly done, invalidate the act or thing done.

Declaration of secrecy

31.—(1) Before the opening of the poll a declaration of secrecy in the form in paragraph (4) of this rule, or in a form as near to it as circumstances admit, shall be made by—

(*a*) the returning officer and the presiding officers;

(*b*) every clerk authorised to attend at a polling station or the counting of the votes;

(*c*) every candidate attending at a polling station or at the counting of the votes and every election agent so attending;

(*d*) every candidate's wife or husband attending at the counting of the votes;

(*e*) every polling agent and counting agent;

(*f*) every person permitted by the returning officer to attend at the counting of the votes, though not entitled to do so,

but the constables on duty at polling stations or at the counting of the votes shall not be required to make the declaration of secrecy.

(2) Notwithstanding anything in paragraph (1) above, the following persons attending at the counting of the votes—

(*a*) any candidate,

(*b*) any election agent, or any candidate's wife or husband attending by virtue of the rule authorising election agents and candidates' wives or husbands to attend as such,

(*c*) any person permitted by the returning officer to attend, though not entitled to do so,

(*d*) any clerk making the declaration in order to attend at the counting of the votes,

need not make the declaration before the opening of the poll but shall make it before he or she is permitted to attend the counting, and a polling or counting agent appointed after the opening of the poll shall make the declaration before acting as such an agent.

(3) The returning officer shall make the declaration in the presence of a justice of the peace, and any other person shall make the declaration in the presence either of a justice of the peace or of

the returning officer, and subsections (1), (2), (3) and (6) of section 66 of this Act shall be read to the declarant by the person taking the declaration or shall be read by the declarant in the presence of that person ; but—

Sch. 1

(*a*) in England and Wales the declaration may be made by the returning officer or any other person before a person who is chairman of the Greater London Council, a county council or a district council or mayor of a London borough, and may be made by a person other than the returning officer before a person who is the proper officer of any such council ; and

(*b*) in Scotland the declaration may be made by a person other than the returning officer before the proper officer of an islands or regional council ; and

(*c*) in Northern Ireland the declaration may be made by a person other than the returning officer before the clerk of a district council.

(4) The declaration shall be as follows—

"I solemnly promise and declare that I will not do anything forbidden by subsections (1), (2), (3) and (6) of section 66 of the Representation of the People Act 1983, which have been read to [*by*] me."

The Poll

Admission to polling station

32.—(1) The presiding officer shall regulate the number of voters to be admitted to the polling station at the same time, and shall exclude all other persons except—

(*a*) the candidates and their election agents ;

(*b*) the polling agents appointed to attend at the polling station ;

(*c*) the clerks appointed to attend at the polling station ;

(*d*) the constables on duty ; and

(*e*) the companions of blind voters.

(2) Not more than one polling agent shall be admitted at the same time to a polling station on behalf of the same candidate.

(3) A constable or person employed by a returning officer shall not be admitted to vote in person elsewhere than at his own polling station under the relevant provision of this Act, except on production and surrender of a certificate as to his employment, which shall be in the prescribed form and signed by the prescribed officer of police or by the returning officer, as the case may be.

(4) Any certificate surrendered under this rule shall forthwith be cancelled.

Keeping of order in station

33.—(1) It is the presiding officer's duty to keep order at his polling station.

SCH. 1

(2) If a person misconducts himself in a polling station, or fails to obey the presiding officer's lawful orders, he may immediately, by the presiding officer's order, be removed from the polling station—

(*a*) by a constable in or near that station, or

(*b*) by any other person authorised in writing by the returning officer to remove him,

and the person so removed shall not, without the presiding officer's permission, again enter the polling station during the day.

(3) Any person so removed may, if charged with the commission in the polling station of an offence, be dealt with as a person taken into custody by a constable for an offence without a warrant.

(4) The powers conferred by this rule shall not be exercised so as to prevent a voter who is otherwise entitled to vote at a polling station from having an opportunity of voting at that station.

Sealing of ballot boxes

34. Immediately before the commencement of the poll, the presiding officer shall show the ballot box empty to such persons, if any, as are present in the polling station, so that they may see that it is empty, and shall then lock it up and place his seal on it in such a manner as to prevent its being opened without breaking the seal, and shall place it in his view for the receipt of ballot papers, and keep it so locked and sealed.

Questions to be put to voters

35.—(1) The presiding officer may, and if required by a candidate or his election or polling agent shall, put to any person applying for a ballot paper at the time of his application, but not afterwards, the following questions, or either of them—

(*a*) in the case of a person applying as an elector—

(i) " Are you the person registered in the register of parliamentary electors for this election as follows? " (*read the whole entry from the register.*)

(ii) " Have you already voted, here or elsewhere, at this by-election [general election], otherwise than as proxy for some other person? "

(*b*) in the case of a person applying as proxy—

(i) " Are you the person whose name appears as A.B. in the list of proxies for this election as entitled to vote as proxy on behalf of C.D.? "

(ii) " Have you already voted here or elsewhere at this by-election [general election] as proxy on behalf of C.D.? "

(2) In the case of a person applying as proxy, the presiding officer may, and if required as mentioned above shall, put the following additional question—

" Are you the husband [wife], parent, grandparent, brother [sister], child or grandchild of C.D.? "

and if that question is not answered in the affirmative the following question—

"Have you at this election already voted in this constituency on behalf of two persons of whom you are not the husband [wife], parent, grandparent, brother [sister], child or grandchild?"

(3) A ballot paper shall not be delivered to any person required to answer the above questions or any of them unless he has answered the questions or question satisfactorily.

(4) Save as by this rule authorised, no inquiry shall be permitted as to the right of any person to vote.

Challenge of voter

36.—(1) If at the time a person applies for a ballot paper for the purpose of voting in person, or after he has applied for a ballot paper for that purpose and before he has left the polling station, a candidate or his election or polling agent—

(*a*) declares to the presiding officer that he has reasonable cause to believe that the applicant has committed an offence of personation, and

(*b*) undertakes to substantiate the charge in a court of law,

the presiding officer may order a constable to arrest the applicant, and the order of the presiding officer shall be sufficient authority for the constable so to do.

(2) A person against whom a declaration is made under this rule shall not by reason of it be prevented from voting.

(3) A person arrested under the provisions of this rule shall be dealt with as a person taken into custody by a constable for an offence without a warrant.

Voting procedure

37.—(1) A ballot paper shall be delivered to a voter who applies for one, and immediately before delivery—

(*a*) the ballot paper shall be stamped with the official mark;

(*b*) the number, name and description of the elector as stated in the copy of the register of electors shall be called out;

(*c*) the number of the elector shall be marked on the counterfoil;

(*d*) a mark shall be placed in the register of electors against the number of the elector to denote that a ballot paper has been received but without showing the particular ballot paper which has been received; and

(*e*) in the case of a person applying for a ballot paper as proxy, a mark shall also be placed against his name in the list of proxies.

(2) The voter, on receiving the ballot paper, shall forthwith proceed into one of the compartments in the polling station and

SCH. 1

there secretly mark his paper and fold it up so as to conceal his vote, and shall then show to the presiding officer the back of the paper, so as to disclose the official mark, and put the ballot paper so folded up into the ballot box in the presiding officer's presence.

(3) The voter shall vote without undue delay, and shall leave the polling station as soon as he has put his ballot paper into the ballot box.

Votes marked by presiding officer

38.—(1) The presiding officer, on the application of a voter—

(*a*) who is incapacitated by blindness or other physical cause from voting in manner directed by these rules, or

(*b*) who declares orally that he is unable to read,

shall, in the presence of the polling agents, cause the voter's vote to be marked on a ballot paper in manner directed by the voter, and the ballot paper to be placed in the ballot box.

(2) The name and number on the register of electors of every voter whose vote is marked in pursuance of this rule, and the reason why it is so marked, shall be entered on a list (in these rules called " the list of votes marked by the presiding officer ").

In the case of a person voting as proxy for an elector, the number to be entered together with the voter's name shall be the elector's number.

Voting by blind persons

39.—(1) If a voter makes an application to the presiding officer to be allowed on the ground of blindness to vote with the assistance of another person by whom he is accompanied (in these rules referred to as " the companion "), the presiding officer shall require the voter to declare orally whether he is so incapacitated by his blindness as to be unable to vote without assistance.

(2) If the presiding officer—

(*a*) is satisfied that the voter is so incapacitated, and

(*b*) is also satisfied by a written declaration made by the companion (in these rules referred to as " the declaration made by the companion of a blind voter ") that the companion—

(i) is a qualified person within the meaning of this rule, and

(ii) has not previously assisted more than one blind person to vote at the election,

the presiding officer shall grant the application, and then anything which is by these rules required to be done to or by that voter in connection with the giving of his vote may be done to, or with the assistance of, the companion.

(3) For the purposes of this rule, a person shall be qualified to assist a blind voter to vote, if that person is either—

(*a*) a person who is entitled to vote as an elector at the election ; or

(b) the father, mother, brother, sister, husband, wife, son or daughter of the blind voter and has attained the age of 18 years.

(4) The name and number in the register of electors of every voter whose vote is given in accordance with this rule and the name and address of the companion shall be entered on a list (in these rules referred to as "the list of blind voters assisted by companions").

In the case of a person voting as proxy for an elector, the number to be entered together with the voter's name shall be the elector's number.

(5) The declaration made by the companion—

(a) shall be in the form in the Appendix;

(b) shall be made before the presiding officer at the time when the voter applies to vote with the assistance of a companion and shall forthwith be given to the presiding officer who shall attest and retain it.

(6) No fee or other payment shall be charged in respect of the declaration

Tendered ballot papers

40.—(1) If a person, representing himself to be—

(a) a particular elector named on the register and not named in the absent voters list, or

(b) a particular person named in the list of proxies as proxy for an elector and not named in the list of persons entitled to vote by post as proxy,

applies for a ballot paper after another person has voted in person either as the elector or his proxy, the applicant shall, on satisfactorily answering the questions permitted by law to be asked at the poll, be entitled, subject to the following provisions of this rule, to mark a ballot paper (in these rules referred to as "a tendered ballot paper") in the same manner as any other voter.

(2) A tendered ballot paper shall—

(a) be of a colour differing from the other ballot papers;

(b) instead of being put into the ballot box, be given to the presiding officer and endorsed by him with the name of the voter and his number in the register of electors, and set aside in a separate packet.

(3) The name of the voter and his number on the register of electors shall be entered on a list (in these rules referred to as the "tendered votes list").

(4) In the case of a person voting as proxy for an elector, the number to be endorsed or entered together with the voter's name shall be the number of that elector.

SCH. 1

Spoilt ballot papers

41. A voter who has inadvertently dealt with his ballot paper in such manner that it cannot be conveniently used as a ballot paper may, on delivering it to the presiding officer and proving to his satisfaction the fact of the inadvertence, obtain another ballot paper in the place of the ballot paper so delivered (in these rules referred to as " a spoilt ballot paper "), and the spoilt ballot paper shall be immediately cancelled.

Adjournment of poll in case of riot

42.—(1) Where the proceedings at any polling station are interrupted or obstructed by riot or open violence, the presiding officer shall adjourn the proceedings till the following day and shall forthwith give notice to the returning officer.

(2) Where the poll is adjourned at any polling station—

(*a*) the hours of polling on the day to which it is adjourned shall be the same as for the original day ; and

(*b*) references in this Act to the close of the poll shall be construed accordingly.

Procedure on close of poll

43.—(1) As soon as practicable after the close of the poll, the presiding officer shall, in the presence of the polling agents, make up into separate packets, sealed with his own seal and the seals of such polling agents as desire to affix their seals—

(*a*) each ballot box in use at the station, sealed so as to prevent the introduction of additional ballot papers and unopened, but with the key attached,

(*b*) the unused and spoilt ballot papers placed together,

(*c*) the tendered ballot papers,

(*d*) the marked copies of the register of electors and of the list of proxies,

(*e*) the counterfoils of the used ballot papers and the certificates as to employment on duty on the day of the poll,

(*f*) the tendered votes list, the list of blind voters assisted by companions, the list of votes marked by the presiding officer, a statement of the number of voters whose votes are so marked by the presiding officer under the heads " physical incapacity " and " unable to read ", and the declarations made by the companions of blind voters,

and shall deliver the packets or cause them to be delivered to the returning officer to be taken charge of by him ; but if the packets are not delivered by the presiding officer personally to the returning officer, the arrangements for their delivery shall require the returning officer's approval.

(2) The marked copies of the register of electors and of the list of proxies shall be in one packet but shall not be in the same packet

as the counterfoils of the used ballot papers and the certificates as to employment on duty on the day of the poll.

(3) The packets shall be accompanied by a statement (in these rules referred to as " the ballot paper account ") made by the presiding officer showing the number of ballot papers entrusted to him, and accounting for them under the heads of ballot papers issued and not otherwise accounted for, unused, spoilt and tendered ballot papers.

COUNTING OF VOTES

Attendance at counting of votes

44.—(1) The returning officer shall make arrangements for counting the votes in the presence of the counting agents as soon as practicable after the close of the poll, and shall give to the counting agents notice in writing of the time and place at which he will begin to count the votes.

(2) No person other than—

(*a*) the returning officer and his clerks,

(*b*) the candidates and their wives or husbands,

(*c*) the election agents,

(*d*) the counting agents,

may be present at the counting of the votes, unless permitted by the returning officer to attend.

(3) A person not entitled to attend at the counting of the votes shall not be permitted to do so by the returning officer unless he—

(*a*) is satisfied that the efficient counting of the votes will not be impeded ; and

(*b*) has either consulted the election agents or thought it impracticable to do so.

(4) The returning officer shall give the counting agents all such reasonable facilities for overseeing the proceedings, and all such information with respect to them, as he can give them consistently with the orderly conduct of the proceedings and the discharge of his duties in connection with them.

(5) In particular, where the votes are counted by sorting the ballot papers according to the candidate for whom the vote is given and then counting the number of ballot papers for each candidate, the counting agents shall be entitled to satisfy themselves that the ballot papers are correctly sorted.

The count

45.—(1) Before the returning officer proceeds to count the votes, he shall—

(*a*) in the presence of the counting agents open each ballot box and, taking out the ballot papers in it, count and record the number of them and in the presence of the election agents verify each ballot paper account ;

SCH. 1

(*b*) count such of the postal ballot papers as have been duly returned and record the number counted ; and

(*c*) then mix together the whole of the ballot papers mentioned in the foregoing sub-paragraphs.

(2) A postal ballot paper shall not be deemed to be duly returned unless it is returned in the proper envelope so as to reach the returning officer before the close of the poll and is accompanied by the declaration of identity duly signed and authenticated.

(3) The returning officer shall not count any tendered ballot paper.

(4) The returning officer, while counting and recording the number of ballot papers and counting the votes, shall keep the ballot papers with their faces upwards and take all proper precautions for preventing any person from seeing the numbers printed on the back of the papers.

(5) The returning officer shall verify each ballot paper account by comparing it with the number of ballot papers recorded by him, and the unused and spoilt ballot papers in his possession and the tendered votes list (opening and resealing the packets containing the unused and spoilt ballot papers and the tendered votes list) and shall draw up a statement as to the result of the verification, which any election agent may copy.

(6) The returning officer shall so far as practicable proceed continuously with counting the votes, allowing only time for refreshment, except that he may, in so far as he and the agents agree, exclude the hours between 7 in the evening and 9 on the following morning.

For the purposes of this exception the agreement of a candidate or his election agent shall be as effective as the agreement of his counting agents.

(7) During the time so excluded the returning officer shall—

(*a*) place the ballot papers and other documents relating to the election under his own seal and the seals of such of the counting agents as desire to affix their seals ; and

(*b*) otherwise take proper precautions for the security of the papers and documents.

Re-count

46.—(1) A candidate or his election agent may, if present when the counting or any re-count of the votes is completed, require the returning officer to have the votes re-counted or again re-counted but the returning officer may refuse to do so if in his opinion the request is unreasonable.

(2) No step shall be taken on the completion of the counting or any re-count of votes until the candidates and election agents present at its completion have been given a reasonable opportunity to exercise the right conferred by this rule.

Rejected ballot papers

SCH. 1

47.—(1) Any ballot paper—

(a) which does not bear the official mark, or

(b) on which votes are given for more than one candidate, or

(c) on which anything is written or marked by which the voter can be identified except the printed number on the back, or

(d) which is unmarked or void for uncertainty,

shall, subject to the provisions of the next following paragraph, be void and not counted.

(2) A ballot paper on which the vote is marked—

(a) elsewhere than in the proper place, or

(b) otherwise than by means of a cross, or

(c) by more than one mark,

shall not for such reason be deemed to be void if an intention that the vote shall be for one or other of the candidates clearly appears, and the way the paper is marked does not itself identify the voter and it is not shown that he can be identified by it.

(3) The returning officer shall endorse the word " rejected " on any ballot paper which under this rule is not to be counted, and shall add to the endorsement the words " rejection objected to " if an objection is made by a counting agent to his decision.

(4) The returning officer shall draw up a statement showing the number of ballot papers rejected under the several heads of—

(a) want of official mark ;

(b) voting for more than one candidate ;

(c) writing or mark by which voter could be identified ;

(d) unmarked or void for uncertainty.

Decisions on ballot papers

48. The decision of the returning officer on any question arising in respect of a ballot paper shall be final, but shall be subject to review on an election petition.

Equality of votes

49. Where, after the counting of the votes (including any re-count) is completed, an equality of votes is found to exist between any candidates and the addition of a vote would entitle any of those candidates to be declared elected, the returning officer shall forthwith decide between those candidates by lot, and proceed as if the candidate on whom the lot falls had received an additional vote.

SCH. 1

PART IV

FINAL PROCEEDINGS IN CONTESTED AND UNCONTESTED ELECTIONS

Declaration of result

50.—(1) In a contested election, when the result of the poll has been ascertained, the returning officer shall forthwith—

(*a*) declare to be elected the candidate to whom the majority of votes has been given ;

(*b*) return his name to the Clerk of the Crown ; and

(*c*) give public notice of his name and of the total number of votes given for each candidate together with the number of rejected ballot papers under each head shown in the statement of rejected ballot papers.

(2) In an uncontested election, the statement of persons nominated, in addition to showing the person standing nominated, shall also declare that person elected, and the returning officer shall forthwith return his name to the Clerk of the Crown.

Return to the writ

51.—(1) The returning officer shall return the name of the member elected by endorsing on the writ a certificate in the form in the Appendix.

(2) Any rule of law or enactment as to the effect of, or manner of dealing with, the return of a member to serve in Parliament applies to the certificate.

(3) The returning officer may, on receiving a receipt, deliver the writ with the certificate endorsed on it to the postmaster of the principal post office of the place of election or the postmaster's deputy.

(4) The postmaster or his deputy shall send the writ so endorsed by the first post, free of charge, under cover to the Clerk of the Crown with the words " Election Writ and Return " endorsed on it.

(5) Any reference in the foregoing provisions of this Part of these rules to the Clerk of the Crown shall be taken, in relation to an election for a constituency in Northern Ireland, as a reference to the Clerk of the Crown for Northern Ireland, but any writ returned to the Clerk of the Crown for Northern Ireland shall be transmitted by him to the Clerk of the Crown in England and the return shall be certified to the House of Commons in the same manner as returns for elections for constituencies in Great Britain.

(6) A copy of each writ returned to the Clerk of the Crown for Northern Ireland and of the certificate endorsed on it shall be attested by the Secretary of State, shall be kept in the office of the Clerk of the Crown for Northern Ireland and may be given in evidence if the originals are lost.

Record of returns at Crown Office

52.—(1) The Clerk of the Crown shall from the certificate on each writ returned to him enter the name of the member returned in a book to be kept by him at the Crown Office.

(2) The Clerk of the Crown shall also enter in the book any alteration or amendment made by him in the certificate endorsed on any writ.

(3) The book shall be open to public inspection at reasonable times and any person may, on payment of a reasonable fee, take copies from the book.

Return or forfeiture of candidate's deposit

53.—(1) The deposit made under rule 9 of these rules shall either be returned to the person making it or his personal representatives or be forfeited to Her Majesty.

(2) Except in the cases mentioned below in this rule, the deposit shall be returned as soon as practicable after the result of the election is declared.

(3) If the candidate is not shown as standing nominated in the statement of persons nominated, or if the poll is countermanded or abandoned by reason of his death, the deposit shall be returned as soon as practicable after the publication of the statement or after his death, as the case may be.

(4) Subject to paragraph (3) above the deposit shall be forfeited if a poll is taken and, after the counting of the votes by the returning officer (including any re-count) is completed, the candidate is found not to have polled more than one-eighth of the total number of votes polled by all the candidates.

(5) Notwithstanding anything in paragraphs (2) to (4) above, if at a general election a candidate is shown as standing nominated in more than one constituency in the statements of persons nominated, not more than one of the deposits shall be returned and, if necessary, the Treasury shall direct which it is to be.

Part V

Disposal of Documents

Sealing up of ballot papers

54.—(1) On the completion of the counting at a contested election the returning officer shall seal up in separate packets the counted and rejected ballot papers.

(2) The returning officer shall not open the sealed packets of tendered ballot papers or of counterfoils and certificates as to employment on duty on the day of the poll, or of marked copies of the register of electors and lists of proxies.

SCH. 1

Delivery of documents to Clerk of the Crown

55.—(1) The returning officer shall then forward to the Clerk of the Crown the following documents—

(*a*) the packets of ballot papers in his possession,

(*b*) the ballot paper accounts and the statements of rejected ballot papers and of the result of the verification of the ballot paper accounts,

(*c*) the tendered votes lists, the lists of blind voters assisted by companions, the lists of votes marked by the presiding officer and the related statements, and the declarations made by the companions of blind voters,

(*d*) the packets of counterfoils and certificates as to employment on duty on the day of the poll,

(*e*) the packets containing marked copies of registers and of lists of proxies,

endorsing on each packet a description of its contents, the date of the election to which they relate and the name of the constituency for which the election was held.

(2) The returning officer may forward the documents either by delivering them by himself or his agent to the Clerk of the Crown or his deputy or by sending them by post in like manner as he may send the writ by post ; but if he sends them by post—

(*a*) he shall send a letter to the Clerk of the Crown by the same post, specifying the number and description of the documents so sent ;

(*b*) a copy of the receipt given him by the postmaster or deputy postmaster shall be signed by him and retained by the postmaster or deputy postmaster.

(3) The Clerk of the Crown shall on receiving the documents give a receipt to the person delivering them, and shall register them in books of the Crown Office specifying the date and time of receipt.

(4) Any receipt to be given for the documents shall show the date and time of their receipt.

Orders for production of documents

56.—(1) An order—

(*a*) for the inspection or production of any rejected ballot papers in the custody of the Clerk of the Crown, or

(*b*) for the opening of a sealed packet of counterfoils and certificates as to employment on duty on the day of the poll or the inspection of any counted ballot papers in his custody,

may be made—

(i) by the House of Commons ; or

(ii) if satisfied by evidence on oath that the order is required for the purpose of instituting or maintaining a prosecution for an offence in relation to ballot papers, or for the purpose of an election petition, by the High Court or a county court. SCH. 1

(2) An order for the opening of a sealed packet of counterfoils and certificates or for the inspection of any counted ballot papers in the Clerk of the Crown's custody may be made by an election court.

(3) An order under this rule may be made subject to such conditions as to—

(*a*) persons,

(*b*) time,

(*c*) place and mode of inspection,

(*d*) production or opening,

as the House of Commons or court making the order may think expedient; but in making and carrying into effect an order for the opening of a packet of counterfoils and certificates or for the inspection of counted ballot papers, care shall be taken that the way in which the vote of any particular elector has been given shall not be disclosed until it has been proved—

(i) that his vote was given; and

(ii) that the vote has been declared by a competent court to be invalid.

(4) An appeal lies to the High Court from any order of a county court under this rule.

(5) Any power given under this rule—

(*a*) to the High Court or, except in Northern Ireland, to a county court, may be exercised by any judge of the court otherwise than in open court; and

(*b*) in Northern Ireland to a county court, may be exercised in such manner as may be provided by rules of court.

(6) Where an order is made for the production by the Clerk of the Crown of any document in his possession relating to any specified election—

(*a*) the production by him or his agent of the document ordered in such manner as may be directed by that order shall be conclusive evidence that the document relates to the specified election; and

(*b*) any endorsement on any packet of ballot papers so produced shall be prima facie evidence that the ballot papers are what they are stated to be by the endorsement.

(7) The production from proper custody of a ballot paper purporting to have been used at any election, and of a counterfoil marked with the same printed number and having a number marked on it in writing, shall be prima facie evidence that the elector whose vote was given by that ballot paper was the person who at the time of the election had affixed to his name in the register of electors the same number as the number written on the counterfoil.

SCH. 1

(8) Save as by this rule provided, no person shall be allowed to inspect any rejected or counted ballot papers in the possession of the Clerk of the Crown or to open any sealed packets of counterfoils and certificates.

Retention and public inspection of documents

57.—(1) The Clerk of the Crown shall retain for a year all documents relating to an election forwarded to him in pursuance of these rules by a returning officer, and then, unless otherwise directed by order of the House of Commons or the High Court, shall cause them to be destroyed.

(2) Those documents, except ballot papers, counterfoils and certificates as to employment on duty on the day of the poll, shall be open to public inspection at such time and subject to such conditions as may be prescribed by the Clerk of the Crown with the consent of the Speaker of the House of Commons.

(3) The Clerk of the Crown shall, on request, supply copies of or extracts from the documents open to public inspection on payment of such fees and subject to such conditions as may be sanctioned by the Treasury.

Disposal of documents in Scotland

58. In Scotland, the documents mentioned in sub-paragraphs (*a*) to (*e*) of paragraph (1) of rule 55 of these rules shall, instead of being forwarded to the Clerk of the Crown—

(*a*) be kept by the sheriff clerk of the sheriff court district comprising the constituency, or

(*b*) if the constituency comprises the whole or part of more sheriff court districts than one, the sheriff clerk of such one of those sheriff court districts as the Secretary of State may by order appoint,

and the provisions of rules 56 and 57 of these rules apply to those documents with the substitution of that sheriff clerk for the Clerk of the Crown.

Disposal of documents in Northern Ireland

59. In relation to an election for a constituency in Northern Ireland, any reference in this Part of these rules to the Clerk of the Crown shall be taken as a reference to the Clerk of the Crown for Northern Ireland.

PART VI

DEATH OF CANDIDATE

Countermand or abandonment of poll on death of candidate

60.—(1) If at a contested election proof is given to the returning officer's satisfaction before the result of the election is declared that one of the persons named or to be named as candidate in the ballot papers has died, then the returning officer shall countermand notice of the poll or, if polling has begun, direct that the poll be abandoned, and all proceedings with reference to the election shall be commenced afresh in all respects as if the writ had been received 28 days after the day on which proof was given to the returning officer of the death except that— Sch. 1

(a) no fresh nomination shall be necessary in the case of a person shown in the statement of persons nominated as standing nominated, and

(b) in the case of a general election, as in the case of a by-election, the time for delivery of nomination papers and the time for polling shall be determined in accordance with the third column in the Timetable in rule 1 of these rules (with the necessary modification of any reference to the date on which the writ is received).

(2) Where the poll is abandoned by reason of a candidate's death the proceedings at or consequent on that poll shall be interrupted, and the presiding officer at any polling station shall take the like steps (so far as not already taken) for the delivery to the returning officer of ballot boxes and of ballot papers and other documents as he is required to take on the close of the poll in due course, and the returning officer shall dispose of ballot papers and other documents in his possession as he is required to do on the completion in due course of the counting of the votes, but—

(a) it shall not be necessary for any ballot paper account to be prepared or verified ; and

(b) the returning officer, without taking any step or further step for the counting of the ballot papers or of the votes shall seal up all the ballot papers, whether the votes on them have been counted or not, and it shall not be necessary to seal up counted and rejected ballot papers in separate packets.

(3) The provisions of these rules as to the inspection, production, retention and destruction of ballot papers and other documents relating to a poll at an election apply to any such documents relating to a poll abandoned by reason of a candidate's death, with the following modifications—

(a) ballot papers on which the votes were neither counted nor rejected shall be treated as counted ballot papers ; and

(b) no order shall be made for the production or inspection of any ballot papers or for the opening of a sealed packet of counterfoils or certificates as to employment on duty on the day of the poll unless the order is made by a court with reference to a prosecution.

SCH. 1

APPENDIX OF FORMS

Note.—The forms contained in this Appendix may be adapted so far as circumstances require.

Form of writ

*The name of the sovereign may be altered when necessary.

* Elizabeth the Second by the Grace of God of the United Kingdom of Great Britain and Northern Ireland and of Our other Realms and Territories Queen Head of the Commonwealth Defender of the Faith to the Returning Officer for the Constituency Greeting

†This preamble to be omitted except in case of a general election.

‡Except in a general election insert here *in the place of A. B., deceased or* otherwise, stating the cause of vacancy.

†Whereas by the advice of Our Council We have ordered a Parliament to be holden at Westminster on the day of next We Command you that due notice being first given you do cause election to be made according to law of a Member to serve in Parliament for the said Constituency [‡in the place of] And that you do cause the name of such Member when so elected, whether he be present or absent, to be certified to Us in Our Chancery without delay

Witness Ourself at Westminster the day of in the year of Our Reign, and in the year of Our Lord 19 .

Label or direction of writ

To the Returning Officer for the Constituency.
A writ of a new election of a Member for the said Constituency.

Endorsement

Received the within Writ on the day of , 19 .

(Signed)

Returning Officer (*or as the case may be.*)

Certificate endorsed on writ

I hereby certify, that the Member elected for the Constituency in pursuance of the within written Writ is of in the County of

(Signed)

Returning Officer (*or as the case may be.*)

Form of notice of election

PARLIAMENTARY ELECTION FOR THE CONSTITUENCY

1. An election is to be held of a Member to serve in Parliament for the said Constituency.

2. Nomination papers may be delivered by the candidate or his proposer or seconder to the returning officer at between the hours of 10 in the morning and 4 in the afternoon on any day after the date of this notice, but not later than the day of

3. Forms of nomination paper may be obtained at the place and times mentioned above. The returning officer will at the request of any elector prepare for signature a nomination paper. SCH. 1

4. If the election is contested, the poll will take place on the day of

(Signed)

Returning Officer (*or as the case may be.*)

day of , 19 .

NOTE

1. The attention of candidates and electors is drawn to the rules for filling up nomination papers and other provisions relating to nomination contained in the parliamentary elections rules in Schedule 1 to the Representation of the People Act 1983.

2. Every person guilty of a corrupt or illegal practice will, on conviction, be liable to the penalties imposed by the Representation of the People Act 1983.

3. Electors and their proxies should take note that applications to be treated as an absent voter and other applications and notices about postal or proxy voting must reach the registration officer by the day of next if they are to be effective for this election.

Form of nomination paper

ELECTION OF A MEMBER to serve in Parliament for the Constituency.

We, the undersigned, being electors for the said Constituency, do hereby nominate the under-mentioned person as a candidate at the said election.

Candidate's surname	Other names in full	Description	Home address in full
BROWN... ...	John Edward ...	Merchant	52, George Street, Bristol

Signatures	Electoral Number (See Note 3) Distinctive letter	Number
Proposer..	....	....
Seconder	....	....
We, the undersigned, being electors for the said Constituency, do hereby assent to the foregoing nomination.		
1	....	....
2	....	....
3	....	....
4	....	....
5	....	....
6	....	....
7	....	....
8	....	....

SCH. 1

NOTE

1. The attention of candidates and electors is drawn to the rules for filling up nomination papers and other provisions relating to nomination contained in the parliamentary elections rules in Schedule 1 to the Representation of the People Act 1983.

2. Where a candidate is commonly known by some title he may be described by his title as if it were his surname.

3. A person's electoral number is his number in the register to be used at the election (including the distinctive letter of the parliamentary polling district in which he is registered) except that before publication of the register his number (if any) in the electors lists for that register shall be used instead.

4. An elector may not subscribe more than one nomination paper for the same election.

5. A person whose name is entered in the register or electors lists may not subscribe a nomination paper if the entry gives as the date on which he will become of voting age a date later than the day fixed for the poll.

Form of Ballot Paper

SCH. 1

Form of Front of Ballot Paper

Counterfoil No.

'he counterfoil ' to have a umber to orrespond with hat on the back f the Ballot 'aper.

1	BROWN (JOHN EDWARD Brown, of 52, George Street, Bristol, merchant.)
2	BROWN (THOMAS WILLIAM Brown, of 136, London Road, Swindon, salesman.)
3	JONES (William David Jones, of High Elms, Wilts., gentleman.)
4	MERTON (Hon. George Travis, commonly called Viscount Merton, of Swansworth, Berks.)
5	SMITH (Mary Smith, of 72 High Street, Bath, married woman.)

Form of Back of Ballot Paper

No.

Election for the Constituency

n 19

Note.—The number on the ballot paper is to correspond with that on the ounterfoil.

SCH. 1

Directions as to printing the ballot paper

1. Nothing is to be printed on the ballot paper except in accordance with these directions.

2. So far as practicable, the following arrangements shall be observed in the printing of the ballot paper—

(*a*) no word shall be printed on the face except the particulars of the candidates ;

(*b*) no rule shall be printed on the face except the horizontal rules separating the particulars of the candidates from one another and the vertical rules separating those particulars from the numbers on the left-hand side and the spaces on the right where the vote is to be marked ;

(*c*) the whole space between the top and bottom of the paper shall be equally divided between the candidates by the rules separating their particulars.

3. The surname of each candidate shall in all cases be printed by itself in large capitals, and his full particulars shall be set out below it and shall be printed in ordinary type except that small capitals shall be used—

(*a*) if his surname is the same as another candidate's, for his other names ; and

(*b*) if his other names are also the same as the other candidate's, either for his home address or for his description unless each of them is the same as that of another candidate with the same surname and other names.

4. The number on the back of the ballot paper shall be printed in small characters.

Form of directions for the guidance of the voters in voting

1. The voter should see that the ballot paper, before it is handed to him, is stamped with the official mark.

2. The voter will go into one of the compartments and, with the pencil provided in the compartment, place a cross on the right-hand side of the ballot paper, opposite the name of the candidate for whom he votes, thus X.

3. The voter will then fold up the ballot paper so as to show the official mark on the back, and leaving the compartment will, without showing the front of the paper to any person, show the official mark on the back to the presiding officer, and then, in the presence of the presiding officer, put the paper into the ballot box, and forthwith leave the polling station.

4. If the voter inadvertently spoils a ballot paper he can return it to the officer, who will, if satisfied of such inadvertence, give him another paper.

5. If the voter votes for more than one candidate, or places any mark on the paper by which he may afterwards be identified his ballot paper will be void, and will not be counted.

6. If the voter fraudulently takes a ballot paper out of a polling station or fraudulently puts into the ballot box any paper other than the one given to him by the officer, he will be liable on conviction to imprisonment for a term not exceeding six months. SCH. 1

Form of declaration to be made by the companion of a blind voter

I, *A. B.*, of , having been requested to assist *C. D.*, (*in the case of a blind person voting as proxy add* voting as proxy for *M. N.*) whose number on the register is to record his vote at the election now being held in this constituency, hereby declare that [I am entitled to vote as an elector at the said election] [I am the * of the said voter and have attained the age of 18 years], and that I have not previously assisted any blind person [except *E. F.*, of] to vote at the said election.

*State the relationship of the companion to the voter.

(Signed) *A. B.*,

day of 19 .

I, the undersigned, being the presiding officer for the polling station for the Constituency, hereby certify that the above declaration, having been first read to the above-named declarant, was signed by the declarant in my presence.

(Signed) *G. H.*,

day of 19 .
minutes past o'clock [a.m.] [p.m.]

NOTE.—If the person making the above declaration knowingly and wilfully makes therein a statement false in a material particular, he will be guilty of an offence.

SCHEDULE 2

Section 53

PROVISIONS WHICH MAY BE CONTAINED IN REGULATIONS AS TO REGISTRATION ETC.

1.—(1) Provisions prescribing the arrangements to be made for the carrying out of his registration duties by a registration officer for part of a constituency, where the constituency is not coterminous with or wholly situated in a district or London borough.

(2) Provisions authorising a registration officer to require persons to give information required for the purpose of his registration duties.

2. Provisions imposing on registration officers the duty of requiring persons to give information required for the purpose of the officer's duty under section 3(1) of the Juries Act 1974. 1974 c. 23.

3. Provisions laying down a timetable for the preparation of the register and other matters, and providing that notices and other documents received by the registration officer out of time may be or shall be disregarded either altogether or for the purposes of a particular register or election.

SCH. 2

4. Provisions as to the manner in which service declarations, and applications and notices from service voters, are to be transmitted to the registration officer.

5.—(1) Provisions as to the evidence which shall or may be required, or be deemed sufficient or conclusive evidence, of a person's service declaration having ceased to be in force.

(2) Provisions as to the evidence of age or nationality which may be required in connection with a person's registration otherwise than as a service voter or with his appointment as a proxy.

(3) Provisions requiring any fee payable in connection with the making for the purpose of the regulations of any statutory declaration to be paid by the registration officer.

(4) Provisions as to the evidence which shall or may be required, or be deemed sufficient or conclusive evidence in connection with a person's application to be treated as an absent voter—

(*a*) of his being subject to any physical incapacity and as to its probable duration ; or

(*b*) of his being bound to any religious observance and of the nature and times of the observance ; or

(*c*) of the fact that he is acting as returning officer at any election ; or

(*d*) of his employment as a constable or by a returning officer, mayor or person acting as mayor and the circumstances of that employment.

6. Provisions as to the cases in which a claim or objection may be determined by the registration officer without a hearing, and as to a person's right in any such cases to make written representations to him.

7. Provisions authorising a registration officer to require any person's evidence at a hearing before him to be given on oath and to administer oaths for the purpose.

8. Provisions as to marking the register so as to distinguish those registered as service voters and others having special rights as to the place or manner of voting at any election.

9. Provisions as to marking the register so as to distinguish those who are registered by virtue of the special provision about residence applying to merchant seamen or who, though not so registered, are merchant seamen within the meaning of that provision.

10. Provisions requiring copies of the electors lists, register and other documents or prescribed parts of them to be available for inspection by the public at such places as may be prescribed.

11. Provisions authorising or requiring the registration officer to supply to such persons as may be prescribed copies of the electors lists, register and other documents or prescribed parts of them, whether free of charge or on payment of a prescribed fee.

12. Provisions as to the proceedings in connection with the issue and receipt of ballot papers for voting by post (including provisions as to the persons who are to be entitled or may be allowed to attend and the rights and obligations of persons attending), and provisions as to the steps to be taken to ensure the secrecy of the voting and the safe custody (before and after the count) of the ballot papers returned and other documents. SCH. 2

13.—(1) Provisions imposing pecuniary penalties (not exceeding level 3 on the standard scale, or, in Northern Ireland, not exceeding £100, for any offence) on persons summarily convicted—

(*a*) of having failed to comply with, or given false information in pursuance of, any such requisition of the registration officer as is mentioned in paragraph 1 or paragraph 2 above.

(*b*) of having, without lawful authority, destroyed, mutilated, defaced or removed any notice published by the registration officer in connection with his registration duties, or any copies of a document which have been made available for inspection in pursuance of those duties.

(2) Any other provisions incidental or supplemental to those mentioned in the foregoing paragraphs of this Schedule.

SCHEDULE 3

Sections 81 and 82.

RETURN AND DECLARATIONS AS TO ELECTION EXPENSES

FORM OF RETURN

Election in the...
constituency (*for a local government election substitute* county of district of , *or as the case may be*)

Date of publication of notice of election.....................................

Name of candidate...

1. I am the election agent of the person named above as a candidate at this election [am the person named above as a candidate at this election and was my own election agent].

(*Where there has been a change of election agent suitable variations may be introduced here and elsewhere in the return.*)

2. I hereby make the following return of the candidate's [my] election expenses at this election.

Receipts

(*Include all money, securities or equivalent of money received in respect of expenses incurred on account of or in connection with or incidental to the above election*).

Received of the above-named candidate (*or, if the candidate is his own election agent*, paid by me) ... ... £

Received of (*set out separately the name and description of each person, club, society or association and the amount received from him or them*) ... ... £

SCH. 3

Expenditure

NOTE.—*The return shall deal under a separate heading or sub-heading with any expenses included in it as respects which a return is required to be made by section 75 of this Act.*

Candidate's personal expenses—
paid by him [by me as candidate] ... ... £
paid by me [by me acting as my election agent] ... £
Received by me for my services as election agent (*omit if candidate is his own election agent*) ... ... £
Paid to * as sub-agent of the polling district of ... ... £
Paid to *† as polling agent ... ... £
Paid to *§ as clerk [messenger] for days services ... ... £
Paid to the following persons in respect of goods supplied or work and labour done—
to *§ (*set out the nature of the goods supplied or work and labour done thus*
[printing], [advertising], [stationery]) ... ... £
Paid to *§ as a speaker at a public meeting at on
19 , as remuneration [expenses] ... £
Paid for the hire of rooms—
for holding public meetings—
paid to *§ for hire of (*identify the rooms by naming or describing them*) ... ... £
for committee rooms—
paid to *§ for hire of (*identify the rooms by naming or describing them*) ... ... £
Paid for postage ... ... £
Paid for telegrams (or any similar means of communication) £
Paid for miscellaneous matters—
to *§ (*set out the reason for the payment*) ... ... £

In addition to the above I am aware (*unless the candidate is his own election agent add* as election agent for the above-named candidate) of the following disputed and unpaid claims—

Disputed claims—
by ‡ for (*set out the goods, work and labour, or other matter on the ground of which the claim is based*) ... £

Unpaid claims allowed by the court to be paid after the proper time or in respect of which application has been or is about to be made to the court (*state in each case whether the High Court or some other court*)—
by ‡ for (*set out the goods, work and labour, or other matter on the ground of which the claim is due*) ... £

Signature of person making return...................................

* *Set out separately the name and description of each person with the amount paid to him.*

† *These particulars may be set out in a separate list annexed to and referred to in the account thus "Paid to* (polling agent) *as per annexed list £*.................".

‡ *Set out separately the name and description of each person with the amount paid to or claimed by him.*

§ *These particulars may be set out in a separate list annexed to and referred to in the account.*

FORM OF DECLARATIONS SCH. 3

Election in the ....
constituency (*for a local government election substitute* county of , district of , *or as the case may be*).

Date of publication of notice of election ....

Name of candidate ....

I solemnly and sincerely declare as follows:—

1. I am the person named above as a candidate at this election [and was my own election agent] *or* was at this election the election agent of the person named above as a candidate.

2. I have examined the return of election expenses [about to be] transmitted by my election agent [by me] to the returning officer, (*at a local government election, substitute* appropriate officer) of which a copy is now shown to me and marked , and to the best of my knowledge and belief it is a complete and correct return as required by law.

3. To the best of my knowledge and belief, all expenses shown in the return as paid were paid by my election agent [by me], except as otherwise stated in relation to my [the candidate's] personal expenses.

4. I understand that the law does not allow any election expenses not mentioned in this return to be defrayed except in pursuance of a court order.

Signature of declarant ....

Signed and declared by the above named declarant on the day of , before me,

(Signed) ....

Justice of the Peace (*or as the case may be*) for ....

(NOTE.—*Where there has been a change of election agent, suitable variations may be introduced into the declaration as to expenses.*)

SCHEDULE 4

Sections 90 and 197.

ELECTION EXPENSES AT CERTAIN LOCAL ELECTIONS IN ENGLAND AND WALES

1.—(1) Any claim against any person in respect of any election expenses incurred by or on behalf of a candidate which is not sent in within 14 days after the day of election shall be barred and not paid, and all election expenses incurred as mentioned above shall be paid within 21 days after the day of election and not otherwise.

(2) If any person makes a payment in contravention of this paragraph he shall be guilty of an illegal practice, but a candidate

SCH. 4 shall not be liable, nor shall his election be avoided, for any illegal practice committed under this sub-paragraph without his consent or connivance.

2. Every agent of a candidate at the election shall, within 23 days after the day of election, make a true return to the candidate in writing of all election expenses incurred by the agent and if he fails so to do he shall be liable on summary conviction to a fine not exceeding level 3 on the standard scale.

3. Within 28 days after the day of election every candidate shall send to the proper officer of the authority for which the election is held a return of all election expenses incurred by the candidate or his agents vouched (except in the case of sums under £1) by bills stating the particulars and receipts and accompanied by a declaration by the candidate as to election expenses.

4.—(1) After the expiry of the time for making the return and declaration, the candidate, if elected, shall not, until he has made the return and declaration or until the date of the allowance of any authorised excuse under paragraph 7 below, sit or vote in the council and if he does so—

(*a*) he shall forfeit £50 for every day on which he so sits or votes ; or

(*b*) instead of civil proceedings for a penalty, proceedings may be instituted in a magistrates' court, and he shall be liable on conviction to a fine of an amount not exceeding the amount of the penalty which would be recoverable in civil proceedings.

(2) In relation to an offence under this paragraph—

(*a*) a proceeding for an offence under this paragraph shall be commenced within one year after the offence was committed and the time so limited by this sub-paragraph shall, in the case of any proceedings under the Magistrates' Courts Act 1980 be substituted for any limitation of time contained in that Act ;

1980 c. 43.

(*b*) the issue of a writ or other process shall be deemed to be a commencement of a proceeding, where the service or execution of the same on or against the alleged offender is prevented by the absconding or concealment or act of the alleged offender, but save as mentioned above the service or execution of the same on or against the alleged offender, and not its issue, shall be deemed to be the commencement of the proceeding.

5. If the candidate fails to make that return and declaration he shall be guilty of an illegal practice, and, if he knowingly makes that declaration falsely, he shall be guilty of a corrupt practice.

6. The High Court, an election court or the county court may, on application either of the candidate or a creditor, allow any claim to be sent in and any expense to be paid after the time limited by this Schedule, and a return of any sum so paid shall forthwith after payment be sent to the proper officer of the authority.

7.—(1) If the candidate applies to the High Court, an election court or the county court and shows that the failure to make that return and declaration or either of them or any error or false statement in them has arisen by reason of— SCH. 4

(*a*) his illness or absence, or

(*b*) the absence, death, illness or misconduct of any agent, clerk or officer, or

(*c*) inadvertence or any reasonable cause of a like nature,

and not by reason of any want of good faith on the applicant's part, the court may—

(i) after such notice of the application as it considers fit, and

(ii) on production of such evidence of the grounds stated in the application, and of the applicant's good faith, and otherwise, as it considers fit,

make such order allowing the authorised excuse for the failure, error or false statement as it considers just.

(2) The order may make the allowance conditional upon compliance with such terms as to the court seem best calculated for carrying into effect the objects of this Schedule, and the order shall relieve the applicant from any liability or consequence under this Act in respect of the matters excused by the order.

(3) The date of the order, or, if conditions and terms are to be complied with, the date on which the applicant fully complies with them, is referred to in this Act as the date of the allowance of the excuse.

8.—(1) The return and declaration shall be kept at the office of the proper officer of the authority and shall at all reasonable times during the twelve months next after they are received by him be open to inspection by any person on payment of the prescribed fee and the proper officer shall, on demand, provide copies of them, or of any part of them, at the prescribed price.

(2) After the expiry of twelve months the proper officer of the authority may cause the return and declaration to be destroyed or, if the candidate so requires, shall return them to him.

9. For the purposes of this Schedule—

(*a*) the jurisdiction vested by paragraph 7 in a county court may be exercised otherwise than in open court; and

(*b*) an appeal lies to the High Court from any order of a county court made by virtue of that paragraph.

SCHEDULE 5

Section 95.

USE FOR PARLIAMENTARY ELECTION MEETINGS OF ROOMS IN SCHOOL PREMISES AND OF MEETING ROOMS

1.—(1) Any arrangements for the use of a room in school premises shall be made with the local education authority maintaining the school.

SCH. 5

(2) Any question as to the rooms in school premises which a candidate in any constituency is entitled to use, or as to the times at which he is entitled to use them, or as to the notice which is reasonable, shall be determined by the Secretary of State.

2.—(1) Every local education authority shall prepare and revise for their area lists of the rooms in school premises which candidates in any constituency are entitled to use.

(2) The list shall include the rooms in premises outside, as well as those in premises in, the constituency.

3.—(1) Every district and London borough council shall prepare and revise for their area lists of the meeting rooms which candidates in any constituency are entitled to use.

(2) The list shall indicate the person to whom applications for the use of the room are to be made in each case.

(3) The list shall not include any room if the person maintaining it disputes the right of candidates in the constituency to use it.

4. The lists of rooms in school premises and of meeting rooms prepared for each constituency shall be kept by the registration officer, and those lists and particulars of any change made on their revision shall (where necessary) be forwarded to him accordingly.

5. In the event of a dissolution, or of a vacancy occurring in the seat for the constituency, any person stating himself to be, or to be authorised by, a candidate or his election agent shall be entitled at all reasonable hours to inspect those lists or a copy of them.

6. In the application of this Schedule to Scotland—

(*a*) for any reference to a local education authority substitute a reference to an education authority ;

(*b*) sub-paragraph (1) of paragraph 2, sub-paragraph (1) of paragraph 3 and paragraph 4 do not apply, and it is the duty of the proper officer of the council of every islands area and district to prepare and keep for each constituency wholly situated in the area of the council and for each part so situated of any other constituency—

(i) a list of rooms in school premises, and

(ii) a list of meeting rooms,

which candidates in the constituency are entitled to use.

SCHEDULE 6

Section 191(2).

Ward Elections in the City

1. Without prejudice to the application of any provision of this Act to elections in the City by virtue of sections 191 to 196 of this Act, this Schedule has effect as regards the operation of Part II of the City of London (Various Powers) Act 1957 (referred to in this Schedule as " the City Act "). 1957 c. x.

2. Notwithstanding anything in section 6(1) of the City Act—

(*a*) a person qualified (age apart) to vote as an elector at a ward election shall be entitled to do so if he is of the age of 18 years or over on the date of the poll, except that,

(*b*) a person registered in the ward list to be used at a ward election shall not be entitled to vote as an elector at the election if his entry in the ward list gives a date later than the date of the poll as the date on which he will attain the age of 18 years.

3. Ward lists and provisional ward lists shall give for any elector the date on which it appears to the town clerk of the City that the elector will attain the age of 18 years, if that date is after the 16th November in the year in which the ward lists are to be published.

4. Claims and objections asking for the omission, insertion or alteration of a date in a ward list as that on which an elector will attain that age may be made as in the case of claims and objections relating to the inclusion of a person's name in the list, and sections 7(4) and 9 of the City Act shall with any necessary modifications apply accordingly.

5. Any power under this Act to prescribe the form of service declaration may be exercised so as to take account of the difference between the qualifying date under this Act and the qualifying date under the City Act.

6. Nothing in this Act affects the operation of subsections (3) and (4) and paragraph (*a*) of subsection (5) of section 5 of the Representation of the People Act 1949 (which contain provisions relating to the yearly value of lands and premises and to cases of their joint occupation) in relation to their application by section 4(2) of the City Act. 1949 c. 68.

SCHEDULE 7

Section 206.

Transitional and Saving Provisions, and Interpretation of other Acts

Part I

Transitional and Saving Provisions

General

1. Where a period of time specified in an enactment repealed by this Act is current at its commencement, this Act has effect as if the provision corresponding to that enactment had been in force when that period began to run.

Sch. 7

2. The imposition or subsistence of an incapacity is not affected by the repeal by this Act of any enactment, and any such incapacity shall for the purposes of this Act be treated as having been imposed under the corresponding provision of this Act.

1962 c. 14 (N.I.).

Electoral Law Act (Northern Ireland) 1962

1977 c. 9.

3. Notwithstanding the repeal by this Act of section 1(3) of the Representation of the People Act 1977, the amendments by that section 1(3) of the Electoral Law Act (Northern Ireland) 1962 continue to have the same effect as they had immediately before the coming into force of this Act.

1964 c. 26.

Licensing Act 1964

1969 c. 15.

4. Notwithstanding the repeal by this Act of section 24(2) of the Representation of the People Act 1969, the amendments by that section 24(2) of the Licensing Act 1964 continue to have the same effect as they had immediately before the coming into force of this Act.

1973 c. 36.

Northern Ireland Constitution Act 1973

5. So far as sections 8(4) and 26 of this Act reproduce any provision derived from the exercise of the power under section 38 of the Northern Ireland Constitution Act 1973 to make an Order in Council that provision has effect as if it were contained in an Order in Council so made.

Variation of limits of candidates' election expenses

S.I. 1981/191.

S.I. 1982/363.

6. Notwithstanding the revocation by this Act of the Representation of the People (Variation of Limits of Candidates' Election Expenses) Order 1981 and the Representation of the People (Variation of Limits of Candidates' Election Expenses) Order 1982, on the commencement of this Act the coming into operation of those orders shall for the purposes of sections 76(3) and 197(3) of this Act be taken (as the case may be) as the last occasion on which the maximum amount of the candidates' expenses was varied by order.

1972 c. 70.

Section 254 of the Local Government Act 1972

7. Any power exercisable under section 254 of the Local Government Act 1972 (consequential and supplementary provision) in relation to a provision of that Act repealed and re-enacted by this Act is exercisable in relation to that provision as so re-enacted to the extent that it would have been exercisable immediately before such repeal.

1982 c. 48.

Criminal Justice Act 1982

8. In the Table below—

(*a*) the first column sets out certain provisions of this Act which specify a fine on summary conviction,

SCH. 7

(*b*) the second column sets out in relation to each corresponding provision in the first column the maximum amount of that fine, and (notwithstanding anything in that provision to the contrary) that maximum amount shall continue to have effect as to any such fine until replaced as mentioned in paragraph (*c*) below,

(*c*) the third column sets out in relation to each corresponding provision in the first column the level on the standard scale which shall replace that maximum amount in relation to any such fine by virtue of an order made under section 80 (commencement) of the Criminal Justice Act 1982 bringing the relevant provisions of that Act into force, 1982 c. 48.

but nothing in paragraphs (*b*) and (*c*) above affects the punishment for an offence committed before the replacement mentioned in those paragraphs.

This paragraph does not apply in Northern Ireland.

TABLE

Provision of this Act	Maximum amount of fine	Level on standard scale
Section 62(1)	£500	4
Section 63(1)	£100	3
Section 64(1)	£100	3
Section 65(4)	£50	2
Section 97(3)	£25	1
Section 99(2)	£200	4
Section 100(2)	£100	3
Section 110(3)	£100	3
Section 169	£100	3
Section 175(1)	£100	3
Section 190	£50	2
Schedule 2, paragraph 13(1) ...	£100	3
Schedule 4, paragraph 2 ...	£50	3

Mental Health (Amendment) Act 1982

1982 c. 51.

9. Notwithstanding the repeal by this Act of section 4(3) of the Representation of the People Act 1949, that subsection shall continue to have effect instead of section 7 of this Act until the coming into force (on 1st April 1983) of section 62 of and Schedule 2 (electoral registration and voting in case of voluntary mental patients) to the Mental Health (Amendment) Act 1982; and the following provisions of this Act shall not have effect until that coming into force— 1949 c. 68.

(*a*) sections 5(3) and 7;

(*b*) section 19(1) and (4), 32(1), 33(2) and 62(1) to the extent that they provide for or refer to a patient's declaration under section 7;

(*c*) paragraph 27 of Schedule 8; and

(*d*) Part II of Schedule 9 to the extent that it repeals certain provisions of the Mental Health (Amendment) Act 1982.

SCH. 7

PART II

INTERPRETATION OF OTHER ACTS

Register, electors, etc.

10.—(1) A reference in any Act (whenever passed) to—

(*a*) the register of parliamentary and local government electors, or

(*b*) the register of parliamentary electors, or

(*c*) the register of local government electors, or

(*d*) the electors lists for such a register,

shall be taken as a reference to—

(i) the register kept under this Act, or

(ii) that register so far as it relates to parliamentary electors, or

(iii) that register so far as it relates to local government electors, or

(iv) the electors lists for such a register,

as the case may be, and references in any Act to a parliamentary or local government elector shall be construed accordingly.

(2) In relation to a person shown in a register or electors list as attaining voting age on a specified date the references in sub-paragraph (1) above do not apply except for the purposes of an election at which the day fixed for the poll falls on or after that date.

Registration and returning officers

11. A reference in any Act (whenever passed) to—

(*a*) the registration officer for the registration of parliamentary or local government electors, or

(*b*) the returning officer for a parliamentary election or constituency,

shall be taken respectively as a reference to the registration officer or returning officer appointed under this Act.

Registration expenses

12. A reference in any Act (whenever passed) to registration expenses in connection with the registration of parliamentary or local government electors shall be taken as a reference to registration expenses under this Act.

Supplemental

13.—(1) Subject to this paragraph, the provisions of paragraphs 10 to 12 of this Schedule apply to a reference—

(*a*) to any of the matters mentioned in those provisions, whatever the terms used in that reference; and

(*b*) to any other matter which was to be construed as a reference to any of those matters by virtue of an enactment repealed by the Representation of the People Act 1948. 1948 c. 65.

(2) Those provisions so far as they relate to this Act or any other Act passed after that Act of 1948 do not apply where the context otherwise requires. Sch. 7

(3) Those provisions so far as they relate to Acts passed before that Act of 1948 may be excluded in whole or in part by an order of the Secretary of State in any particular case where they appear to him to be inappropriate.

(4) That order may make such change in the law which this Act reproduces from the Representation of the People Act 1949 as might 1949 c. 68.
have been made before its commencement under paragraph 8(1)(*c*) of Part I of Schedule 10 to that Act of 1948.

(5) The provisions of paragraphs 10 to 12 may be supplemented by an order made by the Secretary of State in relation to an Act passed previous to the Representation of the People Act 1948— 1948 c. 65.

(*a*) where, in any particular case, such an order appears to him necessary for harmonising the previous Act with the provisions of this Act; and

(*b*) to the extent that the provisions of this Act re-enact such provisions of the Representation of the People Act 1949 as re-enacted provisions of that Act of 1948.

(6) A power conferred by this paragraph to make an order shall be exercisable by statutory instrument, and any such instrument shall be subject to annulment by resolution of either House of Parliament.

(7) Nothing in paragraphs 10 to 12 shall be taken to prejudice the operation in relation to this Act of any provision of the Inter- 1978 c. 30.
pretation Act 1978 as to repeals.

SCHEDULE 8

Section 206.

Consequential Amendments

Acts

Public Meeting Act 1908

1908, 8 Edw. 7 c. 66.

1. After subsection (3) of section 1 of the Public Meeting Act 1908 insert the following subsection—

"(4) This section does not apply as respects meetings to which section 97 of the Representation of the People Act 1983 applies."

City of London (Various Powers) Act 1957

2. In section 4 of the City of London (Various Powers) Act 1957— 1957, 5 & 6 Eliz. 2 c. x.

(*a*) in subsection (1) for "'Act of 1949'" substitute "'Act of 1983'", and for "Representation of the People Act 1949" substitute "Representation of the People Act 1983";

(*b*) in subsection (1), for "set out in the Second Schedule to the Act of 1949" substitute made by the Secretary of State under section 36 of the Act of 1983";

(*c*) in subsection (2), for "Act of 1949" substitute "Representation of the People Act 1949".

SCH. 8

1957, 5 & 6 Eliz. 2 c. x.

3. In section 8 of the City of London (Various Powers) Act 1957—

(*a*) in subsection (1)—

(i) for " Act of 1949 " substitute " Act of 1983 " and for " section 167 " substitute " sections 191 to 196 ";

(ii) for the words after " apply to and in respect of ward elections " to the end substitute the words—

" section 3 (disfranchisement of offenders in prison, etc.);

section 6 (residence: merchant seamen);

sections 14(1) and 15 to 17 (service qualifications and declarations for registration);

section 32 (voting at local government elections);

section 33 (absent voters at local government elections);

section 34 (proxies at local government elections);

section 46 (further provision as to local election voting);

section 59 (supplemental provisions as to members of forces and service voters)."

(*b*) in subsection (2)—

(i) for " section 23 of the 1949 Act " substitute " section 32 of the 1983 Act ";

(ii) for " ' at the polling station allotted to them under the local election rules ' " substitute " ' at the polling station allotted to them by the rules under section 36 or section 42 below ' ".

(*c*) in subsection (3), for " section 25 of the Act of 1949 " substitute " section 34 of the Act of 1983 ";

S.I. 1973/79.

(*d*) in subsection (4), for " Act of 1949 " substitute " Act of 1983 " and for " rule 21 of the local elections rules " substitute " rule 20 of the Local Elections (Principal Areas) Rules 1973 ";

(*e*) in subsection (5), for " Act of 1949 " substitute " Act of 1983 ".

4. In section 9(4) of the City of London (Various Powers) Act 1957 for " Act of 1949 " substitute " Act of 1983 ".

8 & 9 Eliz. 2 c. xxxvi.

City of London (Various Powers) Act 1960

5. In section 39 of the City of London (Various Powers) Act 1960—

1949 c. 68.

(*a*) in paragraph (*b*) of subsection (1), for " Representation of the People Act 1949 " substitute " Representation of the People Act 1983 ";

(*b*) in subsection (2), for " Act of 1949 " substitute " Act of 1983 "

1963 c. 33.

London Government Act 1963

6. In Schedule 3 to the London Government Act 1963—

(*a*) in paragraph 22 of Part II, for " Representation of the People Act 1949 " substitute " Representation of the People Act 1983 ";

(*b*) in paragraph 23 of Part II, for " said Acts of 1949 " substitute " Representation of the People Act 1983 ". SCH. 8

Licensing Act 1964 1964 c. 26.

7. In section 12(2) of the Licensing Act 1964 for " section 146(6) of the Representation of the People Act 1949 " substitute " section 168(7) of the Representation of the People Act 1983 ". 1949 c. 68.

8. In section 67(5) of the Licensing Act 1964, for " Representation of the People Act 1949 " substitute " Representation of the People Act 1983 ", and—

(*a*) in paragraph (*a*) of that subsection, for " section 47, section 48 " substitute " section 60, section 61 ", and for " section 52 " substitute " section 65 ";

(*b*) in paragraph (*b*) of that subsection, for " section 53 " substitute " section 66 ";

(*c*) in paragraph (*c*) of that subsection, for " sections 99 to 101 " substitute " sections 113 to 115 ";

(*d*) in paragraph (*d*) of that subsection, for " sections 146 to 148 and 151 " substitute " sections 168 to 170 and 173 ";

(*e*) in paragraph (i) of that subsection, for " section 53 " substitute " section 66 "; and

(*f*) in paragraph (ii) of that subsection, for " section 99 " substitute " section 113 ".

9. In section 67(6) of the Licensing Act 1964—

(*a*) for " sections 147 and 151 of the Representation of the People Act 1949 " substitute " sections 169 and 173 of the Representation of the People Act 1983 "; and

(*b*) for " section 151 " substitute " section 173 ".

10. In Schedule 8 to the Licensing Act 1964—

(*a*) in paragraph 1, for " section 42 of the Local Government Act 1972 " substitute " section 36 of the Representation of the People Act 1983 "; 1972 c. 70.

(*b*) in paragraph 5—

(i) for " section 42 of the Representation of the People Act 1949 " substitute " section 53 of the Representation of the People Act 1983 ";

(ii) for " section 53(4) of the Representation of the People Act 1949 " substitute " section 66(4) of the Representation of the People Act 1983 ".

Post Office Act 1969 1969 c. 48.

11. In section 72(1) of the Post Office Act 1969 for " Representation of the People Act 1949 " substitute " Representation of the People Act 1983 ".

Local Government Act 1972

12. In the following provisions of the Local Government Act 1972 for " Representation of the People Act 1949 " substitute " Representation of the People Act 1983 "—sections 6(1), 9(5), 11(3)(*b*), 16(2),

SCH. 8 25(1), 28(2), 29(3)(*b*), 35(1), 80(1)(*e*), 86(*b*) and Schedule 2, paragraph 6(1).

1972 c. 70. 13. In section 89(6) of the Local Government Act 1972 for " section 42 above " substitute " section 36 of the Representation of the People Act 1983 ".

14. In paragraphs 18(5) and 34(5) of Schedule 12 to the Local Government Act 1972 for " section 42 above and of the enactments

1949 c. 68. mentioned in section 165(1) of the Representation of the People Act 1949 " substitute " section 36 of the Representation of the People Act 1983 and of the enactments mentioned in section 187(1) of that Act ".

1973 c. 65.

Local Government (Scotland) Act 1973

15. In the Local Government (Scotland) Act 1973—

(*a*) in section 4(1), for " Act of 1949 " substitute " Representation of the People Act 1983 " ;

(*b*) in paragraph (d) of section 31(1), for " Representation of the People Act 1949 " substitute " Representation of the People Act 1983 ".

16. In paragraph (*b*) of section 64(5) of the Local Government (Scotland) Act 1973, for " section 6(3) of the Representation of the People Act 1949 " substitute " section 8(3) of the Representation of the People Act 1983 ".

1974 c. 23.

Juries Act 1974

17. In section 3(1) of the Juries Act 1974, for " Representation of the People Act 1949 " substitute " Representation of the People Act 1983 ".

1975 c. 24.

House of Commons Disqualification Act 1975

18. In section 6(3) of the House of Commons Disqualification Act 1975, for " section 124(5) of the Representation of the People Act 1949 " substitute " section 144(7) of the Representation of the People Act 1983 ".

19. For section 10 of the House of Commons Disqualification Act 1975 substitute—

" Saving as to disqualification of priests in holy orders etc.

10. Nothing in this Act shall be construed as affecting the enactments relating to the disqualification for membership of the House of Commons of priests in holy orders or ministers of any religious denomination."

20. In Part III of Schedule 1 to the House of Commons Disqualification Act 1975—

(*a*) for the reference to " Registration Officer appointed under Part III of the Local Government Act 1972 " substitute " Registration Officer appointed under section 8(2) of the Representation of the People Act 1983 " ;

(*b*) for the reference to "Returning Officer under section 17(2) of the Representation of the People Act 1949 and any Deputy Returning Officer appointed by him" substitute "Returning Officer under section 25(1) of the Representation of the People Act 1983 and any Deputy Returning Officer appointed by him." SCH. 8 1949 c. 68.

European Assembly Elections Act 1978 1978 c. 10.

21. In section 4(2) of the European Assembly Elections Act 1978—

(*a*) for "Representation of the People Act 1949" substitute "Representation of the People Act 1983";

(*b*) for "section 48(2)" substitute "section 61(2)";

(*c*) for "section 48(7)" substitute "section 61(7)"; and

(*d*) for "section 155" substitute "section 178".

22. In paragraph (*b*) of section 7(2) of the European Assembly Elections Act 1978 for "section 43(2) of the Representation of the People Act 1949" substitute "section 54(2) of the Representation of the People Act 1983".

23. In paragraph 4(2) of Schedule 1 to the European Assembly Elections Act 1978, for "section 6 of the Local Government (Scotland) Act 1973" substitute "section 41 of the Representation of the People Act 1983". 1973 c. 65.

Judicature (Northern Ireland) Act 1978 1978 c. 23.

24. In paragraph (*h*) of section 35(2) of the Judicature (Northern Ireland) Act 1978, for "sections 107 to 136 of the Representation of the People Act 1949" substitute "sections 120 to 156 of the Representation of the People Act 1983".

25. In section 108(1) of the Judicature (Northern Ireland) Act 1978 for "section 110 of the Representation of the People Act 1949" substitute "section 123 of the Representation of the People Act 1983".

Supreme Court Act 1981 1981 c. 54.

26. In section 142(1) of the Supreme Court Act 1981, for "Representation of the People Act 1949" substitute "Representation of the People Act 1983".

Mental Health (Amendment) Act 1982 1982 c. 51.

27. In section 70(2) of the Mental Health (Amendment) Act 1982 for "Sections 62 and 64(2) above and Schedule 2 to this Act extend" substitute "Section 64(2) above extends".

ORDER

Legal Aid, Advice and Assistance (Northern Ireland) Order 1981 S.I. 1981/228 (N.I. 8).

28. In Schedule 1 to the Legal Aid, Advice and Assistance (Northern Ireland) Order 1981, in paragraph 5 of Part II, for "Representation of the People Act 1949" substitute "Representation of the People Act 1983".

Section 206.

SCHEDULE 9

Repeals and Revocations

Part I

Repeals of Obsolete Provisions

Chapter	Short title	Extent of repeal
7 & 8 Geo. 5. c. 64.	The Representation of the People Act 1918.	Sections 19 and 43.
12, 13 & 14 Geo. 6. c. 68.	The Representation of the People Act 1949.	In paragraph (*b*) of section 45(11), from the beginning to the words " appeals thereunder, and ". In section 111(2)— (*a*) paragraph (*a*); (*b*) in paragraph (*b*), the words " whose clerk is registration officer ". In section 116(2), the word " gaolers ". Section 132. In section 161(2), the words " a simple contract debt ". In section 163, in the definition of " public office ", the word " municipal " where it first occurs and the word "bailie". In section 168(2), the words " where the poll is taken by means of voting papers ". Section 170. In section 174(1), paragraphs (*b*) and (*c*). In Schedule 2— (*a*) in Part II, rule 4(3); (*b*) in Part IV, in rule 53(2), the words " double return and any ". In paragraph 1(1) of Schedule 8, the words " and local government electors registered under this Act " to the end.
1968 c. xxxvii.	The City of London (Various Powers) Act 1968.	In section 3— (*a*) in subsection (3), the entry relating to the Representation of the People Act 1949; (*b*) subsection (4). Section 4.

Sch. 9

Chapter	Short title	Extent of repeal
1969 c. 39.	The Age of Majority (Scotland) Act 1969.	In paragraph 2 of Schedule 2, the words " The Representation of the People Acts (and any regulations, rules or other instruments thereunder) and".
1969 c. 46.	The Family Law Reform Act 1969.	In paragraph 2 of Schedule 2, the words " The Representation of the People Acts (and any regulations, rules or other instruments thereunder) " and the words " and any statutory provision " to the end.
1973 c. xx.	The City of London (Various Powers) Act 1973.	Section 9.
1973 c. 65.	The Local Government (Scotland) Act 1973.	In section 11— (*a*) subsection (2); (*b*) in subsection (3), the words " Representation of the People Acts and other " and " and local government "; (*c*) subsection (4). In Schedule 2, paragraph 2(4), (5).
1979 c. 40.	The Representation of the People Act 1979.	The whole Act.

Part II

Consequential Repeals

Chapter	Short title	Extent of repeal
12, 13 & 14 Geo. 6 c. 68.	The Representation of the People Act 1949.	The whole Act, so far as unrepealed.
12, 13 & 14 Geo. 6 c. 86.	The Electoral Registers Act 1949.	The whole Act.
2 & 3 Eliz. 2 c. 8.	The Electoral Registers Act 1953.	The whole Act.
6 & 7 Eliz. 2 c. 55.	The Local Government Act 1958.	In Schedule 8, paragraph 31(2) to (4).
6 & 7 Eliz. 2 c. 64.	The Local Government and Miscellaneous Financial Provisions (Scotland) Act 1958.	In Part I of Schedule 4, paragraph 16(2).
1961 c. xxviii.	The City of London (Various Powers) Act 1961.	Section 44.
1963 c. 33.	The London Government Act 1963.	In Schedule 3— (*a*) in Part I, paragraph 16; (*b*) in Part III, paragraphs 27, 31 to 33 and 35.

SCH. 9

Chapter	Short title	Extent of repeal
1964 c. 31.	The Elections (Welsh Forms) Act 1964.	The whole Act.
1968 c. 64.	The Civil Evidence Act 1968.	In the Schedule, the entry relating to the Representation of the People Act 1949.
1969 c. 15.	The Representation of the People Act 1969.	The whole Act.
1969 c. 48.	The Post Office Act 1969.	In Part II of Schedule 4, paragraph 47.
1971 c. 23.	The Courts Act 1971.	In Part II of Schedule 8, paragraph 30.
1971 c. 36. (N.I.).	The Civil Evidence Act (Northern Ireland) 1971.	In the Schedule, the entry relating to the Representation of the People Act 1949.
1972 c. 70.	The Local Government Act 1972.	Part III. In section 243— (*a*) in subsection (2), the words " section 42 above or "; (*b*) in subsection (4), the words " section 44(1) or ". Schedule 6.
1973 c. 65.	The Local Government (Scotland) Act 1973.	Sections 6 to 10. In Schedule 3, paragraphs 2 to 18, and 20 to 23.
1974 c. 23.	The Juries Act 1974.	Section 3(3).
1975 c. 21.	The Criminal Procedure (Scotland) Act 1975.	In Schedule 7A, item 6.
1975 c. 24.	The House of Commons Disqualification Act 1975.	Section 10(1).
1976 c. 29.	The Representation of the People (Armed Forces) Act 1976.	The whole Act.
1976 c. 52.	The Armed Forces Act 1976.	In Schedule 9, paragraph 19.
1976 c. 63.	The Bail Act 1976.	In Schedule 2, paragraph 12.
1977 c. 9.	The Representation of the People Act 1977.	The whole Act.
1977 c. 14.	The Returning Officers (Scotland) Act 1977.	The whole Act.
1977 c. 45.	The Criminal Law Act 1977.	In Schedule 1, item 9. In Schedule 12, the entry relating to the Representation of the People Act 1949.
1978 c. 4.	The Local Government (Scotland) Act 1978.	In the Schedule, paragraph 2.
1978 c. 23.	The Judicature (Northern Ireland) Act 1978.	In Part II of Schedule 5, the entry relating to the Representation of the People Act 1949.
1978 c. 32.	The Representation of the People Act 1978.	The whole Act.
1979 c. 31.	The Prosecution of Offences Act 1979.	In Schedule 1, the entry relating to the Representation of the People Act 1949.

SCH. 9

Chapter	Short title	Extent of repeal
1980 c. 3.	The Representation of the People Act 1980.	The whole Act.
1981 c. 34.	The Representation of the People Act 1981.	Section 3 and the Schedule.
1982 c. 51.	The Mental Health (Amendment) Act 1982.	Section 62. Section 69(5). In section 70(2) the words— (*a*) " 62 and "; (*b*) " and Schedule 2 to this Act ". Schedule 2.

PART III

CONSEQUENTIAL REVOCATIONS

Year and number	Title	Extent of revocation
S.I. 1973/2095.	Local Government Reorganisation (Consequential Provisions) (Northern Ireland) Order 1973.	Article 2(4) to (6).
S.I. 1973/2163.	Northern Ireland (Modification of Enactments—No. 1) Order 1973.	In Schedule 5, paragraph 15.
S.I. 1974/595.	Local Authorities etc. (Miscellaneous Provision) (No. 2) Order 1974.	Article 3(7).
S.I. 1977/293.	Local Authorities etc. (Miscellaneous Provision) Order 1977.	Article 4(2).
S.I. 1981/191.	Representation of the People (Variation of Limits of Candidates' Election Expenses) Order 1981.	The whole Order.
S.I. 1982/363.	Representation of the People (Variation of Limits of Candidates' Election Expenses) Order 1982.	The whole Order.

Agricultural Marketing Act 1983

1983 CHAPTER 3

An Act to establish a body corporate to be known as Food from Britain to improve the marketing of food produced or processed in the United Kingdom and of other agricultural produce of the United Kingdom; to transfer to Food from Britain the functions of the Central Council for Agricultural and Horticultural Co-operation and to dissolve the Central Council; to enable certain other marketing organisations to make contributions to Food from Britain; and to repeal section 61(9) of the Agriculture Act 1967. [1st March 1983]

BE IT ENACTED by the Queen's most Excellent Majesty, by and with the advice and consent of the Lords Spiritual and Temporal, and Commons, in this present Parliament assembled, and by the authority of the same, as follows:—

Food from Britain.

1.—(1) There shall be established in accordance with the provisions of this Act a council to be known as Food from Britain.

(2) The council shall consist of no fewer than thirteen and no more than fifteen members appointed by the Ministers;

and in making any such appointment the Ministers shall have regard to the interests of the agriculture and horticulture industry (including agricultural and horticultural co-operatives) and food manufacturing and distributive industries in the United Kingdom.

(3) The Ministers shall appoint one member to be chairman and another to be deputy chairman of Food from Britain.

(4) Schedule 1 to this Act shall have effect with respect to Food from Britain.

1975 c. 24.
1975 c. 25.

(5) In Part II of Schedule 1 to the House of Commons Disqualification Act 1975 and Part II of Schedule 1 to the Northern Ireland Assembly Disqualification Act 1975 (bodies of which all members are disqualified under those Acts) there shall be inserted at the appropriate place in alphabetical order—

" Food from Britain ".

Functions of Food from Britain.

2.—(1) The functions of the Central Council for Agricultural and Horticultural Co-operation are hereby transferred to Food from Britain.

(2) Food from Britain shall have power to organise, develop, promote, encourage and co-ordinate the marketing in the United Kingdom and elsewhere of—

(*a*) agricultural and horticultural produce of the United Kingdom ;

(*b*) fish, other than sea fish, and fish products made in the United Kingdom ; and

(*c*) any other food produced or processed in the United Kingdom.

(3) Food from Britain shall put itself in a position to advise Ministers on matters connected with any of its functions.

Central Council for Agricultural and Horticultural Co-operation.

3.—(1) Immediately after the coming into force of section 2 above the Central Council for Agricultural and Horticultural Co-operation shall be dissolved.

(2) Schedule 2 to this Act shall have effect with respect to the dissolution of the Central Council and the transfer of functions under section 2(1) above.

Contributions by marketing organisations.

4.—(1) Without prejudice to section 6(2) below, any body to which this section applies may make contributions by way of grant or loan to Food from Britain of such amount as it thinks fit towards the expenses incurred or to be incurred by Food from Britain in connection with any of its functions other than the transferred functions

(2) This section applies to the following bodies, namely—

(*a*) any board established under a scheme made (whether before or after the coming into force of this section) under Part I of the Agricultural Marketing Act 1958 or the Agricultural Marketing Act (Northern Ireland) 1964 or the Agricultural Marketing (Northern Ireland) Order 1982; 1958 c. 47. 1964 c. 13 (N.I.). S.I. 1982/1080 (N.I. 12).

(*b*) the Eggs Authority established under Part I of the Agriculture Act 1970; 1970 c. 40.

(*c*) the Home-Grown Cereals Authority established under Part I of the Cereals Marketing Act 1965; 1965 c. 14.

(*d*) the Meat and Livestock Commission established under Part I of the Agriculture Act 1967; 1967 c. 22.

(*e*) the Livestock Marketing Commission for Northern Ireland established under the Livestock Marketing Commission Act (Northern Ireland) 1967; 1967 c. 21 (N.I.).

(*f*) the Apple and Pear Development Council established under the Apple and Pear Development Council Order 1966; and S.I. 1966/1579.

(*g*) the Scottish Seed Potato Development Council established under the Scottish Seed Potato Development Council Order 1981. S.I. 1981/1767 (S. 183).

(3) The functions of any body to which this section applies for the purposes of which any person or class of persons is or may be required to make contributions (whether by way of levy or otherwise) to the body shall include the function conferred on the body by subsection (1) above and the provisions of any enactment or other instrument relating to such contributions shall have effect accordingly.

Accounts and annual reports.

5.—(1) Food from Britain shall—

(*a*) keep proper accounting records in such form as the Ministers may, with the consent of the Treasury, determine; and

(*b*) prepare a statement of accounts in respect of each financial year.

(2) The statement of accounts shall give a true and fair view of the state of Food from Britain's affairs at the end of the financial year and of its income and expenditure in the financial year, and shall comply with any directions given by the Ministers with the consent of the Treasury as to the information to be contained in the statement or the manner in which it is to be presented or as to the methods and principles according to which the statement is to be prepared.

(3) The statement of accounts shall be audited by persons to be appointed in respect of each financial year by the Ministers, and the auditors shall be furnished by Food from Britain with copies of the statement of accounts for any financial year not later than 30th June following the end of that year.

(4) The auditors shall complete their audit and send the Ministers copies of the statement of accounts and of their report on the statement as soon as possible after the end of the financial year to which they relate and in any event not later than 30th September following the end of that year.

(5) No person shall be qualified to be appointed auditor under this section unless he is a member of one or more of the following bodies—

The Institute of Chartered Accountants in England and Wales;

The Institute of Chartered Accountants of Scotland;

The Association of Certified Accountants;

The Institute of Chartered Accountants in Ireland;

but a Scottish firm may be appointed under this section if each of the partners is qualified to be so appointed.

(6) As soon as possible after the end of any financial year and in any event not later than 30th September following the end of that year Food from Britain shall prepare and submit to the Ministers a report of what has been done in the discharge of its functions in that year.

(7) The Ministers shall lay before Parliament copies of the report for any financial year made under subsection (6) above together with copies of the statement of accounts and of the auditor's report for that year.

(8) The Ministers and the Comptroller and Auditor General shall be entitled to inspect all books, papers and other records of Food from Britain relating to or to matters dealt with in any statement of accounts required to be prepared pursuant to this section.

(9) The first financial year of Food from Britain shall be the period beginning with the coming into force of this section and ending with 31st March 1984; and any subsequent period of twelve months ending with 31st March shall be a financial year of Food from Britain.

Borrowing powers, etc. of Food from Britain.

6.—(1) Food from Britain may borrow money or make loans in accordance with this section but not otherwise.

(2) Food from Britain may borrow temporarily (by way of overdraft or otherwise and in any currency) such sums as it may

require for the purpose of financing any of its functions other than the transferred functions; but the aggregate amount outstanding by way of principal of any sums so borrowed shall not exceed £500,000.

(3) Food from Britain may borrow any such sums—

(*a*) from the Minister of Agriculture, Fisheries and Food or the Secretary of State for Scotland or the Secretary of State for Wales or the Secretary of State for Northern Ireland, or

(*b*) with the consent of the Ministers and the Treasury, from any other person.

(4) Food from Britain may with the consent of the Ministers make such grants or loans as it thinks fit in pursuance of any of its functions other than the transferred functions.

Grants, etc. by Ministers.

7.—(1) The Ministers may with the approval of the Treasury make grants to Food from Britain in respect of any expenses incurred or to be incurred in connection with any of its functions other than the transferred functions.

(2) The Minister may with the approval of the Treasury lend to Food from Britain any sums which it may borrow in accordance with section 6(2) above.

(3) There shall be paid out of money provided by Parliament any sums required for making payments under this section or under paragraph 5 of Schedule 1 to this Act.

(4) In this section " the Minister " means the Minister of Agriculture, Fisheries and Food, the Secretary of State for Scotland, the Secretary of State for Wales or the Secretary of State for Northern Ireland.

Interpretation.

8. In this Act—

" agriculture and horticulture " includes everything included in the expression " agriculture " as defined by section 109(3) of the Agriculture Act 1947 or, as the case may be, section 86(3) of the Agriculture (Scotland) Act 1948 and " agricultural and horticultural " shall be construed accordingly; 1947 c. 48. 1948 c. 45.

" animal " includes any bird or fish ;

" the Central Council " means the Central Council for Agricultural and Horticultural Co-operation ;

" fish " includes crustaceans and molluscs of any kind ;

" fish products " means any food made wholly or partly from fish processed otherwise than solely by filleting or gutting ;

"food" includes any food or drink produced or processed for human or animal consumption (including game of any kind) and any ingredient of such food or drink;

"the Ministers" means the Minister of Agriculture, Fisheries and Food, the Secretary of State for Scotland, the Secretary of State for Wales and the Secretary of State for Northern Ireland acting jointly;

"pension" includes a superannuation allowance or gratuity payable to or in respect of any person on retirement or death;

"processed" means having been subjected to any kind of process including packaging or bottling;

"sea fish" means any fish (excluding crustaceans and molluscs of any kind) found in the sea except any of the salmon species, trout and eels; and

"transferred functions" means functions transferred to Food from Britain by section 2(1) above.

Short title, repeals, commencement and extent.

9.—(1) This Act may be cited as the Agricultural Marketing Act 1983.

(2) Subject to paragraph 3 of Schedule 2 to this Act, the enactments mentioned in Schedule 3 to this Act (which include spent provisions) are hereby repealed to the extent specified in the third column of that Schedule.

(3) This Act shall come into force on such day as the Ministers may by order made by statutory instrument appoint and different days may be appointed for different purposes.

(4) This Act extends to Northern Ireland.

SCHEDULES

SCHEDULE 1

Section 1.

FOOD FROM BRITAIN

1. Food from Britain shall be a body corporate.

2.—(1) Subject to section 6 of this Act, it shall be within the capacity of Food from Britain as a statutory corporation to do such things and to enter into such transactions as are incidental or conducive to the performance of any of its functions.

(2) Without prejudice to the generality of sub-paragraph (1) above—

(*a*) where in the performance of any of its functions Food from Britain renders any services to any person it may make such charges in respect of those services as it may agree with that person ; and

(*b*) Food from Britain may accept contributions from other persons in respect of any expenses incurred or to be incurred in connection with any of its functions other than the transferred functions.

3. The validity of any proceedings of Food from Britain shall not be affected by any vacancy among the members or by any defect in the appointment or any disqualification of any of the members.

4.—(1) Subject to the following provisions of this paragraph, a member of Food from Britain and the chairman and deputy chairman shall hold and vacate office as such in accordance with the terms of his appointment, and previous tenure of any such office shall not affect eligibility for re-appointment.

(2) If the chairman or deputy chairman ceases to be a member of Food from Britain, he shall also cease to be chairman or deputy chairman.

(3) A member may at any time, by notice in writing addressed to the Ministers, or to any of them, resign his membership, and the chairman or deputy chairman may, by the like notice, resign his office as such.

(4) The Ministers may terminate a person's appointment as member of Food from Britain if they are satisfied—

(*a*) that he has been absent from meetings of Food from Britain without the consent of the other members for at least six consecutive months out of the nine months immediately preceding the termination of his appointment ; or

(*b*) that he is an undischarged bankrupt or has made an arrangement with his creditors or has become notour bankrupt or has executed a trust deed for behoof of, or has made a

SCH. 1

composition contract or arrangement with, his creditors; or

(*c*) that he is incapacitated by reason of physical or mental illness; or

(*d*) that he is otherwise unable or unfit to discharge the functions of a member of Food from Britain.

5. The Ministers shall—

(*a*) pay to the members of Food from Britain such travelling or other allowances as the Ministers, with the approval of the Treasury, may determine, and in the case of any member as respects whom the Ministers, with the approval of the Treasury, so determine, may pay such remuneration, whether by way of salary or fees, as the Ministers and the Treasury may determine in his case,

(*b*) in the case of any member of Food from Britain to whom the Ministers, with the approval of the Treasury, determine that this paragraph applies, pay such pension, or make such payments towards the provision of a pension, to or in respect of him as the Ministers and the Treasury may determine in his case,

and if a person ceases to be a member of Food from Britain and it appears to the Ministers that there are special circumstances which make it right that the person should receive compensation the Ministers may, with the approval of the Treasury, pay to that person a sum of such amount as the Ministers may with the approval of the Treasury determine.

6. For the purpose of assisting it in the performance of any of its functions, Food from Britain may appoint committees consisting of or including persons other than members of Food from Britain and may pay those persons such remuneration and such travelling and other allowances as it may with the approval of the Ministers and the Treasury determine.

7.—(1) A member of Food from Britain or any such committee shall, if he has any direct or indirect personal interest in a proposal made or proposed to be made to Food from Britain or the committee in connection with the making of any grant under the Agriculture Act 1967 or any grant or loan under this Act, disclose the nature of his interest at a meeting of Food from Britain or the committee as soon as possible after the relevant circumstances have come to his knowledge.

1967 c. 22.

(2) Any disclosure so made by a member shall be recorded in the minutes of Food from Britain or the committee and that member shall not take part after the disclosure in any decision of Food from Britain or the committee with respect to that proposal, but he may, nevertheless, be taken into account for the purpose of constituting a quorum of Food from Britain or the committee.

SCH. 1

8. In the case of an equality of votes at any meeting of Food from Britain the person who is chairman at that meeting shall have a second or casting vote.

9. Subject to paragraphs 7 and 8 above, the council may determine their own quorum and procedure, and the quorum and procedure of any committee appointed under paragraph 6 above.

10. The Ministers may designate persons to attend on their behalf any meetings of Food from Britain or any of its committees, and it shall be the duty of Food from Britain to afford any person so designated reasonable facilities for taking part in the deliberations of Food from Britain or the committee, and recording the decisions of Food from Britain or the committee; but a person so designated shall not be qualified to vote or otherwise count as a member of Food from Britain or the committee.

11.—(1) Food from Britain may appoint such officers and servants as it thinks fit.

(2) Food from Britain shall—

(*a*) pay to its officers and servants such remuneration and such travelling or other allowances as it may with the approval of the Ministers and the consent of the Treasury determine, and

(*b*) as to any officers or servants in whose case Food from Britain may determine to do so, pay to or in respect of them such pensions, or provide and maintain for them such pension schemes, as Food from Britain may with the approval of the Ministers and the consent of the Treasury determine;

and if a person ceases to be an officer or servant of Food from Britain and it appears to Food from Britain that there are special circumstances which make it right that that person should receive compensation Food from Britain may with the approval of the Ministers and the consent of the Treasury pay to that person a sum of such amount as it may with such approval determine.

12. The application of the seal of Food from Britain shall be authenticated by the signatures of two of its members and of the chief officer of Food from Britain or some other person authorised by Food from Britain to do so in his place.

SCHEDULE 2

Section 3.

TRANSFER OF FUNCTIONS AND DISSOLUTION OF THE CENTRAL COUNCIL FOR AGRICULTURAL AND HORTICULTURAL CO-OPERATION

1. The property, rights and liabilities of the Central Council are hereby transferred to Food from Britain.

2.—(1) Paragraph 1 above has effect to transfer to Food from Britain rights and obligations of the Central Council under contracts of employment with its officers and servants; and for the

SCH. 2 purpose of determining the length of service as an officer or servant of Food from Britain of any person who became such by virtue of paragraph 1 above any service by that person with the Central Council shall be treated as service with Food from Britain.

1967 c. 22. (2) Any determination made under paragraph 9(2)(*b*) of Schedule 6 to the Agriculture Act 1967 in respect of any person shall be treated after the appointed day (so far as may be necessary to preserve its effect) as having been made under paragraph 11(2)(*b*) of Schedule 1 to this Act, and any pension scheme maintained by the Central Council immediately before the appointed day shall be deemed to be a pension scheme provided by Food from Britain under paragraph 11(2)(*b*) of Schedule 1 to this Act and shall continue to be maintained accordingly.

3.—(1) The repeal of section 59 of the Agriculture Act 1967 shall not have effect in respect of any period ending on or before the appointed day which is or is part of a financial year of the Central Council if any function of the Central Council relating to that period has not been performed before that day; and any such function is accordingly transferred by virtue of paragraph 1 above to Food from Britain.

(2) The period beginning with the 1st April preceding the appointed day and ending with the day before the appointed day shall be the last financial year of the Central Council and section 59 shall have effect (by virtue of sub-paragraph (1) above) in relation to that period accordingly but with the substitution for the reference in subsection (3) to the 30th September of a reference to the last day of the period of six months beginning with the appointed day.

4. Any enactment or other instrument passed or made before the appointed day, except section 58(8) of the Agriculture Act 1967, shall have effect as if any reference to the Central Council were a reference to Food from Britain.

5. Anything done by or in relation to the Central Council and having effect immediately before the appointed day shall so far as is required for continuing its effect thereafter be treated as if it had been done by or in relation to Food from Britain, and anything then in the process of being done by or in relation to the Central Council (including in particular any legal proceedings then pending to which the Central Council is a party) may be continued by or in relation to Food from Britain.

6. In section 58(9) of the Agriculture Act 1967 there shall be added at the end the words " under this Part of this Act ".

7. In section 60(3) of that Act for the words " the last foregoing section " there shall be substituted the words " section 5(6) of the Agricultural Marketingt Ac 1983 ".

8. In this Schedule " the appointed day " means the day on which this Schedule comes into force.

SCHEDULE 3

Section 9.

Repeals

Chapter	Short title	Extent of repeal
1967 c. 22.	Agriculture Act 1967.	Section 58(1), (3) to (7), (8)(*a*) and (10). Section 59. Section 61(9). Schedule 6.
1975 c. 24.	House of Commons Disqualification Act 1975.	In Part II of Schedule I, the entry relating to the Central Council for Agricultural and Horticultural Co-operation.
1975 c. 25.	Northern Ireland Assembly Disqualification Act 1975.	In Part II of Schedule I, the entry relating to the Central Council for Agricultural and Horticultural Co-operation.

Pig Industry Levy Act 1983

1983 CHAPTER 4

An Act to authorise the Meat and Livestock Commission to impose a levy for the purpose of meeting costs incurred by the Minister of Agriculture, Fisheries and Food in consequence of exercising any of his powers under the Animal Health Act 1981 in relation to the disease of pigs known as Aujeszky's disease or in relation to pigs which are affected or suspected of being affected with, or have been exposed to the infection of, that disease and for the purpose of making certain additional compensation payments to the owners of such pigs in respect of losses incurred by them in consequence of action taken by the Minister in relation to those pigs under that Act; and to provide for the application of the proceeds of the levy for those and connected purposes and otherwise for the benefit of the pig industry or the pig products industry.

[1st March 1983]

BE IT ENACTED by the Queen's most Excellent Majesty, by and with the advice and consent of the Lords Spiritual and Temporal, and Commons, in this present Parliament assembled, and by the authority of the same, as follows:—

Levy on pig industry to meet costs of eradicating Aujeszky's disease.

1.—(1) The following provisions of this section apply if—

(*a*) the Ministers direct that section 32 of the 1981 Act (slaughter of animals affected by diseases other than those mentioned in section 31) shall apply to the disease of pigs known as Aujeszky's disease ; or

(*b*) that disease is one to which section 32 of that Act applies at the passing of this Act.

(2) Any costs incurred by the Minister (whether before or after the passing of this Act) in consequence of exercising any of his powers under the 1981 Act—

(*a*) in relation to Aujeszky's disease ; or

(*b*) in relation to pigs which are affected or suspected of being affected with, or have been exposed to the infection of, that disease ;

may be met from the proceeds of a levy imposed in accordance with the following provisions of this section.

(3) The Meat and Livestock Commission (referred to below in this Act as " the Commission ") may submit to the Ministers a scheme (referred to below in this Act as a pig industry levy scheme) for the imposition of charges for the purpose of—

(*a*) meeting any costs incurred by the Minister as mentioned in subsection (2) above ; and

(*b*) compensating the owners of any such pigs as are mentioned in that subsection in respect of losses incurred by them in consequence of action taken by the Minister in relation to those pigs under the 1981 Act ;

and for the recovery of such charges by the Commission in such manner and from such persons as may be specified in the scheme.

References below in this Act to the levy purposes are references to the purposes mentioned above in this subsection.

(4) Subsections (2) to (11) of section 13 of the 1967 Act (levy on industries to meet Commission's expenses) and section 14 of that Act (registration, returns and records for purposes of levy scheme under section 13) shall apply for the purposes of a pig industry levy scheme as they apply for the purposes of a levy scheme within the meaning of section 13, except that—

(*a*) references in those provisions to livestock and to livestock products shall be read as references respectively to pigs and to pig products ; and

(*b*) the reference in section 13(8) to that section shall be read as a reference to this section.

(5) Subject to the following provisions of this section and to section 2 of this Act, the proceeds of any levy imposed under a pig industry levy scheme (referred to below in this Act as the levy fund) shall be applied solely in making payments for the levy purposes.

(6) The Commission may make arrangements for payments to be made for the levy purposes by any other person and may for that purpose pay sums collected by them in pursuance of any such scheme to the person for the time being responsible in accordance with any such arrangements for making payments for the levy purposes.

(7) Without prejudice to the inclusion of any other provisions which appear to the Commission to be appropriate in any arrangements made by the Commission by virtue of subsection (6) above, any such arrangements—

(*a*) may provide for payments to be made for the levy purposes by the person so responsible otherwise than out of the levy fund at any time when the fund is insufficient to meet those payments; and

(*b*) may provide for any expenses incurred by the person so responsible in making payments for the levy purposes in accordance with the arrangements (whether out of the levy fund or otherwise) to be met from the levy fund;

and where before the passing of this Act the person so responsible has made payments for the levy purposes in accordance with arrangements made by the Minister, any arrangements made by the Commission by virtue of subsection (6) above may also provide for any expenses incurred by that person in doing so to be met from the levy fund.

(8) Any expenses incurred by the Commission—

(*a*) in collecting charges under any pig industry levy scheme;

(*b*) in making payments themselves for the levy purposes; or

(*c*) for the purpose of any arrangements made by virtue of subsection (6) above;

may be met from the levy fund.

Ministerial control of payments by Commission out of levy.

2.—(1) The Commission may not—

(*a*) make payments themselves for the levy purposes out of sums collected by them in pursuance of a pig industry levy scheme; or

(*b*) pay sums so collected to any person responsible in accordance with any arrangements made by the Commission by virtue of section 1(6) of this Act for making payments for the levy purposes;

except in accordance with directions given by the Minister under this section; and any such arrangements shall be subject to any such directions.

(2) Subject to subsection (3) below, the Minister may, by directions given to the Commission under this section—

(*a*) regulate the application of sums collected by the Commission in pursuance of any such scheme in either manner mentioned in subsection (1) above; and (*b*) require sums so collected which are for the time being surplus to requirements to be applied for such other purposes or dealt with in such other manner as may be specified in any such direction (after deduction of any expenses incurred by the Commission in complying with the direction).

(3) The other purposes or manner mentioned in subsection (2)(*b*) above must be purposes or (as the case may be) a manner appearing to the Minister to be connected with, or beneficial to persons engaged in, the pig industry or the pig products industry.

(4) Without prejudice to the generality of subsection (2)(*a*) above, any direction given by the Minister under this section with respect to the making by the Commission of payments out of sums collected by them in pursuance of any such scheme to any such person as is mentioned in subsection (1)(*b*) above may specify the terms on which any such payments by the Commission are to be made (including terms restricting in any manner specified in the direction the amounts of any payments to be made in pursuance of the arrangements in question for the purpose mentioned in section 1(3)(*b*) of this Act).

(5) Any direction given by the Minister under this section—

(*a*) may relate to payments of any description specified in the direction or to any particular payments so specified ; and

(*b*) may be varied or revoked by a subsequent direction under this section.

(6) It shall be the duty of the Commission to comply with any directions given by the Minister under this section.

(7) Sums collected by the Commission in pursuance of a pig industry levy scheme are surplus to requirements for the purposes of subsection (2)(*b*) above if they are not required for the levy purposes (having regard to any restriction on payments for the purpose mentioned in section 1(3)(*b*) of this Act required to be imposed by virtue of any direction given by the Minister under this section) or for meeting any expenses that may be met from the levy fund in accordance with section 1 of this Act.

(8) In subsection (3) above—

" the pig industry " means any part of the livestock industry (as defined by section 25 of the 1967 Act) that is concerned with pigs ; and

" the pig products industry " means any part of the livestock products industry (as so defined) that is concerned with pig products.

Sums transferred by Commission for payment for the levy purposes to be held on trust for Commission.

3.—(1) This section applies where in accordance with any arrangements made by the Commission by virtue of section 1(6) of this Act any sums collected by the Commission in pursuance of a pig industry levy scheme have been paid to the person for the time being responsible in accordance with those arrangements for making payments for the levy purposes.

(2) In this section " available levy receipts " means any sums so paid which have not been applied in making payments for the levy purposes or in meeting expenses of the person so responsible that may be met from the levy fund and any investments or other property for the time being representing any such sums.

(3) Without prejudice to their application in accordance with the arrangements in making payments for the levy purposes, any available levy receipts for the time being held by the person so responsible (less any expenses of that person that may be met from the levy fund) shall be treated as held by that person on trust for the Commission.

Supplementary provisions.

4.—(1) The duty of the Commission—

(*a*) under section 1A of the 1967 Act (duty to consult representative organisations) ; and

(*b*) under section 2 of that Act (duty to consult Consumers Committee) ;

shall not apply in relation to any matter arising or likely to arise out of the exercise of the Commission's functions under this Act.

(2) Section 15(1)(*b*) of that Act (contributions by the Ministers to initial expenditure of the Commission in performing certain functions) shall not apply in relation to any expenditure incurred by the Commission in performing their functions under this Act.

(3) The reference in section 19(1) of that Act (Commission's annual report) to the Commission's functions under that Act shall be read as including a reference to their functions under this Act.

(4) Section 24 of that Act (disclosure of information) shall apply in relation to returns or other information furnished or obtained by any person in pursuance of a requirement made under a pig industry levy scheme as it applies in relation to returns or other information furnished or obtained by any person in pursuance of a requirement made under a levy scheme within the meaning of section 13 of that Act.

Short title, interpretation and extent.

5.—(1) This Act may be cited as the Pig Industry Levy Act 1983.

(2) In this Act—

" the Commission " has the meaning given by section 1(3) of this Act;

" the levy fund " has the meaning given by section 1(5) of this Act;

" the levy purposes " has the meaning given by section 1(3) of this Act;

" the Minister " and " the Ministers " have the meanings given by section 86(1) of the 1981 Act;

" pig industry levy scheme " has the meaning given by section 1(3) of this Act;

" pig product " means any livestock product (as defined by section 25 of the 1967 Act) derived from pigs;

" the 1967 Act " means the Agriculture Act 1967; and 1967 c. 22.

" the 1981 Act " means the Animal Health Act 1981. 1981 c. 22.

(3) References in this Act to sums collected by the Commission in pursuance of a pig industry levy scheme include references to any investments or other property for the time being representing any sums so collected (and references to the payment of or to payments out of such sums shall be construed accordingly).

(4) Subject to subsection (5) below, this Act does not extend to Northern Ireland.

(5) Section 4(4) of this Act extends to Northern Ireland in so far as it applies in relation to returns or information furnished or obtained in pursuance of a pig industry levy scheme any provision of section 24 of the 1967 Act that extends to Northern Ireland.

Consolidated Fund (No. 2) Act 1983

1983 CHAPTER 5

An Act to apply certain sums out of the Consolidated Fund to the service of the years ending on 31st March 1982 and 1983. [28th March 1983]

Most Gracious Sovereign,

WE, Your Majesty's most dutiful and loyal subjects, the Commons of the United Kingdom in Parliament assembled, towards making good the supply which we have cheerfully granted to Your Majesty in this Session of Parliament, have resolved to grant unto Your Majesty the sums hereinafter mentioned; and do therefore most humbly beseech Your Majesty that it may be enacted, and be it enacted by the Queen's most Excellent Majesty, by and with the advice and consent of the Lords Spiritual and Temporal, and Commons, in this present Parliament assembled, and by the authority of the same, as follows:—

Issue out of the Consolidated Fund for the year ending 31st March 1982.

1. The Treasury may issue out of the Consolidated Fund of the United Kingdom and apply towards making good the supply granted to Her Majesty for the service of the year ending on 31st March 1982 the sum of £68,277,715·78.

Issue out of the Consolidated Fund for the year ending 31st March 1983.

2. The Treasury may issue out of the Consolidated Fund of the United Kingdom and apply towards making good the supply granted to Her Majesty for the service of the year ending on 31st March 1983 the sum of £1,586,910,000.

Short title.

3. This Act may be cited as the Consolidated Fund (No. 2) Act 1983.

British Nationality (Falkland Islands) Act 1983

1983 CHAPTER 6

An Act to provide for the acquisition of British citizenship by persons having connections with the Falkland Islands. [28th March 1983]

BE IT ENACTED by the Queen's most Excellent Majesty, by and with the advice and consent of the Lords Spiritual and Temporal, and Commons, in this present Parliament assembled, and by the authority of the same, as follows:—

Acquisition of British citizenship at commencement of 1981 Act or by birth or adoption.

1.—(1) A person shall at commencement become a British citizen if—

(*a*) that person becomes a British Dependent Territories citizen at commencement under section 23 of the 1981 Act (persons becoming British Dependent Territories citizens at commencement) ; and

(*b*) immediately before commencement either—

(i) that person was a citizen of the United Kingdom and Colonies who had that citizenship by his birth, naturalisation or registration in the Falkland Islands ; or

(ii) one of that person's parents, or a parent of one of that person's parents, was, or but for his death would have been, a citizen of the United Kingdom and Colonies who so had that citizenship ; or

(iii) that person, being a woman, was, or had at any time been, the wife of a man who by virtue of sub-paragraph (i) or (ii) becomes a British citizen at commencement or would have done so but for his death.

(2) A person born in the Falkland Islands after commencement shall be a British citizen if at the time of the birth his father or mother is—

(*a*) a British citizen ; or

(*b*) settled in the Falkland Islands.

(3) A new-born infant who, after commencement, is found abandoned in the Falkland Islands shall, unless the contrary is shown, be deemed for the purposes of subsection (2)—

(*a*) to have been born in the Falkland Islands after commencement ; and

(*b*) to have been born to a parent who at the time of the birth was a British citizen or settled in the Falkland Islands.

(4) Where after commencement an order authorising the adoption of a minor who is not a British citizen is made by a court in the Falkland Islands, he shall be a British citizen as from the date on which the order is made if the adopter or, in the case of a joint adoption, one of the adopters is a British citizen on that date.

(5) Where an order in consequence of which any person became a British citizen by virtue of subsection (4) ceases to have effect, whether on annulment or otherwise, the cesser shall not affect the status of that person as a British citizen.

Acquisition of British citizenship by registration.

2.—(1) If—

(*a*) an application is made for the registration as a British citizen of a person who is a British Dependent Territories citizen by virtue of section 23 of the 1981 Act (persons becoming British Dependent Territories citizens at commencement) ; and

(*b*) that person or a parent of that person was settled in the Falkland Islands either immediately before commencement or, in the case of a parent of that person who died before commencement, immediately before that parent's death,

the Secretary of State may, if he thinks fit, cause the person to whom the application relates to be registered as a British citizen.

(2) If—

(*a*) an application is made for the registration as a British citizen of a person who is a British Dependent Territories citizen by virtue of registration or naturalisation under the 1981 Act ; and

(*b*) either—

(i) that registration or naturalisation was effected in the Falkland Islands in pursuance of arrangements made under section 43 of the 1981 Act (exercise of functions of Secretary of State by Governors and others) ; or

(ii) the Secretary of State is satisfied that the naturalisation or registration was effected wholly or partly by reason of a connection which that person or some other person had with the Falkland Islands,

the Secretary of State may, if he thinks fit, cause the person to whom the application relates to be registered as a British citizen.

Cases in which this Act produces British citizens " by descent ".

3.—(1) A person who is a British citizen by virtue of the application to him of any provision of this Act but not otherwise shall, for the purposes of the 1981 Act, be a British citizen " by descent " if, and only if, being a person who became a British citizen at commencement, he would not be a British citizen by virtue of this Act but for section 1(1)(*b*)(ii) or (iii).

(2) A person who is a British citizen by virtue of the application to him of any of the provisions of the 1981 Act as well as being a British citizen by virtue of the application to him of any provision of this Act shall, for the purposes of that Act, be a British citizen " by descent " if, and only if, being a person who became a British citizen at commencement, he—

(*a*) would have been a British citizen by descent if this Act had not been passed ; and

(*b*) would not be a British citizen by virtue of this Act but for section 1(1)(*b*)(ii) or (iii).

Supplementary provisions.

4.—(1) In this Act—

" the 1981 Act " means the British Nationality Act 1981 ; 1981 c. 61.

" commencement " has the same meaning as in the 1981 Act, that is to say the beginning of 1st January 1983 (that being the day appointed under section 53(2) of that Act for the commencement of all except sections 49 and 53 of that Act) ;

" the Falkland Islands " means the Colony of the Falkland Islands.

(2) The following provisions of the 1981 Act shall apply for the purposes of this Act as they apply for the purposes of that Act, namely—

(*a*) section 41 (regulations and Orders in Council), so far as it relates to the making of regulations;

(*b*) section 42 (registration and naturalisation: general provisions), so far as it relates to registration;

(*c*) section 44 (decisions involving exercise of discretion);

(*d*) section 45 (evidence);

(*e*) section 46 (offences and proceedings);

(*f*) sections 47 and 48 (legitimated and posthumous children); and

(*g*) section 50 (interpretation).

(3) In the following provisions of the 1981 Act, namely—

(*a*) section 37(1)(*a*) (by virtue of which a person who is a British citizen under that Act has the status of a Commonwealth citizen);

(*b*) section 40(2)(*a*)(i) (deprivation of British citizenship of a person registered as a British citizen under that Act); and

(*c*) section 51(3)(*a*)(ii) (meaning of " citizen of United Kingdom and Colonies " in certain contexts),

for the words " this Act " there shall be substituted the words " the British Nationality Acts 1981 and 1983 ".

Citation, provision for retrospective effect, and extent.

1981 c. 61.

5.—(1) This Act may be cited as the British Nationality (Falkland Islands) Act 1983; and this Act and the British Nationality Act 1981 may be cited together as the British Nationality Acts 1981 and 1983.

(2) This Act shall be deemed to have come into force on 1st January 1983 (that is to say at commencement as defined in section 4(1)); and accordingly, subject to subsection (3), where the requirements of any provision of section 1 for the acquisition of British citizenship were satisfied in relation to any person at commencement or at any time between commencement and the passing of this Act, that person shall be treated as having acquired that citizenship at that time.

(3) Nothing in section 1 shall confer British citizenship—

(*a*) on a person in respect of whom a declaration of renunciation of British Dependent Territories citizenship was registered under the 1981 Act at any time before the passing of this Act; or

(*b*) on a person who at any time before the passing of this Act was deprived under the 1981 Act of his British Dependent Territories citizenship.

(4) This Act extends to Northern Ireland.

(5) This Act extends to the Channel Islands and the Isle of Man and to all dependent territories; and it is hereby declared for the purposes of section 3(3) of the West Indies Act 1967 that this Act extends to all associated states. 1967 c. 4.

Conwy Tunnel (Supplementary Powers) Act 1983

1983 CHAPTER 7

An Act to authorise the Secretary of State to acquire certain land and construct and carry out certain works, and to confer on him certain other powers, for or in connection with the construction, maintenance and improvement of a tunnel which he is authorised under the Highways Act 1980 to construct across the Conwy Estuary as part of a special road; and for connected purposes. [28th March 1983]

BE IT ENACTED by the Queen's most Excellent Majesty, by and with the advice and consent of the Lords Spiritual and Temporal, and Commons, in this present Parliament assembled, and by the authority of the same, as follows:—

Preliminary

Purpose of Act.

1980 c. 66.

S.I. 1982 No. 553.

1.—(1) The powers conferred on the Secretary of State by this Act are by way of supplement to those already available to the Secretary of State under the Highways Act 1980 (referred to below in this Act as the 1980 Act) for or in connection with the construction, maintenance and improvement of the tunnel which he is authorised to construct across the Conwy Estuary by the Glan Conwy to Conwy Morfa Special Road and Connecting Roads Scheme 1982.

(2) In this Act—

" the Estuary " means the Conwy Estuary;

" the principal construction works " means—

(*a*) the construction of the tunnel (including works for constructing the tunnel units under section 4 of this Act and works for providing access to the tunnel on either side of the Estuary);

(*b*) the construction of fabrication facilities for constructing those units under that section;

(*c*) the diversion of the waters of the Estuary from any land in accordance with the Scheme; and

(*d*) the construction of the jetty mentioned in section 5 of this Act;

"the Scheme" means the Scheme mentioned in subsection (1) above; and

"the tunnel" means the tunnel that the Secretary of State is authorised by the Scheme to construct (which is a tunnel of the immersed tube type).

(3) References in this Act to the principal works are references to the principal construction works or any of them and any works for the maintenance, improvement or repair of, or other dealing with, the tunnel that are or may be authorised under the 1980 Act (whether by virtue of any provision of Part IV or V of that Act or by virtue of any order made under section 18(1)(*f*) of that Act).

(4) Nothing in this Act shall be read as prejudicing the powers of the Secretary of State under the 1980 Act to acquire land or construct or carry out works for or in connection with the construction, maintenance or improvement of the tunnel.

Land and works

Power to acquire specified land compulsorily.

2.—(1) The Secretary of State is authorised by this section to acquire compulsorily so much of the land shown on the deposited plan within the limits of land to be acquired as may be required for or in connection with the principal works.

1965 c. 56. (2) Part I of the Compulsory Purchase Act 1965 (except sections 4 and 27 and paragraph 3(3) of Schedule 3) shall apply to the acquisition of land under this section as it applies to a
1981 c. 67. compulsory purchase to which Schedule 1 to the Acquisition of Land Act 1981 applies.

(3) A notice to treat under that Part for the purpose of acquiring any land under this section shall not be served after 31st December 1986 or such later date as may for the time being be authorised by an order made by the Secretary of State; and an order under this subsection shall be subject to special parliamentary procedure.

1845 c. 18. (4) The Lands Clauses Consolidation Act 1845 shall not apply to the acquisition of land under this section.

(5) Schedule 1 to this Act (which contains supplementary provisions relating to the acquisition of land for or in connection with the principal works) shall have effect.

Further power to acquire land.

3.—(1) The Secretary of State may acquire compulsorily land required for or in connection with the principal works, not being land which may be acquired under section 2 of this Act.

(2) A compulsory purchase order made in pursuance of this section may provide for the acquisition of rights over land by creating them as well as for the acquisition of rights already in existence.

(3) References in this section and Schedule 1 to this Act to rights over land include references to the right to do, or to place and maintain, anything in, on or under land or in the airspace above its surface.

(4) For the purpose of the acquisition by the Secretary of State of land required for or in connection with the principal works by agreement, Part I of the Compulsory Purchase Act 1965 (so far as applicable and excluding sections 4 to 8, 10, 27 and 31) shall apply; and in that Part, as so applied, " land " has the same meaning as in this Act. 1965 c. 56.

(5) The Acquisition of Land Act 1981 shall apply to the compulsory acquisition of land under this section, and Schedule 3 to that Act shall apply to the compulsory acquisition of a right by virtue of subsection (2) above. 1981 c. 67.

Construction of tunnel units.

4.—(1) The Secretary of State may construct the tunnel units on land acquired under section 2 of this Act or other Crown land shown on the deposited plan within the limits of land to be acquired.

(2) This section is not to be taken as prejudicing the Secretary of State's power to use, in constructing the tunnel, tunnel units constructed by himself or another on land other than land mentioned in subsection (1) above.

Construction of jetty.

5.—(1) The Secretary of State may construct a jetty in the situation and in accordance with the levels shown on the deposited plan and the deposited section.

(2) In constructing the jetty, the Secretary of State may deviate laterally from the situation shown on the deposited plan to the extent of the limits of deviation so shown, and may deviate vertically from the levels shown on the deposited section to the extent of two metres upwards and to any extent downwards.

Subsidiary works and supplementary powers.

6.—(1) Schedule 2 to this Act has effect for authorising certain works to be constructed or carried out in connection with the principal works, and for conferring on the Secretary of State certain other supplementary powers for or in connection with the construction, maintenance or improvement of the tunnel.

(2) References below in this Act to the tunnel works are references to the principal construction works and any works or other action authorised by Schedule 2 to this Act which is undertaken for or in connection with the principal construction works.

(3) References below in this Act to tunnel maintenance works are references to any such works for the maintenance, improvement or repair of, or other dealing with, the tunnel as are mentioned in section 1(3) of this Act and any works or other action authorised by Schedule 2 to this Act which is undertaken for or in connection with any such works.

(4) Without prejudice to the application apart from this subsection of section 6 of the 1980 Act (delegation, etc., of functions with respect to maintenance, etc., of trunk roads) to the powers of the Secretary of State under this Act, that section shall apply to any power under Schedule 2 to this Act exercisable for the purpose of any tunnel maintenance works.

Control of navigation, etc.

Special control during and after the construction period.

7.—(1) If at any time during the construction period it appears to the Secretary of State to be necessary or convenient for the purpose of any of the tunnel works he may give a direction under this section in respect of the harbour area or any part of it.

(2) A direction under this section must specify the area to which it relates.

(3) Without prejudice to the giving of a further direction under this section, any such direction—

(*a*) shall have effect for a limited period only, which must be specified in the direction ; and

(*b*) may be varied or revoked before the end of that period by a further direction under this section.

(4) A direction under this section may apply to the area specified in the direction such of—

(*a*) the powers conferred on the Secretary of State by Part I of Schedule 3 to this Act ; and

(*b*) the prohibitions and restrictions imposed by Part II of that Schedule ;

as may be so specified, whether generally or for such purposes or subject to such exceptions as may be so specified.

(5) A direction under this section may provide—

(*a*) that any powers of the harbour authority or the harbour master under any harbour order shall cease to be exercisable in the area specified in the direction either altogether or to any extent specified in the direction or (as the case may be) shall be so exercisable subject to any restrictions so specified ;

(*b*) that anything authorised or required by any such order or by any byelaws made or directions given under any such order to be done by or to the harbour authority or the harbour master may or shall be done instead in that area by or to the Secretary of State or any person acting on his behalf ; and

(*c*) that any such order, byelaws or directions shall apply within that area subject to any modifications specified in the direction.

(6) A direction under this section may provide that any powers of the harbour authority to levy ship, passenger and goods dues (within the meaning of the Harbours Act 1964) shall cease to be exercisable in the area specified in the direction to any extent so specified. 1964 c. 40.

(7) After the end of the construction period all the powers conferred on the Secretary of State by Part I of Schedule 3 to this Act and the prohibitions and restrictions imposed by Part II of that Schedule shall apply within the tunnel maintenance area.

(8) In this Act—

" the harbour area " means the area comprising—

(*a*) Conwy harbour ; and

(*b*) any land from which the waters of the Estuary have been diverted in accordance with the Scheme ; and

" the tunnel maintenance area " means the area marked by cross-hatching (or by both cross-hatching and dots) on the plan included in Schedule 3 to the Scheme (limit of tunnel backfill).

Provisions supplementary to section 7.

8.—(1) Part III of Schedule 3 to this Act has effect for the purpose of supplementing the provisions of Parts I and II of that Schedule.

(2) References in any provision of that Schedule to the works and to the area affected by the works shall be read as referring respectively—

(*a*) in a case where that provision applies by virtue of a direction given under section 7 of this Act, to the tunnel works and to the area specified in the direction in accordance with subsection (2) of that section; and

(*b*) in a case where that provision applies by virtue of subsection (7) of that section, to any tunnel maintenance works and to the tunnel maintenance area.

(3) Without prejudice to any provision made by a direction under that section, where under or by virtue of that section any prohibition or restriction under Part II of that Schedule applies in any area—

(*a*) any power, right or duty (whether of the harbour authority or any other person) applicable under or by virtue of any other enactment or by virtue of any rule of law shall be subject to that prohibition or restriction; and

(*b*) that prohibition or restriction is additional to any prohibition or restriction under any other enactment.

(4) The Secretary of State shall—

(*a*) publish notice of any direction under section 7 of this Act in a local newspaper circulating in the Conwy area; and

(*b*) give notice of any such direction to the Aberconwy Borough Council and to the Corporation of Trinity House of Deptford Strond;

describing the area to which the direction relates and giving such indication of the effect of the direction as appears to him to be appropriate.

(5) The notice required by subsection (4) above in the case of any direction shall be published or given at least seven days before the direction is given, unless the Secretary of State considers it necessary by reason of any emergency to give the direction without complying with the preceding requirement; and in any such case—

(*a*) the notice required by that subsection shall be published or given as soon as possible after the time by which in accordance with the preceding requirement it should have been published or given; and

(*b*) where it is not possible to publish or give that notice before the direction is given the Secretary of State shall publish or give such advance notice (if any) of the direction as may be possible in the circumstances.

(6) In relation to any advance notice of a direction under section 7 of this Act required by subsection (5) above, references in subsections (4) and (5) above to any such direction shall be read as references to a proposed direction.

(7) In this Act "the construction period" means the period beginning with the date on which the tunnel works are begun and ending with the date on which the tunnel is first open to public traffic.

Remedial action and compensation

Extended right to compensation for injurious affection.

9.—(1) This section applies where any land, or any interest in land, has been injuriously affected by the carrying out of any works or the taking of any other action authorised by Schedule 2 to this Act otherwise than on land acquired for or in connection with the principal works.

(2) Compensation shall be payable in respect of the land or interest injuriously affected under section 10 of the Compulsory Purchase Act 1965, to be assessed in the same manner and subject to the same rules as in the case of other compensation under that section in respect of injurious affection where the injury arises from the execution of works on land acquired in accordance with that Act. 1965 c. 56.

(3) In section 10(1), as it applies for the purposes of this section, the reference to the acquiring authority shall be read as a reference to the Secretary of State.

Expenditure on remedial action.

10.—(1) The Secretary of State is authorised by this section to incur expenditure for or in connection with—

(*a*) the construction or execution of works for mitigating any adverse effects which the tunnel works have or might possibly have on fish or shellfish stocks in Conwy waters;

(*b*) the provision of moorings and other facilities for vessels to replace existing facilities in Conwy harbour which have been or will be removed for the purposes of the tunnel works or to mitigate any adverse effects the tunnel works have or might possibly have on the use of any such existing facilities; and

(*c*) the relocation and reinstatement of any such existing facilities which have been displaced for the purposes of the tunnel works.

In paragraph (*a*) above "Conwy waters" means Conwy harbour and the adjacent sea and the River Conwy and any of its tributaries.

(2) Without prejudice to the generality of subsection (1)(*a*) above, expenditure on any action taken for the purpose of restoring, replenishing or renewing—

(*a*) the mussel beds within the Conwy Mussel Fishery ; or

(*b*) stocks of salmon or migratory trout (within the meaning of the Salmon and Freshwater Fisheries Act 1975) ;

1975 c. 51.

is authorised by that paragraph.

(3) Expenditure by the Secretary of State on works or facilities within subsection (1) above is authorised—

(*a*) irrespective of whether the works or facilities are constructed, carried out or provided by the Secretary of State himself or by any other person ; and

(*b*) in the case of works of construction within paragraph (*a*) or any facilities within paragraph (*b*) of that subsection, irrespective of whether those works or facilities are permanent or temporary.

Compensation for losses arising from the tunnel works.

11.—(1) The Secretary of State may make payments in accordance with this section in respect of losses appearing to him to be losses arising from the tunnel works.

(2) A person is eligible to receive payments under this section in respect of any loss appearing to the Secretary of State to be a loss arising from those works if it appears to the Secretary of State—

(*a*) that he derives a significant part of his income from carrying on a business subject to special damage from works in the Estuary ;

(*b*) that that business had been carried on before the construction period (whether by him or by any other person) for a period of not less than three years extending up to the beginning of the construction period ;

(*c*) that the loss was incurred in respect of that business ; and

(*d*) that the loss was incurred before the end of the relevant period.

(3) For the purposes of this section a loss is a loss arising from the tunnel works if it is a financial loss directly attributable to—

(*a*) the tunnel works ; or

(*b*) the exercise by the Secretary of State for the purposes of those works of any power exercisable by him by virtue of a direction under section 7 of this Act ; or

(*c*) the effect of any prohibition or restriction under Part II of Schedule 3 to this Act which is applicable during the construction period by virtue of any such direction.

(4) For the purposes of this section a business is one subject to special damage from works in the Estuary if it involves or is dependent upon any one or more of the following—

(*a*) the taking of fish or shellfish or other operations or activities carried on in waters within Conwy harbour (whether by the person carrying on the business or by other persons);

(*b*) the use (by that person or by other persons) of facilities in Conwy harbour for the purpose of or in connection with carrying on any operations or activities mentioned in paragraph (*a*) above in waters beyond the limits of Conwy harbour; and

(*c*) the taking of mussels from the Conwy Mussel Fishery by persons licensed to do so under the Conwy Mussel Fishery (Amendment) Order 1948. S.I. 1948 No. 1888.

(5) Any operations or activities shall be regarded for the purposes of subsection (4) above as carried on in waters of any description if carried on in, under or over waters of that description or the land beneath those waters.

(6) For the purposes of this section, the relevant period in relation to any loss—

(*a*) in the case of a loss incurred in respect of a business within subsection (4)(*c*) above, is the period beginning with the date on which the construction period begins and ending five years after the end of the construction period or after the completion of any action taken or financed by the Secretary of State under section 10 of this Act for the purpose of restoring, replenishing or renewing the mussel beds within the Conwy Mussel Fishery (whichever last occurs); and

(*b*) in any other case, is the period beginning with the date on which the construction period begins and ending five years after the end of the construction period.

(7) Subject to subsection (2)(*a*) to (*c*) above, the Secretary of State may make payments under this section in respect of a loss incurred not more than four years after the end of the relevant period if it appears to him that the person who incurred the loss will suffer hardship if no payment is made under this section in respect of it.

(8) Without prejudice to the power of the Secretary of State, in determining whether to make any payment under this section in respect of any loss and the amount of any such payment, to take into account any considerations appearing to him to be relevant, he may in particular have regard to any compensation or financial assistance that in his view is or may be available to the person who suffered the loss under any other enactment.

(9) Payments under this section shall be subject to the consent of the Treasury.

Compensation for losses arising from tunnel maintenance works.

12.—(1) The Secretary of State may make payments in accordance with this section in respect of losses appearing to him to be losses arising from tunnel maintenance works.

(2) A person is eligible to receive payments under this section in respect of any loss appearing to the Secretary of State to be a loss arising from tunnel maintenance works if it appears to the Secretary of State—

(*a*) that he derives a significant part of his income from carrying on a business subject to special damage from works in the Estuary ; and

(*b*) that the loss was incurred in respect of that business.

(3) For the purposes of this section a loss is a loss arising from tunnel maintenance works if it is a financial loss directly attributable to the effect of any prohibition or restriction under Part II of Schedule 3 to this Act as it applies after the end of the construction period by virtue of section 7(7) of this Act.

(4) Subsections (4), (5), (8) and (9) of section 11 of this Act apply for the purposes of this section as they apply for the purposes of that section.

Compensation of harbour authority.

13. The Secretary of State may with the consent of the Treasury make payments to the harbour authority in respect of losses appearing to him to be losses attributable to the tunnel works or tunnel maintenance works.

Compensation for disturbance to apparatus and moorings.

14.—(1) Where—

(*a*) the Secretary of State takes any action in relation to any apparatus under paragraph 1(1)(*a*) or (*b*) of Schedule 3 to this Act ; and

(*b*) any remedial measures rendered reasonably necessary in view of his proposal to take that action are not taken by the Secretary of State before he takes that action ;

the person to whom the apparatus belongs shall be entitled to recover from the Secretary of State any reasonable expenses incurred by that person in, or in connection with, taking those remedial measures.

(2) In subsection (1) above " remedial measures " means—

(*a*) the removal and relaying or replacing, alteration or protection of any apparatus or the provision and construction of any new apparatus ;

(*b*) the cutting off of any apparatus from any other apparatus ; and (*c*) the carrying out of any other work or the doing of any other thing reasonably required for the purposes of or in connection with the operation of any apparatus.

(3) Where the Secretary of State removes any mooring in exercise of his power under paragraph 1(1)(*c*) of Schedule 3 to this Act, the person to whom the mooring belongs shall be entitled to recover from the Secretary of State any reasonable relocation costs incurred by that person in consequence of the removal of the mooring.

(4) In subsection (3) above " relocation costs " means, in relation to any mooring removed by the Secretary of State in exercise of the power mentioned in that subsection—

(*a*) any expenses incurred in relocating the mooring in a new situation or in removing it from the new situation and reinstating it in its original situation ; and

(*b*) any expenses incurred in moving any vessel for which the mooring was used before it was so removed from the original situation of the mooring to a new situation and back again on reinstatement of the mooring in its original situation ;

or, in any case where any such vessel is to be kept on dry land during the period when the site from which the mooring is removed is not available for use in consequence of the carrying out of any works or other action which was the occasion for the removal of the mooring, any expenses incurred for the purpose of lifting the vessel from the water on the removal of the mooring or returning it to the water on reinstatement of the mooring in its original situation.

(5) References in subsection (4) above, in relation to any mooring removed by the Secretary of State as there mentioned, to the mooring include references to any new mooring provided in place of that mooring (whether by the Secretary of State in exercise of his powers under this Act or by the owner of the mooring).

(6) Where the owner of any mooring that the Secretary of State proposes to remove in exercise of his power under paragraph 1(1)(*c*) of Schedule 3 to this Act himself removes it or procures its removal, this section shall apply as if the mooring had been removed by the Secretary of State in exercise of that power.

(7) This section shall be regarded for the purposes of section 37(5) of the Land Compensation Act 1973 (discretionary compensation for disturbance in absence of entitlement to a disturbance payment or to compensation for disturbance under any other enactment) as providing compensation for disturbance for the owners of moorings removed by the Secretary of State in exercise of his power under paragraph 1(1)(*c*) of Schedule 3 to this Act. 1973 c. 26.

Miscellaneous and supplemental

Protection of the tunnel, etc.

15.—(1) A person may not without the consent in writing of the Secretary of State (which may be given subject to conditions)—

(*a*) use, for the purpose of landing or embarking persons or landing or loading goods from or into any vessel, the tunnel, any of the tunnel units, any tunnel approach works or any work constructed in pursuance of Schedule 2 to this Act;

(*b*) interfere with the tunnel, any of the tunnel units or any tunnel approach works; or

(*c*) remove, move or otherwise interfere with any such work or any machinery, apparatus, tools or other things in use or intended for use in constructing or carrying out the tunnel works or any tunnel maintenance works.

(2) A person who without reasonable excuse contravenes subsection (1) above or fails to comply with any condition attached to a consent given by the Secretary of State under that subsection shall be liable on summary conviction to a fine not exceeding level 3 on the standard scale (within the meaning of section 75 of the Criminal Justice Act 1982).

1982 c. 48.

(3) In this section " tunnel approach works " means works for providing access to the tunnel on either side of the Estuary.

Delegation of certain decisions affecting works.

16.—(1) Without prejudice to the power of the Secretary of State to enter into such contracts as he thinks fit with any persons for the purpose of carrying out any works or taking any other action he is authorised by this Act to carry out or take, any contract entered into by the Secretary of State for that purpose may provide for any relevant decision which is reserved by this Act to the Secretary of State to be made instead on his behalf by any person or in any manner specified in or determined in accordance with the contract.

(2) For the purposes of subsection (1) above as it applies to any contract, a decision is a relevant decision reserved by this Act to the Secretary of State if it is a decision with respect to any works or action to which the contract relates that falls to be made by the Secretary of State by virtue of any provision of Schedule 2 or Part I of Schedule 3 to this Act referring (in whatever terms) to the opinion or judgment of the Secretary of State with respect to any matter.

(3) This section shall not be read as prejudicing the power of the Secretary of State to authorise the taking, by any of his officers or servants or in any other manner permitted by law, of any decision or other action that falls to be taken by him for the purposes of this Act.

Employment of local labour.

17. Any contract entered into by the Secretary of State for the purpose of carrying out the tunnel works shall include such provisions as the Secretary of State considers appropriate for securing so far as practicable the maximum employment in carrying out those works of persons normally resident in the area formed by the counties of Gwynedd and Clwyd.

Proof of certain facts by certificate of Secretary of State.

18.—(1) A certificate by the Secretary of State stating the date on which the tunnel works were begun and either—

(*a*) the date on which the tunnel was first open to public traffic; or

(*b*) that the tunnel had not been open to public traffic on any occasion before a date specified in the certificate;

shall be conclusive evidence of the facts stated.

(2) A certificate by the Secretary of State stating the date of completion of any action taken or financed by the Secretary of State under section 10 of this Act for the purpose of restoring, replenishing or renewing the mussel beds within the Conwy Mussel Fishery shall be conclusive evidence that that action was completed on the date stated.

Correction of deposited plan.

19.—(1) If the deposited plan or a book of reference to the plan is inaccurate in its description of any land, or in its statement or description of the ownership or occupation of any land, the Secretary of State, after giving not less than ten days notice to the owner, lessee or occupier of the land in question, may apply to two justices having jurisdiction in the place where the land is situated for the correction of the plan or (as the case may be) the book of reference.

(2) If on any such application it appears to the justices that the misstatement or wrong description arose from mistake or inadvertence, the justices shall certify accordingly and shall in their certificate state in what respect any matter is misstated or wrongly described.

(3) The certificate shall be deposited with the Chief Executive of the Gwynedd County Council and in the Office of the Clerk of the Parliaments and in the Private Bill Office of the House of Commons, and thereupon the deposited plan or the book of reference (as the case may be) shall be deemed to be corrected according to the certificate, and the Secretary of State may proceed under this Act as if the deposited plan or the book of reference had always been in the corrected form.

(4) A person with whom a copy of the certificate is deposited under this section shall keep it with the documents to which it relates.

(5) In this section, " book of reference " means a book deposited in connection with the Bill for this Act with the Chief Executive of the Gwynedd County Council and in the Office of the Clerk of the Parliaments and the Private Bill Office of the

House of Commons containing the names of the owners or reputed owners, lessees or reputed lessees, and occupiers of land which may be acquired under section 2 of this Act.

Provision for expenditure by Secretary of State.

20. Any expenditure incurred by the Secretary of State under this Act shall be defrayed out of money provided by Parliament.

Removal of certain statutory controls.

21.—(1) Where any operation is authorised to be carried out by any provision of this Act, that provision shall not be regarded as limited—

(*a*) by any prohibition on the carrying out of operations of that description or any prohibition on carrying them out without the consent of any person ; or

(*b*) by any restriction on the level of noise which may be emitted in the course of carrying out operations of that description ; or

(*c*) by any prohibition or restriction on the times when or the periods of time for which operations of that description may be carried out.

(2) The powers conferred by paragraph 4 of Schedule 2 to this Act to deal with materials (including liquid) excavated, dredged or pumped in pursuance of that paragraph shall not be regarded as limited by any prohibition or restriction on depositing in or discharging into any waters materials of that description so far as, in the course or in consequence of so dealing with those materials, they are deposited in or discharged into waters within the limits for the exercise of those powers set by paragraph 7 of that Schedule.

(3) This section is not to be taken as prejudicing the generality of any of the powers conferred by this Act.

(4) In this section " operation " means any works or action ; and references to a prohibition or a restriction are references to a prohibition or, as the case may be, a restriction imposed by or under any enactment other than this Act.

Interpretation.

22.—(1) In this Act—

" apparatus " includes any device, structure or work ;

" Conwy harbour " means such part of the Estuary and any land adjacent to it as is for the time being within the limits of the jurisdiction of the harbour authority under any harbour order ;

S.I. 1948 No. 1888.

" Conwy Mussel Fishery " means the fishery comprised in the Conwy Mussel Fishery (Amendment) Order 1948 ;

1971 c. 78.

" Crown land " has the same meaning as in Part XIV of the Town and Country Planning Act 1971 ;

"deposited plan" and "deposited section" mean respectively the plan and the section deposited in connection with the Bill for this Act with the Chief Executive of the Gwynedd County Council and in the Office of the Clerk of the Parliaments and the Private Bill Office of the House of Commons;

"harbour" and "harbour authority" have the same meanings as in the Harbours Act 1964, and "harbour order" means a harbour revision order made under section 14 of that Act; 1964 c. 40.

"land" includes land covered with water, any interest in land and any easement or other right in, to or over land;

"mooring" means any buoy, pile, post, chain, pillar or other apparatus used for the mooring of vessels;

"the harbour authority" means the harbour authority for the harbour formed by the Estuary;

"the harbour master" means the person appointed by the harbour authority as harbour master for Conwy harbour and includes his authorised deputies and assistants and any person authorised by the harbour authority to act as harbour master;

"tunnel units" means sections of concrete, steel or other material (or combination of materials) designed to be attached together so as to constitute the framework of the tunnel;

"vessel" includes a hovercraft within the meaning of the Hovercraft Act 1968. 1968 c. 59.

(2) In this Act, the expressions listed in column 1 below have the meaning given by, or are to be construed in accordance with, the provisions of this Act listed against them in column 2 below.

Expression	*Relevant provision*
construction period	section 8(7)
Estuary	section 1(2)
harbour area	section 7(8)
principal construction works	section 1(2)
principal works	section 1(3)
Scheme	section 1(2)
the 1980 Act	section 1(1)
tunnel	section 1(2)
tunnel maintenance area	section 7(8)
tunnel maintenance works	section 6(3)
tunnel works	section 6(2)

Short title.

23. This Act may be cited as the Conwy Tunnel (Supplementary Powers) Act 1983.

SCHEDULES

Section 2(5).

SCHEDULE 1

Acquisition of Land

Part I

Section 2 Land

Modification of Compulsory Purchase Act 1965

1965 c. 56. 1. Part I of the Compulsory Purchase Act 1965 shall have effect, in its application by virtue of section 2(2) of this Act to the acquisition of land under that section, as if—

1981 c. 67. (*a*) references to an order under section 2(1) of the Acquisition of Land Act 1981 were references to section 2 of this Act; and

(*b*) in section 11(1) (power of acquiring authority having served notice to treat to enter on land after giving fourteen days notice) for the words "fourteen days" there were substituted the words "three months".

Private rights of way

2.—(1) All private rights of way over any land which may be acquired compulsorily under section 2 of this Act shall be extinguished on the acquisition of the land, whether compulsorily or by agreement, or on entry on the land in pursuance of section 11(1) of the Compulsory Purchase Act 1965, whichever is the sooner.

(2) A person who suffers loss by the extinction of any private right under sub-paragraph (1) above shall be entitled to compensation to be determined, in case of dispute, under and in accordance with
1961 c. 33. Part I of the Land Compensation Act 1961.

Part II

Land Other Than Section 2 Land

Objections to compulsory purchase order

3. Where proceedings required by Schedule 1 to the Acquisition of Land Act 1981 to be taken in respect of a compulsory purchase order proposed to be made in pursuance of section 3 of this Act are so taken, the Secretary of State may disregard for the purposes of that Schedule any objection to the draft compulsory purchase order which in his opinion amounts in substance to an objection to the Scheme.

Compulsory acquisition of rights

4.—(1) In relation to the compulsory acquisition of a right by virtue of section 3(2) of this Act, the following provisions of the 1980 Act shall apply—

(*a*) as if references to such a compulsory acquisition were included in references to the compulsory acquisition of a right by virtue of section 250 of that Act; and (*b*) as if a compulsory purchase order providing for such a compulsory acquisition were made in the exercise of highway land acquisition powers. SCH. 1

(2) The provisions mentioned above are—

(*a*) section 250(4) and (5) and Part II of Schedule 19 (adaptations of Compulsory Purchase Act 1965 and the enactments relating to compensation for compulsory purchase); 1965 c. 56.

(*b*) section 251 (rights acquired to be binding on successive owners of the land); and

(*c*) sections 252 and 261(2) (power of landowners affected by rights acquisition to compel acquisition of whole interest).

Commons etc.

5. Where the Secretary of State is authorised under section 3 of this Act to acquire compulsorily land forming part of a common, open space or fuel or field garden allotment (within the meanings of paragraph 6 of Schedule 3 to the Acquisition of Land Act 1981), 1981 c. 67. or rights over such land, he may be authorised under section 3 of this Act to acquire compulsorily land for giving in exchange for the land or rights acquired.

PART III

GENERAL

Compensation

6.—(1) In assessing the compensation payable in respect of the compulsory acquisition of land under section 2 or 3 of this Act, the Lands Tribunal—

(*a*) shall have regard to the extent to which the remaining contiguous lands belonging to the same person may be benefited by the purpose for which the land is authorised to be acquired; and

(*b*) shall take into account, and embody in its award, any undertaking given by the Secretary of State as to the use to which the land, or any part of it, will be put.

(2) In assessing the compensation payable in respect of the compulsory acquisition of rights by virtue of section 3(2) of this Act, the Lands Tribunal—

(*a*) shall have regard to the extent to which the land over which the right in question is, or is to be acquired, or any contiguous land belonging to the same person, may be benefited by the purpose for which the right may be authorised to be acquired; and

(*b*) shall take into account, and embody in its award, any undertaking given by the Secretary of State as to the manner in which the right will be exercised.

(3) Where by a compulsory purchase order made in pursuance of section 3 of this Act the Secretary of State acquires two or more rights over land belonging to the same person, or acquires not only one or more rights but also adjoining or adjacent land so belonging

SCH. 1 then, in applying sub-paragraph (1) or (2) above, the Lands Tribunal shall consider together the compensation payable in respect of both or all of the rights or, as the case may be, in respect of the right or rights and also the adjoining or adjacent land.

(4) In its application in respect of a compulsory acquisition under section 2 or 3 of this Act, section 5 of the Land Compensation Act 1961 shall have effect subject to sub-paragraphs (1) and (2) above. 1961 c. 33.

1965 c. 56. 7. Part I of the Compulsory Purchase Act 1965, in its application to a compulsory acquisition under section 2 or 3 of this Act, shall have effect as if the works authorised to be executed by this Act included the principal construction works (so far as not so authorised).

Statutory undertakers

1971 c. 78. 8.—(1) Sections 230 to 232 of the Town and Country Planning Act 1971 (power to extinguish rights of statutory undertakers and power of statutory undertakers to remove or re-site apparatus) shall apply in relation to land acquired (whether compulsorily or by agreement) for or in connection with the principal works as they apply to land acquired as mentioned in section 230(1) of that Act, but as if—

(*a*) the references in sections 230(1) and 232(1) to the development with a view to which the land was acquired or appropriated or the development to be carried out on the land were references to any of the principal works to be carried out on the land ; and

(*b*) the references in section 232(2) to beginning to carry out the development of the land were references to beginning to carry out any of the principal works on the land ;

and all such other provisions of that Act as apply for the purposes of sections 230 to 232 (including sections 237(2) and (3), 238 and 240, which provide for the payment of compensation, and sections 233 to 236, which contain provisions consequential on the extinguishment of any rights under section 230) shall have effect accordingly.

(2) In the provisions of that Act, as they apply by virtue of sub-paragraph (1) above in relation to land acquired for or in connection with the principal works, references to the undertaking of statutory undertakers shall be read, in relation to the Welsh Water Authority, as including any activities undertaken by the Authority in exercise of any of the functions of the Authority under Part II of
1936 c. 49. the Public Health Act 1936 or under sections 14 to 16 of the Water
1973 c. 37. Act 1973 (sewerage functions).

Section 6(1).

SCHEDULE 2

SUBSIDIARY WORKS AND SUPPLEMENTARY POWERS

Subsidiary construction works, etc.

1. The Secretary of State may, for the purposes of or in connection with the principal works, construct, provide and maintain—

(*a*) all such roads, approaches, bridges, stairs, basins, slipways, ramps, passages, means of ingress or egress, shafts, stages, buildings, walls, fences, pumping works and temporary fabrication facilities ;

(*b*) all such embankments, aprons, abutments, retaining walls, wing walls, drains and culverts ; SCH. 2

(*c*) all such temporary piles, fenders, booms, moorings, dolphins, pontoons, caissons, cofferdams, piers and wharves ; and

(*d*) all such other structures, plant and works ;

as appear to him to be necessary or convenient.

2. The Secretary of State may carry out any works and do any things necessary for the protection of any land adjoining land on which any of the principal works are carried out.

3. The works authorised by paragraphs 1 and 2 above include all necessary and convenient subsidiary and incidental works ; and references below in this Schedule to works so authorised include references to any other action so authorised.

Other subsidiary works and supplementary powers

4.—(1) The Secretary of State may carry out, in any manner and by any means appearing to him to be appropriate, such excavations, such dredging and dumping operations and such pumping operations as appear to him to be necessary or convenient for the purpose of—

(*a*) the principal works ; or

(*b*) any works authorised by paragraph 1 or 2 above.

(2) The Secretary of State may carry out, in any manner and by any means appearing to him to be appropriate, such operations for the purpose of maintaining any channel or trench excavated or dredged in pursuance of this paragraph as appear to him to be necessary or convenient for that purpose.

(3) The Secretary of State may use, appropriate, store, deposit or dispose of any materials (including liquid) excavated, dredged or pumped in pursuance of this paragraph in any manner or by any means appearing to him to be appropriate.

5. The Secretary of State may temporarily alter, interfere with, occupy or use the banks, bed and foreshores of the Estuary in any manner and to any extent appearing to him to be necessary or convenient for the purpose of—

(*a*) the principal works ; or

(*b*) any works authorised by paragraph 1 or 2 above.

6. The Secretary of State may obstruct navigation to any extent appearing to him to be necessary or convenient for the purpose of—

(*a*) the principal works ; or

(*b*) any works authorised by paragraph 1 or 2 above ; or

(*c*) any other works or action authorised by any of the preceding provisions of this Schedule.

Limits for exercise of powers

7.—(1) The powers conferred by paragraphs 1 and 2 above are exercisable for the purposes of or in connection with the principal construction works or any of them anywhere within the limits of the

SCH. 2

land shown on the deposited plan as land the Secretary of State is authorised to acquire under section 2 of this Act.

(2) The powers conferred by paragraph 4 above are exercisable for the purposes of—

(*a*) the principal construction works or any of them ; or

(*b*) any works authorised by paragraph 1 or 2 above undertaken for or in connection with the principal construction works ;

anywhere within the harbour area ; and the power conferred by paragraph 4(1) above is also exercisable for those purposes on any land, or in pursuance of any right over land, acquired by the Secretary of State for or in connection with the principal works.

(3) The power conferred by paragraph 5 above is exercisable for the purposes mentioned in sub-paragraph (2) above anywhere within the harbour area.

(4) The power conferred by paragraph 6 above is exercisable, for the purposes of the principal construction works or any of them or any other works or action mentioned in that paragraph undertaken for or in connection with those works, anywhere within the harbour area.

(5) Without prejudice to sub-paragraphs (2) and (4) above, operations undertaken in pursuance of paragraph 4 above for the purpose of transporting any of the tunnel units constructed elsewhere than on land acquired under section 2 of this Act or other Crown land within the limits mentioned in sub-paragraph (1) above may be carried out on, in, under or over the bed of the sea beyond the harbour area, and the power under paragraph 6 above shall be exercisable beyond the harbour area for the purposes of any such operations.

(6) The powers conferred by any of the preceding provisions of this Schedule, so far as exercisable for the purposes of or in connection with any tunnel maintenance works, are exercisable anywhere within the tunnel maintenance area.

Sections 7 and 8.

SCHEDULE 3

SPECIAL CONTROL OF NAVIGATION, ETC.

PART I

POWERS

1.—(1) Subject to sub-paragraph (2) below, the Secretary of State may raise, lower, divert, alter, remove or otherwise interfere with any of the following, that is to say—

(*a*) any pipe, tube, cable, wire or other apparatus intended or used for carrying water, gas or electricity or for telegraphic, postal or other purposes ;

(*b*) any sewer or drain or other similar works ; and

(*c*) any mooring ;

in any case where it appears to him to be necessary or convenient to do so for the purposes of any of the works.

(2) The Secretary of State may not under sub-paragraph (1)(*a*) or (*b*) above remove from any land acquired for or in connection with

the principal works any apparatus of a description falling within section 230(1)(*b*) of the Town and Country Planning Act 1971 (apparatus vested in or belonging to statutory undertakers for the purpose of carrying on their undertaking) as that paragraph applies by virtue of paragraph 8 of Schedule 1 to this Act in relation to any such land.

Sch. 3

1971 c. 78.

2. If it appears to the Secretary of State to be necessary or convenient for the purposes of any of the works, he may remove any vessel—

(*a*) sunk, stranded or abandoned in the area affected by the works ; or

(*b*) moored or left there (whether lawfully or not) ;

either to another place within that area or to a place outside that area.

Part II

Prohibitions and Restrictions

3.—(1) A person may not navigate within or carry out any other activities or operations on, in, under or over the bed, banks, foreshore or waters of the Estuary within the area affected by the works at any time when that area is closed to navigation in pursuance of this paragraph.

(2) At any time when it appears to the Secretary of State to be necessary or convenient for the purposes of any of the works, he may close the area affected by the works to navigation by a direction given under this paragraph specifying the period during which that area is to be closed.

(3) Subsections (4) to (6) of section 8 of this Act shall apply in relation to a direction under this paragraph as they apply in relation to a direction under section 7 of this Act.

(4) Without prejudice to paragraph 6 of Schedule 2 to this Act, the Secretary of State may take such measures as he thinks fit to prevent access to the area affected by the works at any time when that area is closed to navigation in pursuance of this paragraph.

4. A person may not—

(*a*) cause or permit a vessel to be moored in the area affected by the works ; or

(*b*) lay down or place in that area any apparatus of any description mentioned in paragraph 1 above ;

without the consent in writing of the Secretary of State.

5. A person may not without the consent in writing of the Secretary of State exercise or enjoy within the area affected by the works—

(*a*) any public right of fishery, public right of way or other public or customary right (other than a right of navigation) ;

(*b*) any other privilege, immunity or right conferred by licence or other authority granted or given under any enactment (whenever passed) ;

that would apart from this paragraph be exercisable or available in that area.

SCH. 3

6. A person may not without the consent in writing of the Secretary of State carry out within the area affected by the works—

(*a*) any mining operations ;

(*b*) any blasting or dredging operations ; or

(*c*) any other operations of a similar description in, on, over or under the bed, banks, foreshores or waters of the Estuary.

7. A person may not without the consent in writing of the Secretary of State do anything within the area affected by the works which is capable of preventing or hindering the construction or carrying out of any of the works.

PART III

SUPPLEMENTARY PROVISIONS

8. The Secretary of State may delegate—

(*a*) any of his powers under Part I of this Schedule ; and

(*b*) the giving or withholding of any consent required or the taking of any other action he is authorised to take for the purposes of Part II of this Schedule ;

to the harbour master or to any other person appointed by him for the purpose.

9. Any consent given for the purposes of any provision of Part II of this Schedule by the Secretary of State or by any person exercising a power delegated to him by the Secretary of State in accordance with paragraph 8 above may be given subject to conditions.

10. A person who without reasonable excuse contravenes any provision of Part II of this Schedule or fails to comply with any condition attached to a consent given for the purposes of any such provision shall be liable on summary conviction to a fine not exceeding level 3 on the standard scale (within the meaning of section 75
1982 c. 48. of the Criminal Justice Act 1982).

British Fishing Boats Act 1983

1983 CHAPTER 8

An Act to prohibit the fishing for and trans-shipment of sea fish by or from British fishing boats, in areas specified by order made by the Minister of Agriculture, Fisheries and Food and the Secretaries of State respectively concerned with the sea fishing industry in Scotland, Wales and Northern Ireland, unless those boats satisfy conditions prescribed by an order of those Ministers with respect to the nationality of members of the crew; and to prohibit the landing of sea fish in the United Kingdom from British fishing boats that do not satisfy conditions so prescribed. [28th March 1983]

BE IT ENACTED by the Queen's most Excellent Majesty, by and with the advice and consent of the Lords Spiritual and Temporal, and Commons, in this present Parliament assembled, and by the authority of the same, as follows:—

Restrictions on fishing, etc., by British fishing boats.

1.—(1) The operations mentioned in subsection (2) below may not be carried out by or from a British fishing boat unless the boat is qualified in accordance with an order made by the Ministers under this subsection for use in carrying out operations of that description.

(2) Those operations are—

(*a*) fishing for sea fish in any area for the time being specified in an order made by the Ministers ;

(*b*) the trans-shipment of sea fish in any such area ; and

(*c*) the landing of sea fish in the United Kingdom.

References below in this Act to a restricted fishing area are references to any area for the time being specified in an order made by the Ministers under this subsection.

(3) An order under subsection (1) above prescribing qualifications for British fishing boats for use in carrying out any such operations may prescribe conditions for qualification with respect to the nationality of members of the crew of a fishing boat, or of any proportion of those members specified in the order.

(4) The conditions so prescribed shall be such as appear to the Ministers to be necessary or expedient for the protection of the British sea fishing industry; but any such conditions shall not discriminate between British citizens and persons who are nationals of any other member State.

(5) Where a British fishing boat is not for the time being qualified under this section for use in carrying out operations of any description mentioned in subsection (2)(*a*) or (*b*) above in a restricted fishing area, its fishing gear shall be stowed in accordance with an order made by the Ministers at any time when it is within such an area.

(6) If this section is contravened in the case of any fishing boat the master, the owner and the charterer (if any) of the boat shall be liable on summary conviction to a fine not exceeding £50,000 or on conviction on indictment to a fine.

(7) The court by or before which a person is convicted of an offence under subsection (6) above may order the forfeiture of any fish or fishing gear found in the boat in relation to which the offence was committed or taken or used by any person from the boat; and, in Scotland, any fish or fishing gear forfeited under this subsection may be destroyed or disposed of as the court may direct.

(8) Any power to make an order under this section shall be exercisable by statutory instrument, which shall be subject to annulment in pursuance of a resolution of either House of Parliament.

Powers of British sea-fishery officers in relation to British fishing boats in restricted fishing areas.

2.—(1) The powers conferred by the following provisions of this section are exercisable by British sea-fishery officers, in relation to any British fishing boat within a restricted fishing area, for the purpose of enforcing the provisions of section 1 of this Act.

(2) Any such officer may go on board any such boat, with or without persons assigned to assist him in his duties, and for that purpose may require the boat to stop and do anything else which will facilitate the boarding of the boat.

(3) Any such officer may require the attendance of the master and other persons on board any boat he has boarded under subsection (2) above and may make any examination and inquiry which appears to him to be necessary for the purpose of enforcing the provisions of section 1 of this Act.

(4) Without prejudice to the generality of subsection (3) above, any such officer—

(*a*) may require any person on board any such boat to produce any document he has with him on board that is or may be relevant for determining his nationality and any document relating to the boat, to its fishing operations or other operations ancillary to its fishing operations or to persons on board which is in his custody or possession, and may take copies of any such document;

(*b*) for the purpose of ascertaining whether an offence under section 1 of this Act has been committed in relation to any such boat, may search the boat for any such document and may require any person on board the boat to do anything which appears to him to be necessary for facilitating the search; and

(*c*) if he has reason to suspect that any such offence has been committed in relation to any such boat, may seize and detain any such document produced to him or found on board for the purpose of enabling the document to be used as evidence in proceedings for the offence;

but nothing in paragraph (*c*) above shall permit any document required by law to be carried on board the boat to be seized except while the boat is detained in a port.

(5) Where it appears to any such officer that an offence under section 1 of this Act has been committed in relation to any fishing boat, he may—

(*a*) require the master of the boat to take, or may himself take, the boat and its crew to the port which appears to him to be the nearest convenient port; and

(*b*) detain or require the master to detain the boat in the port;

and where such an officer detains or requires the detention of a boat he shall serve on the master a notice in writing stating that the boat will be or is required to be detained until the notice is withdrawn by the service on the master of a further notice in writing signed by a British sea-fishery officer.

Powers of entry of British sea-fishery officers in relation to premises on land.

3.—(1) Subject to the following provisions of this section, if—

(*a*) in England, Wales or Northern Ireland, a justice of the peace; or

(*b*) in Scotland, the sheriff or a justice of the peace;

is satisfied by information on oath that there is reasonable ground for suspecting that an offence under section 1 of this Act has been committed in relation to any fishing boat, and that any document relevant for determining whether such an offence has been committed in relation to that boat may be found on any premises specified in the information, he may grant a search warrant for the purposes of this section.

(2) The premises specified in any information laid for the purposes of subsection (1) above must be premises (other than a dwelling-house) used for carrying on a business in connection with the operation of fishing boats or activities connected with or ancillary to the operation of fishing boats.

(3) For the purposes of this section, a document shall be regarded as relevant for determining whether an offence under section 1 of this Act has been committed in relation to a fishing boat if it relates—

(*a*) to that boat, to its fishing operations or to other operations ancillary to its fishing operations; or

(*b*) to the nationality of members of the crew of that boat.

(4) A warrant granted under subsection (1) above shall authorise any British sea-fishery officer named in the warrant, with or without any constables, to enter the premises specified in the information and to search the premises for any document relevant for determining whether the suspected offence has been committed.

(5) Any such officer may require any person on any premises he has entered in pursuance of any such warrant to produce any document relevant for determining whether the suspected offence has been committed which is in his custody or possession, and may take copies of any such document.

(6) Any such officer may require any such person to do anything which appears to him to be necessary for facilitating any search carried out by him in pursuance of the warrant.

(7) Any such officer may seize and detain any document relevant for determining whether the suspected offence has been committed which is produced to him or found in the course of any such search, for the purpose of enabling the document to be used as evidence in proceedings for the offence.

(8) A warrant granted under subsection (1) above shall remain in force for a period of one month.

Supplementary provisions with respect to powers of British sea-fishery officers.

4.—(1) Any person who—

(*a*) without reasonable excuse fails to comply with any requirement imposed by a British sea-fishery officer under section 2 or 3 of this Act;

(*b*) prevents, or attempts to prevent, any other person from complying with any such requirement; or

(*c*) assaults any such officer while exercising any of the powers conferred on him under section 2 or 3 of this Act or wilfully obstructs any such officer in the exercise of any of those powers;

shall be liable on summary conviction to a fine not exceeding £5,000 or on conviction on indictment to a fine.

(2) A British sea-fishery officer shall not be liable in any civil or criminal proceedings for anything done in purported exercise of the powers conferred on him by section 2 or 3 of this Act if the court is satisfied that the act was done in good faith and with reasonable skill and care and that there were reasonable grounds for doing it.

Recovery of fines.

5.—(1) Where a fine is imposed by a magistrates' court in England and Wales or Northern Ireland on the master, owner or charterer or a member of the crew of a fishing boat who is convicted by the court of an offence under section 1 or 4 of this Act, the court may—

(*a*) issue a warrant of distress against the boat and its gear and catch and any property of the person convicted for the purpose of levying the amount of the fine; and

(*b*) order the boat to be detained for a period not exceeding three months from the date of the conviction or until the fine is paid or the amount of the fine is levied in pursuance of any such warrant, whichever occurs first.

(2) Where a fine is imposed by a sheriff in Scotland on the master, owner or charterer or a member of the crew of a fishing boat who is convicted by the sheriff of an offence under section 1 or 4 of this Act, the sheriff may—

(*a*) issue a warrant for the poinding and sale of the boat and its gear and catch and any property of the person convicted; and

(*b*) order the boat to be detained for a period not exceeding three months from the date of the conviction or until the fine is paid, whichever occurs first.

(3) Sections 77(1) and 78 of the Magistrates' Courts Act 1980 (postponement of issue of, and defects in, warrants of distress) 1980 c. 43.

shall apply to a warrant of distress issued under this section in England and Wales as they apply to a warrant of distress issued under Part III of that Act.

S.I. 1981/1675 (N.I. 26). (4) Article 114(2) of the Magistrates' Courts (Northern Ireland) Order 1981 (postponement of issue of certain warrants) shall apply to a warrant of distress issued under this section in Northern Ireland as it applies to a warrant referred to in that paragraph.

Offences committed by bodies corporate.

6. Where any offence under section 1 or 4 of this Act committed by a body corporate is proved to have been committed with the consent or approval of any director, manager, secretary or other officer of the body corporate, he, as well as the body corporate, shall be deemed to be guilty of the offence and shall be liable to be proceeded against and punished accordingly.

Jurisdiction to try offences.

7. Proceedings for an offence under section 1 or 4 of this Act may be taken, and the offence may for all incidental purposes be treated as having been committed, in any place in the United Kingdom.

Administrative expenses.

8. Any administrative expenses incurred by the Ministers by virtue of this Act shall be met out of money provided by Parliament.

Interpretation.

9. In this Act—

"British fishing boat" means a fishing boat which is registered in the United Kingdom, exempted from registration by regulations under section 373 of the Merchant Shipping Act 1894 (1894 c. 60.) or owned wholly by a person who is (within the meaning of that Act) a person qualified to own a British ship;

"British sea-fishery officer" means any person who by virtue of section 7 of the Sea Fisheries Act 1968 (1968 c. 77.) is a British sea-fishery officer;

"fishing boat" means any vessel for the time being employed in fishing operations or any operations ancillary to fishing operations;

"master" includes, in relation to any fishing boat, the person for the time being in command or charge of the boat;

"the Ministers" means the Minister of Agriculture, Fisheries and Food and the Secretaries of State respectively concerned with the sea fishing industry in Scotland, Wales and Northern Ireland; and "sea fish" includes shellfish, salmon and migratory trout, and "sea fishing industry" has a corresponding meaning;

and references to a restricted fishing area shall be read in accordance with section 1(2) of this Act.

Isle of Man and Channel Islands.

10. Her Majesty may by Order in Council direct that, subject to such exceptions, adaptations and modifications (if any) as may be specified in the Order, sections 1 to 7, 9 and 11(2) of this Act shall extend to the Isle of Man or any of the Channel Islands.

Short title and consequential amendment.

11.—(1) This Act may be cited as the British Fishing Boats Act 1983.

1894 c. 60.

(2) In section 374 of the Merchant Shipping Act 1894 (fishing boat register to be conclusive evidence for purposes of certain proceedings), after the words "Sea Fisheries Act 1968" there shall be inserted the words "or under the British Fishing Boats Act 1983".

Currency Act 1983

1983 CHAPTER 9

An Act to amend the Coinage Act 1971 and the law relating to issuing and writing off bank notes.

[28th March 1983]

BE IT ENACTED by the Queen's most Excellent Majesty, by and with the advice and consent of the Lords Spiritual and Temporal, and Commons, in this present Parliament assembled, and by the authority of the same, as follows:—

Coinage

Amendments of Coinage Act 1971 in connection with changes in the coinage. 1971 c. 34.

1.—(1) For section 1 of the Coinage Act 1971 (which determines the standards of certain coins) there is substituted—

"Standards of certain coins.

1.—(1) The following provisions of this section have effect with respect to coins made at the Mint.

(2) Gold coins and coins of silver of the Queen's Maundy money shall, if of a denomination mentioned in Schedule 1 to this Act, be of the weight and fineness specified there, but in the making of the coins a remedy (that is, a variation from the standard weight and fineness so specified) shall be

allowed of an amount not exceeding that specified in that Schedule.

(3) Gold coins and coins of silver of the Queen's Maundy money shall, if of any other denomination, be of such weight and fineness as may be specified in a proclamation under section 3 of this Act.

(4) Coins other than gold coins and coins of silver of the Queen's Maundy money shall be of such weight, composition and dimensions as may be specified in a proclamation under that section.

(5) In the making of the coins to which subsections (3) and (4) above apply, such remedy shall be allowed as may be specified in the proclamation.

(6) The variation from the standard weight of any coin (other than a gold coin of a denomination mentioned in Schedule 1 to this Act) specified for that coin in accordance with this section shall be measured as the average of a sample of not more than one kilogram of that coin.

(7) In subsection (5) above " remedy " means—

(*a*) in relation to gold coins and coins of silver of the Queen's Maundy money, a variation from the standard weight and fineness specified in the proclamation of an amount not exceeding that so specified ;

(*b*) in relation to other coins, a variation from the standard weight, composition or dimensions so specified of an amount not exceeding that so specified.".

(2) Part II of Schedule 1 to the Act of 1971 (standards for cupro-nickel and bronze coins) shall cease to have effect; but, until other standards are determined by proclamation under section 3 of that Act with respect to coins of any denomination mentioned in that Part, coins of that denomination shall continue to be circular and of the standards specified in that Part (subject to the remedy allowed).

(3) Section 2 of the Act of 1971 (extent to which coins are legal tender) is amended as follows—

(*a*) for subsection (1) there are substituted the following subsections—

" (1) Gold coins shall be legal tender for payment of any amount, but shall not be legal tender if their weight has become less than that specified in Schedule 1 to this Act, or in the proclamation under which they are made, as the least current weight.

(1A) Subject to any provision made by proclamation under section 3 of this Act, coins of cupro-nickel, silver or bronze shall be legal tender as follows—

(*a*) coins of cupro-nickel or silver of denominations of more than 10 pence, for payment of any amount not exceeding £10 ;

(*b*) coins of cupro-nickel or silver of denominations of not more than 10 pence, for payment of any amount not exceeding £5 ;

(*c*) coins of bronze, for payment of any amount not exceeding 20 pence.

(1B) Other coins, if made current by a proclamation under section 3 of this Act, shall be legal tender in accordance with the provision made by that proclamation or by any later proclamation made under that section." ;

(*b*) in subsection (2) for the words " subsection (1) " there are substituted the words " subsection (1A) " ; and

(*c*) after subsection (2) there is inserted the following subsection—

" (3) In this section " coins " means coins made by the Mint in accordance with this Act and not called in by proclamation under section 3 of this Act."

(4) Section 3 of the Act of 1971 (power to regulate coinage by proclamation) is amended as follows—

(*a*) for paragraph (*c*) there is substituted—

" (*c*) determine the weight and fineness of any gold coins or coins of silver of the Queen's Maundy money, other than those of a denomination mentioned in Schedule 1 to this Act, the remedy to be allowed in making them and (for gold coins) their least current weight ;

(*cc*) determine the weight and composition of any coins, other than gold coins or coins of silver of the Queen's Maundy money, and the remedy (if any) to be allowed in making them ;

(*cd*) provide for the variation from the standard weight specified in Schedule 1 to this Act for a gold coin of a denomination mentioned in that Schedule to be measured in the manner specified in the proclamation ; " ;

(*b*) in paragraph (*d*) the words from " other than " to the end are omitted ;

(*c*) after paragraph (*d*) there is inserted—

" (*dd*) determine the percentage of impurities which coins other than gold coins and coins of silver of the Queen's Maundy money may contain ; " ;

(*d*) in paragraph (*f*) the words from " and be legal tender " to the end are omitted ; and

(*e*) after paragraph (*f*) there is inserted—

" (*ff*) direct that any coin shall be legal tender for payment of any amount not exceeding such amount as may be specified in the proclamation or for payment of any amount (without limit) ; " ;

(*f*) the section as so amended is renumbered so as to become subsection (1) and after that subsection there is inserted the following subsection—

" (2) So far as it relates to the matters mentioned in paragraph (*ff*) of subsection (1) above, a proclamation under this section may make different provision in relation to different parts of the United Kingdom."

(5) Where provision is made by a proclamation under section 3 of the Act of 1971 as to the percentage of impurities which coins of a particular denomination may contain, any coin of that denomination made before the date of the proclamation shall be treated as if that provision had been in force when that coin was made.

(6) In section 6(2) of the Act of 1971 (standard trial plates), in the Table (which sets out descriptions of coins and the composition of plates), for the first entry there is substituted—

" Gold coins of a denomination mentioned in Schedule 1 to this Act.........	Eleven-twelfths fine gold and one-twelfth alloy.
Other gold coins	Gold of the standard fineness specified in the proclamation under which the coins are made."

(7) In section 12(2) of the Act of 1971 (interpretation of references to silver coin in enactments mentioned in Schedule 2 to that Act) for the words " section 3(*c*) " there are substituted the words " section 3(*cc*) " and after the words " not being coin of " there is inserted the word " gold,".

Bank of England note issue

Limit on amount of Bank of England fiduciary note issue.

2.—(1) The Bank shall not cause the limit on the amount of the fiduciary note issue to be exceeded.

(2) For the purposes of this section, the limit is £13,500 million or such other amount as may from time to time be specified in a direction given by the Treasury.

(3) The amount specified in a direction under subsection (2) above shall not be greater than the former limit by more than 25 per cent.

(4) In subsection (3) above " the former limit " means the limit which was in force under this section at the beginning of the period of two years ending with the day on which the direction is given.

(5) A direction under subsection (2) above shall be given by a minute of the Treasury a copy of which shall be laid before each House of Parliament.

(6) The Treasury may by order made by statutory instrument direct that subsection (3) above shall not apply in relation to any direction under subsection (2) above which is given during a specified period not exceeding two years beginning with the day on which the order is made.

(7) A draft of any statutory instrument containing an order under subsection (6) above shall be laid before Parliament.

(8) In the application of subsection (3) above in relation to a direction given during a period of two years beginning with the day on which this Act is passed, " the former limit " means £13,500 million.

1954 c. 12.

(9) Section 2 of the Currency and Bank Notes Act 1954 (which is superseded by this section) shall cease to have effect.

Writing off unpresented bank notes which have ceased to be legal tender.

3.—(1) This section applies to bank notes which, by virtue of section 1(5) of the Currency and Bank Notes Act 1954, have ceased to be legal tender and have not been legal tender for ten years.

(2) Where any bank notes to which this section applies have not been presented for payment, the Bank may write off the amount of the notes from the total amount of notes issued from the issue department of the Bank.

(3) Where any amount is written off under this section—

(*a*) the amount so written off shall be deducted from the amount included in the next weekly account rendered by the Bank under section 6 of the Bank Charter Act

1844 c. 32.

1844 as the amount of bank notes issued by the issue department of the Bank; and

(b) a return of the amount so written off shall be forthwith sent to the Treasury who shall lay a copy of the return before each House of Parliament.

(4) No writing off of an amount under this section shall affect the liability of the Bank to pay any bank note which was included in that amount.

(5) Section 6 of the Bank Act 1892 (which is superseded by this section) shall cease to have effect. 1892 c. 48.

(6) In section 6 of the Currency and Bank Notes Act 1928 (which directs the payment to the Treasury of the annual profits of the issue department of the Bank including the amount of notes written off less the amount of those presented for payment) after the words "section six of the Bank Act 1892, as amended by this Act" there shall be inserted the words "or under section 3 of the Currency Act 1983". 1928 c. 13.

Supplementary

Short title, interpretation, repeals and extent.

4.—(1) This Act may be cited as the Currency Act 1983.

(2) In this Act—

"the Bank" means the Bank of England; and

"bank notes" means notes of the Bank payable to bearer on demand.

(3) The enactments mentioned in the Schedule to this Act (which include a spent provision) are hereby repealed to the extent specified in the third column of that Schedule.

(4) This Act extends to Northern Ireland.

Section 4.

SCHEDULE

ENACTMENTS REPEALED

Chapter	Short title	Extent of repeal
55 & 56 Vict. c. 48.	The Bank Act 1892.	Section 6.
18 & 19 Geo. 5. c. 13.	The Currency and Bank Notes Act 1928.	Section 5. Section 7.
2 & 3 Eliz. 2. c. 12.	The Currency and Bank Notes Act 1954.	Section 2. In section 3, the definitions of " bullion " and " coin ".
1971 c. 24.	The Coinage Act 1971.	In section 3, in paragraph (*d*), the words from " other than " to the end and, in paragraph (*f*), the words from " and be legal tender " to the end. In Schedule 1, Part II.

Transport Act 1983

1983 CHAPTER 10

An Act to make further provision with respect to the finances and management of certain Transport Executives; and to reduce the indebtedness of the National Dock Labour Board in respect of money borrowed from the Secretary of State for financing severance payments to registered dock workers. [28th March 1983]

BE IT ENACTED by the Queen's most Excellent Majesty, by and with the advice and consent of the Lords Spiritual and Temporal, and Commons, in this present Parliament assembled, and by the authority of the same, as follows:—

PART I

TRANSPORT EXECUTIVES

Preliminary

1. In this Part of this Act— Interpretation. of Part I.

" the Act of 1968 " means the Transport Act 1968 ; 1968 c. 73.

" the Act of 1969 " means the Transport (London) Act 1969 ; 1969 c. 35.

" Executive " means—

(*a*) the Passenger Transport Executive for an area which is coterminous with a metropolitan county; and

(*b*) the London Transport Executive ;

PART I

" Authority " means—

(*a*) in relation to any such Passenger Transport Executive, the county council which is the Passenger Transport Authority for the Executive's area ; and

(*b*) in relation to the London Transport Executive, the Greater London Council ;

" revenue grants " means grants under section 13 of the Act of 1968 or section 3(1)(*a*) of the Act of 1969 in aid of the revenues of an Executive (including grants made under those provisions in respect of reductions in fares for children) and accordingly references to the revenues of an Executive include references to sums received by way of revenue grants ;

" year " means a period of twelve months beginning with 1st April.

Financial provisions

Financial duty of Executives.

2.—(1) An Executive shall so perform their functions as to ensure so far as practicable that the combined revenues of the Executive and any subsidiaries of theirs for any accounting period are not less than sufficient to meet their combined charges properly chargeable to revenue account in that period.

(2) If in the case of any accounting period it is not practicable for an Executive to ensure that those revenues are sufficient to meet those charges, subsection (1) above shall have effect in relation to the next following accounting period as if the combined charges there referred to included an amount equal to the amount of the deficit.

(3) For the purposes of this section there shall be disregarded any deficit or potential deficit in an accounting period to the extent to which it is or is to be covered by the appropriation of any reserves of the Executive available for the purpose if the appropriation of those reserves for that purpose has been proposed by the Executive in a plan prepared by them under section 3 below and approved by the Authority under section 4 below.

(4) An Authority in exercising or performing any of their functions under this Part of this Act, under Part II of the Act of 1968 or under the Act of 1969 shall have regard to the duty imposed on an Executive by this section.

1962 c. 46.

(5) In this section " subsidiary " has the meaning given by section 92(1) of the Transport Act 1962, and the provisions of section 51(5) of the Act of 1968 (joint subsidiaries) so far as applying to the London Transport Executive shall accordingly be disregarded.

Part I

Preparation and submission of financial plans.

3.—(1) It shall be the duty of an Executive in each year to prepare in accordance with this section and submit to the Authority a plan containing their proposals for the next three years (" the relevant period ") with respect to—

(*a*) the general level of transport services and facilities to be provided by them or, by agreement with them, by other persons ; and

(*b*) the general level and structure of the fares to be charged for those services, and the general level of charges to be made for those facilities, so far as they are to be charged, made or otherwise determined by the Executive.

(2) The proposals shall be such as to enable the Executive to discharge their duty under section 2 above in the relevant period ; and the plan shall contain particulars of the Executive's financial position and their financial prospects for that period together with an estimate of what would be their annual revenue and expenditure if the proposals were implemented.

(3) To the extent to which the Executive consider it necessary for the discharge of their general duty under section 9(3) of the Act of 1968 or section 5(1) of the Act of 1969, the plan may be formulated on the assumption that the Authority will in the relevant period make revenue grants of such amounts as the Executive may determine ; but if the plan is formulated on that assumption it shall be accompanied by particulars showing the benefits expected to accrue from the grants.

(4) The plan shall be accompanied by estimates of—

(*a*) the cost to the Executive of providing, or arranging the provision of, the services and facilities described in the proposals ;

(*b*) the level of demand for those services and facilities ; and

(*c*) the benefits to potential users of those services and facilities.

(5) In preparing the plan the Executive shall take into account any advice given by the Secretary of State as to the amounts that it would be appropriate for the Executive to determine under subsection (3) above and the method of determining the benefits referred to in that subsection, and generally as to the form and contents of the plan ; and in preparing the estimates referred to in subsection (4) above the Executive shall take into account any advice given by him as to the method of determining the matters referred to in paragraphs (*a*) to (*c*) of that subsection.

PART I

Approval of financial plans and determination of revenue grants.

4.—(1) An Authority shall in each year approve with or without modification the plan submitted to them in that year under section 3 above and, in the light of the provisions of the plan as so approved, determine the amount of the revenue grants, if any, to be made by them to the Executive in the first year of the relevant period.

(2) For the purposes of this section the Authority may require the Executive to supply them with—

(*a*) alternative proposals based on different levels of services, facilities, fares or other charges, or on the assumption that the Authority will in the relevant period make revenue grants of such amounts as the Authority may specify;

(*b*) estimates of the extent to which particular benefits, specified by the Authority, would accrue to the public at large, or to any section of the public so specified, as a result of the making of any such grants as are mentioned in section 3(3) or (as the case may be) paragraph (*a*) above; and

(*c*) such other information as the Authority may specify, including information as to the cost of providing, or arranging the provision by other persons of, services and facilities additional to those proposed in the plan.

(3) In determining whether to approve a plan in a form which would involve the making by the Authority of revenue grants in the relevant period the Authority shall have particular regard to—

(*a*) the matters referred to in paragraphs (*a*) to (*c*) of subsection (4) of section 3 above;

(*b*) any advice given by the Secretary of State under subsection (5) of that section; and

(*c*) the need to achieve a proper balance between the interests of the ratepayers in their area and the interests of transport users.

(4) Before approving a plan in such a form and making any such determination as is mentioned in subsection (1) above the Authority shall—

(*a*) submit the plan and a statement of their proposed determination to the Secretary of State; and

(*b*) take into account the guidance given by him under subsection (5) below.

(5) Where a plan is submitted to the Secretary of State under subsection (4) above he shall give the Authority guidance as to the maximum amount of the revenue grants, if any, which it

would in his opinion be appropriate for the Authority to make in the year in question and, if the amount proposed by them would be greater than that amount, he may indicate to the Authority the respects in which the plan or any modification proposed by them would need to be altered to take account of his guidance.

(6) The matters by reference to which the guidance of the Secretary of State under subsection (5) above may be given shall include—

- (*a*) what appears to him to be the appropriate national level of expenditure by Authorities on revenue grants ;
- (*b*) the benefits which would result from the making of such grants ; and
- (*c*) the levels of present and past expenditure by the Authority on such grants ;

and in giving the guidance the Secretary of State shall have regard to the general duty of the Authority and the Executive under section 9(3) of the Act of 1968 or sections 1 and 5(1) of the Act of 1969, as the case may be.

Payment of revenue grants.

5.—(1) An Authority shall not in any year make any revenue grant to an Executive except in accordance with a determination made by the Authority under section 4(1) above.

(2) To the extent to which the amount of the revenue grants made in any year by an Authority in accordance with any such determination does not exceed the amount specified in guidance given by the Secretary of State under section 4(5) above in relation to that determination, the making of those grants shall, without prejudice to any other proper exercise of the power of the Authority to make revenue grants, be regarded for all purposes as a proper exercise of that power.

Supplementary provisions.

6.—(1) An Executive shall supply the Secretary of State with such information as he may require for the purpose of giving advice under subsection (5) of section 3 above and shall, before preparing any plan under that section, consult the Authority.

(2) An Executive shall, when submitting any plan or supplying any information to an Authority under that section or section 4 above, send a copy of the plan or information to the Secretary of State.

(3) Where the Secretary of State gives an Executive any advice under section 3(5) above he shall communicate that advice to the Authority.

(4) An Authority shall supply the Secretary of State with such information as he may require for the purpose of giving guidance under section 4(5) above.

PART I

(5) Where an Executive's plan is approved by an Authority under section 4 above the Authority shall inform the Executive in writing—

(*a*) of their approval and of any modifications made by them in the plan as approved ; and

(*b*) of any determination made by them under subsection (1) of that section.

(6) The general level and structure of fares and the general level of charges specified in a plan approved by an Authority under section 4 above shall be treated—

(*a*) for the purposes of section 15(2)(*a*) of the Act of 1968 ; and

(*b*) except as respects fares for such journeys as are mentioned in subsection (5) of section 11 of the Act of 1969, for the purposes of subsection (2)(*d*) of that section,

as having been approved by the Authority under that provision.

(7) Before giving or withholding any approval required by section 15(2)(*a*) of the Act of 1968 or section 11(2)(*d*) of the Act of 1969 the Authority shall have regard in particular to the extent to which their decision will affect the amount of revenue grants that will be needed to enable the Executive to comply with their duty under section 2 above and to the need to achieve a proper balance between the interests of the ratepayers in their area and the interests of transport users.

Management

Review of managerial organisation.

7.—(1) An Authority shall, whenever the Secretary of State so requires, cause a review to be made of the organisation of the Executive for the purpose of determining whether, in the interests of managing the activities of the Executive in the most efficient manner, any particular activities of the Executive should be managed as separate units with separate accounts.

(2) The Authority shall inform the Executive in writing of the results of any such review and of the Authority's conclusions arising from it ; and the report under section 16 of the Act of 1968 or section 15 of the Act of 1969 for the accounting period of the Executive in which they are so informed shall contain a statement showing the steps they have taken or propose to take in the light of the Authority's conclusions.

(3) Nothing in this section affects the power of an Authority to cause reviews to be made of the organisation of an Executive under section 15A(3) of the Act of 1968 or section 11(6) of the Act of 1969.

PART I

Tenders for carrying on activities of Executives.

8.—(1) An Executive shall, in the case of such activities carried on by the Executive as they may determine to be appropriate, invite other persons to submit tenders to carry on those activities for such period and on such basis as the Executive may specify in the invitation to tender.

(2) If the Authority so direct, the Executive shall invite tenders to carry on, for such period and on such basis as may be specified in the direction, such activities or descriptions of activities carried on by the Executive as may be so specified.

(3) An Executive shall accept a tender invited pursuant to this section if it appears to them that to do so would result in the relevant activities being carried on in a satisfactory manner and at less cost to them than if they were to continue to carry on those activities themselves.

(4) Any direction under subsection (2) above shall be in writing and it shall be the duty of the Executive to give effect to it.

(5) Every report under section 16 of the Act of 1968 or section 15 of the Act of 1969 for an accounting period of an Executive shall contain a statement showing the steps which the Executive have taken in that period to comply with the requirements of subsections (1) and (2) above.

(6) For the purposes of this section the London Transport Executive shall, in connection with the acceptance of any tender submitted to them pursuant to this section, have the same powers as are conferred on a Passenger Transport Executive by section 10(1)(xv) and (xvi) of the Act of 1968 (powers in connection with agreements for the carrying on of activities by other persons), the reference to the approval of a Passenger Transport Authority being construed as a reference to the written approval of the Greater London Council.

Supplementary

Repeals and minor amendments.

9.—(1) The enactments mentioned in the Schedule to this Act are hereby repealed to the extent specified in the third column of that Schedule.

(2) In relation to a passenger transport area which is coterminous with a metropolitan county, Part II of the Act of 1968 shall have effect with the omission of the following provisions, namely—

(*a*) in section 11, subsection (1);

(*b*) in section 13, subsection (3); and

(*c*) in section 15, in subsection (2) the words following paragraph (*b*), and subsections (3) and (4).

PART I

(3) In section 15(5) of the Act of 1968 (expenditure by an Authority in performing their functions) the reference to Part II of that Act shall include a reference to this Part of this Act.

(4) In section 7(2) of the Act of 1969 (duty to establish general reserve) for the words "shall establish" there shall be substituted the words "may establish".

(5) In section 14(3) of the Act of 1969 for the words "section 7(6) of this Act" there shall be substituted the words "section 2(4) of the Transport Act 1983".

Commencement of Part I and transitional provisions.

10.—(1) In this Part of this Act—

(*a*) the following provisions shall have effect in relation to any accounting period of an Executive ending after 31st March 1983, namely—

sections 2 and 6(7);

section 9(1) and the Schedule so far as they relate to sections 5 and 7 of the Act of 1969;

section 9(2) except so far as it relates to sections 13(3) and 15(3) of the Act of 1968;

section 9(3) to (5);

(*b*) the following provisions shall come into force on 1st April 1983, namely—

sections 3 and 4;

section 6(1) to (6);

section 9(1) and the Schedule so far as they relate to section 11 of the Act of 1969; and

(*c*) the following provisions shall have effect in relation to any year beginning on or after 1st April 1984, namely—

section 5;

section 9(2) so far as it relates to sections 13(3) and 15(3) of the Act of 1968;

but subject to paragraphs (*a*) to (*c*) above this Part shall come into force on the passing of this Act.

(2) An Authority shall not make any revenue grant in the year beginning on 1st April 1983 except in accordance with a determination made by them after the passing of this Act as to the amount of the revenue grants to be made by them in that year; and no such determination shall be made by an Authority unless they have been given guidance by the Secretary of State in relation to the determination and that guidance is taken into account by them in making the determination.

(3) Sections 4(6) and 5(2) above shall apply in relation to any such guidance and determination as are referred to in subsection

(2) above as they apply in relation to any such guidance and determination as are referred to in those provisions.

(4) For the purposes of section 2 above in its application to an accounting period of an Executive ending before 1st April 1984 there shall be disregarded any deficit or potential deficit to the extent to which it is or is to be covered by the appropriation of any reserves of the Executive available for the purpose if, at any time before or after the passing of this Act but before the Secretary of State gives his guidance to the Authority under subsection (2) above, the Executive have notified the Secretary of State of their intention to appropriate those reserves for that purpose.

PART II

NATIONAL DOCK LABOUR BOARD

Reduction of indebtedness of National Dock Labour Board.

11.—(1) The National Dock Labour Board shall not be liable to repay £23·8 million of the money borrowed by them from the Secretary of State and forming part of the Consolidated Loan of 1st April 1982.

(2) The amount mentioned in subsection (1) above (which was used for financing severance payments to registered dock workers in the ports of London and Liverpool in 1981) shall be taken into account for the purposes of subsection (3) of section 1 of the Ports (Financial Assistance) Act 1981 (overall limit on financial assistance for those ports) as if it were a grant made under subsection (1) of that section and not repaid. 1981 c. 21.

PART III

GENERAL

Short title and extent.

12.—(1) This Act may be cited as the Transport Act 1983.

(2) This Act extends to England and Wales only.

Section 9(1)

SCHEDULE

REPEALS

Chapter	Short title	Extent of repeal
1969 c. 35.	The Transport (London) Act 1969.	In section 5(1) the words " Subject always to the requirements of section 7(3) of this Act ". In section 7, subsections (3) and (6) and in subsection (7) the words " and (3) ". In section 11, in subsection (3) the words following the semicolon and in subsection (5) the words " and (3) ".

Civil Aviation (Eurocontrol) Act 1983

1983 CHAPTER 11

An Act to make further provision with respect to the European Organisation for the Safety of Air Navigation known as Eurocontrol and to amend section 73(4) of the Civil Aviation Act 1982. [11 April 1983]

BE IT ENACTED by the Queen's most Excellent Majesty, by and with the advice and consent of the Lords Spiritual and Temporal, and Commons, in this present Parliament assembled, and by the authority of the same, as follows:—

Enforcement of foreign judgments etc. in respect of route charges.
1982 c. 16.

1. After section 74 of the Civil Aviation Act 1982 (supplementary provision about charges for air navigation services), there shall be inserted the following section:—

" Enforcement of foreign judgments etc. in respect of route charges.

74A.—(1) Subject to the following provisions of this section, where a relevant authority in a Contracting State has made a determination as to whether or not any sum is due to Eurocontrol in respect of air navigation services provided by Eurocontrol or by some other person, that determination shall, in the United Kingdom, be enforceable or, as the case may be, recognised in accordance with the following provisions of this section, but not otherwise.

(2) For the purposes of the enforcement in any part of the United Kingdom of any determination which is enforceable by Eurocontrol under this section, the provisions of sections 2, 3(1) and 5(2) and (3) of the Foreign Judgments (Reciprocal Enforcement) Act 1933 (registration of judgments, rules of

1933 c. 13.

court and powers of court on application to set aside registration) shall apply, with the necessary modifications, in relation to the determination as they apply in relation to a judgment to which Part I of that Act applies; and accordingly, for the purposes of this section, in subsection (2) of section 5 of that Act—

(*a*) the reference to subsection (1) of that section shall have effect as a reference to subsection (7) below; and

(*b*) the reference to an appeal shall include a reference to an application for review of a determination.

(3) On an application for the purpose made by any person against whom a determination registered by virtue of subsection (2) above may be enforced, the registration shall (subject to subsection (7) below) be set aside if the court to which the application to register is made is satisfied—

(*a*) that the determination is not a determination to which this section applies;

(*b*) that the determination was registered in contravention of any provision applied by subsection (2) above; or

(*c*) that, by virtue of any of the following provisions of this section, the determination is not to be enforced in the part of the United Kingdom in which it is sought to enforce it.

(4) Subject to subsection (7) below, a determination in respect of any sum by a relevant authority in a Contracting State shall not under this section be enforced or recognised in a part of the United Kingdom if—

(*a*) that Contracting State is not the country, or one of the countries, in which, under subsection (5) below, proceedings in respect of that sum should have been brought; or

(*b*) the determination is not final; or

(*c*) the determination is manifestly contrary to public policy in the part of the United Kingdom in which it is sought to enforce the determination or, as the case may be, in which recognition of the determination is sought; or (*d*) the person against whom the proceedings resulting in the determination were brought did not (notwithstanding that process may have been duly served on him in the Contracting State in which those proceedings were brought) receive notice of the proceedings in sufficient time to enable him to defend them or, as the case may require, to apply for the proceedings to be reviewed ; or

(*e*) proceedings relating to the same sum have been brought previously, and are pending, in any part of the United Kingdom ; or

(*f*) the determination is incompatible with the judgment of any court in any part of the United Kingdom ; or

(*g*) the determination—

(i) involved the application of rules of private international law to a question concerning the status or legal capacity of natural persons, or concerning rights in property arising out of matrimonial relationships or concerning wills or succession (being rules different from the corresponding rules of private international law applicable in the part of the United Kingdom in which it is sought to enforce the determination, or as the case may be, in which recognition of the determination is sought), and

(ii) was different from the determination which would have been made if those corresponding rules had been applied.

(5) For the purposes of this section proceedings in respect of a sum payable to Eurocontrol must be brought against the person liable to pay the sum—

(*a*) in the Contracting State (if any) in which that person's residence or, as the case may be, his registered office is situated ;

(*b*) if that person's residence or, as the case may be, his registered office is not situated in a Contracting State, in any Contracting State in which he has a place of business ;

(*c*) if that person's residence or, as the case may be, his registered office is not situated in a Contracting State and he has no place of business in any Contracting State, in any Contracting State in which he has assets ;

(*d*) if that person's residence or, as the case may be, his registered office is not situated in a Contracting State and he has neither a place of business nor any assets in any Contracting State, in the country in which Eurocontrol for the time being has its headquarters.

(6) For the purposes of this section a determination by a relevant authority in a Contracting State shall be final if neither an appeal from nor an application for review of that determination is pending in that State and it is not possible, for any of the following reasons, for such an appeal to be brought or such an application to be made, that is to say—

(*a*) no appeal or review is provided for in that State in respect of the determination, being a determination made by a court or tribunal;

(*b*) the time within which an appeal must be brought, or an application for review must be made, has expired;

(*c*) an appeal which has been brought, or an application for review which has been made, has been withdrawn; or

(*d*) the determination has been confirmed by, or made in pursuance of a direction contained in, a determination which was made by a relevant authority and is itself final.

(7) If, on an application to set aside the registration by virtue of subsection (2) above of any determination, the applicant satisfies the court to which the application to register is made that the determination is not final, the court may, on such terms as it may think fit, either—

(*a*) set aside the registration; or

(*b*) adjourn the application to set aside the registration until such time as the determination has become final,

but nothing in this section shall require that court to take either of these courses where there is no other ground for setting aside the registration and the court is not satisfied that the applicant intends to continue with any appeal or application for review which is pending or, as the case may be, to bring any appeal or make any such application which it is possible for him to bring or make in respect of the determination.

(8) In this section—

'Contracting State' means a country designated in an Order in Council which has been laid before Parliament as a party to the Multilateral Agreement relating to Route Charges signed at Brussels on 12th February 1981 at the Diplomatic Conference on the Protocol amending the Eurocontrol International Convention relating to Co-operation for the Safety of Air Navigation of 13th December 1960;

'relevant authority', in relation to a Contracting State, means—

(*a*) any court or tribunal which, under the law of the State, has jurisdiction to determine questions as to whether or not a sum is due to Eurocontrol in respect of air navigation services provided by Eurocontrol or some other person;

(*b*) any administrative authority which, under that law, has jurisdiction to make, or is otherwise authorised to make, determinations in respect of such questions, being determinations which in that State are subject to appeal to, or review by, a court or tribunal;

(*c*) any court or tribunal which, under that law, has jurisdiction to determine any appeal from, or carry out any review of, a determination made in respect of any such question by another relevant authority.

(9) This section shall not affect the enforceability or recognition of any determination made before the coming into force of section 1 of the Civil Aviation (Eurocontrol) Act 1983."

Immunities and privileges of Eurocontrol.

2.—(1) Schedule 4 to the Civil Aviation Act 1982 (which makes provision in relation to the organisation known as Eurocontrol) shall be amended as follows.

1982 c. 16.

(2) In paragraph 1(3) (which includes provision according Eurocontrol the same inviolability of archives and premises as an envoy of a foreign sovereign Power accredited to Her Majesty), for the words from " any rule " to " Her Majesty " there shall be substituted the words " the inviolability which, in accordance

with the 1961 Convention Articles, is accorded in respect of the official archives and premises of a diplomatic mission ".

(3) In paragraph 1(4) (which allows constables and other specified persons in certain cases to have access to the premises of Eurocontrol and to inspect its documents) after the word " document " there shall be inserted the words " where the Director-General of the Agency is given advance notice of the exercise of the power conferred by this sub-paragraph and the access or inspection is ".

(4) After paragraph 1(4) there shall be inserted the following sub-paragraphs:—

" (4A) Without prejudice to the preceding provisions of this paragraph, the property and assets of Eurocontrol shall be immune from the exercise by any person of any right or power without the leave of a court to seize or otherwise interfere with such property or assets.

(4B) No court or tribunal in the United Kingdom shall have jurisdiction in respect of any matter involving Eurocontrol and any of its officers or servants, being a matter which by virtue of any international agreement to which the United Kingdom is a party is within the exclusive jurisdiction of the Administrative Tribunal of the International Labour Organisation.

(4C) For the purposes of sub-paragraph (4B) above, a certificate of the Secretary of State that any matter is or is not, as mentioned in that sub-paragraph, within the exclusive jurisdiction of the Administrative Tribunal of the International Labour Organisation shall be conclusive of what is certified.".

(5) In paragraph 1(5) (interpretation of paragraph 1), after the definition of " installations " there shall be inserted the following definition:—

" ' the 1961 Convention Articles ' means the Articles (being certain Articles of the Convention on Diplomatic Relations signed in 1961) which are set out in Schedule 1 to the Diplomatic Privileges Act 1964 ; ".

1964 c. 81.

(6) In sub-paragraph (1) of paragraph 3 (which confers jurisdiction on United Kingdom courts in respect of claims against Eurocontrol), after the words " Subject to " there shall be inserted the words " paragraph 1 above and ".

Minor amendments. 1982 c. 16.

3.—(1) In section 24 of the Civil Aviation Act 1982, in the definition of " the Eurocontrol Convention ", for the words from " and includes any amendment " onwards there shall be substituted the words " as from time to time amended with the agreement of the contracting parties thereto ".

(2) In subsection (4) of section 73 of that Act (under which charges for air navigation services may be imposed on the operator of an aircraft whether or not the aircraft is registered in the United Kingdom and whether or not the services are provided to or from a place in the United Kingdom), after the word " operator " there shall be inserted the words " or owner " ; and that subsection and, in relation to any time before the coming into force of that Act, subsection (3) of section 15 of the Civil Aviation Act 1968 (so far as re-enacted in the said subsection (4)) shall be deemed always to have had effect with that amendment or, as the case may be, with a corresponding amendment. 1968 c. 61.

Short title, commencement and extent.

4.—(1) This Act may be cited as the Civil Aviation (Eurocontrol) Act 1983.

(2) This Act shall come into force on such day as the Secretary of State may by order made by statutory instrument appoint, and different days may be so appointed for different provisions or for different purposes of the same provision.

(3) The power conferred by section 108(1) of the Civil Aviation Act 1982 to extend provisions of that Act to a place outside the United Kingdom includes, in the case of a provision amended by this Act, power so to extend that provision with the amendments made by this Act and includes power so to extend the section inserted in that Act by section 1 above. 1982 c. 16.

(4) This Act extends to Northern Ireland.

Divorce Jurisdiction, Court Fees and Legal Aid (Scotland) Act 1983

1983 CHAPTER 12

An Act to extend the jurisdiction of sheriffs in Scotland in relation to actions for divorce; to make provision as regards the sufficiency of evidence in certain actions for divorce in Scotland; to make new provision in Scotland as to the fees and outlays of counsel and solicitors in relation both to legal aid, and to the giving of legal advice and assistance under the Legal Advice and Assistance Act 1972; to make new provision in relation to the regulation of fees payable in the Scottish courts; and for connected purposes.

[11th April 1983]

BE IT ENACTED by the Queen's most Excellent Majesty, by and with the advice and consent of the Lords Spiritual and Temporal, and Commons, in this present Parliament assembled, and by the authority of the same, as follows:—

PART I

JURISDICTION AND EVIDENCE IN DIVORCE ACTIONS

Sheriffs to have jurisdiction in respect of actions for divorce. 1907 c. 51.

1. In section 5 of the Sheriff Courts (Scotland) Act 1907 (which relates to the jurisdiction of sheriffs), after paragraph (2A) there shall be inserted—

" (2B) Actions for divorce ".

PART I

Rule requiring corroboration not to apply in certain undefended actions for divorce.

2.—(1) Any rule of law whereby in any proceedings evidence tending to establish any fact, unless it is corroborated by other evidence, is not to be taken as sufficient proof of that fact shall cease to have effect in relation to any action to which this section applies, and, accordingly, in any such action the court shall be entitled, if they are satisfied that any fact has been established by evidence which has been given in that action, to find that fact proved by that evidence notwithstanding that the evidence is not corroborated.

(2) This section applies to such class or classes of undefended actions for divorce as the Lord Advocate may by order prescribe.

(3) In this section " undefended action for divorce " means an action for divorce in which the defender has not entered appearance or having entered appearance, has not lodged defences or has withdrawn them.

(4) An order under subsection (2) above shall be made by statutory instrument subject to annulment in pursuance of a resolution of either House of Parliament.

PART II

FEES AND OUTLAYS IN RELATION TO LEGAL AID

Power of Secretary of State to make provision about fees etc. in relation to legal aid.

1967 c. 43.

3. After section 14 of the Legal Aid (Scotland) Act 1967 there shall be inserted the following section—

" Fees and outlays of counsel and solicitors.

14A. In relation to legal aid, the Secretary of State may by regulations make such provision as seems to him appropriate in respect of the fees and outlays of counsel and solicitors, and, in particular, any such regulations may—

(*a*) prescribe, either specifically or otherwise, the work in respect of which fees may be charged ;

(*b*) prescribe, either specifically or otherwise, rates or scales of payment of fees and outlays allowable and the conditions under which such fees and outlays may be allowed ;

(*c*) provide for the assessment and taxation of fees and outlays, and for the review of any such assessment or taxation, either by the Secretary of State or by any other person ;

PART II

(*d*) prescribe general principles in accordance with which those who may be responsible in that regard should conduct any such assessment, taxation or review;

(*e*) prescribe, or provide for the prescription of, the forms to be used for the purposes of any regulations made under this section;

(*f*) make different provision for different cases; and

(*g*) include such supplementary, incidental and procedural provision as the Secretary of State thinks fit.

PART III

COURT FEES

Power of Secretary of State to regulate court fees.

1895 c. 14.

4. For section 2 of the Courts of Law Fees (Scotland) Act 1895 (which enables the High Court of Justiciary and the Court of Session to regulate court fees) there shall be substituted the following section—

"Power of Secretary of State to regulate court fees.

2.—(1) The Secretary of State may, with the concurrence of the Treasury, by order regulate the fees payable—

(*a*) to any officer of any office or department connected with the Scottish courts the expenses of which are paid wholly or partly out of the Consolidated Fund or out of moneys provided by Parliament; and

(*b*) to the district court.

(2) An order under subsection (1) above—

(*a*) may provide as to the times when, places where and persons to whom fees payable by virtue of this section are payable;

(*b*) may, in relation to any such fees, provide—

(i) for exemption from the requirement to pay them;

(ii) for their remission;

(iii) for their modification; and

(iv) as to the circumstances in which and persons by whom such exemptions, remissions and modifications may be made; and

PART III

(c) may make different provision in relation to—

(i) different courts; and

(ii) different cases or classes of case.

(3) In subsection (1) above, " the Scottish courts " means—

(*a*) the Court of Session;

(*b*) the High Court of Justiciary;

(*c*) the sheriff court;

(*d*) the court of commissioners for teinds (provision for which is made in section 8 of the Court of Session Act 1839); 1839 c. 36.

(*e*) the court for hearing appeals under subsection (8)(*b*) of section 45 of the Representation of the People Act 1949 (appeals relating to the registration of electors); 1949 c. 68.

(*f*) the election court constituted under section 110 of the said Act of 1949;

(*g*) the lands valuation appeal court (provision for which is made in section 7 of the Valuation of Lands (Scotland) Amendment Act 1879); and 1879 c. 42.

(*h*) any other court specified as a Scottish court for the purposes of this section in an order made by the Secretary of State.

(4) An order under subsection (1) or (3)(*h*) above shall be made by statutory instrument subject to annulment in pursuance of a resolution of either House of Parliament."

PART IV

SUPPLEMENTAL

Finance.

5. There shall be paid out of moneys provided by Parliament any increase in moneys so payable under any other Act which is attributable to the provisions of this Act.

Minor and consequential amendments and repeals.

6.—(1) The enactments specified in Schedule 1 to this Act shall have effect subject to the amendments specified in that Schedule, being minor amendments and amendments consequential upon the provisions of this Act.

(2) The enactments specified in Schedule 2 to this Act are repealed to the extent specified in the third column of that Schedule.

PART IV

Citation, commencement and extent.

7.—(1) This Act may be cited as the Divorce Jurisdiction, Court Fees and Legal Aid (Scotland) Act 1983.

(2) The following provisions of this Act, that is to say, section 2, this section, and paragraph 2 of Schedule 1 (together with so much of section 6(1) above as relates to that paragraph) shall come into force at the end of the period of two months beginning with the day on which it is passed.

(3) The remaining provisions of this Act shall come into force on such day as the Secretary of State may by order made by statutory instrument appoint and different days may be appointed for different provisions or for different purposes of the same provision.

(4) This Act shall extend to Scotland only.

SCHEDULES

SCHEDULE 1

Section 6 (1).

Minor and Consequential Amendments

The Court of Session Act 1830 c. 69

1. In section 33 (which provides for the Court of Session to have exclusive jurisdiction in respect of certain consistorial actions), for the word "All" there shall be substituted the words "Subject to section 5(2B) of the Sheriff Courts (Scotland) Act 1907, all". 1907 c. 51.

2. In section 36 (which makes provision as to the sufficiency of evidence in consistorial actions)—

(*a*) at the beginning there shall be inserted the words "Subject to section 2 of the Divorce Jurisdiction, Court Fees and Legal Aid (Scotland) Act 1983," and

(*b*) after the word "enumerated" there shall be inserted the words "(including any actions for divorce brought in the sheriff court)".

The Conjugal Rights (Scotland) Amendment Act 1861 c. 86

3. In section 8 (which empowers the Lord Advocate to appear in actions for declarator of nullity of marriage and divorce), after the word "divorce", where it first appears, there shall be inserted the words ", whether (in the case of actions for divorce) in the Court of Session or in the sheriff court".

4. In section 9 (which empowers the Court to make provision for the children of the marriage in any action for separation or divorce), after the word "divorce" there shall be inserted the words ", whether (in the case of actions for divorce) in the Court of Session or in the sheriff court,".

5. In section 10 (which relates to the service of summonses in consistorial actions), after the word "action" where it first appears, there shall be inserted the words "in the Court of Session".

The Crofters Holdings (Scotland) Act 1886 c. 29

6. At the end of section 29 (which provides, among other things, for the fixing of scales of costs and fees, and for their taxation) there shall be added the following—

"Provided that no scale of costs and fees fixed by the Commission, and no regulations made by them as to the taxation of such costs and fees, shall apply in respect of any of the matters which the Secretary of State may regulate under or by virtue of section 14A of the Legal Aid (Scotland) Act 1967". 1967 c. 43.

The Sheriff Courts (Scotland) Act 1907 c. 51

7. In section 40 (which relates to the power of the Court of Session to regulate fees etc.), after the word "agents" there shall be

inserted the words "(other than such of the fees of agents as the Secretary of State may regulate under or by virtue of section 14A
1967 c. 43. of the Legal Aid (Scotland) Act 1967)".

The Administration of Justice (Scotland) Act 1933 c. 41

8. In paragraph (*g*) of section 16 (which relates to the power of the Court of Session to regulate procedure etc. by Act of Sederunt), after the word "fees" there shall be inserted the words "(other than such fees as the Secretary of State may regulate under or by virtue of section 14A of the Legal Aid (Scotland) Act 1967)".

The Juries Act 1949 c. 27

9. In subsection (1) of section 26 (which provides for fees payable by a party applying for a jury trial in a civil cause)—

(*a*) for the words "Act of Sederunt", where they appear for the first time, there shall be substituted the words "an order made by the Secretary of State";

(*b*) after the words "as may be", where they appear for the second time, there shall be inserted the word "so";

(*c*) the words "by Act of Sederunt", where they appear for the second time, shall cease to have effect.

The Summary Jurisdiction (Scotland) Act 1954 c. 48

10. In subsection (3) of section 76 (which relates to the regulation of fees by the High Court of Justiciary), for the words "affect the regulations enacted" there shall be substituted the words "empower the High Court to make any regulation which the Secretary of State is empowered to make".

The Legal Aid (Scotland) Act 1967 c. 43

11. In subsection (7) of section 6 (which relates to the payment of solicitors and counsel appearing for persons receiving legal aid), for the words "not exceed those allowed under Schedule 2 to" there shall be substituted the words "be determined in accordance with regulations made under section 14A of".

The Sheriff Courts (Scotland) Act 1971 c. 58

12. In subsection (2A) of section 37 (which relates to remits from the sheriff court to the Court of Session), after the words "sheriff court" there shall be inserted the words ", being an action for divorce or an action".

The Matrimonial Proceedings (Polygamous Marriages) Act 1972 c. 38

13. In subsection (2)(*c*) of section 2 (which makes provision for matrimonial relief and declarations as to validity in respect of polygamous marriages in relation to Scotland), for the words "section 5 of
1938 c. 50. the Divorce (Scotland) Act 1938" there shall be substituted the words
1977 c. 27. "section 1 of the Presumption of Death (Scotland) Act 1977".

The Legal Advice and Assistance Act 1972 c. 50

14. In subsection (3) of section 3 (which relates to the financial limit on the prospective cost of advice and assistance),—

(*a*) for the word " expenses ", in both places where it occurs, there shall be substituted the word " outlays " ;

(*b*) for the word " disbursements ", wherever it occurs, there shall be substituted the word " outlays " ;

(*c*) the words " charges or ", in both places where they occur, shall cease to have effect ; and

(*d*) for the words " fees payable to ", in both places where they occur, there shall be substituted the words " the fees and outlays of ".

15. In section 4 (which relates to contributions from persons receiving advice or assistance), for the words " charge or fee " and the words " charges or fees " there shall be substituted the words " fees or outlays ".

16. In section 5 (which relates to the payment of charges or fees otherwise than through the client's contribution)—

(*a*) for the words " charges or fees ", wherever they occur, there shall be substituted the words " fees or outlays " ;

(*b*) subsection (6) shall cease to have effect.

17. In section 6 (which provides for certain provisions of the Legal Aid (Scotland) Act 1967 to have effect in relation to legal advice and assistance as they have effect in relation to legal aid)— 1967 c. 43.

(*a*) in subsection (1)(*b*), for the word " 15 " there shall be substituted the words " 14A " ;

(*b*) in subsection (3), before the words " and section 15 " there shall be inserted the words " , 14A ".

The Domicile and Matrimonial Proceedings Act 1973 c. 45

18. In section 8 (which relates to the jurisdiction of the sheriff court),—

(*a*) in subsection (1), at the end there shall be added the words " or divorce " ;

(*b*) in subsection (2) of the said section, after the word " separation " there shall be inserted the words " or divorce " ;

(*c*) in subsection (3) of the said section, after the word " separation " there shall be inserted the words " or divorce " ; and

(*d*) in subsection (4) of the said section, after the word " separation " there shall be inserted the words " or divorce ".

19. In paragraph 8 of Schedule 3 (which relates to the sisting of consistorial actions)—

(*a*) after the words " in the Court of Session " there shall be inserted the words " or in the sheriff court " ;

(*b*) after the word " Court " where it appears for the second time there shall be inserted the word " concerned ".

20. In paragraph 9(3) of the said Schedule the words " on the Court of Session " shall cease to have effect.

The Divorce (Scotland) Act 1976 c. 39

21. In subsection (1)(ii) of section 6 (which empowers the court to make orders relating to settlements and other dealings), for the words " out of the jurisdiction of the court " there shall be substituted the words " furth of Scotland ".

22. In section 13(1) (which defines terms used in the Act), in the definition of " court " for the words from " — (*a*) " to " require " there shall be substituted the words ", in relation to any action, the Court of Session or the sheriff court, as the case may require.".

The Matrimonial Homes (Family Protection) (Scotland) Act 1981 c. 59

23. In subsection (2) of section 13 (which relates to the transfer of a tenancy on the granting of a decree of divorce or nullity of marriage), for the words from the beginning to " marriage," there shall be substituted the words " The Court of Session or a sheriff, in granting decree in an action for divorce, and the Court of Session, in granting decree in an action for nullity of marriage, may ".

The Civil Jurisdiction and Judgments Act 1982 c. 27

1907 c. 51. 24. In Schedule 14 (repeals) in the entry relating to the Sheriff Courts (Scotland) Act 1907, for the words " the first " Provided " " there shall be substituted the words " " Provided that actions " ".

Section 6 (2).

SCHEDULE 2

ENACTMENTS REPEALED

Chapter	Short title	Extent of repeal
1 & 2 Geo. 4. c. 38.	The Court of Session Act 1821.	Section 31.
7 Edw. 7. c. 51.	The Sheriff Courts (Scotland) Act 1907.	In section 40, the words from " and, with the " to " fees of court ".
15 & 16 Geo. 5. c. 33.	The Church of Scotland (Property and Endowments) Act 1925.	In section 11(3), the words from " The Court of Session " to " the said fees.".
1 & 2 Geo. 6. c. 50.	The Divorce (Scotland) Act 1938.	The whole Act.
12 & 13 Geo. 6. c. 27.	The Juries Act 1949.	In section 26(1), the words " by Act of Sederunt " where they appear for the second time.
1967 c. 43.	The Legal Aid (Scotland) Act 1967.	Section 16(1)(*b*)(i),(2) and (4), and Schedule 2.
1972 c. 50.	The Legal Advice and Assistance Act 1972.	In section 3(3) the words " charges or " in both places where they occur. Section 5(6).
1973 c. 45.	The Domicile and Matrimonial Proceedings Act 1973.	In Schedule 3, in paragraph 9(3) the words " on the Court of Session ".

Merchant Shipping Act 1983

1983 CHAPTER 13

An Act to make further provision in respect of the registration of small ships and the appointment of registrars at ports. [11th April 1983]

BE IT ENACTED by the Queen's most Excellent Majesty, by and with the advice and consent of the Lords Spiritual and Temporal, and Commons, in this present Parliament assembled, and by the authority of the same, as follows:—

Measurement for length

Measurement of small ships for length instead of tonnage.

1.—(1) This section applies to any small ship of a class prescribed by regulations made by the Secretary of State.

(2) Where a ship to which this section applies is to be registered under Part I of the 1894 Act in the United Kingdom, the ship may, instead of having her tonnage ascertained in accordance with the tonnage regulations of that Act, be measured for length in accordance with regulations under this section.

(3) If the ship is so measured, the requirements of that Act preliminary to registry shall have effect with the following modifications—

(*a*) the certificate required by section 6 to be granted on survey must specify the ship's length instead of her tonnage;

(*b*) so much of section 7(1)(*b*) as requires the number denoting her registered tonnage to be cut in on her main beam does not apply; and (*c*) the builder's certificate produced under section 10(1)(*a*) must contain a true account of the length of the ship, as estimated by him.

(4) In this Act, " registered ship measured for length " means a ship registered under Part I of the 1894 Act in the United Kingdom the registered particulars of which do not include particulars relating to her tonnage.

(5) Regulations under this section may provide for the survey and measurement for length of ships to which this section applies to be undertaken, in such circumstances as may be specified in the regulations and notwithstanding sections 6 and 86 of that Act, by persons appointed by such organisations as may be authorised in that behalf by the Secretary of State.

(6) Regulations under this section may, in the case of ships measured for length in accordance with the regulations, provide—

(*a*) for the marking of ships with their length ; and

(*b*) for the alteration of the particulars relating to their length ;

and the references in section 7(5) of the 1894 Act (offence of neglecting to mark a ship as required by that section) to the requirements of that section as to the marking of ships include a reference to the requirements of regulations under this section for the marking of ships with their length.

(7) Where a ship to which this section applies is registered under Part I of the 1894 Act in the United Kingdom and is required to be remeasured by virtue of section 82 of that Act (alteration in tonnage of ship or error in computing it) then, instead of having her tonnage determined and registered, she may be measured for length in accordance with regulations under this section and, if she is so measured, her length shall be registered instead of her tonnage.

(8) Regulations under this section—

(*a*) may provide for the payment of fees in connection with the measurement of ships for length or registered ships measured for length, being fees determined with the approval of the Treasury ; and

(*b*) may make different provision for different classes or descriptions of ships and for different circumstances.

Alteration of ships measured for length.

2.—(1) Where a registered ship measured for length ceases by alteration to be a ship to which section 1 of this Act applies (without becoming exempt from registry) subsections (2) to (5) below shall apply instead of section 48 of the 1894 Act (registry of alterations).

(2) The ship must be registered anew or her tonnage (ascertained in accordance with the tonnage regulations of the 1894 Act) must be registered.

(3) Where, on an application to the registrar of the appropriate port—

(*a*) there is delivered to him a certificate granted by a surveyor of ships or a person appointed in pursuance of section 1(4) of the Merchant Shipping Act 1965 specifying the tonnage of the ship ascertained in accordance with the tonnage regulations of the 1894 Act, and 1965 c. 47.

(*b*) the registrar is satisfied that the number denoting her registered tonnage has been cut in on her main beam,

he shall either cause the details comprised in the certificate to be registered or direct that the ship be registered anew.

In this subsection, " appropriate port " means—

(i) where the alteration is made at a port having a registrar, that port; and

(ii) in any other case, the first port having a registrar at which the ship arrives after the alteration.

(4) If subsection (2) above is not complied with in the case of any ship, the owner of the ship shall be guilty of an offence and liable on summary conviction to a fine not exceeding—

(*a*) in England and Wales and Scotland, level 3 on the standard scale (which has the meaning given by section 75 of the Criminal Justice Act 1982); and 1982 c. 48.

(*b*) in Northern Ireland, £200;

and, in addition, to a fine not exceeding £20 for any day during which the offence continues after conviction.

(5) It shall be a defence for a person charged with an offence under subsection (4) above to prove that he took all reasonable precautions and exercised all due diligence to avoid the commission of the offence.

(6) Where a certificate under subsection (3)(*a*) above is delivered to the registrar, sections 49 and 50 of the 1894 Act (registry or provisional certification of alterations) shall apply as if the references to alterations made in a ship included a reference to the details of the ship comprised in the certificate.

Transfer abroad of registry of ships measured for length.

3.—(1) In the case of a registered ship measured for length, the registry of the ship may not be transferred under section 53 of the 1894 Act from a port in the United Kingdom to a port at which her tonnage would require to be registered unless, on the application under subsection (1) of that section—

(*a*) there is delivered to the registrar a certificate granted by a surveyor of ships or a person appointed in pursuance of section 1(4) of the Merchant Shipping Act 1965 specifying the tonnage of the ship ascertained in accordance with the tonnage regulations of the 1894 Act; and

1965 c. 47.

(*b*) the registrar is satisfied that the number denoting her registered tonnage has been cut in on her main beam.

(2) If the requirements of subsection (1)(*a*) and (*b*) above are met, the registrar shall, before transmitting notice of the application to the registrar of the intended port of registry under section 53(2) of the 1894 Act, cause the details comprised in the certificate to be registered; and section 49 of that Act (regulations for registry of alterations) shall apply as if the references to alterations made in the ship were references to the details of the ship comprised in the certificate.

Exemption from registry

Exemption of certain small ships from registry.

4. In section 3 of the 1894 Act (exemptions from registry), in paragraph (1) (exemption for ships not exceeding fifteen tons burden employed in coastal navigation) for the words " not exceeding fifteen tons burden " there are substituted the words " less than 13·7 metres in length " ; and at the end of that section there are inserted the following words—

" For the purposes of this section, the length of a ship is her length determined in accordance with regulations under section 1 of the Merchant Shipping Act 1983."

Small ships register

Separate register for small ships.

5.—(1) The Secretary of State may by regulations make provision for the registration in the United Kingdom of small ships, being ships which—

(*a*) are owned wholly by persons qualified to be owners of British ships ;

(*b*) are not fishing vessels ; and

(*c*) if registered under Part I of the 1894 Act, are so registered in the United Kingdom.

(2) A ship registered under this section is exempt from registry under Part I of the 1894 Act.

(3) Subject to the exceptions mentioned in subsection (4) below, references (however phrased) in any enactment to ships registered under Part I of the 1894 Act in the United Kingdom or to the registered owners of such ships include a reference to ships registered under this section or, as the case may be, to owners registered under this section of such ships; and connected phrases shall be interpreted accordingly.

(4) Those exceptions are—

(*a*) references in Part I of the 1894 Act and in this Act; and

(*b*) references in any enactment prescribed by regulations under this section.

(5) Where an application for the registration under this section of a ship registered under Part I of the 1894 Act is granted—

(*a*) the registrar of the ship's port of registry may, if the requirements of regulations under this section as to the closure of registration under that Part are met, close the registration of the ship under that Part by entering the closure in the register book; and

(*b*) the registration under this section shall not take effect unless the registration under that Part is closed under paragraph (*a*) above and, if it is so closed, shall take effect at the time of closure.

(6) Regulations under this section may provide for the payment of fees determined with the approval of the Treasury in connection with the closure under this section of registration under Part I of the 1894 Act.

(7) The registration of a ship under this section shall, if she is subsequently registered under Part I of the 1894 Act, terminate by virtue of the subsequent registration.

(8) The Schedule to this Act shall have effect for supplementing the provisions of this section.

(9) In this section and the Schedule—

"enactment" includes an enactment comprised in subordinate legislation;

"fishing vessel" has the same meaning as in the Fishing Vessels (Safety Provisions) Act 1970. 1970 c. 27.

Registrars

Registrars at ports.

6. In section 4(1)(*a*) of the 1894 Act (at ports in the United Kingdom approved for the registry of ships, the registrar is the chief officer of customs at that port) for the words " the chief officer of customs " there are substituted the words " any officer (whether at that port or elsewhere) appointed for the purpose by the Commissioners ".

Miscellaneous and supplemental

Regulations.

7. Any power conferred by this Act to make regulations shall be exercisable by statutory instrument which shall be subject to annulment in pursuance of a resolution of either House of Parliament.

Extension to British possessions, etc.

8.—(1) Her Majesty may by Order in Council direct that any of the provisions of this Act and regulations under it shall extend, with such exceptions, adaptations and modifications (if any) as may be specified in the Order, to any of the following countries—

(*a*) the Isle of Man ;

(*b*) any of the Channel Islands ;

(*c*) any colony ; and

(*d*) any country outside Her Majesty's dominions in which Her Majesty has jurisdiction in right of Her Government in the United Kingdom.

(2) Her Majesty may by Order in Council specifying any country referred to in subsection (1) above direct that, with such exceptions, adaptations and modifications (if any) as may be specified in the Order, any of those provisions shall have effect as if references in them to the United Kingdom included a reference to that country.

(3) An Order under subsection (2) above shall be subject to annulment in pursuance of a resolution of either House of Parliament.

Small ships: amendments of Merchant Shipping Acts.

9.—(1) Section 74(1)(*c*) of the 1894 Act (certain ships of 50 tons or more to show colours on entering or leaving British port) does not apply to any registered ship measured for length or any ship registered under section 5 of this Act.

1971 c. 59.

(2) For the purposes of section 503 of the 1894 Act and section 4 of the Merchant Shipping (Oil Pollution) Act 1971 (limitation of owner's liability by reference to tonnage), the tonnage of a registered ship measured for length or a ship registered under section 5 of this Act is her register tonnage ascertained in accordance with the tonnage regulations of the 1894 Act, but without making any deduction required by those regulations of any tonnage allowance for propelling machinery space.

(3) If the tonnage referred to in subsection (2) above cannot be so ascertained, a surveyor of ships shall, if so directed by the court, certify what on the evidence specified in the direction would in his opinion be that tonnage as so ascertained, and the tonnage stated in his certificate shall be taken for the purposes referred to in that subsection to be the tonnage of the ship.

Construction and interpretation.

10.—(1) This Act shall be construed as one with the Merchant Shipping Acts 1894 to 1981.

(2) In this Act—

" small ship " means a ship less than 24 metres in length (and in this definition " length " has the same meaning as in the tonnage regulations of the 1894 Act) ; and

" the 1894 Act " means the Merchant Shipping Act 1894. 1894 c. 60.

(3) In this Act, until the commencement of the provisions referred to in section 75 of the Criminal Justice Act 1982 (construction of references to the standard scale)— 1982 c. 48.

" level 5 on the standard scale " means £1,000 ; and

" level 3 on the standard scale " means £200.

Short title, commencement and extent.

11.—(1) This Act may be cited as the Merchant Shipping Act 1983.

(2) This Act and the Merchant Shipping Acts 1894 to 1981 may be cited together as the Merchant Shipping Acts 1894 to 1983.

(3) This Act shall come into force on such day as the Secretary of State may by order made by statutory instrument appoint, and different days may be appointed for different provisions and for different purposes.

(4) This Act extends to Northern Ireland.

Section 5.

SCHEDULE

Regulations Relating to Registration of Small Ships

1. In this Schedule—

"registered" and "registration" mean registered under section 5 of this Act or, as the case may be, registration under that section;

"regulations" means regulations made under that section; and

"specified" means specified in regulations.

2. Regulations may make provision—

(*a*) for the persons by whom and the manner in which applications in connection with registration are to be made (including provision limiting the persons who may apply for registration, whether by reference to residence or place of business or otherwise);

(*b*) for the information and evidence to be provided in connection with such applications and for such supplementary information or evidence as may be required by any authority specified for the purpose to be so provided;

(*c*) for the issue of certificates of registration, their production and surrender;

(*d*) for the marking of registered ships;

(*e*) for the period for which any registration is to remain effective without renewal;

(*f*) for the refusal of registration where the name of the ship proposed to be registered appears to any authority specified for the purpose to be undesirable;

(*g*) for the termination of registration in specified circumstances (including failure to comply with requirements imposed by or under regulations and circumstances in which any of the requirements applicable to new registrations imposed by or under section 5 of this Act are no longer met);

(*h*) for matters arising out of the expiration or termination of registration (including the removal of marks and the cancellation of certificates);

(*i*) for the inspection of ships registered or to be registered;

(*j*) for the payment of fees in connection with registration or registered ships, being fees determined with the approval of the Treasury;

(*k*) for the discharge of functions under the regulations by persons appointed by such organisations as may be authorised in that behalf by the Secretary of State;

(*l*) excluding from registration specified classes or descriptions of ships; and

(*m*) for any other matters relating to the maintenance of a register of small ships (including its inspection).

3.—(1) Regulations may provide for the creation of offences and their punishment on summary conviction in any of the following cases—

(*a*) where a person with intent to deceive uses, or lends to or allows to be used by another, a certificate of registration which has ceased to have effect;

(*b*) where a person for purposes of registration makes a statement which he knows to be false in a material particular or recklessly makes a statement which is false in a material particular;

(*c*) where a person required by regulations to ensure that any requirement of the regulations as to the marking of a ship is met fails to ensure that that requirement is met;

(*d*) where a person required by regulations to surrender a certificate of registration fails without reasonable excuse to surrender the certificate.

(2) Regulations providing for the creation of an offence by virtue of sub-paragraph (1)(*c*) above shall provide that it shall be a defence for a person charged with the offence to prove that he took all reasonable precautions and exercised all due diligence to avoid the commission of the offence.

(3) Regulations providing for the creation of an offence by virtue of sub-paragraph (1)(*a*) or (*b*) above shall provide for it to be punishable—

(*a*) in England and Wales and Scotland, with a fine not exceeding level 5 on the standard scale (which has the meaning given by section 75 of the Criminal Justice Act 1982); 1982 c. 48.

(*b*) in Northern Ireland, with a fine not exceeding £1,000.

(4) Regulations providing for the creation of an offence by virtue of sub-paragraph (1)(*c*) or (*d*) above shall provide for it to be punishable—

(*a*) in England and Wales and Scotland, with a fine not exceeding level 3 on the standard scale (which has the meaning given by section 75 of the Criminal Justice Act 1982);

(*b*) in Northern Ireland, with a fine not exceeding £200.

4.—(1) Regulations may make different provision for different classes or descriptions of ships and for different circumstances.

(2) Regulations may contain such supplemental and incidental provisions as appear to the Secretary of State to be necessary or expedient.

5. Regulations may provide for their operation within territorial waters adjacent to the United Kingdom.

6. No provision of this Schedule is to be taken to prejudice the generality of section 5 of this Act.

International Transport Conventions Act 1983

1983 CHAPTER 14

An Act to give effect to the Convention concerning International Carriage by Rail signed on behalf of the United Kingdom on 9th May 1980; and to make further provision for the amendment of Acts giving effect to other international transport conventions so as to take account of revisions of the conventions to which they give effect. [11th April 1983]

BE IT ENACTED by the Queen's most Excellent Majesty, by and with the advice and consent of the Lords Spiritual and Temporal, and Commons, in this present Parliament assembled, and by the authority of the same, as follows:—

The Railway Convention

Convention to have the force of law.

1.—(1) The Convention concerning International Carriage by Rail signed on behalf of the United Kingdom on 9th May 1980 shall have the force of law in the United Kingdom.

(2) In this Act " the Convention " means the Convention referred to in subsection (1) above including, except where the context otherwise requires—

(*a*) the protocol on the privileges and immunities of the intergovernmental organisation set up by the Convention; and

(*b*) the uniform rules in Appendix A and Appendix B to the Convention together with the Annexes to Appendix B.

(3) The provisions having the force of law by virtue of this section are—

(*a*) the provisions of the Convention as presented to Parliament in April 1982 and set out in Command Paper 8535; and

(*b*) as respects Annexes I, II and III to Appendix B to the Convention, the provisions referred to in that Command Paper;

and judicial notice shall be taken of those provisions as if they were contained in this Act.

(4) If after the coming into force of this section the provisions referred to in paragraph (*a*) of subsection (3) above are republished in one or more Command Papers in the Treaty Series that subsection shall have effect as if it referred to that or those Command Papers instead of to the Command Paper there mentioned.

Designation of Member States etc.

2.—(1) Her Majesty may by Order in Council from time to time certify who are the Member States for the purposes of the Convention.

(2) An Order in Council under subsection (1) above may also certify whether the United Kingdom or any other Member State has made a reservation under—

(*a*) paragraph 3 of Article 12 of the Convention (arbitration); or

(*b*) paragraph 1 of Article 3 in Appendix A to the Convention (exclusion of own nationals etc.).

(3) Her Majesty may by Order in Council from time to time certify whether the uniform rules referred to in section 1(2)(*b*) above are suspended by virtue of paragraph 3 of Article 20 of the Convention (suspension pending agreement to amendments) in respect of traffic with or between any Member States.

(4) An Order in Council under this section shall, except so far as it has been superseded by a subsequent Order, be conclusive evidence of the matters so certified.

Fatal accidents.

3.—(1) Where by virtue of the Convention any person has a right of action in respect of the death of a passenger by reason of his being a person whom the passenger was under a legal duty to maintain—

(*a*) subject to subsection (2) below, no action in respect of the passenger's death shall be brought for the benefit of that person under the Fatal Accidents Act 1976; but 1976 c. 30.

(*b*) nothing in section 2(3) of that Act (not more than one action in respect of the same subject-matter of complaint) shall prevent an action being brought under that Act for the benefit of any other person.

(2) Nothing in subsection (1)(*a*) above affects the right of any person to claim damages for bereavement under section 1A of the said Act of 1976.

(3) Section 4 of the said Act of 1976 (exclusion of certain benefits in assessment of damages) shall apply in relation to an action brought by any person under the Convention as it applies in relation to an action under that Act.

(4) Where separate proceedings are brought under the Convention and under the said Act of 1976 in respect of the death of a passenger, a court, in awarding damages under that Act, shall take into account any damages awarded in the proceedings brought under the Convention and shall have jurisdiction to make any part of its award conditional on the result of those proceedings.

S.I. 1977/1251 (N.I. 18).

(5) In the application of this section to Northern Ireland references to the said Act of 1976 and to sections 1A, 2(3) and 4 of that Act shall be construed as references to the Fatal Accidents (Northern Ireland) Order 1977 and Articles 3A, 4(3) and 6 of that Order.

(6) The provisions of Schedule 1 to this Act shall, as respects Scotland, have effect in lieu of the foregoing provisions of this section.

Power of court to take account of other proceedings.

4.—(1) A court before which proceedings are brought to enforce a liability which is limited by any of the provisions of the Convention may at any stage of the proceedings make any such order as appears to the court to be just and equitable in view of those provisions and of any other proceedings which have been, or are likely to be, commenced in the United Kingdom or elsewhere to enforce the liability in whole or in part.

(2) Without prejudice to subsection (1) above, a court before which proceedings are brought to enforce a liability which is limited as aforesaid shall, where the liability is or may be partly enforceable in other proceedings in the United Kingdom or elsewhere, have jurisdiction to award an amount less than the court would have awarded if the limitation applied solely to the proceedings before the court, or to make any part of its award conditional on the result of any other proceedings.

Conversion of special drawing rights into sterling.

5.—(1) The special drawing rights by reference to which any liability is limited by the Convention shall, in the case of judicial proceedings or an arbitration in the United Kingdom, be converted into their sterling equivalent on the day of the judgment or award.

(2) For the purposes of this section the value on a particular day of a special drawing right shall be treated as equal to such a

sum in sterling as the International Monetary Fund have fixed as being the equivalent of one special drawing right—

(a) for that day; or

(b) if no sum has been so fixed for that day, for the last day before that day for which a sum has been so fixed.

(3) A certificate given by or on behalf of the Treasury stating—

(a) that a particular sum in sterling has been fixed as aforesaid for a particular day; or

(b) that no sum has been so fixed for a particular day and that a particular sum in sterling has been so fixed for a day which is the last day for which a sum has been so fixed before the particular day,

shall be conclusive evidence of those matters for the purposes of subsection (2) above; and a document purporting to be such a certificate shall in any proceedings be received in evidence and, unless the contrary is proved, be deemed to be such a certificate.

(4) The Treasury may charge a reasonable fee for any certificate given under this section; and any fee received by the Treasury by virtue of this subsection shall be paid into the Consolidated Fund.

Enforcement of judgments. 1933 c. 13.

6.—(1) Subject to subsection (2) below, Part I of the Foreign Judgments (Reciprocal Enforcement) Act 1933 shall apply, whether or not it would otherwise have applied, to any judgment which—

(a) has been pronounced as mentioned in paragraph 1 of Article 18 of the Convention by a court in a Member State other than the United Kingdom; and

(b) has become enforceable under the law applied by that court.

(2) In the application of Part I of the said Act of 1933 in relation to any such judgment section 4 of that Act shall have effect with the omission of subsections (2) and (3).

(3) The registration, in accordance with Part I of the said Act of 1933, of any such judgment shall constitute compliance with the required formalities referred to in paragraph 1 of Article 18 of the Convention.

Examination of luggage.

7. Paragraph 4 of Article 15 and paragraph 2 of Article 22 in Appendix A to the Convention (examination of luggage) shall not in the United Kingdom authorise the opening of any piece of luggage except in the presence of a constable.

Amendments consequential on revision of Convention.

8.—(1) If at any time it appears to Her Majesty in Council that Her Majesty's Government in the United Kingdom have agreed to a revision of the Convention, Her Majesty may by Order in Council make such amendments of this Act as Her Majesty considers appropriate in consequence of the revision.

(2) In subsection (1) above " revision " means an omission from, addition to or alteration of the Convention and includes replacement of the Convention or part of it by another convention.

(3) No recommendation shall be made to Her Majesty to make an Order under this section unless a draft of it has been laid before Parliament and approved by a resolution of each House of Parliament.

(4) An Order under this section may contain such transitional and supplementary provisions as appear to Her Majesty to be expedient.

Other international transport conventions

Power to make amendments consequential on revision of other international transport conventions.

9. The Acts mentioned in Schedule 2 to this Act (which give effect to other international transport conventions) shall have effect with the amendments there specified, being amendments making further provision for enabling those Acts to be modified so as to take account of revisions of the conventions to which they give effect.

Supplementary

Application to Crown.

10. This Act binds the Crown.

Short title, repeals and commencement.

11.—(1) This Act may be cited as the International Transport Conventions Act 1983.

1982 c. 27.

(2) The enactments mentioned in Schedule 3 to this Act are hereby repealed to the extent specified in the third column of that Schedule ; and in section 31(3) and 32(4) of the Civil Jurisdiction and Judgments Act 1982 for the words " section 5 of the Carriage by Railway Act 1972 " there shall be substituted the words " section 6 of the International Transport Conventions Act 1983 ".

(3) Section 1 above shall come into force on such day as Her Majesty may by Order in Council certify to be the day on which the Convention comes into force as regards the United Kingdom ; and subsection (2) above shall have effect from that day.

(4) The provisions having the force of law by virtue of section 1 above do not affect any rights or liabilities arising out of an occurrence before the coming into force of those provisions ; and subsection (2) above does not affect any enactment in its application to any such rights or liabilities.

SCHEDULES

SCHEDULE 1

Section 3(6).

FATAL ACCIDENTS: SCOTLAND

1.—(1) Subject to sub-paragraph (2) below, no enactment or rule of law shall have effect so as to permit a person who has a right of action under the Convention in respect of the death of a passenger by virtue of his being a person whom the passenger was under a legal duty to maintain to raise any other action in that respect for any loss of support suffered by him.

(2) Sub-paragraph (1) above shall not apply in so far as the other action concludes for a loss of society award as defined in section 1(4) of the Damages (Scotland) Act 1976. 1976 c. 13.

2. Section 1(5) of the said Act of 1976 (exclusion of certain items in assessment of damages) shall apply to an action brought under the Convention as it applies to an action brought under that Act; but section 6 of that Act shall not apply to such an action under the Convention.

3. Where separate proceedings in respect of the death of a passenger are brought under the Convention and under any other enactment or rule of law the court, in awarding damages in such other proceedings, shall take into account any damages awarded in the proceedings brought under the Convention and may make any part of its award conditional on the result of those proceedings.

4. In the said Act of 1976—

(*a*) in section 1(7) (restriction on awards of damages to relatives) before the word " no " there shall be inserted the words " or under section 1 of the International Transport Conventions Act 1983 " ;

(*b*) after subsection (1) of section 5 (provisions for avoiding multiplicity of actions) there shall be inserted the following subsection—

" (1A) This section shall not apply to an action brought under section 1 of the International Transport Conventions Act 1983—

(*a*) by a person whom the deceased was under a legal duty to maintain ; or

(*b*) by the deceased's executor.".

SCHEDULE 2

Section 9.

POWER TO MAKE AMENDMENTS CONSEQUENTIAL ON REVISION OF INTERNATIONAL TRANSPORT COVENTIONS

The Carriage by Air Act 1961 1961 c. 27.

1. In section 8A(1) for the words from " provide " to " modifications " there shall be substituted the words " make such amendments of this Act, the Carriage by Air (Supplementary Provisions) Act 1962 and section 5(1) of the Carriage by Air and Road Act 1979 ".

SCH. 2

The Carriage of Goods by Road Act 1965

1965 c. 37. 2. In section 8A(1) for paragraphs (*a*) and (*b*) there shall be substituted—

" (*a*) this Act ; and ".

1974 c. 35. *The Carriage of Passengers by Road Act 1974*

3.—(1) In section 8(1) for paragraphs (*a*) and (*b*) there shall be substituted—

" (*a*) of this Act, and ".

(2) In section 8(2) for paragraphs (*a*) and (*b*) there shall be substituted the words " of this Act ".

1976 c. 58. *The International Carriage of Perishable Foodstuffs Act 1976*

4. For section 16(1) there shall be substituted—

" (1) If at any time it appears to Her Majesty in Council that Her Majesty's Government in the United Kingdom have agreed to any revision of the Agreement on the International Carriage of Perishable Foodstuffs and on the Special Equipment to be Used for such Carriage (ATP) Her Majesty may by Order in Council make such amendments of this Act as Her Majesty considers appropriate in consequence of the revision.

(1A) In subsection (1) above " revision " means an omission from, addition to or alteration of that Agreement and includes replacement of that Agreement or part of it by another agreement."

Section 11(2).

SCHEDULE 3

REPEALS

Chapter etc.	Title	Extent of repeal
1972 c. 33.	The Carriage by Railway Act 1972.	The whole Act.
1976 c. 30.	The Fatal Accidents Act 1976.	In Schedule 1, paragraph 4.
S.I. 1977/1251 (N.I. 18).	The Fatal Accidents (Northern Ireland) Order 1977.	In Schedule 1, paragraph 7.
1978 c. 47.	The Civil Liability (Contribution) Act 1978.	In Schedule 1, paragraph 8.
1982 c. 53.	The Administration of Justice Act 1982.	Section 3(3).

British Shipbuilders Act 1983

1983 CHAPTER 15

An Act to make further provision with respect to the functions and activities of British Shipbuilders.

[9th May 1983]

BE IT ENACTED by the Queen's most Excellent Majesty, by and with the advice and consent of the Lords Spiritual and Temporal, and Commons, in this present Parliament assembled, and by the authority of the same, as follows:—

1.—(1) The Aircraft and Shipbuilding Industries Act 1977 (in this Act referred to as " the 1977 Act ") shall have effect subject to the following amendments (which are designed to remove the general duties of British Shipbuilders and modify its powers). Modification of British Shipbuilders' functions. 1977 c. 3.

(2) Section 2 (which imposes general duties on British Shipbuilders) shall cease to have effect.

(3) For subsection (1) of section 3 (which confers power on British Shipbuilders to carry on activities which it is under a duty to carry on and to carry on certain other activities) there shall be substituted the following subsection—

" (1) Subject to the provisions of this Act, British Shipbuilders shall have power to carry on the following activities, namely—

(*a*) the design, development, production, sale, repair and maintenance of ships and slow speed diesel marine engines;

(*b*) research into matters relating thereto;

(*c*) any activities which were carried on, immediately before the date of transfer, by a company which, by virtue of this Act, becomes a wholly owned subsidiary of British Shipbuilders; and

(*d*) with the consent of, or in accordance with the terms of any general authority given by, the Secretary of State, any other activities to which the consent or authority relates;

and British Shipbuilders may also promote the carrying on of any of those activities to such extent as it thinks fit by other persons none of whom need be a wholly owned subsidiary of British Shipbuilders."

(4) In section 18 subsection (4) (which provides for annual reports to contain statements about the performance of British Shipbuilders' duty under section 2(8)) shall cease to have effect.

(5) In section 48(2) (duty of British Shipbuilders to consult with Northern Ireland state-controlled bodies) for the words "subsection (2) of that section" there shall be substituted the words "section 3(1)(*a*) and (*b*) above".

Organisation etc. of British Shipbuilders' activities.

2.—(1) The following sections shall be inserted after section 4 of the 1977 Act—

"Organisation of British Shipbuilders' activities.

4A.—(1) It shall be the duty of British Shipbuilders so to exercise its powers as to secure that the carrying on of the activities that have fallen to be carried on under its ultimate control is organised, so far as regards the direction thereof, in the most efficient manner.

(2) British Shipbuilders shall not make, or permit to be made, any substantial change in the manner in which the carrying on of the activities that have fallen to be carried on under its ultimate control is organised, so far as regards the direction thereof, except with the consent of the Secretary of State.

Discontinuance and restriction of British Shipbuilders' activities.

4B.—(1) Without prejudice to section 4(2) above but subject as provided in subsection (2) below, the Secretary of State may, after consultation with British Shipbuilders, by order, give to it directions—

(*a*) to discontinue or restrict any of its activities or to dispose of any of its property, rights and liabilities; or

(*b*) to secure the discontinuance or restriction of any of the activities of a wholly owned subsidiary of British Shipbuilders or the disposal of all or any of its property, rights and liabilities or the winding up of any such subsidiary.

(2) The Secretary of State shall not give any direction under subsection (1) above unless he is satisfied that the giving of it will further the national interest.

(3) Subject to subsection (4) below, any direction under subsection (1) above to dispose or secure the disposal of property, rights or liabilities may in particular include a direction—

(*a*) to form a company for the purpose of acquiring the property or rights and assuming the liabilities to be transferred in pursuance of the direction ;

(*b*) prohibiting, except with the consent of the Secretary of State, the disposal to, or acquisition from any person by, any company which will acquire property or rights in pursuance of the direction of assets used or capable of use in the carrying on of activities of a description, or of activities other than activities of a description, specified in the direction.

(4) The powers to direct the formation of a company and to restrict the disposal or acquisition of assets are exercisable subject to the following further limitations, that is to say—

(*a*) no company shall be directed to be formed otherwise than as a wholly owned subsidiary of British Shipbuilders ; and

(*b*) no such restriction shall be imposed except on a company which is, or when formed will be, a wholly owned subsidiary of British Shipbuilders or be binding after it ceases to be such a subsidiary.

(5) So long as the restriction on the disposal or acquisition of assets is binding on British Shipbuilders or any of its wholly owned subsidiaries the provisions of this Act relating to the capacity of British Shipbuilders or of the subsidiary shall have effect subject to the restriction.

(6) Where the Secretary of State gives a direction under subsection (1) above requiring the disposal to an outside person of an interest in a company which

is a wholly owned subsidiary of British Shipbuilders, or gives his consent to such a disposal under section 3(3) above or section 9(3) below, then, without prejudice to section 4(2) above, he may, after consultation with British Shipbuilders, by order give to it directions to secure—

(*a*) that the articles of association of the company are altered in the manner specified in the directions ;

(*b*) that the share capital of the company is increased by the sum and in the manner so specified and that any share or shares representing the whole or any part of that sum are issued to the Secretary of State or to a nominee of his ; and

(*c*) that an employees' share scheme is established in respect of the company in such terms and making such provision as is so specified.

(7) Any power to make orders conferred by this section shall be exercisable by statutory instrument subject to annulment in pursuance of a resolution of either House of Parliament.

(8) In this section—

' employees' share scheme ' means a scheme for encouraging or facilitating the holding of shares or debentures in a company by or for the benefit of—

(*a*) the bona fide employees or former employees of the company or of a subsidiary of the company ; or

(*b*) the wives, husbands, widows, widowers or children or stepchildren under the age of 18 of such employees or former employees ;

' the group ' means British Shipbuilders and all its wholly owned subsidiaries taken together ;

' outside person ' means a person who is not a member of the group."

(2) Section 5 of the 1977 Act (duty of British Shipbuilders to review and report on management of its affairs) shall cease to have effect.

(3) In section 18 of the 1977 Act (annual report) the following subsection shall be inserted after subsection (3)—

" (3A) The report for any accounting year shall also

set out any consent given by the Secretary of State to British Shipbuilders during that year under subsection (2) of section 4A above and shall include a general account of the changes in organisation made during that year by virtue of any consent of his given in that or in any earlier accounting year under that subsection."

(4) In section 53 of the 1977 Act (liabilities of British Shipbuilders etc.), in subsection (1) the words " or has at any time since the cause of action arose been such a subsidiary " and subsection (2) shall cease to have effect ; but nothing in this Act shall affect the operation of that section in a case where the cause of action has arisen, or would (but for this Act) be deemed to have arisen, before the coming into force of this Act.

Short title, interpretation, repeals, commencement and extent.

3.—(1) This Act may be cited as the British Shipbuilders Act 1983.

(2) In this Act " the 1977 Act " means the Aircraft and Shipbuilding Industries Act 1977.

1977 c. 3.

(3) The enactments specified in the Schedule to this Act are hereby repealed to the extent specified in the third column of that Schedule.

(4) This Act shall come into force at the expiry of the period of two months beginning with the day on which it is passed.

(5) This Act extends to Northern Ireland.

Section 3(3).

SCHEDULE

ENACTMENTS REPEALED

Chapter	Short title	Extent of repeal
1977 c. 3.	Aircraft and Shipbuilding Industries Act 1977.	Section 2. Section 5. Section 18(4). In section 53, in subsection (1) the words " or has at any time since the cause of action arose been such a subsidiary" and subsection (2).

Level Crossings Act 1983

1983 CHAPTER 16

An Act to make further provision about level crossings.
[9th May 1983]

BE IT ENACTED by the Queen's most Excellent Majesty, by and with the advice and consent of the Lords Spiritual and Temporal, and Commons, in this present Parliament assembled, and by the authority of the same, as follows:—

Safety arrangements at level crossings.

1.—(1) Subject to the following provisions of this section, the Secretary of State may, in relation to any place where a railway crosses a road on a level (in this section referred to as a " level crossing "), by order provide for the protection of those using the level crossing.

(2) An order under this section may make such provision as the Secretary of State considers necessary or expedient for the safety or convenience of those using the crossing; and, in particular—

(*a*) may require any such barriers or other protective equipment as may be specified in the order to be provided at or near the crossing, and to be maintained and operated, in accordance with the order; and

(*b*) may impose requirements as to the operation of the railway at or near that crossing.

(3) While an order is in force under this section in relation to a level crossing—

(*a*) it shall be the duty of the operator of the crossing to ensure that the order is complied with; and (*b*) subject to any exceptions specified in the order, any provision made by or under any enactment as to the crossing (or level crossings including that crossing) and imposing requirements as to barriers or other protective equipment at or near the crossing, the supervision of the crossing (including the provision of buildings for the purposes of supervision) or the operation of the railway at or near the crossing shall not apply in relation to the crossing.

1967 c. 76. (4) Nothing in subsection (3)(*b*) above affects any provision as to traffic signs made under the Road Traffic Regulation Act 1967; but a traffic sign placed on or near a road in pursuance of an order under this section shall be treated for the purposes of section 54(4) of that Act as having been placed as provided by that Act.

(5) An order under this section—

(*a*) may be varied or revoked by a subsequent order under this section; and

(*b*) may include requirements as to equipment provided before the making of the order.

(6) The Secretary of State may not make an order under this section in respect of a level crossing (other than an order revoking a previous order) unless requested to do so by the operator of the crossing.

(7) A request under subsection (6) above must be accompanied by a draft of the order which the operator desires the Secretary of State to make.

(8) Before making such a request, the operator must give written notice of his intention to do so to each local authority in whose area the level crossing is situated; and the notice—

(*a*) must be accompanied by a copy of the draft order which the operator intends to submit to the Secretary of State; and

(*b*) must specify the period (not being less than two months) within which the local authority may make representations to the Secretary of State in respect of the request.

(9) The Secretary of State must consider any representations in respect of the request made by such a local authority within the period specified in accordance with subsection (8)(*b*) above and may then, if he decides to make the order, make it in accordance with the draft submitted to him or with such modifications as he thinks fit.

(10) This section applies where a Government department is operating a railway at a level crossing as it applies in other cases.

(11) In this section—

" barrier " includes gate;

" local authority ", in relation to England and Wales, means any council of a county, district or London borough, the Greater London Council and the Common Council of the City of London and, in relation to Scotland, means any regional, islands or district council;

" operator ", in relation to a crossing, means the person for the time being operating the railway at the crossing;

" protective equipment " includes lights, traffic signs and telephone and television equipment;

" road " means any highway or other road to which the public has access; and

" traffic sign " has the same meaning as in the Road Traffic Regulation Act 1967. 1967 c. 76.

Short title, commencement and extent.

2.—(1) This Act may be cited as the Level Crossings Act 1983.

(2) This Act shall come into force at the end of the period of three months beginning with the day on which it is passed.

(3) This Act does not extend to Northern Ireland.

Plant Varieties Act 1983

1983 CHAPTER 17

An Act to amend the Plant Varieties and Seeds Act 1964.
[9th May 1983]

BE IT ENACTED by the Queen's most Excellent Majesty, by and with the advice and consent of the Lords Spiritual and Temporal, and Commons, in this present Parliament assembled, and by the authority of the same, as follows:—

Period for which plant breeders' rights are exercisable.
1964 c. 14.

1.—(1) In section 3 (period for which rights are exercisable) of the Plant Varieties and Seeds Act 1964 (in this Act referred to as " the 1964 Act ") there shall be substituted—

(*a*) in subsection (1) for the words " 25 years " the words " 30 years ";

(*b*) in subsection (2) for the words " 18 years " the words " 25 years "; and

(*c*) in subsection (3) for the words " 15 years " the words " 20 years ".

(2) In subsection (2) of that section for the words " fruit trees and their root-stocks, forest and ornamental trees and grapevines " there shall be substituted the words " fruit, forest and ornamental trees and their root-stocks and grapevines and their root-stocks ".

(3) Subsections (5) and (8) of that section and, in subsection (9) of that section, the words " or subsection (8) " shall cease to have effect.

(4) Every scheme made under Part I of the 1964 Act before the commencement of this Act shall be amended as follows—

(*a*) for any period of 25 years prescribed by the scheme there shall be substituted a period of 30 years;

(*b*) for any period of 20 years so prescribed there shall be substituted a period of 25 years; and

(*c*) for any period of 15 or 18 years so prescribed there shall be substituted a period of 20 years;

and the period for which any plant breeders' rights subsisting at the commencement of this Act are exercisable shall be extended by so much (if any) as may be necessary to bring it into conformity with the relevant scheme as so amended.

(5) Nothing in this Act shall affect the operation of subsections (5), (8) and (9) of section 3 of the 1964 Act in relation to applications made, or extensions granted on applications made, before the commencement of this Act.

Plant breeders' rights in special cases.

2. For sub-paragraphs (1) and (2) of paragraph 1 of Schedule 3 to the 1964 Act (sale of cut blooms, fruit etc.) there shall be substituted the following sub-paragraph—

" 1.—(1) If it appears to the Ministers that, in the case of any species or group of plant varieties, plant breeders will not receive adequate remuneration unless there is made such provision as is authorised by this paragraph, and that such provision will be of substantial benefit to plant breeders, they may by a scheme under Part I of this Act provide that, as respects any plant variety of the species or group prescribed by the scheme, plant breeders' rights shall include the exclusive right to do, and to authorise others to do, as follows—

(*a*) to produce or propagate the variety in Great Britain for the purpose of selling such parts or products of the variety as may be prescribed by the scheme; and

(*b*) to sell or offer or expose for sale in Great Britain, so far as they are obtained from plants produced or propagated outside Great Britain, such parts or products of the variety as may be so prescribed."

Compulsory licences.

3.—(1) In subsection (3) of section 7 of the 1964 Act (compulsory licences) for the words from " endeavour to secure " onwards there shall be substituted the words " have regard to the desirability of securing—

(*a*) that the plant variety is available to the public at reasonable prices, is widely distributed and is maintained in quality;

(*b*) that there is reasonable remuneration for the holder of the plant breeders' rights; and

(*c*) where there is a market for the export of the plant variety, that the market is supplied from the production of the variety in Great Britain."

(2) In subsection (5) of that section for paragraph (*a*) there shall be substituted the following paragraph—

" (*a*) the holder of the plant breeders' rights to which an application under subsection (1) of this section relates—

(i) is or includes, or is represented by, a society or other organisation which has as its main object, or one of its main objects, the negotiation or granting of licences to exercise plant breeders' rights, either as the holder of the rights or as agent for holders, or

(ii) is or includes a company any shares of which are held by or on behalf of the Ministers, and ".

Other amendments of the 1964 Act.

4. The 1964 Act shall have effect subject to the further amendments set out in Schedule 1 to this Act, being miscellaneous minor amendments.

Application of Act outside Great Britain.

5.—(1) Section 39 of the 1964 Act (extension of that Act to Northern Ireland) shall have effect as if the provisions of this Act were provisions of the relevant Part of that Act and, with the exception of subsection (2) below, had been extended to Northern Ireland by Order in Council under subsection (2) of that section.

(2) Section 40 of the 1964 Act (extension of that Act to the Isle of Man and Channel Islands) shall have effect as if the provisions of this Act were provisions of that Act.

Short title, repeals and commencement.

6.—(1) This Act may be cited as the Plant Varieties Act 1983.

(2) The enactments mentioned in Schedule 2 to this Act are hereby repealed to the extent specified in the third column of that Schedule.

(3) This Act shall come into force at the expiry of the period of two months beginning with the day on which it is passed.

SCHEDULES

SCHEDULE 1

Section 4.

AMENDMENTS OF THE 1964 ACT

1.—(1) In subsection (1) of section 4 of the 1964 Act (the nature of plant breeders' rights) after the word " sell " there shall be inserted the words " or offer or expose for sale ".

(2) In subsection (2) of that section after the word " sale " there shall be inserted the words " or offer or exposure for sale " and after the word " sold ", in the first place where it occurs, there shall be inserted the words " or offered or exposed for sale ".

(3) In subsection (5) of that section after the word " sell " there shall be inserted the words " or offer or expose for sale ".

2.—(1) In subsection (1) of section 5A of the 1964 Act (requirement to use registered names on sale of reproductive material) after the word " offering " there shall be inserted the words " or exposing ".

(2) In subsection (4) of that section the words " in connection with the registered name of a plant variety " shall be omitted and for the words from " other than " onwards there shall be substituted the words " if—

(*a*) that mark or name and the registered name are juxtaposed; and

(*b*) the registered name is easily recognisable."

(3) In subsection (5) of that section the words " or to imprisonment for a term not exceeding three months, or to both " shall cease to have effect.

3. In subsections (1) and (2) of section 13 of the 1964 Act (false representations as to rights and false information) the words " or to imprisonment for a term not exceeding three months, or to both " shall cease to have effect.

4.—(1) In subsection (1) of section 15 of the 1964 Act (interpretation of Part I), in paragraph (*d*) for the words " ornamental plants and parts of ornamental plants when " there shall be substituted the words " plants or parts of plants of any ornamental variety when plants or parts of plants of that variety are ".

(2) After that subsection there shall be inserted the following subsection—

" (1A) References in this Part of this Act to offering or exposing for sale plants or material of any description include references to publishing, or causing to be published, any advertisement likely to be understood as conveying that the advertiser has plants or material of that description in his possession for the purpose of sale."

5. In subsection (1) of section 38 of the 1964 Act (interpretation) in the definition of " plant variety " for the word "means " there shall be substituted the word " includes ".

SCH. 1

6. In subsection (3)(*b*) of section 39 of the 1964 Act (extension of Act to Northern Ireland) the word "and" immediately following head (iv) shall cease to have effect and after head (v) there shall be inserted the words "and

(vi) in paragraph 9(3) of Schedule 4, after the words 'this Act' there were inserted the words 'or the Seeds Act (Northern Ireland) 1965'".

7. In paragraph 1(3) of Schedule 1 to the 1964 Act (protection of applicant for rights while application is pending) after the word "offer" there shall be inserted the words "or exposure" and the words from "or the exposure" onwards shall cease to have effect.

8.—(1) In paragraph 1(1) of Part I of Schedule 2 to the 1964 Act (priorities between applicants for rights) after the words "those persons" there shall be inserted the words "(and any successors in title of theirs)" and for the words from "in the form" to "section 9 of" there shall be substituted the word "under".

(2) In sub-paragraph (3) of paragraph (2) of that Part of that Schedule for the words from "in the form" to "being a form" there shall be substituted the words "being an application".

9.—(1) In paragraph 1(1) of Part II of Schedule 2 to the 1964 Act (rules for grant of rights) for the words "morphological, physiological or other characteristics" there shall be substituted the words "characteristics which are capable of precise description".

(2) In sub-paragraphs (1) and (2) of paragraph 2 of that Part of that Schedule after the word "offered" there shall be inserted the words "or exposed".

(3) For the proviso to sub-paragraph (2) of that paragraph there shall be substituted the following proviso—

"Provided that the restriction imposed by this sub-paragraph shall not apply to sales or offers or exposures for sale made outside the United Kingdom—

(*a*) in the case of fruit, forest and ornamental trees and their root-stocks and grapevines and their root-stocks, during the period of six years ending with the date of the application;

(*b*) in any other case, during the period of four years ending with that date."

(4) In sub-paragraphs (4)(*a*) and (5) of that paragraph after the word "offer" there shall be inserted the words "or exposure".

SCHEDULE 2

Section 6.

Repeals

Chapter	Short title	Extent of repeal
1964 c. 14.	The Plant Varieties and Seeds Act 1964.	In section 3, subsections (5) and (8) and, in subsection (9), the words " or subsection (8) ". In section 5A, in subsection (4) the words " in connection with the registered name of a plant variety " and in subsection (5) the words " or to imprisonment for a term not exceeding three months, or to both ". In section 13, in subsections (1) and (2) the words " or to imprisonment for a term not exceeding three months, or to both ". In section 39, in subsection (3)(*b*) the word " and " immediately following head (iv). In Schedule 1, in paragraph 1(3) the words from " or the exposure " onwards.

The above repeals have effect subject to section 1(5) above.

Nuclear Material (Offences) Act 1983

1983 CHAPTER 18

An Act to implement the Convention on the Physical Protection of Nuclear Material; and for purposes connected therewith. [9th May 1983]

BE IT ENACTED by the Queen's most Excellent Majesty, by and with the advice and consent of the Lords Spiritual and Temporal, and Commons, in this present Parliament assembled, and by the authority of the same, as follows:—

Extended scope of certain offences.

1.—(1) If a person, whatever his nationality, does outside the United Kingdom, in relation to or by means of nuclear material, any act which, had he done it in any part of the United Kingdom, would have made him guilty of—

(*a*) the offence of murder, manslaughter, culpable homicide, assault to injury, malicious mischief or causing injury, or endangering the life of the lieges, by reckless conduct, or

1861 c. 100. 1971 c. 48. S.I. 1977/426. 1980 c. 62.

(*b*) an offence under section 18 or 20 of the Offences against the Person Act 1861 or section 1 of the Criminal Damage Act 1971 or Article 3 of the Criminal Damage (Northern Ireland) Order 1977 or section 78 of the Criminal Justice (Scotland) Act 1980, or

(*c*) the offence of theft, embezzlement, robbery, assault with intent to rob, burglary or aggravated burglary, or

1968 c. 60. 1969 c. 16 (N.I.).

(*d*) the offence of fraud or extortion or an offence under section 15 or 21 of the Theft Act 1968 or section 15 or 20 of the Theft Act (Northern Ireland) 1969, he shall in any part of the United Kingdom be guilty of such of the offences mentioned in paragraphs (*a*) to (*d*) above as are offences of which the act would have made him guilty had he done it in that part of the United Kingdom.

(2) In this section and in section 2 below, " act " includes omission.

Offences involving preparatory acts and threats.

2.—(1) If a person, whatever his nationality, in the United Kingdom or elsewhere contravenes subsection (2), (3) or (4) below he shall be guilty of an offence.

(2) A person contravenes this subsection if he receives, holds or deals with nuclear material—

(*a*) intending, or for the purpose of enabling another, to do by means of that material an act which is an offence mentioned in paragraph (*a*) or (*b*) of subsection (1) of section 1 above; or

(*b*) being reckless as to whether another would so do such an act.

(3) A person contravenes this subsection if he—

(*a*) makes to another person a threat that he or any other person will do by means of nuclear material such an act as is mentioned in paragraph (*a*) of subsection (2) above; and

(*b*) intends that the person to whom the threat is made shall fear that it will be carried out.

(4) A person contravenes this subsection if, in order to compel a State, international governmental organisation or person to do, or abstain from doing, any act, he threatens that he or any other person will obtain nuclear material by an act which is an offence mentioned in paragraph (*c*) of subsection (1) of section 1 above.

(5) A person guilty of an offence under this section shall be liable on conviction on indictment to imprisonment for a term not exceeding fourteen years and not exceeding the term of imprisonment to which a person would be liable for the offence constituted by doing the contemplated act at the place where the conviction occurs and at the time of the offence to which the conviction relates.

(6) In subsection (5) above " contemplated act " means,—

(*a*) where the conviction relates to an offence under subsection (2) above, the act intended or as to the doing of which the person convicted was reckless, as the case may be; and

(*b*) where the conviction relates to an offence under subsection (3) or (4) above, the act threatened.

(7) In this section references to an act which is an offence mentioned in paragraph (*a*), (*b*) or (*c*) of subsection (1) of section 1 above are references to an act which, by virtue of that subsection or otherwise, is an offence so mentioned.

Supplemental
1978 c. 17.
1978 c. 26.

3.—(1) Proceedings for an offence which (disregarding the provisions of the Internationally Protected Persons Act 1978 and the Suppression of Terrorism Act 1978) would not be an offence apart from the preceding provisions of this Act shall not be begun—

(*a*) in England and Wales, except by or with the consent of the Attorney General; or

(*b*) in Northern Ireland, except by or with the consent of the Attorney General for Northern Ireland.

(2) Without prejudice to any jurisdiction exercisable apart from this subsection, every sheriff court in Scotland shall have jurisdiction to entertain proceedings for an offence which (disregarding the provisions of the Internationally Protected Persons Act 1978 and the Suppression of Terrorism Act 1978) would not be an offence in Scotland apart from the preceding provisions of this Act.

Amendments of other Acts.

4.—(1) In consequence of the provisions of this Act—

(*a*) in subsections (1) and (2) of section 2 of the Internationally Protected Persons Act 1978 (which relates to certain offences committed outside the United Kingdom) after the words " Suppression of Terrorism Act 1978 " there shall be inserted in each place the words " and the Nuclear Material (Offences) Act 1983 "; and

(*b*) in subsections (4) and (5) of section 4 of the Suppression of Terrorism Act 1978 (which also relates to certain offences committed outside the United Kingdom) after the words " Internationally Protected Persons Act 1978 " there shall be inserted in each place the words " and the Nuclear Material (Offences) Act 1983 ".

1952 c. 67.

(2) In the Schedule to the Visiting Forces Act 1952 (which specifies the offences which are offences against the person and against property for the purposes of section 3 of that Act)—

(*a*) at the end of each of paragraphs 1, 2 and 4 there shall be inserted the following sub-paragraph—

" (*d*) an offence under section 2 of the Nuclear Material (Offences) Act 1983, where the circumstances are that—

(i) in the case of a contravention of subsection (2), the act falling within paragraph (*a*) or (*b*) of that subsection would, had it been done, have constituted an offence falling within sub-paragraph (*a*) or (*b*) of this paragraph, or

(ii) in the case of a contravention of subsection (3) or (4), the act threatened would, had it been done, have constituted such an offence " ; and

(*b*) at the end of paragraph 3 there shall be inserted the following sub-paragraph—

" (*k*) an offence under section 2 of the Nuclear Material (Offences) Act 1983, where the circumstances are that—

(i) in the case of a contravention of subsection (2), the act falling within paragraph (*a*) or (*b*) of that subsection would, had it been done, have constituted an offence falling within the foregoing sub-paragraphs, or

(ii) in the case of a contravention of subsection (3) or (4), the act threatened would, had it been done, have constituted such an offence."

(3) In Part I of Schedule 4 to the Northern Ireland (Emergency Provisions) Act 1978 (scheduled offences for the purposes of that Act),— 1978 c. 5.

(*a*) in paragraph 12, for the words " note 4 " there shall be substituted the words " notes 4 and 5 " and at the end there shall be added the following sub-paragraphs—

" (*c*) section 1 (theft) ;

(*d*) section 9 (burglary) ;

(*e*) section 15 (obtaining property by deception) ;

(*f*) section 20 (blackmail) " ;

(*b*) the paragraph inserted by section 2(3) of the Taking of Hostages Act 1982 as paragraph 19A shall be renumbered 19B and after that paragraph there shall be inserted the following— 1982 c. 28.

" *Nuclear Material (Offences) Act 1983*

19C. Offences under section 2 of the Nuclear Material (Offences) Act 1983 (offences involving nuclear material: preparatory acts and threats) " ; and

(*c*) in the Notes, for note 4 there shall be substituted the following notes—

" 4. Robbery and aggravated burglary are scheduled offences only where it is charged—

(*a*) that an explosive, firearm, imitation firearm or weapon of offence was used to commit the offence; or

(*b*) that the offence was committed in relation to or by means of nuclear material within the meaning of the Nuclear Material (Offences) Act 1983;

1969 c. 16. (N.I.). and expressions defined in section 10 of the Theft Act (Northern Ireland) 1969 have the same meaning when used in this note.

5. An offence under section 1, 9, 15 or 20 of the Theft Act (Northern Ireland) 1969 is a scheduled offence only where it is charged that the offence was committed in relation to or by means of nuclear material within the meaning of the Nuclear Material (Offences) Act 1983."

Extradition.

5.—(1) There shall be deemed to be included—

(*a*) in the list of extradition crimes in Schedule 1 to the Extradition Act 1870, and

1870 c. 52.

(*b*) among the description of offences set out in Schedule 1 to the Fugitive Offenders Act 1967,

1967 c. 68.

any offence under section 2 of this Act.

(2) Where no such arrangement as is mentioned in section 2 of the Extradition Act 1870 has been made with a State which is a party to the Convention, an Order in Council applying the Act of 1870 may be made under that section as if the Convention were such an arrangement with that State; but where the Act of 1870 is so applied it shall have effect as if the only extradition crimes within the meaning of that Act were—

(*a*) an offence mentioned in paragraphs (*a*) to (*d*) of subsection (1) of section 1 of this Act which is committed by doing an act in relation to or by means of nuclear material;

(*b*) an offence under section 2 of this Act; and

(*c*) an attempt to commit an offence mentioned in paragraph (*a*) or (*b*) above.

(3) For the purposes of the Extradition Act 1870 any act, wherever committed, which—

(*a*) is an offence mentioned in subsection (2) above, and

(*b*) is an offence against the law of any State in the case of which that Act is applied by an Order in Council under section 2 of that Act,

shall be deemed to be an offence committed within the jurisdiction of that State.

(4) In this section and in section 6 below " the Convention " means the Convention on the Physical Protection of Nuclear Material opened for signature at Vienna and New York on 3rd March 1980.

Material to which the Act applies.

6.—(1) References in this Act to nuclear material are references to material which, within the meaning of the Convention, is nuclear material used for peaceful purposes.

(2) If in any proceedings a question arises whether any material was used for peaceful purposes, a certificate issued by or under the authority of the Secretary of State and stating that it was, or was not, so used at a time specified in the certificate shall be conclusive of that question.

(3) In any proceedings a document purporting to be such a certificate as is mentioned in subsection (2) above shall be taken to be such a certificate unless the contrary is proved.

(4) Paragraphs (*a*) and (*b*) of Article 1 of the Convention (which give the definition of " nuclear material " for the purposes of the Convention) are set out in the Schedule to this Act.

Application to Channel Islands, Isle of Man, etc.

7.—(1) Sections 17 and 22 of the Extradition Act 1870 and sections 16 and 17 of the Fugitive Offenders Act 1967 (application to Channel Islands, Isle of Man and colonies) shall extend respectively to the provisions of this Act amending those Acts.

1870 c. 52.
1967 c. 68.

(2) Her Majesty may by Order in Council make provision for extending the other provisions of this Act, with such exceptions, adaptations or modifications as may be specified in the Order, to any of the Channel Islands, the Isle of Man or any colony.

Short title and commencement.

8.—(1) This Act may be cited as the Nuclear Material (Offences) Act 1983.

(2) This Act shall come into force on such day as Her Majesty may by Order in Council appoint.

Section 6.

SCHEDULE

Article 1(*a*) and (*b*) of the Convention

Article 1

For the purposes of this Convention:

(*a*) " nuclear material " means plutonium except that with isotopic concentration exceeding 80% in plutonium-238; uranium-233; uranium enriched in the isotopes 235 or 233; uranium containing the mixture of isotopes as occurring in nature other than in the form of ore or ore-residue; any material containing one or more of the foregoing;

(*b*) " uranium enriched in the isotope 235 or 233 " means uranium containing the isotopes 235 or 233 or both in an amount such that the abundance ratio of the sum of these isotopes to the isotope 238 is greater than the ratio of the isotope 235 to the isotope 238 occurring in nature.

Matrimonial Homes Act 1983

1983 CHAPTER 19

An Act to consolidate certain enactments relating to the rights of a husband or wife to occupy a dwelling house that has been a matrimonial home. [9th May 1983]

BE IT ENACTED by the Queen's most Excellent Majesty, by and with the advice and consent of the Lords Spiritual and Temporal, and Commons, in this present Parliament assembled, and by the authority of the same, as follows:—

Rights concerning matrimonial home where one spouse has no estate, etc.

1.—(1) Where one spouse is entitled to occupy a dwelling house by virtue of a beneficial estate or interest or contract or by virtue of any enactment giving him or her the right to remain in occupation, and the other spouse is not so entitled, then, subject to the provisions of this Act, the spouse not so entitled shall have the following rights (in this Act referred to as " rights of occupation ")—

(*a*) if in occupation, a right not to be evicted or excluded from the dwelling house or any part thereof by the other spouse except with the leave of the court given by an order under this section ;

(*b*) if not in occupation, a right with the leave of the court so given to enter into and occupy the dwelling house.

(2) So long as one spouse has rights of occupation, either of the spouses may apply to the court for an order—

(*a*) declaring, enforcing, restricting or terminating those rights, or

(*b*) prohibiting, suspending or restricting the exercise by either spouse of the right to occupy the dwelling house, or

(*c*) requiring either spouse to permit the exercise by the other of that right.

(3) On an application for an order under this section, the court may make such order as it thinks just and reasonable having regard to the conduct of the spouses in relation to each other and otherwise, to their respective needs and financial resources, to the needs of any children and to all the circumstances of the case, and, without prejudice to the generality of the foregoing provision—

(*a*) may except part of the dwelling house from a spouse's rights of occupation (and in particular a part used wholly or mainly for or in connection with the trade, business or profession of the other spouse),

(*b*) may order a spouse occupying the dwelling house or any part thereof by virtue of this section to make periodical payments to the other in respect of the occupation,

(*c*) may impose on either spouse obligations as to the repair and maintenance of the dwelling house or the discharge of any liabilities in respect of the dwelling house.

(4) Orders under this section may, in so far as they have a continuing effect, be limited so as to have effect for a period specified in the order or until further order.

(5) Where a spouse is entitled under this section to occupy a dwelling house or any part thereof, any payment or tender made or other thing done by that spouse in or towards satisfaction of any liability of the other spouse in respect of rent, rates, mortgage payments or other outgoings affecting the dwelling house shall, whether or not it is made or done in pursuance of an order under this section, be as good as if made or done by the other spouse.

(6) A spouse's occupation by virtue of this section shall, for
1976 c. 80. the purposes of the Rent (Agriculture) Act 1976, and of the
1977 c. 42. Rent Act 1977 (other than Part V and sections 103 to 106), be treated as possession by the other spouse and for purposes of
1980 c. 51. Chapter II of Part I of the Housing Act 1980 be treated as occupation by the other spouse.

(7) Where a spouse is entitled under this section to occupy a dwelling house or any part thereof and makes any payment in or

towards satisfaction of any liability of the other spouse in respect of mortgage payments affecting the dwelling house, the person to whom the payment is made may treat it as having been made by that other spouse, but the fact that that person has treated any such payment as having been so made shall not affect any claim of the first-mentioned spouse against the other to an interest in the dwelling house by virtue of the payment.

(8) Where a spouse is entitled under this section to occupy a dwelling house or part thereof by reason of an interest of the other spouse under a trust, all the provisions of subsections (5) to (7) above shall apply in relation to the trustees as they apply in relation to the other spouse.

(9) The jurisdiction conferred on the court by this section shall be exercisable by the High Court or by a county court, and shall be exercisable by a county court notwithstanding that by reason of the amount of the net annual value for rating of the dwelling house or otherwise the jurisdiction would not but for this subsection be exercisable by a county court.

(10) This Act shall not apply to a dwelling house which has at no time been a matrimonial home of the spouses in question; and a spouse's rights of occupation shall continue only so long as the marriage subsists and the other spouse is entitled as mentioned in subsection (1) above to occupy the dwelling house, except where provision is made by section 2 of this Act for those rights to be a charge on an estate or interest in the dwelling house.

(11) It is hereby declared that a spouse who has an equitable interest in a dwelling house or in the proceeds of sale thereof, not being a spouse in whom is vested (whether solely or as a joint tenant) a legal estate in fee simple or a legal term of years absolute in the dwelling house, is to be treated for the purpose only of determining whether he or she has rights of occupation under this section as not being entitled to occupy the dwelling house by virtue of that interest.

Effect of rights of occupation as charge on dwelling house.

2.—(1) Where, at any time during the subsistence of a marriage, one spouse is entitled to occupy a dwelling house by virtue of a beneficial estate or interest, then the other spouse's rights of occupation shall be a charge on that estate or interest, having the like priority as if it were an equitable interest created at whichever is the latest of the following dates, that is to say—

(*a*) the date when the spouse so entitled acquires the estate or interest,

(*b*) the date of the marriage, and

(*c*) the 1st January 1968 (which is the date of commencement of the Act of 1967).

(2) If, at any time when a spouse's rights of occupation are a charge on an interest of the other spouse under a trust, there are, apart from either of the spouses, no persons, living or unborn, who are or could become beneficiaries under the trust, then those rights shall be a charge also on the estate or interest of the trustees for the other spouse, having the like priority as if it were an equitable interest created (under powers overriding the trusts) on the date when it arises.

(3) In determining for purposes of subsection (2) above whether there are any persons who are not, but could become, beneficiaries under the trust, there shall be disregarded any potential exercise of a general power of appointment exercisable by either or both of the spouses alone (whether or not the exercise of it requires the consent of another person).

(4) Notwithstanding that a spouse's rights of occupation are a charge on an estate or interest in the dwelling house, those rights shall be brought to an end by—

(*a*) the death of the other spouse, or

(*b*) the termination (otherwise than by death) of the marriage,

unless in the event of a matrimonial dispute or estrangement the court sees fit to direct otherwise by an order made under section 1 above during the subsistence of the marriage.

(5) Where a spouse's rights of occupation are a charge on the estate or interest of the other spouse or of trustees for the other spouse—

(*a*) any order under section 1 above against the other spouse shall, except in so far as the contrary intention appears, have the like effect against persons deriving title under the other spouse or under the trustees and affected by the charge, and

(*b*) subsections (2) to (8) of section 1 above shall apply in relation to any person deriving title under the other spouse or under the trustees and affected by the charge as they apply in relation to the other spouse.

(6) Where—

(*a*) a spouse's rights of occupation are a charge on an estate or interest in the dwelling house, and

(*b*) that estate or interest is surrendered so as to merge in some other estate or interest expectant thereon in such circumstances that, but for the merger, the person taking the estate or interest surrendered would be bound by the charge,

the surrender shall have effect subject to the charge and the persons thereafter entitled to the other estate or interest shall, for so long as the estate or interest surrendered would have endured if not so surrendered, be treated for all purposes of this Act as deriving title to the other estate or interest under the other spouse or, as the case may be, under the trustees for the other spouse, by virtue of the surrender.

(7) Where a spouse's rights of occupation are a charge on the estate or interest of the other spouse or of trustees for the other spouse, and the other spouse—

(*a*) is adjudged bankrupt or makes a conveyance or assignment of his or her property (including that estate or interest) to trustees for the benefit of his or her creditors generally, or

(*b*) dies and his or her estate is insolvent,

then, notwithstanding that it is registered under section 2 of the Land Charges Act 1972 or subsection (8) below, the charge shall 1972 c. 61. be void against the trustee in bankruptcy, the trustees under the conveyance or assignment or the personal representatives of the deceased spouse, as the case may be.

(8) Where the title to the legal estate by virtue of which a spouse is entitled to occupy a dwelling house (including any legal estate held by trustees for that spouse) is registered under the Land Registration Act 1925 or any enactment replaced by that 1925 c. 21. Act—

(*a*) registration of a land charge affecting the dwelling house by virtue of this Act shall be effected by registering a notice under that Act, and

(*b*) a spouse's rights of occupation shall not be an overriding interest within the meaning of that Act affecting the dwelling house notwithstanding that the spouse is in actual occupation of the dwelling house.

(9) A spouse's rights of occupation (whether or not constituting a charge) shall not entitle that spouse to lodge a caution under section 54 of the Land Registration Act 1925.

(10) Where—

(*a*) a spouse's rights of occupation are a charge on the estate of the other spouse or of trustees for the other spouse, and

(*b*) that estate is the subject of a mortgage within the meaning of the Law of Property Act 1925, 1925 c. 20.

then, if, after the date of creation of the mortgage, the charge is registered under section 2 of the Land Charges Act 1972, the charge shall, for the purposes of section 94 of that Act of 1925 (which regulates the rights of mortgagees to make further advances ranking in priority to subsequent mortgages), be deemed to be a mortgage subsequent in date to the first-mentioned mortgage.

1972 c. 61.

(11) It is hereby declared that a charge under subsection (1) or (2) above is not registrable under section 2 of the Land Charges Act 1972 or subsection (8) above unless it is a charge on a legal estate.

Restriction on registration where spouse entitled to more than one charge.

3. Where one spouse is entitled by virtue of section 2 above to a registrable charge in respect of each of two or more dwelling houses, only one of the charges to which that spouse is so entitled shall be registered under section 2 of the Land Charges Act 1972 or section 2(8) above at any one time, and if any of those charges is registered under either of those provisions the Chief Land Registrar, on being satisfied that any other of them is so registered, shall cancel the registration of the charge first registered.

Contract for sale of house affected by registered charge to include term requiring cancellation of registration before completion.

4.—(1) Where one spouse is entitled by virtue of section 2 above to a charge on an estate in a dwelling house and the charge is registered under section 2 of the Land Charges Act 1972 or section 2(8) above, it shall be a term of any contract for the sale of that estate whereby the vendor agrees to give vacant possession of the dwelling house on completion of the contract that the vendor will before such completion procure the cancellation of the registration of the charge at his expense.

(2) Subsection (1) above shall not apply to any such contract made by a vendor who is entitled to sell the estate in the dwelling house freed from any such charge.

(3) If, on the completion of such a contract as is referred to in subsection (1) above, there is delivered to the purchaser or his solicitor an application by the spouse entitled to the charge for the cancellation of the registration of that charge, the term of the contract for which subsection (1) above provides shall be deemed to have been performed.

(4) This section applies only if and so far as a contrary intention is not expressed in the contract.

(5) This section shall apply to a contract for exchange as it applies to a contract for sale.

(6) This section shall, with the necessary modifications, apply to a contract for the grant of a lease or underlease of a dwelling house as it applies to a contract for the sale of an estate in a dwelling house.

5.—(1) Where a spouse's rights of occupation are a charge on an estate in a dwelling house and the charge is registered under section 2 of the Land Charges Act 1972 or section 2(8) above, the Chief Land Registrar shall, subject to subsection (2) below, cancel the registration of the charge if he is satisfied— Cancellation of registration after termination of marriage, etc. 1972 c. 61.

(*a*) by the production of a certificate or other sufficient evidence, that either spouse is dead, or

(*b*) by the production of an official copy of a decree of a court, that the marriage in question has been terminated otherwise than by death, or

(*c*) by the production of an order of the court, that the spouse's rights of occupation constituting the charge have been terminated by the order.

(2) Where—

(*a*) the marriage in question has been terminated by the death of the spouse entitled to an estate in the dwelling house or otherwise than by death, and

(*b*) an order affecting the charge of the spouse not so entitled had been made by virtue of section 2(4) above,

then if, after the making of the order, registration of the charge was renewed or the charge registered in pursuance of subsection (3) below, the Chief Land Registrar shall not cancel the registration of the charge in accordance with subsection (1) above unless he is also satisfied that the order has ceased to have effect.

(3) Where such an order has been made, then, for the purposes of subsection (2) above, the spouse entitled to the charge affected by the order may—

(*a*) if before the date of the order the charge was registered under section 2 of the Land Charges Act 1972 or section 2(8) above, renew the registration of the charge, and

(*b*) if before the said date the charge was not so registered, register the charge under section 2 of the Land Charges Act 1972 or section 2(8) above.

(4) Renewal of the registration of a charge in pursuance of subsection (3) above shall be effected in such manner as may be prescribed, and an application for such renewal or for registration of a charge in pursuance of that subsection shall contain such particulars of any order affecting the charge made by virtue of section 2(4) above as may be prescribed.

(5) The renewal in pursuance of subsection (3) above of the registration of a charge shall not affect the priority of the charge.

(6) In this section " prescribed " means prescribed by rules made under section 16 of the Land Charges Act 1972 or section

1925 c. 21.

144 of the Land Registration Act 1925, as the circumstances of the case require.

Release of rights of occupation and postponement of priority of charge.

1972 c. 61.

6.—(1) A spouse entitled to rights of occupation may by a release in writing release those rights or release them as respects part only of the dwelling house affected by them.

(2) Where a contract is made for the sale of an estate or interest in a dwelling house, or for the grant of a lease or underlease of a dwelling house, being (in either case) a dwelling house affected by a charge registered under section 2 of the Land Charges Act 1972 or section 2(8) above, then, without prejudice to subsection (1) above, the rights of occupation constituting the charge shall be deemed to have been released on the happening of whichever of the following events first occurs—

(*a*) the delivery to the purchaser or lessee, as the case may be, or his solicitor on completion of the contract of an application by the spouse entitled to the charge for the cancellation of the registration of the charge, or

(*b*) the lodging of such an application at Her Majesty's Land Registry.

(3) A spouse entitled by virtue of section 2 above to a charge on an estate or interest may agree in writing that any other charge on, or interest in, that estate or interest shall rank in priority to the charge to which that spouse is so entitled.

Transfer of certain tenancies on divorce, etc.

7. Schedule 1 to this Act shall have effect.

Dwelling house subject to mortgage.

8.—(1) In determining for the purposes of the foregoing provisions of this Act (including Schedule 1) whether a spouse or former spouse is entitled to occupy a dwelling house by virtue of an estate or interest, there shall be disregarded any right to possession of the dwelling house conferred on a mortgagee of the dwelling house under or by virtue of his mortgage, whether the mortgagee is in possession or not; but the other spouse shall not by virtue of the rights of occupation conferred by this Act have any larger right against the mortgagee to occupy the dwelling house than the one first mentioned has by virtue of his or her estate or interest and of any contract with the mortgagee, unless under section 2 above those rights of occupation are a charge, affecting the mortgagee, on the estate or interest mortgaged.

(2) Where a mortgagee of land which consists of or includes a dwelling house brings an action in any court for the enforcement of his security, a spouse who is not a party to the action and who is enabled by section 1(5) or (8) above to meet the mortgagor's liabilities under the mortgage, on applying to the court

at any time before the action is finally disposed of in that court, shall be entitled to be made a party to the action if the court—

(a) does not see special reason against it, and

(b) is satisfied that the applicant may be expected to make such payments or do such things in or towards satisfaction of the mortgagor's liabilities or obligations as might affect the outcome of the proceedings or that the expectation of it should be considered under section 36 of the Administration of Justice Act 1970. 1970 c. 31.

(3) Where a mortgagee of land which consists or substantially consists of a dwelling house brings an action for the enforcement of his security, and at the relevant time there is—

(a) in the case of unregistered land, a land charge of Class F registered against the person who is the estate owner at the relevant time or any person who, where the estate owner is a trustee, preceded him as trustee during the subsistence of the mortgage, or

(b) in the case of registered land, a subsisting registration of a notice under section 2(8) above or a notice or caution under section 2(7) of the Act of 1967,

notice of the action shall be served by the mortgagee on the person on whose behalf the land charge is registered or the notice or caution entered, if that person is not a party to the action.

(4) For the purposes of subsection (3) above, if there has been issued a certificate of the result of an official search made on behalf of the mortgagee which would disclose any land charge of Class F, notice or caution within subsection (3)(a) or (b) above, and the action is commenced within the priority period, the relevant time is the date of that certificate; and in any other case the relevant time is the time when the action is commenced.

(5) In subsection (4) above, " priority period " means, for both registered and unregistered land, the period for which, in accordance with section 11(5) and (6) of the Land Charges Act 1972, a certificate on an official search operates in favour of a purchaser. 1972 c. 61.

Rights concerning matrimonial home where both spouses have estate, etc.

9.—(1) Where each of two spouses is entitled, by virtue of a legal estate vested in them jointly, to occupy a dwelling house in which they have or at any time have had a matrimonial home, either of them may apply to the court, with respect to the exercise during the subsistence of the marriage of the right to occupy the dwelling house, for an order prohibiting, suspending or restricting its exercise by the other or requiring the other to permit its exercise by the applicant.

(2) In relation to orders under this section, section 1(3), (4) and (9) above shall apply as they apply in relation to orders under that section.

(3) Where each of two spouses is entitled to occupy a dwelling house by virtue of a contract, or by virtue of any enactment giving them the right to remain in occupation, this section shall apply as it applies where they are entitled by virtue of a legal estate vested in them jointly.

(4) In determining for the purposes of this section whether two spouses are entitled to occupy a dwelling house, there shall be disregarded any right to possession of the dwelling house conferred on a mortgagee of the dwelling house under or by virtue of his mortgage, whether the mortgagee is in possession or not.

Interpretation.

10.—(1) In this Act—

1967 c. 75. " Act of 1967 " means the Matrimonial Homes Act 1967 ;

1981 c. 24. " Act of 1981 " means the Matrimonial Homes and Property Act 1981 ;

" dwelling house " includes any building or part thereof which is occupied as a dwelling, and any yard, garden, garage or outhouse belonging to the dwelling house and occupied therewith ;

" mortgage " includes a charge and " mortgagor " and " mortgagee " shall be construed accordingly ;

" mortgagor " and " mortgagee " includes any person deriving title under the original mortgagor or mortgagee ;

" rights of occupation " has the meaning assigned to it in section 1(1) above.

(2) It is hereby declared that this Act applies as between a husband and a wife notwithstanding that the marriage in question was entered into under a law which permits polygamy (whether or not either party to the marriage in question has for the time being any spouse additional to the other party).

(3) References in this Act to registration under section 2(8) above include (as well as references to registration by notice under section 2(7) of the Act of 1967) references to registration by caution duly lodged under the said section 2(7) before the 14th February 1983 (the date of commencement of section 4(2) of the Act of 1981).

Transitional provision.

11. Neither section 2(9) above, nor the repeal by section 4(2) of the Act of 1981 of the words " or caution " in section 2(7) of the Act of 1967, affects a caution duly lodged as respects any estate of interest before the said 14th February 1983.

12.—(1) The Acts specified in Schedule 2 to this Act shall have effect subject to the amendments specified in that Schedule.

Consequential amendments and repeals.

(2) The Acts specified in Schedule 3 to this Act are repealed to the extent specified in the third column of that Schedule.

13.—(1) This Act may be cited as the Matrimonial Homes Act 1983.

Short title, commencement and extent.

(2) This Act shall come into force at the end of the period of three months beginning with the day on which it is passed.

(3) This Act does not extend to Scotland or Northern Ireland.

SCHEDULES

Section 7.

SCHEDULE 1

Transfer of Certain Tenancies on Divorce, Etc.

Part I

General

1.—(1) Where one spouse is entitled, either in his or her own right or jointly with the other spouse, to occupy a dwelling house by virtue of—

(*a*) a protected tenancy or statutory tenancy within the meaning of the Rent Act 1977, or

1977 c. 42.

1976 c. 80.

(*b*) a statutory tenancy within the meaning of the Rent (Agriculture) Act 1976, or

(*c*) a secure tenancy within the meaning of section 28 of the Housing Act 1980,

1980 c. 51.

then, on granting a decree of divorce, a decree of nullity of marriage or a decree of judicial separation, or at any time thereafter (whether, in the case of a decree of divorce or nullity of marriage, before or after the decree is made absolute), the court by which the decree is granted may make an order under Part II below.

(2) References in this Schedule to a spouse being entitled to occupy a dwelling house by virtue of a protected, statutory or secure tenancy apply whether that entitlement is in his or her own right, or jointly with the other spouse.

Part II

Protected or secure tenancy

2.—(1) Where a spouse is entitled to occupy the dwelling house by virtue of a protected tenancy within the meaning of the Rent Act 1977, or a secure tenancy within the meaning of the Housing Act 1980, the court may by order direct that, as from such date as may be specified in the order, there shall, by virtue of the order and without further assurance, be transferred to, and vested in, the other spouse—

(*a*) the estate or interest which the spouse so entitled had in the dwelling house immediately before that date by virtue of the lease or agreement creating the tenancy and any assignment of that lease or agreement, with all rights, privileges and appurtenances attaching to that estate or interest but subject to all covenants, obligations, liabilities and incumbrances to which it is subject; and

(*b*) where the spouse so entitled is an assignee of such lease or agreement, the liability of that spouse under any covenant of indemnity by the assignee expressed or implied in the assignment of the lease or agreement to that spouse.

(2) Where an order is made under this paragraph, any liability or obligation to which the spouse so entitled is subject under any covenant having reference to the dwelling house in the lease or agreement, being a liability or obligation falling due to be discharged or performed on or after the date so specified, shall not be enforceable against that spouse. SCH. 1

(3) Where the spouse so entitled is a successor within the meaning of Chapter II of Part I of the Housing Act 1980, his or her former spouse (or, in the case of judicial separation, his or her spouse) shall be deemed also to be a successor within the meaning of that Chapter. 1980 c. 51.

Statutory tenancy within the meaning of the Rent Act 1977

3.—(1) Where the spouse is entitled to occupy the dwelling house by virtue of a statutory tenancy within the meaning of the Rent Act 1977, the court may by order direct that, as from such date as may be specified in the order, that spouse shall cease to be entitled to occupy the dwelling house and that the other spouse shall be deemed to be the tenant or, as the case may be, the sole tenant under that statutory tenancy. 1977 c. 42.

(2) The question whether the provisions of paragraphs 1 to 3 or, as the case may be, paragraphs 5 to 7 of Schedule 1 to the Rent Act 1977 as to the succession by the surviving spouse of a deceased tenant, or by a member of the deceased tenant's family, to the right to retain possession are capable of having effect in the event of the death of the person deemed by an order under this paragraph to be the tenant or sole tenant under the statutory tenancy shall be determined according as those provisions have or have not already had effect in relation to the statutory tenancy.

Statutory tenancy within the meaning of the Rent (Agriculture) Act 1976

4. Where the spouse is entitled to occupy the dwelling house by virtue of a statutory tenancy within the meaning of the Rent (Agriculture) Act 1976, the court may by order direct that, as from such date as may be specified in the order, that spouse shall cease to be entitled to occupy the dwelling house and that the other spouse shall be deemed to be the tenant or, as the case may be, the sole tenant under that statutory tenancy; and a spouse who is deemed as aforesaid to be the tenant under a statutory tenancy shall be (within the meaning of that Act) a statutory tenant in his own right, or a statutory tenant by succession, according as the other spouse was a statutory tenant in his own right or a statutory tenant by succession. 1976 c. 80.

PART III

Ancillary jurisdiction

5. Where the court makes an order under Part II of this Schedule, it may by the order direct that both spouses shall be jointly and severally liable to discharge or perform any or all of the liabilities and obligations in respect of the dwelling house (whether arising under the tenancy or otherwise) which have at the date of the order

SCH. 1 fallen due to be discharged or performed by one only of the spouses or which, but for the direction, would before the date specified as the date on which the order is to take effect fall due to be discharged or performed by one only of them; and where the court gives such a direction it may further direct that either spouse shall be liable to indemnify the other in whole or in part against any payment made or expenses incurred by the other in discharging or performing any such liability or obligation.

Date when order is to take effect

6. In the case of a decree of divorce or nullity of marriage, the date specified in an order under Part II of this Schedule as the date on which the order is to take effect shall not be earlier than the date on which the decree is made absolute.

Remarriage of either spouse

7. If after the grant of a decree dissolving or annulling a marriage either spouse remarries, that spouse shall not be entitled to apply, by reference to the grant of that decree, for an order under Part II of this Schedule.

Rules of court

8.—(1) Rules of court shall be made requiring the court before it makes an order under this Schedule to give the landlord of the dwelling house to which the order will relate an opportunity of being heard.

(2) Rules of court may provide that an application for an order under this Schedule shall not, without the leave of the court by which the decree of divorce, nullity of marriage or judicial separation was granted, be made after the expiration of such period from the grant of the decree as may be prescribed by the rules.

(3) Rules of court may provide for the transfer of proceedings pending by virtue of this Schedule in the court which granted the decree of divorce, nullity of marriage or judicial separation as follows—

(*a*) if the proceedings are pending in the High Court, for the transfer of the proceedings to a divorce county court;

(*b*) if the proceedings are pending in a divorce county court, for the transfer of the proceedings to the High Court or to some other divorce county court;

and a court shall have jurisdiction to entertain any proceedings transferred to the court by virtue of rules made in pursuance of this sub-paragraph.

(4) For the purposes of sub-paragraph (3) above—

(*a*) any proceedings in the divorce registry shall be treated as pending in a divorce county court; and

(*b*) the power to provide for the transfer of proceedings to a divorce county court shall include power to provide for the transfer of proceedings to the divorce registry.

Savings for sections 1 *and* 2 *of this Act* SCH. 1

9. Where a spouse is entitled to occupy a dwelling house by virtue of a tenancy, this Schedule shall not affect the operation of sections 1 and 2 of this Act in relation to the other spouse's rights of occupation, and the court's power to make orders under this Schedule shall be in addition to the powers conferred by those sections.

Interpretation

10.—(1) In this Schedule—

" divorce county court " means a county court designated under section 1 of the Matrimonial Causes Act 1967 ; 1967 c. 56.

" divorce registry " means the principal registry of the Family Division of the High Court ;

" landlord " includes any person from time to time deriving title under the original landlord and also includes, in relation to any dwelling house, any person other than the tenant who is, or but for Part VII of the Rent Act 1977 or Part II of the Rent (Agriculture) Act 1976 would be, entitled to possession of the dwelling house ; 1977 c. 42. 1976 c. 80.

" tenancy " includes sub-tenancy.

(2) For the avoidance of doubt it is hereby declared that the reference in paragraph 7 above to remarriage includes a reference to a marriage which is by law void or voidable.

SCHEDULE 2

Section 12.

CONSEQUENTIAL AMENDMENTS

LAND REGISTRATION ACT 1925

1925 c. 21.

In sections 64(5) and 112B, for " section 2(7) of the Matrimonial Homes Act 1967 " substitute in each case " section 2(8) of the Matrimonial Homes Act 1983 ".

MATRIMONIAL HOMES ACT 1967

1967 c. 75.

In paragraph 4 of the Schedule, for " Matrimonial Homes Act 1967 " substitute " Matrimonial Homes Act 1983 ".

LAND CHARGES ACT 1972

1972 c. 61.

In section 2(7), for " Matrimonial Homes Act 1967 " substitute " Matrimonial Homes Act 1983 ".

MATRIMONIAL CAUSES ACT 1973

1973 c. 18.

In section 4(4)(*b*) (inserted by section 62 of the Domestic Proceedings and Magistrates' Courts Act 1978), for subparagraphs (i) and (ii) substitute " section 1 or 9 of the Matrimonial Homes Act 1983 ".

In section (50)(1)(*b*), for the words from " section 7 " to the end of the paragraph substitute " Schedule 1 to the Matrimonial Homes Act 1983 (transfer of certain tenancies on divorce, etc.) ".

In section 50(1)(*c*), for " Matrimonial Homes Act 1967 " substitute " Matrimonial Homes Act 1983 "

SCH. 2

DOMESTIC PROCEEDINGS AND MAGISTRATES' COURTS ACT 1978

1978 c. 22. In section 28(2)(*a*), for " Matrimonial Homes Act 1967 " substitute " Matrimonial Homes Act 1983 ".

In section 28(2)(*b*), for " section 4 of the Domestic Violence and Matrimonial Proceedings Act 1976 " substitute " section 9 of the Matrimonial Homes Act 1983 ".

Section 12.

SCHEDULE 3

REPEALS

Chapter	Short title	Extent of repeal
1967 c. 75.	Matrimonial Homes Act 1967.	The whole Act except section 2(6) so far as it relates to paragraph 4 of the Schedule, and except that paragraph.
1970 c. 45.	Matrimonial Proceedings and Property Act 1970.	Section 38.
1972 c. 61.	Land Charges Act 1972.	In Schedule 3, paragraphs 8 to 12.
1976 c. 50.	Domestic Violence and Matrimonial Proceedings Act 1976.	Sections 3 and 4.
1977 c. 42.	Rent Act 1977.	In Schedule 23, paragraph 40.
1980 c. 51.	Housing Act 1980.	In Schedule 25, paragraph 14.
1981 c. 24.	Matrimonial Homes and Property Act 1981.	Sections 1 to 3. In section 4, subsections (2) and (3). Sections 5 and 6. Schedules 1 and 2.

Mental Health Act 1983

1983 CHAPTER 20

An Act to consolidate the law relating to mentally disordered persons. [9th May 1983]

BE IT ENACTED by the Queen's most Excellent Majesty, by and with the advice and consent of the Lords Spiritual and Temporal, and Commons, in this present Parliament assembled, and by the authority of the same, as follows:—

PART I

APPLICATION OF ACT

1.—(1) The provisions of this Act shall have effect with respect to the reception, care and treatment of mentally disordered patients, the management of their property and other related matters. Application of Act: "mental disorder".

(2) In this Act—

"mental disorder" means mental illness, arrested or incomplete development of mind, psychopathic disorder and any other disorder or disability of mind and "mentally disordered" shall be construed accordingly;

"severe mental impairment" means a state of arrested or incomplete development of mind which includes severe impairment of intelligence and social functioning and is associated with abnormally aggressive or seriously irresponsible conduct on the part of the person concerned and "severely mentally impaired" shall be construed accordingly;

PART I

"mental impairment" means a state of arrested or incomplete development of mind (not amounting to severe mental impairment) which includes significant impairment of intelligence and social functioning and is associated with abnormally aggressive or seriously irresponsible conduct on the part of the person concerned and "mentally impaired" shall be construed accordingly;

"psychopathic disorder" means a persistent disorder or disability of mind (whether or not including significant impairment of intelligence) which results in abnormally aggressive or seriously irresponsible conduct on the part of the person concerned;

and other expressions shall have the meanings assigned to them in section 145 below.

(3) Nothing in subsection (2) above shall be construed as implying that a person may be dealt with under this Act as suffering from mental disorder, or from any form of mental disorder described in this section, by reason only of promiscuity or other immoral conduct, sexual deviancy or dependence on alcohol or drugs.

PART II

COMPULSORY ADMISSION TO HOSPITAL AND GUARDIANSHIP

Procedure for hospital admission

Admission for assessment.

2.—(1) A patient may be admitted to a hospital and detained there for the period allowed by subsection (4) below in pursuance of an application (in this Act referred to as "an application for admission for assessment") made in accordance with subsections (2) and (3) below.

(2) An application for admission for assessment may be made in respect of a patient on the grounds that—

(*a*) he is suffering from mental disorder of a nature or degree which warrants the detention of the patient in a hospital for assessment (or for assessment followed by medical treatment) for at least a limited period; and

(*b*) he ought to be so detained in the interests of his own health or safety or with a view to the protection of other persons.

PART II

(3) An application for admission for assessment shall be founded on the written recommendations in the prescribed form of two registered medical practitioners, including in each case a statement that in the opinion of the practitioner the conditions set out in subsection (2) above are complied with.

(4) Subject to the provisions of section 29(4) below, a patient admitted to hospital in pursuance of an application for admission for assessment may be detained for a period not exceeding 28 days beginning with the day on which he is admitted, but shall not be detained after the expiration of that period unless before it has expired he has become liable to be detained by virtue of a subsequent application, order or direction under the following provisions of this Act.

Admission for treatment.

3.—(1) A patient may be admitted to a hospital and detained there for the period allowed by the following provisions of this Act in pursuance of an application (in this Act referred to as " an application for admission for treatment ") made in accordance with this section.

(2) An application for admission for treatment may be made in respect of a patient on the grounds that—

(*a*) he is suffering from mental illness, severe mental impairment, psychopathic disorder or mental impairment and his mental disorder is of a nature or degree which makes it appropriate for him to receive medical treatment in a hospital ; and

(*b*) in the case of psychopathic disorder or mental impairment, such treatment is likely to alleviate or prevent a deterioration of his condition ; and

(*c*) it is necessary for the health or safety of the patient or for the protection of other persons that he should receive such treatment and it cannot be provided unless he is detained under this section.

(3) An application for admission for treatment shall be founded on the written recommendations in the prescribed form of two registered medical practitioners, including in each case a statement that in the opinion of the practitioner the conditions set out in subsection (2) above are complied with ; and each such recommendation shall include—

(*a*) such particulars as may be prescribed of the grounds for that opinion so far as it relates to the conditions set out in paragraphs (*a*) and (*b*) of that subsection ; and

(*b*) a statement of the reasons for that opinion so far as it relates to the conditions set out in paragraph (*c*) of that subsection, specifying whether other methods of dealing with the patient are available and, if so, why they are not appropriate.

PART II

Admission for assessment in cases of emergency.

4.—(1) In any case of urgent necessity, an application for admission for assessment may be made in respect of a patient in accordance with the following provisions of this section, and any application so made is in this Act referred to as " an emergency application ".

(2) An emergency application may be made either by an approved social worker or by the nearest relative of the patient; and every such application shall include a statement that it is of urgent necessity for the patient to be admitted and detained under section 2 above, and that compliance with the provisions of this Part of this Act relating to applications under that section would involve undesirable delay.

(3) An emergency application shall be sufficient in the first instance if founded on one of the medical recommendations required by section 2 above, given, if practicable, by a practitioner who has previous acquaintance with the patient and otherwise complying with the requirements of section 12 below so far as applicable to a single recommendation, and verifying the statement referred to in subsection (2) above.

(4) An emergency application shall cease to have effect on the expiration of a period of 72 hours from the time when the patient is admitted to the hospital unless—

(*a*) the second medical recommendation required by section 2 above is given and received by the managers within that period; and

(*b*) that recommendation and the recommendation referred to in subsection (3) above together comply with all the requirements of section 12 below (other than the requirement as to the time of signature of the second recommendation).

(5) In relation to an emergency application, section 11 below shall have effect as if in subsection (5) of that section for the words " the period of 14 days ending with the date of the application " there were substituted the words " the previous 24 hours ".

Application in respect of patient already in hospital.

5.—(1) An application for the admission of a patient to a hospital may be made under this Part of this Act notwithstanding that the patient is already an in-patient in that hospital or, in the case of an application for admission for treatment, that the patient is for the time being liable to be detained in the hospital in pursuance of an application for admission for assessment; and where an application is so made the patient shall be treated for the purposes of this Part of this Act as if he had been admitted to the hospital at the time when that application was received by the managers.

(2) If, in the case of a patient who is an in-patient in a hospital, it appears to the registered medical practitioner in charge of the treatment of the patient that an application ought to be made under this Part of this Act for the admission of the patient to hospital, he may furnish to the managers a report in writing to that effect; and in any such case the patient may be detained in the hospital for a period of 72 hours from the time when the report is so furnished.

(3) The registered medical practitioner in charge of the treatment of a patient in a hospital may nominate one (but not more than one) other registered medical practitioner on the staff of that hospital to act for him under subsection (2) above in his absence.

(4) If, in the case of a patient who is receiving treatment for mental disorder as an in-patient in a hospital, it appears to a nurse of the prescribed class—

(*a*) that the patient is suffering from mental disorder to such a degree that it is necessary for his health or safety or for the protection of others for him to be immediately restrained from leaving the hospital; and

(*b*) that it is not practicable to secure the immediate attendance of a practitioner for the purpose of furnishing a report under subsection (2) above,

the nurse may record that fact in writing; and in that event the patient may be detained in the hospital for a period of six hours from the time when that fact is so recorded or until the earlier arrival at the place where the patient is detained of a practitioner having power to furnish a report under that subsection.

(5) A record made under subsection (4) above shall be delivered by the nurse (or by a person authorised by the nurse in that behalf) to the managers of the hospital as soon as possible after it is made; and where a record is made under that subsection the period mentioned in subsection (2) above shall begin at the time when it is made.

(6) The reference in subsection (1) above to an in-patient does not include an in-patient who is liable to be detained in pursuance of an application under this Part of this Act and the references in subsections (2) and (4) above do not include an in-patient who is liable to be detained in a hospital under this Part of this Act.

(7) In subsection (4) above " prescribed " means prescribed by an order made by the Secretary of State.

PART II

Effect of application for admission.

6.—(1) An application for the admission of a patient to a hospital under this Part of this Act, duly completed in accordance with the provisions of this Part of this Act, shall be sufficient authority for the applicant, or any person authorised by the applicant, to take the patient and convey him to the hospital at any time within the following period, that is to say—

(*a*) in the case of an application other than an emergency application, the period of 14 days beginning with the date on which the patient was last examined by a registered medical practitioner before giving a medical recommendation for the purposes of the application;

(*b*) in the case of an emergency application, the period of 24 hours beginning at the time when the patient was examined by the practitioner giving the medical recommendation which is referred to in section 4(3) above, or at the time when the application is made, whichever is the earlier.

(2) Where a patient is admitted within the said period to the hospital specified in such an application as is mentioned in subsection (1) above, or, being within that hospital, is treated by virtue of section 5 above as if he had been so admitted, the application shall be sufficient authority for the managers to detain the patient in the hospital in accordance with the provisions of this Act.

(3) Any application for the admission of a patient under this Part of this Act which appears to be duly made and to be founded on the necessary medical recommendations may be acted upon without further proof of the signature or qualification of the person by whom the application or any such medical recommendation is made or given or of any matter of fact or opinion stated in it.

(4) Where a patient is admitted to a hospital in pursuance of an application for admission for treatment, any previous application under this Part of this Act by virtue of which he was liable to be detained in a hospital or subject to guardianship shall cease to have effect.

Guardianship

Application for guardianship.

7.—(1) A patient who has attained the age of 16 years may be received into guardianship, for the period allowed by the following provisions of this Act, in pursuance of an application (in this Act referred to as " a guardianship application ") made in accordance with this section.

(2) A guardianship application may be made in respect of a patient on the grounds that—

(*a*) he is suffering from mental disorder, being mental illness, severe mental impairment, psychopathic disorder or mental impairment and his mental disorder is of a nature or degree which warrants his reception into guardianship under this section ; and

(b) it is necessary in the interests of the welfare of the patient or for the protection of other persons that the patient should be so received.

(3) A guardianship application shall be founded on the written recommendations in the prescribed form of two registered medical practitioners, including in each case a statement that in the opinion of the practitioner the conditions set out in subsection (2) above are complied with ; and each such recommendation shall include—

(a) such particulars as may be prescribed of the grounds for that opinion so far as it relates to the conditions set out in paragraph (a) of that subsection ; and

(b) a statement of the reasons for that opinion so far as it relates to the conditions set out in paragraph (b) of that subsection.

(4) A guardianship application shall state the age of the patient or, if his exact age is not known to the applicant, shall state (if it be the fact) that the patient is believed to have attained the age of 16 years.

(5) The person named as guardian in a guardianship application may be either a local social services authority or any other person (including the applicant himself) ; but a guardianship application in which a person other than a local social services authority is named as guardian shall be of no effect unless it is accepted on behalf of that person by the local social services authority for the area in which he resides, and shall be accompanied by a statement in writing by that person that he is willing to act as guardian.

Effect of guardianship application, etc.

8.—(1) Where a guardianship application, duly made under the provisions of this Part of this Act and forwarded to the local social services authority within the period allowed by subsection (2) below is accepted by that authority, the application shall, subject to regulations made by the Secretary of State, confer on the authority or person named in the application as guardian, to the exclusion of any other person—

(a) the power to require the patient to reside at a place specified by the authority or person named as guardian ;

(b) the power to require the patient to attend at places and times so specified for the purpose of medical treatment, occupation, education or training ;

PART II

(*c*) the power to require access to the patient to be given, at any place where the patient is residing, to any registered medical practitioner, approved social worker or other person so specified.

(2) The period within which a guardianship application is required for the purposes of this section to be forwarded to the local social services authority is the period of 14 days beginning with the date on which the patient was last examined by a registered medical practitioner before giving a medical recommendation for the purposes of the application.

(3) A guardianship application which appears to be duly made and to be founded on the necessary medical recommendations may be acted upon without further proof of the signature or qualification of the person by whom the application or any such medical recommendation is made or given, or of any matter of fact or opinion stated in the application.

(4) If within the period of 14 days beginning with the day on which a guardianship application has been accepted by the local social services authority the application, or any medical recommendation given for the purposes of the application, is found to be in any respect incorrect or defective, the application or recommendation may, within that period and with the consent of that authority, be amended by the person by whom it was signed; and upon such amendment being made the application or recommendation shall have effect and shall be deemed to have had effect as if it had been originally made as so amended.

(5) Where a patient is received into guardianship in pursuance of a guardianship application, any previous application under this Part of this Act by virtue of which he was subject to guardianship or liable to be detained in a hospital shall cease to have effect.

Regulations as to guardianship.

9.—(1) Subject to the provisions of this Part of this Act, the Secretary of State may make regulations—

(*a*) for regulating the exercise by the guardians of patients received into guardianship under this Part of this Act of their powers as such; and

(*b*) for imposing on such guardians, and upon local social services authorities in the case of patients under the guardianship of persons other than local social services authorities, such duties as he considers necessary or expedient in the interests of the patients.

(2) Regulations under this section may in particular make provision for requiring the patients to be visited, on such occasions or at such intervals as may be prescribed by the regulations, on behalf of such local social services authorities as may be so prescribed, and shall provide for the appointment, in the case of every patient subject to the guardianship of a person other than a local social services authority, of a registered medical practitioner to act as the nominated medical attendant of the patient.

Transfer of guardianship in case of death, incapacity, etc., of guardian.

10.—(1) If any person (other than a local social services authority) who is the guardian of a patient received into guardianship under this Part of this Act—

(*a*) dies ; or

(*b*) gives notice in writing to the local social services authority that he desires to relinquish the functions of guardian,

the guardianship of the patient shall thereupon vest in the local social services authority, but without prejudice to any power to transfer the patient into the guardianship of another person in pursuance of regulations under section 19 below.

(2) If any such person, not having given notice under subsection (1)(*b*) above, is incapacitated by illness or any other cause from performing the functions of guardian of the patient, those functions may, during his incapacity, be performed on his behalf by the local social services authority or by any other person approved for the purposes by that authority.

(3) If it appears to the county court, upon application made by an approved social worker, that any person other than a local social services authority having the guardianship of a patient received into guardianship under this Part of this Act has performed his functions negligently or in a manner contrary to the interests of the welfare of the patient, the court may order that the guardianship of the patient be transferred to the local social services authority or to any other person approved for the purpose by that authority.

(4) Where the guardianship of a patient is transferred to a local social services authority or other person by or under this section, subsection (2)(*c*) of section 19 below shall apply as if the patient had been transferred into the guardianship of that authority or person in pursuance of regulations under that section.

General provisions as to applications and recommendations

General provisions as to applications.

11.—(1) Subject to the provisions of this section, an application for admission for assessment, an application for admission for treatment and a guardianship application may be made

PART II

either by the nearest relative of the patient or by an approved social worker; and every such application shall specify the qualification of the applicant to make the application.

(2) Every application for admission shall be addressed to the managers of the hospital to which admission is sought and every guardianship application shall be forwarded to the local social services authority named in the application as guardian, or, as the case may be, to the local social services authority for the area in which the person so named resides.

(3) Before or within a reasonable time after an application for the admission of a patient for assessment is made by an approved social worker, that social worker shall take such steps as are practicable to inform the person (if any) appearing to be the nearest relative of the patient that the application is to be or has been made and of the power of the nearest relative under section 23(2)(*a*) below.

(4) Neither an application for admission for treatment nor a guardianship application shall be made by an approved social worker if the nearest relative of the patient has notified that social worker, or the local social services authority by whom that social worker is appointed, that he objects to the application being made and, without prejudice to the foregoing provision, no such application shall be made by such a social worker except after consultation with the person (if any) appearing to be the nearest relative of the patient unless it appears to that social worker that in the circumstances such consultation is not reasonably practicable or would involve unreasonable delay.

(5) None of the applications mentioned in subsection (1) above shall be made by any person in respect of a patient unless that person has personally seen the patient within the period of 14 days ending with the date of the application.

(6) An application for admission for treatment or a guardianship application, and any recommendation given for the purposes of such an application, may describe the patient as suffering from more than one of the following forms of mental disorder, namely mental illness, severe mental impairment, psychopathic disorder or mental impairment; but the application shall be of no effect unless the patient is described in each of the recommendations as suffering from the same form of mental disorder, whether or not he is also described in either of those recommendations as suffering from another form.

(7) Each of the applications mentioned in subsection (1) above shall be sufficient if the recommendations on which it is founded are given either as separate recommendations, each signed by a registered medical practitioner, or as a joint recommendation signed by two such practitioners.

PART II

General provisions as to medical recommendations.

12.—(1) The recommendations required for the purposes of an application for the admission of a patient under this Part of this Act (in this Act referred to as " medical recommendations ") shall be signed on or before the date of the application, and shall be given by practitioners who have personally examined the patient either together or separately, but where they have examined the patient separately not more than five days must have elapsed between the days on which the separate examinations took place.

(2) Of the medical recommendations given for the purposes of any such application, one shall be given by a practitioner approved for the purposes of this section by the Secretary of State as having special experience in the diagnosis or treatment of mental disorder; and unless that practitioner has previous acquaintance with the patient, the other such recommendation shall, if practicable, be given by a registered medical practitioner who has such previous acquaintance.

(3) Subject to subsection (4) below, where the application is for the admission of the patient to a hospital which is not a mental nursing home, one (but not more than one) of the medical recommendations may be given by a practitioner on the staff of that hospital, except where the patient is proposed to be accommodated under section 65 or 66 of the National Health Service Act 1977 (which relate to accommodation for private patients). 1977 c. 49.

(4) Subsection (3) above shall not preclude both the medical recommendations being given by practitioners on the staff of the hospital in question if—

(*a*) compliance with that subsection would result in delay involving serious risk to the health or safety of the patient; and

(*b*) one of the practitioners giving the recommendations works at the hospital for less than half of the time which he is bound by contract to devote to work in the health service; and

(*c*) where one of those practitioners is a consultant, the other does not work (whether at the hospital or elsewhere) in a grade in which he is under that consultant's directions.

(5) A medical recommendation for the purposes of an application for the admission of a patient under this Part of this Act shall not be given by—

(*a*) the applicant;

(*b*) a partner of the applicant or of a practitioner by whom another medical recommendation is given for the purposes of the same application;

PART II

(*c*) a person employed as an assistant by the applicant or by any such practitioner;

(*d*) a person who receives or has an interest in the receipt of any payments made on account of the maintenance of the patient; or

(*e*) except as provided by subsection (3) or (4) above, a practitioner on the staff of the hospital to which the patient is to be admitted,

or by the husband, wife, father, father-in-law, mother, mother-in-law, son, son-in-law, daughter, daughter-in-law, brother, brother-in-law, sister or sister-in-law of the patient, or of any person mentioned in paragraphs (*a*) to (*e*) above, or of a practitioner by whom another medical recommendation is given for the purposes of the same application.

(6) A general practitioner who is employed part-time in a hospital shall not for the purposes of this section be regarded as a practitioner on its staff.

(7) Subsections (1), (2) and (5) above shall apply to applications for guardianship as they apply to applications for admission but with the substitution for paragraph (*e*) of subsection (5) above of the following paragraph—

" (*e*) the person named as guardian in the application.".

Duty of approved social workers to make applications for admission or guardianship.

13.—(1) It shall be the duty of an approved social worker to make an application for admission to hospital or a guardianship application in respect of a patient within the area of the local social services authority by which that officer is appointed in any case where he is satisfied that such an application ought to be made and is of the opinion, having regard to any wishes expressed by relatives of the patient or any other relevant circumstances, that it is necessary or proper for the application to be made by him.

(2) Before making an application for the admission of a patient to hospital an approved social worker shall interview the patient in a suitable manner and satisfy himself that detention in a hospital is in all the circumstances of the case the most appropriate way of providing the care and medical treatment of which the patient stands in need.

(3) An application under this section by an approved social worker may be made outside the area of the local social services authority by which he is appointed.

(4) It shall be the duty of a local social services authority, if so required by the nearest relative of a patient residing in their area, to direct an approved social worker as soon as practicable to take the patient's case into consideration under subsection (1)

PART II

above with a view to making an application for his admission to hospital; and if in any such case that approved social worker decides not to make an application he shall inform the nearest relative of his reasons in writing.

(5) Nothing in this section shall be construed as authorising or requiring an application to be made by an approved social worker in contravention of the provisions of section 11(4) above, or as restricting the power of an approved social worker to make any application under this Act.

Social reports.

14. Where a patient is admitted to a hospital in pursuance of an application (other than an emergency application) made under this Part of this Act by his nearest relative, the managers of the hospital shall as soon as practicable give notice of that fact to the local social services authority for the area in which the patient resided immediately before his admission; and that authority shall as soon as practicable arrange for a social worker of their social services department to interview the patient and provide the managers with a report on his social circumstances.

Rectification of applications and recommendations.

15.—(1) If within the period of 14 days beginning with the day on which a patient has been admitted to a hospital in pursuance of an application for admission for assessment or for treatment the application, or any medical recommendation given for the purposes of the application, is found to be in any respect incorrect or defective, the application or recommendation may, within that period and with the consent of the managers of the hospital, be amended by the person by whom it was signed; and upon such amendment being made the application or recommendation shall have effect and shall be deemed to have had effect as if it had been originally made as so amended.

(2) Without prejudice to subsection (1) above, if within the period mentioned in that subsection it appears to the managers of the hospital that one of the two medical recommendations on which an application for the admission of a patient is founded is insufficient to warrant the detention of the patient in pursuance of the application, they may, within that period, give notice in writing to that effect to the applicant; and where any such notice is given in respect of a medical recommendation, that recommendation shall be disregarded, but the application shall be, and shall be deemed always to have been, sufficient if—

(*a*) a fresh medical recommendation complying with the relevant provisions of this Part of this Act (other than the provisions relating to the time of signature and the interval between examinations) is furnished to the managers within that period; and

PART II

(*b*) that recommendation, and the other recommendation on which the application is founded, together comply with those provisions.

(3) Where the medical recommendations upon which an application for admission is founded are, taken together, insufficient to warrant the detention of the patient in pursuance of the application, a notice under subsection (2) above may be given in respect of either of those recommendations; but this subsection shall not apply in a case where the application is of no effect by virtue of section 11(6) above.

(4) Nothing in this section shall be construed as authorising the giving of notice in respect of an application made as an emergency application, or the detention of a patient admitted in pursuance of such an application, after the period of 72 hours referred to in section 4(4) above, unless the conditions set out in paragraphs (*a*) and (*b*) of that section are complied with or would be complied with apart from any error or defect to which this section applies.

Position of patients subject to detention or guardianship

Reclassification of patients.

16.—(1) If in the case of a patient who is for the time being detained in a hospital in pursuance of an application for admission for treatment, or subject to guardianship in pursuance of a guardianship application, it appears to the appropriate medical officer that the patient is suffering from a form of mental disorder other than the form or forms specified in the application, he may furnish to the managers of the hospital, or to the guardian, as the case may be, a report to that effect; and where a report is so furnished, the application shall have effect as if that other form of mental disorder were specified in it.

(2) Where a report under subsection (1) above in respect of a patient detained in a hospital is to the effect that he is suffering from psychopathic disorder or mental impairment but not from mental illness or severe mental impairment the appropriate medical officer shall include in the report a statement of his opinion whether further medical treatment in hospital is likely to alleviate or prevent a deterioration of the patient's condition; and if he states that in his opinion such treatment is not likely to have that effect the authority of the managers to detain the patient shall cease.

(3) Before furnishing a report under subsection (1) above the appropriate medical officer shall consult one or more other persons who have been professionally concerned with the patient's medical treatment.

(4) Where a report is furnished under this section in respect of a patient, the managers or guardian shall cause the patient and the nearest relative to be informed.

(5) In this section " appropriate medical officer " means—

(*a*) in the case of a patient who is subject to the guardianship of a person other than a local social services authority, the nominated medical attendant of the patient ; and

(*b*) in any other case, the responsible medical officer.

Leave of absence from hospital.

17.—(1) The responsible medical officer may grant to any patient who is for the time being liable to be detained in a hospital under this Part of this Act leave to be absent from the hospital subject to such conditions (if any) as that officer considers necessary in the interests of the patient or for the protection of other persons.

(2) Leave of absence may be granted to a patient under this section either indefinitely or on specified occasions or for any specified period ; and where leave is so granted for a specified period, that period may be extended by further leave granted in the absence of the patient.

(3) Where it appears to the responsible medical officer that it is necessary so to do in the interests of the patient or for the protection of other persons, he may, upon granting leave of absence under this section, direct that the patient remain in custody during his absence ; and where leave of absence is so granted the patient may be kept in the custody of any officer on the staff of the hospital, or of any other person authorised in writing by the managers of the hospital or, if the patient is required in accordance with conditions imposed on the grant of leave of absence to reside in another hospital, of any officer on the staff of that other hospital.

(4) In any case where a patient is absent from a hospital in pursuance of leave of absence granted under this section, and it appears to the responsible medical officer that it is necessary so to do in the interests of the patient's health or safety or for the protection of other persons, that officer may, subject to subsection (5) below, by notice in writing given to the patient or to the person for the time being in charge of the patient, revoke the leave of absence and recall the patient to the hospital.

(5) A patient to whom leave of absence is granted under this section shall not be recalled under subsection (4) above after he has ceased to be liable to be detained under this Part of this Act ; and without prejudice to any other provision of this Part of this Act any such patient shall cease to be so liable at the

PART II

expiration of the period of six months beginning with the first day of his absence on leave unless either—

(*a*) he has returned to the hospital, or has been transferred to another hospital under the following provisions of this Act, before the expiration of that period; or

(*b*) he is absent without leave at the expiration of that period.

Return and readmission of patients absent without leave.

18.—(1) Where a patient who is for the time being liable to be detained under this Part of this Act in a hospital—

(*a*) absents himself from the hospital without leave granted under section 17 above; or

(*b*) fails to return to the hospital on any occasion on which, or at the expiration of any period for which, leave of absence was granted to him under that section, or upon being recalled under that section; or

(*c*) absents himself without permission from any place where he is required to reside in accordance with conditions imposed on the grant of leave of absence under that section,

he may, subject to the provisions of this section, be taken into custody and returned to the hospital or place by any approved social worker, by any officer on the staff of the hospital, by any constable, or by any person authorised in writing by the managers of the hospital.

(2) Where the place referred to in paragraph (*c*) of subsection (1) above is a hospital other than the one in which the patient is for the time being liable to be detained, the references in that subsection to an officer on the staff of the hospital and the managers of the hospital shall respectively include references to an officer on the staff of the first-mentioned hospital and the managers of that hospital.

(3) Where a patient who is for the time being subject to guardianship under this Part of this Act absents himself without the leave of the guardian from the place at which he is required by the guardian to reside, he may, subject to the provisions of this section, be taken into custody and returned to that place by any officer on the staff of a local social services authority, by any constable, or by any person authorised in writing by the guardian or a local social services authority.

(4) A patient shall not be taken into custody under this section after the expiration of the period of 28 days beginning with the first day of his absence without leave; and a patient who has not returned or been taken into custody under this section within the said period shall cease to be liable to be

detained or subject to guardianship, as the case may be, at the expiration of that period.

(5) A patient shall not be taken into custody under this section if the period for which he is liable to be detained is that specified in section 2(4), 4(4) or 5(2) or (4) above and that period has expired.

(6) In this Act " absent without leave " means absent from any hospital or other place and liable to be taken into custody and returned under this section, and related expressions shall be construed accordingly.

Regulations as to transfer of patients.

19.—(1) In such circumstances and subject to such conditions as may be prescribed by regulations made by the Secretary of State—

(*a*) a patient who is for the time being liable to be detained in a hospital by virtue of an application under this Part of this Act may be transferred to another hospital or into the guardianship of a local social services authority or of any person approved by such an authority ;

(*b*) a patient who is for the time being subject to the guardianship of a local social services authority or other person by virtue of an application under this Part of this Act may be transferred into the guardianship of another local social services authority or person, or be transferred to a hospital.

(2) Where a patient is transferred in pursuance of regulations under this section, the provisions of this Part of this Act (including this subsection) shall apply to him as follows, that is to say—

(*a*) in the case of a patient who is liable to be detained in a hospital by virtue of an application for admission for assessment or for treatment and is transferred to another hospital, as if the application were an application for admission to that other hospital and as if the patient had been admitted to that other hospital at the time when he was originally admitted in pursuance of the application ;

(*b*) in the case of a patient who is liable to be detained in a hospital by virtue of such an application and is transferred into guardianship, as if the application were a guardianship application duly accepted at the said time ;

(*c*) in the case of a patient who is subject to guardianship by virtue of a guardianship application and its transferred into the guardianship of another authority or

PART II

person, as if the application were for his reception into the guardianship of that authority or person and had been accepted at the time when it was originally accepted;

(*d*) in the case of a patient who is subject to guardianship by virtue of a guardianship application and is transferred to a hospital, as if the guardianship application were an application for admission to that hospital for treatment and as if the patient had been admitted to the hospital at the time when the application was originally accepted.

(3) Without prejudice to subsections (1) and (2) above, any patient, who is for the time being liable to be detained under this Part of this Act in a hospital vested in the Secretary of State for the purposes of his functions under the National Health Service Act 1977 or any accommodation used under Part I of that Act by the managers of such a hospital, may at any time be removed to any other such hospital or accommodation for which the managers of the first-mentioned hospital are also the managers; and paragraph (*a*) of subsection (2) above shall apply in relation to a patient so removed as it applies in relation to a patient transferred in pursuance of regulations made under this section.

1977 c. 49.

(4) Regulations made under this section may make provision for regulating the conveyance to their destination of patients authorised to be transferred or removed in pursuance of the regulations or under subsection (3) above.

Duration of detention or guardianship and discharge

Duration of authority.

20.—(1) Subject to the following provisions of this Part of this Act, a patient admitted to hospital in pursuance of an application for admission for treatment, and a patient placed under guardianship in pursuance of a guardianship application, may be detained in a hospital or kept under guardianship for a period not exceeding six months beginning with the day on which he was so admitted, or the day on which the guardianship application was accepted, as the case may be, but shall not be so detained or kept for any longer period unless the authority for his detention or guardianship is renewed under this section.

(2) Authority for the detention or guardianship of a patient may, unless the patient has previously been discharged, be renewed—

(*a*) from the expiration of the period referred to in subsection (1) above, for a further period of six months;

(b) from the expiration of any period of renewal under paragraph (a) above, for a further period of one year,

and so on for periods of one year at a time.

(3) Within the period of two months ending on the day on which a patient who is liable to be detained in pursuance of an application for admission for treatment would cease under this section to be so liable in default of the renewal of the authority for his detention, it shall be the duty of the responsible medical officer—

(a) to examine the patient; and

(b) if it appears to him that the conditions set out in subsection (4) below are satisfied, to furnish to the managers of the hospital where the patient is detained a report to that effect in the prescribed form;

and where such a report is furnished in respect of a patient the managers shall, unless they discharge the patient, cause him to be informed.

(4) The conditions referred to in subsection (3) above are that—

(a) the patient is suffering from mental illness, severe mental impairment, psychopathic disorder or mental impairment, and his mental disorder is of a nature or degree which makes it appropriate for him to receive medical treatment in a hospital; and

(b) such treatment is likely to alleviate or prevent a deterioration of his condition; and

(c) it is necessary for the health or safety of the patient or for the protection of other persons that he should receive such treatment and that it cannot be provided unless he continues to be detained;

but, in the case of mental illness or severe mental impairment, it shall be an alternative to the condition specified in paragraph (b) above that the patient, if discharged, is unlikely to be able to care for himself, to obtain the care which he needs or to guard himself against serious exploitation.

(5) Before furnishing a report under subsection (3) above the responsible medical officer shall consult one or more other persons who have been professionally concerned with the patient's medical treatment.

(6) Within the period of two months ending with the day on which a patient who is subject to guardianship under this Part of this Act would cease under this section to be so liable in default of the renewal of the authority for his guardianship, it shall be the duty of the appropriate medical officer—

(a) to examine the patient; and

PART II

(*b*) if it appears to him that the conditions set out in subsection (7) below are satisfied, to furnish to the guardian and, where the guardian is a person other than a local social services authority, to the responsible local social services authority a report to that effect in the prescribed form ;

and where such a report is furnished in respect of a patient, the local social services authority shall, unless they discharge the patient, cause him to be informed.

(7) The conditions referred to in subsection (6) above are that—

(*a*) the patient is suffering from mental illness, severe mental impairment, psychopathic disorder or mental impairment and his mental disorder is of a nature or degree which warrants his reception into guardianship ; and

(*b*) it is necessary in the interests of the welfare of the patient or for the protection of other persons that the patient should remain under guardianship.

(8) Where a report is duly furnished under subsection (3) or (6) above, the authority for the detention or guardianship of the patient shall be thereby renewed for the period prescribed in that case by subsection (2) above.

(9) Where the form of mental disorder specified in a report furnished under subsection (3) or (6) above is a form of disorder other than that specified in the application for admission for treatment or, as the case may be, in the guardianship application, that application shall have effect as if that other form of mental disorder were specified in it ; and where on any occasion a report specifying such a form of mental disorder is furnished under either of those subsections the appropriate medical officer need not on that occasion furnish a report under section 16 above.

(10) In this section " appropriate medical officer " has the same meaning as in section 16(5) above.

Special provisions as to patients absent without leave.

21.—(1) If on the day on which, apart from this section, a patient would cease to be liable to be detained or subject to guardianship under this Part of this Act or, within the period of one week ending with that day, the patient is absent without leave, he shall not cease to be so liable or subject—

(*a*) in any case, until the expiration of the period during which he can be taken into custody under section 18 above or the day on which he is returned or returns himself to the hospital or place where he ought to be, whichever is the earlier ; and (*b*) if he is so returned or so returns himself within the period first mentioned in paragraph (*a*) above, until the expiration of the period of one week beginning with the day on which he is so returned or so returns.

(2) Where the period for which a patient is liable to be detained or subject to guardianship is extended by virtue of this section, any examination and report to be made and furnished under section 20(3) or (6) above may be made and furnished within that period as so extended.

(3) Where the authority for the detention or guardianship of a patient is renewed by virtue of this section after the day on which, apart from this section, that authority would have expired under section 20 above, the renewal shall take effect as from that day.

Special provisions as to patients sentenced to imprisonment, etc.

22.—(1) Where a patient who is liable to be detained by virtue of an application for admission for treatment or is subject to guardianship by virtue of a guardianship application is detained in custody in pursuance of any sentence or order passed or made by a court in the United Kingdom (including an order committing or remanding him in custody), and is so detained for a period exceeding, or for successive periods exceeding in the aggregate, six months, the application shall cease to have effect at the expiration of that period.

(2) Where any such patient is so detained in custody but the application does not cease to have effect under subsection (1) above, then—

(*a*) if apart from this subsection the patient would have ceased to be liable to be so detained or subject to guardianship on or before the day on which he is discharged from custody, he shall not cease and shall be deemed not to have ceased to be so liable or subject until the end of that day; and

(*b*) in any case, sections 18 and 21 above shall apply in relation to the patient as if he had absented himself without leave on that day.

Discharge of patients.

23.—(1) Subject to the provisions of this section and section 25 below, a patient who is for the time being liable to be detained or subject to guardianship under this Part of this Act shall cease to be so liable or subject if an order in writing discharging him from detention or guardianship (in this Act referred to as " an order for discharge ") is made in accordance with this section.

(2) An order for discharge may be made in respect of a patient—

(*a*) where the patient is liable to be detained in a hospital in pursuance of an application for admission for assess-

PART II

ment or for treatment by the responsible medical officer, by the managers or by the nearest relative of the patient;

(*b*) where the patient is subject to guardianship, by the responsible medical officer, by the responsible local social services authority or by the nearest relative of the patient.

(3) Where the patient is liable to be detained in a mental nursing home in pursuance of an application for admission for assessment or for treatment, an order for his discharge may, without prejudice to subsection (2) above, be made by the Secretary of State and, if the patient is maintained under a contract with a Regional Health Authority, District Health Authority or special health authority, by that authority.

(4) The powers conferred by this section on any authority or body of persons may be exercised by any three or more members of that authority or body authorised by them in that behalf or by three or more members of a committee or sub-committee of that authority or body which has been authorised by them in that behalf.

Visiting and examination of patients.

24.—(1) For the purpose of advising as to the exercise by the nearest relative of a patient who is liable to be detained or subject to guardianship under this Part of this Act of any power to order his discharge, any registered medical practitioner authorised by or on behalf of the nearest relative of the patient may, at any reasonable time, visit the patient and examine him in private.

(2) Any registered medical practitioner authorised for the purposes of subsection (1) above to visit and examine a patient may require the production of and inspect any records relating to the detention or treatment of the patient in any hospital.

(3) Where application is made by the Secretary of State or a Regional Health Authority, District Health Authority or special health authority to exercise, in respect of a patient liable to be detained in a mental nursing home, any power to make an order for his discharge, the following persons, that is to say—

(*a*) any registered medical practitioner authorised by the Secretary of State or, as the case may be, that authority; and

(*b*) any other person (whether a registered medical practitioner or not) authorised under the Nursing Homes Act 1975 to inspect the home,

1975 c. 37.

may at any reasonable time visit the patient and interview him in private.

(4) Any person authorised for the purposes of subsection (3) above to visit a patient may require the production of and inspect any documents constituting or alleged to constitute the authority for the detention of the patient under this Part of this Act; and any person so authorised, who is a registered medical practitioner, may examine the patient in private, and may require the production of and inspect any other records relating to the treatment of the patient in the home.

Restrictions on discharge by nearest relative.

25.—(1) An order for the discharge of a patient who is liable to be detained in a hospital shall not be made by his nearest relative except after giving not less than 72 hours' notice in writing to the managers of the hospital; and if, within 72 hours after such notice has been given, the responsible medical officer furnishes to the managers a report certifying that in the opinion of that officer the patient, if discharged, would be likely to act in a manner dangerous to other persons or to himself—

(*a*) any order for the discharge of the patient made by that relative in pursuance of the notice shall be of no effect; and

(*b*) no further order for the discharge of the patient shall be made by that relative during the period of six months beginning with the date of the report.

(2) In any case where a report under subsection (1) above is furnished in respect of a patient who is liable to be detained in pursuance of an application for admission for treatment the managers shall cause the nearest relative of the patient to be informed.

Functions of relatives of patients

Definition of " relative " and " nearest relative ".

26.—(1) In this Part of this Act " relative " means any of the following persons:—

(*a*) husband or wife;

(*b*) son or daughter;

(*c*) father or mother;

(*d*) brother or sister;

(*e*) grandparent;

(*f*) grandchild;

(*g*) uncle or aunt;

(*h*) nephew or niece.

(2) In deducing relationships for the purposes of this section, any relationship of the half-blood shall be treated as a relation-

PART II

ship of the whole blood, and an illegitimate person shall be treated as the legitimate child of his mother.

(3) In this Part of this Act, subject to the provisions of this section and to the following provisions of this Part of this Act, the " nearest relative " means the person first described in subsection (1) above who is for the time being surviving, relatives of the whole blood being preferred to relatives of the same description of the half-blood and the elder or eldest of two or more relatives described in any paragraph of that subsection being preferred to the other or others of those relatives, regardless of sex.

(4) Subject to the provisions of this section and to the following provisions of this Part of this Act, where the patient ordinarily resides with or is cared for by one or more of his relatives (or, if he is for the time being an in-patient in a hospital, he last ordinarily resided with or was cared for by one or more of his relatives) his nearest relative shall be determined—

(*a*) by giving preference to that relative or those relatives over the other or others ; and

(*b*) as between two or more such relatives, in accordance with subsection (3) above.

(5) Where the person who, under subsection (3) or (4) above, would be the nearest relative of a patient—

(*a*) in the case of a patient ordinarily resident in the United Kingdom, the Channel Islands or the Isle of Man, is not so resident ; or

(*b*) is the husband or wife of the patient, but is permanently separated from the patient, either by agreement or under an order of a court, or has deserted or has been deserted by the patient for a period which has not come to an end ; or

(*c*) is a person other than the husband, wife, father or mother of the patient, and is for the time being under 18 years of age ; or

(*d*) is a person against whom an order divesting him of authority over the patient has been made under section 38 of the Sexual Offences Act 1956 (which relates to incest with a person under eighteen) and has not been rescinded,

1956 c. 69.

the nearest relative of the patient shall be ascertained as if that person were dead.

(6) In this section " husband " and " wife " include a person who is living with the patient as the patient's husband or wife, as the case may be (or, if the patient is for the time being an in-patient in a hospital, was so living until the patient was

PART II

admitted), and has been or had been so living for a period of not less than six months; but a person shall not be treated by virtue of this subsection as the nearest relative of a married patient unless the husband or wife of the patient is disregarded by virtue of paragraph (*b*) of subsection (5) above.

(7) A person, other than a relative, with whom the patient ordinarily resides (or, if the patient is for the time being an in-patient in a hospital, last ordinarily resided before he was admitted), and with whom he has or had been ordinarily residing for a period of not less than five years, shall be treated for the purposes of this Part of this Act as if he were a relative but—

(*a*) shall be treated for the purposes of subsection (3) above as if mentioned last in subsection (1) above; and

(*b*) shall not be treated by virtue of this subsection as the nearest relative of a married patient unless the husband or wife of the patient is disregarded by virtue of paragraph (*b*) of subsection (5) above.

Children and young persons in care of local authority.

27. In any case where the rights and powers of a parent of a patient, being a child or young person, are vested in a local authority or other person by virtue of—

(*a*) section 3 of the Child Care Act 1980 (which relates to the assumption by a local authority of parental rights and duties in relation to a child in their care); 1980 c. 5.

(*b*) section 10 of that Act (which relates to the powers and duties of local authorities with respect to persons committed to their care under the Children and Young Persons Act 1969); or 1969 c. 54.

(*c*) section 17 of the Social Work (Scotland) Act 1968 (which makes corresponding provision for Scotland), 1968 c. 49.

that authority or person shall be deemed to be the nearest relative of the patient in preference to any person except the patient's husband or wife (if any) and except, in a case where the said rights and powers are vested in a local authority by virtue of subsection (1) of the said section 3, any parent of the patient not being the person on whose account the resolution mentioned in that subsection was passed.

Nearest relative of minor under guardianship, etc.

28.—(1) Where a patient who has not attained the age of 18 years—

(*a*) is, by virtue of an order made by a court in the exercise of jurisdiction (whether under any enactment or otherwise) in respect of the guardianship of minors (including an order under section 38 of the Sexual Offences Act 1956), or by virtue of a deed or will executed by his father or mother, under the guardianship of 1956 c. 69.

PART II

a person who is not his nearest relative under the foregoing provisions of this Act, or is under the joint guardianship of two persons of whom one is such a person; or

(*b*) is, by virtue of an order made by a court in the exercise of such jurisdiction or in matrimonial proceedings, or by virtue of a separation agreement between his father and mother, in the custody of any such person,

the person or persons having the guardianship or custody of the patient shall, to the exclusion of any other person, be deemed to be his nearest relative.

(2) Subsection (5) of section 26 above shall apply in relation to a person who is, or who is one of the persons, deemed to be the nearest relative of a patient by virtue of this section as it applies in relation to a person who would be the nearest relative under subsection (3) of that section.

(3) A patient shall be treated for the purposes of this section as being in the custody of another person if he would be in that other person's custody apart from section 8 above.

(4) In this section "court" includes a court in Scotland or Northern Ireland, and "enactment" includes an enactment of the Parliament of Northern Ireland, a Measure of the Northern Ireland Assembly and an Order in Council under Schedule 1 of the Northern Ireland Act 1974.

1974 c. 28.

Appointment by court of acting nearest relative.

29.—(1) The county court may, upon application made in accordance with the provisions of this section in respect of a patient, by order direct that the functions of the nearest relative of the patient under this Part of this Act and sections 66 and 69 below shall, during the continuance in force of the order, be exercisable by the applicant, or by any other person specified in the application, being a person who, in the opinion of the court, is a proper person to act as the patient's nearest relative and is willing to do so.

(2) An order under this section may be made on the application of—

(*a*) any relative of the patient;

(*b*) any other person with whom the patient is residing (or, if the patient is then an in-patient in a hospital, was last residing before he was admitted); or

(*c*) an approved social worker;

but in relation to an application made by such a social worker, subsection (1) above shall have effect as if for the words "the applicant" there were substituted the words "the local social services authority".

(3) An application for an order under this section may be made upon any of the following grounds, that is to say—

(*a*) that the patient has no nearest relative within the meaning of this Act, or that it is not reasonably practicable to ascertain whether he has such a relative, or who that relative is ;

(*b*) that the nearest relative of the patient is incapable of acting as such by reason of mental disorder or other illness ;

(*c*) that the nearest relative of the patient unreasonably objects to the making of an application for admission for treatment or a guardianship application in respect of the patient ; or

(*d*) that the nearest relative of the patient has exercised without due regard to the welfare of the patient or the interests of the public his power to discharge the patient from hospital or guardianship under this Part of this Act, or is likely to do so.

(4) If, immediately before the expiration of the period for which a patient is liable to be detained by virtue of an application for admission for assessment, an application under this section, which is an application made on the ground specified in subsection (3)(*c*) or (*d*) above, is pending in respect of the patient, that period shall be extended—

(*a*) in any case, until the application under this section has been finally disposed of ; and

(*b*) if an order is made in pursuance of the application under this section, for a further period of seven days ;

and for the purposes of this subsection an application under this section shall be deemed to have been finally disposed of at the expiration of the time allowed for appealing from the decision of the court or, if notice of appeal has been given within that time, when the appeal has been heard or withdrawn, and " pending " shall be construed accordingly.

(5) An order made on the ground specified in subsection (3)(*a*) or (*b*) above may specify a period for which it is to continue in force unless previously discharged under section 30 below.

(6) While an order made under this section is in force, the provisions of this Part of this Act (other than this section and section 30 below) and sections 66, 69, 132(4) and 133 below shall apply in relation to the patient as if for any reference to the nearest relative of the patient there were substituted a reference to the person having the functions of that relative and (without prejudice to section 30 below) shall so apply notwithstanding that the person who was the patient's nearest relative when the order

PART II

was made is no longer his nearest relative ; but this subsection shall not apply to section 66 below in the case mentioned in paragraph (*h*) of subsection (1) of that section.

Discharge and variation of orders under s. 29.

30.—(1) An order made under section 29 above in respect of a patient may be discharged by the county court upon application made—

(*a*) in any case, by the person having the functions of the nearest relative of the patient by virtue of the order ;

(*b*) where the order was made on the ground specified in paragraph (*a*) or paragraph (*b*) of section 29(3) above, or where the person who was the nearest relative of the patient when the order was made has ceased to be his nearest relative, on the application of the nearest relative of the patient.

(2) An order made under section 29 above in respect of a patient may be varied by the county court, on the application of the person having the functions of the nearest relative by virtue of the order or on the application of an approved social worker, by substituting for the first-mentioned person a local social services authority or any other person who in the opinion of the court is a proper person to exercise those functions, being an authority or person who is willing to do so.

(3) If the person having the functions of the nearest relative of a patient by virtue of an order under section 29 above dies—

(*a*) subsections (1) and (2) above shall apply as if for any reference to that person there were substituted a reference to any relative of the patient, and

(*b*) until the order is discharged or varied under those provisions the functions of the nearest relative under this Part of this Act and sections 66 and 69 below shall not be exercisable by any person.

(4) An order under section 29 above shall, unless previously discharged under subsection (1) above, cease to have effect at the expiration of the period, if any, specified under subsection (5) of that section or, where no such period is specified—

(*a*) if the patient was on the date of the order liable to be detained in pursuance of an application for admission for treatment or by virtue of an order or direction under Part III of this Act (otherwise than under section 35, 36 or 38) or was subject to guardianship under this Part of this Act or by virtue of such an order or direction, or becomes so liable or subject within the period of three months beginning with that date, when he ceases to be so liable or subject (otherwise than on being transferred in pursuance of regulations under section 19 above);

(*b*) if the patient was not on the date of the order, and has not within the said period become, so liable or subject, at the expiration of that period.

(5) The discharge or variation under this section of an order made under section 29 above shall not affect the validity of anything previously done in pursuance of the order.

Supplemental

Procedure on applications to county court.

31. County court rules which relate to applications authorised by this Part of this Act to be made to a county court may make provision—

(*a*) for the hearing and determination of such applications otherwise than in open court;

(*b*) for the admission on the hearing of such applications of evidence of such descriptions as may be specified in the rules notwithstanding anything to the contrary in any enactment or rule of law relating to the admissibility of evidence;

(*c*) for the visiting and interviewing of patients in private by or under the directions of the court.

Regulations for purposes of Part II.

32.—(1) The Secretary of State may make regulations for prescribing anything which, under this Part of this Act, is required or authorised to be prescribed, and otherwise for carrying this Part of this Act into full effect.

(2) Regulations under this section may in particular make provision—

(*a*) for prescribing the form of any application, recommendation, report, order, notice or other document to be made or given under this Part of this Act;

(*b*) for prescribing the manner in which any such application, recommendation, report, order, notice or other document may be proved, and for regulating the service of any such application, report, order or notice;

(*c*) for requiring the managers of hospitals and local social services authorities to keep such registers or other records as may be prescribed by the regulations in respect of patients liable to be detained or subject to guardianship under this Part of this Act, and to furnish or make available to those patients, and their relatives, such written statements of their rights and powers under this Act as may be so prescribed;

(*d*) for the determination in accordance with the regulations of the age of any person whose exact age cannot be

PART II

1953 c. 20.

ascertained by reference to the registers kept under the Births and Deaths Registration Act 1953 ; and

(*e*) for enabling the functions under this Part of this Act of the nearest relative of a patient to be performed, in such circumstances and subject to such conditions (if any) as may be prescribed by the regulations, by any person authorised in that behalf by that relative ;

and for the purposes of this Part of this Act any application, report or notice the service of which is regulated under paragraph (*b*) above shall be deemed to have been received by or furnished to the authority or person to whom it is authorised or required to be furnished, addressed or given if it is duly served in accordance with the regulations.

(3) Without prejudice to subsections (1) and (2) above, but subject to section 23(4) above, regulations under this section may determine the manner in which functions under this Part of this Act of the managers of hospitals, local social services authorities, Regional Health Authorities, District Health Authorities or special health authorities are to be exercised, and such regulations may in particular specify the circumstances in which, and the conditions subject to which, any such functions may be performed by officers of or other persons acting on behalf of those managers and authorities.

Special provisions as to wards of court.

33.—(1) An application for the admission to hospital of a minor who is a ward of court may be made under this Part of this Act with the leave of the court ; and section 11(4) above shall not apply in relation to an application so made.

(2) Where a minor who is a ward of court is liable to be detained in a hospital by virtue of an application for admission under this Part of this Act, any power exercisable under this Part of this Act or under section 66 below in relation to the patient by his nearest relative shall be exercisable by or with the leave of the court.

(3) Nothing in this Part of this Act shall be construed as authorising the making of a guardianship application in respect of a minor who is a ward of court, or the transfer into guardianship of any such minor.

Interpretation of Part II.

34.—(1) In this Part of this Act—

" the nominated medical attendant ", in relation to a patient who is subject to the guardianship of a person other than a local social services authority, means the person appointed in pursuance of regulations made under section 9(2) above to act as the medical attendant of the patient ;

"the responsible medical officer" means—

(a) in relation to a patient liable to be detained by virtue of an application for admission for assessment or an application for admission for treatment, the registered medical practitioner in charge of the treatment of the patient;

(b) in relation to a patient subject to guardianship, the medical officer authorised by the local social services authority to act (either generally or in any particular case or for any particular purpose) as the responsible medical officer.

(2) Except where otherwise expressly provided, this Part of this Act applies in relation to a mental nursing home, being a home in respect of which the particulars of registration are for the time being entered in the separate part of the register kept for the purposes of section 3(4)(b) of the Nursing Homes Act 1975, as it applies in relation to a hospital, and references in this Part of this Act to a hospital, and any reference in this Act to a hospital to which this Part of this Act applies, shall be construed accordingly. 1975 c. 37.

(3) In relation to a patient who is subject to guardianship in pursuance of a guardianship application, any reference in this Part of this Act to the responsible local social services authority is a reference—

(a) where the patient is subject to the guardianship of a local social services authority, to that authority;

(b) where the patient is subject to the guardianship of a person other than a local social services authority, to the local social services authority for the area in which that person resides.

PART III

PATIENTS CONCERNED IN CRIMINAL PROCEEDINGS OR UNDER SENTENCE

Remands to hospital

Remand to hospital for report on accused's mental condition.

35.—(1) Subject to the provisions of this section, the Crown Court or a magistrates' court may remand an accused person to a hospital specified by the court for a report on his mental condition.

(2) For the purposes of this section an accused person is—

(a) in relation to the Crown Court, any person who is awaiting trial before the court for an offence punishable with imprisonment or who has been arraigned before

PART III

the court for such an offence and has not yet been sentenced or otherwise dealt with for the offence on which he has been arraigned;

(*b*) in relation to a magistrates' court, any person who has been convicted by the court of an offence punishable on summary conviction with imprisonment and any person charged with such an offence if the court is satisfied that he did the act or made the omission charged or he has consented to the exercise by the court of the powers conferred by this section.

(3) Subject to subsection (4) below, the powers conferred by this section may be exercised if—

(*a*) the court is satisfied, on the written or oral evidence of a registered medical practitioner, that there is reason to suspect that the accused person is suffering from mental illness, psychopathic disorder, severe mental impairment or mental impairment; and

(*b*) the court is of the opinion that it would be impracticable for a report on his mental condition to be made if he were remanded on bail;

but those powers shall not be exercised by the Crown Court in respect of a person who has been convicted before the court if the sentence for the offence of which he has been convicted is fixed by law.

(4) The court shall not remand an accused person to a hospital under this section unless satisfied, on the written or oral evidence of the registered medical practitioner who would be responsible for making the report or of some other person representing the managers of the hospital, that arrangements have been made for his admission to that hospital and for his admission to it within the period of seven days beginning with the date of the remand; and if the court is so satisfied it may, pending his admission, give directions for his conveyance to and detention in a place of safety.

(5) Where a court has remanded an accused person under this section it may further remand him if it appears to the court, on the written or oral evidence of the registered medical practitioner responsible for making the report, that a further remand is necessary for completing the assessment of the accused person's mental condition.

(6) The power of further remanding an accused person under this section may be exercised by the court without his being brought before the court if he is represented by counsel or a solicitor and his counsel or solicitor is given an opportunity of being heard.

PART III

(7) An accused person shall not be remanded or further remanded under this section for more than 28 days at a time or for more than 12 weeks in all; and the court may at any time terminate the remand if it appears to the court that it is appropriate to do so.

(8) An accused person remanded to hospital under this section shall be entitled to obtain at his own expense an independent report on his mental condition from a registered medical practitioner chosen by him and to apply to the court on the basis of it for his remand to be terminated under subsection (7) above.

(9) Where an accused person is remanded under this section—

(*a*) a constable or any other person directed to do so by the court shall convey the accused person to the hospital specified by the court within the period mentioned in subsection (4) above; and

(*b*) the managers of the hospital shall admit him within that period and thereafter detain him in accordance with the provisions of this section.

(10) If an accused person absconds from a hospital to which he has been remanded under this section, or while being conveyed to or from that hospital, he may be arrested without warrant by any constable and shall, after being arrested, be brought as soon as practicable before the court that remanded him; and the court may thereupon terminate the remand and deal with him in any way in which it could have dealt with him if he had not been remanded under this section.

Remand of accused person to hospital for treatment.

36.—(1) Subject to the provisions of this section, the Crown Court may, instead of remanding an accused person in custody, remand him to a hospital specified by the court if satisfied, on the written or oral evidence of two registered medical practitioners, that he is suffering from mental illness or severe mental impairment of a nature or degree which makes it appropriate for him to be detained in a hospital for medical treatment.

(2) For the purposes of this section an accused person is any person who is in custody awaiting trial before the Crown Court for an offence punishable with imprisonment (other than an offence the sentence for which is fixed by law) or who at any time before sentence is in custody in the course of a trial before that court for such an offence.

(3) The court shall not remand an accused person under this section to a hospital unless it is satisfied, on the written or oral evidence of the registered medical practitioner who would be in charge of his treatment or of some other person representing the managers of the hospital, that arrangements have been made

PART III

for his admission to that hospital and for his admission to it within the period of seven days beginning with the date of the remand; and if the court is so satisfied it may, pending his admission, give directions for his conveyance to and detention in a place of safety.

(4) Where a court has remanded an accused person under this section it may further remand him if it appears to the court, on the written or oral evidence of the responsible medical officer, that a further remand is warranted.

(5) The power of further remanding an accused person under this section may be exercised by the court without his being brought before the court if he is represented by counsel or a solicitor and his counsel or solicitor is given an opportunity of being heard.

(6) An accused person shall not be remanded or further remanded under this section for more than 28 days at a time or for more than 12 weeks in all; and the court may at any time terminate the remand if it appears to the court that it is appropriate to do so.

(7) An accused person remanded to hospital under this section shall be entitled to obtain at his own expense an independent report on his mental condition from a registered medical practitioner chosen by him and to apply to the court on the basis of it for his remand to be terminated under subsection (6) above.

(8) Subsections (9) and (10) of section 35 above shall have effect in relation to a remand under this section as they have effect in relation to a remand under that section.

Hospital and guardianship orders

Powers of courts to order hospital admission or guardianship.

37.—(1) Where a person is convicted before the Crown Court of an offence punishable with imprisonment other than an offence the sentence for which is fixed by law, or is convicted by a magistrates' court of an offence punishable on summary conviction with imprisonment, and the conditions mentioned in subsection (2) below are satisfied, the court may by order authorise his admission to and detention in such hospital as may be specified in the order or, as the case may be, place him under the guardianship of a local social services authority or of such other person approved by a local social services authority as may be so specified.

(2) The conditions referred to in subsection (1) above are that—

(*a*) the court is satisfied, on the written or oral evidence of two registered medical practitioners, that the offender is suffering from mental illness, psychopathic disorder, severe mental impairment or mental impairment and that either— PART III

(i) the mental disorder from which the offender is suffering is of a nature or degree which makes it appropriate for him to be detained in a hospital for medical treatment and, in the case of psychopathic disorder or mental impairment, that such treatment is likely to alleviate or prevent a deterioration of his condition ; or

(ii) in the case of an offender who has attained the age of 16 years, the mental disorder is of a nature or degree which warrants his reception into guardianship under this Act ; and

(*b*) the court is of the opinion, having regard to all the circumstances including the nature of the offence and the character and antecedents of the offender, and to the other available methods of dealing with him, that the most suitable method of disposing of the case is by means of an order under this section.

(3) Where a person is charged before a magistrates' court with any act or omission as an offence and the court would have power, on convicting him of that offence, to make an order under subsection (1) above in his case as being a person suffering from mental illness or severe mental impairment, then, if the court is satisfied that the accused did the act or made the omission charged, the court may, if it thinks fit, make such an order without convicting him.

(4) An order for the admission of an offender to a hospital (in this Act referred to as " a hospital order ") shall not be made under this section unless the court is satisfied on the written or oral evidence of the registered medical practitioner who would be in charge of his treatment or of some other person representing the managers of the hospital that arrangements have been made for his admission to that hospital in the event of such an order being made by the court, and for his admission to it within the period of 28 days beginning with the date of the making of such an order ; and the court may, pending his admission within that period, give such directions as it thinks fit for his conveyance to and detention in a place of safety.

(5) If within the said period of 28 days it appears to the Secretary of State that by reason of an emergency or other special circumstances it is not practicable for the patient to be received into the hospital specified in the order, he may give directions for the admission of the patient to such other hospital

PART III

as appears to be appropriate instead of the hospital so specified; and where such directions are given—

(*a*) the Secretary of State shall cause the person having the custody of the patient to be informed, and

(*b*) the hospital order shall have effect as if the hospital specified in the directions were substituted for the hospital specified in the order.

(6) An order placing an offender under the guardianship of a local social services authority or of any other person (in this Act referred to as "a guardianship order") shall not be made under this section unless the court is satisfied that that authority or person is willing to receive the offender into guardianship.

(7) A hospital order or guardianship order shall specify the form or forms of mental disorder referred to in subsection (2)(*a*) above from which, upon the evidence taken into account under that subsection, the offender is found by the court to be suffering; and no such order shall be made unless the offender is described by each of the practitioners whose evidence is taken into account under that subsection as suffering from the same one of those forms of mental disorder, whether or not he is also described by either of them as suffering from another of them.

(8) Where an order is made under this section, the court shall not pass sentence of imprisonment or impose a fine or make a probation order in respect of the offence or make any such order as is mentioned in paragraph (*b*) or (*c*) of section 7(7) of the Children and Young Persons Act 1969 in respect of the offender, but may make any other order which the court has power to make apart from this section; and for the purposes of this subsection "sentence of imprisonment" includes any sentence or order for detention.

1969 c. 54.

Interim hospital orders.

38.—(1) Where a person is convicted before the Crown Court of an offence punishable with imprisonment (other than an offence the sentence for which is fixed by law) or is convicted by a magistrates' court of an offence punishable on summary conviction with imprisonment and the court before or by which he is convicted is satisfied, on the written or oral evidence of two registered medical practitioners—

(*a*) that the offender is suffering from mental illness, psychopathic disorder, severe mental impairment or mental impairment; and

(*b*) that there is reason to suppose that the mental disorder from which the offender is suffering is such that it may be appropriate for a hospital order to be made in his case,

the court may, before making a hospital order or dealing with him in some other way, make an order (in this Act referred to as "an interim hospital order") authorising his admission to such hospital as may be specified in the order and his detention there in accordance with this section. PART III

(2) In the case of an offender who is subject to an interim hospital order the court may make a hospital order without his being brought before the court if he is represented by counsel or a solicitor and his counsel or solicitor is given an opportunity of being heard.

(3) At least one of the registered medical practitioners whose evidence is taken into account under subsection (1) above shall be employed at the hospital which is to be specified in the order.

(4) An interim hospital order shall not be made for the admission of an offender to a hospital unless the court is satisfied, on the written or oral evidence of the registered medical practitioner who would be in charge of his treatment or of some other person representing the managers of the hospital, that arrangements have been made for his admission to that hospital and for his admission to it within the period of 28 days beginning with the date of the order; and if the court is so satisfied the court may, pending his admission, give directions for his conveyance to and detention in a place of safety.

(5) An interim hospital order—

(*a*) shall be in force for such period, not exceeding 12 weeks, as the court may specify when making the order; but

(*b*) may be renewed for further periods of not more than 28 days at a time if it appears to the court, on the written or oral evidence of the responsible medical officer, that the continuation of the order is warranted;

but no such order shall continue in force for more than six months in all and the court shall terminate the order if it makes a hospital order in respect of the offender or decides after considering the written or oral evidence of the responsible medical officer to deal with the offender in some other way.

(6) The power of renewing an interim hospital order may be exercised without the offender being brought before the court if he is represented by counsel or a solicitor and his counsel or solicitor is given an opportunity of being heard.

(7) If an offender absconds from a hospital in which he is detained in pursuance of an interim hospital order, or while being conveyed to or from such a hospital, he may be arrested without warrant by a constable and shall, after being arrested, be brought as soon as practicable before the court that made the order; and the court may thereupon terminate the order and deal

PART III

with him in any way in which it could have dealt with him if no such order had been made.

Information as to hospitals.

39.—(1) Where a court is minded to make a hospital order or interim hospital order in respect of any person it may request—

(*a*) the Regional Health Authority for the region in which that person resides or last resided ; or

(*b*) any other Regional Health Authority that appears to the court to be appropriate,

to furnish the court with such information as that Authority has or can reasonably obtain with respect to the hospital or hospitals (if any) in its region or elsewhere at which arrangements could be made for the admission of that person in pursuance of the order, and that Authority shall comply with any such request.

(2) In its application to Wales subsection (1) above shall have effect as if for any reference to any such Authority as is mentioned in paragraph (*a*) or (*b*) of that subsection there were substituted a reference to the Secretary of State, and as if for the words " in its region or elsewhere " there were substituted the words " in Wales ".

Effect of hospital orders, guardianship orders and interim hospital orders.

40.—(1) A hospital order shall be sufficient authority—

(*a*) for a constable, an approved social worker or any other person directed to do so by the court to convey the patient to the hospital specified in the order within a period of 28 days ; and

(*b*) for the managers of the hospital to admit him at any time within that period and thereafter detain him in accordance with the provisions of this Act.

(2) A guardianship order shall confer on the authority or person named in the order as guardian the same powers as a guardianship application made and accepted under Part II of this Act.

(3) Where an interim hospital order is made in respect of an offender—

(*a*) a constable or any other person directed to do so by the court shall convey the offender to the hospital specified in the order within the period mentioned in section 38(4) above ; and

(*b*) the managers of the hospital shall admit him within that period and thereafter detain him in accordance with the provisions of section 38 above.

(4) A patient who is admitted to a hospital in pursuance of a hospital order, or placed under guardianship by a guardianship order, shall, subject to the provisions of this subsection, be treated

for the purposes of the provisions of this Act mentioned in Part I of Schedule 1 to this Act as if he had been so admitted or placed on the date of the order in pursuance of an application for admission for treatment or a guardianship application, as the case may be, duly made under Part II of this Act, but subject to any modifications of those provisions specified in that Part of that Schedule.

(5) Where a patient is admitted to a hospital in pursuance of a hospital order, or placed under guardianship by a guardianship order, any previous application, hospital order or guardianship order by virtue of which he was liable to be detained in a hospital or subject to guardianship shall cease to have effect; but if the first-mentioned order, or the conviction on which it was made, is quashed on appeal, this subsection shall not apply and section 22 above shall have effect as if during any period for which the patient was liable to be detained or subject to guardianship under the order, he had been detained in custody as mentioned in that section.

Restriction orders

Power of higher courts to restrict discharge from hospital.

41.—(1) Where a hospital order is made in respect of an offender by the Crown Court, and it appears to the court, having regard to the nature of the offence, the antecedents of the offender and the risk of his committing further offences if set at large, that it is necessary for the protection of the public from serious harm so to do, the court may, subject to the provisions of this section, further order that the offender shall be subject to the special restrictions set out in this section, either without limit of time or during such period as may be specified in the order; and an order under this section shall be known as " a restriction order ".

(2) A restriction order shall not be made in the case of any person unless at least one of the registered medical practitioners whose evidence is taken into account by the court under section 37(2)(*a*) above has given evidence orally before the court.

(3) The special restrictions applicable to a patient in respect of whom a restriction order is in force are as follows—

(*a*) none of the provisions of Part II of this Act relating to the duration, renewal and expiration of authority for the detention of patients shall apply, and the patient shall continue to be liable to be detained by virtue of the relevant hospital order until he is duly discharged under the said Part II or absolutely discharged under section 42, 73, 74 or 75 below;

(*b*) no application shall be made to a Mental Health Review Tribunal in respect of a patient under section 66 or 69(1) below;

PART III

(*c*) the following powers shall be exercisable only with the consent of the Secretary of State, namely—

(i) power to grant leave of absence to the patient under section 17 above;

(ii) power to transfer the patient in pursuance of regulations under section 19 above; and

(iii) power to order the discharge of the patient under section 23 above;

and if leave of absence is granted under the said section 17 power to recall the patient under that section shall vest in the Secretary of State as well as the responsible medical officer; and

(*d*) the power of the Secretary of State to recall the patient under the said section 17 and power to take the patient into custody and return him under section 18 above may be exercised at any time;

and in relation to any such patient section 40(4) above shall have effect as if it referred to Part II of Schedule 1 to this Act instead of Part I of that Schedule.

(4) A hospital order shall not cease to have effect under section 40(5) above if a restriction order in respect of the patient is in force at the material time.

(5) Where a restriction order in respect of a patient ceases to have effect while the relevant hospital order continues in force, the provisions of section 40 above and Part I of Schedule 1 to this Act shall apply to the patient as if he had been admitted to the hospital in pursuance of a hospital order (without a restriction order) made on the date on which the restriction order ceased to have effect.

(6) While a person is subject to a restriction order the responsible medical officer shall at such intervals (not exceeding one year) as the Secretary of State may direct examine and report to the Secretary of State on that person; and every report shall contain such particulars as the Secretary of State may require.

Powers of Secretary of State in respect of patients subject to restriction orders.

42.—(1) If the Secretary of State is satisfied that in the case of any patient a restriction order is no longer required for the protection of the public from serious harm, he may direct that the patient shall cease to be subject to the special restrictions set out in section 41(3) above; and where the Secretary of State so directs, the restriction order shall cease to have effect, and section 41(5) above shall apply accordingly.

(2) At any time while a restriction order is in force in respect of a patient, the Secretary of State may, if he thinks fit, by warrant discharge the patient from hospital, either absolutely

or subject to conditions; and where a person is absolutely discharged under this subsection, he shall thereupon cease to be liable to be detained by virtue of the relevant hospital order, and the restriction order shall cease to have effect accordingly.

(3) The Secretary of State may at any time during the continuance in force of a restriction order in respect of a patient who has been conditionally discharged under subsection (2) above by warrant recall the patient to such hospital as may be specified in the warrant.

(4) Where a patient is recalled as mentioned in subsection (3) above—

(*a*) if the hospital specified in the warrant is not the hospital from which the patient was conditionally discharged, the hospital order and the restriction order shall have effect as if the hospital specified in the warrant were substituted for the hospital specified in the hospital order;

(*b*) in any case, the patient shall be treated for the purposes of section 18 above as if he had absented himself without leave from the hospital specified in the warrant, and, if the restriction order was made for a specified period, that period shall not in any event expire until the patient returns to the hospital or is returned to the hospital under that section.

(5) If a restriction order in respect of a patient ceases to have effect after the patient has been conditionally discharged under this section, the patient shall, unless previously recalled under subsection (3) above, be deemed to be absolutely discharged on the date when the order ceases to have effect, and shall cease to be liable to be detained by virtue of the relevant hospital order accordingly.

(6) The Secretary of State may, if satisfied that the attendance at any place in Great Britain of a patient who is subject to a restriction order is desirable in the interests of justice or for the purposes of any public inquiry, direct him to be taken to that place; and where a patient is directed under this subsection to be taken to any place he shall, unless the Secretary of State otherwise directs, be kept in custody while being so taken, while at that place and while being taken back to the hospital in which he is liable to be detained.

Power of magistrates' courts to commit for restriction order.

43.—(1) If in the case of a person of or over the age of 14 years who is convicted by a magistrates' court of an offence punishable on summary conviction with imprisonment—

(*a*) the conditions which under section 37(1) above are required to be satisfied for the making of a hospital order are satisfied in respect of the offender; but

PART III

(*b*) it appears to the court, having regard to the nature of the offence, the antecedents of the offender and the risk of his committing further offences if set at large, that if a hospital order is made a restriction order should also be made,

the court may, instead of making a hospital order or dealing with him in any other manner, commit him in custody to the Crown Court to be dealt with in respect of the offence.

(2) Where an offender is committed to the Crown Court under this section, the Crown Court shall inquire into the circumstances of the case and may—

(*a*) if that court would have power so to do under the foregoing provisions of this Part of this Act upon the conviction of the offender before that court of such an offence as is described in section 37(1) above, make a hospital order in his case, with or without a restriction order ;

(*b*) if the court does not make such an order, deal with the offender in any other manner in which the magistrates' court might have dealt with him.

(3) The Crown Court shall have the same power to make orders under sections 35, 36 and 38 above in the case of a person committed to the court under this section as the Crown Court has under those sections in the case of an accused person within the meaning of section 35 or 36 above or of a person convicted before that court as mentioned in section 38 above.

1980 c. 43.

(4) The power of a magistrates' court under section 38 of the Magistrates' Courts Act 1980 (which enables such a court to commit an offender to the Crown Court where the court is of the opinion that greater punishment should be inflicted for the offence than the court has power to inflict) shall also be exercisable by a magistrates' court where it is of the opinion that greater punishment should be inflicted as aforesaid on the offender unless a hospital order is made in his case with a restriction order.

1824 c. 83.

(5) The power of the Crown Court to make a hospital order, with or without a restriction order, in the case of a person convicted before that court of an offence may, in the same circumstances and subject to the same conditions, be exercised by such a court in the case of a person committed to the court under section 5 of the Vagrancy Act 1824 (which provides for the committal to the Crown Court of persons who are incorrigible rogues within the meaning of that section).

Committal to hospital under s. 43.

44.—(1) Where an offender is committed under section 43(1) above and the magistrates' court by which he is committed is satisfied on written or oral evidence that arrangements have been made for the admission of the offender to a hospital in the event of an order being made under this section, the court may, instead of committing him in custody, by order direct him to be admitted to that hospital, specifying it, and to be detained there until the case is disposed of by the Crown Court, and may give such directions as it thinks fit for his production from the hospital to attend the Crown Court by which his case is to be dealt with.

(2) The evidence required by subsection (1) above shall be given by the registered medical practitioner who would be in charge of the offender's treatment or by some other person representing the managers of the hospital in question.

(3) The power to give directions under section 37(4) above, section 37(5) above and section 40(1) above shall apply in relation to an order under this section as they apply in relation to a hospital order, but as if references to the period of 28 days mentioned in section 40(1) above were omitted; and subject as aforesaid an order under this section shall, until the offender's case is disposed of by the Crown Court, have the same effect as a hospital order together with a restriction order, made without limitation of time.

Appeals from magistrates' courts.

45.—(1) Where on the trial of an information charging a person with an offence a magistrates' court makes a hospital order or guardianship order in respect of him without convicting him, he shall have the same right of appeal against the order as if it had been made on his conviction; and on any such appeal the Crown Court shall have the same powers as if the appeal had been against both conviction and sentence.

(2) An appeal by a child or young person with respect to whom any such order has been made, whether the appeal is against the order or against the finding upon which the order was made, may be brought by him or by his parent or guardian on his behalf.

Detention during Her Majesty's pleasure

Persons ordered to be kept in custody during Her Majesty's pleasure.

46.—(1) The Secretary of State may by warrant direct that any person who, by virtue of any enactment to which this subsection applies, is required to be kept in custody during Her Majesty's pleasure or until the directions of Her Majesty are known shall be detained in such hospital (not being a mental nursing home) as may be specified in the warrant and, where that person is not already detained in the hospital, give directions for his removal there.

PART III

1968 c. 20. 1955 c. 18. 1955 c. 19. 1957 c. 53.

(2) The enactments to which subsection (1) above applies are section 16 of the Courts-Martial (Appeals) Act 1968, section 116 of the Army Act 1955, section 116 of the Air Force Act 1955 and section 63 of the Naval Discipline Act 1957.

(3) A direction under this section in respect of any person shall have the same effect as a hospital order together with a restriction order, made without limitation of time; and where such a direction is given in respect of a person while he is in the hospital, he shall be deemed to be admitted in pursuance of, and on the date of, the direction.

Transfer to hospital of prisoners, etc.

Removal to hospital of persons serving sentences of imprisonment, etc.

47.—(1) If in the case of a person serving a sentence of imprisonment the Secretary of State is satisfied, by reports from at least two registered medical practitioners—

(*a*) that the said person is suffering from mental illness, psychopathic disorder, severe mental impairment or mental impairment; and

(*b*) that the mental disorder from which that person is suffering is of a nature or degree which makes it appropriate for him to be detained in a hospital for medical treatment and, in the case of psychopathic disorder or mental impairment, that such treatment is likely to alleviate or prevent a deterioration of his condition;

the Secretary of State may, if he is of the opinion having regard to the public interest and all the circumstances that it is expedient so to do, by warrant direct that that person be removed to and detained in such hospital (not being a mental nursing home) as may be specified in the direction; and a direction under this section shall be known as "a transfer direction".

(2) A transfer direction shall cease to have effect at the expiration of the period of 14 days beginning with the date on which it is given unless within that period the person with respect to whom it was given has been received into the hospital specified in the direction.

(3) A transfer direction with respect to any person shall have the same effect as a hospital order made in his case.

(4) A transfer direction shall specify the form or forms of mental disorder referred to in paragraph (*a*) of subsection (1) above from which, upon the reports taken into account under that subsection, the patient is found by the Secretary of State to be suffering; and no such direction shall be given unless the patient is described in each of those reports as suffering from the same form of disorder, whether or not he is also described in either of them as suffering from another form.

PART III

(5) References in this Part of this Act to a person serving a sentence of imprisonment include references—

(*a*) to a person detained in pursuance of any sentence or order for detention made by a court in criminal proceedings (other than an order under any enactment to which section 46 above applies);

(*b*) to a person committed to custody under section 115(3) of the Magistrates' Courts Act 1980 (which relates to persons who fail to comply with an order to enter into recognisances to keep the peace or be of good behaviour); and 1980 c. 43.

(*c*) to a person committed by a court to a prison or other institution to which the Prison Act 1952 applies in default of payment of any sum adjudged to be paid on his conviction. 1952 c. 52.

Removal to hospital of other prisoners.

48.—(1) If in the case of a person to whom this section applies the Secretary of State is satisfied by the same reports as are required for the purposes of section 47 above that that person is suffering from mental illness or severe mental impairment of a nature or degree which makes it appropriate for him to be detained in a hospital for medical treatment and that he is in urgent need of such treatment, the Secretary of State shall have the same power of giving a transfer direction in respect of him under that section as if he were serving a sentence of imprisonment.

(2) This section applies to the following persons, that is to say—

(*a*) persons detained in a prison or remand centre, not being persons serving a sentence of imprisonment or persons falling within the following paragraphs of this subsection;

(*b*) persons remanded in custody by a magistrates' court;

(*c*) civil prisoners, that is to say, persons committed by a court to prison for a limited term (including persons committed to prison in pursuance of a writ of attachment), who are not persons falling to be dealt with under section 47 above;

(*d*) persons detained under the Immigration Act 1971. 1971 c. 77.

(3) Subsections (2) to (4) of section 47 above shall apply for the purposes of this section and of any transfer direction given by virtue of this section as they apply for the purposes of that section and of any transfer direction under that section.

Restriction on discharge of prisoners removed to hospital.

49.—(1) Where a transfer direction is given in respect of any person, the Secretary of State, if he thinks fit, may by warrant further direct that that person shall be subject to the special

PART III

restrictions set out in section 41 above; and where the Secretary of State gives a transfer direction in respect of any such person as is described in paragraph *(a)* or *(b)* of section 48(2) above, he shall also give a direction under this section applying those restrictions to him.

(2) A direction under this section shall have the same effect as a restriction order made under section 41 above and shall be known as " a restriction direction ".

(3) While a person is subject to a restriction direction the responsible medical officer shall at such intervals (not exceeding one year) as the Secretary of State may direct examine and report to the Secretary of State on that person; and every report shall contain such particulars as the Secretary of State may require.

Further provisions as to prisoners under sentence.

50.—(1) Where a transfer direction and a restriction direction have been given in respect of a person serving a sentence of imprisonment and before the expiration of that person's sentence the Secretary of State is notified by the responsible medical officer, any other registered medical practitioner or a Mental Health Review Tribunal that that person no longer requires treatment in hospital for mental disorder or that no effective treatment for his disorder can be given in the hospital to which he has been removed, the Secretary of State may—

(*a*) by warrant direct that he be remitted to any prison or other institution in which he might have been detained if he had not been removed to hospital, there to be dealt with as if he had not been so removed; or

(*b*) exercise any power of releasing him on licence or discharging him under supervision which would have been exercisable if he had been remitted to such a prison or institution as aforesaid,

and on his arrival in the prison or other institution or, as the case may be, his release or discharge as aforesaid, the transfer direction and the restriction direction shall cease to have effect.

(2) A restriction direction in the case of a person serving a sentence of imprisonment shall cease to have effect on the expiration of the sentence.

(3) Subject to subsection (4) below, references in this section to the expiration of a person's sentence are references to the expiration of the period during which he would have been liable to be detained in a prison or other institution if the transfer direction had not been given and that period shall be treated as expiring on the date on which he could have been discharged if he had not forfeited remission of any part of the sentence after his removal pursuant to the direction.

PART III

(4) For the purposes of section 49(2) of the Prison Act 1952 (which provides for discounting from the sentences of certain prisoners periods while they are unlawfully at large) a patient who, having been transferred in pursuance of a transfer direction from any such institution as is referred to in that section, is at large in circumstances in which he is liable to be taken into custody under any provision of this Act, shall be treated as unlawfully at large and absent from that institution.

1952 c. 52.

Further provisions as to detained persons.

51.—(1) This section has effect where a transfer direction has been given in respect of any such person as is described in paragraph (*a*) of section 48(2) above and that person is in this section referred to as " the detainee ".

(2) The transfer direction shall cease to have effect when the detainee's case is disposed of by the court having jurisdiction to try or otherwise deal with him, but without prejudice to any power of that court to make a hospital order or other order under this Part of this Act in his case.

(3) If the Secretary of State is notified by the responsible medical officer, any other registered medical practitioner or a Mental Health Review Tribunal at any time before the detainee's case is disposed of by that court—

(*a*) that the detainee no longer requires treatment in hospital for mental disorder ; or

(*b*) that no effective treatment for his disorder can be given at the hospital to which he has been removed,

the Secretary of State may by warrant direct that he be remitted to any place where he might have been detained if he had not been removed to hospital, there to be dealt with as if he had not been so removed, and on his arrival at the place to which he is so remitted the transfer direction shall cease to have effect.

(4) If (no direction having been given under subsection (3) above) the court having jurisdiction to try or otherwise deal with the detainee is satisfied on the written or oral evidence of the responsible medical officer—

(*a*) that the detainee no longer requires treatment in hospital for mental disorder ; or

(*b*) that no effective treatment for his disorder can be given at the hospital to which he has been removed,

the court may order him to be remitted to any such place as is mentioned in subsection (3) above or released on bail and on his arrival at that place or, as the case may be, his release on bail the transfer direction shall cease to have effect.

PART III

(5) If (no direction or order having been given or made under subsection (3) or (4) above) it appears to the court having jurisdiction to try or otherwise deal with the detainee—

(*a*) that it is impracticable or inappropriate to bring the detainee before the court; and

(*b*) that the conditions set out in subsection (6) below are satisfied,

the court may make a hospital order (with or without a restriction order) in his case in his absence and, in the case of a person awaiting trial, without convicting him.

(6) A hospital order may be made in respect of a person under subsection (5) above if the court—

(*a*) is satisfied, on the written or oral evidence of at least two registered medical practitioners, that the detainee is suffering from mental illness or severe mental impairment of a nature or degree which makes it appropriate for the patient to be detained in a hospital for medical treatment; and

(*b*) is of the opinion, after considering any depositions or other documents required to be sent to the proper officer of the court, that it is proper to make such an order.

(7) Where a person committed to the Crown Court to be dealt with under section 43 above is admitted to a hospital in pursuance of an order under section 44 above, subsections (5) and (6) above shall apply as if he were a person subject to a transfer direction.

Further provisions as to persons remanded by magistrates' courts.

52.—(1) This section has effect where a transfer direction has been given in respect of any such person as is described in paragraph (*b*) of section 48(2) above; and that person is in this section referred to as " the accused ".

(2) Subject to subsection (5) below, the transfer direction shall cease to have effect on the expiration of the period of remand unless the accused is committed in custody to the Crown Court for trial or to be otherwise dealt with.

1980 c. 43.

(3) Subject to subsection (4) below, the power of further remanding the accused under section 128 of the Magistrates' Courts Act 1980 may be exercised by the court without his being brought before the court; and if the court further remands the accused in custody (whether or not he is brought before the court) the period of remand shall, for the purposes of this section, be deemed not to have expired.

(4) The court shall not under subsection (3) above further remand the accused in his absence unless he has appeared before the court within the previous six months.

PART III

(5) If the magistrates' court is satisfied, on the written or oral evidence of the responsible medical officer—

(*a*) that the accused no longer requires treatment in hospital for mental disorder ; or

(*b*) that no effective treatment for his disorder can be given in the hospital to which he has been removed,

the court may direct that the transfer direction shall cease to have effect notwithstanding that the period of remand has not expired or that the accused is committed to the Crown Court as mentioned in subsection (2) above.

(6) If the accused is committed to the Crown Court as mentioned in subsection (2) above and the transfer direction has not ceased to have effect under subsection (5) above, section 51 above shall apply as if the transfer direction given in his case were a direction given in respect of a person falling within that section.

(7) The magistrates' court may, in the absence of the accused, inquire as examining justices into an offence alleged to have been committed by him and commit him for trial in accordance with section 6 of the Magistrates' Courts Act 1980 if— 1980 c. 43.

(*a*) the court is satisfied, on the written or oral evidence of the responsible medical officer, that the accused is unfit to take part in the proceedings ; and

(*b*) where the court proceeds under subsection (1) of that section, the accused is represented by counsel or a solicitor.

Further provisions as to civil prisoners and persons detained under the Immigration Act 1971. 1971 c. 77.

53.—(1) Subject to subsection (2) below, a transfer direction given in respect of any such person as is described in paragraph (*c*) or (*d*) of section 48(2) above shall cease to have effect on the expiration of the period during which he would, but for his removal to hospital, be liable to be detained in the place from which he was removed.

(2) Where a transfer direction and a restriction direction have been given in respect of any such person as is mentioned in subsection (1) above, then, if the Secretary of State is notified by the responsible medical officer, any other registered medical practitioner or a Mental Health Review Tribunal at any time before the expiration of the period there mentioned—

(*a*) that that person no longer requires treatment in hospital for mental disorder; or

(*b*) that no effective treatment for his disorder can be given in the hospital to which he has been removed,

the Secretary of State may by warrant direct that he be remitted to any place where he might have been detained if he

PART III

had not been removed to hospital, and on his arrival at the place to which he is so remitted the transfer direction and the restriction direction shall cease to have effect.

Supplemental

Requirements as to medical evidence.

54.—(1) The registered medical practitioner whose evidence is taken into account under section 35(3)(*a*) above and at least one of the registered medical practitioners whose evidence is taken into account under sections 36(1), 37(2)(*a*), 38(1) and 51(6)(*a*) above and whose reports are taken into account under sections 47(1) and 48(1) above shall be a practitioner approved for the purposes of section 12 above by the Secretary of State as having special experience in the diagnosis or treatment of mental disorder.

(2) For the purposes of any provision of this Part of this Act under which a court may act on the written evidence of—

(*a*) a registered medical practitioner or a registered medical practitioner of any description ; or

(*b*) a person representing the managers of a hospital,

a report in writing purporting to be signed by a registered medical practitioner or a registered medical practitioner of such a description or by a person representing the managers of a hospital may, subject to the provisions of this section, be received in evidence without proof of the signature of the practitioner or that person and without proof that he has the requisite qualifications or authority or is of the requisite description ; but the court may require the signatory of any such report to be called to give oral evidence.

(3) Where, in pursuance of a direction of the court, any such report is tendered in evidence otherwise than by or on behalf of the person who is the subject of the report, then—

(*a*) if that person is represented by counsel or a solicitor, a copy of the report shall be given to his counsel or solicitor ;

(*b*) if that person is not so represented, the substance of the report shall be disclosed to him or, where he is a child or young person, to his parent or guardian if present in court ; and

(*c*) except where the report relates only to arrangements for his admission to a hospital, that person may require the signatory of the report to be called to give oral evidence, and evidence to rebut the evidence contained in the report may be called by or on behalf of that person.

PART III

Interpretation of Part III.

55.—(1) In this Part of this Act—

" child " and " young person " have the same meaning as in the Children and Young Persons Act 1933 ; 1933 c. 12.

" civil prisoner " has the meaning given to it by section 48(2)(*c*) above ;

" guardian ", in relation to a child or young person, has the same meaning as in the Children and Young Persons Act 1933 ;

" place of safety ", in relation to a person who is not a child or young person, means any police station, prison or remand centre, or any hospital the managers of which are willing temporarily to receive him, and in relation to a child or young person has the same meaning as in the Children and Young Persons Act 1933 ;

" responsible medical officer ", in relation to a person liable to be detained in a hospital within the meaning of Part II of this Act, means the registered medical practitioner in charge of the treatment of the patient.

(2) Any reference in this Part of this Act to an offence punishable on summary conviction with imprisonment shall be construed without regard to any prohibition or restriction imposed by or under any enactment relating to the imprisonment of young offenders.

(3) Where a patient who is liable to be detained in a hospital in pursuance of an order or direction under this Part of this Act is treated by virtue of any provision of this Part of this Act as if he had been admitted to the hospital in pursuance of a subsequent order or direction under this Part of this Act or a subsequent application for admission for treatment under Part II of this Act, he shall be treated as if the subsequent order, direction or application had described him as suffering from the form or forms of mental disorder specified in the earlier order or direction or, where he is treated as if he had been so admitted by virtue of a direction under section 42(1) above, such form of mental disorder as may be specified in the direction under that section.

(4) Any reference to a hospital order, a guardianship order or a restriction order in section 40(2), (4) or (5), section 41(3) to (5), or section 42 above or section 69(1) below shall be construed as including a reference to any order or direction under this Part of this Act having the same effect as the first-mentioned order ; and the exceptions and modifications set out in Schedule 1 to this Act in respect of the provisions of this Act described in that Schedule accordingly include those which are consequential on the provisions of this subsection.

PART III

(5) Section 34(2) above shall apply for the purposes of this Part of this Act as it applies for the purposes of Part II of this Act.

(6) References in this Part of this Act to persons serving a sentence of imprisonment shall be construed in accordance with section 47(5) above.

1933 c. 12.

(7) Section 99 of the Children and Young Persons Act 1933 (which relates to the presumption and determination of age) shall apply for the purposes of this Part of this Act as it applies for the purposes of that Act.

PART IV

CONSENT TO TREATMENT

Patients to whom Part IV applies.

56.—(1) This Part of this Act applies to any patient liable to be detained under this Act except—

(*a*) a patient who is liable to be detained by virtue of an emergency application and in respect of whom the second medical recommendation referred to in section 4(4)(*a*) above has not been given and received ;

(*b*) a patient who is liable to be detained by virtue of section 5(2) or (4) or 35 above or section 135 or 136 below or by virtue of a direction under section 37(4) above ; and

(*c*) a patient who has been conditionally discharged under section 42(2) above or section 73 or 74 below and has not been recalled to hospital.

(2) Section 57 and, so far as relevant to that section, sections 59, 60 and 62 below, apply also to any patient who is not liable to be detained under this Act.

Treatment requiring consent and a second opinion.

57.—(1) This section applies to the following forms of medical treatment for mental disorder—

(*a*) any surgical operation for destroying brain tissue or for destroying the functioning of brain tissue ; and

(*b*) such other forms of treatment as may be specified for the purposes of this section by regulations made by the Secretary of State.

(2) Subject to section 62 below, a patient shall not be given any form of treatment to which this section applies unless he has consented to it and—

(*a*) a registered medical practitioner appointed for the purposes of this Part of this Act by the Secretary of State (not being the responsible medical officer) and two other persons appointed for the purposes of this paragraph by the Secretary of State (not being registered medical practitioners) have certified in writing that the patient is capable of understanding the nature, purpose and likely effects of the treatment in question and has consented to it; and

(*b*) the registered medical practitioner referred to in paragraph (*a*) above has certified in writing that, having regard to the likelihood of the treatment alleviating or preventing a deterioration of the patient's condition, the treatment should be given.

(3) Before giving a certificate under subsection (2)(*b*) above the registered medical practitioner concerned shall consult two other persons who have been professionally concerned with the patient's medical treatment, and of those persons one shall be a nurse and the other shall be neither a nurse nor a registered medical practitioner.

(4) Before making any regulations for the purpose of this section the Secretary of State shall consult such bodies as appear to him to be concerned.

Treatment requiring consent or a second opinion.

58.—(1) This section applies to the following forms of medical treatment for mental disorder—

(*a*) such forms of treatment as may be specified for the purposes of this section by regulations made by the Secretary of State;

(*b*) the administration of medicine to a patient by any means (not being a form of treatment specified under paragraph (*a*) above or section 57 above) at any time during a period for which he is liable to be detained as a patient to whom this Part of this Act applies if three months or more have elapsed since the first occasion in that period when medicine was administered to him by any means for his mental disorder.

(2) The Secretary of State may by order vary the length of the period mentioned in subsection (1)(*b*) above.

(3) Subject to section 62 below, a patient shall not be given any form of treatment to which this section applies unless—

(*a*) he has consented to that treatment and either the responsible medical officer or a registered medical practitioner appointed for the purposes of this Part of this Act by the Secretary of State has certified in writing that the patient is capable of understanding its nature, purpose and likely effects and has consented to it; or

(*b*) a registered medical practitioner appointed as aforesaid (not being the responsible medical officer) has

PART IV

certified in writing that the patient is not capable of understanding the nature, purpose and likely effects of that treatment or has not consented to it but that, having regard to the likelihood of its alleviating or preventing a deterioration of his condition, the treatment should be given.

(4) Before giving a certificate under subsection (3)(*b*) above the registered medical practitioner concerned shall consult two other persons who have been professionally concerned with the patient's medical treatment, and of those persons one shall be a nurse and the other shall be neither a nurse nor a registered medical practitioner.

(5) Before making any regulations for the purposes of this section the Secretary of State shall consult such bodies as appear to him to be concerned.

Plans of treatment.

59. Any consent or certificate under section 57 or 58 above may relate to a plan of treatment under which the patient is to be given (whether within a specified period or otherwise) one or more of the forms of treatment to which that section applies.

Withdrawal of consent.

60.—(1) Where the consent of a patient to any treatment has been given for the purposes of section 57 or 58 above, the patient may, subject to section 62 below, at any time before the completion of the treatment withdraw his consent, and those sections shall then apply as if the remainder of the treatment were a separate form of treatment.

(2) Without prejudice to the application of subsection (1) above to any treatment given under the plan of treatment to which a patient has consented, a patient who has consented to such a plan may, subject to section 62 below, at any time withdraw his consent to further treatment, or to further treatment of any description, under the plan.

Review of treatment.

61.—(1) Where a patient is given treatment in accordance with section 57(2) or 58(3)(*b*) above a report on the treatment and the patient's condition shall be given by the responsible medical officer to the Secretary of State—

(*a*) on the next occasion on which the responsible medical officer furnishes a report in respect of the patient under section 20(3) above; and

(*b*) at any other time if so required by the Secretary of State.

(2) In relation to a patient who is subject to a restriction order or restriction direction subsection (1) above shall have effect as if paragraph (*a*) required the report to be made—

(*a*) in the case of treatment in the period of six months beginning with the date of the order or direction, at the end of that period;

(*b*) in the case of treatment at any subsequent time, on the next occasion on which the responsible medical officer makes a report in respect of the patient under section 41(6) or 49(3) above.

(3) The Secretary of State may at any time give notice to the responsible medical officer directing that, subject to section 62 below, a certificate given in respect of a patient under section 57(2) or 58(3)(*b*) above shall not apply to treatment given to him after a date specified in the notice and sections 57 and 58 above shall then apply to any such treatment as if that certificate had not been given.

Urgent treatment.

62.—(1) Sections 57 and 58 above shall not apply to any treatment—

(*a*) which is immediately necessary to save the patient's life; or

(*b*) which (not being irreversible) is immediately necessary to prevent a serious deterioration on his condition; or

(*c*) which (not being irreversible or hazardous) is immediately necessary to alleviate serious suffering by the patient; or

(*d*) which (not being irreversible or hazardous) is immediately necessary and represents the minimum interference necessary to prevent the patient from behaving violently or being a danger to himself or to others.

(2) Sections 60 and 61(3) above shall not preclude the continuation of any treatment or of treatment under any plan pending compliance with section 57 or 58 above if the responsible medical officer considers that the discontinuance of the treatment or of treatment under the plan would cause serious suffering to the patient.

(3) For the purposes of this section treatment is irreversible if it has unfavourable irreversible physical or psychological consequences and hazardous if it entails significant physical hazard.

Treatment not requiring consent.

63. The consent of a patient shall not be required for any medical treatment given to him for the mental disorder from which he is suffering, not being treatment falling within section 57 or 58 above, if the treatment is given by or under the direction of the responsible medical officer.

Supplementary provisions for Part IV.

64.—(1) In this Part of this Act " the responsible medical officer " means the registered medical practitioner in charge of the treatment of the patient in question and " hospital " includes a mental nursing home.

(2) Any certificate for the purposes of this Part of this Act shall be in such form as may be prescribed by regulations made by the Secretary of State.

Part V

Mental Health Review Tribunals

Constitution etc.

Mental Health Review Tribunals. 1977 c. 49.

65.—(1) There shall continue to be a tribunal known as a Mental Health Review Tribunal for every region for which a Regional Health Authority is established in pursuance of the National Health Service Act 1977 and for Wales, for the purpose of dealing with applications and references by and in respect of patients under the provisions of this Act.

(2) The provisions of Schedule 2 to this Act shall have effect with respect to the constitution of Mental Health Review Tribunals.

(3) Subject to the provisions of Schedule 2 to this Act, and to rules made by the Lord Chancellor under this Act, the jurisdiction of a Mental Health Review Tribunal may be exercised by any three or more of its members, and references in this Act to a Mental Health Review Tribunal shall be construed accordingly.

(4) The Secretary of State may pay to the members of Mental Health Review Tribunals such remuneration and allowances as he may with the consent of the Treasury determine, and defray the expenses of such tribunals to such amount as he may with the consent of the Treasury determine, and may provide for each such tribunal such officers and servants, and such accommodation, as the tribunal may require.

Applications and references concerning Part II patients

Applications to tribunals.

66.—(1) Where—

(*a*) a patient is admitted to a hospital in pursuance of an application for admission for assessment; or

(*b*) a patient is admitted to a hospital in pursuance of an application for admission for treatment; or

(*c*) a patient is received into guardianship in pursuance of a guardianship application; or

(*d*) a report is furnished under section 16 above in respect of a patient; or

(*e*) a patient is transferred from guardianship to a hospital in pursuance of regulations made under section 19 above; or

(*f*) a report is furnished under section 20 above in respect of a patient and the patient is not discharged; or

(*g*) a report is furnished under section 25 above in respect of a patient who is detained in pursuance of an application for admission for treatment; or

PART V

(*h*) an order is made under section 29 above in respect of a patient who is or subsequently becomes liable to be detained or subject to guardianship under Part II of this Act,

an application may be made to a Mental Health Review Tribunal within the relevant period—

(i) by the patient (except in the cases mentioned in paragraphs (*g*) and (*h*) above) or, in the case mentioned in paragraph (*d*) above, by his nearest relative, and

(ii) in the cases mentioned in paragraphs (*g*) and (*h*) above, by his nearest relative.

(2) In subsection (1) above " the relevant period " means—

(*a*) in the case mentioned in paragraph (*a*) of that subsection, 14 days beginning with the day on which the patient is admitted as so mentioned ;

(*b*) in the case mentioned in paragraph (*b*) of that subsection, six months beginning with the day on which the patient is admitted as so mentioned ;

(*c*) in the case mentioned in paragraph (*c*) of that subsection, six months beginning with the day on which the application is accepted ;

(*d*) in the cases mentioned in paragraphs (*d*) and (*g*) of that subsection, 28 days beginning with the day on which the applicant is informed that the report has been furnished ;

(*e*) in the case mentioned in paragraph (*e*) of that subsection, six months beginning with the day on which the patient is transferred ;

(*f*) in the case mentioned in paragraph (*f*) of that subsection, the period for which authority for the patient's detention or guardianship is renewed by virtue of the report ;

(*g*) in the case mentioned in paragraph (*h*) of that subsection, 12 months beginning with the date of the order, and in any subsequent period of 12 months during which the order continues in force.

(3) Section 32 above shall apply for the purposes of this section as it applies for the purposes of Part II of this Act.

References to tribunals by Secretary of State concerning Part II patients.

67.—(1) The Secretary of State may, if he thinks fit, at any time refer to a Mental Health Review Tribunal the case of any patient who is liable to be detained or subject to guardianship under Part II of this Act.

PART V

(2) For the purpose of furnishing information for the purposes of a reference under subsection (1) above any registered medical practitioner authorised by or on behalf of the patient may, at any reasonable time, visit the patient and examine him in private and require the production of and inspect any records relating to the detention or treatment of the patient in any hospital.

(3) Section 32 above shall apply for the purposes of this section as it applies for the purposes of Part II of this Act.

Duty of managers of hospitals to refer cases to tribunal.

68.—(1) Where a patient who is admitted to a hospital in pursuance of an application for admission for treatment or a patient who is transferred from guardianship to hospital does not exercise his right to apply to a Mental Health Review Tribunal under section 66(1) above by virtue of his case falling within paragraph (*b*) or, as the case may be, paragraph (*e*) of that section, the managers of the hospital shall at the expiration of the period for making such an application refer the patient's case to such a tribunal unless an application or reference in respect of the patient has then been made under section 66(1) above by virtue of his case falling within paragraph (*d*), (*g*) or (*h*) of that section or under section 67(1) above.

(2) If the authority for the detention of a patient in a hospital is renewed under section 20 above and a period of three years (or, if the patient has not attained the age of sixteen years, one year) has elapsed since his case was last considered by a Mental Health Review Tribunal, whether on his own application or otherwise, the managers of the hospital shall refer his case to such a tribunal.

(3) For the purpose of furnishing information for the purposes of any reference under this section, any registered medical practitioner authorised by or on behalf of the patient may at any reasonable time visit and examine the patient in private and require the production of and inspect any records relating to the detention or treatment of the patient in any hospital.

(4) The Secretary of State may by order vary the length of the periods mentioned in subsection (2) above.

(5) For the purposes of subsection (1) above a person who applies to a tribunal but subsequently withdraws his application shall be treated as not having exercised his right to apply, and where a person withdraws his application on a date after the expiration of the period mentioned in that subsection, the managers shall refer the patient's case as soon as possible after that date.

Applications and references concerning Part III patients PART V

69.—(1) Without prejudice to any provision of section 66(1) above as applied by section 40(4) above, an application to a Mental Health Review Tribunal may also be made— Applications to tribunals concerning patients subject to hospitals and guardianship orders.

(*a*) in respect of a patient admitted to a hospital in pursuance of a hospital order, by the nearest relative of the patient in the period between the expiration of six months and the expiration of 12 months beginning with the date of the order and in any subsequent period of 12 months ; and

(*b*) in respect of a patient placed under guardianship by a guardianship order—

(i) by the patient, within the period of six months beginning with the date of the order ;

(ii) by the nearest relative of the patient, within the period of 12 months beginning with the date of the order and in any subsequent period of 12 months.

(2) Where a person detained in a hospital—

(*a*) is treated as subject to a hospital order or transfer direction by virtue of section 41(5) above, 82(2) or 85(2) below, section 73(2) of the Mental Health (Scotland) Act 1960 or section 5(1) of the Criminal Procedure (Insanity) Act 1964 ; or 1960 c. 61. 1964 c. 84.

(*b*) is subject to a direction having the same effect as a hospital order by virtue of section 46(3), 47(3) or 48(3) above,

then, without prejudice to any provision of Part II of this Act as applied by section 40 above, that person may make an application to a Mental Health Review Tribunal in the period of six months beginning with the date of the order or direction mentioned in paragraph (*a*) above or, as the case may be, the date of the direction mentioned in paragraph (*b*) above.

70. A patient who is a restricted patient within the meaning of section 79 below and is detained in a hospital may apply to a Mental Health Review Tribunal— Applications to tribunals concerning restricted patients.

(*a*) in the period between the expiration of six months and the expiration of 12 months beginning with the date of the relevant hospital order or transfer direction ; and

(*b*) in any subsequent period of 12 months.

71.—(1) The Secretary of State may at any time refer the case of a restricted patient to a Mental Health Review Tribunal. References by Secretary of State concerning restricted patients.

(2) The Secretary of State shall refer to a Mental Health Review Tribunal the case of any restricted patient detained in a

PART V

hospital whose case has not been considered by such a tribunal, whether on his own application or otherwise, within the last three years.

(3) The Secretary of State may by order vary the length of the period mentioned in subsection (2) above.

(4) Any reference under subsection (1) above in respect of a patient who has been conditionally discharged and not recalled to hospital shall be made to the tribunal for the area in which the patient resides.

(5) Where a person who is treated as subject to a hospital order and a restriction order by virtue of an order under section 5(1) of the Criminal Procedure (Insanity) Act 1964 does not exercise his right to apply to a Mental Health Review Tribunal in the period of six months beginning with the date of that order, the Secretary of State shall at the expiration of that period refer his case to a tribunal.

1964 c. 84.

(6) For the purposes of subsection (5) above a person who applies to a tribunal but subsequently withdraws his application shall be treated as not having exercised his right to apply, and where a patient withdraws his application on a date after the expiration of the period there mentioned the Secretary of State shall refer his case as soon as possible after that date.

Discharge of patients

Powers of tribunals.

72.—(1) Where application is made to a Mental Health Review Tribunal by or in respect of a patient who is liable to be detained under this Act, the tribunal may in any case direct that the patient be discharged, and—

(*a*) the tribunal shall direct the discharge of a patient liable to be detained under section 2 above if they are satisfied—

(i) that he is not then suffering from mental disorder or from mental disorder of a nature or degree which warrants his detention in a hospital for assessment (or for assessment followed by medical treatment) for at least a limited period; or

(ii) that his detention as aforesaid is not justified in the interests of his own health or safety or with a view to the protection of other persons;

(*b*) the tribunal shall direct the discharge of a patient liable to be detained otherwise than under section 2 above if they are satisfied—

(i) that he is not then suffering from mental illness, psychopathic disorder, severe mental impairment or mental impairment or from any of those forms of disorder of a nature or degree which makes it appropriate for him to be liable to be detained in a hospital for medical treatment; or

(ii) that it is not necessary for the health or safety of the patient or for the protection of other persons that he should receive such treatment; or

(iii) in the case of an application by virtue of paragraph (*g*) of section 66(1) above, that the patient, if released, would not be likely to act in a manner dangerous to other persons or to himself.

(2) In determining whether to direct the discharge of a patient detained otherwise than under section 2 above in a case not falling within paragraph (*b*) of subsection (1) above, the tribunal shall have regard—

(*a*) to the likelihood of medical treatment alleviating or preventing a deterioration of the patient's condition; and

(*b*) in the case of a patient suffering from mental illness or severe mental impairment, to the likelihood of the patient, if discharged, being able to care for himself, to obtain the care he needs or to guard himself against serious exploitation.

(3) A tribunal may under subsection (1) above direct the discharge of a patient on a future date specified in the direction; and where a tribunal do not direct the discharge of a patient under that subsection the tribunal may—

(*a*) with a view to facilitating his discharge on a future date, recommend that he be granted leave of absence or transferred to another hospital or into guardianship; and

(*b*) further consider his case in the event of any such recommendation not being complied with.

(4) Where application is made to a Mental Health Review Tribunal by or in respect of a patient who is subject to guardianship under this Act, the tribunal may in any case direct that the patient be discharged, and shall so direct if they are satisfied—

(*a*) that he is not then suffering from mental illness, psychopathic disorder, severe mental impairment or mental impairment; or

(*b*) that it is not necessary in the interests of the welfare of the patient, or for the protection of other persons, that the patient should remain under such guardianship.

(5) Where application is made to a Mental Health Review Tribunal under any provision of this Act by or in respect of

PART V

a patient and the tribunal do not direct that the patient be discharged, the tribunal may, if satisfied that the patient is suffering from a form of mental disorder other than the form specified in the application, order or direction relating to him, direct that that application, order or direction be amended by substituting for the form of mental disorder specified in it such other form of mental disorder as appears to the tribunal to be appropriate.

(6) Subsections (1) to (5) above apply in relation to references to a Mental Health Review Tribunal as they apply in relation to applications made to such a tribunal by or in respect of a patient.

(7) Subsection (1) above shall not apply in the case of a restricted patient except as provided in sections 73 and 74 below.

Power to discharge restricted patients.

73.—(1) Where an application to a Mental Health Review Tribunal is made by a restricted patient who is subject to a restriction order, or where the case of such a patient is referred to such a tribunal, the tribunal shall direct the absolute discharge of the patient if satisfied—

(*a*) as to the matters mentioned in paragraph (*b*)(i) or (ii) of section 72(1) above; and

(*b*) that it is not appropriate for the patient to remain liable to be recalled to hospital for further treatment.

(2) Where in the case of any such patient as is mentioned in subsection (1) above the tribunal are satisfied as to the matters referred to in paragraph (*a*) of that subsection but not as to the matter referred to in paragraph (*b*) of that subsection the tribunal shall direct the conditional discharge of the patient.

(3) Where a patient is absolutely discharged under this section he shall thereupon cease to be liable to be detained by virtue of the relevant hospital order, and the restriction order shall cease to have effect accordingly.

(4) Where a patient is conditionally discharged under this section—

(*a*) he may be recalled by the Secretary of State under subsection (3) of section 42 above as if he had been conditionally discharged under subsection (2) of that section; and

(*b*) the patient shall comply with such conditions (if any) as may be imposed at the time of discharge by the tribunal or at any subsequent time by the Secretary of State.

(5) The Secretary of State may from time to time vary any condition imposed (whether by the tribunal or by him) under subsection (4) above.

(6) Where a restriction order in respect of a patient ceases to have effect after he has been conditionally discharged under this section the patient shall, unless previously recalled, be deemed to be absolutely discharged on the date when the order ceases to have effect and shall cease to be liable to be detained by virtue of the relevant hospital order.

(7) A tribunal may defer a direction for the conditional discharge of a patient until such arrangements as appear to the tribunal to be necessary for that purpose have been made to their satisfaction; and where by virtue of any such deferment no direction has been given on an application or reference before the time when the patient's case comes before the tribunal on a subsequent application or reference, the previous application or reference shall be treated as one on which no direction under this section can be given.

(8) This section is without prejudice to section 42 above.

Restricted patients subject to restriction directions.

74.—(1) Where an application to a Mental Health Review Tribunal is made by a restricted patient who is subject to a restriction direction, or where the case of such a patient is referred to such a tribunal, the tribunal—

(*a*) shall notify the Secretary of State whether, in their opinion, the patient would, if subject to a restriction order, be entitled to be absolutely or conditionally discharged under section 73 above; and

(*b*) if they notify him that the patient would be entitled to be conditionally discharged, may recommend that in the event of his not being discharged under this section he should continue to be detained in hospital.

(2) If in the case of a patient not falling within subsection (4) below—

(*a*) the tribunal notify the Secretary of State that the patient would be entitled to be absolutely or conditionally discharged; and

(*b*) within the period of 90 days beginning with the date of that notification the Secretary of State gives notice to the tribunal that the patient may be so discharged,

the tribunal shall direct the absolute or, as the case may be, the conditional discharge of the patient.

(3) Where a patient continues to be liable to be detained in a hospital at the end of the period referred to in subsection (2)(*b*) above because the Secretary of State has not given the notice there mentioned, the managers of the hospital shall, unless

PART V

the tribunal have made a recommendation under subsection (1)(*b*) above, transfer the patient to a prison or other institution in which he might have been detained if he had not been removed to hospital, there to be dealt with as if he had not been so removed.

(4) If, in the case of a patient who is subject to a transfer direction under section 48 above, the tribunal notify the Secretary of State that the patient would be entitled to be absolutely or conditionally discharged, the Secretary of State shall, unless the tribunal have made a recommendation under subsection (1)(*b*) above, by warrant direct that the patient be remitted to a prison or other institution in which he might have been detained if he had not been removed to hospital, there to be dealt with as if he had not been so removed.

(5) Where a patient is transferred or remitted under subsection (3) or (4) above the relevant transfer direction and the restriction direction shall cease to have effect on his arrival in the prison or other institution.

(6) Subsections (3) to (8) of section 73 above shall have effect in relation to this section as they have effect in relation to that section, taking references to the relevant hospital order and the restriction order as references to the transfer direction and the restriction direction.

(7) This section is without prejudice to sections 50 to 53 above in their application to patients who are not discharged under this section.

Applications and references concerning conditionally discharged restricted patients.

75.—(1) Where a restricted patient has been conditionally discharged under section 42(2), 73 or 74 above and is subsequently recalled to hospital—

(*a*) the Secretary of State shall, within one month of the day on which the patient returns or is returned to hospital, refer his case to a Mental Health Review Tribunal; and

(*b*) section 70 above shall apply to the patient as if the relevant hospital order or transfer direction had been made on that day.

(2) Where a restricted patient has been conditionally discharged as aforesaid but has not been recalled to hospital he may apply to a Mental Health Review Tribunal—

(*a*) in the period between the expiration of 12 months and the expiration of two years beginning with the date on which he was conditionally discharged; and

(*b*) in any subsequent period of two years.

(3) Sections 73 and 74 above shall not apply to an application under subsection (2) above but on any such application the tribunal may—

(*a*) vary any condition to which the patient is subject in connection with his discharge or impose any condition which might have been imposed in connection therewith; or

(*b*) direct that the restriction order or restriction direction to which he is subject shall cease to have effect;

and if the tribunal give a direction under paragraph (*b*) above the patient shall cease to be liable to be detained by virtue of the relevant hospital order or transfer direction.

General

Visiting and examination of patients.

76.—(1) For the purpose of advising whether an application to a Mental Health Review Tribunal should be made by or in respect of a patient who is liable to be detained or subject to guardianship under Part II of this Act or of furnishing information as to the condition of a patient for the purposes of such an application, any registered medical practitioner authorised by or on behalf of the patient or other person who is entitled to make or has made the application—

(*a*) may at any reasonable time visit the patient and examine him in private, and

(*b*) may require the production of and inspect any records relating to the detention or treatment of the patient in any hospital.

(2) Section 32 above shall apply for the purposes of this section as it applies for the purposes of Part II of this Act.

General provisions concerning tribunal applications.

77.—(1) No application shall be made to a Mental Health Review Tribunal by or in respect of a patient except in such cases and at such times as are expressly provided by this Act.

(2) Where under this Act any person is authorised to make an application to a Mental Health Review Tribunal within a specified period, not more than one such application shall be made by that person within that period but for that purpose there shall be disregarded any application which is withdrawn in accordance with rules made under section 78 below.

(3) Subject to subsection (4) below an application to a Mental Health Review Tribunal authorised to be made by or in respect of a patient under this Act shall be made by notice in writing addressed to the tribunal for the area in which the hospital in

PART V

which the patient is detained is situated or in which the patient is residing under guardianship as the case may be.

(4) Any application under section 75(2) above shall be made to the tribunal for the area in which the patient resides.

Procedure of tribunals.

78.—(1) The Lord Chancellor may make rules with respect to the making of applications to Mental Health Review Tribunals and with respect to the proceedings of such tribunals and matters incidental to or consequential on such proceedings.

(2) Rules made under this section may in particular make provision—

(*a*) for enabling a tribunal, or the chairman of a tribunal, to postpone the consideration of any application by or in respect of a patient, or of any such application of any specified class, until the expiration of such period (not exceeding 12 months) as may be specified in the rules from the date on which an application by or in respect of the same patient was last considered and determined by that or any other tribunal under this Act;

(*b*) for the transfer of proceedings from one tribunal to another in any case where, after the making of the application, the patient is removed out of the area of the tribunal to which it was made;

(*c*) for restricting the persons qualified to serve as members of a tribunal for the consideration of any application, or of an application of any specified class;

(*d*) for enabling a tribunal to dispose of an application without a formal hearing where such a hearing is not requested by the applicant or it appears to the tribunal that such a hearing would be detrimental to the health of the patient;

(*e*) for enabling a tribunal to exclude members of the public, or any specified class of members of the public, from any proceedings of the tribunal, or to prohibit the publication of reports of any such proceedings or the names of any persons concerned in such proceedings;

(*f*) for regulating the circumstances in which, and the persons by whom, applicants and patients in respect of whom applications are made to a tribunal may, if not desiring to conduct their own case, be represented for the purposes of those applications;

(*g*) for regulating the methods by which information relevant to an application may be obtained by or furnished to the tribunal, and in particular for authorising the members of a tribunal, or any one or more of them, to visit and interview in private any patient by or in respect of whom an application has been made; PART V

(*h*) for making available to any applicant, and to any patient in respect of whom an application is made to a tribunal, copies of any documents obtained by or furnished to the tribunal in connection with the application, and a statement of the substance of any oral information so obtained or furnished except where the tribunal considers it undesirable in the interests of the patient or for other special reasons;

(*i*) for requiring a tribunal, if so requested in accordance with the rules, to furnish such statements of the reasons for any decision given by the tribunal as may be prescribed by the rules, subject to any provision made by the rules for withholding such a statement from a patient or any other person in cases where the tribunal considers that furnishing it would be undesirable in the interests of the patient or for other special reasons;

(*j*) for conferring on the tribunals such ancillary powers as the Lord Chancellor thinks necessary for the purposes of the exercise of their functions under this Act;

(*k*) for enabling any functions of a tribunal which relate to matters preliminary or incidental to an application to be performed by the chairman of the tribunal.

(3) Subsections (1) and (2) above apply in relation to references to Mental Health Review Tribunals as they apply in relation to applications to such tribunals by or in respect of patients.

(4) Rules under this section may make provision as to the procedure to be adopted in cases concerning restricted patients and, in particular—

(*a*) for restricting the persons qualified to serve as president of a tribunal for the consideration of an application or reference relating to a restricted patient;

(*b*) for the transfer of proceedings from one tribunal to another in any case where, after the making of a reference or application in accordance with section 71(4) or 77(4) above, the patient ceases to reside in the area of the tribunal to which the reference or application was made.

(5) Rules under this section may be so framed as to apply to all applications or references or to applications or references of any specified class and may make different provision in relation to different cases.

PART V

(6) Any functions conferred on the chairman of a Mental Health Review Tribunal by rules under this section may, if for any reason he is unable to act, be exercised by another member of that tribunal appointed by him for the purpose.

(7) A Mental Health Review Tribunal may pay allowances in respect of travelling expenses, subsistence and loss of earnings to any person attending the tribunal as an applicant or witness, to the patient who is the subject of the proceedings if he attends otherwise than as the applicant or a witness and to any person (other than counsel or a solicitor) who attends as the representative of an applicant.

(8) A Mental Health Review Tribunal may, and if so required by the High Court shall, state in the form of a special case for determination by the High Court any question of law which may arise before them.

1950 c. 27.

(9) The Arbitration Act 1950 shall not apply to any proceedings before a Mental Health Review Tribunal except so far as any provisions of that Act may be applied, with or without modifications, by rules made under this section.

Interpretation of Part V.

79.—(1) In this Part of this Act " restricted patient " means a patient who is subject to a restriction order or restriction direction and this Part of this Act shall, subject to the provisions of this section, have effect in relation to any person who—

(*a*) is subject to a direction which by virtue of section 46(3) above has the same effect as a hospital order and a restriction order ; or

1964 c. 84.
1968 c. 19.

(*b*) is treated as subject to a hospital order and a restriction order by virtue of an order under section 5(1) of the Criminal Procedure (Insanity) Act 1964 or section 6 or 14(1) of the Criminal Appeal Act 1968 ; or

1960 c. 61.

(*c*) is treated as subject to a hospital order and a restriction order or to a transfer direction and a restriction direction by virtue of section 82(2) or 85(2) below or section 73(2) of the Mental Health (Scotland) Act 1960,

as it has effect in relation to a restricted patient.

(2) Subject to the following provisions of this section, in this Part of this Act " the relevant hospital order " and " the relevant transfer direction ", in relation to a restricted patient, mean the hospital order or transfer direction by virtue of which he is liable to be detained in a hospital.

(3) In the case of a person within paragraph (*a*) of subsection (1) above, references in this Part of this Act to the relevant hospital order or restriction order shall be construed as references to the direction referred to in that paragraph.

(4) In the case of a person within paragraph (*b*) of subsection (1) above, references in this Part of this Act to the relevant hospital order or restriction order shall be construed as references to the order under the provisions mentioned in that paragraph.

(5) In the case of a person within paragraph (*c*) of subsection (1) above, references in this Part of this Act to the relevant hospital order, the relevant transfer direction, the restriction order or the restriction direction or to a transfer direction under section 48 above shall be construed as references to the hospital order, transfer direction, restriction order, restriction direction or transfer direction under that section to which that person is treated as subject by virtue of the provisions mentioned in that paragraph.

(6) In this Part of this Act, unless the context otherwise requires, "hospital" means a hospital within the meaning of Part II of this Act.

PART VI

REMOVAL AND RETURN OF PATIENTS WITHIN UNITED KINGDOM, ETC.

Removal to Scotland

Removal of patients to Scotland.

80.—(1) If it appears to the Secretary of State, in the case of a patient who is for the time being liable to be detained or subject to guardianship under this Act (otherwise than by virtue of section 35, 36 or 38 above), that it is in the interests of the patient to remove him to Scotland, and that arrangements have been made for admitting him to a hospital or, as the case may be, for receiving him into guardianship there, the Secretary of State may authorise his removal to Scotland and may give any necessary directions for his conveyance to his destination.

(2) Subject to the provisions of subsection (4) below, where a patient liable to be detained under this Act by virtue of an application, order or direction under any enactment in force in England and Wales is removed under this section and admitted to a hospital in Scotland, he shall be treated as if on the date of his admission he had been so admitted in pursuance of an application forwarded to the Health Board responsible for the administration of the hospital, or an order or direction made

PART VI

or given, on that date under the corresponding enactment in Scotland, and, where he is subject to a restriction order or restriction direction under any enactment in this Act, as if he were subject to an order or direction under the corresponding enactment in force in Scotland.

(3) Where a patient subject to guardianship under this Act by virtue of an application, order or direction under any enactment in force in England and Wales is removed under this section and received into guardianship in Scotland, he shall be treated as if on the date on which he arrives at the place where he is to reside he had been so received in pursuance of an application, order or direction under the corresponding enactment in force in Scotland, and as if the application had been forwarded or, as the case may be, the order or direction had been made or given on that date.

(4) Where a person removed under this section was immediately before his removal liable to be detained by virtue of an application for admission for assessment under this Act, he shall, on his admission to a hospital in Scotland, be treated as if he had been admitted to the hospital in pursuance of an emergency recommendation under the Mental Health (Scotland) Act 1960 made on the date of his admission.

1960 c. 61.

(5) Where a patient removed under this section was immediately before his removal liable to be detained under this Act by virtue of a transfer direction given while he was serving a sentence of imprisonment (within the meaning of section 47(5) above) imposed by a court in England and Wales, he shall be treated as if the sentence had been imposed by a court in Scotland.

(6) Where a person removed under this section was immediately before his removal subject to a restriction order or restriction direction of limited duration, the order or direction restricting his discharge to which he is subject by virtue of subsection (2) above shall expire on the date on which the restriction order or restriction direction would have expired if he had not been so removed.

(7) In this section "hospital" has the same meaning as in the Mental Health (Scotland) Act 1960.

Removal to and from Northern Ireland

Removal of patients to Northern Ireland.

81.—(1) If it appears to the Secretary of State, in the case of a patient who is for the time being liable to be detained or subject to guardianship under this Act (otherwise than by virtue of section 35, 36 or 38 above), that it is in the interests of the patient to remove him to Northern Ireland, and that arrangements have been made for admitting him to a hospital or, as the case may be, for receiving him into guardianship there, the Secretary of State may authorise his removal to Northern Ireland and may give any necessary directions for his conveyance to his destination. PART VI

(2) Subject to the provisions of subsections (4) and (5) below, where a patient liable to be detained under this Act by virtue of an application, order or direction under any enactment in force in England and Wales is removed under this section and admitted to a hospital in Northern Ireland, he shall be treated as if on the date of his admission he had been so admitted in pursuance of an application made, or an order or direction made or given, on that date under the corresponding enactment in force in Northern Ireland, and, where he is subject to a restriction order or restriction direction under any enactment in this Act, as if he were subject to an order or direction under the corresponding enactment in force in Northern Ireland.

(3) Where a patient subject to guardianship under this Act by virtue of an application, order or direction under any enactment in force in England and Wales is removed under this section and received into guardianship in Northern Ireland, he shall be treated as if on the date on which he arrives at the place where he is to reside he had been so received in pursuance of an application, order or direction under the corresponding enactment in force in Northern Ireland, and as if the application had been accepted or, as the case may be, the order or direction had been made or given on that date.

(4) Where a person removed under this section was immediately before his removal liable to be detained by virtue of an application for admission for assessment under this Act, he shall, on his admission to a hospital in Northern Ireland, be treated as if he had been admitted to the hospital in pursuance of an application for admission under section 12 of the Mental Health Act (Northern Ireland) 1961 made on the date of his admission. 1961 c. 15 (N.I.).

(5) Where a person removed under this section was immediately before his removal liable to be detained by virtue of an application for admission for treatment under this Act, he shall, on his admission to a hospital in Northern Ireland, be treated as if—

(*a*) he had been admitted to the hospital in pursuance of an application for admission under section 12 of the Mental Health Act (Northern Ireland) 1961 made on the date of his admission; and

(*b*) a medical report under section 19 of that Act had been made in respect of him on that date.

PART VI

(6) Where a patient removed under this section was immediately before his removal liable to be detained under this Act by virtue of a transfer direction given while he was serving a sentence of imprisonment (within the meaning of section 47(5) above) imposed by a court in England and Wales, he shall be treated as if the sentence had been imposed by a court in Northern Ireland.

(7) Where a person removed under this section was immediately before his removal subject to a restriction order or restriction direction of limited duration, the order or direction restricting his discharge to which he is subject by virtue of subsection (2) above shall expire on the date on which the restriction order or restriction direction would have expired if he had not been so removed.

(8) In this section " hospital " has the same meaning as in the Mental Health Act (Northern Ireland) 1961.

1961 c. 15 (N.I.).

Removal to England and Wales of patients from Northern Ireland.

82.—(1) If it appears to the responsible authority, in the case of a patient who is for the time being liable to be detained or subject to guardianship under the Mental Health Act (Northern Ireland) 1961, that it is in the interests of the patient to remove him to England and Wales, and that arrangements have been made for admitting him to a hospital or, as the case may be, for receiving him into guardianship there, the responsible authority may authorise his removal to England and Wales and may give any necessary directions for his conveyance to his destination.

(2) Subject to the provisions of subsection (4) below, where a patient who is liable to be detained under the said Act of 1961 by virtue of an application, order or direction under any enactment in force in Northern Ireland is removed under this section and admitted to a hospital in England and Wales, he shall be treated as if on the date of his admission he had been so admitted in pursuance of an application made, or an order or direction made or given, on that date under the corresponding enactment in force in England and Wales and, where he is subject to an order or direction under any enactment in the said Act of 1961 restricting his discharge, as if he were subject to a restriction order or restriction direction.

(3) Where a patient subject to guardianship under the said Act of 1961 by virtue of an application, order or direction under any enactment in force in Northern Ireland is removed under this section and received into guardianship in England and Wales, he shall be treated as if on the date on which he arrives at the place where he is to reside he had been so received in

pursuance of an application, order or direction under the corresponding enactment in force in England and Wales and as if the application had been accepted or, as the case may be, the order or direction had been made or given on that date.

(4) Where a person removed under this section was immediately before his removal liable to be detained by virtue of an application for admission under section 12 of the said Act of 1961 he shall—

(*a*) if a report under section 19 of that Act has not been made in respect of him, be treated, on his admission to a hospital in England and Wales, as if he had been admitted to the hospital in pursuance of an application for admission for assessment made on the date of his admission ;

(*b*) if a report under the said section 19 has been made in respect of him, be treated, on his admission to a hospital in England and Wales, as if he had been admitted to the hospital in pursuance of an application for admission for treatment made on the date of his admission.

(5) Where a patient removed under this section was immediately before his removal liable to be detained under the said Act of 1961 by virtue of a transfer direction given while he was serving a sentence of imprisonment (within the meaning of section 58(6) of that Act) imposed by a court in Northern Ireland, he shall be treated as if the sentence had been imposed by a court in England and Wales.

(6) Where a person removed under this section was immediately before his removal subject to an order or direction restricting his discharge, being an order or direction of limited duration, the restriction order or restriction direction to which he is subject by virtue of subsection (2) above shall expire on the date on which the first-mentioned order or direction would have expired if he had not been so removed.

(7) In this section " the responsible authority " means the Department of Health and Social Services for Northern Ireland or, in relation to a patient who is subject to an order or direction restricting his discharge, the Secretary of State.

Removal to and from Channel Islands and Isle of Man

Removal of patients to Channel Islands or Isle of Man.

83. If it appears to the Secretary of State, in the case of a patient who is for the time being liable to be detained or subject to guardianship under this Act (otherwise than by virtue of section 35, 36 or 38 above), that it is in the interests of the patient to remove him to any of the Channel Islands or to the

PART VI

Isle of Man, and that arrangements have been made for admitting him to a hospital or, as the case may be, for receiving him into guardianship there, the Secretary of State may authorise his removal to the island in question and may give any necessary directions for his conveyance to his destination.

Removal to England and Wales of offenders found insane in Channel Islands and Isle of Man.

84.—(1) The Secretary of State may by warrant direct that any offender found by a court in any of the Channel Islands or in the Isle of Man to be insane or to have been insane at the time of the alleged offence, and ordered to be detained during Her Majesty's pleasure, be removed to a hospital in England and Wales.

(2) A patient removed under subsection (1) above shall, on his reception into the hospital in England and Wales, be treated as if he had been removed to that hospital in pursuance of a direction under section 46 above.

(3) The Secretary of State may by warrant direct that any patient removed under this section from any of the Channel Islands or from the Isle of Man be returned to the island from which he was so removed, there to be dealt with according to law in all respects as if he had not been removed under this section.

Patients removed from Channel Islands or Isle of Man.

85.—(1) This section applies to any patient who is removed to England and Wales from any of the Channel Islands or the Isle of Man under a provision corresponding to section 83 above and who immediately before his removal was liable to be detained or subject to guardianship in the island in question under a provision corresponding to an enactment contained in this Act (other than section 35, 36 or 38 above).

(2) Where the patient is admitted to a hospital in England and Wales he shall be treated as if on the date of his admission he had been so admitted in pursuance of an application made, or an order or direction made or given, on that date under the corresponding enactment contained in this Act and, where he is subject to an order or direction restricting his discharge, as if he were subject to a restriction order or restriction direction.

(3) Where the patient is received into guardianship in England and Wales, he shall be treated as if on the date on which he arrives at the place where he is to reside he had been so received in pursuance of an application, order or direction under the corresponding enactment contained in this Act and as if the application had been accepted or, as the case may be, the order or direction had been made or given on that date.

(4) Where the patient was immediately before his removal liable to be detained by virtue of a transfer direction given while he was serving a sentence of imprisonment imposed by a court in the island in question, he shall be treated as if the sentence had been imposed by a court in England and Wales.

(5) Where the patient was immediately before his removal subject to an order or direction restricting his discharge, being an order or direction of limited duration, the restriction order or restriction direction to which he is subject by virtue of subsection (2) above shall expire on the date on which the first-mentioned order or direction would have expired if he had not been removed.

(6) While being conveyed to the hospital referred to in subsection (2) or, as the case may be, the place referred to in subsection (3) above, the patient shall be deemed to be in legal custody, and section 138 below shall apply to him as if he were in legal custody by virtue of section 137 below.

(7) In the case of a patient removed from the Isle of Man the reference in subsection (4) above to a person serving a sentence of imprisonment includes a reference to a person detained as mentioned in section 60(6)(*a*) of the Mental Health Act 1974 (an Act of Tynwald).

Removal of aliens

86.—(1) This section applies to any patient who is neither a British citizen nor a Commonwealth citizen having the right of abode in the United Kingdom by virtue of section 2(1)(*b*) of the Immigration Act 1971, being a patient who is receiving treatment for mental illness as an in-patient in a hospital in England and Wales or a hospital within the meaning of the Mental Health Act (Northern Ireland) 1961 and is detained pursuant to—

Removal of alien patients.

1971 c. 77.

1961 c. 15 (N.I.).

(*a*) an application for admission for treatment or an application under section 12 of the said Act of 1961 ;

(*b*) a hospital order under section 37 above or section 48 of the said Act of 1961 ; or

(*c*) an order or direction under this Act (other than under section 35, 36 or 38 above) or the said Act of 1961 having the same effect as such a hospital order.

(2) If it appears to the Secretary of State that proper arrangements have been made for the removal of a patient to whom this section applies to a country or territory outside the United Kingdom, the Isle of Man and the Channel Islands and for his care or treatment there and that it is in the interests of the

PART VI

patient to remove him, the Secretary of State may, subject to subsection (3) below—

(*a*) by warrant authorise the removal of the patient from the place where he is receiving treatment as mentioned in subsection (1) above, and

(*b*) give such directions as the Secretary of State thinks fit for the conveyance of the patient to his destination in that country or territory and for his detention in any place or on board any ship or aircraft until his arrival at any specified port or place in any such country or territory.

(3) The Secretary of State shall not exercise his powers under subsection (2) above in the case of any patient except with the approval of a Mental Health Review Tribunal or, as the case may be, of the Mental Health Review Tribunal for Northern Ireland.

Return of patients absent without leave

Patients absent from hospitals in Northern Ireland.

1961 c. 15 (N.I.).

87.—(1) Any person who—

(*a*) under section 30 or section 108 of the Mental Health Act (Northern Ireland) 1961 (which provide, respectively, for the retaking of patients absent without leave and for the retaking of patients escaping from custody); or

(*b*) under the said section 30 as applied by section 34 of the said Act of 1961 (which makes special provision as to persons sentenced to imprisonment),

may be taken into custody in Northern Ireland, may be taken into custody in, and returned to Northern Ireland from, England and Wales by an approved social worker, by any constable or by any person authorised by or by virtue of the said Act of 1961 to take him into custody.

(2) This section does not apply to any person who is subject to guardianship.

Patients absent from hospitals in England and Wales.

88.—(1) Subject to the provisions of this section, any person who, under section 18 above or section 138 below or under the said section 18 as applied by section 22 above, may be taken into custody in England and Wales may be taken into custody in, and returned to England and Wales from, any other part of the United Kingdom or the Channel Islands or the Isle of Man.

(2) For the purposes of the enactments referred to in subsection (1) above, in their application by virtue of this section to Scotland, Northern Ireland, the Channel Islands or the Isle

PART VI

of Man, the expression "constable" includes a Scottish constable, an officer or constable of the Royal Ulster Constabulary, a member of the police in Jersey, an officer of police within the meaning of section 43 of the Larceny (Guernsey) Law 1958 or any corresponding law for the time being in force, or a constable in the Isle of Man, as the case may be.

(3) For the purposes of the said enactments in their application by virtue of this section to Scotland or Northern Ireland, any reference to an approved social worker shall be construed as including a reference—

(a) in Scotland, to any mental health officer within the meaning of the Mental Health (Scotland) Act 1960; 1960 c. 61.

(b) in Northern Ireland, to any social worker within the meaning of the Mental Health Act (Northern Ireland) 1961. 1961 c. 15 (N.I.).

(4) This section does not apply to any person who is subject to guardianship.

Patients absent from hospitals in the Channel Islands or Isle of Man.

89.—(1) Any person who under any provision corresponding to section 18 above or 138 below may be taken into custody in any of the Channel Islands or the Isle of Man may be taken into custody in, and returned to the island in question from, England and Wales by an approved social worker or a constable.

(2) This section does not apply to any person who is subject to guardianship.

General

Regulations for purposes of Part VI.

90. Section 32 above shall have effect as if references in that section to Part II of this Act included references to this Part of this Act and to Part VI of the Mental Health (Scotland) Act 1960, so far as those Parts apply to patients removed to England and Wales thereunder.

General provisions as to patients removed from England and Wales.

91.—(1) Subject to subsection (2) below, where a patient liable to be detained or subject to guardianship by virtue of an application, order or direction under Part II or III of this Act (other than section 35, 36 or 38 above) is removed from England and Wales in pursuance of arrangements under this Part of this Act, the application, order or direction shall cease to have effect when he is duly received into a hospital or other institution, or placed under guardianship, in pursuance of those arrangements.

(2) Where the Secretary of State exercises his powers under section 86(2) above in respect of a patient who is detained pursuant to a hospital order under section 37 above and in

PART VI

respect of whom a restriction order is in force, those orders shall continue in force so as to apply to the patient if he returns to England and Wales at any time before the end of the period for which those orders would have continued in force.

Interpretation of Part VI.

92.—(1) References in this Part of this Act to a hospital, being a hospital in England and Wales, shall be construed as references to a hospital within the meaning of Part II of this Act.

(2) Where a patient is treated by virtue of this Part of this Act as if he had been removed to a hospital in England and Wales in pursuance of a direction under Part III of this Act, that direction shall be deemed to have been given on the date of his reception into the hospital.

1960 c. 61.

(3) A patient removed to England and Wales under this Part of this Act or under Part VI of the Mental Health (Scotland) Act 1960 shall be treated for the purposes of this Act as suffering from such form of mental disorder as may be recorded in his case in pursuance of regulations made by virtue of section 90 above, and references in this Act to the form or forms of mental disorder specified in the relevant application, order or direction shall be construed as including references to the form or forms of mental disorder so recorded.

PART VII

MANAGEMENT OF PROPERTY AND AFFAIRS OF PATIENTS

Judicial authorities and Court of Protection.

93.—(1) The Lord Chancellor shall from time to time nominate one or more judges of the Supreme Court (in this Act referred to as " nominated judges ") to act for the purposes of this Part of this Act.

1981 c. 54.

(2) There shall continue to be an office of the Supreme Court, called the Court of Protection, for the protection and management, as provided by this Part of this Act, of the property and affairs of persons under disability ; and there shall continue to be a Master of the Court of Protection appointed by the Lord Chancellor under section 89 of the Supreme Court Act 1981.

1868 c. 72.

(3) The Master of the Court of Protection shall take the oath of allegiance and judicial oath in the presence of the Lord Chancellor ; and the Promissory Oaths Act 1868 shall have effect as if the officers named in the Second Part of the Schedule to that Act included the Master of the Court of Protection.

(4) The Lord Chancellor may nominate other officers of the Court of Protection (in this Part of this Act referred to as "nominated officers") to act for the purposes of this Part of this Act.

Exercise of the judge's functions: "the patient".

94.—(1) The functions expressed to be conferred by this Part of this Act on the judge shall be exercisable by the Lord Chancellor or by any nominated judge, and shall also be exercisable by the Master of the Court of Protection or by any nominated officer, but—

(*a*) in the case of the Master or any nominated officer, subject to any express provision to the contrary in this Part of this Act or any rules made under this Part of this Act,

(*b*) in the case of any nominated officer, subject to any directions of the Master and so far only as may be provided by the instrument by which he is nominated;

and references in this Part of this Act to the judge shall be construed accordingly.

(2) The functions of the judge under this Part of this Act shall be exercisable where, after considering medical evidence, he is satisfied that a person is incapable, by reason of mental disorder, of managing and administering his property and affairs; and a person as to whom the judge is so satisfied is referred to in this Part of this Act as a patient.

General functions of the judge with respect to property and affairs of patient.

95.—(1) The judge may, with respect to the property and affairs of a patient, do or secure the doing of all such things as appear necessary or expedient—

(*a*) for the maintenance or other benefit of the patient,

(*b*) for the maintenance or other benefit of members of the patient's family,

(*c*) for making provision for other persons or purposes for whom or which the patient might be expected to provide if he were not mentally disordered, or

(*d*) otherwise for administering the patient's affairs.

(2) In the exercise of the powers conferred by this section regard shall be had first of all to the requirements of the patient, and the rules of law which restricted the enforcement by a creditor of rights against property under the control of the judge in lunacy shall apply to property under the control of the judge; but, subject to the foregoing provisions of this subsection, the judge shall, in administering a patient's affairs, have regard to

PART VII

the interests of creditors and also to the desirability of making provision for obligations of the patient notwithstanding that they may not be legally enforceable.

Powers of the judge as to patient's property and affairs.

96.—(1) Without prejudice to the generality of section 95 above, the judge shall have power to make such orders and give such directions and authorities as he thinks fit for the purposes of that section and in particular may for those purposes make orders or give directions or authorities for—

(*a*) the control (with or without the transfer or vesting of property or the payment into or lodgment in the Supreme Court of money or securities) and management of any property of the patient;

(*b*) the sale, exchange, charging or other disposition of or dealing with any property of the patient;

(*c*) the acquisition of any property in the name or on behalf of the patient;

(*d*) the settlement of any property of the patient, or the gift of any property of the patient to any such persons or for any such purposes as are mentioned in paragraphs (*b*) and (*c*) of section 95(1) above;

(*e*) the execution for the patient of a will making any provision (whether by way of disposing of property or exercising a power or otherwise) which could be made by a will executed by the patient if he were not mentally disordered;

(*f*) the carrying on by a suitable person of any profession, trade or business of the patient;

(*g*) the dissolution of a partnership of which the patient is a member;

(*h*) the carrying out of any contract entered into by the patient;

(*i*) the conduct of legal proceedings in the name of the patient or on his behalf;

(*j*) the reimbursement out of the property of the patient, with or without interest, of money applied by any person either in payment of the patient's debts (whether legally enforceable or not) or for the maintenance or other benefit of the patient or members of his family or in making provision for other persons or purposes for whom or which he might be expected to provide if he were not mentally disordered;

(*k*) the exercise of any power (including a power to consent) vested in the patient, whether beneficially, or as guardian or trustee, or otherwise.

(2) If under subsection (1) above provision is made for the settlement of any property of a patient, or the exercise of a power vested in a patient of appointing trustees or retiring from a trust, the judge may also make as respects the property settled or trust property such consequential vesting or other orders as the case may require, including (in the case of the exercise of such a power) any order which could have been made in such a case under Part IV of the Trustee Act 1925. 1925 c. 19.

(3) Where under this section a settlement has been made of any property of a patient, and the Lord Chancellor or a nominated judge is satisfied, at any time before the death of the patient, that any material fact was not disclosed when the settlement was made, or that there has been any substantial change in circumstances, he may by order vary the settlement in such manner as he thinks fit, and give any consequential directions.

(4) The power of the judge to make or give an order, direction or authority for the execution of a will for a patient—

(*a*) shall not be exercisable at any time when the patient is a minor, and

(*b*) shall not be exercised unless the judge has reason to believe that the patient is incapable of making a valid will for himself.

(5) The powers of a patient as patron of a benefice shall be exercisable by the Lord Chancellor only.

Supplementary provisions as to wills executed under s. 96.

97.—(1) Where under section 96(1) above the judge makes or gives an order, direction or authority requiring or authorising a person (in this section referred to as " the authorised person ") to execute a will for a patient, any will executed in pursuance of that order, direction or authority shall be expressed to be signed by the patient acting by the authorised person, and shall be—

(*a*) signed by the authorised person with the name of the patient, and with his own name, in the presence of two or more witnesses present at the same time, and

(*b*) attested and subscribed by those witnesses in the presence of the authorised person, and

(*c*) sealed with the official seal of the Court of Protection.

(2) The Wills Act 1837 shall have effect in relation to any such will as if it were signed by the patient by his own hand, except that in relation to any such will— 1837 c. 26.

(*a*) section 9 of that Act (which makes provision as to the signing and attestation of wills) shall not apply, and

PART VII

(*b*) in the subsequent provisions of that Act any reference to execution in the manner required by the previous provisions of that Act shall be construed as a reference to execution in the manner required by subsection (1) above.

(3) Subject to the following provisions of this section, any such will executed in accordance with subsection (1) above shall have the same effect for all purposes as if the patient were capable of making a valid will and the will had been executed by him in the manner required by the Wills Act 1837.

1837 c. 26.

(4) So much of subsection (3) above as provides for such a will to have effect as if the patient were capable of making a valid will—

(*a*) shall not have effect in relation to such a will in so far as it disposes of any immovable property, other than immovable property in England or Wales, and

(*b*) where at the time when such a will is executed the patient is domiciled in Scotland or Northern Ireland or in a country or territory outside the United Kingdom, shall not have effect in relation to that will in so far as it relates to any other property or matter, except any property or matter in respect of which, under the law of his domicile, any question of his testamentary capacity would fall to be determined in accordance with the law of England and Wales.

Judge's powers in cases of emergency.

98. Where it is represented to the judge, and he has reason to believe, that a person may be incapable, by reason of mental disorder, of managing and administering his property and affairs, and the judge is of the opinion that it is necessary to make immediate provision for any of the matters referred to in section 95 above, then pending the determination of the question whether that person is so incapable the judge may exercise in relation to the property and affairs of that person any of the powers conferred on him in relation to the property and affairs of a patient by this Part of this Act so far as is requisite for enabling that provision to be made.

Power to appoint receiver.

99.—(1) The judge may by order appoint as receiver for a patient a person specified in the order or the holder for the time being of an office so specified.

(2) A person appointed as receiver for a patient shall do all such things in relation to the property and affairs of the patient as the judge, in the exercise of the powers conferred on him by

sections 95 and 96 above, orders or directs him to do and may do any such thing in relation to the property and affairs of the patient as the judge, in the exercise of those powers, authorises him to do.

PART VII

(3) A receiver appointed for any person shall be discharged by order of the judge on the judge being satisfied that that person has become capable of managing and administering his property and affairs, and may be discharged by order of the judge at any time if the judge considers it expedient to do so; and a receiver shall be discharged (without any order) on the death of the patient.

Vesting of stock in curator appointed outside England and Wales.

100.—(1) Where the judge is satisfied—

(*a*) that under the law prevailing in a place outside England and Wales a person has been appointed to exercise powers with respect to the property or affairs of any other person on the ground (however formulated) that that other person is incapable, by reason of mental disorder, of managing and administering his property and affairs, and

(*b*) that having regard to the nature of the appointment and to the circumstances of the case it is expedient that the judge should exercise his powers under this section,

the judge may direct any stock standing in the name of the said other person or the right to receive the dividends from the stock to be transferred into the name of the person so appointed or otherwise dealt with as requested by that person, and may give such directions as the judge thinks fit for dealing with accrued dividends from the stock.

(2) In this section " stock " includes shares and also any fund, annuity or security transferable in the books kept by any body corporate or unincorporated company or society, or by an instrument of transfer either alone or accompanied by other formalities, and " dividends " shall be construed accordingly.

Preservation of interests in patient's property.

101.—(1) Where any property of a person has been disposed of under this Part of this Act, and under his will or his intestacy, or by any gift perfected or nomination taking effect on his death, any other person would have taken an interest in the property but for the disposal—

(*a*) he shall take the same interest, if and so far as circumstances allow, in any property belonging to the estate of the deceased which represents the property disposed of; and

PART VII

(*b*) if the property disposed of was real property any property representing it shall so long as it remains part of his estate be treated as if it were real property.

(2) The judge, in ordering, directing or authorising under this Part of this Act any disposal of property which apart from this section would result in the conversion of personal property into real property, may direct that the property representing the property disposed of shall, so long as it remains the property of the patient or forms part of his estate, be treated as if it were personal property.

(3) References in subsections (1) and (2) above to the disposal of property are references to—

(*a*) the sale, exchange, charging or other dealing (otherwise than by will) with property other than money,

(*b*) the removal of property from one place to another,

(*c*) the application of money in acquiring property, or

(*d*) the transfer of money from one account to another;

and references to property representing property disposed of shall be construed accordingly and as including the result of successive disposals.

(4) The judge may give such directions as appear to him necessary or expedient for the purpose of facilitating the operation of subsection (1) above, including the carrying of money to a separate account and the transfer of property other than money.

(5) Where the judge has ordered, directed or authorised the expenditure of money for the carrying out of permanent improvements on, or otherwise for the permanent benefit of, any property of the patient, he may order that the whole or any part of the money expended or to be expended shall be a charge upon the property, whether without interest or with interest at a specified rate; and an order under this subsection may provide for excluding or restricting the operation of subsection (1) above.

(6) A charge under subsection (5) above may be made in favour of such person as may be just, and in particular, where the money charged is paid out of the patient's general estate, may be made in favour of a person as trustee for the patient; but no charge under that subsection shall confer any right of sale or foreclosure during the lifetime of the patient.

Lord Chancellor's Visitors.

102.—(1) There shall continue to be the following panels of Lord Chancellor's Visitors of patients constituted in accordance with this section, namely—

(*a*) a panel of Medical Visitors;

(*b*) a panel of Legal Visitors ; and

(*c*) a panel of General Visitors (being Visitors who are not required by this section to possess either a medical or legal qualification for appointment).

(2) Each panel shall consist of persons appointed to it by the Lord Chancellor, the appointment of each person being for such term and subject to such conditions as the Lord Chancellor may determine.

(3) A person shall not be qualified to be appointed—

(*a*) to the panel of Medical Visitors unless he is a registered medical practitioner who appears to the Lord Chancellor to have special knowledge and experience of cases of mental disorder ;

(*b*) to the panel of Legal Visitors unless he is a barrister or solicitor of not less than 10 years' standing.

(4) If the Lord Chancellor so determines in the case of any Visitor appointed under this section, he shall be paid out of money provided by Parliament such remuneration and allowances as the Lord Chancellor may, with the concurrence of the Treasury, determine.

Functions of Visitors.

103.—(1) Patients shall be visited by Lord Chancellor's Visitors in such circumstances, and in such manner, as may be prescribed by directions of a standing nature given by the Master of the Court of Protection with the concurrence of the Lord Chancellor.

(2) Where it appears to the judge in the case of any patient that a visit by a Lord Chancellor's Visitor is necessary for the purpose of investigating any particular matter or matters relating to the capacity of the patient to manage and administer his property and affairs, or otherwise relating to the exercise in relation to him of the functions of the judge under this Part of this Act, the judge may order that the patient shall be visited for that purpose.

(3) Every visit falling to be made under subsection (1) or (2) above shall be made by a General Visitor unless, in a case where it appears to the judge that it is in the circumstances essential for the visit to be made by a Visitor with medical or legal qualifications, the judge directs that the visit shall be made by a Medical or a Legal Visitor.

(4) A Visitor making a visit under this section shall make such report on the visit as the judge may direct.

(5) A Visitor making a visit under this section may interview the patient in private.

PART VII

(6) A Medical Visitor making a visit under this section may carry out in private a medical examination of the patient and may require the production of and inspect any medical records relating to the patient.

(7) The Master of the Court of Protection may visit any patient for the purpose mentioned in subsection (2) above and may interview the patient in private.

(8) A report made by a Visitor under this section, and information contained in such a report, shall not be disclosed except to the judge and any person authorised by the judge to receive the disclosure.

(9) If any person discloses any report or information in contravention of subsection (8) above, he shall be guilty of an offence and liable on summary conviction to imprisonment for a term not exceeding three months or to a fine not exceeding level 3 on the standard scale or both.

(10) In this section references to patients include references to persons alleged to be incapable, by reason of mental disorder, of managing and administering their property and affairs.

General powers of the judge with respect to proceedings.

104.—(1) For the purposes of any proceedings before him with respect to persons suffering or alleged to be suffering from mental disorder, the judge shall have the same powers as are vested in the High Court in respect of securing the attendance of witnesses and the production of documents.

(2) Subject to the provisions of this section, any act or omission in the course of such proceedings which, if occurring in the course of proceedings in the High Court would have been a contempt of the Court, shall be punishable by the judge in any manner in which it could have been punished by the High Court.

(3) Subsection (2) above shall not authorise the Master, or any other officer of the Court of Protection to exercise any power of attachment or committal, but the Master or officer may certify any such act or omission to the Lord Chancellor or a nominated judge, and the Lord Chancellor or judge may upon such certification inquire into the alleged act or omission and take any such action in relation to it as he could have taken if the proceedings had been before him.

1981 c. 54.

(4) Subsections (1) to (4) of section 36 of the Supreme Court Act 1981 (which provides a special procedure for the issue of writs of subpoena ad testificandum and duces tecum so as to be enforceable throughout the United Kingdom) shall apply in relation to proceedings under this Part of this Act with the

substitution for references to the High Court of references to the judge and for references to such writs of references to such document as may be prescribed by rules under this Part of this Act for issue by the judge for securing the attendance of witnesses or the production of documents. PART VII

Appeals.

105.—(1) Subject to and in accordance with rules under this Part of this Act, an appeal shall lie to a nominated judge from any decision of the Master of the Court of Protection or any nominated officer.

(2) The Court of Appeal shall continue to have the same jurisdiction as to appeals from any decision of the Lord Chancellor or from any decision of a nominated judge, whether given in the exercise of his original jurisdiction or on the hearing of an appeal under subsection (1) above, as they had immediately before the coming into operation of Part VIII of the Mental Health Act 1959 as to appeals from orders in lunacy made by the Lord Chancellor or any other person having jurisdiction in lunacy. 1959 c. 72.

Rules of procedure.

106.—(1) Proceedings before the judge with respect to persons suffering or alleged to be suffering from mental disorder (in this section referred to as "proceedings") shall be conducted in accordance with the provisions of rules made under this Part of this Act.

(2) Rules under this Part of this Act may make provision as to—

(*a*) the carrying out of preliminary or incidental inquiries;

(*b*) the persons by whom and manner in which proceedings may be instituted and carried on;

(*c*) the persons who are to be entitled to be notified of, to attend, or to take part in proceedings;

(*d*) the evidence which may be authorised or required to be given in proceedings and the manner (whether on oath or otherwise and whether orally or in writing) in which it is to be given;

(*e*) the administration of oaths and taking of affidavits for the purposes of proceedings; and

(*f*) the enforcement of orders made and directions given in proceedings.

(3) Without prejudice to the provisions of section 104(1) above, rules under this Part of this Act may make provision for authorising or requiring the attendance and examination of persons suffering or alleged to be suffering from mental disorder, the furnishing of information and the production of documents.

PART VII

(4) Rules under this Part of this Act may make provision as to the termination of proceedings, whether on the death or recovery of the person to whom the proceedings relate or otherwise, and for the exercise, pending the termination of the proceedings, of powers exercisable under this Part of this Act in relation to the property or affairs of a patient.

(5) Rules under this Part of this Act made with the consent of the Treasury may—

(*a*) make provision as to the scale of costs, fees and percentages payable in relation to proceedings, and as to the manner in which and funds out of which such costs, fees and percentages are to be paid ;

(*b*) contain provision for charging any percentage upon the estate of the person to whom the proceedings relate and for the payment of costs, fees and percentages within such time after the death of the person to whom the proceedings relate or the termination of the proceedings as may be provided by the rules ; and

(*c*) provide for the remission of fees and percentages.

(6) A charge upon the estate of a person created by virtue of subsection (5) above shall not cause any interest of that person in any property to fail or determine or to be prevented from recommencing.

(7) Rules under this Part of this Act may authorise the making of orders for the payment of costs to or by persons attending, as well as persons taking part in, proceedings.

Security and accounts.

107.—(1) Rules under this Part of this Act may make provision as to the giving of security by a receiver and as to the enforcement and discharge of the security.

(2) It shall be the duty of a receiver to render accounts in accordance with the requirements of rules under this Part of this Act, as well after his discharge as during his receivership ; and rules under this Part of this Act may make provision for the rendering of accounts by persons other than receivers who are ordered, directed or authorised under this Part of this Act to carry out any transaction.

General provisions as to rules under Part VII.

108.—(1) Any power to make rules conferred by this Part of this Act shall be exercisable by the Lord Chancellor.

(2) Rules under this Part of this Act may contain such incidental and supplemental provisions as appear requisite for the purposes of the rules.

PART VII

Effect and proof of orders, etc.
1925 c. 20.

109.—(1) Section 204 of the Law of Property Act 1925 (by which orders of the High Court are made conclusive in favour of purchasers) shall apply in relation to orders made and directions and authorities given by the judge as it applies in relation to orders of the High Court.

(2) Office copies of orders made, directions or authorities given or other instruments issued by the judge and sealed with the official seal of the Court of Protection shall be admissible in all legal proceedings as evidence of the originals without any further proof.

Reciprocal arrangements in relation to Scotland and Northern Ireland as to exercise of powers.

110.—(1) This Part of this Act shall apply in relation to the property and affairs in Scotland or Northern Ireland of a patient in relation to whom powers have been exercised under this Part of this Act, or a person as to whom powers are exercisable and have been exercised under section 98 above as it applies in relation to his property and affairs in England and Wales unless a curator bonis, tutor, judicial factor, committee, receiver or guardian has been appointed for him in Scotland or, as the case may be, Northern Ireland.

(2) Where under the law in force in Scotland or Northern Ireland with respect to the property and affairs of persons suffering from mental disorder a curator bonis, tutor, judicial factor, committee, receiver or guardian has been appointed for any person, the provisions of that law shall apply in relation to that person's property and affairs in England and Wales unless he is a patient in relation to whom powers have been exercised under this Part of this Act, or a person as to whom powers are exercisable and have been exercised under section 98 above.

(3) Nothing in this section shall affect any power to execute a will under section 96(1)(*e*) above or the effect of any will executed in the exercise of such a power.

(4) In this section references to property do not include references to land or interests in land but this subsection shall not prevent the receipt of rent or other income arising from land or interests in land.

Construction of references in other Acts to judge or authority having jurisdiction under Part VII.

111.—(1) The functions expressed to be conferred by any enactment not contained in this Part of this Act on the judge having jurisdiction under this Part of this Act shall be exercisable by the Lord Chancellor or by a nominated judge.

(2) Subject to subsection (3) below, the functions expressed to be conferred by any such enactment on the authority having jurisdiction under this Part of this Act shall, subject to any express provision to the contrary, be exercisable by the Lord Chancellor, a nominated judge, the Master of the Court of Protection or a nominated officer.

PART VII

(3) The exercise of the functions referred to in subsection (2) above by a nominated officer shall be subject to any directions of the Master and they shall be exercisable so far only as may be provided by the instrument by which the officer is nominated.

(4) Subject to the foregoing provisions of this section—

(*a*) references in any enactment not contained in this Part of this Act to the judge having jurisdiction under this Part of this Act shall be construed as references to the Lord Chancellor or a nominated judge, and

(*b*) references in any such enactment to the authority having jurisdiction under this Part of this Act shall be construed as references to the Lord Chancellor, a nominated judge, the Master of the Court of Protection or a nominated officer.

Interpretation of Part VII.

112. In this Part of this Act, unless the context otherwise requires—

"nominated judge" means a judge nominated in pursuance of subsection (1) of section 93 above;

"nominated officer" means an officer nominated in pursuance of subsection (4) of that section;

"patient" has the meaning assigned to it by section 94 above;

"property" includes any thing in action, and any interest in real or personal property;

"the judge" shall be construed in accordance with section 94 above;

"will" includes a codicil.

Disapplication of certain enactments in relation to persons within the jurisdiction of the judge.

113. The provisions of the Acts described in Schedule 3 to this Act which are specified in the third column of that Schedule, so far as they make special provision for persons suffering from mental disorder, shall not have effect in relation to patients and to persons as to whom powers are exercisable and have been exercised under section 98 above.

PART VIII

MISCELLANEOUS FUNCTIONS OF LOCAL AUTHORITIES AND THE SECRETARY OF STATE

Approved social workers

Appointment of approved social workers.

114.—(1) A local social services authority shall appoint a sufficient number of approved social workers for the purpose of discharging the functions conferred on them by this Act.

(2) No person shall be appointed by a local social services authority as an approved social worker unless he is approved by the authority as having appropriate competence in dealing with persons who are suffering from mental disorder.

(3) In approving a person for appointment as an approved social worker a local social services authority shall have regard to such matters as the Secretary of State may direct.

Powers of entry and inspection.

115. An approved social worker of a local social services authority may at all reasonable times after producing, if asked to do so, some duly authenticated document showing that he is such a social worker, enter and inspect any premises (not being a hospital) in the area of that authority in which a mentally disordered patient is living, if he has reasonable cause to believe that the patient is not under proper care.

Visiting patients

Welfare of certain hospital patients.

116.—(1) Where a patient to whom this section applies is admitted to a hospital or nursing home in England and Wales (whether for treatment for mental disorder or for any other reason) then, without prejudice to their duties in relation to the patient apart from the provisions of this section, the authority shall arrange for visits to be made to him on behalf of the authority, and shall take such other steps in relation to the patient while in the hospital or nursing home as would be expected to be taken by his parents.

(2) This section applies to—

(*a*) a child or young person in respect of whom the rights and powers of a parent are vested in a local authority by virtue of—

(i) section 3 of the Child Care Act 1980 (which relates to the assumption by a local authority of parental rights and duties in relation to a child in their care), 1980 c. 5

(ii) section 10 of that Act (which relates to the powers and duties of local authorities with respect to persons committed to their care under the Children and Young Persons Act 1969), or 1969 c. 54.

(iii) section 17 of the Social Work (Scotland) Act 1968 (which makes corresponding provision for Scotland); 1968 c. 49.

(*b*) a person who is subject to the guardianship of a local social services authority under the provisions of this Act or the Mental Health (Scotland) Act 1960; or 1960 c. 61.

PART VIII

(*c*) a person the functions of whose nearest relative under this Act or under the Mental Health (Scotland) Act 1960 are for the time being transferred to a local social services authority.

After-care

After-care.

117.—(1) This section applies to persons who are detained under section 3 above, or admitted to a hospital in pursuance of a hospital order made under section 37 above, or transferred to a hospital in pursuance of a transfer direction made under section 47 or 48 above, and then cease to be detained and leave hospital.

(2) It shall be the duty of the District Health Authority and of the local social services authority to provide, in co-operation with relevant voluntary agencies, after-care services for any person to whom this section applies until such time as the District Health Authority and the local social services authority are satisfied that the person concerned is no longer in need of such services.

(3) In this section " the District Health Authority " means the District Health Authority for the district, and " the local social services authority " means the local social services authority for the area in which the person concerned is resident or to which he is sent on discharge by the hospital in which he was detained.

Functions of the Secretary of State

Code of practice.

118.—(1) The Secretary of State shall prepare, and from time to time revise, a code of practice—

(*a*) for the guidance of registered medical practitioners, managers and staff of hospitals and mental nursing homes and approved social workers in relation to the admission of patients to hospitals and mental nursing homes under this Act ; and

(*b*) for the guidance of registered medical practitioners and members of other professions in relation to the medical treatment of patients suffering from mental disorder.

(2) The code shall, in particular, specify forms of medical treatment in addition to any specified by regulations made for the purposes of section 57 above which in the opinion of the Secretary of State give rise to special concern and which should accordingly not be given by a registered medical practitioner unless the patient has consented to the treatment (or to a plan of treatment including that treatment) and a certificate in writing as to the matters mentioned in subsection (2)(*a*) and (*b*) of that

section has been given by another registered medical practitioner, being a practitioner appointed for the purposes of this section by the Secretary of State.

(3) Before preparing the code or making any alteration in it the Secretary of State shall consult such bodies as appear to him to be concerned.

(4) The Secretary of State shall lay copies of the code and of any alteration in the code before Parliament; and if either House of Parliament passes a resolution requiring the code or any alteration in it to be withdrawn the Secretary of State shall withdraw the code or alteration and, where he withdraws the code, shall prepare a code in substitution for the one which is withdrawn.

(5) No resolution shall be passed by either House of Parliament under subsection (4) above in respect of a code or alteration after the expiration of the period of 40 days beginning with the day on which a copy of the code or alteration was laid before that House; but for the purposes of this subsection no account shall be taken of any time during which Parliament is dissolved or prorogued or during which both Houses are adjourned for more than four days.

(6) The Secretary of State shall publish the code as for the time being in force.

Practitioners approved for Part IV and s. 118.

119.—(1) The Secretary of State may make such provision as he may with the approval of the Treasury determine for the payment of remuneration, allowances, pensions or gratuities to or in respect of registered medical practitioners appointed by him for the purposes of Part IV of this Act and section 118 above and to or in respect of other persons appointed for the purposes of section 57 (2)(*a*) above.

(2) A registered medical practitioner or other person appointed by the Secretary of State for the purposes of the provisions mentioned in subsection (1) above may, for the purpose of exercising his functions under those provisions, at any reasonable time—

(*a*) visit and interview and, in the case of a registered medical practitioner, examine in private any patient detained in a mental nursing home; and

(*b*) require the production of and inspect any records relating to the treatment of the patient in that home.

General protection of detained patients.

120.—(1) The Secretary of State shall keep under review the exercise of the powers and the discharge of the duties conferred or imposed by this Act so far as relating to the detention of

PART VIII

patients or to patients liable to be detained under this Act and shall make arrangements for persons authorised by him in that behalf—

(*a*) to visit and interview in private patients detained under this Act in hospitals and mental nursing homes; and

(*b*) to investigate—

(i) any complaint made by a person in respect of a matter that occurred while he was detained under this Act in a hospital or mental nursing home and which he considers has not been satisfactorily dealt with by the managers of that hospital or mental nursing home; and

(ii) any other complaint as to the exercise of the powers or the discharge of the duties conferred or imposed by this Act in respect of a person who is or has been so detained.

(2) The arrangements made under this section in respect of the investigation of complaints may exclude matters from investigation in specified circumstances and shall not require any person exercising functions under the arrangements to undertake or continue with any investigation where he does not consider it appropriate to do so.

(3) Where any such complaint as is mentioned in subsection (1)(*b*)(ii) above is made by a Member of Parliament and investigated under the arrangements made under this section the results of the investigation shall be reported to him.

(4) For the purpose of any such review as is mentioned in subsection (1) above or of carrying out his functions under arrangements made under this section any person authorised in that behalf by the Secretary of State may at any reasonable time—

(*a*) visit and interview and, if he is a registered medical practitioner, examine in private any patient in a mental nursing home; and

(*b*) require the production of and inspect any records relating to the detention or treatment of any person who is or has been detained in a mental nursing home.

1975 c. 37.

(5) The matters in respect of which regulations may be made under section 6 of the Nursing Homes Act 1975 shall include the keeping of records relating to the detention and treatment of persons detained under this Act in a mental nursing home.

(6) The Secretary of State may make such provision as he may with the approval of the Treasury determine for the payment of remuneration, allowances, pensions or gratuities to or in

respect of persons exercising functions in relation to any such review as is mentioned in subsection (1) above or functions under arrangements made under this section.

(7) The powers and duties referred to in subsection (1) above do not include any power or duty conferred or imposed by Part VII of this Act.

Mental Health Act Commission. 1977 c. 49.

121.—(1) Without prejudice to section 126(3) of the National Health Service Act 1977 (power to vary or revoke orders or directions) there shall continue to be a special health authority known as the Mental Health Act Commission established under section 11 of that Act.

(2) Without prejudice to the generality of his powers under section 13 of that Act, the Secretary of State shall direct the Commission to perform on his behalf—

(*a*) the function of appointing registered medical practitioners for the purposes of Part IV of this Act and section 118 above and of appointing other persons for the purposes of section 57(2)(*a*) above; and

(*b*) the functions of the Secretary of State under sections 61 and 120(1) and (4) above.

(3) The registered medical practitioners and other persons appointed for the purposes mentioned in subsection (2)(*a*) above may include members of the Commission.

(4) The Secretary of State may, at the request of or after consultation with the Commission and after consulting such other bodies as appear to him to be concerned, direct the Commission to keep under review the care and treatment, or any aspect of the care and treatment, in hospitals and mental nursing homes of patients who are not liable to be detained under this Act.

(5) For the purpose of any such review as is mentioned in subsection (4) above any person authorised in that behalf by the Commission may at any reasonable time—

(*a*) visit and interview and, if he is a registered medical practitioner, examine in private any patient in a mental nursing home; and

(*b*) require the production of and inspect any records relating to the treatment of any person who is or has been a patient in a mental nursing home.

(6) The Secretary of State may make such provision as he may with the approval of the Treasury determine for the payment of remuneration, allowances, pensions or gratuities to or in respect of persons exercising functions in relation to any such review as is mentioned in subsection (4) above.

PART VIII

(7) The Commission shall review any decision to withhold a postal packet (or anything contained in it) under subsection (1)(*b*) or (2) of section 134 below if an application in that behalf is made—

(*a*) in a case under subsection (1)(*b*), by the patient; or

(*b*) in a case under subsection (2), either by the patient or by the person by whom the postal packet was sent;

and any such application shall be made within six months of the receipt by the applicant of the notice referred to in subsection (6) of that section.

(8) On an application under subsection (7) above the Commission may direct that the postal packet which is the subject of the application (or anything contained in it) shall not be withheld and the managers in question shall comply with any such direction.

(9) The Secretary of State may by regulations make provision with respect to the making and determination of applications under subsection (7) above, including provision for the production to the Commission of any postal packet which is the subject of such an application.

(10) The Commission shall in the second year after its establishment and subsequently in every second year publish a report on its activities; and copies of every such report shall be sent by the Commission to the Secretary of State who shall lay a copy before each House of Parliament.

(11) Paragraph 9 of Schedule 5 to the said Act of 1977 (pay and allowances for chairmen and members of health authorities) shall have effect in relation to the Mental Health Act Commission as if references in sub-paragraphs (1) and (2) to the chairman included references to any member and as if subparagraphs (4) and (5) were omitted.

Provision of pocket money for in-patients in hospital.

122.—(1) The Secretary of State may pay to persons who are receiving treatment as in-patients (whether liable to be detained or not) in special hospitals or other hospitals being hospitals wholly or mainly used for the treatment of persons suffering from mental disorder, such amounts as he thinks fit in respect of their occasional personal expenses where it appears to him that they would otherwise be without resources to meet those expenses.

1977 c. 49.

(2) For the purposes of the National Health Service Act 1977, the making of payments under this section to persons for whom hospital services are provided under that Act shall be treated as included among those services.

Transfers to and from special hospitals.

123.—(1) Without prejudice to any other provisions of this Act with respect to the transfer of patients, any patient who is for the time being liable to be detained in a special hospital under this Act (other than under section 35, 36 or 38 above) may, upon the directions of the Secretary of State, at any time be removed into any other special hospital.

(2) Without prejudice to any such provision, the Secretary of State may give directions for the transfer of any patient who is for the time being liable to be so detained into a hospital which is not a special hospital.

(3) Subsections (2) and (4) of section 19 above shall apply in relation to the transfer or removal of a patient under this section as they apply in relation to the transfer or removal of a patient from one hospital to another under that section.

Default powers of Secretary of State.

124.—(1) Where the Secretary of State is of the opinion, on complaint or otherwise, that a local social services authority have failed to carry out functions conferred or imposed on the authority by or under this Act or have in carrying out those functions failed to comply with any regulations relating to those functions, he may after such inquiry as he thinks fit make an order declaring the authority to be in default.

(2) Subsections (3) to (5) of section 85 of the National Health Service Act 1977 (which relates to orders declaring, among others, a local social services authority to be in default under that Act) shall apply in relation to an order under this section as they apply in relation to an order under that section. 1977 c. 49.

Inquiries.

125.—(1) The Secretary of State may cause an inquiry to be held in any case where he thinks it advisable to do so in connection with any matter arising under this Act.

(2) Subsections (2) to (5) of section 250 of the Local Government Act 1972 shall apply to any inquiry held under this Act, except that no local authority shall be ordered to pay costs under subsection (4) of that section in the case of any inquiry unless the authority is a party to the inquiry. 1972 c. 70.

PART IX

OFFENCES

Forgery, false statements, etc.

126.—(1) Any person who without lawful authority or excuse has in his custody or under his control any document to which this subsection applies, which is, and which he knows or believes to be, false within the meaning of Part I of the Forgery and Counterfeiting Act 1981, shall be guilty of an offence. 1981 c. 45.

PART IX

(2) Any person who without lawful authority or excuse makes or has in his custody or under his control, any document so closely resembling a document to which subsection (1) above applies as to be calculated to deceive shall be guilty of an offence.

(3) The documents to which subsection (1) above applies are any documents purporting to be—

(*a*) an application under Part II of this Act;

(*b*) a medical recommendation or report under this Act; and

(*c*) any other document required or authorised to be made for any of the purposes of this Act.

(4) Any person who—

(*a*) wilfully makes a false entry or statement in any application, recommendation, report, record or other document required or authorised to be made for any of the purposes of this Act; or

(*b*) with intent to deceive, makes use of any such entry or statement which he knows to be false,

shall be guilty of an offence.

(5) Any person guilty of an offence under this section shall be liable—

(*a*) on summary conviction, to imprisonment for a term not exceeding six months or to a fine not exceeding the statutory maximum, or to both;

(*b*) on conviction on indictment, to imprisonment for a term not exceeding two years or to a fine of any amount, or to both.

Ill-treatment of patients.

127.—(1) It shall be an offence for any person who is an officer on the staff of or otherwise employed in, or who is one of the managers of, a hospital or mental nursing home—

(*a*) to ill-treat or wilfully to neglect a patient for the time being receiving treatment for mental disorder as an in-patient in that hospital or home; or

(*b*) to ill-treat or wilfully to neglect, on the premises of which the hospital or home forms part, a patient for the time being receiving such treatment there as an out-patient.

(2) It shall be an offence for any individual to ill-treat or wilfully to neglect a mentally disordered patient who is for the time being subject to his guardianship under this Act or otherwise in his custody or care (whether by virtue of any legal or moral obligation or otherwise).

(3) Any person guilty of an offence under this section shall be liable—

(*a*) on summary conviction, to imprisonment for a term not exceeding six months or to a fine not exceeding the statutory maximum, or to both;

(*b*) on conviction on indictment, to imprisonment for a term not exceeding two years or to a fine of any amount, or to both.

(4) No proceedings shall be instituted for an offence under this section except by or with the consent of the Director of Public Prosecutions.

Assisting patients to absent themselves without leave, etc.

128.—(1) Where any person induces or knowingly assists another person who is liable to be detained in a hospital within the meaning of Part II of this Act or is subject to guardianship under this Act to absent himself without leave he shall be guilty of an offence.

(2) Where any person induces or knowingly assists another person who is in legal custody by virtue of section 137 below to escape from such custody he shall be guilty of an offence.

(3) Where any person knowingly harbours a patient who is absent without leave or is otherwise at large and liable to be retaken under this Act or gives him any assistance with intent to prevent, hinder or interfere with his being taken into custody or returned to the hospital or other place where he ought to be he shall be guilty of an offence.

(4) Any person guilty of an offence under this section shall be liable—

(*a*) on summary conviction, to imprisonment for a term not exceeding six months or to a fine not exceeding the statutory maximum, or to both;

(*b*) on conviction on indictment, to imprisonment for a term not exceeding two years or to a fine of any amount, or to both.

Obstruction.

129.—(1) Any person who without reasonable cause—

(*a*) refuses to allow the inspection of any premises; or

(*b*) refuses to allow the visiting, interviewing or examination of any person by a person authorised in that behalf by or under this Act; or

(*c*) refuses to produce for the inspection of any person so authorised any document or record the production of which is duly required by him; or

PART IX

(*d*) otherwise obstructs any such person in the exercise of his functions,

shall be guilty of an offence.

(2) Without prejudice to the generality of subsection (1) above, any person who insists on being present when required to withdraw by a person authorised by or under this Act to interview or examine a person in private shall be guilty of an offence.

(3) Any person guilty of an offence under this section shall be liable on summary conviction to imprisonment for a term not exceeding three months or to a fine not exceeding level 4 on the standard scale or to both.

Prosecutions by local authorities.

130. A local social services authority may institute proceedings for any offence under this Part of this Act, but without prejudice to any provision of this Part of this Act requiring the consent of the Director of Public Prosecutions for the institution of such proceedings.

PART X

MISCELLANEOUS AND SUPPLEMENTARY

Miscellaneous provisions

Informal admission of patients.

131.—(1) Nothing in this Act shall be construed as preventing a patient who requires treatment for mental disorder from being admitted to any hospital or mental nursing home in pursuance of arrangements made in that behalf and without any application, order or direction rendering him liable to be detained under this Act, or from remaining in any hospital or mental nursing home in pursuance of such arrangements after he has ceased to be so liable to be detained.

(2) In the case of a minor who has attained the age of 16 years and is capable of expressing his own wishes, any such arrangements as are mentioned in subsection (1) above may be made, carried out and determined notwithstanding any right of custody or control vested by law in his parent or guardian.

Duty of managers of hospitals to give information to detained patients.

132.—(1) The managers of a hospital or mental nursing home in which a patient is detained under this Act shall take such steps as are practicable to ensure that the patient understands—

(*a*) under which of the provisions of this Act he is for the time being detained and the effect of that provision; and

(*b*) what rights of applying to a Mental Health Review Tribunal are available to him in respect of his detention under that provision;

and those steps shall be taken as soon as practicable after the commencement of the patient's detention under the provision in question.

(2) The managers of a hospital or mental nursing home in which a patient is detained as aforesaid shall also take such steps as are practicable to ensure that the patient understands the effect, so far as relevant in his case, of sections 23, 25, 56 to 64, 66(1)(*g*), 118 and 120 above and section 134 below; and those steps shall be taken as soon as practicable after the commencement of the patient's detention in the hospital or nursing home.

(3) The steps to be taken under subsections (1) and (2) above shall include giving the requisite information both orally and in writing.

(4) The managers of a hospital or mental nursing home in which a patient is detained as aforesaid shall, except where the patient otherwise requests, take such steps as are practicable to furnish the person (if any) appearing to them to be his nearest relative with a copy of any information given to him in writing under subsections (1) and (2) above; and those steps shall be taken when the information is given to the patient or within a reasonable time thereafter.

Duty of managers of hospitals to inform nearest relatives of discharge.

133.—(1) Where a patient liable to be detained under this Act in a hospital or mental nursing home is to be discharged otherwise than by virtue of an order for discharge made by his nearest relative, the managers of the hospital or mental nursing home shall, subject to subsection (2) below, take such steps as are practicable to inform the person (if any) appearing to them to be the nearest relative of the patient; and that information shall, if practicable, be given at least seven days before the date of discharge.

(2) Subsection (1) above shall not apply if the patient or his nearest relative has requested that information about the patient's discharge should not be given under this section.

Correspondence of patients.

134.—(1) A postal packet addressed to any person by a patient detained in a hospital under this Act and delivered by the patient for dispatch may be withheld from the Post Office—

(*a*) if that person has requested that communications addressed to him by the patient should be withheld; or

(*b*) subject to subsection (3) below, if the hospital is a special hospital and the managers of the hospital consider that the postal packet is likely—

(i) to cause distress to the person to whom it is addressed or to any other person (not being a person on the staff of the hospital); or

PART X

(ii) to cause danger to any person;

and any request for the purposes of paragraph (*a*) above shall be made by a notice in writing given to the managers of the hospital, the registered medical practitioner in charge of the treatment of the patient or the Secretary of State.

(2) Subject to subsection (3) below, a postal packet addressed to a patient detained in a special hospital under this Act may be withheld from the patient if, in the opinion of the managers of the hospital, it is necessary to do so in the interests of the safety of the patient or for the protection of other persons.

(3) Subsections (1)(*b*) and (2) above do not apply to any postal packet addressed by a patient to, or sent to a patient by or on behalf of—

(*a*) any Minister of the Crown or Member of either House of Parliament;

(*b*) the Master or any other officer of the Court of Protection or any of the Lord Chancellor's Visitors;

(*c*) the Parliamentary Commissioner for Administration, the Health Service Commissioner for England, the Health Service Commissioner for Wales or a Local Commissioner within the meaning of Part III of the Local Government Act 1974;

1974 c. 7.

(*d*) a Mental Health Review Tribunal;

1977 c. 49.

(*e*) a health authority within the meaning of the National Health Service Act 1977, a local social services authority, a Community Health Council or a probation and after-care committee appointed under paragraph 2 of Schedule 3 to the Powers of Criminal Courts Act 1973;

1973 c. 62.

(*f*) the managers of the hospital in which the patient is detained;

(*g*) any legally qualified person instructed by the patient to act as his legal adviser; or

(*h*) the European Commission of Human Rights or the European Court of Human Rights.

(4) The managers of a hospital may inspect and open any postal packet for the purposes of determining—

(*a*) whether it is one to which subsection (1) or (2) applies, and

(*b*) in the case of a postal packet to which subsection (1) or (2) above applies, whether or not it should be withheld under that subsection;

and the power to withhold a postal packet under either of those subsections includes power to withhold anything contained in it.

PART X

(5) Where a postal packet or anything contained in it is withheld under subsection (1) or (2) above the managers of the hospital shall record that fact in writing.

(6) Where a postal packet or anything contained in it is withheld under subsection (1)(*b*) or (2) above the managers of the hospital shall within seven days give notice of that fact to the patient and, in the case of a packet withheld under subsection (2) above, to the person (if known) by whom the postal packet was sent ; and any such notice shall be given in writing and shall contain a statement of the effect of section 121(7) and (8) above.

(7) The functions of the managers of a hospital under this section shall be discharged on their behalf by a person on the staff of the hospital appointed by them for that purpose and different persons may be appointed to discharge different functions.

(8) The Secretary of State may make regulations with respect to the exercise of the powers conferred by this section.

(9) In this section " hospital " has the same meaning as in Part II of this Act, " postal packet " has the same meaning as in the Post Office Act 1953 and the provisions of this section shall have effect notwithstanding anything in section 56 of that Act. 1953 c. 36.

Warrant to search for and remove patients.

135.—(1) If it appears to a justice of the peace, on information on oath laid by an approved social worker, that there is reasonable cause to suspect that a person believed to be suffering from mental disorder—

(*a*) has been, or is being, ill-treated, neglected or kept otherwise than under proper control, in any place within the jurisdiction of the justice, or

(*b*) being unable to care for himself, is living alone in any such place,

the justice may issue a warrant authorising any constable named in the warrant to enter, if need be by force, any premises specified in the warrant in which that person is believed to be, and, if thought fit, to remove him to a place of safety with a view to the making of an application in respect of him under Part II of this Act, or of other arrangements for his treatment or care.

(2) If it appears to a justice of the peace, on information on oath laid by any constable or other person who is authorised by or under this Act or under section 83 of the Mental Health (Scotland) Act 1960 to take a patient to any place, or to take into custody or retake a patient who is liable under this Act or under the said section 83 to be so taken or retaken— 1960 c. 61.

PART X

(*a*) that there is reasonable cause to believe that the patient is to be found on premises within the jurisdiction of the justice; and

(*b*) that admission to the premises has been refused or that a refusal of such admission is apprehended,

the justice may issue a warrant authorising any constable named in the warrant to enter the premises, if need be by force, and remove the patient.

(3) A patient who is removed to a place of safety in the execution of a warrant issued under this section may be detained there for a period not exceeding 72 hours.

(4) In the execution of a warrant issued under subsection (1) above, the constable to whom it is addressed shall be accompanied by an approved social worker and by a registered medical practitioner, and in the execution of a warrant issued under subsection (2) above the constable to whom it is addressed may be accompanied—

(*a*) by a registered medical practitioner;

(*b*) by any person authorised by or under this Act or under section 83 of the Mental Health (Scotland) Act 1960 to take or retake the patient.

(5) It shall not be necessary in any information or warrant under subsection (1) above to name the patient concerned.

(6) In this section "place of safety" means residential accommodation provided by a local social services authority under Part III of the National Assistance Act 1948 or under paragraph 2 of Schedule 8 to the National Health Service Act 1977, a hospital as defined by this Act, a police station, a mental nursing home or residential home for mentally disordered persons or any other suitable place the occupier of which is willing temporarily to receive the patient.

1948 c. 29.
1977 c. 49.

Mentally disordered persons found in public places.

136.—(1) If a constable finds in a place to which the public have access a person who appears to him to be suffering from mental disorder and to be in immediate need of care or control, the constable may, if he thinks it necessary to do so in the interests of that person or for the protection of other persons, remove that person to a place of safety within the meaning of section 135 above.

(2) A person removed to a place of safety under this section may be detained there for a period not exceeding 72 hours for the purpose of enabling him to be examined by a registered medical practitioner and to be interviewed by an approved social worker and of making any necessary arrangements for his treatment or care.

PART X

Provisions as to custody, conveyance and detention.

137.—(1) Any person required or authorised by or by virtue of this Act to be conveyed to any place or to be kept in custody or detained in a place of safety or at any place to which he is taken under section 42(6) above shall, while being so conveyed, detained or kept, as the case may be, be deemed to be in legal custody.

(2) A constable or any other person required or authorised by or by virtue of this Act to take any person into custody, or to convey or detain any person shall, for the purposes of taking him into custody or conveying or detaining him, have all the powers, authorities, protection and privileges which a constable has within the area for which he acts as constable.

(3) In this section " convey " includes any other expression denoting removal from one place to another.

Retaking of patients escaping from custody.

138.—(1) If any person who is in legal custody by virtue of section 137 above escapes, he may, subject to the provisions of this section, be retaken—

(*a*) in any case, by the person who had his custody immediately before the escape, or by any constable or approved social worker ;

(*b*) if at the time of the escape he was liable to be detained in a hospital within the meaning of Part II of this Act, or subject to guardianship under this Act, by any other person who could take him into custody under section 18 above if he had absented himself without leave.

(2) A person to whom paragraph (*b*) of subsection (1) above applies shall not be retaken under this section after the expiration of the period within which he could be retaken under section 18 above if he had absented himself without leave on the day of the escape unless he is subject to a restriction order under Part III of this Act or an order or direction having the same effect as such an order ; and subsection (4) of the said section 18 shall apply with the necessary modifications accordingly.

(3) A person who escapes while being taken to or detained in a place of safety under section 135 or 136 above shall not be retaken under this section after the expiration of the period of 72 hours beginning with the time when he escapes or the period during which he is liable to be so detained, whichever expires first.

(4) This section, so far as it relates to the escape of a person liable to be detained in a hospital within the meaning of Part II of this Act, shall apply in relation to a person who escapes—

(*a*) while being taken to or from such a hospital in pursuance of regulations under section 19 above, or of any

PART X

order, direction or authorisation under Part III or VI of this Act (other than under section 35, 36, 38, 53, 83 or 85) or under section 123 above ; or

(*b*) while being taken to or detained in a place of safety in pursuance of an order under Part III of this Act (other than under section 35, 36 or 38 above) pending his admission to such a hospital,

as if he were liable to be detained in that hospital and, if he had not previously been received in that hospital, as if he had been so received.

(5) In computing for the purposes of the power to give directions under section 37(4) above and for the purposes of sections 37(5) and 40(1) above the period of 28 days mentioned in those sections, no account shall be taken of any time during which the patient is at large and liable to be retaken by virtue of this section.

(6) Section 21 above shall, with any necessary modifications, apply in relation to a patient who is at large and liable to be retaken by virtue of this section as it applies in relation to a patient who is absent without leave and references in that section to section 18 above shall be construed accordingly.

Protection for acts done in pursuance of this Act.

139.—(1) No person shall be liable, whether on the ground of want of jurisdiction or on any other ground, to any civil or criminal proceedings to which he would have been liable apart from this section in respect of any act purporting to be done in pursuance of this Act or any regulations or rules made under this Act, or in, or in pursuance of anything done in, the discharge of functions conferred by any other enactment on the authority having jurisdiction under Part VII of this Act, unless the act was done in bad faith or without reasonable care.

(2) No civil proceedings shall be brought against any person in any court in respect of any such act without the leave of the High Court ; and no criminal proceedings shall be brought against any person in any court in respect of any such act except by or with the consent of the Director of Public Prosecutions.

(3) This section does not apply to proceedings for an offence under this Act, being proceedings which, under any other provision of this Act, can be instituted only by or with the consent of the Director of Public Prosecutions.

(4) This section does not apply to proceedings against the Secretary of State or against a health authority within the meaning of the National Health Service Act 1977.

1977 c. 49.

(5) In relation to Northern Ireland the reference in this section to the Director of Public Prosecutions shall be construed as a reference to the Director of Public Prosecutions for Northern Ireland.

Notification of hospitals having arrangements for reception of urgent cases.

140. It shall be the duty of every Regional Health Authority and in Wales every District Health Authority to give notice to every local social services authority for an area wholly or partly comprised within the region or district, as the case may be, of the Authority specifying the hospital or hospitals administered by the Authority in which arrangements are from time to time in force for the reception, in case of special urgency, of patients requiring treatment for mental disorder.

Members of Parliament suffering from mental illness.

141.—(1) Where a member of the House of Commons is authorised to be detained on the ground (however formulated) that he is suffering from mental illness, it shall be the duty of the court, authority or person on whose order or application, and of any registered medical practitioner upon whose recommendation or certificate, the detention was authorised, and of the person in charge of the hospital or other place in which the member is authorised to be detained, to notify the Speaker of the House of Commons that the detention has been authorised.

(2) Where the Speaker receives a notification under subsection (1) above, or is notified by two members of the House of Commons that they are credibly informed that such an authorisation has been given, the Speaker shall cause the member to whom the notification relates to be visited and examined by two registered medical practitioners appointed in accordance with subsection (3) below.

(3) The registered medical practitioners to be appointed for the purposes of subsection (2) above shall be appointed by the President of the Royal College of Psychiatrists and shall be practitioners appearing to the President to have special experience in the diagnosis or treatment of mental disorders.

(4) The registered medical practitioners appointed in accordance with subsection (3) above shall report to the Speaker whether the member is suffering from mental illness and is authorised to be detained as such.

(5) If the report is to the effect that the member is suffering from mental illness and authorised to be detained as aforesaid, the Speaker shall at the expiration of six months from

the date of the report, if the House is then sitting, and otherwise as soon as may be after the House next sits, again cause the member to be visited and examined by two such registered medical practitioners as aforesaid, and the registered medical practitioners shall report as aforesaid.

(6) If the second report is that the member is suffering from mental illness and authorised to be detained as mentioned in subsection (4) above, the Speaker shall forthwith lay both reports before the House of Commons, and thereupon the seat of the member shall become vacant.

(7) Any sums required for the payment of fees and expenses to registered medical practitioners acting in relation to a member of the House of Commons under this section shall be defrayed out of moneys provided by Parliament.

Pay, pensions, etc., of mentally disordered persons.

142.—(1) Where a periodic payment falls to be made to any person by way of pay or pension or otherwise in connection with the service or employment of that or any other person, and the payment falls to be made directly out of moneys provided by Parliament or the Consolidated Fund, or other moneys administered by or under the control or supervision of a government department, the authority by whom the sum in question is payable, if satisfied after considering medical evidence that the person to whom it is payable (referred to in this section as " the patient ") is incapable by reason of mental disorder of managing and administering his property and affairs, may, instead of paying the sum to the patient, apply it in accordance with subsection (2) below.

(2) The authority may pay the sum or such part of it as they think fit to the institution or person having the care of the patient, to be applied for his benefit and may pay the remainder (if any) or such part of the remainder as they think fit—

(*a*) to or for the benefit of persons who appear to the authority to be members of the patient's family or other persons for whom the patient might be expected to provide if he were not mentally disordered, or

(*b*) in reimbursement, with or without interest, of money applied by any person either in payment of the patient's debts (whether legally enforceable or not) or for the maintenance or other benefit of the patient or such persons as are mentioned in paragraph (*a*) above.

(3) In this section " government department " does not include a Northern Ireland department.

Supplemental PART X

143.—(1) Any power of the Secretary of State or the Lord Chancellor to make regulations, orders or rules under this Act shall be exercisable by statutory instrument.

General provisions as to regulations, orders and rules.

(2) Any Order in Council under this Act and any statutory instrument containing regulations or rules made under this Act shall be subject to annulment in pursuance of a resolution of either House of Parliament.

(3) No order shall be made under section 68(4) or 71(3) above unless a draft of it has been approved by a resolution of each House of Parliament.

144. Her Majesty may by Order in Council repeal or amend any local enactment so far as appears to Her Majesty to be necessary in consequence of this Act.

Power to amend local Acts.

145.—(1) In this Act, unless the context otherwise requires—

Interpretation.

" absent without leave " has the meaning given to it by section 18 above and related expressions shall be construed accordingly ;

" application for admission for assessment " has the meaning given in section 2 above ;

" application for admission for treatment " has the meaning given in section 3 above ;

" approved social worker " means an officer of a local social services authority appointed to act as an approved social worker for the purposes of this Act ;

" hospital " means—

(*a*) any health service hospital within the meaning of the National Health Service Act 1977 ; and 1977 c. 49.

(*b*) any accommodation provided by a local authority and used as a hospital by or on behalf of the Secretary of State under that Act ;

and " hospital within the meaning of Part II of this Act " has the meaning given in section 34 above ;

" hospital order " and " guardianship order " have the meanings respectively given in section 37 above ;

" interim hospital order " has the meaning given in section 38 above ;

" local social services authority " means a council which is a local authority for the purpose of the Local Authority Social Services Act 1970 ; 1970 c. 42.

PART X

"the managers" means—

(*a*) in relation to a hospital vested in the Secretary of State for the purposes of his functions under the National Health Service Act 1977, and in relation to any accommodation provided by a local authority and used as a hospital by or on behalf of the Secretary of State under that Act, the District Health Authority or special health authority responsible for the administration of the hospital; (1977 c. 49.)

(*b*) in relation to a special hospital, the Secretary of State;

(*c*) in relation to a mental nursing home registered in pursuance of the Nursing Homes Act 1975, the person or persons registered in respect of the home; (1975 c. 37.)

and in this definition "hospital" means a hospital within the meaning of Part II of this Act;

"medical treatment" includes nursing, and also includes care, habilitation and rehabilitation under medical supervision;

"mental disorder", "severe mental impairment", "mental impairment" and "psychopathic disorder" have the meanings given in section 1 above;

"mental nursing home" has the same meaning as in the Nursing Homes Act 1975;

"nearest relative", in relation to a patient, has the meaning given in Part II of this Act;

"patient" (except in Part VII of this Act) means a person suffering or appearing to be suffering from mental disorder;

"restriction direction" has the meaning given to it by section 49 above;

"restriction order" has the meaning given to it by section 41 above;

"special hospital" has the same meaning as in the National Health Service Act 1977; (1977 c. 49.)

"standard scale" has the meaning given in section 75 of the Criminal Justice Act 1982; (1982 c. 48.)

"transfer direction" has the meaning given to it by section 47 above.

(2) "Statutory maximum" has the meaning given in section 74 of the Criminal Justice Act 1982 and for the purposes of section 128(4)(*a*) above—

(*a*) subsection (1) of section 74 shall have effect as if after the words "England and Wales" there were inserted the words "or Northern Ireland"; and

(b) section 32 of the Magistrates' Courts Act 1980 shall extend to Northern Ireland. 1980 c. 43.

(3) In relation to a person who is liable to be detained or subject to guardianship by virtue of an order or direction under Part III of this Act (other than under section 35, 36 or 38), any reference in this Act to any enactment contained in Part II of this Act or in section 66 or 67 above shall be construed as a reference to that enactment as it applies to that person by virtue of Part III of this Act.

Application to Scotland.

146. Sections 42(6), 80, 88 (and so far as applied by that section sections 18, 22 and 138), 104(4), 110 (and so much of Part VII of this Act as is applied in relation to Scotland by that section), 116, 122, 128 (except so far as it relates to patients subject to guardianship), 137, 139(1), 141, 142, 143 (so far as applicable to any Order in Council extending to Scotland) and 144 above shall extend to Scotland together with any amendment or repeal by this Act of or any provision of Schedule 5 to this Act relating to any enactment which so extends; but, except as aforesaid and except so far as it relates to the interpretation or commencement of the said provisions, this Act shall not extend to Scotland.

Application to Northern Ireland.

147. Sections 81, 82, 86, 87, 88 (and so far as applied by that section sections 18, 22 and 138), 104(4), 110 (and so much of Part VII as is applied in relation to Northern Ireland by that section), section 128 (except so far as it relates to patients subject to guardianship), 137, 139, 141, 142, 143 (so far as applicable to any Order in Council extending to Northern Ireland) and 144 above shall extend to Northern Ireland together with any amendment or repeal by this Act of or any provision of Schedule 5 to this Act relating to any enactment which so extends; but except as aforesaid and except so far as it relates to the interpretation or commencement of the said provisions, this Act shall not extend to Northern Ireland.

Consequential and transitional provisions and repeals.

148.—(1) Schedule 4 (consequential amendments) and Schedule 5 (transitional and saving provisions) to this Act shall have effect but without prejudice to the operation of sections 15 to 17 of the Interpretation Act 1978 (which relate to the effect of repeals). 1978 c. 30.

(2) Where any amendment in Schedule 4 to this Act affects an enactment amended by the Mental Health (Amendment) Act 1982 the amendment in Schedule 4 shall come into force immediately after the provision of the Act of 1982 amending that enactment. 1982 c. 51.

PART X

(3) The enactments specified in Schedule 6 to this Act are hereby repealed to the extent mentioned in the third column of that Schedule.

Short title, commencement and application to Scilly Isles.

149.—(1) This Act may be cited as the Mental Health Act 1983.

(2) Subject to subsection (3) below and Schedule 5 to this Act, this Act shall come into force on 30th September 1983.

(3) Sections 35, 36, 38 and 40(3) above shall come into force on such day (not being earlier than the said 30th September) as may be appointed by the Secretary of State and a different day may be appointed for each of those sections or for different purposes of any of those sections.

1977 c. 49.

(4) Section 130(4) of the National Health Service Act 1977 (which provides for the extension of that Act to the Isles of Scilly) shall have effect as if the references to that Act included references to this Act.

SCHEDULES

SCHEDULE 1

Sections 40(4), 41(3) and (5), and 55(4).

Application of Certain Provisions to Patients Subject to Hospital and Guardianship Orders

Part I

Patients Not Subject to Special Restrictions

1. Sections 9, 10, 17, 21, 24(3) and (4), 26 to 28, 31, 32, 34, 67 and 76 shall apply in relation to the patient without modification.

2. Sections 16, 18, 19, 20, 22, 23 and 66 shall apply in relation to the patient with the modifications specified in paragraphs 3 to 9 below.

3. In section 16(1) for references to an application for admission or a guardianship application there shall be substituted references to the order or direction under Part III of this Act by virtue of which the patient is liable to be detained or subject to guardianship.

4. In section 18 subsection (5) shall be omitted.

5. In section 19(2) for the words from " as follows " to the end of the subsection there shall be substituted the words " as if the order or direction under Part III of this Act by virtue of which he was liable to be detained or subject to guardianship before being transferred were an order or direction for his admission or removal to the hospital to which he is transferred, or placing him under the guardianship of the authority or person into whose guardianship he is transferred, as the case may be ".

6. In section 20—

(*a*) in subsection (1) for the words from " day on which he was " to " as the case may be " there shall be substituted the words " date of the relevant order or direction under Part III of this Act " ; and

(*b*) in subsection (9) for the words " the application for admission for treatment or, as the case may be, in the guardianship application, that application " there shall be substituted the words " the relevant order or direction under Part III of this Act, that order or direction ".

7. In section 22 for references to an application for admission or a guardianship application there shall be substituted references to the order or direction under Part III of this Act by virtue of which the patient is liable to be detained or subject to guardianship.

8. In section 23(2)—

(*a*) in paragraph (*a*) the words " for assessment or " shall be omitted ; and

(*b*) in paragraphs (*a*) and (*b*) the references to the nearest relative shall be omitted.

SCH. 1

9. In section 66—

(*a*) in subsection (1), paragraphs (*a*), (*b*), (*c*), (*g*) and (*h*), the words in parenthesis in paragraph (i) and paragraph (ii) shall be omitted; and

(*b*) in subsection (2), paragraphs (*a*), (*b*), (*c*) and (*g*) shall be omitted and in paragraph (*d*) for the words "cases mentioned in paragraphs (*d*) and (*g*)" there shall be substituted the words "case mentioned in paragraph (*d*)".

PART II

PATIENTS SUBJECT TO SPECIAL RESTRICTIONS

1. Sections 24(3) and (4), 32 and 76 shall apply in relation to the patient without modification.

2. Sections 17 to 19, 22, 23 and 34 shall apply in relation to the patient with the modifications specified in paragraphs 3 to 8 below.

3. In section 17—

(*a*) in subsection (1) after the word "may" there shall be inserted the words "with the consent of the Secretary of State";

(*b*) in subsection (4) after the words "the responsible medical officer" and after the words "that officer" there shall be inserted the words "or the Secretary of State"; and

(*c*) in subsection (5) after the word "recalled" there shall be inserted the words "by the responsible medical officer", and for the words from "he has ceased" to the end of the subsection there shall be substituted the words "the expiration of the period of six months beginning with the first day of his absence on leave".

4. In section 18 there shall be omitted—

(*a*) in subsection (1) the words "subject to the provisions of this section"; and

(*b*) subsections (3), (4) and (5).

5. In section 19—

(*a*) in subsection (1) after the word "may" in paragraph (*a*) there shall be inserted the words "with the consent of the Secretary of State", and the words from "or into" to the end of the subsection shall be omitted; and

(*b*) in subsection (2) for the words from "as follows" to the end of the subsection there shall be substituted the words "as if the order or direction under Part III of this Act by virtue of which he was liable to be detained before being transferred were an order or direction for his admission or removal to the hospital to which he is transferred".

6. In section 22 subsection (1) and paragraph (*a*) of subsection (2) shall not apply.

Sch. 1

7. In section 23—

(*a*) in subsection (1) references to guardianship shall be omitted and after the word " made " there shall be inserted the words " with the consent of the Secretary of State and ", and

(*b*) in subsection (2)—

(i) in paragraph (*a*) the words " for assessment or " and " or by the nearest relative of the patient " shall be omitted ; and

(ii) paragraph (*b*) shall be omitted.

8. In section 34, in subsection (1) the definition of " the nominated medical attendant " and subsection (3) shall be omitted.

SCHEDULE 2

Section 65(2).

Mental Health Review Tribunals

1. Each of the Mental Health Review Tribunals shall consist of—

(*a*) a number of persons (referred to in this Schedule as " the legal members ") appointed by the Lord Chancellor and having such legal experience as the Lord Chancellor considers suitable ;

(*b*) a number of persons (referred to in this Schedule as " the medical members ") being registered medical practitioners appointed by the Lord Chancellor after consultation with the Secretary of State ; and

(*c*) a number of persons appointed by the Lord Chancellor after consultation with the Secretary of State and having such experience in administration, such knowledge of social services or such other qualifications or experience as the Lord Chancellor considers suitable.

2. The members of Mental Health Review Tribunals shall hold and vacate office under the terms of the instrument under which they are appointed, but may resign office by notice in writing to the Lord Chancellor ; and any such member who ceases to hold office shall be eligible for re-appointment.

3. One of the legal members of each Mental Health Review Tribunal shall be appointed by the Lord Chancellor as chairman of the Tribunal.

4. Subject to rules made by the Lord Chancellor under section 78(2)(*c*) above, the members who are to constitute a Mental Health Review Tribunal for the purposes of any proceedings or class or group of proceedings under this Act shall be appointed by the chairman of the tribunal or, if for any reason he is unable to act, by another member of the tribunal appointed for the purpose by the chairman ; and of the members so appointed—

(*a*) one or more shall be appointed from the legal members ;

SCH. 2

(*b*) one or more shall be appointed from the medical members; and

(*c*) one or more shall be appointed from the members who are neither legal nor medical members.

5. A member of a Mental Health Review Tribunal for any area may be appointed under paragraph 4 above as one of the persons to constitute a Mental Health Review Tribunal for any other area for the purposes of any proceedings or class or group of proceedings; and for the purposes of this Act, a person so appointed shall, in relation to the proceedings for which he was appointed, be deemed to be a member of that other tribunal.

6. Subject to any rules made by the Lord Chancellor under section 78(4)(*a*) above, where the chairman of the tribunal is included among the persons appointed under paragraph 4 above, he shall be president of the tribunal; and in any other case the president of the tribunal shall be such one of the members so appointed (being one of the legal members) as the chairman may nominate.

Section 113.

SCHEDULE 3

ENACTMENTS DISAPPLIED IN RESPECT OF PERSONS WITHIN JURISDICTION UNDER PART VII

Session and Chapter	Short Title	Enactments
13 Geo. 3. c.81.	The Inclosure Act 1773.	Sections 22 and 24.
7 Geo. 4. c. 16.	The Chelsea and Kilmainham Hospitals Act 1826.	Sections 44 to 48.
2 & 3 Will. 4. c. 80.	The Ecclesiastical Corporations Act 1832.	Section 3.
1 & 2 Vict. c. 106.	The Pluralities Act 1838.	Section 127.
4 & 5 Vict. c. 38.	The School Sites Act 1841.	Section 5.
5 & 6 Vict. c. 26.	The Ecclesiastical Houses of Residence Act 1842.	Section 12.
5 & 6 Vict. c. 108.	The Ecclesiastical Leasing Act 1842.	Section 24.
8 & 9 Vict. c. 16.	The Companies Clauses Consolidation Act 1845.	Section 79.
8 & 9 Vict. c. 18.	The Lands Clauses Consolidation Act 1845.	Section 9.
8 & 9 Vict. c. 118.	The Inclosure Act 1845.	Sections 20, 133, 134 and 137.
9 & 10 Vict. c. 73.	The Tithe Act 1846.	Sections 5, 9 and 10.
17 & 18 Vict. c. 112.	The Literary and Scientific Institutions Act 1854.	Section 5.
25 & 26 Vict. c. 53.	The Land Registry Act 1862.	Section 116.

Sch. 3

Session and Chapter	Short Title	Enactments
27 & 28 Vict. c. 114.	The Improvement of Land Act 1864.	Section 24.
29 & 30 Vict. c. 122.	The Metropolitan Commons Act 1866.	Section 28.
31 & 32 Vict. c. 109.	The Compulsory Church Rate Abolition Act 1868.	Section 7.
36 & 37 Vict. c. 50.	The Places of Worship Sites Act 1873.	Sections 1 and 3.
40 & 41 Vict. c. 59.	The Colonial Stock Act 1877.	Section 6.
57 & 58 Vict. c. 60.	The Merchant Shipping Act 1894.	In section 55, subsection (1).

SCHEDULE 4

Section 148.

Consequential Amendments

1. In the Fines and Recoveries Act 1833— 1833 c. 74.

(*a*) in section 33 for the words "the Mental Health Act 1959" and "Part VIII" there shall be substituted respectively the words "the Mental Health Act 1983" and "Part VII"; 1959 c. 72.

(*b*) in sections 48 and 49 for the references to the judge having jurisdiction under Part VIII of the Mental Health Act 1959 there shall be substituted references to the judge having jurisdiction under Part VII of this Act.

2. In section 68 of the Improvement of Land Act 1864 for the words "Part VIII of the Mental Health Act 1959" there shall be substituted the words "Part VII of the Mental Health Act 1983". 1864 c. 114.

3. In section 10(3) of the Colonial Prisoners Removal Act 1884 for the words "section seventy-one of the Mental Health Act 1959", "section seventy-two" and "section seventy-four" there shall be substituted respectively the words "section 46 of the Mental Health Act 1983", "section 47" and "section 49". 1884 c. 31.

4. In the Trustee Act 1925— 1925 c. 19.

(*a*) in section 36(9) for the words "the Mental Health Act 1959" and "Part VIII of the Mental Health Act 1959" there shall be substituted respectively the words "the Mental Health Act 1983" and "Part VII of the Mental Health Act 1983";

(*b*) in section 41(1) for the words "the Mental Health Act 1959" there shall be substituted the words "the Mental Health Act 1983";

(*c*) in section 54—

(i) in subsection (1) for the words "Part VIII of the Mental Health Act 1959" there shall be substituted the words "Part VII of the Mental Health Act 1983"; and

SCH. 4

(ii) in subsection (3) for the words "section one hundred and one of the Mental Health Act 1959" and "exercisable and have been exercised under section one hundred and four" there shall be substituted respectively the words "section 94 of the Mental Health Act 1983" and "exercisable under section 98 of that Act and have been exercised under that section or section 104 of the Mental Health Act 1959";

(*d*) in section 55 except so far as it applies to existing orders made before the commencement of this Act, for the words "Part VIII of the Mental Health Act 1959" there shall be substituted the words "Part VII of the Mental Health Act 1983".

1925 c. 20. 5. In the Law of Property Act 1925—

(*a*) in section 22(1) for the words "Part VIII of the Mental Health Act 1959" there shall be substituted the words "Part VII of the Mental Health Act 1983";

(*b*) in section 205(1)(xiii) for the words "section four of the Mental Health Act 1959" and "Part VIII" there shall be substituted respectively the words "section 1 of the Mental Health Act 1983" and "Part VIII of the Mental Health Act 1959 or Part VII of the said Act of 1983".

1925 c. 21. 6. In section 111 of the Land Registration Act 1925—

(*a*) in subsection (5) for the words "the Mental Health Act 1959" and "Part VIII of the Mental Health Act 1959" there shall be substituted respectively the words "the Mental Health Act 1983" and "Part VII of the Mental Health Act 1983"; and

(*b*) in subsection (6) for the words "Part VIII of the Mental Health Act 1959" there shall be substituted the words "Part VII of the Mental Health Act 1983".

1925 c. 23. 7. In paragraph (ii) of the proviso to section 41(1) of the Administration of Estates Act 1925 for the words "the Mental Health Act 1959" there shall be substituted the words "the Mental Health Act 1983".

1947 c. 19. 8. In sections 4(1) and 11(3)(*b*) of the Polish Resettlement Act 1947 for the words "the Mental Health Act 1959" there shall be substituted the words "the Mental Health Act 1983".

1949 c. 45. 9. In section 1(4) of the U.S.A. Veterans' Pensions (Administration) Act 1949 after the words "curator bonis" there shall be inserted the words "or for whom a receiver has been appointed under section 105 of the Mental Health Act 1959 or section 99 of the Mental Health Act 1983".

1955 c. 18. 10. In section 116(7) of the Army Act 1955 for the words "section 71 of the Mental Health Act 1959" and "within the meaning of the Mental Health Act 1959" there shall be substituted respectively the words "section 46 of the Mental Health Act 1983" and "within the meaning of the Mental Health Act 1983".

SCH. 4

11. In section 116(7) of the Air Force Act 1955 for the words "section 71 of the Mental Health Act 1959" and "within the meaning of the Mental Health Act 1959" there shall be substituted respectively the words "section 46 of the Mental Health Act Act 1983" and "within the meaning of the Mental Health Act 1983". 1955 c. 19.

12. In section 38(4) of the Sexual Offences Act 1956 for the words "the Mental Health Act 1959" there shall be substituted the words "the Mental Health Act 1983". 1956 c. 69.

13. In section 71(6) of the Naval Discipline Act 1957 for the words "section 71 of the Mental Health Act 1959" and "within the meaning of the Mental Health Act 1959" there shall be substituted respectively the words "section 46 of the Mental Health Act 1983" and "within the meaning of the Mental Health Act 1983". 1957 c. 53.

14. In section 1 of the Variation of Trusts Act 1958— 1958 c. 53.

(*a*) in subsection (3) for the words "Part VIII of the Mental Health Act 1959" and "the said Part VIII" there shall be substituted respectively the words "Part VII of the Mental Health Act 1983" and "the said Part VII"; and

(*b*) in subsection (6) for the words "Part VIII of the Mental Health Act 1959" there shall be substituted the words "Part VII of the Mental Health Act 1983".

15. In section 128(1)(*b*) of the Mental Health Act 1959 for the words "this Act" in both places where they occur there shall be substituted the words "the Mental Health Act 1983". 1959 c. 72.

16. In the Mental Health (Scotland) Act 1960— 1960 c. 61

(*a*) in section 10(1)(*b*) and (*c*) for the words "the Mental Health Act 1959" there shall be substituted the words "the Mental Health Act 1983";

(*b*) in section 73(5) for the words "Part IV of the Mental Health Act 1959" there shall be substituted the words "Part II of the Mental Health Act 1983";

(*c*) in section 75 for the words "Part IV of the Mental Health Act 1959", "section forty-nine of the said Act of 1959", "Part IV of that Act", "Part IV of the said Act of 1959", and "section fifty-two" wherever they occur there shall be substituted respectively the words "Part II of the Mental Health Act 1983", "section 26 of the said Act of 1983", "Part II of that Act", "Part II of the said Act of 1983" and "section 29";

(*d*) in section 76—

(i) in subsection (1) for the words "the Mental Health Act 1959 as amended by this Act" and "Part IV of that Act" there shall be substituted respectively the words "the Mental Health Act 1983" and "Part II of that Act";

(ii) in subsection (2) for the words "sections forty-nine to fifty-one of the said Act of 1959" and "Part IV of that Act" there shall be substituted respectively the

SCH. 4

words " sections 26 to 28 of the said Act of 1983 " and " Part II of that Act " ; and

(iii) in subsection (3) after the words " the Mental Health Act 1959 " there shall be inserted the words " or section 29 or 30 of the Mental Health Act 1983 ".

(*e*) in section 83(3)(*a*) for the words " mental welfare officer within the meaning of the Mental Health Act 1959 " there shall be substituted the words " approved social worker within the meaning of the Mental Health Act 1983 " ;

(*f*) in sections 85 and 87 for the words " the Mental Health Act 1959 " there shall be substituted the words " the Mental Health Act 1983 ".

(*g*) in section 88(2) after " 1959 " there shall be inserted the words " or Part VI of the Mental Health Act 1983 " ;

(*h*) in section 103(3) and (5) for the words " section ninety-three of the Mental Health Act 1959 " there shall be substituted the words " section 88 of the Mental Health Act 1983 " ;

(*i*) in section 107(2) for the words " section one hundred and forty-one of the Mental Health Act 1959 " there shall be substituted the words " section 139 of the Mental Health Act 1983 ".

1960 c. 65.

17. In section 5 of the Administration of Justice Act 1960—

(*a*) in subsection (4) for the words " Part V of the Mental Health Health Act 1959 " and the words " the said Part V " there shall be substituted respectively the words " Part III of the Mental Health Act 1983 (other than under section 35, 36 or 38) " and " the said Part III " ; and

(*b*) in subsection (4A) for the words " section 31 of the Mental Health (Amendment) Act 1982 ", " Part V of the said Act of 1959 " and " the said section 31 " there shall be substituted respectively " section 38 of the Mental Health Act 1983 ", " Part III of the said Act of 1983 " and " the said section 38 ".

1964 c. 84.

18. In the Criminal Procedure (Insanity) Act 1964—

(*a*) in section 8(2) for the words " the Mental Health Act 1959 ", " Part V " and " sections 139 to 141 " there shall be substituted respectively the words " the Mental Health Act 1983 ", " Part III " and " sections 137 to 139 " ;

(*b*) in Schedule 1—

(i) in paragraph 1(3) for the words " sections 60 and 65 of the Mental Health Act 1959 " there shall be substituted the words " sections 37 and 41 of the Mental Health Act 1983 " ;

(ii) in paragraph 2(1) for the words " the Mental Health Act 1959 ", " section 60 " and " section 65 " there shall be substituted respectively " the Mental Health Act 1983 ", " section 37 " and " section 41 " ;

(iii) in paragraph 2(2) for the words " section 66 of the said Act of 1959 " and " section 65 " there shall be substituted respectively the words " section 42 of the said Act of 1983 " and " section 41 " ;

(iv) in paragraph 2(3) for the words " section 63(5) of the Mental Health Act 1959 " and the words from " the proviso " to " the reference " there shall be substituted respectively the words " section 40(5) of the Mental Health Act 1983 " and " the reference in the said section 40(5) " ; Sch. 4

19. In section 18 of the Administration of Justice Act 1965 for the words " Part VIII of the Mental Health Act 1959 " there shall be substituted the words " Part VII of the Mental Health Act 1983 ". 1965 c. 2.

20. In paragraph 1(2)(*b*) of Schedule 1 to the Compulsory Purchase Act 1965 at the end there shall be inserted the words " or section 98 of the Mental Health Act 1983 ". 1965 c. 56.

21. In the Criminal Justice Act 1967— 1967 c. 80.

(*a*) in section 72(1)(*b*) for the words " section 40 or 140 of the Mental Health Act 1959 or section 31(8) of the Mental Health (Amendment) Act 1982 " there shall be substituted the words " section 18, 38(7) or 138 of the Mental Health Act 1983 " ;

(*b*) in section 72(3) for the words " Section 139 of the Mental Health Act 1959 " and " the said Act of 1959 " there shall be substituted respectively the words " Section 137 of the Mental Health Act 1983 " and " the said Act of 1983 " ;

(*c*) in section 72(4) for the words " Part V of the Mental Health Act 1959 ", " section 31 of the Mental Health (Amendment) Act 1982 " and " Part V of the said Act of 1959 " there shall be substituted respectively the words " Part III of the Mental Health Act 1983 ", " section 38 of the said Act of 1983 " and " Part III of the said Act of 1983 ".

22. In section 26(2) of the Leasehold Reform Act 1967 for the words " the Mental Health Act 1959 ", " appointed under Part VIII of that Act " and " having jurisdiction under Part VIII of that Act " there shall be substituted respectively the words " Mental Health Act 1983 ", " appointed under Part VII of the said Act of 1983 or Part VIII of the Mental Health Act 1959 " and " having jurisdiction under Part VII of the said Act of 1983 ". 1967 c. 88.

23. In the Criminal Appeal Act 1968— 1968 c. 19.

(*a*) in section 6(4) for the words " section 72 of the Mental Health Act 1959 " and " subsection (6) " there shall be substituted respectively the words " section 47 of the Mental Health Act 1983 " and " subsection (5) " ;

(*b*) in section 8(3) after the words " Part V of the Mental Health Act 1959 " there shall be inserted the words " or under Part III of the Mental Health Act 1983 (other than under section 35, 36 or 38 of that Act) " ;

(*c*) in section 8(3A)—

(i) for the words " section 30 of the Mental Health (Amendment) Act 1982 " there shall be substituted the words " section 36 of the Mental Health Act 1983 " ;

SCH. 4

(ii) for the words " section 31 of that Act " there shall be substituted the words " section 38 of that Act " ; and

(iii) for the words " Part V of the Mental Health Act 1959 " there shall be substituted the words " Part III of that Act " ;

(*d*) in section 11—

(i) in subsection (5) for the words "the Mental Health (Amendment) Act 1982 " there shall be substituted the words " the Mental Health Act 1983 " ; and

(ii) in subsection (6)(*b*) for the words " section 31(8) of the said Act of 1982 " there shall be substituted the words " section 38(7) of the said Act of 1983 ".

(*e*) in section 14(5) for the words " section 72 of the Mental Health Act 1959 " and " subsection (6) " there shall be substituted respectively the words " section 47 of the Mental Health Act 1983 " and " subsection (5) " ;

(*f*) in section 16(3) for the words " the Mental Health Act 1959 " and " Part V " there shall be substituted respectively the words " the Mental Health Act 1983 " and " Part III " ;

(*g*) in section 37(4) for the words " Part V of the Mental Health Act 1959 " and " the Mental Health Act 1959 " there shall be substituted respectively the words " Part III of the Mental Health Act 1983 (otherwise than under section 35, 36 or 38 of that Act) " and " the Mental Health Act 1983 " ;

(*h*) in section 37(4A) for the words " section 30 of the Mental Health (Amendment) Act 1982 ", " section 31 " and " Part V of the said Act of 1959 " wherever they occur there shall be substituted respectively the words " section 36 of the Mental Health Act 1983 ", " section 38 " and " Part III of the said Act of 1983 " ;

(*i*) in section 50(1), for the words from " Part V " to " 1982 " there shall be substituted the words " Part III of the Mental Health Act 1983, with or without a restriction order, and an interim hospital order under that Part " ;

(*j*) in section 51(2) for the words " section 147(1) of the Mental Health Act 1959 " there shall be substituted the words " section 145(1) of the Mental Health Act 1983 " ;

(*k*) in paragraph 1(3) of Schedule 1 for the words " the Mental Health Act 1959 " there shall be substituted the words " the Mental Health Act 1983 " ;

(*l*) in paragraph 2 of Schedule 1 for the words " the Mental Health Act 1959 ", " section 60 " and " section 65 " there shall be substituted respectively the words " the Mental Health Act 1983 ", " section 37 " and " section 41 " ;

(*m*) in paragraph 3 of Schedule 1 for the words " Part IV of the Mental Health Act 1959 " and " the said Part IV " there shall be substituted respectively the words " Part II of the Mental Health Act 1983 " and " the said Part II " ;

(n) in Schedule 3— Sch. 4

(i) in the heading to the Schedule for the words " PART V OF MENTAL HEALTH ACT 1959 " there shall be substituted the words " PART III OF MENTAL HEALTH ACT 1983 " ; and

(ii) for paragraph 2 there shall be substituted—

" *Order for continued detention under Act of 1983*

2. Where an order is made by the Court of Appeal under section 16(3) of this Act for a person's continued detention under the Mental Health Act 1983, Part III of that Act (patients concerned in criminal proceedings or under sentence) shall apply to him as if he had been ordered under the said section 16(3) to be kept in custody pending trial and were detained in pursuance of a transfer direction together with a restriction direction.".

24. In the Courts-Martial (Appeals) Act 1968— 1968 c. 20.

(a) in sections 20(4) and 43(4) for the words " Part V of the Mental Health Act 1959 " there shall be substituted the words " Part III of the Mental Health Act 1983 " ;

(b) in section 23, in subsection (1) for the words " section 71 of the Mental Health Act 1959 " there shall be substituted the words " section 46 of the Mental Health Act 1983 " and in subsection (2) for the words " the Mental Health Act 1959 " there shall be substituted the words " the Mental Health Act 1983 " ;

(c) in section 25(4) for the words " the Mental Health Act 1959 " there shall be substituted the words " the Mental Health Act 1983 ".

25. In section 21(4) of the Family Law Reform Act 1969 for the words " the Mental Health Act 1959 " there shall be substituted the words " the Mental Health Act 1983 ". 1969 c. 46.

26. In the Children and Young Persons Act 1969— 1969 c. 54.

(a) in section 1(3) for the words " Part V of the Mental Health Act 1959 " there shall be substituted the words " Part III of the Mental Health Act 1983 " ;

(b) in section 1(5) for the words " section 60 of the said Act of 1959 " there shall be substituted the words " section 37 of the said Act of 1983 " ;

(c) in section 2(10) for the words " section 31 of the Mental Health (Amendment) Act 1982 " and " the said section 31 " there shall be substituted respectively the words " section 38 of the Mental Health Act 1983 " and " the said section 38 ".

(d) in section 12(4) for the words " section 28 of the Mental Health Act 1959 ", " Part V " and " the said Act of 1959 " there shall be substituted respectively the words " section 12 of the Mental Health Act 1983 ", " Part III " and " the said Act of 1983 " ;

(e) in paragraph 7(7) of Schedule 4 for the words from the beginning to " 1959 " there shall be substituted the words " A

SCH. 4

restriction direction which was given under section 49 of the Mental Health Act 1983 ".

1970 c. 42

27. In Schedule 1 to the Local Authorities Social Services Act 1970—

(*a*) in the entry relating to the Mental Health Act 1959, in the first column for the words " Parts II to VI and IX " there shall be substituted the words " sections 8 and 9 " and for the entry in the second column there shall be substituted the words " Welfare and accommodation of mentally disordered persons." ;

(*b*) there shall be inserted at the end—

" Mental Health Act 1983 (c. 20)	
Parts II, III and VI	Welfare of the mentally disordered; guardianship of persons suffering from mental disorder including such persons removed to England and Wales from Scotland or Northern Ireland ; exercise of functions of nearest relative of person so suffering.
Sections 66, 67, 69(1)	Exercise of functions of nearest relative in relation to applications and references to Mental Health Review Tribunals.
Section 114	Appointment of approved social workers.
Section 115	Entry and inspection.
Section 116	Welfare of certain hospital patients.
Section 117	After-care of detained patients.
Section 130	Prosecutions." ;

1982 c. 51. (*c*) the entry relating to the Mental Health (Amendment) Act 1982 shall cease to have effect.

1971 c. 23.

28. In section 57(1) of the Courts Act 1971 for the words " Part V of the Mental Health Act 1959 " there shall be substituted the words " Part III of the Mental Health Act 1983 ".

1971 c. 62.

29. In Schedule 1 to the Tribunals and Inquiries Act 1971, in the second column of the entry relating to the Mental Health Review Tribunals for the words following " Tribunals " there shall be substituted the words " constituted or having effect as if constituted under section 65 of the Mental Health Act 1983 (c. 20).".

Sch. 4

30. In section 30(2) of the Immigration Act 1971 for the words from the beginning to " 1960) " there shall be substituted the words " Under section 82 of the Mental Health (Scotland) Act 1960 " and the words from " and accordingly " onwards shall be omitted. 1971 c. 77.

31. In section 20(2) of the Parliamentary and other Pensions Act 1972 for the words " Section 138 of the Mental Health Act 1959 " there shall be substituted the words " Section 142 of the Mental Health Act 1983 ". 1972 c. 48.

32. In section 118 of the Local Government Act 1972— 1972 c. 70.

(*a*) in subsection (1) for the words " the Mental Health Act 1959 " there shall be substituted the words " the Mental Health Act 1983 " ; and

(*b*) in subsection (4) for the words " Part VIII of the said Act of 1959 " there shall be substituted the words " Part VII of the said Act of 1983 ".

33. In the Costs in Criminal Cases Act 1973— 1973 c. 14.

(*a*) in section 3(7) for the words from " under Part V " to " 1982 " there shall be substituted the words " and an interim hospital order under Part III of the Mental Health Act 1983 " ; and

(*b*) in section 18(1)(*c*) for the words " Part V of the Mental Health Act 1959 " there shall be substituted the words " Part III of the Mental Health Act 1983 ".

34. In section 12(*d*) of the Matrimonial Causes Act 1973 for the words " the Mental Health Act 1959 " there shall be substituted the words " the Mental Health Act 1983 ". 1973 c. 18.

35. In section 1 of the Guardianship Act 1973— 1973 c. 29.

(*a*) in subsection (8), the words from " and " to the end of the subsection shall be omitted ; and

(*b*) after subsection (8) there shall be inserted—

" (9) Nothing in this section shall be taken to affect the provisions of the Mental Health Act 1983 as to the person who is ' the nearest relative ' for the purposes of that Act.".

36. In section 3 of the Powers of Criminal Courts Act 1973— 1973 c. 62.

(*a*) in subsection (1) for the words " section 28 of the Mental Health Act 1959 " and " Part V of that Act " there shall be substituted respectively the words " section 12 of the Mental Health Act 1983 " and " Part III of that Act " ;

(*b*) in subsection (2) for the words " hospital or mental nursing home within the meaning of the Mental Health Act 1959 " and " that Act " there shall be substituted respectively the words " hospital within the meaning of the Mental Health Act 1983 or mental nursing home within the meaning of the Nursing Homes Act 1975 " and " the National Health Service Act 1977 " ; and

(*c*) in subsection (7) for the words " Subsections (2) and (3) of section 62 of the Mental Health Act 1959 " and " section

SCH. 4 60(1)(*a*)" there shall be substituted respectively the words "Subsections (2) and (3) of section 54 of the Mental Health Act 1983" and "section 37(2)(*a*)".

1974 c. 23. 37. In Group D in Schedule 1 to the Juries Act 1974 for the words "section 33 of the Mental Health Act 1959", "Part VIII of that Act" and "the said Act of 1959" there shall be substituted respectively the words "section 7 of the Mental Health Act 1983", "Part VII of that Act" and "the said Act of 1983".

1974 c. 47. 38. In the Solicitors Act 1974—

(*a*) in section 12(1)(*j*) for the words "section 101 of the Mental Health Act 1959" and "section 104 of that Act" there shall be substituted respectively the words "section 94 of the Mental Health Act 1983" and "section 104 of the Mental Health Act 1959 or section 98 of the said Act of 1983";

(*b*) in section 62(4)(*c*) for the words "under Part VIII of the Mental Health Act 1959" there shall be substituted the words "appointed under Part VII of the Mental Health Act 1983";

(*c*) in paragraph 1(1)(*f*) of Schedule 1 for the words "section 104 (emergency powers) or 105 (appointment of receiver) of the Mental Health Act 1959" there shall be substituted the words "section 104 of the Mental Health Act 1959 or section 98 of the Mental Health Act 1983 (emergency powers) or section 105 of the said Act of 1959 or section 99 of the said Act of 1983 (appointment of receiver)".

1974 c. 53. 39. In section 5(7) of the Rehabilitation of Offenders Act 1974 for the words "Part V of the Mental Health Act 1959" there shall be substituted the words "Part III of the Mental Health Act 1983".

1975 c. 7. 40. In paragraph 19(4) of Schedule 5 to the Finance Act 1975 for the words "the Mental Health Act 1959" there shall be substituted the words "the Mental Health Act 1983".

1975 c. 21. 41. In the Criminal Procedure (Scotland) Act 1975—

(*a*) in sections 13(1)(*b*) and 322(1)(*b*) for the words "section 40 or 140 of the Mental Health Act 1959, section 31(8) of the Mental Health (Amendment) Act 1982" there shall be substituted the words "section 18, 38(7) or 138 of the Mental Health Act 1983";

(*b*) in sections 13(3) and 322(3) for the words "Section 139 of the Mental Health Act 1959" and "the said Act of 1959" there shall be substituted respectively "Section 137 of the Mental Health Act 1983" and "the said Act of 1983";

(*c*) in sections 13(4) and 322(4) for the words "Part V of the Mental Health Act 1959", "section 31 of the Mental Health (Amendment) Act 1982" and "Part V of the said Act of 1959" there shall be substituted respectively the words "Part III of the Mental Health Act 1983", "section 38 of the said Act of 1983" and "Part III of the said Act of 1983".

42. In Part II of Schedule 1 to the House of Commons Disqualification Act 1975 in the entry relating to Mental Health Review Tribunals for the words " constituted under the Mental Health Act 1959 " there shall be substituted the words " constituted or having effect as if constituted under the Mental Health Act 1983 ". SCH. 4 1975 c. 24.

43. In the Nursing Homes Act 1975— 1975 c. 37.

(*a*) in sections 3(2)(*c*) and 10(2) for the words " the Mental Health Act 1959 or the Mental Health (Amendment) Act 1982 " there shall be substituted the words " the Mental Health Act 1983 " ;

(*b*) in section 20(1) for the words " section 4 of the Mental Health Act 1959 " there shall be substituted the words " section 1 of the Mental Health Act 1983 " ;

(*c*) in section 21 for the words " those sections " there shall be substituted the words " the sections of the Mental Health Act 1983 corresponding to those sections, namely sections 126, 139 and 125 respectively ".

44. In section 98(4) of the Children Act 1975 for the words " or residential home within the meaning of Part III of the Mental Health Act 1959 " there shall be substituted the words " residential home for mentally disordered persons within the meaning of the Nursing Homes Act 1975 or the Residential Homes Act 1980 ". 1975 c. 72. 1980 c. 7.

45. In section 32(6)(*c*) of the Adoption Act 1976 for the words " the Mental Health Act 1959 or the Mental Health (Amendment) Act 1982 " there shall be substituted the words " the Mental Health Act 1983 ". 1976 c. 36.

46. In section 3(6B) of the Bail Act 1976 for the words " section 28 of the Mental Health Act 1959 " there shall be substituted the words " section 12 of the Mental Health Act 1983 ". 1976 c. 63.

47. In the National Health Service Act 1977— 1977 c. 49.

(*a*) in section 4 for the words " the Mental Health Act 1959 of the Mental Health (Amendment) Act 1982 " there shall be substituted the words " the Mental Health Act 1983 " ;

(*b*) in section 105(1) for the words " Part IV of the Mental Health Act 1959 " there shall be substituted the words " Part II of the Mental Health Act 1983 " ;

(*c*) in section 105(3) the words " or the Mental Health Act 1959 " shall be omitted ;

(*d*) in section 128(1), in the definition of " illness ", for the words " the Mental Health Act 1959 " there shall be substituted the words " the Mental Health Act 1983 " ;

(*e*) in paragraph 2 of Schedule 8—

(i) for sub-paragraph (1)(*d*) there shall be substituted—

" (*d*) for the exercise of the functions of the authority in respect of persons suffering from mental disorder who are received into guardianship under

SCH. 4

Part II or III of the Mental Health Act 1983 (whether the guardianship of the local social services authority or of other persons). ";

(ii) in sub-paragraph (2)(*b*)(i) for the words "the Mental Health Act 1959" there shall be substituted the words "the Mental Health Act 1983"; and

(iii) in sub-paragraph (3) for the words "that Act of 1959" there shall be substituted the words "that Act of 1983";

(*f*) in paragraph 13(1)(*b*) of Schedule 14 for the words "80 to 83, 86 to 91, 93 and 96" there shall be substituted "80 to 82, 96".

1978 c. 29.

48. In section 16A(1)(*b*)(ii) of the National Health Service (Scotland) Act 1978 for the words "section 10 of the Mental Health Act 1959" there shall be substituted the words "section 116 of the Mental Health Act 1983".

1979 c. 14.

49. In paragraph 5(2) of Schedule 1 to the Capital Gains Tax Act 1979 for the words "the Mental Health Act 1959" there shall be substituted the words "the Mental Health Act 1983".

1980 c. 5.

50. In the Child Care Act 1980—

(*a*) in section 3(1)(*b*)(iii) for the words "the Mental Health Act 1959" there shall be substituted the words "the Mental Health Act 1983"; and

(*b*) in section 79(5)(*c*) for the words "section 10 of that Act" and "subsection (1)(*a*)" there shall be substituted respectively the words "section 116 of the Mental Health Act 1983" and "subsection (2)(*a*)".

1980 c. 6.

51. In section 2(5) of the Foster Children Act 1980 for the words "the Mental Health Act 1959 or the Mental Health (Amendment) Act 1982" there shall be substituted the words "the Mental Health Act 1983".

1980 c. 7.

52. In the Residential Homes Act 1980—

(*a*) in section 1(3)(*a*) for the words "section 147(1) of the Mental Health Act 1959" there shall be substituted the words "section 145(1) of the Mental Health Act 1983"; and

(*b*) in section 10(1) for the words "the Mental Health Act 1959" there shall be substituted the words "the Mental Health Act 1983".

1980 c. 9.

53. In paragraph 2(*a*) of Schedule 2 to the Reserve Forces Act 1980 for the words "the Mental Health Act 1959" there shall be substituted the words "the Mental Health Act 1983".

1980 c. 34.

54. In section 31(2)(*c*) of the Transport Act 1980 for the words "Part VIII of the Mental Health Act 1959" there shall be substituted the words "Part VII of the Mental Health Act 1983".

1980 c. 58.

55. In section 38 of the Limitation Act 1980—

(*a*) in subsection (3) for the words "Mental Health Act 1959" there shall be substituted the words "Mental Health Act 1983"; and (*b*) in subsection (4)— SCH. 4

(i) in paragraph (*a*), for the words " the Mental Health Act 1959 or section 30 or 31 of the Mental Health (Amendment) Act 1982 " there shall be substituted the words " the Mental Health Act 1983 (otherwise than by virtue of section 35 or 89) " ; and

(ii) for paragraph (*b*) there shall be substituted—

" (*b*) while he is receiving treatment as an in-patient in any hospital within the meaning of the Mental Health Act 1983 or mental nursing home within the meaning of the Nursing Homes Act 1975 without being liable to be detained under the said Act of 1983 (otherwise than by virtue of section 35 or 89), being treatment which follows without any interval a period during which he was liable to be detained or subject to guardianship under the Mental Health Act 1959, or the said Act of 1983 (otherwise than by virtue of section 35 or 89) or by virtue of any enactment repealed or excluded by the Mental Health Act 1959 ". 1975 c. 37.

56. In section 57(2)(*c*) of the Public Passenger Vehicles Act 1981 for the words " Part VIII of the Mental Health Act 1959 " there shall be substituted the words " Part VII of the Mental Health Act 1983 ". 1981 c. 14.

57. In the Contempt of Court Act 1981— 1981 c. 49.

(*a*) in section 14(4) for the words " section 60 of the Mental Health Act 1959 " and " section 31 of the Mental Health (Amendment) Act 1982 " there shall be substituted respectively the words " section 37 of the Mental Health Act 1983 " and " section 38 of that Act " ; and

(*b*) in section 14(4A) for the words " section 29 of the said Act of 1982 " there shall be substituted the words "section 35 of the said Act of 1983 ".

(*c*) in paragraph 10(*b*) of Schedule 1 for the words " paragraph (*b*) of subsection (2) of section 76 of the Mental Health Act 1959 " there shall be substituted the words " section 51(5) of the Mental Health Act 1983 ".

58. In the Supreme Court Act 1981— 1981 c. 54.

(*a*) in section 48(6)(*a*) for the words " Part V of the Mental Health Act 1959 " and " the Mental Health (Amendment) Act 1982 " there shall be substituted respectively the words " Part III of the Mental Health Act 1983 " and " that Act " ;

(*b*) in section 48(7) for the words " the said Act of 1982 " there shall be substituted the words " the said Act of 1983 " ; and

(*c*) in section 48(8)(*b*) for the words " section 31(8) of the said Act of 1982 " there shall be substituted the words " section 38(7) of the said Act of 1983 ".

SCH. 4

1981 c. 55. 59. In section 13(9) of the Armed Forces Act 1981 or the words "the Mental Health Act 1959" there shall be substituted the words "the Mental Health Act 1983".

1981 c. 61. 60. In paragraph 9 of Schedule 1 to the British Nationality Act 1981—

(*a*) in sub-paragraph (1)(*b*) for the words "Part V of the Mental Health Act 1959" there shall be substituted the words "Part III of the Mental Health Act 1983"; and

(*b*) in sub-paragraph (2)(*b*) for the words "Part V of the Mental Health Act 1959" there shall be substituted the words "Part III of the Mental Health Act 1983".

1982 c. 51. 61. In the Mental Health (Amendment) Act 1982—

(*a*) in section 70(2)—

(i) for the words "Sections 62 and 64(2)" there shall be substituted the words "Section 62", and

(ii) the words "sections 35(1) and (2) and 64(6) above extend to Northern Ireland" shall be omitted;

(*b*) in section 70(3) for the words "Section 154(2) of the principal Act" there shall be substituted the words "Section 149(4) of the Mental Health Act 1983".

Section 148.

SCHEDULE 5

TRANSITIONAL AND SAVING PROVISIONS

1. Where any period of time specified in an enactment repealed by this Act is current at the commencement of this Act, this Act shall have effect as if the corresponding provision of this Act had been in force when that period began to run.

1959 c. 72. 2. Nothing in this Act shall affect the interpretation of any provision of the Mental Health Act 1959 which is not repealed by this Act and accordingly sections 1 and 145(1) of this Act shall apply to any such provision as if it were contained in this Act.

3. Where, apart from this paragraph, anything done under or for the purposes of any enactment which is repealed by this Act would cease to have effect by virtue of that repeal it shall have effect as if it had been done under or for the purposes of the corresponding provision of this Act.

4.—(1) Until the expiration of the period of two years beginning with the day on which the Mental Health (Amendment) Act 1982 was passed this Act shall have effect as if—

(*a*) section 114 were omitted;

(*b*) in section 145(1) the definition of an approved social worker were omitted and there were inserted in the appropriate place the following definition:—

"'mental welfare officer' means an officer of a local

Sch. 5

social services authority appointed to act as mental welfare officer for the purposes of the Mental Health Act 1959 or this Act "; 1959 c. 72.

(c) for paragraph 16(e) of Schedule 4 there were substituted—

" (e) in section 83(3)(a) for the words ' the Mental Health Act 1959 ' there were substituted the words ' the Mental Health Act 1983 ' ";

(d) for paragraph 47(e)(i) of Schedule 4 there were substituted—

" (i) in sub-paragraph (1)(d) for the words ' the Mental Health Act 1959 ' and ' Part IV or Part V ' there were substituted respectively the words ' the Mental Health Act 1983 ' and ' Part II or III ' "; and

(e) for any reference to an approved social worker there were substituted a reference to a mental welfare officer.

(2) Any appointment of a person as a mental welfare officer for the purposes of the Mental Health Act 1959 or this Act shall terminate at the expiration of the period mentioned in sub-paragraph (1) above but without prejudice to anything previously done by that person or to the continuation by an approved social worker of anything which is then in process of being done by that person.

5. If no order has been made under section 11 of the National Health Service Act 1977 before 30th September 1983 establishing the Mental Health Act Commission the following shall be substituted for subsection (1) of section 121 of this Act— 1977 c. 49.

" (1) The Secretary of State shall under section 11 of the National Health Service Act 1977 establish a special health authority to be known as the Mental Health Act Commission.".

6. This Act shall apply in relation to any authority for the detention or guardianship of a person who was liable to be detained or subject to guardianship under the Mental Health Act 1959 immediately before 30th September 1983 as if the provisions of this Act which derive from provisions amended by section 1 or 2 of the Mental Health (Amendment) Act 1982 and the amendments in Schedule 3 to that Act which are consequential on those sections were included in this Act in the form the provisions from which they derive would take if those amendments were disregarded but this provision shall not apply to any renewal of that authority on or after that date. 1982 c. 51.

7. This Act shall apply to any application made before 30th September 1983 as if the provisions of this Act which derive from provisions amended by sections 3 to 5 of the Mental Health (Amendment) Act 1982 and the amendments in Schedule 3 to that Act which are consequential on those sections were included in this Act in the form the provisions from which they derive would take if those amendments were disregarded.

8.—(1) Where on 30th September 1983 a person who has not attained the age of sixteen years is subject to guardianship by virtue of a guardianship application the authority for his guardianship shall terminate on that day.

SCH. 5

1959 c. 72. (2) Section 8(1) of this Act has effect (instead of section 34(1) of the Mental Health Act 1959) in relation to a guardianship application made before the coming into force of this Act as well as in relation to one made later.

9.—(1) Section 20(1) of this Act shall have effect in relation to any application for admission for treatment and to any guardianship application made before 1st October 1983 with the substitution for the words " six months " of the words " one year ".

(2) Section 20(2) of this Act shall have effect in relation to any authority renewed before 1st October 1983 with the substitution for the words " six months " of the words " one year " and for the words " one year " in both places they occur of the words " two years ".

(3) Where an authority has been renewed on or before 30th September 1983 for a period of two years of which less than 16 months has expired on that date that period shall expire at the end of 18 months from the date on which it began.

10. Section 23(2)(*a*) of this Act shall have effect in relation to a patient liable to be detained in pursuance of an application under section 25 of the Mental Health Act 1959 made before 30th September 1983 as if the reference to the nearest relative of the patient were omitted.

11. Where at any time before 30th September 1983 an application to a Mental Health Review Tribunal has been made by a person who at that time was the patient's nearest relative and the application has not then been determined and by reason of the coming into force of section 26 of this Act that person ceased to be the patient's nearest relative on that date, that person shall nevertheless be treated for the purposes of the application as continuing to be his nearest relative.

12. A person—

(*a*) who was admitted to hospital in pursuance of an application for admission for treatment ; or

(*b*) in respect of whom a guardianship application was accepted ; or

(*c*) in respect of whom a hospital order was made,

before 30th September 1983 may make application to a tribunal under section 66 of this Act in the cases mentioned in subsection (1)(*b*) and (*c*) of that section and under section 69(1)(*b*) of this Act within the period of six months beginning with the day on which he attains the age of 16 years if that period is later than that which would otherwise apply to an application in his case.

13. Subsection (1) of section 68 of this Act does not apply to any patient admitted or transferred to hospital more than six months before 30th September 1983 ; and subsection (2) of that section applies only in relation to a renewal of authority for detention after that date.

14. Section 69(1)(*b*) of this Act shall have effect in relation to patients liable to be detained immediately before 30th September 1983 as if after the words " in respect of a patient " there were inserted the words " admitted to a hospital in pursuance of a hospital order or ". SCH. 5

15. The provisions of this Act which derive from sections 24 to 27 of the Mental Health (Amendment) Act 1982 shall have effect in relation to a transfer direction given before 30th September 1983 as well as in relation to one given later, but where, apart from this paragraph, a transfer direction given before 30th September 1983 would by virtue of the words in section 50(3) of this Act which are derived from section 24(3) of the Mental Health (Amendment) Act 1982 have ceased to have effect before that date it shall cease to have effect on that date. 1982 c. 51.

16. The words in section 42(1) of this Act which derive from the amendment of section 66(1) of the Mental Health Act 1959 by section 28(1) of the Mental Health (Amendment) Act 1982 and the provisions of this Act which derive from section 28(3) of and Schedule 1 to that Act have effect in relation to a restriction order or, as the case may be, a restriction direction made or given before 30th September 1983 as well as in relation to one made or given later, but— 1959 c. 72.

(*a*) any reference to a tribunal under section 66(6) of the said Act of 1959 in respect of a patient shall be treated for the purposes of subsections (1) and (2) of section 77 of this Act in their application to sections 70 and 75(2) of this Act as an application made by him ; and

(*b*) sections 71(5) and 75(1)(*a*) of this Act do not apply where the period in question has expired before 30th September 1983.

17. Section 91(2) of this Act shall not apply in relation to a patient removed from England and Wales before 30th September 1983.

18.—(1) Subsection (3) of section 58 of this Act shall not apply to any treatment given to a patient in the period of six months beginning with 30th September 1983 if—

(*a*) the detention of the patient began before the beginning of that period ; and

(*b*) that subsection has not been complied with in respect of any treatment previously given to him in that period.

(2) The Secretary of State may by order reduce the length of the period mentioned in sub-paragraph (1) above.

19. In the case of a patient who is detained at the time when section 132 of this Act comes into force, the steps required by that section shall be taken as soon as practicable after that time.

20. The repeal by the Mental Health (Amendment) Act 1982 of section 77 of the Mental Health Act 1959 does not affect subsection (4) of that section in its application to a transfer direction given

SCH. 5

before 30th September 1983, but after the coming into force of this Act that subsection shall have effect for that purpose as if for the references to subsection (6) of section 60, Part IV of that Act and the provisions of that Act there were substituted respectively references to section 37(8), Part II and the provisions of this Act.

1959 c. 72.

21. Section 46(3) of this Act shall apply to any direction to which section 71(4) of the Mental Health Act 1959 applied immediately before the commencement of this Act.

22. Notwithstanding the repeal by this Act of section 53(5) of the Mental Health Act 1959, the discharge or variation under that section of an order made under section 52 of that Act shall not affect the validity of anything previously done in pursuance of the order.

23. For any reference in any enactment, instrument, deed or other document to a receiver under Part VIII of the Mental Health Act 1959 there shall be substituted a reference to a receiver under Part VII of this Act.

24. Nothing in this Act shall affect the operation of the proviso to section 107(5) of the Mental Health Act 1959 in relation to a charge created before the commencement of this Act under that section.

25. Nothing in this Act shall affect the operation of subsection (6) of section 112 of the Mental Health Act 1959 in relation to a charge created before the commencement of this Act by virtue of subsection (5) of that section.

26. If the person who is the Master of the Court of Protection at the commencement of this Act has before that time duly taken the oaths required by section 115(1) of the Mental Health Act 1959 he shall not be obliged to take those oaths again by virtue of section 93(3) of this Act.

27. Nothing in this Act shall affect the operation of section 116 of the Mental Health Act 1959 in relation to orders made, directions or authorities given or other instruments issued before the commencement of this Act.

28. References to applications, recommendations, reports and other documents in section 126 of this Act shall include those to which section 125 of the Mental Health Act 1959 applied immediately before the commencement of this Act and references in section 139 of this Act to the acts to which that section applies shall include those to which section 141 of the said Act of 1959 applied at that time.

1930 c. 23.

29. The repeal by the Mental Health Act 1959 of the Mental Treatment Act 1930 shall not affect any amendment effected by section 20 of that Act in any enactment not repealed by the said Act of 1959.

1890 c. 5.
1913 c. 28.

30. The repeal by the Mental Health Act 1959 of the provisions of the Lunacy Act 1890 and of the Mental Deficiency Act 1913 relating to the superannuation of officers or employees shall not affect any arrangements for the payment of allowances or other benefits made in accordance with those provisions and in force on 1st November 1960.

31.—(1) Any patient who immediately before the commencement of this Act was liable to be detained in a hospital or subject to guardianship by virtue of paragraph 9 of Schedule 6 to the Mental Health Act 1959 shall unless previously discharged continue to be so liable for the remainder of the period of his treatment current on 1st November 1960. 1959 c. 72.

(2) The patient may before the expiration of the period of treatment referred to in sub-paragraph (1) above apply to a Mental Health Review Tribunal.

32. Any patient who immediately before the commencement of this Act was liable to be detained or subject to guardianship by virtue of an authority which had been renewed under paragraph 11 of Schedule 6 to the Mental Health Act 1959 shall unless previously discharged continue to be so liable during the period for which that authority was so renewed.

33.—(1) This paragraph applies to patients who at the commencement of this Act are liable to be detained or subject to guardianship by virtue of paragraph 31 or 32 above.

(2) Authority for the detention or guardianship of the patient may on the expiration of the relevant period, unless the patient has previously been discharged, be renewed for a further period of two years.

(3) Sections 20(3) to (10) and 66(1)(*f*) of this Act shall apply in relation to the renewal of authority for the detention or guardianship of a patient under this paragraph as they apply in relation to the renewal of authority for the detention or guardianship of the patient under section 20(2).

(4) In this paragraph " the relevant period " means—

(*a*) in relation to a patient liable to be detained or subject to guardianship by virtue of the said paragraph 31, the period of his treatment referred to in that paragraph ;

(*b*) in relation to a patient detained by virtue of the said paragraph 32, the period for which authority for the detention or guardianship of the patient has been renewed under paragraph 11 of Schedule 6 to the 1959 Act ;

(*c*) in relation to a patient the authority for whose detention or guardianship has previously been renewed under this paragraph, the latest period for which it has been so renewed.

34.—(1) Any patient who is liable to be detained in a hospital or subject to guardianship by virtue of paragraph 31 above shall (subject to the exceptions and modifications specified in the following provisions of this paragraph) be treated as if he had been admitted to the hospital in pursuance of an application for admission for treatment under Part II of this Act or had been received into guardianship in pursuance of a guardianship application under the said Part II and had been so admitted or received as a patient suffering from the form or forms of mental disorder recorded under paragraph

SCH. 5 7 of Schedule 6 to the Mental Health Act 1959 or, if a different form or forms have been specified in a report under section 38 of that Act as applied by that paragraph, the form or forms so specified.

1959 c. 72.

(2) Section 20 of this Act shall not apply in relation to the patient, but the provisions of paragraph 33 above shall apply instead.

(3) Any patient to whom paragraph 9(3) of Schedule 6 to the Mental Health Act 1959 applied at the commencement of this Act who fell within paragraph (*b*) of that paragraph shall cease to be liable to be detained on attaining the age of 25 years unless, during the period of two months ending on the date when he attains that age, the responsible medical officer records his opinion under the following provisions of this Schedule that the patient is unfit for discharge.

(4) If the patient was immediately before 1st November 1960 liable to be detained by virtue of section 6, 8(1) or 9 of the Mental Deficiency Act 1913, the power of discharging him under section 23 of this Act shall not be exercisable by his nearest relative, but his nearest relative may make one application in respect of him to a Mental Health Review Tribunal in any period of 12 months.

1913 c. 28.

35.—(1) The responsible medical officer may record for the purposes of paragraph 34(3) above his opinion that a patient detained in a hospital is unfit for discharge if it appears to the responsible medical officer—

(*a*) that if that patient were released from the hospital he would be likely to act in a manner dangerous to other persons or to himself, or would be likely to resort to criminal activities; or

(*b*) that that patient is incapable of caring for himself and that there is no suitable hospital or other establishment into which he can be admitted and where he would be likely to remain voluntarily;

and where the responsible medical officer records his opinion as aforesaid he shall also record the grounds for his opinion.

(2) Where the responsible medical officer records his opinion under this paragraph in respect of a patient, the managers of the hospital or other persons in charge of the establishment where he is for the time being detained or liable to be detained shall cause the patient to be informed, and the patient may, at any time before the expiration of the period of 28 days beginning with the date on which he is so informed, apply to a Mental Health Review Tribunal.

(3) On any application under sub-paragraph (2) above the tribunal shall, if satisfied that none of the conditions set out in paragraphs (*a*) and (*b*) of sub-paragraph (1) above are fulfilled, direct that the patient be discharged, and subsection (1) of section 72 of this Act shall have effect in relation to the application as if paragraph (*b*) of that subsection were omitted.

36. Any person who immediately before the commencement of this Act was deemed to have been named as the guardian of any patient under paragraph 14 of Schedule 6 to the Mental Health Act 1959

shall be deemed for the purposes of this Act to have been named as the guardian of the patient in an application for his reception into guardianship under Part II of this Act accepted on that person's behalf by the relevant local authority. SCH. 5

37.—(1) This paragraph applies to patients who immediately before the commencement of this Act were transferred patients within the meaning of paragraph 15 of Schedule 6 to the Mental Health Act 1959. 1959 c. 72.

(2) A transferred patient who immediately before the commencement of this Act was by virtue of sub-paragraph (2) of that paragraph treated for the purposes of that Act as if he were liable to be detained in a hospital in pursuance of a direction under section 71 of that Act shall be treated as if he were so liable in pursuance of a direction under section 46 of this Act.

(3) A transferred patient who immediately before the commencement of this Act was by virtue of sub-paragraph (3) of that paragraph treated for the purposes of that Act as if he were liable to be detained in a hospital by virtue of a transfer direction under section 72 of that Act and as if a direction restricting his discharge had been given under section 74 of that Act shall be treated as if he were so liable by virtue of a transfer direction under section 47 of this Act and as if a restriction direction had been given under section 49 of this Act.

(4) Section 84 of this Act shall apply to a transferred patient who was treated by virtue of sub-paragraph (5) of that paragraph immediately before the commencement of this Act as if he had been removed to a hospital under section 89 of that Act as if he had been so removed under the said section 84.

(5) Any person to whom sub-paragraph (6) of that paragraph applied immediately before the commencement of this Act shall be treated for the purposes of this Act as if he were liable to be detained in a hospital in pursuance of a transfer direction given under section 48 of this Act and as if a restriction direction had been given under section 49 of this Act, and he shall be so treated notwithstanding that he is not suffering from a form of mental disorder mentioned in the said section 48.

38. Any patient who immediately before the commencement of this Act was treated by virtue of sub-paragraph (1) of paragraph 16 of Schedule 6 to the Mental Health Act 1959 as if he had been conditionally discharged under section 66 of that Act shall be treated as if he had been conditionally discharged under section 42 of this Act and any such direction as is mentioned in paragraph (*b*) of that sub-paragraph shall be treated as if it had been given under the said section 42.

39. Upon a restriction direction in respect of a patient who immediately before the commencement of this Act was a transferred patient within the meaning of paragraph 15 of Schedule 6 to the Mental Health Act 1959 ceasing to have effect, the responsible medical officer shall record his opinion whether the patient is suffering from mental illness, severe mental impairment, psycho-

SCH. 5 pathic disorder or mental impairment, and references in this Act to the form or forms of mental disorder specified in the relevant application, order or direction shall be construed as including references to the form or forms of mental disorder recorded under this paragraph or under paragraph 17 of the said Schedule 6.

40. A person who immediately before the commencement of this Act was detained by virtue of paragraph 19 of Schedule 6 to the Mental Health Act 1959 may continue to be detained until the expiration of the period of his treatment current on 1st November 1960 or until he becomes liable to be detained or subject to guardianship under this Act, whichever occurs first, and may be so detained in any place in which he might have been detained under that paragraph.

1959 c. 72.

41. Any opinion recorded by the responsible medical officer under the foregoing provisions of this Schedule shall be recorded in such form as may be prescribed by regulations made by the Secretary of State.

42.—(1) In the foregoing provisions of this Schedule—

(*a*) references to the period of treatment of a patient that was current on 1st November 1960 are to the period for which he would have been liable to be detained or subject to guardianship by virtue of any enactment repealed or excluded by the Mental Health Act 1959, or any enactment repealed or replaced by any such enactment as aforesaid, being a period which began but did not expire before that date; and

(*b*) " the responsible medical officer " means—

(i) in relation to a patient subject to guardianship, the medical officer authorised by the local social services authority to act (either generally or in any particular case or for any particular purpose) as the responsible medical officer;

(ii) in relation to any other class of patient, the registered medical practitioner in charge of the treatment of the patient.

(2) Subsection (2) of section 34 of this Act shall apply for the purposes of the foregoing provisions of this Schedule as it applies for the purposes of Part II of this Act.

(3) The sentence or other period of detention of a person who was liable to be detained or subject to guardianship immediately before 1st November 1960 by virtue of an order under section 9 of the Mental Deficiency Act 1913 shall be treated for the purposes of the foregoing provisions of this Schedule as expiring at the end of the period for which that person would have been liable to be detained in a prison or other institution if the order had not been made.

1913 c. 28.

(4) For the purposes of the foregoing provisions of this Schedule, an order sending a person to an institution or placing a person under guardianship made before 9th March 1956 on a petition presented under the Mental Deficiency Act 1913 shall be deemed to be

valid if it was so deemed immediately before the commencement of this Act by virtue of section 148(2) of the Mental Health Act 1959. SCH. 5 1959 c. 72.

43.—(1) Any order or appointment made, direction or authority given, or thing done which by virtue of paragraph 25 of Schedule 6 to the Mental Health Act 1959 had effect immediately before the commencement of this Act as if made, given or done under any provision of Part VIII of that Act shall have effect as if made, given or done under Part VII of this Act.

(2) Where at the commencement of this Act Part VIII of the Mental Health Act 1959 applied in any person's case by virtue of paragraph 25 of Schedule 6 to that Act as if immediately after the commencement of that Act it had been determined that he was a patient within the meaning of the said Part VIII, Part VII of this Act shall apply in his case as if immediately after the commencement of this Act it had been determined that he was a patient within the meaning of the said Part VII.

44. Where a person who immediately before 1st November 1960 was the committee of the estate of a person of unsound mind so found by inquisition was immediately before the commencement of this Act deemed by virtue of paragraph 26 of Schedule 6 to the Mental Health Act 1959 to be a receiver appointed under section 105 of that Act for that person, he shall be deemed to be a receiver appointed under section 99 of this Act for that person and shall continue to have the same functions in relation to that person's property and affairs as were exercisable by him immediately before the commencement of that Act as committee of the estate and references in any document to the committee of the estate of that person shall be construed accordingly.

45. Section 101(1) of this Act shall apply in relation to any disposal of property (within the meaning of that section) of a person living on 1st November 1960, being a disposal effected under the Lunacy Act 1890 as it applies in relation to the disposal of property of a person effected under Part VII of this Act. 1890 c. 5.

46. For the purposes of section 15 of the National Health Service Reorganisation Act 1973 (preservation of certain boards of governors) any provision of this Act which corresponds to a provision amended by that Act shall be treated as if it were such a provision and any reference in any order for the time being in force under that section to such a provision shall have effect as if it were a reference to the corresponding provision of this Act. 1973 c. 32.

Section 134.

SCHEDULE 6

Repeals

Chapter	Short title	Extent of repeal
7 & 8 Eliz. 2. c. 72.	The Mental Health Act 1959.	Sections 1 to 5. Section 10. Section 22. Sections 25 to 35. Sections 37 to 43. Sections 45 to 60. Sections 62 to 68. Sections 70 to 76. Sections 80 and 81. Section 85. Section 87. Sections 89 and 90. Sections 92 to 96. Sections 99 to 119. Sections 121 to 126. Sections 129 and 130. Sections 132 and 133. Sections 135 to 141. In section 144, in subsection (1), paragraph (*b*). Section 145(2). Sections 147 and 148. Section 149(3) to (5). In section 150, the words from " section ten " to " section one hundred and forty one " and from " section one hundred and forty six " to " Schedules ". In section 152, the words from " sections eighty-five " to " Northern Ireland by that section ", from " section one hundred and twenty-nine " to " Schedules " and the words " Part II of the Seventh Schedule; Part II of the Eighth Schedule ". Section 153. Schedule 1. Schedule 3. Schedule 5. Schedule 6, except paragraph 15(4). In Schedule 7, in Part I the entry relating to sections 48 and 49 of the Fines and Recoveries Act 1833 and in Part II the entries relating to the Polish Resettlement Act 1947 and the USA Veterans' Pensions (Administration) Act 1949.

Chapter	Short title	Extent of repeal
1960 c. 61.	The Mental Health (Scotland) Act 1960.	Section 74. In Schedule 4, all the entries relating to the Mental Health Act 1959 except those relating to section 9 and Schedule 7.
1961 (N.I.) c. 15.	The Mental Health Act (Northern Ireland) 1961.	In Schedule 5, paragraphs 1 to 4.
1964 c. 84.	The Criminal Procedure (Insanity) Act 1964.	Section 4(7).
1965 c. 2.	The Administration of Justice Act 1965.	In Schedule 1, the entry relating to the Mental Health Act 1959.
1968 c. 20.	The Courts-Martial (Appeals) Act 1968.	In Schedule 4, the entry relating to the Mental Health Act 1959.
1968 c. 49.	The Social Work (Scotland) Act 1968.	In Schedule 8, paragraphs 48 and 49.
1969 c. 46.	The Family Law Reform Act 1969.	In Schedule 1 the entries relating to the Mental Health Act 1959.
1969 c. 54.	The Children and Young Persons Act 1969.	In Schedule 5, paragraphs 38 to 40.
1969 c. 58.	The Administration of Justice Act 1969.	Sections 17 to 19.
1970 c. 42.	The Local Authority Social Services Act 1970.	In Schedule 1, the entry relating to the Mental Health (Amendment) Act 1982.
1971 c. 23.	The Courts Act 1971.	In Schedule 8, paragraph 38. In Part I of Schedule 9, the entry relating to the Mental Health Act 1959.
1971 c. 77.	The Immigration Act 1971.	In section 30(2), the words from " and accordingly " onwards.
1972 c. 70.	The Local Government Act 1972.	In Schedule 23, in paragraph 9, in sub-paragraph (1) the words " 35, 56(2)(*c*) and 56(3) ", in sub-paragraph (2) the words " 10(1), 22, 27(2), 33, 34, 38(3), 40 to 43, 47(2), 52, 53, 59, 60 " and " 132 ", sub-paragraphs (4), (5) and (6).
1973 c. 29.	The Guardianship Act 1973.	In section 1(8), the words from " and " to the end of the subsection.
1975 c. 37.	The Nursing Homes Act 1975.	In Schedule 1, paragraphs 1 to 4.
1977 c. 45.	The Criminal Law Act 1977.	In Schedule 6, the entry relating to section 130(3) of the Mental Health Act 1959.
1977 c. 49.	The National Health Service Act 1977.	In section 105(3), the words " or the Mental Health Act 1959 ". In Schedule 15, paragraphs 23, 26 to 28, 30, 31 and 33.

SCH. 6

Chapter	Short title	Extent of repeal
1978 c. 29.	The National Health Service (Scotland) Act 1978.	In paragraph 10(*b*) of Schedule 15, the figure " 102 ".
1980 c. 5.	The Child Care Act 1980.	In Schedule 5, paragraphs 13 and 14.
1980 c. 43.	The Magistrates' Courts Act 1980.	In Schedule 7, paragraphs 31 and 32.
1980 c. 53.	The Health Services Act 1980.	In Schedule 1, paragraph 13.
1981 c. 45.	The Forgery and Counterfeiting Act 1981.	Section 11(1).
1981 c. 54.	The Supreme Court Act 1981.	Section 144. In Schedule 5, paragraphs 2 and 3 of the entry relating to the Mental Health Act 1959. In Schedule 6, paragraph 4.
1981 c. 61.	The British Nationality Act 1981.	In section 39(7) the words " section 90 of the Mental Health Act 1959 and ".
1982 c. 51.	The Mental Health (Amendment) Act 1982.	Sections 1 to 33. Sections 35 to 61. In section 63, subsection (1) and in subsection (2) the words from the beginning to " Act and ". Section 64(1), (2), (3), (5) and (6). Section 66. Section 68(2) and (3). Section 69(2), (3), and (4). In section 70(2), the words " sections 35(1) and (2) and 64(6) above extend to Northern Ireland ". Schedule 1. In Schedule 3, in Part I paragraphs 1 to 26, in paragraph 35 sub-paragraph (*a*), paragraphs 40, 42, 45 and 46, in paragraph 50 sub-paragraph (*a*), in paragraph 51 sub-paragraph (*a*), paragraphs 52 to 55, 57 and 58 and Part II. In Schedule 5, paragraphs 2 to 15.

Pilotage Act 1983

1983 CHAPTER 21

An Act to consolidate the Pilotage Acts 1913 and 1936 and certain provisions of the Merchant Shipping Act 1979. [9th May 1983]

BE IT ENACTED by the Queen's most Excellent Majesty, by and with the advice and consent of the Lords Spiritual and Temporal, and Commons, in this present Parliament assembled, and by the authority of the same, as follows:—

PART I

ADMINISTRATION

Introductory

Continuation in being of existing organisation. 1979 c. 39.

1.—(1) There shall continue to be a body corporate called the Pilotage Commission (in this Act referred to as " the Commission ") and the Commission constituted under the Merchant Shipping Act 1979 and in being immediately before the commencement of this Act shall continue in being as the Commission for the purposes of this Act.

1913 c. 31.

(2) Subject to the provisions of any pilotage order made under section 9 of this Act, every pilotage district and every pilotage authority established, constituted or incorporated under the Pilotage Act 1913 and in being immediately before the commencement of this Act shall continue in being as a pilotage district or, as the case may be, a pilotage authority for the purposes of this Act.

PART I

The Pilotage Commission

Constitution of Commission.

2.—(1) The Commission shall consist of not less than 10 and not more than 15 persons appointed by the Secretary of State from among the following, namely—

(*a*) licensed pilots;

(*b*) persons appearing to the Secretary of State to have wide practical experience of the management of ships;

(*c*) persons appearing to the Secretary of State to have wide practical experience of the administration of pilotage services;

(*d*) persons appearing to the Secretary of State to have wide practical experience of the management of docks or harbours;

(*e*) other persons appearing to the Secretary of State to have special knowledge or experience likely to be of value to the Commission in connection with the performance of its functions;

and it shall be the duty of the Secretary of State to appoint as members of the Commission at least one person from each of the categories of persons mentioned in paragraphs (*a*) to (*d*) of this subsection and to appoint one member to be the chairman of the Commission.

(2) It shall be the duty of the Secretary of State—

(*a*) before appointing as a member a person in any category of persons which is mentioned in paragraphs (*a*) to (*d*) of subsection (1) above, to consult on the appointment such persons as the Secretary of State considers are representative of the persons in the United Kingdom in the category in question;

(*b*) before appointing as a member a person in the category of persons which is mentioned in paragraph (*e*) of that subsection, to consult on the appointment—

(i) such persons as the Secretary of State considers are representative of the persons in the United Kingdom in all the categories of persons mentioned in the said paragraphs (*a*) to (*d*), and

(ii) such other persons, if any, as he considers appropriate;

(*c*) before appointing a member to be the chairman of the Commission, to consult on the appointment such persons as the Secretary of State considers are representative of the persons in the United Kingdom in all the categories of persons mentioned in the said paragraphs (*a*) to (*d*).

(3) the provisions of Schedule 1 to this Act shall have effect with respect to the Commission.

(4) It is hereby declared that the Commission is not to be regarded as the servant or agent of the Crown or as enjoying any status, privilege or immunity of the Crown or as exempt from any tax, duty, rate, levy or other charge whatsoever, whether general or local, and that its property is not to be regarded as property of or held on behalf of the Crown.

(5) In Part II of Schedule 1 to the House of Commons Disqualification Act 1975, after the entry relating to the Performing Right Tribunal there shall be inserted the words " The Pilotage Commission " ; and in Part II of Schedule 1 to the Northern Ireland Assembly Disqualification Act 1975, after the entry relating to the said Tribunal there shall be inserted the words aforesaid.

1975 c. 24.

1975 c. 25.

Payments by pilotage authorities to Commission.

3.—(1) The Commission may make a scheme or schemes requiring pilotage authorities to pay to the Commission from time to time, in respect of the expenses of the Commission in performing its functions, such sums as are determined under the scheme or schemes ; and such a scheme—

(*a*) may provide for the payment of different sums by different authorities ;

(*b*) must contain provision requiring the Commission to indicate how the sums to be payable under the scheme for periods determined under it are related to the Commission's estimates of its expenditure during those periods ;

(*c*) may be revoked or varied by a subsequent scheme made by virtue of this subsection ;

but a scheme made by virtue of this subsection shall not come into force unless it has been confirmed by the Secretary of State.

(2) It shall be the duty of the Commission, immediately after it has submitted such a scheme to the Secretary of State for confirmation—

(*a*) to send a copy of the scheme to each pilotage authority by which sums are to be payable under the scheme ; and

(*b*) to publish in a manner approved by the Secretary of State a notice which—

(i) states that the scheme has been so submitted, and

(ii) specifies a place where a copy of the scheme may be obtained free of charge by any licensed pilot, any harbour authority and any shipowner, and

(iii) states that any person mentioned in paragraph (*a*) or sub-paragraph (ii) above and any

PART I

person appearing to the Secretary of State to represent any persons so mentioned may, within a period specified in the notice of not less than 42 days beginning with the date of first publication of the notice, object to the scheme by giving to the Secretary of State a statement in writing setting out his objections to the scheme and the reasons for the objections.

(3) The Secretary of State may, after considering any statement of objections and of reasons for objections to a scheme which is given to him by a person and within the period mentioned in paragraph (*b*)(iii) of subsection (2) above, by order confirm the scheme either without modification or, after consulting the Commission about any modifications he proposes to make to the scheme, with such modifications as he thinks fit; but the Secretary of State shall not have power to make a modification of a scheme which would increase the amount of any sum payable in pursuance of the scheme.

(4) Any sum payable to the Commission by a pilotage authority in pursuance of a scheme made by virtue of this section may be recovered by the Commission in any court of competent jurisdiction.

(5) In this section "modifications" includes additions, omissions and alterations.

Other financial provisions relating to Commission.

4.—(1) The Commission may borrow in sterling any sum which it requires for the purpose of carrying out its functions, but the aggregate amount of the principal of sums borrowed by the Commission which is outstanding at any time shall not exceed £200,000 or such larger amount, not exceeding £500,000, as the Secretary of State may specify by order.

(2) The Secretary of State may out of money provided by Parliament lend to the Commission, with the consent of the Treasury and on such terms as he may determine with the consent of the Treasury, any sum which the Commission has power to borrow in pursuance of subsection (1) above; and any sum received by the Secretary of State by way of interest on or the payment of a loan made by virtue of this subsection shall be paid into the Consolidated Fund.

(3) It shall be the duty of the Commission—

(*a*) to keep proper accounts and proper records in relation to the accounts; and

(*b*) to prepare in respect of the period of 12 months ending with the 31st March in each year a statement of those accounts in such form as the Secretary of State may direct with the approval of the Treasury; and

PART I

(c) to cause the accounts kept and the statement prepared for each such period to be audited by auditors appointed by the Commission with the approval of the Secretary of State.

(4) A person shall not be qualified to be appointed as an auditor in pursuance of subsection (3) above unless he is a member of one or more of the following bodies—

the Institute of Chartered Accountants in England and Wales;

the Institute of Chartered Accountants of Scotland;

the Association of Certified Accountants;

the Institute of Chartered Accountants in Ireland;

any other body of accountants established in the United Kingdom and for the time being recognised for the purposes of section 161(1)(*a*) of the Companies Act 1948 by the Secretary of State; 1948 c. 38.

but a Scottish firm may be so appointed if each of the partners in the firm is qualified to be so appointed.

Functions of Commission

General functions of Commission.

5.—(1) It shall be the duty of the Commission to give to the Secretary of State, and to pilotage authorities, dock and harbour authorities, pilots and shipowners, such advice as the Commission considers appropriate for any of the following purposes, namely—

(*a*) securing by means of pilotage the safety of navigation in ports of, and waters off the coasts of, the United Kingdom;

(*b*) ensuring that efficient pilotage services are provided for those ports and waters and, in particular, that suitable equipment is provided in connection with those services;

(*c*) ensuring that the terms of service of pilots providing those services are fair; and

(*d*) promoting standards, in the qualifications which entitle persons to apply for pilots' licences and in the training of pilots, which are uniform for areas which the Commission considers are of the same kind.

(2) The Secretary of State may by order confer on the Commission such functions, in addition to the functions conferred on the Commission by this Act, as he considers appropriate for any of the purposes mentioned in subsection (1) above.

(3) Without prejudice to the generality of subsection (2) above, an order in pursuance of that subsection may in particular provide for the making of schemes under which payments may be

PART I

made by the Commission for the purpose of compensating pilots and their assistants for loss of employment or reductions in earnings suffered by them in consequence of changes in the organisation of pilotage services or of the granting of pilotage certificates to nationals of member States of the Economic Community other than the United Kingdom.

(4) The Commission shall have power to do anything which is calculated to facilitate, or is conducive or incidental to, the performance of any of its functions.

Review of pilotage services and non-compulsory pilotage areas.

6.—(1) It shall be the duty of the Commission—

(*a*) to keep under consideration the organisation of pilotage services at ports of, and waters off the coasts of, the United Kingdom, to consider suggestions for changes in the organisation of those services which are made to the Commission by persons appearing to the Commission to be interested in the organisation of them and to make proposals for such changes in the organisation of those services as the Commission considers appropriate;

(*b*) without prejudice to the generality of paragraph (*a*) above, to consider what numbers of pilots are needed in order to provide efficient pilotage services in pilotage districts and to make to the pilotage authorities concerned such recommendations about the numbers as the Commission considers appropriate; and

(*c*) to carry out such investigations as the Commission considers appropriate in order to ascertain whether pilotage should be made compulsory at places in, or off the coasts of, the United Kingdom where it is not compulsory and to make proposals for pilotage to be made compulsory at such places as the Commission considers appropriate in consequence of the investigations.

(2) If the Commission considers that a pilotage order or byelaws should be made for the purpose of giving effect to such a proposal as is mentioned in paragraph (*a*) or paragraph (*c*) of subsection (1) above and that an application for such an order or for confirmation of byelaws which are appropriate for that purpose has not been made to the Secretary of State by a pilotage authority affected by the proposal within a period which the Commission considers reasonable in the circumstances, the Commission may apply to the Secretary of State for a pilotage order for that purpose or, as the case may be, may exercise for that purpose the power to make byelaws which is conferred on the pilotage authority by section 15(1) of this Act.

PART I

(3) It shall be the duty of the Commission before it performs a function conferred on it by subsection (1) above, to consult such persons in the United Kingdom as the Commission considers are likely to be affected by the performance of the function or to consult persons appearing to the Commission to represent those persons.

Pilots' pension and compensation schemes.

7.—(1) The Commission may establish and maintain a scheme for the payment of pensions and other benefits to and in respect of pilots and former pilots.

(2) Such a scheme may include provision for the assets and liabilities of any pilots' benefit fund established by virtue of section 17(1)(*j*) of the Pilotage Act 1913 or section 15(1)(*i*) of this Act to become, with the consent of the managers of the fund, assets and liabilities of the scheme instead of assets and liabilities of the fund; and the managers of any such fund shall have power to give their consent for the purposes of this subsection and to wind up the fund to which their consent relates. 1913 c. 31.

(3) The Commission may establish and maintain a scheme under which payments may be made for the purpose of compensating pilots and their assistants for loss of employment or reductions in earnings suffered by them in consequence of incidents over which they have no control.

Annual report.

8. It shall be the duty of the Commission—

(*a*) to prepare and publish, as soon as possible after the 31st March in each year, a report on the performance of its functions during the period of 12 months ending with that date;

(*b*) to include in the report a copy of the statement of accounts prepared in respect of that period in pursuance of section 4(3)(*b*) of this Act and a copy of the auditors' report on the statement and on the accounts to which the statement relates; and

(*c*) to deliver a copy of the report to the Secretary of State before it is published;

and it shall be the duty of the Secretary of State to lay before Parliament copies of each report of which he receives a copy in pursuance of this section.

Pilotage orders

Power of Secretary of State to make pilotage orders.

9.—(1) The Secretary of State may, by order made under this Act (in this Act referred to as a pilotage order),—

(*a*) make such rearrangement of pilotage districts and pilotage authorities as he thinks necessary or expedient;

PART I

(*b*) establish new pilotage districts and new pilotage authorities and abolish existing pilotage districts and existing pilotage authorities in cases where it appears to him necessary or expedient;

(*c*) define the limits of pilotage districts;

(*d*) provide for the incorporation of any pilotage authority, and make such alteration in the constitution of any pilotage authority with reference to their powers and duties as pilotage authority;

(*e*) make such provisions as to the appointment of committees (including, if the Secretary of State thinks fit, the appointment of persons not members of the authority), and, as to the relations between the authority and the committee, as he thinks necessary or expedient;

(*f*) empower a pilotage authority to delegate to a committee of the authority any of their powers and duties, and provide, if it appears necessary or desirable, that the decisions of the committee on questions so delegated shall not require confirmation by the pilotage authority;

(*g*) make such provision for the direct representation of pilots and shipowners on any pilotage authority or committee of a pilotage authority as the Secretary of State thinks necessary or expedient;

(*h*) in cases where a pilotage authority have powers and duties relating to matters other than pilotage, provide for their accounts as pilotage authority being kept separate from their accounts in relation to those other matters;

(*i*) make provision as to the circumstances in which pilotage in a pilotage district is to be compulsory, subject to provision being also made, in a case where pilotage ceases to be compulsory in connection with the rearrangement of the district, for the payment of compensation to the pilots concerned for any loss or damage which may be incurred by them in consequence of such rearrangement;

(*j*) authorise, where it appears to the Secretary of State to be expedient, any pilotage authority to make byelaws providing for the grant of certificates (in this Act referred to as deep sea certificates) certifying that persons are qualified to act as pilots of ships for any part of the sea or channels outside the district of any pilotage authority, so, however, that a pilot holding such a certificate shall not be entitled to supersede any other person as pilot of a ship;

(*k*) provide that any Act (other than this Act), order, charter, custom, byelaw, regulation, or provision shall, so far as it relates to pilotage, cease to have effect within any pilotage district or as respects any pilotage authority, but may re-enact the whole or any part thereof so far as is not inconsistent with the provisions of this Act; PART I

(*l*) provide for compensation being paid to any pilots for any loss or damage which may be incurred by them in consequence of any order abolishing or rearranging any pilotage districts;

(*m*) make any provisions which appear to the Secretary of State to be necessary or expedient for the purpose of giving full effect to the order.

(2) A pilotage order in dealing with any Act, order, charter, custom, byelaw, regulation, or provision shall not provide for abolishing or diminishing any power of a pilotage authority to acquire, own, hire, build, renew, maintain, or work pilot boats.

(3) Provision shall be made by pilotage order for the direct representation of pilots either on the pilotage authority or on the committee of the pilotage authority of any district where there are not less than six licensed pilots if a majority of the pilots licensed for the district signify in writing to the Secretary of State that they desire such representation, and, where such provision is made, provision shall also be made for the representation of shipowners on the authority or committee, as the case may be.

(4) A pilotage order establishing a pilotage authority for any pilotage district shall provide for any dock or harbour authority wishing to be represented on the pilotage authority to be so represented if—

(*a*) the dock or harbour authority has jurisdiction in the district, and

(*b*) the authority was represented on the pilotage authority for the district in existence on 7th March 1913 (the date of the passing of the Pilotage Act 1913). 1913 c. 31.

(5) A pilotage order shall not be made by the Secretary of State except—

(*a*) on an application in writing by any person interested in the pilotage of any pilotage district or in the operation of the laws relating to pilotage in that district or the administration of those laws; or

(*b*) on an application by the Commission made under section 6(2) of this Act.

(6) Until such day as the Secretary of State may by order

PART I

appoint, paragraph (*c*) of subsection (1) above shall have effect as if for that paragraph there were substituted—

"(*c*) define the limits of pilotage districts distinguishing as respects any pilotage district in part of which pilotage is compulsory and in part of which pilotage is not compulsory, the part of the district in which pilotage is compulsory;".

(7) Different days may be appointed under subsection (6) above for different purposes.

Procedure connected with making and coming into force of pilotage orders.

10.—(1) The Secretary of State may by regulations make provision as to the notices to be given, the other steps to be taken and the payments to be made in connection with an application for a pilotage order, and the regulations must include provision for notice of the application to be advertised and for any person who objects to the application and who appears to the Secretary of State to have a substantial interest in the pilotage services in the area to which the application relates to be given an opportunity of making representations in writing to the Secretary of State about the application.

(2) Where the Secretary of State makes a pilotage order in consequence of such an application, then—

(*a*) if before the order is made either—

(i) no objection to the application has been made in accordance with regulations made by virtue of subsection (1) above, or

(ii) every objection so made to the application has been withdrawn,

the statutory instrument containing the order shall be subject to annulment in pursuance of a resolution of either House of Parliament; and

(*b*) if an objection so made to the application has not been withdrawn before the order is made the order shall be subject to special parliamentary procedure, and the Statutory Orders (Special Procedure) Act 1945 shall have effect accordingly but as if—

1945 c. 18.

(i) sections 2 and 10(2) of that Act (which relate to preliminary proceedings) were omitted, and

(ii) that Act extended to Northern Ireland and, in the application of section 7(3) of that Act to Northern Ireland, for any reference to a local authority and the Secretary of State there were substituted respectively a reference to a district council and the Department of the Environment for Northern Ireland.

PART I

(3) Any Act confirming a pilotage order made under this Act may be repealed, altered or amended by any subsequent pilotage order made under this Act.

Powers of Pilotage Authorities

General powers of pilotage authorities.

11. Subject to the provisions of this Act, a pilotage authority may do all such things as may be necessary or expedient for the performance of their powers and duties.

Licensing of pilots.

12.—(1) Subject to the provisions of this Act, a pilotage authority may license pilots for their district.

(2) The required fee shall be payable on the examination for a pilot's licence and on the grant, renewal or alteration of any such licence.

In this subsection the " required fee " means the fee fixed by byelaw made in pursuance of paragraph (*o*) of section 15(1) of this Act.

Employment of pilots by pilotage authorities.

13.—(1) A pilotage authority shall have and be deemed always to have had—

(*a*) power to employ pilots licensed by the authority and, as assistants for such pilots, persons who are or are not pilots so licensed; and

(*b*) power to make arrangements with shipowners and other persons under which payments are made to the authority in respect of services of persons employed by the authority by virtue of paragraph (*a*) above.

(2) If a majority of the persons who for the time being hold pilots' licences for the district of a pilotage authority and are not employed by the authority resolve that the authority shall not be entitled to exercise the power mentioned in subsection (1) above to employ, as pilots or assistants, any pilots licensed by the authority, the authority shall not be entitled to exercise that power until the resolution is revoked by a majority of such persons as aforesaid ; and

(*a*) the Secretary of State may by regulations make provision with respect to the passing and revocation of resolutions for the purposes of this subsection and with respect to records of resolutions and of the revocation of them ; but

(*b*) nothing in the preceding provisions of this subsection shall affect any contract of employment in force when a resolution is passed in pursuance of those provisions.

Pilotage charges.

14.—(1) A pilotage authority may make in the prescribed form a list of the charges to be paid, by persons who make use

PART I

in the district of the authority of the services of a pilot licensed by the authority, for the services of the pilot and in respect of the pilotage services of the district; and without prejudice to the generality of the preceding provisions of this subsection—

(*a*) the charges for the services of a pilot may be or include charges in respect of an assistant for the pilot and in respect of the fees and expenses of the pilot and any assistant of his during periods spent outside the district of the authority in anticipation or in consequence of his activities as a pilot or assistant;

(*b*) the charges for the services of a pilot, in a case where the master of the relevant ship has not complied with the requirements of byelaws made under this Act by the authority about requests for pilots, may be greater than, but not more than one and a half times, the charges for those services in a case where the master has so complied;

(*c*) the charges in respect of the pilotage services of the district may be or include charges in respect of the cost of providing, maintaining and operating pilot boats for the district, charges in respect of other costs of providing and maintaining the pilotage organisation provided by the authority and charges in respect of sums payable or paid by the authority to the Commission by virtue of section 3 of this Act; and

(*d*) the list may provide for the payment of different charges in connection with different circumstances, may provide for a charge which is not paid within a prescribed period after it becomes due to be increased periodically in accordance with a prescribed scale and may alter or cancel any previous list made by the authority by virtue of this section.

(2) The charges specified in a list made in pursuance of this section shall not be payable in respect of any use of the services of a pilot before the expiration of the period of 28 days beginning with the day when the list was first published in the prescribed manner; and if at any time after that day an objection to the list is made in writing to the Commission in accordance with subsection (3) below the Commission may, after giving the authority which made the list an opportunity of commenting in writing to the Commission on the objection and considering any comments then made by the authority, serve in a prescribed manner on the authority a notice in writing cancelling the list or altering the list in a manner specified in the notice and providing that the cancellation or alteration shall have effect on and after a day so specified which is not earlier than the date of service of the notice.

(3) An objection to a list must—

(*a*) be made by—

(i) a majority of the pilots licensed for the district to which the list relates by the authority which made the list or, if the objection is to a particular charge in the list, by a majority of those pilots who are customarily employed in providing the services to which the charge relates, or

(ii) three or more persons who are owners of ships which are customarily navigated in the district of the authority, or

(iii) a dock or harbour authority whose area lies within the district of the authority, or

(iv) any other person appearing to the Commission to have a substantial interest in the list; and

(*b*) be so made on one or more of the following grounds, namely—

(i) that one or more of the charges in the list should not be payable or should not be payable in a case specified in the objection;

(ii) that the amount of one or more of the charges in the list should be reduced or increased or should be reduced or increased in a case so specified.

(4) The alteration or cancellation of a list made in pursuance of this section shall not affect charges payable in pursuance of the list in respect of the use of the services of a pilot before the alteration or cancellation took effect.

(5) If the Secretary of State directs the Commission to give to an authority by which a list has been made in pursuance of this section a notice in writing cancelling the list, or altering it in a manner specified in the direction, with effect from a day so specified, it shall be the duty of the Commission to comply with the direction.

(6) It shall be the duty of an authority which has made a list in pursuance of this section to send copies of the list to the Secretary of State and the Commission and, unless it has been cancelled, to keep copies of the list, or if it has been altered of the altered list, available during office hours at the principal office of the authority for inspection free of charge and purchase at a reasonable price by members of the public.

(7) In this section " prescribed " means prescribed by regulations made by the Secretary of State.

Power of pilotage authorities to make byelaws.

15.—(1) A pilotage authority may by byelaws made under this Act—

(*a*) determine the qualification in respect of age, physical fitness, time of service, local knowledge, skill, character,

PART I

and otherwise to be required from persons applying to be licensed by them as pilots, provide for the examination of such persons, and fix the term for which a licence is to be in force, and the conditions under which a licence may be renewed ;

(*b*) fix the limit (if any) on the number of pilots to be licensed, and provide for the method in which and the conditions under which the list of pilots is to be filled up ;

(*c*) provide generally for the good government of pilots licensed by the authority, and of apprentices, and in particular for ensuring their good conduct and constant attendance to and effectual performance of their duties, whether at sea or on shore ;

(*d*) determine the system to be adopted with respect to the supply and employment of pilots, and provide, so far as necessary, for the approval, licensing, and working of pilot boats in the district, and for the establishment and regulation of pilot boat companies ;

(*e*) provide for the punishment of any breach of any byelaws made by the authority for the good government of pilots or apprentices by the imposition of fines not exceeding—

(i) in England and Wales and in Scotland, £20 ;

(ii) in Northern Ireland, £50.

Such fines to be recoverable as fines are recoverable under the Merchant Shipping Acts 1894 to 1981 ;

(*f*) provide for the collection (either before or after the performance of services to which they relate) and for the distribution of pilotage charges ;

(*g*) if, and so far as, it appears to the authority to be generally desired by the pilots concerned, provide for the pooling of pilotage charges earned by the licensed pilots or by any class of pilots in the district ;

(*h*) provide for a deduction to be made from any sums received by pilots of any contributions required for any fund established for the payment of pensions or other benefits to pilots, their widows or children (in this Act referred to as a pilots' benefit fund) ;

(*i*) establish, either alone or in conjunction with any other pilotage authority, pilots' benefit funds, and provide for the direct payment to any such fund of any contributions by pilots towards the fund, or of any part of the ordinary receipts of the pilotage authority, and also for the administration of any such fund and for the conditions of participation in any such fund ;

PART I

(*j*) provide for the method of conducting the examination of masters and first mates applying for pilotage certificates so as to maintain a proper standard of efficiency;

(*k*) prohibit the grant of pilotage certificates to masters or first mates who do not hold at least such certificate issued under the Merchant Shipping Act 1970 as may be specified in the byelaws; 1970 c. 36.

(*l*) provide that a pilotage certificate shall not be renewed without re-examination unless the master or first mate has made not less than a specified number of visits to the port as master or first mate of any ship in respect of which the certificate is granted;

(*m*) if the pilotage authority are an authority authorised to grant deep sea certificates by virtue of a pilotage order made with reference to that authority, provide for the grant of deep sea certificates;

(*n*) apply, with any necessary modifications, any byelaws made under this section for the good government of pilots and the punishment of any breach of any such byelaws to masters and mates holding pilotage certificates;

(*o*) fix the fees payable on the examination for a pilot's licence, or for a pilotage certificate, and on the grant, renewal, or alteration of any such licence or certificate;

(*p*) require the owners of ships, whose masters or first mates hold pilotage certificates, to contribute towards the pilot fund or account of the pilotage district, and require the holders of such certificates to make a periodical return to them of the pilotage services rendered by them; but the contribution so required from an owner shall not exceed such proportion of the pilotage charges which would have been payable in respect of the ship if the master or first mate had not held a pilotage certificate, as may be fixed by the Secretary of State;

(*q*) provide for any matter for which provision is to be made or may be made under this Act by byelaw.

(2) Nothing in paragraph (*e*) of subsection (1) above prejudices the powers of a pilotage authority under this Act to revoke or suspend a licence in the case of any breach of any byelaw made by the authority.

(3) A byelaw shall not take effect unless it has been submitted to the Secretary of State and confirmed by him with or without modifications.

(4) Notice of any byelaw proposed to be submitted for confirmation under this section shall, before it is so submitted, be published in such manner as the Secretary of State directs.

PART I

(5) A byelaw may make different provision for different circumstances.

Power of Secretary of State as respects byelaws.

16.—(1) If at any port either—

(*a*) a majority of the licensed pilots belonging to the port; or

(*b*) not less than 6 persons, being masters, owners, or insurers of vessels using the port; or

(*c*) a dock or harbour authority not being the pilotage authority; or

(*d*) the Commission;

object to any byelaw in force at the port, or desire that any byelaw should be in force at the port which is not in force therein, they may make a representation to the Secretary of State to that effect.

(2) If (after he has given the pilotage authority concerned and, if he thinks fit, any other persons an opportunity to make representations on the subject) the representation appears to the Secretary of State reasonable, he may by order—

(*a*) revoke, vary or add to any byelaw to which the representation objects, or

(*b*) require the pilotage authority concerned to submit to him for confirmation a byelaw for the purpose of giving effect to the representation.

(3) Any byelaw revoked by any such order shall cease to have effect, and any byelaw to which additions are made or which is varied or added to, shall have effect with the variations or additions made by the order.

(4) If a pilotage authority fail to submit to the Secretary of State for confirmation a byelaw in accordance with an order made under this section, the Secretary of State may treat the byelaw which he has required the pilotage authority to submit to him as a byelaw submitted to him by the authority, and confirm it accordingly, and the byelaw so confirmed shall have effect as if it had been made and confirmed in accordance with this Act.

Other provisions relating to pilotage authorities

Licensing of pilots by pilotage authority not to involve any liability.

17. The grant or renewal of a licence to a pilot by a pilotage authority under the powers given to them by this Act does not impose any liability on the authority for any loss occasioned by any act or default of the pilot.

Receipts and expenses of pilotage authority.

18.—(1) All receipts of a pilotage authority in their capacity as such (other than any money received by them on behalf of and paid over to any pilot, or if the authority administer a pilots' benefit fund, any sums received by them as direct payments for that fund), shall be paid into a separate fund or account, to be called the pilot fund or account of the pilotage district. **Part I**

(2) All expenses incurred by a pilotage authority in the exercise of their powers or performance of their duties as such authority shall be paid out of their pilot fund or account, and, except so far as may be provided to the contrary by byelaw, the balance remaining after the payment of those expenses shall in each year be applied for the purposes of any pilots' benefit fund established in the district and so far as not required for that purpose shall be applied for the benefit of pilots in such manner as may be determined by the pilotage authority with the approval of the Secretary of State.

(3) A separate account shall be kept by any pilotage authority who administer a pilots' benefit fund of all moneys received by them as payments to that fund, or for the benefit of that fund, and money standing to the credit of that account shall not be applicable to any purpose other than the purposes of the fund.

(4) Nothing in this section shall prevent a pilotage authority which owns or hires the pilot boats for the district from keeping a separate account in respect of such boats.

Returns and statements of accounts of pilotage authorities.

19.—(1) Every pilotage authority shall deliver triennially or, if the Secretary of State so directs, at shorter intervals, to the Commission, in the form and at the time required by the Secretary of State, returns giving such particulars as the Secretary of State may by order prescribe with respect to pilotage in their district.

(2) Every pilotage authority shall in addition furnish annually to the Commission, at such time as the Secretary of State directs, a statement of their accounts in the form prescribed by the Secretary of State, duly audited, including a statement of the average gross and net earnings of pilots during the past year, and, where the authority administer a pilots' benefit fund, the separate accounts of that fund, including particulars of the investments if any.

(3) Every pilotage authority shall allow the Commission or any person appointed by the Commission for the purpose, to inspect any books or documents in the possession of that authority relating to any matter in respect of which a return is required to be delivered or a statement is required to be furnished under this section.

(4) If a pilotage authority refuse or fail without reasonable cause to deliver any return or furnish any statement to the Commission in accordance with this section, Her Majesty may by Order in Council suspend the pilotage authority for such time as Her Majesty may direct, and thereupon the Secretary of State shall by order direct that, in the meantime, the powers of the

PART I

authority shall be exercised, and the duties of the authority shall be performed by such person as he may appoint for the purpose.

(5) It shall be the duty of the Commission to send to the Secretary of State and to publish in such manner as the Commission thinks fit, copies of the returns and statements received by the Commission under this section.

(6) It shall be the duty of the Secretary of State to lay before Parliament copies of any document he receives in pursuance of subsection (5) above.

Masters' and First Mates' Certificates

Grant of masters' and first mates' certificates by pilotage authorities.

20.—(1) Subject to subsection (2) below, a pilotage authority may grant a certificate (in this Act referred to as a pilotage certificate) to any person who is bona fide the master or first mate of any ship if that person applies for such a certificate, and if, after examination, they are satisfied that, having regard to his skill, experience, and local knowledge, he is capable of piloting the ship of which he is master or first mate within their district.

(2) A pilotage certificate shall not be granted—

(*a*) to the master or first mate of a ship unless he is a—

(i) Commonwealth citizen or,

(ii) citizen of the Republic of Ireland or,

(iii) national of a member State of the Economic Community other than the United Kingdom,

and the ship is registered under the law of a member State of the Economic Community;

(*b*) in any district where a byelaw is in force prohibiting the grant of pilotage certificates to masters or first mates who do not hold at least such certificate issued under the Merchant Shipping Act 1970 as is specified in the byelaw except to a master or first mate holding a certificate so specified;

1970 c. 36.

(*c*) in any district where a byelaw is in force prohibiting the grant of a pilotage certificate in respect of a vessel of a description specified in the byelaw, in respect of such a vessel.

(3) A pilotage certificate shall be in a form approved for the time being by the Secretary of State, and shall contain (in addition to any other particulars which may be required) the name of the person to whom the certificate is granted, the name and draught of water of the ship or ships in respect of which it is granted, the limits of the district in respect of which the certificate is granted, and the date on which it was granted.

PART I

(4) A pilotage certificate shall not be in force for more than a year from the date on which it is granted, but may, if held by the master or first mate of a ship, be renewed annually by the pilotage authority, subject to the provisions of any byelaw made by that authority as to re-examination.

(5) A pilotage certificate may be granted so as to extend to more than one ship belonging to the same owner, while the master or first mate is bona fide acting as master or first mate of any such ship, provided that they are ships of substantially the same class and registered as mentioned in paragraph *(a)* of subsection (2) above.

(6) A pilotage authority may, on the application of the master or first mate of a ship, alter his pilotage certificate so as to relate to any other ship or ships of a not substantially greater draught of water or tonnage than that to which the certificate formerly related, to which the master or first mate may be transferred, or so as to cover any ships of substantially the same class and which are registered as mentioned in paragraph *(a)* of subsection (2) above and belong to the same owner as the ships to which the certificate already relates.

(7) A pilotage authority may, for the purposes of this section, treat ships which are shown to their satisfaction to be bona fide under the management of the same person as manager, managing owner, demisee, or time charterer, as being ships owned by that person.

(8) The required fee shall be payable on the examination for a pilotage certificate and on the grant, renewal or alteration of any such certificate.

In this subsection the " required fee " means the fee fixed by byelaw made in pursuance of paragraph *(o)* of section 15(1) of this Act.

Refusal and revocation of pilotage certificates.

21.—(1) A pilotage authority shall not be obliged to grant a pilotage certificate if the Commission considers—

(a) that, without the certificate, the number of persons holding pilots' licences for the authority's district and the number of persons holding pilotage certificates for the district are appropriate for the district ; or

(b) that, if the certificate were granted, functions by virtue of it would probably be performed wholly or mainly in a particular area in the authority's district, and that, without the certificate, the number of persons holding pilots' licences by virtue of which functions are performed wholly or mainly in that area and the number

PART I

of persons holding pilotage certificates by virtue of which functions are so performed are adequate for the area.

(2) If—

(*a*) a majority of the persons holding pilots' licences for the district of a pilotage authority; or

(*b*) a majority of the persons who hold pilots' licences for the district of a pilotage authority and appear to the Commission to perform functions by virtue of the licences wholly or mainly within a particular area in the district,

make representations in writing to the Secretary of State, within the period of two months beginning with the day when a pilotage certificate is granted by the authority, requesting him to revoke the certificate—

(i) on the ground, in the case of a request by a majority mentioned in paragraph (*a*) above, that apart from the holder of the certificate the number of persons holding pilots' licences for the district and the number of persons holding pilotage certificates for the district are in the opinion of the Commission appropriate for the district; or

(ii) on the ground, in the case of a request by a majority mentioned in paragraph (*b*) above, that in the opinion of the Commission the holder of the certificate is likely to perform functions by virtue of the certificate wholly or mainly within the area in question and that, apart from him, the number of persons who hold pilots' licences by virtue of which functions are in the opinion of the Commission performed wholly or mainly in that area and the number of persons who hold pilotage certificates by virtue of which functions are in the opinion of the Commission so performed are in the opinion of the Commission appropriate for that area,

the Secretary of State may, after giving to the holder of the certificate and the authority an opportunity of making representations in writing to him about the request, give to the holder a notice in writing revoking the certificate; and the certificate shall cease to have effect when the holder receives the notice.

(3) The Secretary of State may, by an order made after the expiration of the period of ten years beginning on 4th July

1979 c. 39. 1980 (the date on which section 10 of the Merchant Shipping Act 1979 came into force), repeal subsections (1) and (2) above and subsection (3) of section 25 of this Act (which subsection makes provision consequential on subsections (1) and (2) of this section); and such an order may contain such transitional provisions as the Secretary of State considers are appropriate in connection with the repeal.

PART I

Provision with respect to foreign certificates of competency.

22. For the purposes of this Act, references to certificates issued under the Merchant Shipping Act 1970 shall be deemed to include references to any certificate of competency granted by the government of a foreign country, being a certificate of a class approved by the Secretary of State for the purpose.

1970 c. 36.

Supplementary Provisions as to Licences and Certificates

Form of pilot's licence, and production and return of licence to pilotage authority.

23.—(1) A pilot's licence shall be in a form approved for the time being by the Secretary of State.

(2) A licensed pilot shall, when required by the pilotage authority by whom the licence has been granted, produce his licence to the authority, and, in a case where his licence is revoked or suspended, shall deliver up his licence to the authority.

(3) On the death of a licensed pilot, the person into whose hands his licence comes shall without delay transmit it to the pilotage authority by whom it was granted.

(4) If any licensed pilot or other person fails without reasonable excuse, to comply with the requirements of this section, he shall be liable on summary conviction in respect of each offence to a fine not exceeding—

(*a*) in England and Wales and in Scotland, level 3 on the standard scale,

(*b*) in Northern Ireland, £200.

Suspension or revocation of a pilot's licence or a pilotage certificate.

24.—(1) A pilotage authority may suspend or revoke any pilot's licence or any pilotage certificate granted by them if it appears to them, after giving the holder thereof an opportunity of being heard,—

(*a*) that he has been guilty of any offence under this Act, or

(*b*) that he has been guilty of any breach of any byelaw made by the authority, or

(*c*) that he has been guilty of any other misconduct affecting his capability as a pilot, or

(*d*) that he has failed in or neglected his duty as a pilot, or

(*e*) that he has become incompetent to act as pilot;

and a licence or certificate, if so revoked, shall cease to have effect, and, if so suspended, shall cease to have effect for the period for which it is suspended.

(2) In any case where pilots are directly represented on a committee of a pilotage authority, that committee may, until a pilotage order is made regulating the relations between the authority and the committee, exercise the powers conferred on a pilotage authority by this section with respect to pilots' licences as though they were the pilotage authority.

PART I

Appeal to Secretary of State by pilot, master or first mate, against action of pilotage authority.

25.—(1) If a complaint is made to the Secretary of State that a pilotage authority have—

(*a*) without reasonable cause refused or failed to examine any candidate for a pilot's licence, or a master or first mate for a pilotage certificate, or to grant such a licence or certificate after examination; or

(*b*) conducted any examination for a pilot's licence or a pilotage certificate improperly or unfairly; or

(*c*) imposed conditions on the granting of a pilot's licence or a pilotage certificate which they have no power to impose or which are unreasonable ; or

(*d*) without reasonable cause refused or failed to renew a pilotage certificate, or, having obtained possession of any such certificate, refused or failed to return it; or

(*e*) without reasonable cause suspended or revoked a pilotage certificate; or

(*f*) in any other manner failed properly to perform their duties under this Act with respect to the matters above-mentioned in this section, or improperly exercised any of their powers under this Act with respect to those matters;

the Secretary of State shall consider the complaint, and if he is of the opinion that the complaint is in any respect well founded, shall make such order as he thinks fit for the purpose of redressing the matter complained of, and the pilotage authority shall give effect to any order so made by the Secretary of State.

(2) The Secretary of State may—

(*a*) before he considers a complaint as required by subsection (1) above, ask the Commission for its advice on the complaint; and

(*b*) when considering the complaint as so required, have regard to the Commission's advice on the complaint.

(3) For the purposes of subsection (1)(*a*) above a pilotage authority shall have reasonable cause for refusing or failing to grant a pilotage certificate if by virtue of section 21 of this Act the authority are not obliged to grant it.

(4) If a pilotage authority refuse or fail to give effect to any order of the Secretary of State under subsection (1) above, the Secretary of State may, for the purpose of giving effect to the order, exercise any powers of the pilotage authority, and anything done by the Secretary of State in the exercise of those powers shall have the same effect as if it had been done by the pilotage authority.

Appeal to court by pilot against action of pilotage authority.

26.—(1) A pilot may appeal to the relevant court against—

(*a*) the suspension or revocation of his licence by the pilotage authority,

(*b*) the refusal or failure of the pilotage authority to renew his licence,

(*c*) the refusal or failure of the pilotage authority who have obtained possession of his licence to return it to him,

(*d*) the imposition upon him by the pilotage authority of a fine exceeding £2.

(2) In this section the expression " the relevant court " means—

(*a*) in the case of an appeal by a pilot licensed for a district in England or Wales, either a judge of county courts having jurisdiction within the port for which the pilot is licensed or a stipendiary magistrate having jurisdiction within that port; and the expression "stipendiary magistrate " includes a metropolitan stipendiary magistrate,

(*b*) in the case of an appeal by a pilot licensed for a district in Scotland, the sheriff having jurisdiction at the port where the decision is given,

(*c*) in the case of an appeal by a pilot licensed for a district in Northern Ireland, either a judge of the county court having jurisdiction within the port for which the pilot is licensed or a court of summary jurisdiction having jurisdiction within that port,

and the expression " court " shall be construed accordingly.

(3) For the purpose of hearing the appeal, the court shall sit with an assessor of nautical and pilotage experience selected and summoned by the court.

(4) Objection may be taken to any person proposed to be summoned as an assessor, either personally or in respect of his qualification, and by either party to the appeal.

(5) The court may confirm or reverse the suspension or revocation of the licence, or make such order in the case as may seem just, and its decision shall be final, unless special leave to appeal from the same to the High Court on a question of law or a question of mixed law and fact is given by the court, or by the High Court, and in such case the decision of the High Court shall be final.

In the application of this subsection to Scotland, references to the Court of Session shall be substituted for references to the High Court.

PART I

(6) The costs incurred by a pilotage authority under this section shall be payable out of any fund applicable to the general expenses of the pilotage authority.

(7) Rules of Court with respect to the procedure under this section (including costs and the remuneration of assessors) may be made, with the concurrence of the Treasury as to fees.

This subsection does not extend to Northern Ireland.

Special Provisions as to the Trinity House

Trinity House outport districts.

27.—(1) For the purposes of this Act, any district which at the time of the passing of this Act is under the authority of sub-commissioners appointed by the Trinity House and any pilotage district which may be declared after the passing of this Act to be a Trinity House outport district, shall be deemed to be a Trinity House outport district.

(2) The powers and duties of the Trinity House under this Act as the pilotage authority of an outport district shall be exercised and performed through a committee appointed for the district in such manner and subject to such conditions as may be determined by a pilotage order, under the name of sub-commissioners or such other name as may be fixed by the order, and any such order may be made so as to apply to all or any one or more of the outport districts.

Trinity House Pilot Fund.

28. Nothing in this Act shall oblige the Trinity House to maintain separate pilot funds for each of the pilotage districts of which they are the authority, and, if they maintain a single pilot fund for all those districts, the provisions of this Act as to pilot funds shall apply as if all the districts of which they are the pilotage authority were a single pilotage district.

Collection of pilotage charges in Port of London by officers of Customs and Excise.

29.—(1) The following pilotage charges in respect of foreign ships, not being excepted ships, trading to and from the port of London, namely:—

(*a*) as to ships inwards, the full amount of pilotage charges for the distance piloted; and

(*b*) as to ships outwards, the full amount of charges for the distance required by law;

shall be paid to the chief officer of Customs and Excise in the port of London by the master, or by any consignees or agents of the ship who have paid, or made themselves liable to pay, any other charge for the ship in the port of London.

(2) The chief officer of Customs and Excise, on receiving any pilotage charges in respect of foreign ships, shall give to the

person paying the charges a receipt in writing for the charges, and in the port of London the ship may be detained until the receipt is produced to the proper officer of Customs and Excise of the port.

(3) The chief officer of Customs and Excise shall pay over to the Trinity House the pilotage charges received by him under this section, and the Trinity House shall apply the charges so received—

(*a*) in paying to any licensed pilot who produces to them sufficient proof of his having piloted the ship such charges as would have been payable to him for pilotage services if the ship had been a British ship, after making any deductions which they are authorised to make by byelaw under this Act;

(*b*) in paying to any person not being a licensed pilot who produces to them sufficient proof of his having, in the absence of a licensed pilot, piloted the ship, such amount as the Trinity House think proper, not exceeding the amount which would, under similar circumstances, have been payable to a licensed pilot after making the said deductions;

(*c*) in paying over to the Trinity House pilot fund the residue, together with the amount of any deductions made as aforesaid.

(4) Nothing in this section shall affect the application of the provisions of this Act as to the recovery of pilotage charges.

PART II

PRINCIPAL PILOTAGE PROVISIONS

Compulsory Pilotage

30.—(1) On the day appointed under subsection (7) below for the coming into force of this section or for the coming into force for a particular purpose, this section shall be substituted for section 31 of this Act to the extent (if any) specified in the order. Compulsory pilotage.

(2) Subject to subsection (4) below, a ship which is being navigated in a pilotage district in circumstances which the pilotage order for the district specifies as circumstances in which pilotage in the district is compulsory shall be—

(*a*) under the pilotage of a licensed pilot of the district who, in any such case as is specified in byelaws made under this Act by the pilotage authority for the district, is accompanied by an assistant who is also a licensed pilot of the district or, if the byelaws so provide, has a qualification specified in the byelaws; or

PART II

(*b*) under the pilotage of a master or first mate who possesses a pilotage certificate for the district and is bona fide acting as master or first mate of the ship.

(3) Without prejudice to the generality of subsection (2) above but subject to the following subsection, a ship which is being navigated in a port in a pilotage district at a time when—

(*a*) there is a defect in its hull, machinery or equipment which might affect materially the navigation of the ship; and

(*b*) the pilotage authority for the district have, at the request of the body managing or regulating the port, given notice to the master of the ship stating that the ship is to be under pilotage,

shall be under such pilotage as is mentioned in paragraph (*a*) or paragraph (*b*) of subsection (2) above.

(4) Subsections (2) and (3) above shall not apply to a ship belonging to Her Majesty, and a pilotage authority may by byelaws under this Act provide that a ship which is of a kind described in the byelaws by reference to its type, size or cargo shall not be required by virtue of the pilotage order for the authority's district to be under such pilotage as is mentioned in subsection (2) above; and in this Act " excepted ship " means, in relation to a pilotage district, a ship belonging to Her Majesty and any other ship of a kind described in byelaws made by virtue of this subsection by the pilotage authority for the district.

(5) If any ship is not under pilotage as required by subsection (2) or (3) above, and either—

(*a*) the master of the ship has not complied with the requirements of byelaws made under this Act, by the pilotage authority for the district in question, about requests for pilots; or

(*b*) a licensed pilot of the district has offered to take charge of the ship,

then, subject to the following subsection, the master of the ship shall be guilty of an offence and liable on summary conviction to a fine not exceeding whichever of the following is the greater, namely—

(i) in England and Wales and in Scotland, level 5 on the standard scale,

(ii) in Northern Ireland, £1,000,

or double the amount of the pilotage charges which would have been payable in respect of the ship if it had been under pilotage as so required and, where the master has not complied as aforesaid, if he had so complied.

(6) It shall be a defence in proceedings for an offence under subsection (5) above to prove that on the occasion to which

the charge relates the ship was being navigated in the pilotage district in question only so far as was necessary to avoid serious danger to the ship.

PART II

(7) This section shall come into force on such day as the Secretary of State may by order appoint; and different days may be appointed under this subsection for different purposes.

(8) Without prejudice to the generality of subsection (7) above, an order under that subsection may appoint a day for the coming into force of this section in relation only to such pilotage districts as are specified in the order.

Compulsory pilotage; transitory provisions.

31.—(1) Every ship (other than an excepted ship) while navigating in a pilotage district in which pilotage is compulsory for the purpose of entering, leaving, or making use of any port in the district, and every ship carrying passengers (other than an excepted ship), while navigating for any such purpose as aforesaid in any pilotage district (whether pilotage is compulsory or not compulsory in that district) shall be either—

(*a*) under the pilotage of a licensed pilot of the district; or

(*b*) under the pilotage of a master or mate possessing a pilotage certificate for the district who is bona fide acting as master or mate of the ship.

(2) If any ship (other than an excepted ship) in circumstances in which pilotage is compulsory under this section, is not under pilotage as required by this section, after a licensed pilot of the district has offered to take charge of the ship, the master of that ship shall be liable on summary conviction in respect of each offence to a fine not exceeding double the amount of the pilotage charges that (disregarding any increase in the charges attributable to failure to comply with the requirements of byelaws in force in the district about requests for pilots) would have been payable in respect of the ship if it had been under pilotage as so required.

(3) For the purposes of this Act the following ships are excepted ships:—

(*a*) ships belonging to Her Majesty;

(*b*) fishing vessels of which the registered length is less than 47·5 metres;

(*c*) ferry boats plying as such exclusively within the limits of a harbour authority;

(*d*) ships of less than fifty tons gross tonnage;

(*e*) ships exempted from compulsory pilotage by byelaw in force by virtue of paragraph 1 of Schedule 2 to this Act.

PART II

Exemption from compulsory pilotage of ships belonging to certain public authorities.

32.—(1) Subject to the provisions of this section the provisions of this Act relating to compulsory pilotage shall not apply to tugs, dredgers, sludge-vessels, barges, and other similar craft—

(*a*) belonging to or hired by a dock, harbour or water authority whilst employed in the exercise of the statutory powers or duties of the authority and navigating within any pilotage district which includes within its limits the whole or any part of the area of the authority; or

(*b*) belonging to a local authority whilst employed in the exercise of the statutory powers or duties of the authority and navigating within the pilotage district within which the port to which they belong is situated.

(2) Where in any pilotage district any of the classes of craft mentioned in subsection (1) above were at the time of the passing of this Act in practice subject to compulsory pilotage, the pilotage authority may by byelaw provide that any of such classes of craft shall continue to be so subject.

(3) The Secretary of State may by order provide that the provisions of this Act relating to compulsory pilotage shall apply to such of the craft mentioned in subsection (1) above as may be specified in the order.

(4) Until such day as the Secretary of State may by order appoint, subsection (3) above shall be omitted; and different days may be appointed under this subsection for different purposes.

Provision as to ships calling at a port for the purpose only of taking pilot; transitory provisions.

33.—(1) A ship calling at a port in a pilotage district for the purpose only of taking on board or landing a pilot belonging to some other pilotage district shall not, for the purpose of the provisions of this Act relating to compulsory pilotage, be deemed to be navigating in the first-mentioned district for the purpose of entering, leaving, or making use of that port.

(2) Subsection (1) above shall cease to have effect on such day as the Secretary of State may by order appoint; and different days may be appointed under this subsection for different purposes

Construction of references to pilotage district in which pilotage is compulsory; transitory provisions.

34.—(1) Any reference in this Act to a pilotage district in which pilotage is compulsory shall, in the case of a district in which pilotage is compulsory only in part of the district, be construed, if the context so requires, as a reference to that part of the district only.

PART II

(2) Subsection (1) above shall cease to have effect on such day as the Secretary of State may by order appoint; and different days may be appointed under this subsection for different purposes.

Liability of owner or master in case of a vessel under pilotage.

35. Notwithstanding anything in any public or local Act, the owner or master of a vessel navigating under circumstances in which pilotage is compulsory shall be answerable for any loss or damage caused by the vessel or by any fault of the navigation of the vessel in the same manner as he would if pilotage were not compulsory.

Provisions with respect to Licensed Pilots

Right of licensed pilot to supersede unlicensed persons.

36.—(1) A pilot licensed for a district may supersede any pilot not so licensed who is employed to pilot a ship in the district.

(2) Where a licensed pilot supersedes an unlicensed pilot the master of the ship shall pay to the latter an appropriate proportion of the pilotage charges payable in respect of the ship.

Any question as to the proportion payable to the person whom the licensed pilot has superseded shall be referred to the pilotage authority by whom the licensed pilot has been licensed, and their decision on the question shall be final.

(3) If in any pilotage district a pilot not licensed for the district pilots or attempts to pilot a ship when he knows that a pilot licensed for that district has offered to pilot the ship, he shall be liable on summary conviction in respect of each offence to a fine not exceeding—

(*a*) in England and Wales and in Scotland, level 4 on the standard scale,

(*b*) in Northern Ireland, £500.

(4) If the master of a ship knowingly employs or continues to employ a pilot not licensed for the district to pilot the ship within any pilotage district after a pilot licensed for that district has offered to pilot the ship, or, in the case of an outward bound ship, without having taken reasonable steps (proof whereof shall lie on the master) to obtain a licensed pilot, he shall be liable on summary conviction in respect of each offence to a fine not exceeding—

(*a*) in England and Wales and in Scotland, level 4 on the standard scale,

(*b*) in Northern Ireland, £500.

(5) If any person other than the master or a seaman being bona fide one of the crew of the ship is on the bridge of a ship, or in any other position (whether on board the ship or elsewhere) from which the ship is navigated, that person shall, for the purposes of this section, be deemed to be piloting the ship unless the contrary is proved.

PART II

(6) In this section, " ship " does not include a ship which a person is piloting or ordered to pilot, in a dockyard port within the meaning of the Dockyard Ports Regulation Act 1865, in the course of his duties as a servant of the Crown; but nothing in this subsection shall be construed as derogating from any immunity which affects a ship apart from this subsection.

1865 c. 125.

Declaration as to draught etc. of ship.

37.—(1) A licensed pilot may require the master of any ship which he is piloting to declare her draught of water, length and beam, and to provide him with such other information relating to the ship or its cargo as the pilot specifies and is necessary to enable him to carry out his duties as the pilot of the ship, and the master shall comply with any such request.

(2) It shall be the duty of the master of a ship to bring to the notice of each licensed pilot who pilots the ship any defects in, and any matter peculiar to, the ship and its machinery and equipment of which the master knows and which might affect materially the navigation of the ship.

(3) The master of a ship who—

(*a*) refuses to comply with a request made to him in pursuance of subsection (1) above; or

(*b*) makes a statement which he knows is false, or recklessly makes a statement which is false, in answer to such a request or is privy to the making by another person in answer to such a request of a statement which the master knows is false; or

(*c*) fails without reasonable excuse to perform the duty imposed on him by subsection (2) above,

shall be guilty of an offence.

(4) The master of a ship who is guilty of an offence under this section shall be liable on summary conviction—

(*a*) in the case of an offence under subsection (3)(*b*) above, to a fine not exceeding—

(i) in England and Wales and in Scotland, level 5 on the standard scale,

(ii) in Northern Ireland, £1,000;

(*b*) in any other case, to a fine not exceeding—

(i) in England and Wales and in Scotland, level 4 on the standard scale,

(ii) in Northern Ireland, £500.

Provision as to ships within a harbour, dock, etc.

38.—(1) A ship while being moved within a harbour which forms part of a pilotage district shall be deemed to be being navigated in a pilotage district, except so far as may be provided by byelaw in the case of ships being so moved for the

PART II

purpose of changing from one mooring to another mooring or of being taken into or out of any dock: and a byelaw shall in every case be made for the purpose aforesaid in any pilotage district where any class of persons other than licensed pilots were in practice employed on 7th March 1913 (the date of the passing of the Pilotage Act 1913) for the purpose of changing the moorings of ships or of taking ships into or out of dock. 1913 c. 31.

(2) Until such day as the Secretary of State may by order appoint, subsection (1) above shall have effect as if for the words " being navigated " there were substituted the words " a ship navigating "; and different days may be appointed under this subsection for different purposes.

Provision as to ships in closed dock etc.; transitory provisions.

39.—(1) A ship whilst being navigated within any closed dock, lock or other closed work in a pilotage district shall, notwithstanding anything in this Act, be deemed to be navigating in a district in which pilotage is not compulsory.

(2) Subsection (1) above shall cease to have effect on such day as the Secretary of State may by order appoint; and different days may be appointed under this subsection for different purposes.

(3) Without prejudice to the generality of subsection (2) above, an order under that subsection may appoint a day for subsection (1) above to cease to have effect in relation only to such pilotage districts as may be specified in the order.

Copies of pilotage provisions to be furnished to pilots.

40. The pilotage authority shall cause every pilot licensed by them to be furnished with a copy of this Act as amended for the time being, and with a copy of any pilotage order for the time being in force in the district, and of any byelaws so in force.

Licensed pilot not to be taken out of his district.

41. A master of a ship shall not, except in circumstances of unavoidable necessity, take a licensed pilot without his consent beyond the district for which he is licensed, or beyond the point up to which he has been engaged to pilot the ship, and if a master of a ship acts in contravention of this section, he shall be liable on summary conviction in respect of each offence to a fine not exceeding—

(*a*) in England and Wales and in Scotland, level 5 on the standard scale,

(*b*) in Northern Ireland, £1,000.

PART II

Limitation of liability of pilots, and of pilotage authorities as employers.

42.—(1) A licensed pilot, a person authorised to act as the assistant of a licensed pilot by the authority who licensed the pilot and the pilotage authority who employ a licensed pilot or such an assistant shall not be liable—

(*a*) in the case of a pilot or assistant, for neglect or want of skill ; and

(*b*) in the case of a pilotage authority, for neglect or want of skill by the pilot or assistant or by the authority in employing the pilot or assistant,

beyond the amount of £100 and the amount of the pilotage charges in respect of the voyage during which the liability arose.

(2) Where any proceedings are taken against a pilot, assistant or pilotage authority for any neglect or want of skill in respect of which liability is limited as provided by this section, and other claims are made or apprehended in respect of the same neglect or want of skill, the court in which the proceedings are taken may—

(*a*) determine the amount of the liability,

(*b*) upon payment by the pilot, assistant or pilotage authority of that amount into court, distribute that amount rateably among the several claimants,

(*c*) stay or, in Scotland, sist any proceedings pending in any other court in relation to the same matter,

(*d*) proceed in such manner and subject to such requirements—

(i) as to making persons interested parties to the proceedings,

(ii) as to the exclusion of any claimants who do not come in within a certain time,

(iii) as to requiring security from the pilot, assistant or pilotage authority,

(iv) as to payment of any costs,

as the court thinks just.

Obligation on licensed pilot to produce his licence to employer.

43.—(1) Every licensed pilot when acting as such shall be provided with his licence, and shall, if requested, produce it to any person by whom he is employed, or to whom he offers his services as pilot.

(2) If a licensed pilot refuses without reasonable excuse to produce his licence in accordance with this section, he shall be liable on summary conviction in respect of each offence to a fine not exceeding—

(*a*) in England and Wales and in Scotland, level 3 on the standard scale,

(*b*) in Northern Ireland, £200.

PART II

Penalty on fraudulent use of licence.

44. If any person not being a licensed pilot for a district falsely represents himself to be a licensed pilot for that district, either by means of using a licence which he is not entitled to use or by any other means, he shall be liable on summary conviction in respect of each offence to a fine not exceeding—

(*a*) in England and Wales and in Scotland, level 5 on the standard scale,

(*b*) in Northern Ireland, £1,000.

Pilot Boats and Pilot Signals

Approval of pilot boats.

45. All vessels regularly employed in the pilotage service of any pilotage district (in this Act referred to as " pilot boats ") shall be approved and licensed by the pilotage authority of the district, and that authority may, at their discretion, appoint and remove the masters of those pilot boats.

Pilot boats to fly pilot flag.

46.—(1) Every pilot boat shall when afloat fly a flag (in this Act called a " pilot flag ") of large dimensions compared with the size of the pilot boat, and of two colours, the upper horizontal half white, and the lower horizontal half red, to be placed at the mast head, or on a sprit or staff, or in some equally conspicuous situation.

(2) It shall be the duty of the master of the pilot boat to see that the pilot flag is kept clean and distinct, so as to be easily discerned at a reasonable distance ; and if a master fails, without reasonable cause, to comply with the requirements of this section, he shall be liable on summary conviction in respect of each offence to a fine not exceeding—

(*a*) in England and Wales and in Scotland, level 2 on the standard scale,

(*b*) in Northern Ireland, £50.

Display of pilot flag when pilot is on board ship.

47. When a ship is navigating in a pilotage district, and has on board a pilot licensed for that district, or a master or mate holding a pilotage certificate for that district, the master of the ship shall cause a pilot flag to be exhibited ; and if he fails, without reasonable cause, to do so, he shall be liable on summary conviction in respect of each offence to a fine not exceeding—

(*a*) in England and Wales and in Scotland, level 4 on the standard scale,

(*b*) in Northern Ireland, £500.

Penalty on ordinary boat displaying pilot flag.

48.—(1) A pilot flag shall not be displayed on any ship or boat not having on board a licensed pilot or a master or mate holding a pilotage certificate and if any such flag is displayed on any

PART II

such ship or boat, the master of that vessel shall, unless he proves that he took all reasonable precautions and exercised all due diligence to avoid displaying the flag, be liable on summary conviction for each offence to a fine not exceeding—

(*a*) in England and Wales and in Scotland, level 4 on the standard scale,

(*b*) in Northern Ireland, £500.

(2) A flag so nearly resembling a pilot flag as to be likely to deceive shall not be displayed on any ship or boat not having on board a licensed pilot or a master or mate holding a pilotage certificate and, if any such flag is displayed on any such ship or boat, the master of that vessel shall, unless he proves that he had no intention to deceive, be liable on summary conviction for each offence to a fine not exceeding—

(*a*) in England and Wales and in Scotland, level 4 on the standard scale,

(*b*) in Northern Ireland, £500.

Signals to be displayed by ships requiring a pilot.

49.—(1) Her Majesty may by Order in Council make rules as to the signals to be used or displayed where the services of a pilot are required on any vessel, and those signals are in this Act referred to as " pilot signals ".

(2) If a vessel requires the services of a pilot, the master of that vessel shall use or display the pilot signals.

(3) If without reasonable excuse a master of a vessel uses or displays, or causes or permits any person under his authority to use or display, any of the pilot signals for any other purpose than that of summoning a pilot, or uses or causes or permits any person under his authority to use any other signal for a pilot, he shall be liable on summary conviction in respect of each offence to a fine not exceeding—

(*a*) in England and Wales and in Scotland, level 2 on the standard scale,

(*b*) in Northern Ireland, £50.

Obligation to display signal for pilot in certain circumstances.

50.—(1) The master of a ship (other than an excepted ship) shall when navigating in circumstances in which pilotage is compulsory under this Act, display a pilot signal, and keep the signal displayed until a licensed pilot comes on board.

(2) The master of a ship, whether navigating in circumstances in which pilotage is compulsory or not, which is being piloted in a pilotage district by a pilot not licensed for the district, shall display a pilot signal and keep the signal displayed until a licensed pilot comes on board.

PART II

(3) If the master of any ship fails without reasonable excuse to comply with this section, he shall be liable on summary conviction in respect of each offence to a fine not exceeding—

(*a*) in England and Wales and in Scotland, level 2 on the standard scale,

(*b*) in Northern Ireland, £50.

(4) In subsection (2) above, " ship " does not include a ship which a person is piloting or ordered to pilot, in a dockyard port within the meaning of the Dockyard Ports Regulation Act 1865, in the course of his duties as a servant of the Crown ; but nothing in this subsection shall be construed as derogating from any immunity which affects a ship apart from this subsection.

1865 c. 125.

Facilities to be given for pilot getting on board and leaving ship.

51.—(1) The master of a ship (other than an excepted ship) which, in circumstances in which pilotage is compulsory under this Act, is not under pilotage as required in these circumstances, shall, if a licensed pilot of the district makes a signal for the purpose of offering his services as pilot, by any practical means consistent with the safety of his ship, facilitate the pilot getting on board the ship, and shall give the charge of piloting the ship to that pilot, or, if there are two or more licensed pilots offering at the same time, to such one of them as may, according to any byelaws for the time being in force in the district, be entitled or required to take charge of the ship.

(2) Where the master of a ship, whether in circumstances in which pilotage is compulsory or not, accepts the services of a licensed pilot, he shall, by any practical means consistent with the safety of his ship, facilitate the pilot and any assistant of his getting on board and subsequently leaving the ship.

(3) If the master of any ship fails without reasonable excuse to comply with the provisions of this section, he shall be liable on summary conviction in respect of each offence to a fine not exceeding—

(*a*) double the amount of pilotage charges that (disregarding any increase in the charges attributable to failure to comply with the requirements of byelaws in force in the district about requests for pilots) are payable in respect of the ship or would have been so payable if he had complied with those provisions, or

(*b*) in England and Wales and in Scotland, level 4 on the standard scale,

(*c*) in Northern Ireland, £500,

whichever is the greater.

PART II

Offences by Pilots

Penalty on pilot endangering ship, life, or limb.

52. If, when piloting a ship, any pilot by wilful breach of duty or by neglect of duty, or by reason of drunkenness—

(*a*) does any act tending to the immediate loss or destruction of or serious damage to the ship, or tending immediately to endanger the life or limb of any person on board the ship ; or

(*b*) refuses or omits to do any lawful act proper and requisite to be done by him for preserving the ship from loss, destruction, or serious damage, or for preserving any person belonging to or on board the ship from danger to life or limb ;

that pilot shall be guilty of an offence and liable—

(i) on summary conviction, to imprisonment for a term not exceeding 3 months or a fine of an amount not exceeding the statutory maximum or both ;

(ii) on conviction on indictment, to imprisonment for a term not exceeding two years or a fine or both.

Penalty on person obtaining charge of a ship by misrepresentation.

53. If any person, by wilful misrepresentation of circumstances upon which the safety of a ship may depend, obtains, or endeavours to obtain, the charge of that ship, that person and every person procuring, abetting or conniving at the commission of the offence shall, in addition to any liability for damages, be liable on summary conviction in respect of each offence to a fine not exceeding—

(*a*) in England and Wales and in Scotland, level 5 on the standard scale,

(*b*) in Northern Ireland, £1,000.

Offences by pilots.

54.—(1) If a licensed pilot, either within or outside the district for which he is licensed,—

(*a*) is in any way directly or indirectly concerned in any corrupt practices relating to ships, their tackle, furniture, cargoes, crews, or passengers, or to persons in distress at sea or by shipwreck, or to their moneys, goods, or chattels ;

(*b*) lends his licence ;

(*c*) acts as pilot when he knows he is suspended ;

(*d*) acts as pilot when in a state of intoxication ;

(*e*) employs, or causes to be employed, on board any ship which he is piloting any boat, anchor, cable, or other store, matter, or thing beyond what is necessary for the service of that ship, with intent to enhance the expenses of pilotage for his own gain or for the gain of any other person ;

(*f*) refuses, or wilfully delays, without reasonable cause, to pilot any ship within the district for which he is licensed, upon the signal for a pilot being made by that ship, or upon being required to do so by the master, owner, agent, or consignee thereof, or by any officer of the pilotage authority by whom the pilot is licensed, or by any chief officer of Customs and Excise ;

(*g*) unnecessarily cuts or slips, or causes to be cut or slipped, any cable belonging to any ship ;

(*h*) refuses, otherwise than on reasonable ground of danger to the ship, when requested by the master, to conduct the ship which he is piloting into any port or place within the district for which he is licensed ; or

(*i*) quits the ship, which he is piloting, before the service for which he was engaged has been performed and without the consent of the master of the ship ;

that pilot shall, in addition to any liability for damages, be liable on summary conviction in respect of each offence to a fine not exceeding—

(i) in England and Wales and in Scotland, level 4 on the standard scale,

(ii) in Northern Ireland, £500.

(2) If any person procures, aids, abets or connives at the commission of any offence under this section he shall, in addition to any liability for damages, be liable on summary conviction to a fine not exceeding—

(*a*) in England and Wales and in Scotland, level 4 on the standard scale,

(*b*) in Northern Ireland, £500.

(3) The provisions of the law relating to customs or excise with respect to the recovery of penalties under that law, and the application of such penalties, shall apply in the case of any prosecution by any officer of Customs and Excise for the recovery of a fine in respect of any offence against this section.

PART III

LIABILITY OF PILOTAGE AUTHORITIES FOR LOSS OR DAMAGE TO VESSELS OR GOODS, ETC.

Limitation of liability

55.—(1) Where, without any such personal act or omission of theirs as is mentioned in Article 4 of the Convention in Part I of Schedule 4 to the Merchant Shipping Act 1979, any loss or damage is caused— Limitation of liability. 1979 c. 39.

(*a*) to any vessel or vessels, or

PART III

(*b*) to any goods, merchandise or other things whatsoever on board any vessel or vessels, or

(*c*) to any other property or rights of any kind, whether on land or on water or whether fixed or movable,

a pilotage authority shall not be liable to damages beyond the amount of £100 multiplied by the number of pilots holding licences from the pilotage authority under section 12 of this Act for the pilotage district of the pilotage authority at the date when the loss or damage occurs.

(2) The limit of liability under subsection (1) above shall apply whether the liability arises at common law or under any public general or local Act of Parliament and notwithstanding anything contained in any such Act passed before 16th July 1936 (the date of the passing of the Pilotage Authorities (Limitation of Liability) Act 1936).

1936 c. 36.

(3) Nothing in this section shall impose any liability in respect of any such loss or damage on any pilotage authority in any case where no such liability would have existed if this Part of this Act had not been enacted.

(4) Until such day as the Secretary of State may by order appoint, subsection (1) above shall have effect in the United Kingdom as if for the words from " any such " to " 1979 " there were substituted the words " their fault or privity ".

Limitation of liability where several claims on one occasion.

56. The limit of liability under section 55 of this Act shall relate to the whole of any losses and damages which may arise upon any one distinct occasion although such losses and damages may be sustained by more than one person.

Power of courts to consolidate claims.

57.—(1) Where any liability is alleged to have been incurred by a pilotage authority in respect of any loss or damage to which section 55 of this Act applies and several claims are made or apprehended in respect of that liability, then the pilotage authority may apply to the court.

(2) On an application under subsection (1) above, the court may—

(*a*) determine the amount of liability of the pilotage authority,

(*b*) distribute that amount rateably among the several claimants,

(*c*) stay or, in Scotland, sist any proceedings pending in any other court in relation to the same matter,

(*d*) proceed in such manner and subject to such requirements—

(i) as to making persons interested parties to the proceedings,

(ii) as to the exclusion of any claimants who do not come in within a certain time,

(iii) as to requiring security from the pilotage authority,

(iv) as to the payment of any costs,

as the court thinks just.

(3) In this section, " the court " means—

(*a*) in England and Wales, the High Court,

(*b*) in Scotland, the Court of Session,

(*c*) in Northern Ireland, the High Court.

Rights of pilotage authorities as owners of ships.

58.—(1) Where any pilotage authority are the owners of any ship, nothing in this Part of this Act shall affect any limitation of liability conferred on them or other rights to which they are entitled as such owners under section 17 or 18 of the Merchant Shipping Act 1979, and accordingly the foregoing provisions of this Part of this Act shall not apply to any loss or damage the liability of which can be limited under the said sections.

1979 c. 39.

(2) Until such day as the Secretary of State may by order appoint, subsection (1) above has effect in the United Kingdom as if—

(*a*) for the words " under section 17 or 18 of the Merchant Shipping Act 1979 " there were substituted the words " by or under Part VIII of the Merchant Shipping Act 1894, and the Merchant Shipping (Liability of Shipowners and Others) Act 1900 ",

1894 c. 60.
1900 c. 32.

(*b*) for the word " sections " there were substituted the word " enactments ".

An order under this subsection may appoint different days for different purposes.

Exclusion of funds for benefit of pilots etc.

59. No pilots' benefit fund, pilotage annuity fund or other fund formed or maintained by a pilotage authority for the benefit of pilots, their widows or children, shall be capable of being charged or attached or taken in execution or made available by any legal process or otherwise for meeting any liability of or any claim against the pilotage authority.

Exclusion of funds of authorities acting in dual capacity.

60. If any body of persons corporate or unincorporate are the owners of any dock or canal (including any body of persons having the control or management of any dock or canal) or are a harbour authority or a conservancy authority and that body or a committee of that body are also a pilotage authority, then—

(i) no funds, revenues, moneys or other property whatsoever belonging to such body in any capacity other than as pilotage authority shall be capable of being charged

PART III

or attached or taken in execution or made available by any legal process or otherwise for meeting any liability of, or any claim against, such body or any committee of such body in their capacity as pilotage authority; and

(ii) no funds, revenues, moneys or other property whatsoever belonging to such body or a committee of such body in their capacity as pilotage authority shall be capable of being charged or attached or taken in execution or made available by any legal process or otherwise for meeting any liability of, or any claim against, such body in any capacity other than as pilotage authority.

Exclusion of funds of certain Trinity Houses.

61.—(1) No funds, revenues, moneys or other property whatsoever belonging to the Trinity House or the Trinity House of Newcastle-upon-Tyne, in any capacity other than as pilotage authority, shall be capable of being charged or attached or taken in execution or made available by any legal process or otherwise for meeting any liability of, or any claim against, either such body in their capacity as pilotage authority.

(2) No funds, revenues, moneys or other property whatsoever belonging to the Trinity House or any committee or sub-commissioners of the Trinity House or the Trinity House of Newcastle-upon-Tyne, in their capacity as pilotage authority, shall be capable of being charged or attached or taken in execution or made available by any legal process or otherwise for meeting any liability of, or any claim against, any such body in any capacity other than as pilotage authority.

Interpretation

Provision for pilotage authority for more than one district.

62. Where a pilotage authority are the pilotage authority for more than one pilotage district, this Part of this Act shall have effect as though the authority were a separate pilotage authority for each separate pilotage district.

PART IV

MISCELLANEOUS AND GENERAL

Recovery, etc. of Pilotage Charges

Recovery of pilotage charges.

63.—(1) The following persons shall be liable to pay pilotage charges for any ship for which the services of a licensed pilot are obtained, namely:—

(*a*) the owner or master;

PART IV

(b) as to pilotage inwards, such consignees or agents as have paid or made themselves liable to pay any other charge on account of the ship in the port of her arrival or discharge;

(c) as to pilotage outwards, such consignees or agents as have paid or made themselves liable to pay any other charge on account of the ship in the port of her departure;

and those charges may be recovered in the same manner as fines of like amount under the Merchant Shipping Act 1894, but that recovery shall not take place until a previous demand has been made in writing. 1894 c. 60.

(2) Any consignee or agent (not being the owner or master of the ship) who is hereby made liable for the payment of pilotage charges in respect of any ship may, out of any moneys received by him on account of that ship or belonging to the owner thereof, retain the amount of all charges paid by him, together with any reasonable expenses he may have incurred by reason of the payment of the charges or his liability to pay the charges.

Receiving or offering improper rates of pilotage.

64. A licensed pilot shall not demand or receive, and a master shall not offer or pay to any licensed pilot, pilotage charges of amounts which he knows are greater or less than the amounts authorised by law, and, if a pilot or master acts in contravention of this section, he shall be liable on summary conviction in respect of each offence to a fine not exceeding—

(a) in England and Wales and in Scotland, level 3 on the standard scale,

(b) in Northern Ireland, £200.

Pilotage rate for leading ships.

65. If any boat or ship, having on board a licensed pilot, leads another ship which has not a licensed pilot on board when that other ship cannot be boarded due to particular circumstances, the same pilotage charges shall be payable in respect of the ship so led as if the pilot had actually been on board and had charge of that ship.

Supplementary

Application of Board of Trade Arbitrations, etc. Act 1874.

66. The Board of Trade Arbitrations etc. Act 1874, shall apply as if this Act were a special Act within the meaning of the said Act of 1874.

1874 c. 40.

Orders, rules and regulations.

67.—(1) All powers to make orders, rules or regulations conferred on the Secretary of State by this Act except those conferred by sections 16(2), 19(4) and 25(1) of this Act shall be exercisable by statutory instrument.

PART IV

(2) No order shall be made in pursuance of section 4(1), 5(2), 21(3) or 32(3) of this Act unless a draft of the order has been approved by resolution of each House of Parliament.

(3) Any statutory instrument containing an order made by virtue of section 3(3) of this Act or containing regulations made by virtue of section 13(2)(*a*) of this Act shall be subject to annulment in pursuance of a resolution by either House of Parliament.

Interpretation.

68.—(1) In this Act—

"the Commission" means the Pilotage Commission;

"excepted ship" has the meaning assigned to it by section 30, or, as the case may require, section 31 of this Act;

"functions" includes powers and duties;

"pilotage authority" means, without prejudice to section 1(2) of this Act, an authority established, constituted or incorporated as a pilotage authority—

(*a*) by pilotage order made under this Act, or

(*b*) for the purposes of this Act;

"pilot boat" has the meaning assigned to it by section 45 of this Act;

"pilotage charges" means the charges payable by virtue of section 14 of this Act;

"pilotage district" means, without prejudice to section 1(2) of this Act, a district established as a pilotage district—

(*a*) under a pilotage order made under this Act, or

(*b*) for the purposes of this Act;

"pilot flag" has the meaning assigned to it by section 46 of this Act;

1982 c. 48.

"standard scale" shall be construed in accordance with section 75 of the Criminal Justice Act 1982;

"statutory maximum" shall be construed in accordance with section 74 of the said Act of 1982;

"the Trinity House of Newcastle-upon-Tyne" means the Corporation of the Master Pilots and Seamen of the Trinity House of Newcastle-upon-Tyne;

1980 c. 45.

"water authority" in relation to Scotland means a water authority within the meaning of section 3 of the Water (Scotland) Act 1980.

(2) This Act shall be construed as one with the Merchant Shipping Acts 1894 to 1981.

PART IV

(3) Without prejudice to subsection (2) above, any expression to which a meaning is given by the Merchant Shipping Act 1894 has, unless the context otherwise requires, the same meaning as in that Act; and for ease of reference the Table below indicates the expressions used in this Act to which a meaning is given by that Act— 1894 c. 60.

" chief officer of Customs "
" conservancy authority "
" harbour "
" harbour authority "
" master "
" pilot "
" port "
" seaman "
" ship "
" the Trinity House "
" vessel "

(4) Any reference in this Act to failure to do any act or thing includes a reference to refuse to do that act or thing.

Transitional provisions, savings, amendments and repeals.

69.—(1) Schedule 2 to this Act, which contains transitional and saving provisions, shall have effect.

(2) The enactments mentioned in Schedule 3 to this Act shall have effect subject to the amendments there specified.

(3) The enactments specified in Schedule 4 to this Act are hereby repealed to the extent specified in the third column of that Schedule.

Short title, citation, extent and commencement.

70.—(1) This Act may be cited as the Pilotage Act 1983 and shall be included among the Acts that may be cited as the Merchant Shipping Acts 1894 to 1983.

(2) This Act extends to Northern Ireland and applies to all ships, British and foreign.

(3) It is hereby declared that this Act does not extend to the Isle of Man.

(4) This Act shall come into force at the expiration of the period of three months beginning with the date on which it is passed.

SCHEDULES

Section 2(3).

SCHEDULE 1

FURTHER PROVISIONS RELATING TO CONSTITUTION ETC. OF PILOTAGE COMMISSION

Tenure of members

1. Subject to paragraphs 2 to 4 below, a person shall hold and vacate office as a Commissioner or the Chairman in accordance with the terms of the instrument appointing him to that office.

2. A person shall not be appointed as a Commissioner and a Commissioner shall not be appointed as the Chairman for a term of more than three years; but a person may be reappointed as a Commissioner and a Commissioner may be reappointed as the Chairman on or after the date on which he ceases to be a Commissioner or, as the case may be, ceases to be the Chairman.

3.—(1) A person may at any time resign his office as a Commissioner or the Chairman by giving to the Secretary of State a notice in writing signed by that person and stating that he resigns that office.

(2) If the Chairman ceases to be a Commissioner he shall cease to be the Chairman.

4. If the Secretary of State is satisfied that a Commissioner—

(*a*) has been absent from the meetings of the Commission for a period longer than six consecutive months without the permission of the Commission; or

(*b*) is incapacitated by physical or mental illness; or

(*c*) is otherwise unable or unfit to discharge the functions of a Commissioner,

the Secretary of State may declare his office as a Commissioner to be vacant and shall notify the declaration in such manner as the Secretary of State thinks fit; and thereupon the office shall become vacant.

Remuneration of members

5. The Commission shall pay to each Commissioner such remuneration and allowances as the Secretary of State may determine with the consent of the Treasury.

6. Where a person ceases to be a Commissioner otherwise than on the expiry of his term of office and it appears to the Secretary of State that there are special circumstances which make it right for that person to receive compensation, the Secretary of State may with the consent of the Treasury direct the Commission to make to that person a payment of such amount as the Secretary of State may determine with the consent of the Treasury; and it shall be the duty of the Commission to comply with that direction.

Proceedings

Sch. 1

7. The quorum of the Commission and the arrangements relating to meetings of the Commission shall be such as the Commission may determine.

8.—(1) A Commissioner who is in any way directly or indirectly interested in a contract made or proposed to be made by the Commission, or in any other matter whatsoever which falls to be considered by the Commission, shall disclose the nature of his interest at a meeting of the Commission and the disclosure shall be recorded in the minutes of the meeting ; and the Commissioner shall not—

(*a*) in the case of a contract, take part in any deliberation or decision of the Commission with respect to the contract; and

(*b*) in the case of any other matter, take part in any decision of the Commission with respect to the matter if the Commission decides that the interest in question might affect prejudicially the Commissioner's consideration of the matter.

(2) A notice given by a Commissioner at a meeting of the Commission to the effect that he is a member or employee of a specified company or firm and is to be regarded as interested in any contract which is made after the date of the notice with the company or firm shall, for the purposes of the preceding sub-paragraph, be a sufficient disclosure of his interest in relation to any contract so made.

(3) A Commissioner need not attend in person at a meeting of the Commission in order to make a disclosure which he is required to make under this paragraph if he takes reasonable steps to secure that the disclosure is made by a notice which is taken into consideration and read at such a meeting.

9. The validity of any proceedings of the Commission shall not be affected by any vacancy among the Commissioners or by any defect in the appointment of a Commissioner.

Staff

10. The Commission may employ such persons as it considers are needed to assist the Commission in the performance of its functions and may pay to them such remuneration and allowances as the Commission considers appropriate.

11. The Commission may—

(*a*) pay, to or in respect of persons formerly employed by the Commission, pensions, allowances or gratuities of such amounts as the Commission may determine ;

(*b*) make such payments towards the provision of any of the said benefits as the Commission may determine ;

(*c*) maintain such schemes as the Commission may determine, whether contributory or not, for the payment of any of the said benefits.

SCH. 1

12. If a person employed by the Commission becomes a Commissioner and was by reference to his employment by the Commission a participant in a pension scheme maintained by the Commission in pursuance of the preceding paragraph, the Commission may determine that his service as a Commissioner shall be treated for the purposes of the scheme as service as an employee of the Commission.

Instruments

13. The fixing of the common seal of the Commission shall be authenticated by the signature of the Chairman or of another Commissioner authorised by the Commission to authenticate it.

14. A document purporting to be duly executed under the seal of the Commission shall be received in evidence and shall, unless the contrary is proved, be deemed to be so executed.

Interpretation

15. In the preceding provisions of this Schedule " the Chairman " and " a Commissioner " mean respectively the chairman of the Commission and a member of the Commission.

Section 69(1).

SCHEDULE 2

TRANSITIONAL AND SAVING PROVISIONS

Byelaws

1. Notwithstanding the repeal by this Act of section 8(2) of the
1979 c. 39. Merchant Shipping Act 1979, any byelaws in force immediately before 4th July 1980 (the date of commencement of section 8(1)(*b*) of the Merchant Shipping Act 1979) by virtue of section 11(4) of the
1913 c. 31. Pilotage Act 1913 shall, if in force immediately before the commencement of this Act, continue in force thereafter and may be revoked as if the said subsection (4) were still in force.

2. Notwithstanding the repeal by this Act of section 9(8) of the Merchant Shipping Act 1979, any byelaws made before 1st September 1980 (the date of commencement of section 9(8) of the Merchant Shipping Act 1979) by a pilotage authority by virtue of section 17(1)(*f*) of the Pilotage Act 1913 shall, if in force immediately before the commencement of this Act, continue in force but—

(*a*) may be revoked by byelaws made by the authority and confirmed by the Secretary of State ; and

(*b*) shall not apply to services provided or to be provided after the date when charges first became payable by reference to a list made by the authority in pursuance of section 9 of the Merchant Shipping Act 1979 or section 14 of this Act.

Acts confirming pilotage orders

3. Any Act confirming a pilotage order made under an enactment repealed by this Act and in force immediately before the commencement of this Act may be repealed, altered or amended by a pilotage order made under this Act.

Penalties

4. Notwithstanding the repeal by this Act of section 13(4) of the Merchant Shipping Act 1979, that subsection (which makes transitional provision relating to the alteration, by virtue of subsections (1), (2) and (3) of that section, of punishments specified in the Pilotage Act 1913) continues to have effect in relation to the punishment for any offence committed before 1st January 1980 (being the date on which the provisions to which that subsection relates came into force).

1979 c. 39.

1913 c. 31.

Licences and certificates

5. Nothing in paragraph (*a*) of section 20(2) of this Act affects the validity or prevents the renewal of any pilotage certificate in force immediately before 4th July 1980 (the commencement date of paragraph 8(1)(*b*) of Schedule 2 to the Merchant Shipping Act 1979) in respect of a ship which is not registered under the law of a member State of the Economic Community.

1979 c. 39.

6. Any licence or certificate granted under any enactment repealed by this Act shall, subject to the provisions of this Act, continue in force as if it had been made or granted under this Act.

Appointments etc.

7. Any officer appointed, any body elected or constituted and any office established under any enactment repealed by this Act shall continue and be deemed to have been appointed, elected, constituted or established, as the case may be, under this Act.

Sections 55(4) and 58(2)

8. Nothing in any order made in pursuance of section 55(4) or section 58(2) of this Act shall affect the operation of either of those sections in relation to any occurrence which took place before the coming into force of any such order.

Orders under sections 18(1), 22(4) and 27(1) of the Pilotage Act 1913

1913 c. 31.

9. The repeal by this Act of sections 18(1), 22(4) and 27(1) of the Pilotage Act 1913 does not affect the operation of any order made under any of those provisions.

Periods of time

10. Where a period of time specified in any enactment repealed by this Act is current at the commencement of this Act, this Act has effect as if the corresponding provision of this Act had been in force when that period began to run.

Section 69(2).

SCHEDULE 3

AMENDMENTS

1939 c. 83.

The Pensions (Navy, Army, Air Force and Mercantile Marine) Act 1939

1. In section 4(4) of the Pensions (Navy, Army, Air Force and Mercantile Marine) Act 1939 for the words " section thirty eight of the Pilotage Act 1913 " there shall be substituted the words " section 45 of the Pilotage Act 1983 ".

1950 c. 9.

The Merchant Shipping Act 1950

2. In section 7(1) of the Merchant Shipping Act 1950, the definition of " pilotage authority " shall be omitted.

1968 c. 59.

The Hovercraft Act 1968

3. The enactments and instruments with respect to which provision may be made by an Order in Council under section 1(1)(*h*) of the Hovercraft Act 1968 shall include this Act and any instrument made under it.

1971 c. 68.

The Finance Act 1971

4. In Part VI of Schedule 14 to the Finance Act 1971, the entry relating to the Pilotage Act 1913 shall be omitted.

1975 c. 8.

The Offshore Petroleum Development (Scotland) Act 1975

5. In section 18 of the Offshore Petroleum Development (Scotland) Act 1975 for paragraph (*c*) there shall be substituted the following paragraph—

" (*c*) the Pilotage Act 1983 ; "

1979 c. 2.

The Customs and Excise Management Act 1979

6. In Part I of the Table in Schedule 4 to the Customs and Excise Management Act 1979 the entry relating to the Pilotage Act 1913 shall be omitted.

1979 c. 39.

The Merchant Shipping Act 1979

7. In section 50(2) of the Merchant Shipping Act 1979 in the definition of " the Merchant Shipping Acts " after the word " 1977 " there shall be inserted the words " and the Pilotage Act 1983 ".

1979 c. 55.

The Justices of the Peace Act 1979

8. In section 33(3) of the Justices of the Peace Act 1979 in paragraph (*b*) for the words " section 28 of the Pilotage Act 1913 " there shall be substituted the words " section 26 of the Pilotage Act 1983 ".

The Magistrates' Courts Act 1980 SCH. 3

9. In Part III of Schedule 6 to the Magistrates' Courts Act 1980 in paragraph 4 for the words " section 28 of the Pilotage Act 1913 " there shall be substituted the words " section 26 of the Pilotage Act 1983 ". 1980 c. 43.

The Finance Act 1980 1980 c. 48.

10. In section 35(4) of the Finance Act 1980 for the words " section 17(1)(*j*) of the Pilotage Act 1913 " there shall be substituted the words " section 15(1)(*i*) of the Pilotage Act 1983 ".

The Oil and Gas (*Enterprise*) *Act* 1982 1982 c. 23.

11. In section 27(2)(*a*) of the Oil and Gas (Enterprise) Act 1982 after the word " 1979 " there shall be inserted the words " the Pilotage Act 1983,".

SCHEDULE 4

Section 69(3).

REPEALS

Chapter	Short Title	Extent of Repeal
2 & 3 Geo. 5. c. 31.	The Pilotage Act 1913.	The whole Act.
1936 c. 36.	The Pilotage Authorities (Limitation of Liability) Act 1936.	The whole Act.
1950 c. 9.	The Merchant Shipping Act 1950.	In section 7(1), the definition of " pilotage authority ".
1971 c. 68.	The Finance Act 1971.	In Part VI of Schedule 14, the entry relating to the Pilotage Act 1913.
1979 c. 2.	The Customs and Excise Management Act 1979.	In Part I of the Table in Schedule 4, the entry relating to the Pilotage Act 1913.
1979 c. 39.	The Merchant Shipping Act 1979.	Sections 1 to 13. Schedule 2. In Schedule 5, paragraph 2. In Schedule 7, in Part II, the entries relating to the Pilotage Act 1913.

Ports (Reduction of Debt) Act 1983

1983 CHAPTER 22

An Act to make provision for reducing the indebtedness of the Port of London Authority and the Mersey Docks and Harbour Company. [9th May 1983]

BE IT ENACTED by the Queen's most Excellent Majesty, by and with the advice and consent of the Lords Spiritual and Temporal, and Commons, in this present Parliament assembled, and by the authority of the same, as follows:—

Reduction of indebtedness.

1.—(1) The Secretary of State may with the consent of the Treasury—

(*a*) release the Port of London Authority from its liability to repay such part, not exceeding £26 million, as he may determine of the money lent to it under the provisions of section 11 of the Harbours Act 1964 and section 1 of the Ports (Financial Assistance) Act 1981; 1964 c. 40. 1981 c. 21.

(*b*) release the Mersey Docks and Harbour Company from its liability to repay such part, not exceeding £36 million, as he may determine of the money lent to it under those provisions.

(2) The Secretary of State may with the consent of the Treasury make out of money provided by Parliament a grant not exceeding £22 million to the Port of London Authority for enabling it to repay such loan or loans guaranteed by him under section 1 of the said Act of 1981 as he may determine.

(3) For the purposes of section 1(3) of the said Act of 1981 (limit on financial assistance to the Port of London Authority and the Mersey Docks and Harbour Company)—

(*a*) the amounts that cease to be repayable by virtue of subsection (1) above; and

(*b*) any grant under subsection (2) above,

shall be taken into account as if they were grants made under section 1(1) of that Act and not repaid; and the assets of the National Loans Fund shall be reduced by so much of the amounts mentioned in paragraph (*a*) of this subsection as is attributable to money lent under the said Act of 1964.

Short title.

2. This Act may be cited as the Ports (Reduction of Debt) Act 1983.

Water Act 1983

1983 CHAPTER 23

An Act to make provision as to the constitution and procedure of water authorities and their borrowing and other powers and as to arrangements for the carrying out of their sewerage functions; to enable water authorities and statutory water companies to provide advice and assistance outside the United Kingdom; to provide for the dissolution of the National Water Council and the Water Space Amenity Commission; and to repeal the Water Charges Equalisation Act 1977; and for connected purposes. [9th May 1983]

BE IT ENACTED by the Queen's most Excellent Majesty, by and with the advice and consent of the Lords Spiritual and Temporal, and Commons, in this present Parliament assembled, and by the authority of the same, as follows:—

Constitution and procedure of water authorities

Constitution and procedure of water authorities.

1.—(1) For section 3 of the principal Act (members of water authorities) there is substituted the following section—

" Constitution and procedure of water authorities.

3.—(1) Each of the regional water authorities shall consist of the following members—

(*a*) a chairman appointed by the Secretary of State,

(*b*) two members appointed by the Minister, and

(*c*) not less than six nor more than twelve other members appointed by the Secretary of State.

(2) The Welsh authority shall consist of a chairman, and not less than eight nor more than fourteen other members, appointed by the Secretary of State.

(3) The Secretary of State shall designate a member of each water authority as deputy chairman of that authority.

(4) The members appointed by the Minister shall be persons who appear to him to have had experience of, and shown capacity in, agriculture, land drainage or fisheries.

(5) In the case of the regional water authorities, the members appointed by the Secretary of State shall be persons who appear to him to have had experience of, and shown capacity in, some matter relevant to the functions of water authorities.

(6) In the case of the Welsh authority—

(*a*) at least two members shall be persons who appear to the Secretary of State to have had experience of, and shown capacity in, land drainage or fisheries ; and

(*b*) the remaining members shall be persons who appear to him to have had experience of, and shown capacity in, some other matter relevant to the functions of water authorities.

(7) In appointing the members of a water authority, regard shall be had to the desirability of members of the authority being familiar with the requirements and circumstances of the authority's area.".

1975 c. 24. (2) In Part II of Schedule 1 to the House of Commons Disqualification Act 1975 (bodies of which all members are disqualified), the following entries are inserted at the appropriate places—

"A regional water authority established in accordance with
1973 c. 37. section 2 of the Water Act 1973";

"The Welsh Water Authority".

(3) For Part I of Schedule 3 to the principal Act (supplementary provisions as to administration etc, of water authorities) there are substituted the provisions set out in Schedule 1 to this Act.

Borrowing powers

Borrowing powers of water authorities.

2.—(1) In paragraph 34(3)(*b*) of Schedule 3 to the principal Act (water authorities to borrow from persons other than the Secretary of State, otherwise than by way of temporary loan, only in a currency other than sterling) after the word "Treasury," there are inserted the words "either in sterling or".

(2) In paragraph 34(5) of Schedule 3 to the principal Act (which limits the aggregate amount outstanding in respect of the principal of sums borrowed by water authorities and sums borrowed or treated as borrowed by certain other bodies to £3,750 million or such greater sum not exceeding £5,000 million as the Secretary of State may by order specify) for the words "£3,750 million" and "£5,000 million" there are substituted respectively the words "£6,000 million" and "£7,500 million".

(3) Paragraph 34(5) and (6) of Schedule 3 to the principal Act shall have effect as if any sum borrowed by the National Water Council the liability to repay which is or has been transferred to a water authority were borrowed by that authority and not by the Council.

Dissolution of National Water Council and Water Space Amenity Commission

Dissolution of National Water Council and Water Space Amenity Commission.

3.—(1) On such day as the Secretary of State may by order appoint, the functions of the National Water Council shall determine and all the property, rights and liabilities which immediately before the day so appointed were property, rights and liabilities of the Council shall, by virtue of this section, become property, rights and liabilities of the Secretary of State for the Environment.

(2) On such day as the Secretary of State may by order appoint, the functions of the Water Space Amenity Commission shall determine.

(3) This section has effect subject to Schedule 2 to this Act which makes further provision in relation to the Council and Commission, including provision for their dissolution.

(4) The Secretary of State may by order transfer to any authority, or to any person who in his opinion acts or will act on behalf of one or more authorities—

(*a*) such of the property, rights and liabilities of the Council, or

(*b*) in the case of an order having effect after the day appointed under subsection (1) above, such of the property, rights and liabilities vested in him by virtue of that subsection,

as he considers expedient.

(5) In subsection (4) above "authority" means—

(*a*) a water authority,

(*b*) a statutory water company,

(*c*) a regional or islands council,

(*d*) a river purification board, or

(*e*) a water development board.

Expenses of Secretary of State occasioned by section 3.

4.—(1) Any sums received by the Secretary of State by virtue of the transfer of property, rights and liabilities effected by section 3 of this Act shall be paid by him into the Consolidated Fund.

(2) The Secretary of State may levy from water authorities such contributions (which need not be the same for each authority) as appear to him, when taken together, necessary to meet the net expenses incurred by him—

(*a*) in discharging any liabilities to which he becomes subject by virtue of section 3 of this Act, or

(*b*) otherwise in connection with the dissolution of the National Water Council and Water Space Amenity Commission.

(3) In subsection (2) above " net expenses " means the amount of the expenses in question reduced by the amount paid by the Secretary of State into the Consolidated Fund in accordance with subsection (1) above.

(4) Any sums received by the Secretary of State by way of levy under subsection (2) above shall be paid by him into the Consolidated Fund.

Miscellaneous

Overseas activities of water authorities and statutory water companies.

5.—(1) Subject to subsection (2) below, a water authority or statutory water company may provide for any person outside the United Kingdom advice or assistance, including training facilities, as respects any matter in which they have skill or experience ; and for the purposes of this section, statutory water companies shall have the same powers as water authorities have by virtue of paragraph 2(1) of Schedule 3 to the principal Act.

(2) The power conferred by subsection (1) above shall not be exercised except—

(*a*) with the consent in writing of the Secretary of State ; and

(*b*) if the exercise of that power involves capital expenditure by the authority or company, or the guaranteeing by the authority or company of any liability, with that consent given with the approval of the Treasury.

(3) Subsections (1) and (2) above are without prejudice to any power of a water authority or statutory water company apart from subsection (1) above to provide advice or assistance of the kind mentioned in that subsection.

(4) Any consent under this section may be given subject to such conditions as the Secretary of State thinks fit.

(5) The Secretary of State shall issue guidance as to the criteria by reference to which he will determine any request for consent under this section.

Arrangements for carrying out sewerage functions.

6.—(1) The following section is substituted for section 15 of the principal Act—

" Arrangements for carrying out sewerage functions.

15.—(1) It shall be the duty of every water authority and of every relevant authority whose area is wholly or partly in the area of the water authority to endeavour to make arrangements for the relevant authority to discharge, as respects their area, the sewerage functions of the water authority.

(2) Schedule 4A to this Act shall have effect for the purpose of supplementing this section."

(2) After Schedule 4 to the principal Act there are inserted, as Schedule 4A, the provisions set out in Schedule 3 to this Act.

Arrangements by water authorities for representation of consumers' interests.

7. The following section is inserted after section 24 of the principal Act—

" Arrangements for representation of consumers' interests.

24A.—(1) It shall be the duty of each water authority to submit to the Secretary of State, before such date as he may appoint for the purposes of this section by order made by statutory instrument or such later date as he may specify in any particular case, a report on the arrangements which they propose to make for the representation of the interests of consumers in their area.

(2) In preparing a report under this section, a water authority shall have regard to any guidelines issued by the Secretary of State.

(3) On receiving a report under this section the Secretary of State may—

(*a*) approve the proposed arrangements ; or

(*b*) modify them and approve them as modified ; or

(*c*) reject the proposed arrangements and either—

(i) require the water authority to modify them and to submit a further report, or

(ii) require them to formulate new proposals and to submit a further report.

(4) Any report required under subsection (3)(*c*) above shall be submitted to the Secretary of State

before such date as he may specify when notifying the water authority concerned that he has rejected their proposed arrangements.

(5) Where proposed arrangements under this section have been approved by the Secretary of State it shall be the duty of the water authority—

(*a*) to put the arrangements into effect, subject to any variations approved by the Secretary of State under subsection (6) below, before the date specified by the Secretary of State in his approval of the arrangements ; and

(*b*) subsequently to maintain the arrangements, subject to any such variations and any variations required by the Secretary of State under subsection (7) below.

(6) At any time after the approval by the Secretary of State of proposed arrangements under this section (whether or not the arrangements have been put into effect) the water authority may apply to the Secretary of State for his approval of a variation of the arrangements.

(7) Where arrangements under this section have been put into effect by a water authority, the Secretary of State may at any time direct the authority to vary the arrangements in such manner, and before such date, as may be specified in the direction.

(8) Before submitting any report under this section, a water authority shall consult about the proposals in question those statutory water companies (if any) through whom they discharge duties.

(9) In subsection (1) above ' consumers ' includes persons who use or are likely to use, for the purposes of recreation, any water or land associated with water in respect of which the water authority in question are under the duty imposed by section 20 above.

(10) The Secretary of State shall lay before each House of Parliament a copy of any guidelines issued by him for the purposes of this section."

Repeal of Water Charges Equalisation Act 1977.
1977 c. 41.

8.—(1) The Water Charges Equalisation Act 1977 shall cease to have effect.

(2) If the Secretary of State is satisfied—

(*a*) that, had the Act of 1977 not ceased to have effect, he would have been required to make adjustments under section 3(3) of that Act on making the next orders under sections 1 and 2, and (*b*) that it is expedient to make provision in lieu of those adjustments,

he shall comply with subsection (3) below in relation to every statutory water undertaker as respects which such an adjustment would, in his opinion, have been so required.

(3) Where the Secretary of State is required to comply with this subsection in relation to any statutory water undertaker, he shall—

(*a*) in a case where the adjustment would have been by way of a reduction in the equalisation levy payable by, or an increase in the equalisation payment payable to, the undertaker, pay to that undertaker out of money provided by Parliament the appropriate amount, or

(*b*) in any other case, by order direct that undertaker to pay to him the appropriate amount.

(4) In subsection (3) above " appropriate amount " means an amount equal to the adjustment which, in the opinion of the Secretary of State, would have been required under section 3(3) in the case of the undertaker in question.

(5) No order shall be made under subsection (3) above unless a draft of the order has been laid before, and approved by a resolution of, the House of Commons.

(6) Any sums received by the Secretary of State under this section shall be paid by him into the Consolidated Fund.

Supplemental

Orders and regulations.

9.—(1) Any power of the Secretary of State to make an order or regulations under this Act shall be exercisable by statutory instrument which, except in the case of an order under section 3(1) or (2), 8(3) or 11(5) of this Act or paragraphs 3(2) or 10(2) of Schedule 2 to this Act, shall be subject to annulment in pursuance of a resolution of either House of Parliament.

(2) Any order or regulations under this Act may make different provision for different cases or descriptions of case, including different provision for different areas, and may contain such incidental or supplemental provision as the Secretary of State thinks fit.

Interpretation.

10.—In this Act—

" appointed day " means, in relation to the Council or, as the case may be, Commission, the day appointed under section 3 of this Act in relation to that body,

" Commission " means the Water Space Amenity Commission,

" Council " means the National Water Council,

" principal Act " means the Water Act 1973, 1973 c. 37.

"river purification board" means a board established under section 135 of the Local Government (Scotland) Act 1973, (1973 c. 65.)

"statutory water company" has the same meaning as in the principal Act, and

"water development board" has the meaning given by section 109(1) of the Water (Scotland) Act 1980. (1980 c. 45.)

Short title and commencement, etc.

11.—(1) This Act may be cited as the Water Act 1983.

(2) Schedule 4 to this Act (which makes minor and consequential amendments) shall have effect.

(3) The enactments and instruments specified in Schedule 5 to this Act are hereby repealed or, as the case may be, revoked to the extent specified in the third column of that Schedule.

(4) The following provisions of this Act—

(*a*) sections 2 to 6;

(*b*) sections 9 and 10;

(*c*) this section, except subsections (2) and (3);

(*d*) Schedule 2;

(*e*) Schedule 3;

(*f*) paragraphs 8 and 9 of Schedule 4 and subsection (2) of this section so far as relating to those paragraphs; and

(*g*) the revocation by Schedule 5 of the Water Authorities and National Water Council (Limit on Borrowing) Order 1982 and subsection (3) of this section so far as relating to that revocation; (S.I. 1982/944)

shall come into force on the passing of this Act.

(5) The remaining provisions of this Act shall come into force on such day as the Secretary of State may by order appoint; and different days may be appointed for different purposes.

(6) An order under subsection (5) above appointing a day for the commencement of section 1 of this Act may make provision for the existing members of water authorities, other than the chairmen, to vacate office before that day; but no such provision shall be taken as preventing the re-appointment of any such person under the provisions substituted by that section.

(7) The following provisions of this Act—

(*a*) section 1(2);

(*b*) section 3(1) and (3) to (5);

(*c*) this section;

(*d*) Part I of Schedule 2;

extend to Scotland and Northern Ireland and any repeal by Schedule 5 to this Act of an enactment which extends to Scotland or Northern Ireland has the same extent as that enactment, but otherwise this Act extends to England and Wales only.

SCHEDULES

SCHEDULE 1

Section 1(3).

PROVISIONS SUBSTITUTED FOR PART I OF SCHEDULE 3 TO THE WATER ACT 1973

The following are the provisions substituted for Part I of Schedule 3 to the principal Act by virtue of section 1 of this Act.

" PART I

WATER AUTHORITIES

General

1. A water authority shall be a body corporate.

2.—(1) A water authority shall have power to do anything (whether or not involving the expenditure, borrowing or lending of money or the acquisition or disposal of any property or rights) which in the opinion of the authority is calculated to facilitate, or is conducive or incidental to, the discharge of any of their functions.

(2) A water authority shall not—

(*a*) make arrangements for the discharge of any of their functions which are exercisable by their regional land drainage committee or any of their local land drainage committees otherwise than in accordance with the provisions of section 1(1) of the Land Drainage Act 1976 (general supervision by water authorities of land drainage), or 1976 c. 70.

(*b*) make arrangements for the discharge by any other body, or by any committee, of any of their functions with respect to—

(i) issuing precepts,

(ii) making drainage charges,

(iii) applying for a water charges option order pursuant to section 62 of the Act of 1976, or

(iv) borrowing money.

3.—(1) The Secretary of State may by regulations make provision as to—

(*a*) the appointment of members of water authorities and the terms on which they are to hold and vacate office,

(*b*) the execution of instruments and the mode of entering into contracts by and on behalf of water authorities,

(*c*) the proof of documents purporting to be executed, issued or signed by a water authority or by one of their members or officers, and

(*d*) such supplemental and incidental matters as the Secretary of State considers appropriate,

SCH. 1 but subject to any provision so made, each water authority shall regulate their own procedure.

(2) Regulations under this paragraph shall be subject to annulment in pursuance of a resolution of either House of Parliament.

Remuneration and allowances, superannuation and compensation

4. A water authority shall pay to their members such remuneration and allowances as may be determined by the appropriate Minister with the consent of the Treasury.

5.—(1) A water authority shall pay such pensions in relation to persons who are or have been members of the authority, or make such provision for the payment of pensions in relation to such persons, as may be determined by the appropriate Minister with the consent of the Treasury.

(2) Where an employee of a water authority—

(*a*) becomes a member of that or any other water authority, and

(*b*) immediately before becoming such a member was, by reference to his employment with that authority, participating in a superannuation scheme,

the authority of which he becomes a member may make provision for him to continue to participate in that scheme, on terms and conditions determined by the authority with the consent of the appropriate Minister, as if his service as a member were service as an employee; and any such superannuation scheme shall have effect subject to any provision made under this sub-paragraph.

(3) In this paragraph "pension", in relation to any person, means a pension (whether contributory or not) of any kind payable to or in respect of him, and includes an allowance, gratuity or lump sum so payable and a return of contributions with or without interest or any other addition.

6. If a person ceases to be a member of a water authority and it appears to the appropriate Minister that there are special circumstances which make it right that that person should receive compensation, that Minister may require the authority to pay that person such sum as he may, with the consent of the Treasury, determine.

7. In paragraphs 4 to 6 above "appropriate Minister" means—

(*a*) the Minister, in the case of members appointed by him, and

(*b*) the Secretary of State, in any other case.

Validity of proceedings

8. The validity of any proceedings of a water authority shall not be affected by any vacancy among the members of the authority or by any defect in the appointment of any such member.

Housing accommodation for employees

9. Without prejudice to paragraph 2 above, a water authority may—

(*a*) provide housing accommodation for persons employed by them (whether by constructing, converting, enlarging or acquiring any buildings and whether by selling such accommodation or letting or permitting it to be occupied with or without requiring the payment of rent or other charges), and

(*b*) permit a person for whom the authority provided housing accommodation while employed by them to occupy such accommodation provided by them after ceasing to be so employed."

SCHEDULE 2

Section 3(3).

PROVISIONS RELATING TO DISSOLUTION OF NATIONAL WATER COUNCIL AND WATER SPACE AMENITY COMMISSION

PART I

NATIONAL WATER COUNCIL

General duty of Council

1. It shall be the duty of the Council to give to the Secretary of State all such information, to prepare all such documents and to do all such other things, as appear to him to be necessary or expedient for facilitating the carrying into effect of section 3 of this Act and this Schedule and for enabling him to exercise any function conferred or imposed on him by, or by virtue of, that section or this Schedule.

Final accounts and reports

2.—(1) The Council shall (if they have not done so before the appointed day)—

(*a*) comply with paragraph 38 of Schedule 3 to the principal Act (statement of accounts) in relation to the last accounting year before the appointed day, and

(*b*) comply with paragraph 40 of that Schedule (annual reports) in relation to that year,

and shall also comply with those paragraphs in respect of the interval (if any) between the end of that accounting year and the appointed day, that interval being treated for the purposes of those paragraphs and of paragraphs 39 to 39G of Schedule 3 as an accounting year in relation to the Council.

(2) The Secretary of State shall lay before each House of Parliament a copy of—

(*a*) any statement of accounts, and any report, sent to him by the Council in compliance with this paragraph, and

(*b*) any report made by the auditors on the statement or on the accounts to which it relates.

SCH. 2

Continuance of Council until residual functions completed to Secretary of State's satisfaction

3.—(1) No amendment or repeal made by this Act shall affect—

(*a*) the continuance of the Council for the purposes of paragraphs 1 or 2 above or their powers and duties under those paragraphs, or

(*b*) the continued operation for those purposes of the provisions of the principal Act relating to the constitution and proceedings of the Council.

(2) The Council shall cease to exist when the Secretary of State, being satisfied that their duties under paragraphs 1 and 2 above have been discharged, so directs by order.

(3) Section 3(1) of this Act does not affect the continuance of employment with the Council, but on the Council ceasing to exist—

(*a*) any contract of employment with the Council then in force shall cease to have effect, except as regards rights previously accrued and liabilities previously incurred, and

(*b*) subject to any provision made under paragraph 6(1)(*b*) or 8(1) below, any rights and liabilities of the Council then existing shall by virtue of this paragraph become rights and liabilities of the Secretary of State.

(4) The Secretary of State shall pay to the appointed members of the Council (within the meaning of paragraph 27(2) of Schedule 3 to the principal Act), in respect of the period beginning with the appointed day and ending with the Council ceasing to exist, such remuneration (whether by way of salary or fees) and such allowances as, with the approval of the Treasury, he may determine.

(5) The Secretary of State shall, as soon as possible after determining the amount of any remuneration or allowances payable under sub-paragraph (4) above, lay a statement of his determination before each House of Parliament.

(6) As from the appointed day, the Secretary of State shall make available to the Council such facilities as the Council or their auditors may reasonably require for performing duties imposed on them by or by virtue of paragraphs 1 and 2 above ; and the remuneration of the auditors and any other expenses incurred by the Council in connection with the performance of those duties on and after the appointed day shall be defrayed by the Secretary of State out of money provided by Parliament.

Modification of agreements and documents

4.—(1) Subject to sub-paragraph (3) below, every agreement, other than a contract of employment or an agreement under section 26(2) of the principal Act, to which the Council are a party immediately before the appointed day, whether in writing or not and whether or not of such a nature that rights and liabilities under the agreement could be assigned by the Council, shall have effect as from that date as if—

(*a*) the Secretary of State had been a party to the agreement, and

(b) for any reference to the Council there were substituted, as respects anything falling to be done on or after the appointed day, a reference to the Secretary of State. SCH. 2

(2) Other documents (not being enactments) which refer to the Council shall be construed in accordance with sub-paragraph (1) above so far as applicable.

(3) An order under section 3(4) of this Act which transfers any property, rights or liabilities may contain consequential provision for the construction of references in—

(a) agreements (other than contracts of employment) to which the Council are a party at the date of the order or, in a case of an order made after the appointed day, were a party immediately before the appointed day, and

(b) other documents (not being enactments) which refer to the Council.

Legal remedies and pending proceedings

5.—(1) Where any right or liability is transferred by virtue of any provision of this Act, the transferee and all other persons shall have the same rights, powers and remedies (and, in particular, the same rights as to the taking or resisting of legal proceedings) for ascertaining, perfecting or enforcing that right or liability as they would have had if it had at all times been a right or liability of the transferee.

(2) Any pending legal proceedings by or against the Council which relate to any property, right or liability so transferred may be continued by or against the transferee.

(3) Any reference in sub-paragraph (1) or (2) above to legal proceedings shall be construed as including a reference to any application to an authority, and any reference to the taking or resisting of legal proceedings shall be construed accordingly.

Superannuation

6.—(1) The Secretary of State may, with the consent of the Treasury, make regulations providing for—

(a) the payment by such water authority as may be designated by the regulations (the "pension authority") of pensions, allowances or gratuities to or in respect of persons who have been members of the Council;

(b) the transfer to the pension authority of such pension liabilities of the Council as may be specified in the regulations.

(2) The regulations shall provide for the recovery by the pension authority from each of the other water authorities of such proportion of the cost incurred by the pension authority in discharging their functions under the regulations as the Secretary of State may from time to time determine.

(3) The proportions determined by the Secretary of State need not be the same for each water authority.

SCH. 2

(4) In sub-paragraph (1) above "pension liabilities" means any liability in connection with the payment of pensions, allowances or gratuities imposed on or assumed by the Council and includes the liability to make any payment by way of an increase in a pension.

7.—(1) The classes of person in whose interests water authorities may exercise their powers under section 27(1) of the principal Act (power to establish and administer pension schemes etc.) shall include—

(a) persons who have been employed by the Council, and

(b) persons who are or have been employed in such other appropriate employment as the Secretary of State may by order prescribe.

(2) No scheme shall be established by a water authority under section 27(1) of the principal Act, and no variation of any scheme established by a water authority under that section shall be effected, without the consent in writing of the Secretary of State.

(3) In sub-paragraph (1) above "appropriate employment" means employment in respect of which it would, in the opinion of the Secretary of State, be appropriate for provision to be made under section 27 of the principal Act.

Compensation

8.—(1) The Secretary of State may by regulations transfer to such water authority as may be designated by the regulations ("the compensation authority") the liabilities of the Council relating to—

(a) the payment of benefits or compensation in respect of early retirement or for loss of employment, or

(b) redundancy payments within the meaning of the Employment Protection (Consolidation) Act 1978.

1978 c. 44.

(2) The regulations may provide for the exercise by the compensation authority of such of the functions of the Council which immediately before the passing of this Act were functions relating to compensation in respect of early retirement or for loss of employment as may be specified in the regulations.

(3) The regulations may provide for the recovery by the compensation authority from each of the other water authorities of such proportion of the cost incurred by the compensation authority in consequence of the regulations as the Secretary of State may from time to time determine.

(4) The proportions determined by the Secretary of State need not be the same for each water authority.

PART II

WATER SPACE AMENITY COMMISSION

Final reports

9.—(1) The Commission shall comply with paragraph 40 of Schedule 3 to the principal Act (annual reports) in relation to the period between the end of the period to which their last annual report relates and the appointed day.

(2) The Secretary of State shall lay before each House of Parliament a copy of any annual report sent to him by the Commission in compliance with this paragraph. SCH. 2

Continuance of Commission until residual functions completed to Secretary of State's satisfaction

10.—(1) No amendment or repeal made by this Act shall affect—

(*a*) the continuance of the Commission for the purpose of paragraph 9 above or their duty under that paragraph, or

(*b*) the continued operation for those purposes of the provisions of the principal Act relating to the constitution of the Commission.

(2) The Commission shall cease to exist when the Secretary of State, being satisfied that their duty under paragraph 9 above has been discharged, so directs by order.

(3) The Secretary of State shall pay to members of the Commission, other than the chairmen of water authorities, in respect of the period beginning with the appointed day and ending with the Commission ceasing to exist, such allowances as he may with the consent of the Treasury determine.

(4) The Secretary of State shall, as soon as possible after determining the amount of any allowances payable under sub-paragraph (3) above, lay a statement of his determination before each House of Parliament.

(5) As from the appointed day, the Secretary of State shall make available to the Commission such facilities as the Commission may reasonably require for performing the duty imposed on them by paragraph 9 above; and any expenses incurred by the Commission in connection with the performance of that duty on and after the appointed day shall be defrayed by the Secretary of State out of money provided by Parliament.

SCHEDULE 3

Section 6.

ARRANGEMENTS FOR CARRYING OUT SEWERAGE FUNCTIONS

The following is the Schedule inserted in the principal Act by section 6(2) of this Act—

"SCHEDULE 4A

ARRANGEMENTS FOR CARRYING OUT SEWERAGE FUNCTIONS

1. In this Schedule "arrangements" means arrangements (whenever made) under section 15 of this Act.

General

2. Arrangements entered into by a water authority shall be made with a view to ensuring that their sewerage functions, taken as a whole, are carried out efficiently.

SCH. 3

3.—(1) All arrangements shall comply with the requirements of such regulations as may be made by the Secretary of State for the purposes of this paragraph.

(2) Any such regulations may, in particular, include requirements as to the obligations to be imposed by any arrangements on the parties to those arrangements.

(3) Regulations under this paragraph shall be subject to annulment in pursuance of a resolution of either House of Parliament.

(4) Where arrangements are in force at the time when the first regulations made under this paragraph come into force, the parties to those arrangements shall, within such period as may be specified by the Secretary of State, make such alterations in the arrangements as are necessary to ensure that they comply with the regulations; and where, on the expiry of that period, any arrangements fail to comply with the regulations those arrangements shall have effect subject to such alterations as the Secretary of State may direct.

Cases where duty to make arrangements does not apply

4.—(1) The duty imposed by section 15(1) of this Act shall not apply in relation to any sewerage functions where—

(*a*) the water authority and relevant authority concerned agree that it would be inexpedient for arrangements to be made in respect of those functions;

(*b*) arrangements in respect of those functions have been brought to an end within the previous five years and either the water authority or relevant authority concerned are of the opinion that it would be inexpedient for arrangements to be so made; or

(*c*) any relevant authority requesting the making of arrangements have had a similar request refused by the water authority concerned within that period and the water authority are of that opinion.

(2) A water authority may refuse to enter into arrangements with a relevant authority where they are of the opinion that it would be inexpedient to do so, but where a water authority so refuse, in a case which does not fall within sub-paragraph (1) above, the relevant authority may apply to the Secretary of State for the decision to be reviewed.

(3) On any such review the Secretary of State may confirm the water authority's decision or give a direction requiring them to enter into arrangements with the relevant authority; and any such direction may specify the provision to be made by the arrangements (either in substitution for or in addition to any provision required by regulations under paragraph 3 above).

Variation and termination of arrangements

5.—(1) Any arrangements may—

(*a*) be varied or brought to an end by agreement between the parties;

(*b*) be brought to an end by the relevant authority giving reasonable notice to the water authority ; and Sch. 3

(*c*) subject to sub-paragraph (2) below, be varied or brought to an end by the water authority giving reasonable notice to the relevant authority.

(2) Where a notice has been served under sub-paragraph (1) (*c*) above, the Secretary of State may, on an application made to him by the relevant authority before the expiry of the notice, review the proposed variation or ending of the arrangements ; and on any such review the Secretary of State may confirm the proposals or give a direction—

(*a*) requiring the arrangements to be brought to an end, or varied, in accordance with the terms of the direction ; or

(*b*) requiring the notice to be withdrawn.

(3) The matters to which the Secretary of State must have regard in conducting a review under paragraph 4(2) or sub-paragraph (2) above, include the likely financial consequences for the parties of the proposed action.

(4) Where a review is conducted under sub-paragraph (2) above the notice in question shall not take effect except in accordance with a confirmation or direction under that sub-paragraph.

Local authority committees etc.

6.—(1) Where by virtue of any arrangements functions of a water authority are to be discharged by a local authority, then subject to the provision made by the arrangements, the local authority may arrange for the discharge of those functions by a committee, sub-committee or officer of theirs.

(2) Where by virtue of sub-paragraph (1) above any such functions may be discharged by a committee of a local authority, then, unless the water authority or local authority otherwise direct, the committee may arrange for the discharge of any of those functions by a sub-committee or an officer of the local authority.

(3) Where by virtue of sub-paragraph (1) above any such functions may be discharged by a sub-committee of a local authority, then, unless the water authority, the local authority or the committee otherwise direct, the sub-committee may arrange for the discharge of any of those functions by an officer of the local authority.

(4) Any arrangements made by a local authority or committee under this paragraph for the discharge of any functions by a committee, sub-committee or officer shall not prevent the authority or committee by whom those arrangements are made from discharging those functions.

SCH. 3

Transfer of officers

7. Where arrangements are made, varied or brought to an end, provision may be made by the parties to the arrangements for the transfer of any officers of either party to the other.

Compensation

8.—(1) Where an authority who are party to any arrangements have compensated any officer of theirs who has suffered loss as a result of the making, variation or ending of those arrangements, the authority who are the other party to those arrangements may make such payment to the compensating authority, by way of total or partial reimbursement, as they consider appropriate.

(2) The application, by section 34 of this Act, of section 259 of the Local Government Act 1972 (compensation for loss of
1972 c. 70. office), and accordingly the Local Government (Compensation)
S.I. 1974/463. Regulations 1974, shall cease to have effect in relation to any loss of employment or loss or diminution of emoluments resulting, after the passing of the Water Act 1983, from the making, varying or ending of any arrangements.

Interpretation

9. In this Schedule, and in section 15 of this Act—

" council " means the council of a district or London borough or the Common Council of the City of London ;

" relevant authority " means a council or—

(*a*) in relation to a new town as respects which an
1981 c. 64. order is in force under section 34 of the New Towns Act 1981 (provision of sewers and sewage disposal works by development corporation), the development corporation or any council within whose area the town is wholly or partly situated ;

(*b*) in relation to a new town as respects which an order is in force under paragraph 51 of Schedule 3
1976 c. 75. to the Development of Rural Wales Act 1976 (provision of sewers and sewage disposal works by Development Board for Rural Wales), the Board or any council within whose area the town is wholly or partly situated ;

(*c*) in relation to an area designated as an urban
1980 c. 65. development area under Part XVI of the Local Government, Planning and Land Act 1980, the urban development corporation or any council within whose area the urban development area is wholly or partly situated ; and

" sewerage functions " means, in relation to a water authority, the functions of the authority under Part
1936 c. 49. II of the Public Health Act 1936, other than those relating to sewage disposal."

SCHEDULE 4

Section 11(2).

Minor and Consequential Amendments

Water Act 1973 (*c.* 37)

1. In section 7(1) of the principal Act (supply of goods and services to public bodies), in paragraph (*a*), for the words " and the Council were each " there is substituted the word " were ".

2. In section 26(1) of the principal Act (duties of statutory water undertakers to their staff), after the word " make " there is inserted the word " such " and for the words from " and in doing so " to the end there are substituted the words " as they consider to be appropriate ".

Control of Pollution Act 1974 (*c.* 40)

3. In section 52(1) of the Control of Pollution Act 1974 (charges in respect of certain discharges in England and Wales) for the words " an order made after consultation with the National Water Council ", there is substituted the word " order ".

Salmon and Freshwater Fisheries Act 1975 (*c.* 51)

4.—(1) In section 28 of the Salmon and Freshwater Fisheries Act 1975 (general powers and duties of water authorities in relation to fisheries) after subsection (2) there is inserted the following subsection—

> " (2A) A water authority may pay to any member of an advisory committee established by it in accordance with paragraph (*b*) of subsection (1) above such allowances as may be determined by the Minister with the consent of the Treasury.".

(2) In section 41 of that Act (interpretation) after subsection (2) there is inserted the following subsection—

> " (2A) In section 28(2A) above, the reference to the Minister shall be construed, in relation to the Welsh Water Authority, as a reference to the Secretary of State.".

Land Drainage Act 1976 (*c.* 70)

5. For paragraph 10 of Schedule 1 to the Land Drainage Act 1976 (payments to chairmen of regional and local land drainage committees) there is substituted the following paragraph—

> " 10—(1) A water authority shall pay to any person who, not being a member of the authority, is chairman of one of their local land drainage committees such remuneration and allowances as may be determined by the appropriate Minister with the consent of the Treasury and, if that Minister so determines in the case of any such person who is or has been chairman of such a committee, shall pay or make arrangements for the payment of a pension in relation to that person in accordance with the determination.
>
> (2) If a person ceases to be chairman of the regional land drainage committee or of a local land drainage committee of a water authority and it appears to the appropriate Minister that there are special circumstances which make it right that that

SCH. 4 person should receive compensation in respect of his ceasing to be chairman (whether or not he becomes or remains a member of the authority), the appropriate Minister may require the authority to pay to that person a sum of such amount as that Minister may determine with the consent of the Treasury.

(3) A water authority may pay to any person who, not being a member of the authority, is a member of their regional land drainage committee or of one of their local land drainage committees such allowances as may be determined by the appropriate Minister with the consent of the Treasury.

(4) In this paragraph—

'the appropriate Minister' means—

(*a*) in the case of the Welsh Water Authority, the Secretary of State; and

(*b*) in any other case, the Minister; and

'pension', in relation to any person, means a pension (whether contributory or not) of any kind payable to or in respect of him, and includes an allowance, gratuity or lump sum so payable and a return of contributions with or without interest or any other addition."

6. In Schedule 1 to the Act of 1976 (members and proceedings of regional and local land drainage committees), after paragraph 14, there are inserted the following paragraphs—

"14A. The validity of any proceedings of a regional land drainage committee or local land drainage committee shall not be affected by any vacancy among the members of the committee or by any defect in the appointment of such a member.

1972 c. 70. 14B.—(1) Subject to the following provisions of this paragraph, the provisions of sections 94 to 98 of the Local Government Act 1972 (pecuniary interests of members of local authorities) shall apply in relation to members of a regional land drainage committee and those of a local land drainage committee as those provisions apply in relation to members of local authorities.

(2) In their application by virtue of this paragraph those provisions shall have effect in accordance with the following provisions—

(*a*) for references to meetings of the local authority there shall be substituted references to meetings of the committee,

(*b*) in section 94(4) for the reference to provision being made by standing orders of a local authority there shall be substituted a reference to provisions being made by direction of the committee,

(*c*) in section 96 for references to the proper officer of the local authority there shall be substituted a reference to an officer of the committee appointed for the purposes of this paragraph,

(*d*) section 97 shall apply as it applies to a local authority other than a parish or community council.

14C. A minute of the proceedings of a meeting of a regional land drainage committee or local land drainage committee, purporting to be signed at that or the next ensuing meeting by the chairman of the meeting to the proceedings of which the minute relates or by the chairman of the next ensuing meeting, shall be evidence of the proceedings and shall be received in evidence without further proof; and, until the contrary is proved, every meeting in respect of the proceedings of which a minute has been so signed shall be deemed to have been duly convened and held, and all the proceedings had at the meeting to have been duly had, and that committee or subcommittee shall be deemed to have been duly constituted and have had power to deal with the matters referred to in the minute." SCH. 4

Local Government, Planning and Land Act 1980 (*c.* 65)

7. In section 25(3) of the Local Government, Planning and Land Act 1980 (allowances in relation to meetings etc. of water authorities) for the words from the beginning to "(3B)" there are substituted the words "The following subsection shall be inserted after section 175(3) of the said Act of 1972:—"(3B)".

Transitional provisions

8. The repeals contained in Schedule 5 below shall not affect the operation of paragraph 31(1) and (2) of Schedule 3 to the principal Act in relation to any period before the day appointed for the purposes of section 3(1) of this Act.

9. In any case where—

(*a*) the Treasury have given a guarantee under paragraph 36(1) of Schedule 3 to the principal Act in respect of any sum borrowed by the Council; and

(*b*) any liability of the Council relating to repayment of the principal of, or payment of interest on, the sum so borrowed (or any part of that sum) has become a liability of one or more water authorities, whether by virtue of an order under section 3(4) of this Act or otherwise;

paragraph 36(1) of Schedule 3 shall have effect as if it empowered the Treasury to give a new guarantee in respect of that liability.

Section 11(3).

SCHEDULE 5

Repeals and Revocations

Part 1

Enactments Repealed

Chapter	Short title	Extent of repeal
1960 c. 67.	The Public Bodies (Admission to Meetings) Act 1960.	In the Schedule, paragraph 1(*c*).
1961 c. 64.	The Public Health Act 1961.	In section 9(3), the words from " (including " to the end.
1972 c. 70.	The Local Government Act 1972.	Section 175 (3A). Section 177(1)(*aa*).
1973 c. 37.	The Water Act 1973.	Section 4. In section 5(3), the words from " but before " to the end. Section 6. In section 17(5), the words " under section 6 above ". Section 23. In section 24(12)(*a*), the words " and to the Water Space Amenity Commission ". Section 25(5)(*a*). In section 26, subsections (2) to (4). In section 29(2), the words " and after consultation with the Council ". In section 30(6), the words " after consultation with the Council ". In section 38(1), the definitions of " the Council ", " regional water board " and " water development board ". In Schedule 3, paragraphs 22 to 30; in paragraph 31(1), the words from " and including " to the end; in paragraph 31(2), the words " and of any payment to the Council under paragraph 33 below "; in paragraph 32(1), the words " and after consultation with the Council "; paragraph 33; in paragraph 34, 39F(1), 40(1) and 41, the words " and the Council ", wherever they occur; in paragraphs 34(6) and 40(6), the words " or of the Council "; in paragraphs 35(2) and 39E(1), the words " or to the Council "; in paragraphs 36, 38(5) and

SCH. 5

Chapter	Short title	Extent of repeal
		(6), 39(1), 39E(1)(*b*) and 39F(1)(*a*), the words " or the Council ", wherever they occur; in paragraph 36(4), the words " or, as the case may be, the Council "; in paragraph 38(1), the words " and of the Council "; paragraph 39F(2); in paragraph 40(1), paragraph (*b*) and the word " and " immediately preceding it; in paragraph 40(3) the words " to the Council and ", sub-paragraphs (4) and (5) and in sub-paragraph (8) the words from " the Council " to " Commission ". In Schedule 8, paragraph 90.
1973 c. 65.	The Local Government (Scotland) Act 1973.	In Schedule 17, paragraph 64.
1974 c. 37.	The Health and Safety at Work etc. Act 1974.	In section 66(4), the words from " (including " to the end. In Schedule 6, paragraph 8.
1975 c. 24.	The House of Commons Disqualification Act 1975.	In Part III of Schedule 1, the entries relating to the National Water Council, a regional water authority and the Welsh Water Authority.
1976 c. 70.	The Land Drainage Act 1976.	In Schedule 5, in paragraph 8(1), the words " section 4(5)(*a*) and (*b*) ".
1976 c. 75.	The Development of Rural Wales Act 1976.	In Schedule 7, paragraph 11.
1977 c. 41.	The Water Charges Equalisation Act 1977.	The whole Act.
1980 c. 45.	The Water (Scotland) Act 1980.	In Schedule 10, the entry relating to the Water Act 1973.
1980 c. 65.	The Local Government, Planning and Land Act 1980.	Section 25(4). In section 158, subsections (1) and (2).
1981 c. 64.	The New Towns Act 1981.	In Schedule 12, paragraph 12.

PART II
INSTRUMENTS REVOKED

Number	Name of Instrument	Extent of revocation
S.I. 1973/1287	The North West Water Authority Constitution Order 1973.	Article 4. Schedule 2.
S.I. 1973/1288	The Northumbrian Water Authority Constitution Order 1973.	Article 4 Schedule 1.

SCH. 5

Number	Name of Instrument	Extent of revocation
S.I. 1973/1289	The Yorkshire Water Authority Constitution Order 1973.	Article 4. Schedule 1.
S.I. 1973/1306	The Wessex Water Authority Constitution Order 1973.	Article 4. Schedule 2.
S.I. 1973/1307	The South West Water Authority Constitution Order 1973.	Article 4. Schedule 2.
S.I. 1973/1345	The Welsh National Water Development Authority (Establishment and Constitution) Order 1973.	Article 4. Article 5. Schedule 2.
S.I. 1973/1359	The Anglian Water Authority Constitution Order 1973.	Article 4. Schedule 2.
S.I. 1973/1360	The Thames Water Authority Constitution Order 1973.	Article 4. Schedule 2.
S.I. 1973/1361	The Southern Water Authority Constitution Order 1973.	Article 4. Schedule 2.
S.I. 1973/1437	The Severn–Trent Water Authority Constitution Order 1973.	Article 4. Schedule 2.
S.I. 1974/1208	The Severn–Trent Water Authority Constitution (Amendment) Order 1974.	The whole Order.
S.I. 1974/2077	The Thames Water Authority Constitution (Amendment) Order 1974.	The whole Order.
S.I. 1977/724	The Welsh National Water Development Authority (Establishment and Constitution) (Variation) Order 1977.	The whole Order.
S.I. 1979/466	The Anglian Water Authority Constitution (Amendment) Order 1979.	The whole Order.
S.I. 1979/467	The Northumbrian Water Authority Constitution (Amendment) Order 1979.	The whole Order.
S.I. 1979/468	The North West Water Authority Constitution (Amendment) Order 1979.	The whole Order.
S.I. 1979/469	The Severn–Trent Water Authority Constitution (Amendment) Order 1979.	The whole Order.
S.I. 1979/470	The Southern Water Authority Constitution (Amendment) Order 1979.	The whole Order.
S.I. 1979/471	The South West Water Authority Constitution (Amendment) Order 1979.	The whole Order.
S.I. 1979/472	The Thames Water Authority Constitution (Amendment) Order 1979.	The whole Order.
S.I. 1979/473	The Wessex Water Authority Constitution (Amendment) Order 1979.	The whole Order.
S.I. 1979/474	The Yorkshire Water Authority Constitution (Amendment) Order 1979.	The whole Order.
S.I. 1981/1883	The Welsh Water Authority (Constitution) (Variation) Order 1981.	The whole Order.
S.I. 1982/944	The Water Authorities and National Water Council (Limit for Borrowing) Order 1982.	The whole Order.

Licensing (Occasional Permissions) Act 1983

1983 CHAPTER 24

An Act to empower licensing justices in England and Wales to grant to representatives of organisations not carried on for private gain occasional permissions authorising the sale of intoxicating liquor at functions connected with the activities of such organisations.

[9th May 1983]

BE IT ENACTED by the Queen's most Excellent Majesty, by and with the advice and consent of the Lords Spiritual and Temporal, and Commons, in this present Parliament assembled, and by the authority of the same, as follows:—

Grant of occasional permissions.

1.—(1) Licensing justices may, if satisfied as to the matters mentioned in subsection (2) below, grant to an officer of an eligible organisation or of a branch of such an organisation a permission (referred to in this Act as an occasional permission) authorising him to sell intoxicating liquor during a period not exceeding twenty-four hours at a function held by the organisation or branch in connection with the organisation's activities.

(2) The matters as to which the licensing justices must be satisfied are—

(*a*) that the officer is a fit and proper person to sell intoxicating liquor and is resident in their licensing district;

(*b*) that the place where the function is to be held will be a suitable place for intoxicating liquor to be sold and is situated in that district ; and

(*c*) that the sale of intoxicating liquor at the function is not likely to result in disturbance or annoyance being caused to residents in the neighbourhood of that place, or in any disorderly conduct.

(3) An occasional permission shall be in writing and shall specify—

(*a*) the place where intoxicating liquor may be sold by virtue of the permission ;

(*b*) the kind or kinds of intoxicating liquor that may be sold there by virtue of the permission ; and

(*c*) the hours between which such liquor may be so sold and the date (or dates) on which those hours fall ;

and the licensing justices may attach to the permission any condition that they think proper.

(4) Not more than four occasional permissions may be granted in a licensing district in any period of twelve months in respect of functions held by the same organisation or branch.

(5) An occasional permission shall not authorise the sale of intoxicating liquor on a Sunday in a district in Wales or Monmouthshire to which section 66(1) of the principal Act for the time being applies.

(6) In this section " eligible organisation " means any organisation not carried on for purposes of private gain ; and, except in the case of an organisation carrying on a commercial undertaking, a purpose which is calculated to benefit an organisation as a whole shall not be taken to be a purpose of private gain by reason only that action in fulfilment of the purpose would result in benefit to any person as an individual.

Applications for occasional permissions.

2.—(1) An application for an occasional permission shall be in writing and shall contain the following particulars—

(*a*) the name and address of the applicant and the date and place of his birth ;

(*b*) the name of the organisation in connection with whose activities the function in question is to be held, the purposes for which the organisation is carried on, and (where appropriate) the name of the branch holding the function ;

(*c*) the nature of the applicant's office in the organisation or branch holding the function ;

(*d*) the date and nature of the function and the place where it is to be held ;

(*e*) the kind or kinds of intoxicating liquor proposed to be sold at the function and the hours between which it is proposed that such liquor should be sold ;

(*f*) details of any occasional permissions granted by the licensing justices in the twelve months preceding the date of the application in respect of functions held by the organisation or branch holding the function.

(2) An application for an occasional permission shall be made by serving two copies of the application on the clerk to the licensing justices not less than one month before the date of the function in respect of which the application is made.

(3) On receiving an application under subsection (2) above the clerk shall serve notice of the application on the chief officer of police by sending him a copy of it.

(4) An application for an occasional permission shall be heard by the licensing justices at the next licensing sessions following its receipt by the clerk or, where those sessions are to be held fifteen days or less after its receipt, at the licensing sessions next following those sessions.

(5) The clerk shall send to an applicant notice of the date, time and place of the licensing sessions at which his application is to be heard in accordance with subsection (4) above ; and the list kept for those sessions under paragraph 6 of Schedule 2 to the principal Act shall show the name and address of the applicant, the nature of the application and the place where the function in question is to be held.

(6) On the consideration of an application for an occasional permission the applicant shall, if so required by the licensing justices, attend in person, and licensing justices may postpone consideration of such an application until the applicant does attend.

(7) Subsections (1), (3) and (4) of section 97 of the Magistrates' Courts Act 1980 (summons to witness and warrant for his arrest) shall apply in relation to licensing justices and to an application for an occasional permission as if they were a magistrates' court for the petty sessions area constituting the licensing district and the application were a complaint. 1980 c. 43.

3. The Schedule to this Act (which provides for offences in relation to occasional permissions and applications for such permissions, and in relation to the conduct of premises where the sale of intoxicating liquor is authorised by such permissions) shall have effect. **Offences.**

Interpretation and other supplementary provisions.

4.—(1) In this Act—

" occasional permission " means a permission granted under section 1 above;

" organisation " includes any society, club, institution or association of persons;

1964 c. 26.

" the principal Act " means the Licensing Act 1964.

(2) The following provisions of the principal Act, namely—

(*a*) section 2 (licensing justices and districts);

(*b*) section 29 (fees);

(*c*) sections 192 and 193 (jurisdiction and disqualification of justices);

(*d*) section 197 (service of notices, etc.);

(*e*) section 201 (interpretation),

shall have effect as if the provisions of this Act were contained in that Act.

(3) In section 160 of the principal Act (selling liquor without a licence)—

(*a*) in subsection (1) there shall be inserted after the words " canteen licence ", in both places, the words " or occasional permission ", and after the words " that licence " the words " or permission "; and

(*b*) after subsection (6) there shall be inserted—

" (7) In subsection (1) of this section " occasional permission " means a permission granted under the Licensing (Occasional Permissions) Act 1983."

(4) In section 202 of that Act (application to Isles of Scilly), in subsection (1)(*b*), after the words " Part III of this Act " there shall be inserted the words " , under the Licensing (Occasional Permissions) Act 1983 ".

Short title, commencement and extent.

5.—(1) This Act may be cited as the Licensing (Occasional Permissions) Act 1983.

(2) This Act shall come into force at the end of the period of three months beginning with the day on which it is passed.

(3) This Act shall extend to England and Wales only.

SCHEDULE

Section 3.

Offences

Interpretation

1.—(1) In this Schedule " authorised premises ", in relation to an occasional permission, means any place where the sale of intoxicating liquor is for the time being authorised by the permission.

(2) Any reference in this Schedule to an agent of the holder of an occasional permission includes a reference to any person assisting the holder of the permission with the sale of intoxicating liquor in the authorised premises.

False statements in applications

2. Any person who in an application for an occasional permission knowingly or recklessly makes any statement which is false in a material respect shall be guilty of an offence.

Failure to comply with conditions or produce permission

3. Any holder of an occasional permission who—

(*a*) fails to comply with a condition attached to it under section 1(3) of this Act, or

(*b*) on being ordered by a constable to produce it for examination, fails to do so within a reasonable time,

shall be guilty of an offence.

Sale of liquor to persons under 18

4.—(1) In any authorised premises the holder of the occasional permission or any agent of his shall not—

(*a*) knowingly sell intoxicating liquor to a person under eighteen, or

(*b*) knowingly allow a person under eighteen to consume intoxicating liquor in a bar,

and in those premises the holder of the permission shall not knowingly allow any person to sell intoxicating liquor to a person under eighteen.

(2) A person under eighteen shall not in any authorised premises buy or attempt to buy intoxicating liquor, nor consume intoxicating liquor in a bar.

(3) No person shall buy or attempt to buy intoxicating liquor for consumption in a bar in any authorised premises by a person under eighteen.

(4) Sub-paragraphs (1) and (2) above do not prohibit the sale to or purchase by a person who has attained the age of sixteen of beer, porter, cider or perry for consumption at a meal in a part of the premises which is set apart for the service of meals and is not a bar.

(5) Any person who contravenes any provision of this paragraph shall be guilty of an offence.

(6) Where, as regards any authorised premises, the holder of the occasional permission is charged with an offence under sub-paragraph (1) above in a case in which it is proved or admitted that he did not personally have the knowledge required for the commission of the offence charged, he shall not be convicted of the offence on the basis of another's knowledge if he proves that he exercised all due diligence to avoid the commission of an offence under that sub-paragraph.

(7) References in sub-paragraphs (1) to (3) above to a bar do not include a bar at any time when it is—

(*a*) set apart for the service of table meals ; and

(*b*) not used for the sale or supply of intoxicating liquor otherwise than to persons having table meals there and for consumption by such persons as ancillary to their meals.

Sale or serving of liquor by persons under 18

5.—(1) Any holder of an occasional permission who allows any person under eighteen to sell or serve any intoxicating liquor in the authorised premises shall be guilty of an offence.

(2) Where in any proceedings under this paragraph it is alleged that a person was at any time under eighteen, and he appears to the court to have then been under that age, he shall be deemed for the purposes of the proceedings to have then been under that age unless the contrary is proved.

Holder of permission not to allow drunkenness etc.

6.—(1) The holder of an occasional permission shall not permit drunkenness or any violent, quarrelsome or riotous conduct to take place in the authorised premises.

(2) The holder of an occasional permission shall not sell intoxicating liquor to a drunken person.

(3) Any person who contravenes this paragraph shall be guilty of an offence.

(4) Where, as regards any authorised premises, the holder of the occasional permission is charged with permitting drunkenness contrary to sub-paragraph (1) above in a case in which it is proved that any person was drunk in the premises, the burden of proving that the holder of the permission and his agents took all reasonable steps for preventing drunkenness in the premises shall lie upon him.

Procuring drink for drunken person

7. Any person who—

(*a*) in any authorised premises procures or attempts to procure any intoxicating liquor for consumption by a drunken person, or (*b*) aids a drunken person in obtaining or consuming intoxicating liquor in any authorised premises,

shall be guilty of an offence.

Power to exclude drunkards etc. from authorised premises

8.—(1) Without prejudice to any other right to refuse a person admission to premises or to expel a person from premises, the holder of an occasional permission may refuse to admit to, or may expel from, the authorised premises any person who is drunken, violent, quarrelsome or disorderly or whose presence in the authorised premises would subject the holder of the permission to a penalty under this Schedule.

(2) Any person liable to be expelled from any authorised premises under this paragraph who, when requested by the holder of the occasional permission or any agent of his or any constable to leave the premises, fails to do so shall be guilty of an offence.

(3) Any constable shall, on the demand of the holder of an occasional permission or any agent of his, help to expel from the authorised premises any person liable to be expelled from them under this paragraph, and may use such force as may be required for the purpose.

Right of constables to enter premises

9.—(1) For the purpose of preventing or detecting the commission of any offence under this Schedule a constable may enter any authorised premises at any time during the hours specified in the occasional permission under section 1(3)(*c*) of this Act.

(2) Any person who, whether himself or by any person acting with his consent, fails to admit a constable who demands entry to premises in pursuance of this paragraph shall be guilty of an offence.

Penalties for offences

10. Any person guilty of an offence under this Schedule shall be liable on summary conviction—

(*a*) in the case of an offence under paragraph 2, 3(*a*) or 4(2) or (3) above, to a fine not exceeding the third level on the standard scale (as defined by section 75 of the Criminal Justice Act 1982); **1982 c.** 48

(*b*) in the case of an offence under paragraph 4(1), 5 or 6 above, to a fine not exceeding the second level on that scale; and

(*c*) in the case of an offence under paragraph 3(*b*), 7, 8(2) or 9(2) above, to a fine not exceeding the first level on that scale.

Proof of sale or consumption of intoxicating liquor

11.—(1) Evidence that a transaction in the nature of a sale of intoxicating liquor took place shall, in any proceedings relating to an offence under this Schedule, be evidence of the sale of the liquor without proof that money passed.

(2) Evidence that consumption of intoxicating liquor was about to take place shall in any such proceedings be evidence of the consumption of intoxicating liquor without proof of actual consumption.

(3) Evidence that any person, other than the holder of an occasional permission or any agent of his, consumed or intended to consume intoxicating liquor in the authorised premises shall be evidence that the liquor was sold by or on behalf of the holder of the permission to that person.

Energy Act 1983

1983 CHAPTER 25

An Act to amend the law relating to electricity so as to facilitate the generation and supply of electricity by persons other than Electricity Boards, and for certain other purposes; and to amend the law relating to the duties of persons responsible for nuclear installations and to compensation for breach of those duties.

[9th May 1983]

BE IT ENACTED by the Queen's most Excellent Majesty, by and with the advice and consent of the Lords Spiritual and Temporal, and Commons, in this present Parliament assembled, and by the authority of the same, as follows:—

PART I

ELECTRICITY

Private generation and supply

1. Section 23 of the Electric Lighting Act 1909 (which prohibits persons other than Electricity Boards from commencing to supply or distribute electricity) and section 11 of the Electricity (Supply) Act 1919 (which restricts the establishment and extension of generating stations) shall cease to have effect.

Removal of restrictions on supply etc.
1909 c. 34.
1919 c. 100.

PART I

Notice of construction or extension of generating stations.

2.—(1) Subject to subsection (5) below, any person other than an Electricity Board or a local authority who proposes—

(*a*) to construct or extend an electricity generating station having plant with a rating exceeding 10 megawatts, or

(*b*) to extend an existing electricity generating station in such a way that it will have plant with such a rating,

shall give written notice of his proposal to the Area Board for the area in which the station is or will be or, if it is or will be within the district of a Scottish Board, to that Board.

(2) The Secretary of State may make regulations as to the time when a notice under this section is to be given and the particulars which it is to contain.

(3) A person who is required to give a notice under this section shall be guilty of an offence if the work of construction or extension begins without the required notice having been given.

(4) A person guilty of an offence under this section shall be liable—

(*a*) on conviction on indictment, to a fine, or

(*b*) on summary conviction, to a fine not exceeding the statutory maximum.

(5) This section shall not apply in a case in which section 35 of the Electricity (Scotland) Act 1979 applies.

1979 c. 11.

(6) References in this section to extending a generating station are references to increasing the rating of its plant.

Nuclear-powered generating stations.

3.—(1) Subject to subsection (5) below, no person shall construct, extend or become the operator of a nuclear-powered generating station without the consent of the Secretary of State.

(2) A consent given for the purposes of this section may be subject to such conditions as the Secretary of State thinks fit.

(3) A person who contravenes subsection (1) above, or any condition of a consent given for the purposes of this section, shall be guilty of an offence.

(4) A person guilty of an offence under this section shall be liable—

(*a*) on conviction on indictment, to a fine, or

(*b*) on summary conviction, to a fine not exceeding the statutory maximum.

(5) This section shall not apply to the construction, extension or operation of a generating station by an Electricity Board.

PART I

(6) In this section " nuclear-powered generating station " means an electricity generating station the operation of which requires a licence under section 1 of the Nuclear Installations Act 1965; and references to extending a generating station are references to increasing the rating of its plant.

1965 c. 57.

Hydro-electric generating stations in Scotland.

1979 c. 11.

4.—(1) In section 35(1) of the Electricity (Scotland) Act 1979 (which relates to the control of private hydro-electric generating stations)—

(*a*) for the word " establish " there shall be substituted the words " construct or extend ";

(*b*) the word " new " shall cease to have effect;

(*c*) the word " private ", in both places where it occurs, shall cease to have effect; and

(*d*) for the words " 50 kilowatts ", in both places where they occur, there shall be substituted the words " 1 megawatt ".

(2) Section 35(2) of that Act shall cease to have effect.

Private generators and Electricity Boards.

5.—(1) In this section " private generator or supplier " means a person other than an Electricity Board or local authority who—

(*a*) generates electricity, or

(*b*) supplies electricity generated otherwise than by an Electricity Board or local authority.

(2) Where a private generator or supplier requests an Electricity Board—

(*a*) to give and continue to give a supply of electricity to premises where he generates electricity or from which he supplies electricity to others, or

(*b*) to purchase electricity generated by him, or

(*c*) to permit him to use the Board's transmission and distribution system for the purpose of giving a supply of electricity to any premises,

the Board shall offer to comply with the request unless on technical grounds it would not be reasonably practicable to do so.

(3) Subject to sections 6 to 8 below, an offer under this section may include such reasonable terms and may be made subject to such reasonable conditions as the Board may determine, including—

(*a*) terms requiring security to be given for the payment of any sums that may become payable to the Board, and

(*b*) the condition that any necessary planning or other consents are obtained (including, in the case of an offer by

PART I

1957 c. 48.

the Central Electricity Generating Board, the consent of the Secretary of State under section 2(6) of the Electricity Act 1957).

(4) Every offer under this section shall include such reasonable terms and conditions as the Board may consider necessary to secure that the control by Electricity Boards of the operation of the electricity supply system is not impaired.

(5) If, before a request under this section can be complied with, it is necessary for any electric lines or other electrical plant to be provided, or for any other works to be carried out, the terms of an offer under this section—

(*a*) shall include an undertaking by the Board to provide the lines or other plant or carry out the works, and

(*b*) may require the person making the request to make payments to the Board in respect of any expenditure incurred by the Board in carrying out the undertaking.

(6) A request under this section shall contain such particulars, and shall be in such form, as may be prescribed by regulations made by the Secretary of State ; and such regulations may make provision for the payment to the Board by the person making the request of fees to meet the Board's administrative expenses in dealing with the request.

Charges for supplies by Electricity Boards.

1947 c. 54.

1979 c. 11.

6.—(1) Subject to subsection (2) below, the price to be paid for electricity supplied by an Electricity Board in compliance with requests under section 5 above shall be in accordance with tariffs fixed under section 37 of the Electricity Act 1947 or section 22 of the Electricity (Scotland) Act 1979.

(2) Where, owing to special circumstances, the tariffs fixed under section 37 of the Electricity Act 1947 or section 22 of the Electricity (Scotland) Act 1979 are not appropriate to a supply requested under section 5 above, the terms of the Board's offer under section 5 shall specify the price proposed by the Board and any arrangements proposed for its revision.

Charges for purchases by Electricity Boards.

7.—(1) Each Electricity Board other than the Central Electricity Generating Board shall as soon as practicable after the commencement of this section fix tariffs of prices that will be paid by the Board for electricity purchased by it in compliance with requests under section 5 above.

(2) In the case of any purchase in respect of which—

(*a*) there is no tariff in force under this section which is applicable, or

(*b*) the tariff applicable is not appropriate owing to special circumstances, the terms of the offer made by the Board under section 5 above shall specify the price proposed by the Board and any arrangements proposed for its revision. PART I

(3) The principles on which tariffs are fixed and prices proposed by an Electricity Board in accordance with this section shall include the principle that a purchase by the Board in compliance with a request under section 5 above should be on terms which—

(*a*) will not increase the prices payable by customers of the Board for electricity supplied to them by the Board, and

(*b*) will reflect the costs that would have been incurred by the Board but for the purchase.

(4) The terms of an offer to purchase electricity in compliance with a request under section 5 above may include a requirement that the vendor shall make to the Board from time to time such reasonable payments as the Board may determine in respect of the costs of maintenance, operation and depreciation of the assets employed, and of the administrative expenses incurred, by the Board in complying with the request.

(5) The amount of the payments to be made to the Board in accordance with subsection (4) above may include an amount designed to give the Board a return on the assets there referred to (taking into account any payment of the kind referred to in section 5(5) above) which is not greater than any return that the Board expects to receive on comparable assets.

Charges for use of transmission and distribution systems.

8.—(1) Each Electricity Board shall as soon as practicable after the commencement of this section prepare tariffs of charges that will be made by the Board to persons permitted to use the Board's transmission and distribution system in pursuance of requests under section 5 above.

(2) In any case where—

(*a*) there is no tariff in force under this section which is applicable to the use requested, or

(*b*) the tariff applicable is not appropriate owing to special circumstances,

the terms of the offer made by the Board under section 5 above shall specify the charge proposed by the Board and any arrangements proposed for its revision.

(3) The principles on which tariffs are fixed and charges proposed by an Electricity Board in accordance with this section shall include the principle that charges should be no more than sufficient to provide a return on the relevant assets (taking into account any payments of the kind referred to in section 5(5) above) comparable to any return that the Board expects to receive on comparable assets; and for this purpose "relevant

PART I

assets" means the assets employed by the Board in complying with requests for permission to use the Board's transmission and distribution system.

Disputes as to offers under section 5 etc.

9.—(1) Any dispute as to—

(*a*) whether it would be reasonably practicable for an Electricity Board to comply with a request made to it under section 5 above, or

(*b*) whether a tariff which is applicable in the case of any supply, purchase or use requested under section 5 above is appropriate to that case, or

(*c*) the price or charge proposed by an Electricity Board in a case in which no tariff is applicable and appropriate, or

(*d*) the reasonableness of any other term or condition of an offer made by the Board under section 5 above, or

(*e*) the reasonableness of any payment demanded by an Electricity Board in accordance with section 7(4) above,

may be referred to the Secretary of State for determination by him or, if he thinks fit, by an arbitrator (or in Scotland an arbiter) appointed by him.

(2) The Secretary of State may make regulations as to the conduct of proceedings for the determination of disputes under this section; and the Arbitration Act 1950 and the Arbitration Act 1979 shall, in their application to disputes determined by an arbitrator appointed under this section, have effect subject to the provisions of such regulations.

1950 c. 27.
1979 c. 42.

(3) Regulations under this section relating to the determination of disputes by the Secretary of State may include provision—

(*a*) enabling the Secretary of State to require a party to the dispute to pay a sum determined by the Secretary of State towards any administrative expenses incurred by him in connection with the determination of the dispute, and

(*b*) as to awards of costs or expenses as between the parties to the dispute.

(4) Any sums paid to the Secretary of State by virtue of this section shall be paid into the Consolidated Fund.

(5) Subsections (6) to (8) below shall have effect in relation to Scotland, but subject to the provisions of regulations made by the Secretary of State under this section.

(6) Any arbiter appointed by the Secretary of State shall have the like powers for securing the attendance of witnesses and the production of documents and with regard to the examination of witnesses on oath and the awarding of expenses as if the arbitration were on a submission.

(7) The arbiter may, and if so directed by the Court of Session shall, state a case for the opinion of that Court on any question of law arising in the proceedings.

(8) Any award of the Secretary of State or of an arbiter under this section may be recorded in the Books of Council and Session for execution and may be enforced accordingly.

Further provisions as to charges under sections 7 and 8.

10.—(1) The tariffs fixed under section 7 or 8 above shall be so framed as to show the methods by which and the principles on which the charges are to be made as well as their amount, and shall be published in such manner as in the opinion of the Electricity Board concerned will secure adequate publicity.

(2) Tariffs fixed under section 7 or 8 above by an Electricity Board other than a Scottish Board shall be fixed after consultation with the Electricity Council, which shall consult the Secretary of State as to the methods by which and the principles on which charges are to be made.

(3) Tariffs fixed under section 7 or 8 above by a Scottish Board shall be fixed after consultation with the Secretary of State as to the methods by which and the principles on which charges are to be made.

(4) The tariffs required by sections 7 and 8 above may be altered or replaced from time to time, and need not be exhaustive.

(5) Before proposing a price in accordance with section 7(2) above or a charge in accordance with section 8(2) above an Electricity Board other than a Scottish Board shall consult the Electricity Council.

(6) An Electricity Board, in fixing tariffs and proposing prices or charges in accordance with section 7 or 8 above, shall not show undue preference to any person or class of persons and shall not exercise any undue discrimination against any person or class of persons.

Arrangements between Electricity Boards.

11.—(1) Where a request is made to an Electricity Board under section 5 above and that Board (" the first Board ") considers that the request could more appropriately be met by another Electricity Board (" the second Board "), the first Board may propose to the second Board that the second Board meet the request.

(2) If the second Board does not agree to a proposal under subsection (1) above, the first Board may refer the dispute to the Secretary of State for determination by him.

(3) If—

(*a*) the second Board agrees to a proposal under subsection (1) above ; or

PART I

(*b*) the Secretary of State, on a reference under subsection (2) above, determines that the request is to be met by the second Board,

the request shall be treated as if it had been made to the second Board.

Meters to be of approved pattern.

12.—(1) Subject to subsection (5) below, no person shall use a meter for measuring the amount of electrical energy supplied by him to another person, or the electrical quantity contained in the supply, unless it is of an approved pattern.

(2) A meter is of an approved pattern for the purposes of this section if it is of a pattern for the time being approved by the Secretary of State or by a person who, for the purpose of implementing any Community obligation, is responsible for giving pattern approval in a member State other than the United Kingdom.

(3) A person who uses a meter in contravention of this section shall be guilty of an offence unless he believes, on reasonable grounds, that the meter is of an approved pattern.

(4) A person guilty of an offence under this section shall be liable on summary conviction to a fine not exceeding level 2 on the standard scale.

(5) This section shall not apply—

(*a*) in relation to a supply by an Electricity Board, or

(*b*) in relation to a meter installed before (and not moved since) the commencement of this section.

Duty of Boards to supply.

1899 c. 19.

1947 c. 54.

13. In section 27 of the Schedule to the Electric Lighting (Clauses) Act 1899 as incorporated with the Electricity Act 1947 (duty to supply premises within fifty yards of a distributing main) after subsection (1) there shall be inserted—

" (1A) Subsection (1) of this section shall not apply in relation to premises to which a supply of energy is already given, directly from electric lines belonging to the Undertakers, by a private supplier.".

Inspection and testing of lines etc.

1882 c. 56.

14.—(1) In section 24 of the Electric Lighting Act 1882 (which empowers Electricity Boards to enter premises to which electricity is supplied by them) for the words " by the undertakers " in the second place where they occur there shall be substituted the words " (whether by the undertakers or by any other person) directly through electric lines belonging to the undertakers ".

(2) In section 36(1)(*a*) of the Schedule to the Electric Lighting (Clauses) Act 1899 (which provides for inspectors appointed under that Schedule to inspect and test the lines and works of

Electricity Boards and the supply of energy given by them), for the words " Undertakers' electric lines and works " there shall be substituted the words " electric lines and works of persons who supply energy ".

(3) Sections 39 and 42 to 48 of that Schedule (which make further provision as to testing and inspection, including provision giving inspectors the right of access to the premises of suppliers for the purpose of testing electric lines and instruments and provision penalising suppliers who fail to comply with the Schedule's requirements) shall apply in relation to suppliers of electricity other than Electricity Boards as they apply in relation to Area Boards and Scottish Boards.

(4) References in this section to the Schedule to the Electric Lighting (Clauses) Act 1899 are references to that Schedule as incorporated with the Electricity Act 1947.

1899 c. 19.
1947 c. 54.

Miscellaneous and general

Amendments relating to meters.

15. The enactments mentioned in Schedule 1 to this Act shall have effect subject to the amendments specified in that Schedule.

Regulations relating to supply and safety.

16.—(1) The Secretary of State may make such regulations as he thinks fit for the purpose of—

(*a*) securing that supplies of electricity by Electricity Boards or other persons are regular and efficient; and

(*b*) eliminating or reducing the risks of personal injury, or damage to property or interference with its use, arising from the supply of electricity by an Electricity Board or any other person, from the use of electricity so supplied or from the installation, maintenance or use of any electrical plant.

(2) Without prejudice to the generality of subsection (1) above, regulations under this section may—

(*a*) make provision for relieving an Electricity Board from any obligation to supply or purchase electricity, or to permit the use of the Board's transmission and distribution system, in cases where electrical plant or fittings or their use do not comply with the regulations;

(*b*) prohibit the supply of electricity except by means of a system approved by the Secretary of State;

(*c*) make provision requiring compliance with notices given by the Secretary of State specifying action to be taken in relation to any electrical plant or fittings for the purpose of—

(i) preventing or ending a breach of regulations under this section, or

PART I

(ii) eliminating or reducing a risk of personal injury or damage to property or interference with its use;

(*d*) make provision requiring notice to be given to the Secretary of State, in such cases as may be specified in the regulations, of accidents and of failures of supplies of electricity;

(*e*) make provision as to the keeping, by persons who supply electricity, of maps, plans and sections and as to their production (on payment, if so required, of a reasonable fee) for inspection or copying;

(*f*) provide for particular requirements of the regulations to be deemed to be complied with in the case of electrical plant or fittings complying with specified standards or requirements;

(*g*) provide for the granting of exemptions from any requirement of the regulations.

(3) Regulations under this section may provide that any person who contravenes any specified provision of the regulations, or any person who does so in specified circumstances, shall be guilty of an offence under this section.

(4) A person guilty of an offence under this section shall be liable on summary conviction to a fine not exceeding level 5 on the standard scale.

Charges for availability of supply.

1947 c. 54.

17.—(1) In section 37 of the Electricity Act 1947 (tariffs), after subsection (4) there shall be inserted—

" (4A) Tariffs fixed under this section may include charges in respect of the availability of a supply of electricity, and such a charge may vary according to the extent to which the supply is taken up.

(4B) Where the Electricity Council is consulted as to a tariff which includes a charge of the kind referred to in subsection (4A) of this section, the Council shall consult the Secretary of State as to the methods by which and the principles on which the charge is to be made.";

1922 c. 46.

and section 23 of the Electricity (Supply) Act 1922 (annual payments for standby supplies) shall cease to have effect.

1979 c. 11.

(2) In section 22 of the Electricity (Scotland) Act 1979 after subsection (3) there shall be inserted—

" (3A) Tariffs fixed under this section may include charges in respect of the availability of a supply of electricity, and such a charge may vary according to the extent to which the supply is taken up.

(3B) Before fixing under subsection (1) a tariff which includes a charge of the kind referred to in subsection

(3A), a Board shall consult the Secretary of State as to the methods by which and the principles on which the charge is to be made.". PART I

Purchases by Electricity Boards from local authorities.

18.—(1) This section applies to any purchase of electricity by an Electricity Board in accordance with arrangements made in pursuance of—

(*a*) section 21(2) of the Control of Pollution Act 1974 (production of heat and electricity from waste etc.), or 1974 c. 40.

(*b*) section 11(2) of the Local Government (Miscellaneous Provisions) Act 1976 (production of heat etc. by local authorities). 1976 c. 57.

(2) The price at which a purchase to which this section applies is made shall be the same as it would be by virtue of section 7 above if the purchase were made in compliance with a request under section 5 above; and subsections (4) and (5) of section 7 shall apply to a purchase to which this section applies as they apply to a purchase made in compliance with such a request.

(3) Section 9 above shall apply to a dispute as to—

(*a*) the price at which a purchase to which this section applies is to be made, or

(*b*) the reasonableness of any payment demanded by an Electricity Board in accordance with section 7(4) above as applied by this section,

as it applies to disputes within section 9(1)(*a*) to (*e*).

Combined heat and power.

19.—(1) For subsections (1) and (2) of section 50 of the Electricity Act 1947 (use of heat from generating stations) there shall be substituted— 1947 c. 54.

" (1) It shall be the duty of every Electricity Board to adopt and support schemes—

(*a*) for the combined production of heat and electricity, and

(*b*) for the use of heat produced in combination with electricity, or incidentally from its generation, for the heating of buildings or for other useful purposes.

(2) Nothing in subsection (1) of this section—

(*a*) shall remove the need for an Area Board to obtain the approval of the Secretary of State under section 6 of the Electricity Act 1957 to proposals for the generation of electricity by the Board, or 1957 c. 48.

(*b*) shall require an Electricity Board to undertake expenditure in connection with a scheme which

PART I

does not meet the financial criteria applied by the Board in relation to other expenditure of the Board.".

(2) In subsection (3) of section 50 for the words " the last foregoing subsection " there shall be substituted the words " subsection (1) of this section ".

1979 c. 11.

(3) For section 15 of the Electricity (Scotland) Act 1979 (research into heating from electricity) there shall be substituted—

" Production and use of heat and electricity.

15.—(1) It shall be the duty of each Board to adopt and support schemes—

(a) for the combined production of heat and electricity, and

(b) for the use of heat produced in combination with electricity, or incidentally from its generation, for the heating of buildings or for other useful purposes.

(2) For the purposes of a scheme under subsection (1), a Board may, in accordance with a scheme submitted by them to the Secretary of State and approved by order made with or without modification by him, exercise the powers conferred by section 13(8) for the purposes of that section, and section 13(9) shall apply in relation to the manner in which the powers are exercisable.

(3) Nothing in subsection (1) shall require a Board to undertake expenditure in connection with a scheme which does not meet the financial criteria applied by the Board in relation to other expenditure of the Board.".

Abolition of rights of entry.
1899 c. 19.
1947 c. 54.

20. In the Schedule to the Electric Lighting (Clauses) Act 1899 (as incorporated with the Electricity Act 1947 or any other enactment), the following provisions (which give rights to enter premises for purposes connected with the supply and maintenance of meters) shall cease to have effect—

(a) in section 52 the words from " and for those purposes " to " acts ", and

(b) section 54(2).

The Electricity Consumers' Council.

21.—(1) There shall be a consumers' council for England and Wales (in this section referred to as " the Council ") to be known as the Electricity Consumers' Council.

(2) The Council shall consist of a chairman appointed by the Secretary of State, and not more than thirty other members made up of—

(a) the chairmen for the time being of the Consultative Councils established under section 7 of the Electricity Act 1947 for the areas of Area Boards, and

(b) such other persons as the Secretary of State may appoint. **Part I**

(3) It shall be the duty of the Council to consider any matter affecting the interests of consumers generally of electricity supplied by Electricity Boards in England and Wales, or of any class of such consumers, being a matter which—

(a) is referred to the Council by the Secretary of State or the Electricity Council, or

(b) is the subject of a report or representations made to the Council by one of the Consultative Councils mentioned in subsection (2) above, or

(c) appears to the Council to be a matter to which consideration ought to be given apart from any such reference, report or representations.

(4) The Council shall report to the Secretary of State or, as the case may be, the Electricity Council on any matter considered by them by virtue of subsection (3)(a) above, and where it appears to them that action ought to be taken concerning any other matter considered by them under subsection (3) they shall make representations to the Electricity Council on that matter.

(5) The Council may, after consulting the Electricity Council, make representations to the Secretary of State on any matter considered by them under this section otherwise than on a reference by the Secretary of State.

(6) The Council shall consider any plans, arrangements or proposals of which they are informed under section 22 below and may make representations on them to the Electricity Council.

(7) The Council may refer to any of the Consultative Councils mentioned in subsection (2) above any matter which affects the interests of consumers of electricity in the area for which the Consultative Council is established or the interests of any class of those consumers.

(8) The Secretary of State may, after consultation with the Board concerned and with the Electricity Council, give such directions as he thinks fit to an Electricity Board in England or Wales with respect to matters arising out of representations made to him by the Council under this section, and shall send to the Council a copy of any such directions; and section 40(2) of the Electricity Act 1957 shall apply in relation to such directions as it applies in relation to directions under that Act. **1957 c. 48.**

(9) The Council shall make to the Secretary of State, as soon as possible after the end of each financial year of the Electricity Council, a report on the performance by the Council of their

PART I

functions during that year; and the Secretary of State shall lay a copy of the report before each House of Parliament.

(10) In this section references to consumers of electricity include references to prospective consumers.

(11) Schedule 2 to this Act shall have effect with respect to the Council.

Functions of other bodies in relation to Electricity Consumers' Council.

22.—(1) It shall be the duty of the Electricity Council to inform the Electricity Consumers' Council of the general plans and arrangements of the Electricity Council and of the Central Electricity Generating Board for performing their functions in relation to the supply of electricity, and in particular of any proposal of the Central Electricity Generating Board to vary a tariff.

(2) The Electricity Council may refer any matter to the Electricity Consumers' Council and shall consider any representations or report made to them by the Electricity Consumers' Council.

1947 c. 54.

(3) In section 7 of the Electricity Act 1947 (which establishes Consultative Councils for the area of every Area Board) after subsection (4) there shall be inserted—

"(4A) Each of the said Councils—

(*a*) may make representations to the Electricity Consumers' Council on any matter which has been considered by them under subsection (4) of this section and affects the interests of consumers or prospective consumers of electricity in the area or of any class of those consumers, and

(*b*) shall consider and report to the Electricity Consumers' Council on any matter which may be referred to them by that Council.".

Offences.

23.—(1) Proceedings for an offence under this Part of this Act shall not, in England and Wales, be instituted except by or with the consent of the Secretary of State or the Director of Public Prosecutions.

(2) Where an offence committed by a body corporate under this Part of this Act is proved to have been committed with the consent or connivance of, or to be attributable to any neglect on the part of, any director, manager, secretary or other similar officer of the body corporate or any person who was purporting to act in any such capacity, he as well as the body corporate shall be guilty of that offence and shall be liable to be proceeded against and punished accordingly.

PART I

(3) Where the affairs of a body corporate are managed by its members, subsection (2) above shall apply in relation to acts and defaults of a member in connection with his functions of management as if he were a director of the body corporate.

Regulations: general.

24. Any power to make regulations conferred on the Secretary of State by this Part of this Act—

(*a*) shall include power to make different provision for different areas or in relation to different cases or circumstances ; and

(*b*) shall be exercisable by statutory instrument, which shall be subject to annulment in pursuance of a resolution of either House of Parliament.

Amendments.

25. The enactments mentioned in Schedule 3 to this Act shall have effect subject to the amendments specified in that Schedule (being minor amendments and amendments consequential on the preceding provisions of this Part of this Act).

Interpretation of Part I.

26. In this Part of this Act—

" Area Board " has the same meaning as in the Electricity Act 1947 ; 1947 c. 54.

" electrical fittings " and " electrical plant " have the same meanings as in the Electricity Act 1947 ;

" electric line " has the same meaning as in the Electric Lighting Act 1882 ; 1882 c. 56.

" Electricity Board " means an Area Board, a Scottish Board or the Central Electricity Generating Board ;

" local authority " means any of the following—

(*a*) a county or district council in England or Wales, the Greater London Council, a London borough council, the Common Council of the City of London, and the Council of the Isles of Scilly ;

(*b*) a regional, islands or district council in Scotland ;

" Scottish Board " means the North of Scotland Hydro-Electric Board or the South of Scotland Electricity Board ;

" standard scale " has the meaning given by section 75 of the Criminal Justice Act 1982 ; 1982 c. 48.

" statutory maximum " has the meaning given by section 74 of the Criminal Justice Act 1982.

PART II

NUCLEAR INSTALLATIONS

Limitation of operators' liability.
1965 c. 57.

27.—(1) In section 16 of the Nuclear Installations Act 1965 (below called " the 1965 Act "), in subsection (1) (limitation of operator's liability in respect of any occurrence to £5 million) for the words " five million pounds " there shall be substituted the words " £20 million or, in the case of the licensees of such sites as may be prescribed, £5 million ".

(2) After subsection (1) of that section there shall be inserted—

" (1A) The Secretary of State may with the approval of the Treasury by order increase or further increase either or both of the amounts specified in subsection (1) of this section ; but an order under this subsection shall not affect liability in respect of any occurrence before (or beginning before) the order comes into force.".

(3) In subsection (5) of section 13 of that Act (claim by a person who has himself paid compensation) for the words from " not exceeding the " to " pounds " there shall be substituted the words " (subject to subsection (5A) of this section) " ; and after subsection (5) there shall be inserted—

" (5A) The amount that a person may claim by virtue of subsection (5) of this section shall not exceed the amount of the payment made by him and, in the case of a claim made by virtue of paragraph (*b*) of that subsection, shall not exceed the amount applicable under section 16(1) or (2) of this Act to the person subject to the duty in question.".

(4) In subsection (1) of section 19 of that Act (special cover for licensee's liability), for the words " an aggregate amount of five million pounds " there shall be substituted the words " the required amount " ; and after that subsection there shall be inserted—

" (1A) In this section " the required amount ", in relation to the provision to be made by a licensee in respect of a cover period, means an aggregate amount equal to the amount applicable under section 16(1) of this Act to the licensee, as licensee of the site in question, in respect of an occurrence within that period.".

(5) In subsection (2) of section 19 of that Act, after the word " means " there shall be inserted the words " subject to subsection (2A) of this section " ; and after subsection (2) there shall be inserted—

" (2A) When the amount applicable under section 16(1) of this Act to a licensee of a site changes as a result of—

(*a*) the coming into force of an order under section 16(1A) or of regulations made for the purposes of section 16(1), or

PART II

(*b*) an alteration relating to the site which brings it within, or takes it outside, the description prescribed by such regulations,

the current cover period relating to him as licensee of that site shall end and a new cover period shall begin.".

(6) In section 20(1) of that Act (duty to notify Secretary of State when claims reach £3 million), for the words " three million pounds " there shall be substituted the words " three-fifths of the required amount within the meaning of section 19 ".

(7) In section 26(1) of that Act, in the definition of " occurrence ", after " 16(1) " there shall be inserted " and (1A) ".

(8) Subsection (1) above shall not affect liability in respect of any occurrence before (or beginning before) the commencement of this section; and where the amount applicable under section 16(1) of the 1965 Act to the licensee of a site is increased by virtue of subsection (1) above, then for the purposes of section 19 of that Act the cover period relating to him as licensee of that site and current at the commencement of this section shall end and a new cover period shall begin.

General cover for compensation.

28.—(1) In subsection (1) of section 18 of the 1965 Act (general cover for compensation)—

(*a*) for the words " and (3) " there shall be substituted the words " to (4B) ", and

(*b*) for the words from " an aggregate " to the end there shall be substituted the words " the aggregate amount specified in subsection (1A) of this section ".

(2) After subsection (1) of that section there shall be inserted—

" (1A) The aggregate amount referred to in subsection (1) of this section is the equivalent in sterling of 300 million special drawing rights on—

(*a*) the day (or first day) of the occurrence in question, or

(*b*) if the Secretary of State certifies that another day has been fixed in relation to the occurrence in accordance with an international agreement, that other day.

(1B) The Secretary of State may with the approval of the Treasury by order increase or further increase the sum expressed in special drawing rights in subsection (1A) of this section; but an order under this subsection shall not have effect in respect of an occurrence before (or beginning before) the order comes into force.".

PART II

(3) For subsection (4) of that section there shall be substituted—

"(4) In relation to liability by virtue of any relevant foreign law, there shall be left out of account for the purposes of subsection (1) of this section any claim which, though made within the relevant period, was made after the expiration of any period of limitation imposed by that law and permitted by a relevant international agreement.

(4A) Where—

(*a*) a relevant foreign law provides in pursuance of a relevant international agreement for sums additional to those referred to in subsection (1)(*a*) of this section to be made available out of public funds, but

(*b*) the maximum aggregate amount of compensation for which it provides in respect of an occurrence in pursuance of that agreement is less than that specified in subsection (1A) of this section,

then, in relation to liability by virtue of that law in respect of the occurrence, subsection (1) of this section shall have effect as if for the reference to the amount so specified there were substituted a reference to the maximum aggregate amount so provided.

(4B) Where a relevant foreign law does not make the provision mentioned in subsection (4A)(*a*) of this section, then in relation to liability by virtue of that law in respect of any occurrence—

(*a*) subsection (1) of this section shall not have effect unless the person (or one of the persons) liable is a licensee, the Authority or the Crown; and

(*b*) if a licensee, the Authority or the Crown is liable, subsection (1) shall have effect as if for the reference to the amount specified in subsection (1A) there were substituted a reference to the amount which would be applicable to that person under section 16(1) of this Act in respect of the occurrence (or, if more than one such person is liable, to the aggregate of the amounts which would be so applicable) if it had constituted a breach of duty under section 7, 8 or 9 of this Act.".

(4) In section 17(3)(*b*) of the 1965 Act (which restricts the cover required under section 18 in cases of shared liability)—

(*a*) in sub-paragraph (i), for the words " of five million pounds " there shall be substituted the words " equal to that applicable to the person in question under section 16(1) of this Act "; and

(*b*) in sub-paragraph (ii), the words "not being less than £2,100,000 " shall cease to have effect.

(5) This section shall not have effect in respect of any occurrence before (or beginning before) the commencement of this section.

Carriage of nuclear matter.

29.—(1) In subsection (1) of section 21 of the 1965 Act (compensation in respect of carriage), for the words " of £2,100,000 " there shall be substituted the words " which is the equivalent in sterling (on the day, or first day, of that occurrence) of 5 million special drawing rights ".

(2) After that subsection there shall be inserted—

" (1A) The Secretary of State may with the approval of the Treasury by order increase or further increase the sum expressed in special drawing rights in subsection (1) of this section ; but an order under this subsection shall not have effect in respect of any occurrence before (or beginning before) the order comes into force.".

(3) After subsection (4) of that section there shall be inserted—

" (4A) Subsection (3) of this section shall not apply where the carriage in question is wholly within the territorial limits of the United Kingdom.".

(4) This section shall not have effect in respect of any occurrence before (or beginning before) the commencement of this section.

Provisions supplementary to sections 27 to 29.

30. After section 25 of the 1965 Act there shall be inserted—

" Orders. 25A. The power to make orders under section 16(1A), 18(1B) or 21(1A) of this Act shall be exercisable by statutory instrument ; but no such order shall be made unless a draft of it has been laid before and approved by resolution of the House of Commons.

Special drawing rights. 25B.—(1) In this Act " special drawing rights " means special drawing rights as defined by the International Monetary Fund ; and for the purpose of determining the equivalent in sterling on any day of a sum expressed in special drawing rights, one special drawing right shall be treated as equal to such a sum in sterling as the International Monetary Fund have fixed as being the equivalent of one special drawing right—

(*a*) for that day, or

(*b*) if no sum has been so fixed for that day, for the last day before that day for which a sum has been so fixed.

PART II

(2) A certificate given by or on behalf of the Treasury stating—

(*a*) that a particular sum in sterling has been so fixed for a particular day, or

(*b*) that no sum has been so fixed for a particular day and that a particular sum in sterling has been so fixed for a day which is the last day for which a sum has been so fixed before the particular day,

shall be conclusive evidence of those matters for the purposes of subsection (1) of this section ; and a document purporting to be such a certificate shall in any proceedings be received in evidence and, unless the contrary is proved, be deemed to be such a certificate.

(3) The Treasury may charge a reasonable fee for any certificate given in pursuance of subsection (2) of this section and any fee received by the Treasury by virtue of this subsection shall be paid into the Consolidated Fund.".

Reciprocal enforcement of judgments.

31. In subsection (5) of section 17 of the 1965 Act (foreign judgments), at the beginning there shall be inserted the words " Subject to subsection (5A) of this section " ; and after subsection (5) there shall be inserted—

" (5A) Subsection (5) of this section shall not have effect where the judgment in question is enforceable in the United Kingdom in pursuance of an international agreement.".

Meaning of " excepted matter ".

32. In section 26(1) of the 1965 Act (interpretation), in paragraph (*a*) of the definition of " excepted matter ", for the words " or scientific " there shall be substituted the words " scientific or educational ".

Extension to territories outside United Kingdom.

33. The provisions in respect of which the power conferred by section 28 of the 1965 Act is exercisable shall include the provisions of that Act as amended by this Act.

United Kingdom Atomic Energy Authority.

1954 c. 32.

34. Section 5(3) of the Atomic Energy Authority Act 1954 (which imposes a duty on the United Kingdom Atomic Energy Authority similar to that imposed by section 8 of the 1965 Act) shall cease to have effect.

Part III

General

35. There shall be paid out of money provided by Parliament— Financial provisions.

(*a*) any administrative expenses of the Secretary of State attributable to this Act, and

(*b*) any increase attributable to this Act in the sums payable out of money so provided under the Nuclear Installations Act 1965. 1965 c. 57.

36. The enactments mentioned in Schedule 4 to this Act are hereby repealed to the extent specified in the third column of that Schedule. Repeals.

37.—(1) This Act shall come into force on such day as the Secretary of State may appoint by order made by statutory instrument, and different days may be so appointed for different purposes. Commencement.

(2) An order under subsection (1) above may make such transitional provision and savings as appear to the Secretary of State to be necessary or expedient.

(3) If section 17(5) of the Nuclear Installations Act 1965 has not been brought into force under section 30(2) of that Act before the day appointed under subsection (1) above for the coming into force of section 31 of this Act, it shall come into force on that day.

38.—(1) This Act may be cited as the Energy Act 1983. Short title and extent.

(2) The following provisions of this Act, namely—

(*a*) Part I (except paragraph 11 of Schedule 2), and

(*b*) Part I of Schedule 4,

do not extend to Northern Ireland; but otherwise this Act does extend there.

SCHEDULES

Section 15

SCHEDULE 1

ELECTRICITY: AMENDMENTS RELATING TO METERS

The Electric Lighting (Clauses) Act 1899

1899 c. 19.
1947 c. 54.

1. The Schedule to the Electric Lighting (Clauses) Act 1899 (as incorporated with the Electricity Act 1947) shall be amended in accordance with paragraphs 2 to 14 below.

2. At the end of section 1 (interpretation) there shall be added—

" the expression " private supplier " means a person other than an Electricity Board who supplies electricity generated otherwise than by an Electricity Board.".

3. In section 2 (definition of " the Undertakers ") the words from " forty-nine " to " fifty-eight " shall cease to have effect.

4. For section 49 there shall be substituted—

" Meters to be used except by agreement.

49.—(1) This section applies to—

(*a*) a supply by the Undertakers to an ordinary consumer, and

(*b*) a supply by a private supplier to a person (other than the Undertakers) who takes the supply directly from electric lines belonging to the Undertakers,

unless otherwise agreed between the Undertakers and (in a case within paragraph (*a*) above), the consumer or (in a case within paragraph (*b*) above) the private supplier.

(2) The value of a supply to which this section applies shall be ascertained by means of an appropriate meter duly certified under the provisions of this Schedule, and fixed and connected with the Undertakers' lines in some manner approved by the Secretary of State.

(3) References in this section and the following sections to the value of a supply are references to the amount of energy supplied or (according to the method of charging) the electrical quantity contained in the supply.".

5. In section 50 (certification of meters) for the words " electric inspector appointed under this Schedule " there shall be substituted the words " authorised person ".

6. After section 50 there shall be inserted—

" Persons authorised to certify meters.

50A.—(1) The reference in section 50 above to an authorised person is a reference to—

1936 c. 20.

(*a*) a meter examiner appointed under the Electricity Supply (Meters) Act 1936, or

(*b*) a person authorised by the Secretary of State under this section.

Sch. 1

(2) The Secretary of State may authorise a person who manufactures or repairs meters to certify, in accordance with section 50 above, meters manufactured or repaired by him.

(3) An authorisation under this section may be given subject to such conditions as the Secretary of State thinks fit and may be withdrawn before the end of the period for which it is given if any of those conditions is not satisfied.

(4) The Secretary of State may make regulations prescribing fees to be paid to him by applicants for or holders of authorisations under this section towards administrative expenses incurred by him by virtue of this section; and different fees may be prescribed in relation to different areas and different cases.

Uncertified meters—offences.

50B.—(1) If the Undertakers or a private supplier install a meter for the purpose of ascertaining the value of a supply to which section 49 above applies and that meter, at the time when it is installed, is not a certified meter, the Undertakers or the supplier shall be guilty of an offence.

(2) Where a meter used for the purpose of ascertaining the value of a supply to which section 49 above applies ceases to be a certified meter, the person providing the supply shall as soon as practicable take all reasonable steps either for causing the meter to be recertified or for causing it to be removed or (if its removal is not reasonably practicable) for ceasing to supply energy through it.

(3) A person who fails to take the steps required of him by subsection (2) above shall be guilty of an offence unless he shows that the meter ceased to be a duly certified meter by reason only of its being altered or moved without his knowledge.

(4) A person guilty of an offence under this section shall be liable on summary conviction to a fine not exceeding level 2 on the standard scale (within the meaning of section 75 of the Criminal Justice Act 1982). 1982 c. 48.

(5) Proceedings for an offence under this section shall not, in England and Wales, be instituted except by or with the consent of the Secretary of State or the Director of Public Prosecutions.".

7. In section 51 (meter examiners to certify meters)—

(a) for the words "or by any consumer" there shall be substituted the words ", the person supplied with energy or, where the supply is by a private supplier, that supplier";

(b) for the words "the supply" there shall be substituted the words "a supply to which section 49 above applies"; and

(c) for the word "service" in both places where it occurs there shall be substituted the word "Undertakers'".

Sch. 1

8. In section 52 (Undertakers to supply meters if required to do so) for the words " the supply " there shall be substituted the words " a supply by the Undertakers ".

9. For section 53 there shall be substituted—

" Meters not to be connected or disconnected without notice.

53.—(1) No meter used or to be used for ascertaining the value of a supply to which section 49 above applies shall be connected with, or disconnected from, any electric line belonging to the Undertakers by the Undertakers, the person supplied (or to be supplied) with energy or, where the supply is by a private supplier, that supplier unless the person intending to connect or disconnect the meter has given to the other person or persons mentioned above not less than forty-eight hours' notice in writing of the intention to do so.

(2) A person who contravenes this section shall be guilty of an offence and liable on summary conviction to a fine not exceeding level 2 on the standard scale (within the meaning of section 75 of the Criminal Justice Act 1982).".

1982 c. 48.

10. In section 54(1) (consumer to keep meters in order) for the words " the supply " there shall be substituted the words " a supply by the Undertakers ".

11. In section 55 (power of Undertakers to let meters) for the words " the supply " there shall be substituted the words " a supply of energy ".

12. In section 56 (Undertakers to keep meters let for hire in repair) for the words " the supply " there shall be substituted the words " a supply by the Undertakers ".

13. For section 57 there shall be substituted—

" Questions as to correctness of meter to be determined by meter examiner.

57.—(1) Any question—

(*a*) whether a meter, by which there is ascertained the value of a supply to which section 49 above applies, is in proper order for correctly registering that value, or

(*b*) whether the value of such a supply has been correctly registered by any meter,

may be referred by any of the persons concerned to a meter examiner appointed under the Electricity Supply (Meters) Act 1936 for determination by him; and in this section " the persons concerned " means the Undertakers, the person supplied and, where the supply is by a private supplier, that supplier.

1936 c. 20.

(2) Before determining a question referred to him under this section, the meter examiner shall give notice to the other person or persons concerned; and his decision shall be final and binding upon all the persons concerned.

(3) A meter examiner determining a question referred to him under this section may make awards of costs or expenses as between the persons concerned.

(4) In the case of a supply by the Undertakers the register of the meter used to ascertain the value of the supply shall, except as provided by this section, be conclusive evidence in the absence of fraud of that value.

(5) The Secretary of State may by regulations—

(*a*) prescribe a fee to be paid to the Secretary of State by a person other than the Undertakers referring a question for determination under this section ;

(*b*) specify circumstances in which the fee may be refunded ; and

(*c*) make provision requiring the Undertakers to pay sums determined by the Secretary of State towards any administrative expenses incurred by him (and not recovered as mentioned in paragraph (*a*) above) in connection with the determination of questions under this section.".

14. For section 59 there shall be substituted—

"Undertakers may place meters to measure supply or to check measurement.

59.—(1) Subject to subsection (2) below, the Undertakers may place upon the premises of any person supplied with energy directly from electric lines belonging to them such meter or other apparatus (in addition to any meter to ascertain the value of the supply) as they may desire for the purpose of ascertaining or regulating the amount of energy supplied to him, the number of hours during which the supply is given, the maximum power taken by him or any other quantity or time connected with the supply.

(2) A meter or apparatus placed upon premises under this section—

(*a*) shall be of a construction and pattern approved by the Secretary of State and shall be fixed and connected with the Undertakers' lines in a manner so approved ;

(*b*) shall, where the supply of energy is by the Undertakers, be supplied and maintained entirely at the cost of the Undertakers ; and

(*c*) shall be placed between the Undertakers' mains and the ends of the Undertakers' lines at which the supply of energy is delivered unless otherwise agreed between the Undertakers, the person supplied with energy and, where the supply is by a private supplier, that supplier.".

SCH. 1

The Electricity Supply (Meters) Act 1936

1936 c. 20.

15.—(1) Section 1 of the Electricity Supply (Meters) Act 1936 shall be amended as follows.

(2) In subsection (1)—

(*a*) after the words " charged with ", there shall be inserted the words " such duties as the Secretary of State may determine in connection with " ; and

(*b*) the words " by authorised undertakers " shall cease to have effect.

(3) In subsection (3), the words " by any consumer or the undertakers as the case may be " shall cease to have effect.

16.—(1) Section 2 of that Act shall be amended as follows.

(2) In subsection (1), for the words " by those undertakers " there shall be substituted the words " (whether by the undertakers or by another person) directly through lines belonging to the undertakers ".

(3) In subsection (2), for the words " by the other parties " (in both places where those words occur) there shall be substituted the words " through lines belonging to the other parties ".

(4) In subsection (3), for the words " by the undertakers " there shall be substituted the words " through lines belonging to the undertakers ".

The Electricity Act 1957

1957 c. 48.

17.—(1) Section 30 of the Electricity Act 1957 shall be amended as follows.

(2) In subsection (1)(*c*), for the words " the supply " there shall be substituted the words " a supply ".

(3) After subsection (4) there shall be inserted—

" (4A) Where a person other than an Electricity Board submits a meter to a meter examiner for certification under the provisions of the Schedule of 1899, the meter examiner may certify the meter, notwithstanding that he has not himself examined or tested it, if—

(*a*) the meter was manufactured or repaired by the person submitting it ;

(*b*) that person has obtained the consent of the Secretary of State to the submission ; and

(*c*) any conditions subject to which the consent was given have been satisfied."

(4) Subsections (5) to (8) shall cease to have effect.

(5) In subsection (9), for the words " the supply " there shall be substituted the words " a supply ".

SCHEDULE 2

Section 21.

The Electricity Consumers' Council

The chairman

1. If the Secretary of State so determines, there shall be paid to the chairman of the Council such remuneration as the Secretary of State may determine.

2. If the Secretary of State so determines in the case of a person who has been remunerated under paragraph 1 above, a pension shall be paid to or in respect of that person, or payments towards the provision of a pension to or in respect of that person shall be made, in accordance with the determination.

3. If a person in receipt of remuneration under paragraph 1 above as chairman ceases to hold that office, and it appears to the Secretary of State that there are special circumstances which make it right that that person should receive compensation, he shall be paid by way of compensation a sum of such amount as the Secretary of State may determine.

Administration, personnel, etc.

4. The Council may, subject to the approval of the Secretary of State as to numbers, appoint such officers as appear to the Council to be requisite for the performance of their functions.

5. The Secretary of State shall provide the Council with funds—

(*a*) with which to pay—

(i) to their members, such travelling and other allowances as the Secretary of State may determine ; and

(ii) to their officers, such remuneration and such travelling and other allowances, as the Council may with the approval of the Secretary of State determine ; and

(*b*) with which to defray such other expenses in connection with the Council's functions as the Secretary of State may determine to be appropriate.

6. The Secretary of State may make arrangements for the Council to be provided with office accommodation.

7.—(1) There shall be paid such pensions, or arrangements shall be made for the payment of such pensions, as the Secretary of State may determine to or in respect of such persons who are or have been officers of the Council as the Secretary of State may determine.

(2) The Secretary of State shall provide the Council with funds with which to pay any such pension or to finance any such arrangements.

Constitution and procedure

8.—(1) The Secretary of State may make regulations with respect to—

(*a*) the appointment of, and the tenure and vacation of office by, members of the Council ;

SCH. 2

(*b*) the appointment of one or more members of the Council as deputy chairman or deputy chairmen;

(*c*) the quorum, proceedings, meetings and determinations of the Council;

(*d*) the execution of documents and the mode of entering into contracts by and on behalf of the Council, and the proof of documents purporting to be executed, issued or signed by the Council or a member or officer of the Council; and

(*e*) any other matters supplementary or incidental to those mentioned in paragraphs (*a*) to (*d*) for which provision appears to him to be necessary or expedient.

(2) Subject to any regulations made under this paragraph, the Council shall have power to regulate their own procedure.

9. The validity of any proceedings of the Council shall not be affected by any vacancy amongst the members or by any defect in the appointment of a member.

Amendment of other Acts

1970 c. 44. 10. In section 14(1) of the Chronically Sick and Disabled Persons Act 1970, after the words " Electricity Consultative Councils " there shall be inserted the words " the Electricity Consumers' Council ".

1975 c. 24. 11. In Part III of Schedule 1 to the House of Commons Disqualification Act 1975, there shall be inserted at the appropriate place in alphabetical order—

" Chairman in receipt of remuneration of the Electricity Consumers' Council ".

Supplementary

12. The consent of the Treasury shall be required for any determination or approval by the Secretary of State under this Schedule.

13. Any payments to be made under paragraphs 1 to 3 above shall be made by the Secretary of State, and they and any other payments made by him under this Schedule shall be defrayed out of money provided by Parliament.

14. In this Schedule " pension " includes an allowance or gratuity payable on retirement or otherwise.

Section 25.

SCHEDULE 3

ELECTRICITY: MINOR AND CONSEQUENTIAL AMENDMENTS

The Electric Lighting Act 1882

1882 c. 56. 1. In section 25 of the Electric Lighting Act 1882, for the words from " supplying " to " special Act " there shall be substituted the words " a supply of electricity (whether by the undertakers or any other person) directly through electric lines belonging to them ".

The Electric Lighting (Clauses) Act 1899 SCH. 3

2.—(1) The Schedule to the Electric Lighting (Clauses) Act 1899 (as incorporated with the Electricity Act 1947) shall be amended as follows. 1899 c. 19. 1947 c. 54.

(2) In section 1, in the definition of "Electricity regulations", for the words from "by" to the end there shall be substituted the words "under section 60 of the Electricity Act 1947 or section 16 of the Energy Act 1983".

(3) In section 27—

(*a*) in subsection (4), after the word "electrical" in each place where it occurs there shall be inserted the words "plant or"; and

(*b*) in subsections (5) and (6), after the word "lines" there shall be inserted the word "plant".

(4) In section 36(1)(*c*), for the words from "in" to "regulations" there shall be substituted the words "as the Secretary of State may determine".

The Electricity Act 1947

3.—(1) Section 1 of the Electricity Act 1947 shall be amended as follows.

(2) In subsection (4)—

(*a*) for paragraph (*b*) there shall be substituted—

"(*b*) by agreement with any person other than an Electricity Board, acquire supplies of electricity from that person"; and

(*b*) in paragraph (*c*), after the words "any other Area Board" there shall be inserted the words "or in compliance with a request under section 5 of the Energy Act 1983".

(3) At the end of subsection (6)(*c*) there shall be inserted the words "and in complying with requests under section 5 of the Energy Act 1983".

4.—(1) Section 2 of that Act shall be amended as follows.

(2) In subsection (4)(*b*), the words "under the foregoing section" shall cease to have effect.

(3) In the proviso to subsection (4), for the words from "exercise or" to the end there shall be inserted the words "manufacture electrical fittings or to manufacture, sell, hire or otherwise supply electrical plant."

(4) In subsection (5), the words from "under" where it first occurs to "this section" and the words from "but" to the end shall cease to have effect.

5.—(1) Section 37 of that Act shall be amended as follows.

(2) After subsection (1) there shall be inserted—

"(1A) The prices to be charged by the Generating Board for any supply of electricity given in compliance with a request under section 5 of the Energy Act 1983 shall be in accor-

SCH. 3 dance with such tariffs as may be fixed from time to time by the Generating Board after consultation with the Electricity Council.".

(3) In subsection (2), for the words "the last foregoing subsection" there shall be substituted the words "subsection (1) or (1A) of this section".

(4) In subsection (7)—

(*a*) for the words "an Area Board", in each place where they occur, there shall be substituted the words "a Board", and

(*b*) for the word "consumer" there shall be substituted the word "person".

(5) In subsection (8)—

(*a*) for the words "An Area Board" there shall be substituted the words "A Board"; and

(*b*) after the word "section" there shall be inserted the words "and in proposing prices in accordance with section 6(2) of the Energy Act 1983".

6. In section 63 of that Act, after the words "the Electricity Act 1957" there shall be inserted the words "or Part I of the Energy Act 1983 or regulations made thereunder".

7. In subsections (1) and (2) of section 64 of that Act, after the word "Act" there shall be inserted the words "or by Part I of the Energy Act 1983".

8. In section 66(1) of that Act, after the words "the Electricity Act 1957" there shall be added the words "or Part I of the Energy Act 1983".

The Clean Air Act 1956

1956 c. 52. 9. In section 10(4) of the Clean Air Act 1956, for the words from "a generating" to the end there shall be substituted the words "an electricity generating station by an Electricity Board (as defined in section 26 of the Energy Act 1983)".

The Electricity Act 1957

1957 c. 48. 10. In section 2(7)(*c*) of the Electricity Act 1957, the words "under the preceding provisions of this section" shall cease to have effect.

The Clean Air Act 1968

1968 c. 62. 11. In section 6(10) of the Clean Air Act 1968, for the words from "a generating" to the end there shall be substituted the words "an electricity generating station occupied by an Electricity Board (as defined in section 26 of the Energy Act 1983)".

The Electricity (Scotland) Act 1979

1979 c. 11. 12. In section 4 of the Electricity (Scotland) Act 1979, at the end of paragraph (*c*) there shall be added the words "and in complying with requests under section 5 of the Energy Act 1983".

13. For section 8(1) of that Act there shall be substituted— SCH. 3

"8.—(1) Subject to this section and to section 9 either of the Boards may—

(*a*) supply electricity to consumers in the district of the other Board, either—

(i) in compliance with a request under section 5 of the Energy Act 1983 ; or

(ii) by agreement with the other Board ;

(*b*) by agreement with the other Board give to or acquire from the other Board bulk supplies of electricity ;

(*c*) by agreement with any person acquire from that person supplies of electricity ;

(*d*) by agreement with the Generating Board or with any person or body of persons carrying on an electricity undertaking outside Great Britain, provide bulk supplies of electricity for the Generating Board or for that undertaking.".

14. In section 22 of that Act—

(*a*) at the end of subsection (1) there shall be added the words " after consultation with the Consultative Council established for the district of that Board " ;

(*b*) in subsection (4), for the word " consumer " there shall be substituted the word " person " ; and

(*c*) in subsection (5), after the word " section " there shall be inserted the words " and in proposing prices in accordance with section 6(2) of the Energy Act 1983 ".

15. In section 38(1) of that Act, after the words " the Act of 1957 " there shall be inserted the words ", Part I of the Energy Act 1983 ".

16. In section 40(6) of that Act—

(*a*) after the words " Schedule 7 " there shall be inserted the words " or by virtue of Part I of the Energy Act 1983 " ;

(*b*) in paragraph (*d*), after the word " regulations " there shall be inserted the words " other than regulations made by virtue of Part I of the Energy Act 1983 ".

17. In Schedule 9 to that Act, after the words " by this Act " there shall be inserted the words " or by or under Part I of the Energy Act 1983, or regulations made thereunder, ".

Section 36.

SCHEDULE 4

Enactments Repealed

Part I

Electricity

Chapter	Short title	Extent of repeal
51 & 52 Vict. c. 12.	The Electric Lighting Act 1888.	The whole Act.
62 & 63 Vict. c. 19.	The Electric Lighting (Clauses) Act 1899.	In the Schedule (as incorporated with the Electricity Act 1947 or any other enactment)— in section 2, the words from " forty-nine " to " fifty-eight "; in section 10, paragraph (*a*), paragraph (*c*) and the word " and " immediately preceding paragraph (*c*); section 38; in section 52, the words from " and for those purposes " to " acts "; section 54(2); section 60; in section 69(1), in paragraph (*a*) the words from " are " to " Schedule " and the words from " permitted " to " earth or ", paragraph (*b*) (and the word " or " preceding it) and paragraph (*c*); in section 69(2), the words " or work " in each place where they occur.
9 Edw. 7. c. 34.	The Electric Lighting Act 1909.	Section 23.
9 & 10 Geo. 5. c. 100.	The Electricity (Supply) Act 1919.	Section 11. In section 36, the definition of " private generating station ".
12 & 13 Geo. 5. c. 46.	The Electricity (Supply) Act 1922.	Section 23.
16 & 17 Geo. 5. c. 51.	The Electricity (Supply) Act 1926.	Section 24.
26 Geo. 5. & 1 Edw. 8. c. 20.	The Electricity Supply (Meters) Act 1936.	In section 1(1), the words " by authorised undertakers ". In section 1(3), the words " by any consumer or the undertakers as the case may be ".
9 & 10 Geo. 6. c. 49.	The Acquisition of Land (Authorisation Procedure) Act 1946.	In Schedule 4, the entry relating to the Electricity (Supply) Act 1919.

Sch. 4

Chapter	Short title	Extent of repeal
10 & 11 Geo. 6. c. 54.	The Electricity Act 1947.	In section 2(4)(*b*), the words " under the foregoing section ". In section 2(5), the words from " under " where it first occurs to " this section " and the words from " but " to the end. In section 37(4), the words " on the premises of the consumer ". Section 60. In Schedule 4— in Part I, the entries relating to section 23 of the Electric Lighting Act 1909, section 11 of the Electricity (Supply) Act 1919 and section 24 of the Electricity (Supply) Act 1926; and in Part III, the entries relating to sections 49 and 60 of the Schedule to the Electric Lighting (Clauses) Act 1899.
2 & 3 Eliz. 2. c. 60.	The Electricity Reorganisation (Scotland) Act 1954.	Section 1(3). In Part III of Schedule 1, the entry relating to the Electric Lighting Act 1888.
4 & 5 Eliz. 2. c. xciv.	The South of Scotland Electricity Order Confirmation Act 1956.	Section 40.
5 & 6 Eliz. 2. c. 48.	The Electricity Act 1957.	In section 2(7)(*c*), the words " under the preceding provisions of this section ". Section 30(5) to (8). In Schedule 4— in Part I, the entries relating to sections 50 and 60 of the Electricity Act 1947; and in Part II, the entry relating to the Electricity (Supply) Act 1919.
7 Eliz. 2. c. ii.	The North of Scotland Electricity Order Confirmation Act 1958.	Section 27.
1969 c. 48.	The Post Office Act 1969.	In Schedule 4— in paragraph 8, sub-paragraph (*b*), in sub-paragraph (*c*) the references to sections 10, 60 and 69 of the Schedule to the Electric Lighting (Clauses) Act 1899 and sub-paragraph (*g*); paragraph 11.
1976 c. 76.	The Energy Act 1976	Section 14(6)(*b*).

SCH. 4

Chapter	Short title	Extent of repeal
1979 c. 11.	The Electricity (Scotland) Act 1979.	In section 7(3), the words " under this Act ". In section 9(2), the words from " but " to the end. In section 22(3), the words " on the premises of the consumer ". In section 35(1), the word " private " in both places where it occurs and the word " new ". Section 35(2). In paragraph 13 of Schedule 10, the reference to section 60 of the Electricity Act 1947.
1981 c. 67.	The Acquisition of Land Act 1981.	In paragraph 1 of Schedule 4, the entry relating to the Electricity (Supply) Act 1919.

PART II

NUCLEAR INSTALLATIONS

Chapter	Short title	Extent of repeal
2 & 3 Eliz. 2. c. 32.	The Atomic Energy Authority Act 1954.	Section 5(3).
1965 c. 57.	The Nuclear Installations Act 1965.	In section 17(3)(*b*)(ii), the words "not being less than £2,100,000 ".
1969 c. 18.	The Nuclear Installations Act 1969.	Section 2.

Pet Animals Act 1951 (Amendment) Act 1983

1983 CHAPTER 26

An Act to amend the Pet Animals Act 1951 regulating the sale of pet animals. [9th May 1983]

BE IT ENACTED by the Queen's most Excellent Majesty, by and with the advice and consent of the Lords Spiritual and Temporal, and Commons, in this present Parliament assembled, and by the authority of the same, as follows:—

1. The Pet Animals Act 1951 shall be amended as follows:— Amendment of 1951 Act. 1951 c. 35.

(*a*) in section 2 (Pets not to be sold in streets, etc.), there shall be substituted for the word " except " the word " or ";

(*b*) in subsection (3) of section 7 (Interpretation) there shall be omitted the words " " premises " includes any stall or barrow in a market, but save as aforesaid does not include any stall or barrow or any part of a street or public place ".

2.—(1) This Act may be cited as the Pet Animals Act 1951 (Amendment) Act 1982. Short title, commencement and extent.

(2) This Act shall come into operation at the end of a period of six months beginning with the day on which it is passed.

(3) This Act does not apply to Northern Ireland.

Appropriation Act 1983

1983 CHAPTER 27

An Act to apply a sum out of the Consolidated Fund to the service of the year ending on 31st March 1984, to appropriate the supplies granted in this Session of Parliament, and to repeal certain Consolidated Fund and Appropriation Acts. [13th May 1983]

Most Gracious Sovereign,

WE, Your Majesty's most dutiful and loyal subjects the Commons of the United Kingdom in Parliament assembled, towards making good the supply which we have cheerfully granted to Your Majesty in this Session of Parliament, have resolved to grant unto Your Majesty the sum hereinafter mentioned; and do therefore most humbly beseech Your Majesty that it may be enacted, and be it enacted by the Queen's Most Excellent Majesty, by and with the advice and consent of the Lords Spiritual and Temporal, and Commons, in this present Parliament assembled, and by the authority of the same, as follows:—

Grant out of the Consolidated Fund

1. The Treasury may issue out of the Consolidated Fund of the United Kingdom and apply towards making good the supply granted to Her Majesty for the service of the year ending on 31st March 1984 the sum of £49,416,525,100.

Issue out of the Consolidated Fund for the year ending 31st March 1984.

Appropriation of Grants

Appropriation of sums voted for supply services.

2. All sums granted by this Act and the other Acts mentioned in Schedule (A) annexed to this Act out of the said Consolidated Fund towards making good the supply granted to Her Majesty amounting, as appears by the said schedule, in the aggregate, to the sum of £88,537,459,315·78 are appropriated, and shall be deemed to have been appropriated as from the date of the passing of the Acts mentioned in the said Schedule (A), for the services and purposes expressed in Schedule (B) annexed hereto.

The abstract of schedules and schedules annexed hereto, with the notes (if any) to such schedules, shall be deemed to be part of this Act in the same manner as if they had been contained in the body thereof.

1891 c. 24.

In addition to the said sums granted out of the Consolidated Fund, there may be applied out of any money directed, under section 2 of the Public Accounts and Charges Act 1891, to be applied as appropriations in aid of the grants for the services and purposes specified in Schedule (B) annexed hereto the sums respectively set forth in the last column of the said schedule.

Repeals.

3. The enactments mentioned in Schedule (C) annexed to this Act are hereby repealed.

Short title.

4. This Act may be cited as the Appropriation Act 1983.

ABSTRACT

OF

SCHEDULES (A) and (B) to which this Act refers

SCHEDULE (A)

Section 2.

Grants out of the Consolidated Fund ... ... £88,537,459,315·78

SCHEDULE (B)—Appropriation of Grants

Section 2.

	Supply Grants	Appropriations in Aid
	£	£
1981–82 and 1982–83		
Part 1. Defence and Civil (Excesses), 1981–82	68,277,715·78	8,074,207·67
Part 2. Defence (Supplementary), 1982–83	598,441,000·00	*—241,998,000·00*
Part 3. Civil Departments (Supplementary), 1982–83	2,498,230,000·00	117,797,000·00
	£3,164,948,715·78	*—116,126,792·33*

SCHEDULE (B)—APPROPRIATION OF GRANTS—*continued*

1983–84	Supply Grants	Appropriations in Aid
	£	£
Part 4. Defence, Class I	15,791,503,000·00	1,742,622,000·00
Part 5. Civil, Class II	1,768,692,000·00	49,440,000·00
Part 6. Civil, Class III	841,987,000·00	193,317,000·00
Part 7. Civil, Class IV	5,451,533,000·00	1,637,651,000·00
Part 8. Civil, Class V	366,000,000·00	—
Part 9. Civil, Class VI	2,024,825,000·00	76,594,000·00
Part 10. Civil, Class VII	1,666,213,000·00	—
Part 11. Civil, Class VIII	674,839,000·00	36,053,000·00
Part 12. Civil, Class IX	2,786,712,000·00	166,855,000·00
Part 13. Civil, Class X	3,045,915,000·00	8,759,000·00
Part 14. Civil, Class XI	10,914,409,000·00	1,607,683,000·00
Part 15. Civil, Class XII	14,691,073,000·00	654,395,000·00
Part 16. Civil, Class XIII	1,591,739,600·00	113,880,300·00
Part 17. Civil, Class XIIIA	16,521,000·00	152,000·00
Part 18. Civil, Class XIV	2,030,191,000·00	403,241,000·00
Part 19. Civil, Class XV	3,029,267,000·00	216,723,000·00

Part II

Part 20. Civil, Class XVI	-	1,195,857,000·00	99,188,000·00
Part 21. Civil, Class XVII	-	1,170,313,000·00	2,739,000·00
Part 22. Civil, Class XVIII	-	16,314,921,000·00	1,660,093,000·00
TOTAL, DEFENCE AND CIVIL	-	85,372,510,600·00	8,669,385,300·00
GRAND TOTAL	£	88,537,459,315·78	8,553,258,507·67

SCHEDULE (A)

GRANTS OUT OF THE CONSOLIDATED FUND

	£
For the service of the year ended 31st March 1982—	
Under Act 1983 c. 5 ...	68,277,715·78
For the service of the year ended 31st March 1983—	
Under Act 1983 c. 1 ...	1,509,761,000·00
Under Act 1983 c. 5 ...	1,586,910,000·00
For the service of the year ending on 31st March 1984—	
Under Act 1983 c. 1 ...	35,955,985,500·00
Under this Act ...	49,416,525,100·00
TOTAL ...	88,537,459,315·78

SCHEDULE (B)—PART 1

Defence and Civil (Excesses), 1981–82.

DEFENCE AND CIVIL (EXCESSES), 1981–82

SUMS granted, and sums which may be applied as appropriations in aid in addition thereto, to make good excesses on certain grants for Defence and Civil Services for the year ended 31st March 1982, viz.:—

Vote	Supply Grants	Surplus receipts available to be applied as Appropriations in Aid
	£	£
CLASS I		
1. DEFENCE: PAY, &C. OF THE ARMED FORCES AND CIVILIANS, STORES, SUPPLIES AND MISCELLANEOUS SERVICES	10·00	5,323,384·36
2. DEFENCE PROCUREMENT	19,585,348·43	2,585,187·17
CLASS VI		
6. NATIONAL FREIGHT COMPANY LIMITED	611,483·25	—
CLASS XII		
1. PENSION BENEFITS (NON-CONTRIBUTORY)	48,041,285·68	—
CLASS XV		
1. AGRICULTURAL SUPPORT, SCOTLAND	39,588·42	165,636·14
TOTAL, DEFENCE AND CIVIL (EXCESSES) 1981–82 £	68,277,715·78	8,074,207·67

SCHEDULE (B)—PART 2

DEFENCE (SUPPLEMENTARY), 1982–83

Defence (Supplementary), 1982–83.

SCHEDULE OF SUPPLEMENTARY SUMS granted, and of the sums which may be applied as appropriations in aid in addition thereto, to defray the charges for the Defence Services herein particularly mentioned for the year ended 31st March 1983, viz.:—

	Supply Grants	Appropriations in Aid
	£	£
CLASS I		
Vote		
1. For expenditure by the Ministry of Defence on pay, allowances etc of the Armed Forces and their Reserves and Cadet Forces etc, pay etc of Defence Ministers and certain civilian staff employed by the Ministry of Defence; on movements; certain stores; supplies and services; plant and machinery; charter and contract repair of ships; certain research; lands and buildings; sundry grants; payments abroad including contributions and subscriptions to international organisations; and grants in aid	531,541,000	**−74,423,000*
2. For expenditure by the Procurement Executive of the Ministry of Defence in operating its Headquarters and Establishments and for its other common services; for research etc by contract; lands and buildings; for development by contract, production, repair etc and purchases for sale abroad of sea systems, land systems, air systems and associated equipment; for reservation of capacity in Royal Ordnance Factories; for certain contingent liabilities, and for sundry other Procurement Executive services including those on repayment terms to non-exchequer customers	1,000	**−113,929,000*
3. For expenditure by the Ministry of Defence on retired pay, pensions etc	18,253,000	258,000
4. For expenditure including loans by the Property Services Agency of the Department of the Environment on public building work and certain accommodation services etc for defence purposes	23,310,000	**−53,692,000*
5. For operating the Royal Dockyards and for the repair of ships by contract including work undertaken on repayment terms for exchequer and non-exchequer customers	25,336,000	**−212,000*
TOTAL, DEFENCE (SUPPLEMENTARY), 1982–83 £	598,441,000	**−241,998,000*

* Deficit.

SCHEDULE (B)—PART 3

Civil Departments (Supplementary), 1982–83.

CIVIL DEPARTMENTS (SUPPLEMENTARY), 1982–83

SCHEDULE OF SUPPLEMENTARY SUMS granted, and of the sums which may be applied as appropriations in aid in addition thereto, to defray the charges for the Civil Services herein particularly mentioned for the year ended 31st March 1983, viz.:—

	Supply Grants	Appropriations in Aid
	£	£
CLASS II		
Vote		
3. For expenditure by the Foreign and Commonwealth Office on grants in aid of the British Broadcasting Corporation for external broadcasting and monitoring services	2,086,000	18,000
4. For expenditure by the Foreign and Commonwealth Office on a grant in aid of the British Council	3,190,000	—
5. For expenditure by the Foreign and Commonwealth Office on official information services, military aid, certain grants in aid and sundry other grants and services	2,000	—
6. For expenditure by the Foreign and Commonwealth Office on grants and subscriptions, etc, to certain international organisations, special payments and assistance, a loan to Yugoslavia and sundry other grants and services	44,100,000	687,000
9. For expenditure by the Foreign and Commonwealth Office (Overseas Development Administration) on pensions and superannuation payments etc in respect of overseas service, pensions in respect of service with the Cotton Research Corporation and sundry other services and expenses	2,431,000	*—*4,033,000*
10. For expenditure by the Foreign and Commonwealth Office (Overseas Development Administration) on the official United Kingdom aid programme including pensions and allowances in respect of overseas service, assistance to certain refugee students, grants in aid, certain subscriptions to international organisations and certain payments under the Commonwealth Scholarship and Fellowship Plan	8,601,000	—

* Deficit.

Vote	Supply Grants	Appropriations in Aid
	£	£
CLASS III		
1. For expenditure by the Intervention Board for Agricultural Produce on carrying out the obligations of the United Kingdom under the Common Agricultural Policy of the European Community in connection with arrangements for import and export, support for certain agricultural and other products including fish, assistance to producers, and arrangements for food aid; and for certain other services - -	303,682,000	1,345,000
2. For expenditure by the Ministry of Agriculture, Fisheries and Food on price guarantees, production grants and subsidies, grants and loans for capital and other improvements, support for agriculture in special areas, animal health and support services, land drainage, flood protection, water supply and certain other services - -	57,850,000	***–13,050,000*
3. For expenditure by the Ministry of Agriculture, Fisheries and Food on educational, advisory, research and development services, livestock services and pest control, food services and assistance to marketing and processing, land management and smallholdings, emergency and strategic food services, some central, special and other services, including grants in aid and subscriptions to certain international organisations - - - - - - - - - - - -	2,000	—
5. For expenditure by the Ministry of Agriculture, Fisheries and Food on assistance to the fishing industry, research and development, protective and other services including subscriptions to certain international organisations - - - -	2,740,000	—
7. For expenditure by the Ministry of Agriculture, Fisheries and Food on departmental administration and certain other services - - - - - - - -	1,000	***–186,000*
CLASS IV		
1. For expenditure by the Department of Industry on regional development grants, selective assistance to industry, certain other services including the provision of public dividend capital to the National Enterprise Board, UK contributions to the funding of buffer stock operations of international commodity agreements, a strategic mineral stockpile and on investment grants - - - - -	208,550,000	—

* Deficit.

2. For expenditure by the Department of Industry on provision of land and buildings, assistance for publicity, and other support services including grants in aid	2,000	—
3. For expenditure by the Department of Energy in connection with the energy industries, including selective assistance to industry and the nationalised industries, financial assistance to certain classes of energy consumers and certain other services	1,000	6,002,000
5. For expenditure by the Department of Energy in connection with the energy industries including related research and development, the nationalised industries, energy conservation, oil storage, and certain other services including grants in aid and an international subscription	1,000	10,000
8. For expenditure by the Department of Industry on support for the aerospace, shipbuilding, steel and vehicle manufacturing industries, including loans, grants and the purchase of assets, and assistance to redundant steel workers	65,734,000	12,000,000
10. For expenditure by the Export Credits Guarantee Department in connection with export credits guarantees including an international subscription, special guarantees, refinancing and financing arrangements made for facilitating trade with other countries and assistance towards the cost of financing export credits, the purchase of securities, overseas investment insurance and cost escalation guarantees	1,000	49,584,000
11. For expenditure by the Registry of Friendly Societies	35,000	—
13. For expenditure by the Department of Employment on general labour market services, on services for seriously disabled people and on an international subscription	5,642,000	—
14. For expenditure by the Department of Employment on demand determined measures to promote and preserve employment opportunities, the National Dock Labour Board, payments towards expenses of trade union ballots, compensation for persons disabled by pneumoconiosis, byssinosis and diffuse mesothelioma and compensation to persons for certain dismissals	1,000	—
18. For expenditure by the Department of Industry on central and miscellaneous services, on those common services shared with the Department of Trade, on services provided by the Ministry of Defence (Procurement Executive) Headquarters, on international subscriptions and on British Telecommunications Civil Defence	4,768,000	—
21. For expenditure by the Department of Energy in connection with the sale of shares in Britoil	1,000	14,999,000

Vote	Supply Grants	Appropriations in Aid
	£	£
CLASS V		
1. For Government investment in the British Steel Corporation and British Shipbuilders	260,000,000	—
CLASS VI		
1. For expenditure by the Department of Transport on roads and certain associated services including lighting and road safety, including a grant in aid, and certain grants	45,000,000	5,000,000
2. For expenditure by the Department of Transport on support to nationalised transport industries, assistance to local transport, research and certain other transport services, including civil defence and international subscriptions	1,000	—
3. For expenditure by the Department of Transport on support to nationalised transport industries and assistance to local transport and ports	33,001,000	—
4. For expenditure by the Department of Transport on central and other administration, certain licensing and testing schemes and certain other services	1,660,000	*—*2,000,000*
6. For expenditure by the Department of Transport in connection with the sale of shares in the Associated British Ports	601,000	2,399,000
CLASS VII		
1. For expenditure by the Department of the Environment on subsidies, the option mortgage scheme, improvements and investment, grants to housing associations and the Housing Corporation and sundry other housing services	196,151,000	—
CLASS VIII		
1. For expenditure by the Department of the Environment on assistance to the construction industry, other water supply, conservation and sewerage, local authority and other environmental services including recreation	9,855,000	—
2. For expenditure by the Department of the Environment on other environmental services including grants in aid and international subscriptions, on grants in aid to the British Waterways Board and Development Fund, on bridgeworks, on certain categories of derelict land and on developing Civil Defence water supply services	2,808,000	—

* Deficit

4. For expenditure by the Department of the Environment on royal palaces, royal parks etc., historic buildings, ancient monuments and the national heritage, on certain public buildings, on grants in aid, other grants and on payments to Inland Revenue covering assets accepted in lieu of tax	3,969,000	100,000
Class IX		
4. For grants to the Legal Aid Fund and for expenditure by the Lord Chancellor's Department on legal aid in criminal cases, court services, and costs paid from central funds	20,000,000	—
6. For expenditure by the Home Office on court services, compensation for criminal injuries, including a grant in aid, and probation and after-care	6,909,000	700,000
10. For expenditure by the Home Office on grants to local and police authorities and the Metropolitan Police Fund for police, civil defence, and community services and for police and fire services superannuation payments	39,228,000	—
12. For expenditure by the Departments of the Director of Public Prosecutions, the Law Officers and the Treasury Solicitor on central and certain other services	1,000	186,000
Class X		
3. For expenditure by the Department of Education and Science on student awards and compensation payments to redundant teachers and staff of certain institutions	37,639,000	*—*2,000*
8. For a grant in aid of the Natural Environment Research Council	500,000	—
15. For the expenditure of the Victoria and Albert Museum including purchase grants in aid	130,000	—
21. For the expenditure of the Wallace Collection	6,000	—
22. For certain grants and services for the benefit of the arts, for grants in aid to the Arts Council and certain other institutions and for a grant in aid to the National Heritage Memorial Fund and for payments to the Inland Revenue covering assets accepted in lieu of tax, and for expenditure on the Government Art Collection	10,500,000	—

* Deficit

Vote	Supply Grants	Appropriations in Aid
	£	£
CLASS XI		
1. For expenditure by the Department of Health and Social Security on the provision of services under the national health service in England, on other health and personal social services including certain services in relation to the United Kingdom, and on research, exports, services for the disabled and certain other services; including grants in aid and international subscriptions	37,301,000	9,178,000
2. For expenditure by the Department of Health and Social Security on the provision of services under the national health service in England, on other health and personal social services, on welfare food and certain other services including grants under Section 8 of the Industry Act 1972	132,924,000	40,296,000
CLASS XII		
1. For expenditure by the Department of Health and Social Security on pensions, etc., for disablement or death arising out of war or service in the armed forces after 2 September 1939 and on certain associated services, on attendance allowances, invalid care allowance, old persons' retirement pensions, non-contributory invalidity pensions, lump sum payments to pensioners, and mobility allowance, etc.	135,000,000	—
2. For expenditure by the Department of Health and Social Security on supplementary pensions and allowances	550,000,000	*—*30,000,000*
3. For expenditure by the Department of Health and Social Security on child benefit, one parent benefit, family income supplements and non-contributory maternity grants	19,000,000	—
4. For expenditure by the Department of Health and Social Security on administration and certain other services including an international subscription	9,435,000	14,898,000
5. For expenditure for the payment of rate rebate and rent rebate subsidies to rating and housing authorities respectively and the administrative costs of the housing benefits scheme incurred by the rating, housing and local authorities	62,000,000	—

* Deficit

Class XIII		
1. For the expenditure of the House of Lords	135,000	—
4. For expenditure by the Treasury on the management of the economy, and for certain other services including grants in aid to certain Parliamentary bodies and others	1,000	—
13. For expenditure by the Central Computer and Telecommunications Agency (Treasury) in connection with computers and general telecommunications	1,000	945,000
18. For the expenditure of the Charity Commission for England and Wales	298,000	—
22. For payment to Her Majesty's Stationery Office Trading Fund to compensate for the provision of reports of Parliamentary Debates at less than full cost, and for price concessions to public libraries	393,000	—
23. For expenditure by Her Majesty's Stationery Office on the reimbursement of their trading fund in respect of stationery and printing supplied to the Houses of Parliament and to United Kingdom members of the European Assembly	414,000	*—*40,000*
Class XIV		
1. For expenditure including loans by the Property Services Agency of the Department of the Environment on public building works and accommodation services, etc., for civil purposes in the United Kingdom, transport services and sundry other services, including those on repayment terms	7,000,000	2,000,000
Class XV		
1. For expenditure by the Department of Agriculture and Fisheries for Scotland on price guarantees, production grants and subsidies, grants and loans for capital and other improvements, support for agriculture in special areas and certain other services including services relating to livestock diseases	12,250,000	*—*4,983,000*

* Deficit

Class XV—*continued*	Supply Grants	Appropriations in Aid
Vote	£	£
2. For expenditure by the Department of Agriculture and Fisheries for Scotland on educational, advisory, livestock services and pest control, assistance to marketing and processing, administration, land management and land settlement, the Royal Botanic and associated gardens, assistance to crofters, assistance to the Scottish fishing industry, protective and certain other services including research development and special services	7,485,000	—
5. For expenditure by the Scottish Economic Planning Department on selective assistance to industry; on compensation to nationalised industries and private industry, and on state owned harbours	1,827,000	*—*3,401,000*
6. For expenditure by the Scottish Development Department in connection with acquisition of land and related services, on roads and certain associated services, including lighting and road safety, on assistance to local transport, on support for transport services in the Highlands and Islands, piers and harbours and on certain other transport services and grants, on housing subsidies, Royal Palaces and Royal Parks, historic buildings and ancient monuments, other central environmental services and grants in aid	1,000	—
8. For expenditure by the Scottish Development Department on subsidies, the option mortgage scheme, improvements and investment, certain rent registration expenses, capital grants to housing associations, loans and grants to first-time purchasers and sundry other housing services	10,951,000	—
9. For expenditure by the Scottish Economic Planning Department on grants to New Town Development Corporations in connection with housing and other services	1,612,000	—
10. For expenditure by the Scottish Development Department in connection with water supply, sewerage, land drainage and flood protection, town and country planning (including compensation), recreation, land reclamation, coast protection, urban programme and other local environmental services	1,432,000	—
11. For expenditure by the Scottish Courts Administration on Court services, the Scottish Law Commission and certain other legal services, including grants in aid	1,000	44,000

* Deficit.

12. For expenditure by the Scottish Home and Health Department on legal aid and criminal injuries compensation (excluding administration), on police and fire services superannuation and police and civil defence grants - - - -	1,978,000	38,000
14. For expenditure by the Scottish Home and Health Department on legal aid administration, certain services relating to crime, treatment of offenders, and on fire services, police and civil defence (excluding grants and superannuation), on the provision of services under the National Health Service, on other health services, on research, services for the disabled and certain other services including a grant in aid - -	5,280,000	—
15. For expenditure by the Scottish Education Department on schools, and certain grants to local authorities, higher and further education, libraries, miscellaneous educational services including compensation payments for redundant staff at colleges of education, research and administration, the Royal Scottish Museum, certain grants for the arts, including purchase grants in aid, sport, social work and other grants in aid - - - - - - - - - - - - - -	1,000	—
16. For expenditure by the Scottish Education Department on awards to students receiving higher and further education - - - - - - - - - -	4,700,000	—
17. For expenditure by the National Library of Scotland, including a purchase grant in aid - - - - - - - - - - - - - -	94,000	*—*100,000*
20. For expenditure by the Scottish Home and Health Department on the provision of services under the National Health Service in Scotland, on welfare food and certain other services - - - - - - - - - - - -	8,842,000	*—*167,000*
CLASS XVI		
1. For expenditure by the Welsh Office on tourism; roads and certain associated services including road safety; housing subsidies and administration; historic buildings and ancient monuments, other environmental services; schools, higher and further education, grants in aid of the National Library of Wales and the National Museum of Wales, miscellaneous educational services and other arts; services under the National Health Service, other health and personal social services, services for the disabled; grants in aid, other grants and certain other services including research	2,420,000	—

* Deficit.

Vote	Supply Grants	Appropriations in Aid
	£	£
CLASS XVI—*continued*		
2. For expenditure by the Welsh Office on production grants and subsidies, grants and loans for capital and other improvements, support for agriculture in special areas, assistance to marketing and processing, animal health and support services, land drainage and certain other services	7,577,000	**—2,445,000*
5. For expenditure by the Welsh Office on assistance to marketing and processing, pest control, land management and smallholdings, research, support to the fishing industry, protective and other services to the fishing industry, special assistance for rural and highland areas, on the Welsh Development Agency and some special and other services including grants in aid	275,000	—
6. For expenditure by the Welsh Office on subsidies, the option mortgage scheme, improvements, investment, grants to housing associations, and sundry other housing services	1,000,000	—
7. For expenditure by the Welsh Office on central administration and certain other services	101,000	—
8. For expenditure by the Welsh Office in connection with water supply, sewerage, town and country planning (including compensation), recreation, other local services, coast protection, urban programme, schools, student awards, miscellaneous educational services, services under the National Health Service, on other health and personal social services, including welfare food	8,218,000	2,247,000
CLASS XVII		
1. For expenditure by the Northern Ireland Office on crown prosecutions and other legal services, services related to crime, compensation for criminal injuries, prisons, probation, training schools and after-care etc, police, central and miscellaneous services, grant in aid to the Police Complaints Board, and certain other grants	14,001,000	—

* Deficit.

CLASS XVIII		
6. For rate rebates and domestic rate relief grants to local authorities in England and for additional rate support grants and payments of compensation for loss of rates to local authorities in England and Wales	50,000,000	—
7. For rate rebate grants and additional rate support grants in Wales	4,000,000	—
8. For rate rebate grants to local authorities in Scotland	5,760,000	—
9. For expenditure by the Home Office on grants to the British Broadcasting Corporation for home broadcasting and sundry other services	5,300,000	—
12. For the expenditure by the Scottish Home and Health Department on superannuation allowances and gratuities etc, in respect of teachers, and the widows and dependants of deceased teachers	8,819,000	1,999,000
13. For expenditure by the Department of Health and Social Security on pensions, allowances, gratuities, etc to or in respect of persons engaged in health services or in other approved employment	1,000	13,111,000
15. For the salaries and expenses of the Crown Estate Office	21,000	—
17. For payment of pensions, etc, to members of the United Kingdom Atomic Energy Authority's superannuation schemes and other related expenditure	1,000	418,000
18. For payment to the Trustees of the Post Office Pensions Fund in respect of former civil servants	3,000,000	—
TOTAL, CIVIL DEPARTMENTS (SUPPLEMENTARY) 1982–83 £	2,498,230,000	117,797,000

SCHEDULE (B).—PART 4

DEFENCE.—CLASS I

Defence, Class I, 1983–84.

SCHEDULE OF SUMS granted, and of the sums which may be applied as appropriations in aid in addition thereto, to defray the charges of the several Defence Services herein particularly mentioned, which will come in course of payment during the year ending on 31st March 1984, including provision for numbers of personnel as set out hereunder, viz.:—

Vote	Sums not exceeding	
	Supply Grants	Appropriations in Aid
	£	£
1. For expenditure by the Ministry of Defence on pay, allowances etc of the Armed Forces and their Reserves and Cadet Forces etc, (including provision for Naval Service to a number not exceeding 75,000, provision for Army Service to a number not exceeding 185,000, for the Individual Reserves to a number not exceeding 134,500, for the Territorial Army to a number not exceeding 86,000, and for the Ulster Defence Regiment to a number not exceeding 12,600, and provision for Air Force Service to a number not exceeding 94,750, for RAF Reserves to a number not exceeding 12,675, and for the Royal Auxiliary Air Force to a number not exceeding 1,120); pay etc of Defence Ministers and of certain civilian staff employed by the Ministry of Defence; on movements; certain stores; supplies and services; plant and machinery; charter and contract repair of ships; certain research; lands and buildings; sundry grants; payments abroad including contributions and subscriptions to international organisations; and grants in aid - - - -	6,134,884,000	838,195,000
2. For expenditure by the Procurement Executive of the Ministry of Defence in operating its Headquarters and Establishments and for its other common services; for research etc by contract; lands and buildings; for development by contract, production, repair etc and purchases for sale abroad of sea systems, land systems, air systems and associated equipment; for reservation of capacity in Royal Ordnance Factories; for certain contingent liabilities, and for sundry other Procurement Executive services including those on repayment terms to non-exchequer customers	7,557,940,000	731,321,000

Vote		
3. For expenditure by the Ministry of Defence on retired pay, pensions etc	755,163,000	1,731,000
4. For expenditure including loans by the Property Services Agency of the Department of the Environment on public building work and certain accommodation services etc for defence purposes	915,996,000	169,157,000
5. For operating the Royal Dockyards and for the repair of ships by contract including work undertaken on repayment terms for exchequer and non-exchequer customers	427,520,000	2,218,000
TOTAL, DEFENCE, CLASS I £	15,791,503,000	1,742,622,000

SCHEDULE (B).—PART 5

Civil Class II, 1983–84.

CIVIL.—CLASS II

SCHEDULE OF SUMS granted, and of the sums which may be applied as appropriations in aid in addition thereto, to defray the charges of the several Civil Services herein particularly mentioned, which will come in course of payment during the year ending on 31st March 1984, viz.:—

	Sums not exceeding	
	Supply Grants	Appropriations in Aid
Vote	£	£
1. For expenditure by the Foreign and Commonwealth Office on the salaries, building and other accommodation services, and administration of Her Majesty's Diplomatic Service, official information services, military aid, certain grants in aid, and sundry other grants, services and loans	328,904,000	40,297,000
2. For expenditure by the Foreign and Commonwealth Office on grants and subscriptions, etc, to certain international organisations, special payments and assistance, and sundry other grants and services	78,505,000	1,773,000
3. For expenditure by the Foreign and Commonwealth Office on grants in aid of the British Broadcasting Corporation for external broadcasting and monitoring services	77,177,000	1,191,000
4. For expenditure by the Foreign and Commonwealth Office on a grant in aid of the British Council	40,233,000	—
5. For a grant in aid of the Commonwealth War Graves Commission	8,540,000	—
6. For Her Majesty's foreign and other secret services	71,500,000	—
7. For expenditure by the Foreign and Commonwealth Office (Overseas Development Administration) on pensions and superannuation payments etc in respect of overseas service, pensions in respect of service with the Cotton Research Corporation and sundry other services and expenses	111,027,000	1,169,000

Vote		
8. For expenditure by the Foreign and Commonwealth Office (Overseas Development Administration) on the official United Kingdom aid programme including pensions and allowances in respect of overseas service, assistance to certain refugee students, grants in aid, certain subscriptions to international organisations and certain payments under the Commonwealth Scholarship and Fellowship Plan - - -	1,027,362,000	4,920,000
9. For expenditure by the Foreign and Commonwealth Office (Overseas Development Administration) on administration - - - - - - - - -	25,444,000	90,000
TOTAL, CIVIL, CLASS II - - - - - - - - - £	1,768,692,000	49,440,000

SCHEDULE (B).—PART 6

Civil, Class III, 1983–84.

CIVIL.—CLASS III

SCHEDULE OF SUMS granted, and of the sums which may be applied as appropriations in aid in addition thereto, to defray the charges of the several Civil Services herein particularly mentioned, which will come in course of payment during the year ending on 31st March 1984, viz.:—

	Sums not exceeding	
	Supply Grants	Appropriations in Aid
	£	£
Vote 1. For expenditure by the Intervention Board for Agricultural Produce in giving effect in the United Kingdom to the agricultural support provisions of the Common Agricultural Policy of the European Community and to Community food aid measures and for certain other services	205,114,000	137,042,000
2. For expenditure by the Ministry of Agriculture, Fisheries and Food on price guarantees, production grants and subsidies, grants and loans for capital and other improvements, support for agriculture in special areas, animal health and support services, land drainage, flood protection, water supply and certain other services	241,115,000	39,981,000
3. For expenditure by the Ministry of Agriculture, Fisheries and Food on educational, advisory, research and development services, livestock services, plant health and pest control, food services and assistance to marketing and processing, land management and smallholdings, emergency and strategic food services, some central, special and other services, including grants in aid and subscriptions to certain international organisations	97,824,000	10,272,000
4. For expenditure by the Intervention Board for Agricultural Produce on central administration and miscellaneous services	18,155,000	340,000

Vote		
5. For expenditure by the Ministry of Agriculture, Fisheries and Food on assistance to the fishing industry, research and development, protective and other services including subscriptions to certain international organisations - - - -	26,703,000	52,000
6. For a grant in aid of the Forestry Fund - - - - - - - -	59,521,000	—
7. For expenditure by the Ministry of Agriculture, Fisheries and Food on departmental administration and certain other services - - - - - - -	193,555,000	5,630,000
TOTAL, CIVIL, CLASS III - - - - - - - - -	841,987,000	193,317,000

SCHEDULE (B).—PART 7

CIVIL.—CLASS IV

Civil, Class IV, 1983–84.

SCHEDULE OF SUMS granted, and of the sums which may be applied as appropriations in aid in addition thereto, to defray the charges of the several Civil Services herein particularly mentioned, which will come in course of payment during the year ending on 31st March 1984, viz.:—

	Sums not exceeding	
	Supply Grants	Appropriations in Aid
Vote	£	£
1. For expenditure by the Department of Industry on regional development grants, selective assistance to industry, certain other services including the provision of public dividend capital to the National Enterprise Board, U.K. contributions to the funding of buffer stock operations of international commodity agreements, a strategic mineral stockpile, and on investment grants - - - - -	606,489,000	18,065,000
2. For expenditure by the Department of Industry on provision of land and buildings, assistance for publicity, and other support services including grants in aid - -	32,491,000	9,570,000
3. For expenditure by the Department of Energy on assistance to the coal industry including grants to the National Coal Board and payments to redundant workers	624,384,000	13,000,000
4. For expenditure by the Department of Trade on promotion of tourism, export promotion, trade co-operation, protection of innovation, regulation of trading practices and consumer protection, standards, central and miscellaneous services, shipping and civil aviation and certain other services including grants in aid and international subscriptions, and other grants - - - - - - - - -	196,604,000	82,889,000

Vote		
5. For expenditure by the Department of Energy in connection with the energy industries including related research and development, selective assistance to industry, energy conservation, oil storage, and certain other services including grants in aid and an international subscription	85,283,000	18,864,000
6. For expenditure by the Department of Industry on the Department's research establishments; industrial research and development and other support; general research and development on civil aeronautics and aero-engines and associated equipment; national and international space technology programmes; loans, grants in aid, international subscriptions and a grant to the National Research Development Corporation and certain other grants	309,661,000	30,600,000
7. For expenditure by the United Kingdom Atomic Energy Authority and the Department of Energy in connection with nuclear energy including research and development, other research and development, the purchase of nuclear and other materials, subscriptions and contributions to international organisations and projects, grants in aid, loans, guarantees, and for sundry other services	210,570,000	201,967,000
8. For expenditure by the Department of Industry on support for the aerospace, shipbuilding, steel and vehicle manufacturing industries, including loans, grants, and the purchase of assets, and assistance to redundant steel workers	271,396,000	59,234,000
9. For expenditure by the Export Credits Guarantee Department on administration	25,855,000	300,000
10. For expenditure by the Export Credits Guarantee Department in connection with export credits guarantees including an international subscription, special guarantees, refinancing and financing arrangements made for facilitating trade with other countries and assistance towards the cost of financing export credits, the purchase of securities, overseas investment insurance and cost escalation guarantees	536,192,000	416,227,000
11. For expenditure by the Registry of Friendly Societies	1,695,000	340,000
12. For expenditure by the Office of Fair Trading	6,609,000	—
13. For expenditure by the Department of Employment on general labour market services, on services for seriously disabled people and on an international subscription	499,140,000	70,000

SCHEDULE (B).—PART 7—*continued*

Vote	Sums not exceeding	
	Supply Grants	Appropriations in Aid
	£	£
14. For expenditure by the Department of Employment on demand determined measures to promote and preserve employment opportunities, compensation to persons for certain dismissals, payments towards expenses of trade union ballots and compensation for persons disabled by pneumoconiosis, byssinosis and diffuse mesothelioma	445,493,000	10,000
15. For expenditure by the Department of Employment on a grant in aid to the Advisory, Conciliation and Arbitration Service	12,629,000	—
16. For expenditure by the Department of Employment on a grant in aid to the Manpower Services Commission	1,211,441,000	211,397,000
17. For expenditure by the Department of Employment on the administration of benefit services and on central and miscellaneous services	187,013,000	120,452,000
18. For expenditure by the Department of Industry on central and miscellaneous services, on those common services shared with the Department of Trade, on services provided by the Ministry of Defence (Procurement Executive) Headquarters, on international subscriptions, on British Telecommunications Civil Defence, on the fund for sub-postmasters and on the World Communication Year	75,815,000	29,753,000
19. For expenditure by the Department of Energy on salaries and other services	22,778,000	4,060,000
20. For expenditure by the Department of Energy in connection with the sale of shares in Britoil	1,000	499,000

Vote		
21. For refunds and repayments of petroleum licensing proceeds, and other payments in connection with such proceeds, to be made by the Department of Energy out of income received from application fees; from annual and other payments for exploration, production, mining and methane drainage licences; from royalty; and from the disposal of petroleum taken as royalty in kind	1,000	420,354,000
22. For expenditure by the Department of Energy to meet preliminary expenses, including loans, incurred in transferring to the private sector oil interests of the British Gas Corporation (BGC)	2,000,000	—
23. For expenditure by the Department of Employment as a grant in aid to the Health and Safety Commission	87,993,000	—
TOTAL, CIVIL, CLASS IV £	5,451,533,000	1,637,651,000

SCHEDULE (B).—PART 8

CIVIL.—CLASS V

Civil, Class V, 1983–84.

SCHEDULE OF SUMS granted, and of the sums which may be applied as appropriations in aid in addition thereto, to defray the charges of the several Civil Services herein particularly mentioned, which will come in course of payment during the year ending on 31st March 1984, viz.:—

	Sums not exceeding	
	Supply Grants	Appropriations in Aid
	£	£
Vote 1. For Government investment in the British Steel Corporation and British Shipbuilders	366,000,000	—
TOTAL, CIVIL, CLASS V - - - - - - - - - £	366,000,000	—

SCHEDULE (B).—PART 9

CIVIL.—CLASS VI

Civil, Class VI, 1983–84.

SCHEDULE OF SUMS granted, and of the sums which may be applied as appropriations in aid in addition thereto, to defray the charges of the several Civil Services herein particularly mentioned, which will come in course of payment during the year ending on 31st March 1984, viz.:—

	Sums not exceeding	
	Supply Grants	Appropriations in Aid
Vote	£	£
1. For expenditure by the Department of Transport on roads and certain associated services including lighting and road safety, including a grant in aid, and certain grants	732,308,000	16,476,000
2. For expenditure by the Department of Transport on assistance to local transport; central administration; certain licensing and testing schemes including privatisation of vehicle testing; research and development; and certain other transport services including civil defence and international subscriptions	114,854,000	55,112,000
3. For expenditure by the Department of Transport on support to nationalised transport industries and assistance to local transport and ports	1,077,648,000	303,000
4. For expenditure by the Department of Transport in connection with driver and motor vehicle registration and licensing and the collection of revenue	100,015,000	4,703,000
TOTAL, CIVIL, CLASS VI £	2,024,825,000	76,594,000

SCHEDULE (B).—PART 10

CIVIL.—CLASS VII

Civil, Class VII, 1983–84.

SCHEDULE OF SUMS granted, and of the sums which may be applied as appropriations in aid in addition thereto, to defray the charges of the several Civil Services herein particularly mentioned, which will come in course of payment during the year ending on 31st March 1984, viz.:—

	Sums not exceeding	
	Supply Grants	Appropriations in Aid
	£	£
Vote 1. For expenditure by the Department of the Environment on subsidies, the option mortgage scheme, improvements and investments, grants to housing associations and the Housing Corporation and sundry other housing services	1,666,213,000	—
TOTAL, CIVIL, CLASS VII £	1,666,213,000	—

SCHEDULE (B).—PART 11

CIVIL.—CLASS VIII

Civil, Class VIII, 1983–84.

SCHEDULE OF SUMS granted, and of the sums which may be applied as appropriations in aid in addition thereto, to defray the charges of the several Civil Services herein particularly mentioned, which will come in course of payment during the year ending on 31st March 1984, viz.:—

Vote	Sums not exceeding	
	Supply Grants	Appropriations in Aid
	£	£
1. For expenditure by the Department of the Environment on assistance to the construction industry, other water supply, conservation and sewerage, local authority and other environmental services including recreation	40,981,000	—
2. For expenditure by the Department of the Environment on other environmental services including grants in aid and international subscriptions, on grants in aid to the British Waterways Board and Development Fund, on bridgeworks, on certain categories of derelict land, and on Civil Defence water services	117,708,000	19,000
3. For expenditure by the Department of the Environment on town and country planning (including compensation), certain categories of derelict land, and other local services	66,110,000	—
4. For expenditure by the Department of the Environment on royal palaces, etc, royal parks, etc, historic buildings, ancient monuments and certain public buildings, the national heritage, on grants in aid, other grants and on payments to Inland Revenue covering assets accepted in lieu of tax, and on the administration of those activities	72,633,000	10,328,000

SCHEDULE (B).—PART 11—*continued*

	Sums not exceeding	
	Supply Grants	Appropriations in Aid
	£	£
Vote		
5. For expenditure by the Department of the Environment on housing subsidies; housing administration; housing tenancy exchanges; central administration including royal commissions, committees etc; building and construction research; environmental research and surveys; payments in connection with licence fees, certain transfers to the private sector and the winding up of redundant functions; and the audit commission	170,762,000	25,706,000
6. For expenditure by the Department of the Environment on the urban programme	140,000,000	—
7. For expenditure by the Department of the Environment on grants in aid to Urban Development Corporations	66,645,000	—
TOTAL, CIVIL, CLASS VIII £	674,839,000	36,053,000

SCHEDULE (B).—PART 12

CIVIL.—CLASS IX

Civil, Class IX, 1983–84.

SCHEDULE OF SUMS granted, and of the sums which may be applied as appropriations in aid in addition thereto, to defray the charges of the several Civil Services herein particularly mentioned, which will come in course of payment during the year ending on 31st March 1984, viz.:—

Vote	Sums not exceeding	
	Supply Grants	Appropriations in Aid
	£	£
1. For expenditure by the Lord Chancellor's Department on court services, the Law Commission, Legal Aid Administration, the Public Trustee Office and certain other legal services	85,554,000	88,809,000
2. For expenditure by the Northern Ireland Court Service on court services, certain other legal services including a grant in aid, accommodation services, and legal aid administration in Northern Ireland	7,942,000	2,593,000
3. For expenditure by the Departments of the Director of Public Prosecutions, and the Treasury Solicitor on Crown prosecutions and other legal services	6,042,000	530,000
4. For grants to the Legal Aid Fund and for expenditure by the Lord Chancellor's Department on legal aid in criminal cases, court services, and costs paid from central funds	319,597,000	4,700,000
5. For expenditure by the Crown Office on crown prosecutions and certain other legal services	3,898,000	2,000
6. For expenditure by the Home Office on court services, compensation for criminal injuries, including a grant in aid, and probation and after-care	256,490,000	5,900,000
7. For expenditure by the Home Office on court services, other services related to crime, probation and after-care, community services, and wireless telegraphy and other miscellaneous services, including grants in aid	39,849,000	8,743,000

SCHEDULE (B).—PART 12—*continued*

Vote	Sums not exceeding	
	Supply Grants	Appropriations in Aid
	£	£
8. For expenditure by the Home Office on prisons (including central administrative staff) and associated stores in England and Wales	538,376,000	24,166,000
9. For expenditure by the Home Office on police, fire, control of immigration and nationality, and of gaming and other protective services, and civil defence, including grants in aid and international subscriptions	79,550,000	17,289,000
10. For expenditure by the Home Office on grants to local and police authorities and the Metropolitan Police Fund for police and community services and for police and fire services superannuation payments	1,257,190,000	616,000
11. For expenditure by the Home Office on administrative and operational staff (excluding prisons) and on central services	164,986,000	12,375,000
12. For expenditure by the Departments of the Director of Public Prosecutions, the Law Officers and the Treasury Solicitor on central and certain other services	10,761,000	1,085,000
13. For expenditure by the Lord Advocate's Departments on central and miscellaneous services	12,013,000	47,000
14. For expenditure by the Northern Ireland Court Service on legal aid and court services	4,464,000	—
TOTAL, CIVIL, CLASS IX £	2,786,712,000	166,855,000

SCHEDULE (B).—PART 13

Civil, Class X, 1983–84.

CIVIL.—CLASS X

SCHEDULE OF SUMS granted, and of the sums which may be applied as appropriations in aid in addition thereto, to defray the charges of the several Civil Services herein particularly mentioned, which will come in course of payment during the year ending on 31st March 1984, viz.:—

	Sums not exceeding	
	Supply Grants	Appropriations in Aid
Vote	£	£
1. For expenditure by the Department of Education and Science on schools, further education, teacher training, adult education, miscellaneous educational services and research, including grants in aid and international subscriptions - - -	180,089,000	5,784,000
2. For expenditure by the Department of Education and Science on the assisted places scheme, student awards and compensation payments to redundant teachers and staff of certain institutions - - - - - - - - - -	654,094,000	10,000
3. For expenditure by the Department of Education and Science on universities and certain other institutions, grants for higher and further education, grants in aid and a subscription to an international organisation - - - - - -	1,441,559,000	1,456,000
4. For expenditure by the Department of Education and Science and the University Grants Committee on administration - - - - - - - -	47,317,000	1,504,000
5. For a grant in aid of the Agricultural Research Council - - - - -	45,982,000	—
6. For grants in aid of the Medical Research Council including subscriptions to certain international organisations - - - - - - - - - -	113,709,000	—
7. For a grant in aid of the Natural Environment Research Council - - - -	62,500,000	—

SCHEDULE (B).—PART 13—*continued*

Vote	Sums not exceeding	
	Supply Grants	Appropriations in Aid
	£	£
8. For grants in aid of the Science and Engineering Research Council including subscriptions to certain international organisations	254,495,000	—
9. For a grant in aid of the Social Science Research Council	22,440,000	—
10. For the expenditure of the British Museum (Natural History), including a purchase grant in aid	9,429,000	—
11. For a grant in aid of the Royal Society	4,951,000	—
12. For the expenditure of the British Museum including a purchase grant in aid	12,536,000	—
13. For the expenditure of the Science Museum, including purchase grants in aid	7,728,000	—
14. For the expenditure of the Victoria and Albert Museum including purchase grants in aid	10,456,000	—
15. For the expenditure of the Imperial War Museum including a purchase grant in aid	4,140,000	—
16. For the expenditure of the National Gallery including a purchase grant in aid	6,797,000	—
17. For the expenditure of the National Maritime Museum, including a purchase grant in aid	4,080,000	—
18. For the expenditure of the National Portrait Gallery including a purchase grant in aid	1,789,000	—
19. For the expenditure of the Tate Gallery including a purchase grant in aid	5,375,000	—

20. For the expenditure of the Wallace Collection	791,000	—
21. For certain grants and services for the benefit of the arts, for grants in aid to the Arts Council and certain other institutions, payments in respect of Public Lending Right, for a grant in aid to the National Heritage Memorial Fund and for payments to the Inland Revenue covering assets accepted in lieu of tax, and for expenditure on the Government Art Collection	109,359,000	5,000
22. For grants in aid to the British Library and certain other institutions and for the expenses of the Royal Commission on Historical Manuscripts	46,299,000	—
TOTAL, CIVIL, CLASS X £	3,045,915,000	8,759,000

SCHEDULE (B).—PART 14

Civil, Class XI, 1983–84.

CIVIL.—CLASS XI

SCHEDULE OF SUMS granted, and of the sums which may be applied as appropriations in aid in addition thereto, to defray the charges of the several Civil Services herein particularly mentioned, which will come in course of payment during the year ending on 31st March 1984, viz.:—

	Sums not exceeding	
	Supply Grants	Appropriations in Aid
Vote	£	£
1. For expenditure by the Department of Health and Social Security on the provision of services under the national health service in England, on other health and personal social services including certain services in relation to the Unitcd Kingdom, and on research, exports, services for the disabled and certain other services; including grants in aid and international subscriptions	8,552,823,000	1,294,539,000
2. For expenditure by the Department of Health and Social Security on the provision of services under the national health service in England, on other health and personal social services, on welfare food and certain other services including grants under Section 8 of the Industry Act 1972	2,361,586,000	313,144,000
TOTAL, CIVIL, CLASS XI £	10,914,409,000	1,607,683,000

SCHEDULE (B).—PART 15

Civil, Class XII, 1983–84.

CIVIL.—CLASS XII

SCHEDULE OF SUMS granted, and of the sums which may be applied as appropriations in aid in addition thereto, to defray the charges of the several Civil Services herein particularly mentioned, which will come in course of payment during the year ending on 31st March 1984, viz.:—

	Sums not exceeding	
	Supply Grants	Appropriations in Aid
Vote	£	£
1. For expenditure by the Department of Health and Social Security on non-contributory retirement pensions, Christmas bonus payments to pensioners, pensions etc for disablement or death arising out of war or service in the armed forces after 2 September 1939 and on certain associated services, on attendance allowances, invalid care allowance, non-contributory invalidity pensions, and mobility allowance	1,522,000,000	—
2. For expenditure by the Department of Health and Social Security on supplementary pensions and allowances	5,053,000,000	118,000,000
3. For expenditure by the Department of Health and Social Security on child benefit, one parent benefit, family income supplements and non-contributory maternity grants	4,134,000,000	—
4. For expenditure by the Department of Health and Social Security for the payment of rate rebate, rent rebate and rent allowance subsidies to rating and housing and local authorities respectively and the additional administrative costs incurred by these authorities in operating the housing benefit scheme	3,267,900,000	—
5. For expenditure by the Department of Health and Social Security on administration and certain other services including an international subscription	714,173,000	536,395,000
TOTAL, CIVIL, CLASS XII £	14,691,073,000	654,395,000

SCHEDULE (B).—PART 16

CIVIL.—CLASS XIII

Civil, Class XIII, 1983–84.

SCHEDULE OF SUMS granted, and of the sums which may be applied as appropriations in aid in addition thereto, to defray the charges of the several Civil Services, herein particularly mentioned, which will come in course of payment during the year ending on 31st March 1984, viz.:—

	Sums not exceeding	
	Supply Grants	Appropriations in Aid
Vote	£	£
1. For the expenditure of the House of Lords	7,541,000	220,000
2. For the expenditure of the House of Commons on members' salaries, allowances, pensions, etc, financial assistance to opposition parties and a grant in aid	24,371,000	—
3. For the expenditure of the Department of Her Majesty's Most Honourable Privy Council	917,000	15,000
4. For expenditure by the Treasury on the management of the economy, and for certain other services including grants in aid to certain Parliamentary bodies and others	42,941,000	2,055,000
5. For expenditure by the Customs and Excise Department including the expenses of value added tax tribunals and an international subscription	321,723,000	14,715,000
6. For the expenditure of the Inland Revenue Department	753,481,000	39,417,000
7. For the expenditure of the Inland Revenue Department on life assurance premium relief and mortgage interest relief	68,000,000	—
8. For the expenditure of the Department of the Comptroller and Auditor General, including an international subscription	11,236,000	2,924,000

Vote			
9.	For the expenditure of the National Debt Office, Pensions Commutation Board and Public Works Loan Commission	1,000	984,000
10.	For the expenditure of the Department for National Savings	144,542,000	803,000
11.	For expenditure by the Treasury in connection with the manufacture, storage and distribution of coinage for use in the United Kingdom	22,795,600	2,808,000
12.	For the expenditure by the Management and Personnel Office on the central management of the civil service, on the Office of the Parliamentary Counsel, and certain other services, including grants in aid	30,749,000	530,000
13.	For expenditure by the Central Computer and Telecommunications Agency (Treasury) in connection with computers and general telecommunications including an international subscription	11,380,000	19,013,000
14.	For the expenditure of the Civil Service Catering Organisation (Treasury) in connection with the provision of catering services	301,000	1,591,000
15.	For the expenditure of the Public Record Office	8,496,000	443,000
16.	For the expenditure of the Office of Population Censuses and Surveys, including a grant in aid	23,889,000	6,717,000
17.	For the expenditure of the Land Registry	64,933,000	82,000
18.	For the expenditure of the Charity Commission for England and Wales	4,865,000	7,300
19.	For the expenditure of the Cabinet Office and grants in aid to international organisations	13,996,000	73,000
20.	For the expenditure of the Office of the Parliamentary Commissioner for Administration and the Health Service Commissioners for England, Scotland and Wales, including an international subscription	1,696,000	—
21.	For payment to Her Majesty's Stationery Office Trading Fund to compensate for the provision of reports of Parliamentary debates at less than full cost, and for the price concessions to public libraries	6,997,000	—

SCHEDULE (B).—PART 16—*continued*

Vote	Sums not exceeding	
	Supply Grants	Appropriations in Aid
	£	£
22. For expenditure by Her Majesty's Stationery Office on the reimbursement of their trading fund in respect of stationery and printing supplied to the Houses of Parliament and to United Kingdom members of the European Assembly	9,530,000	103,000
23. For expenditure by the Ordnance Survey on the survey of Great Britain and other mapping services	17,359,000	21,380,000
TOTAL, CIVIL, CLASS XIII £	1,591,739,600	113,880,300

SCHEDULE (B).—PART 17

CIVIL.—CLASS XIIIA

Civil, Class XIIIA, 1983–84.

SCHEDULE OF SUMS granted, and of the sums which may be applied as appropriations in aid in addition thereto, to defray the charges of the several Civil Services herein particularly mentioned, which will come in course of payment during the year ending on 31st March 1984, viz.:—

	Sums not exceeding	
	Supply Grants	Appropriations in Aid
Vote	£	£
1. For the expenditure of the House of Commons Commission	16,521,000	152,000
TOTAL, CIVIL, CLASS XIIIA £	16,521,000	152,000

SCHEDULE (B).—PART 18

Civil, Class XIV, 1983–84.

CIVIL.—CLASS XIV

SCHEDULE OF SUMS granted, and of the sums which may be applied as appropriations in aid in addition thereto, to defray the charges of the several Civil Services herein particularly mentioned, which will come in course of payment during the year ending on 31st March 1984, viz.:—

	Sums not exceeding	
	Supply Grants	Appropriations in Aid
Vote	£	£
1. For recoverable expenditure, including loans, by the Property Services Agency of the Department of the Environment on acquisitions, public building work and accommodation services, etc, for civil purposes in the United Kingdom	278,235,000	48,472,000
2. For expenditure by the Property Services Agency of the Department of the Environment on administration and certain other services	314,746,000	—
3. For expenditure which is not recoverable from departments including loans by the Property Services Agency of the Department of the Environment on acquisitions, public building work and accommodation services, etc, for civil purposes in the United Kingdom	165,907,000	13,639,000
4. For expenditure by the Central Office of Information on home and overseas publicity	49,081,000	13,005,000
5. For expenditure by the Paymaster General's Office on the superannuation of civil servants, pensions, etc, in respect of former members of the Royal Irish Constabulary and other pensions and non-recurrent payments; and for certain other services	1,091,832,000	76,300,000

6. For rates and contributions in lieu of rates paid by the Rating of Government Property Department in respect of property occupied by the Crown and premises occupied by representatives of Commonwealth and foreign countries and international organisations - - - - - - - - - - - -	119,000,000	250,000,000
7. For the expenditure of the Department of the Government Actuary - - -	1,030,000	513,000
8. For expenditure by the Paymaster General's Office - - - - - -	10,360,000	1,312,000
TOTAL, CIVIL, CLASS XIV - - - - - - - - - - -£	2,030,191,000	403,241,000

Civil, Class XV, 1983–84.

SCHEDULE (B).—PART 19

CIVIL.—CLASS XV

SCHEDULE OF SUMS granted, and of the sums which may be applied as appropriations in aid in addition thereto, to defray the charges of the several Civil Services herein particularly mentioned, which will come in course of payment during the year ending on 31st March 1984, viz.:—

	Sums not exceeding	
	Supply Grants	Appropriations in Aid
Vote	£	£
1. For expenditure by the Department of Agriculture and Fisheries for Scotland on price guarantees, production grants and subsidies, grants and loans for capital and other improvements, support for agriculture in special areas and certain other services including services relating to livestock diseases	57,367,000	19,086,000
2. For expenditure by the Department of Agriculture and Fisheries for Scotland on educational, advisory, livestock services, plant health and pest control, assistance to marketing and processing, administration, land management and land settlement, the Royal Botanic and associated gardens, assistance to crofters, assistance to the Scottish fishing industry, protective and certain other services including research and development and special services	58,888,000	5,507,000
3. For expenditure by the Scottish Economic Planning Department on grants in aid to the Scottish Development Agency and to the Highlands and Islands Development Board; on the promotion of tourism including a grant in aid; on financial assistance to nationalised industries; on employment services in Scotland; on consumer protection, and on sundry other services in connection with trade and industry	132,276,000	380,000

Vote			
4.	For expenditure by the Scottish Economic Planning Department on Manpower Services Commission activities in Scotland	137,255,000	—
5.	For expenditure by the Scottish Economic Planning Department on selective assistance to industry; on compensation to private industry and on state owned harbours	22,301,000	4,995,000
6.	For expenditure by the Scottish Development Department in connection with acquisition of land and related services, on roads and certain associated services, including lighting and road safety, on assistance to local transport, on support for transport services in the Highlands and Islands, piers and harbours and on certain other transport services and grants, on housing subsidies, Royal Palaces and Royal Parks, historic buildings and ancient monuments, other central environmental services and grants in aid	148,003,000	4.807,000
7.	For expenditure by the Scottish Development Department on assistance to local transport, and on piers and harbours	8,085,000	—
8.	For expenditure by the Scottish Development Department on subsidies, the option mortgage scheme, improvements and investment, certain rent registration expenses, capital grants to housing associations, loans and grants to first time purchasers and sundry other housing services	236,931,000	1,000
9.	For expenditure by the Scottish Economic Planning Department on grants to New Town Development Corporations in connection with housing and other services	39,303,000	—
10.	For expenditure by the Scottish Development Department in connection with water supply and sewerage, land drainage and flood protection, town and country planning (including compensation), recreation, land reclamation, coast protection, urban programme and other local environmental services	36,275,000	—

SCHEDULE (B).—PART 19—*continued*

Vote	Sums not exceeding	
	Supply Grants	Appropriations in Aid
	£	£
11. For expenditure by the Scottish Courts Administration on court services, the Scottish Law Commission and certain other legal services, including a grant in aid	7,616,000	4,840,000
12. For expenditure by the Scottish Home and Health Department on legal aid and criminal injuries compensation (excluding administration), on police and fire services superannuation and police and civil defence grants	163,087,000	880,000
13. For expenditure by the Scottish Courts Administration on costs and fees in connection with legal proceedings	2,064,000	—
14. For expenditure by the Scottish Home and Health Department on legal aid administration, certain services relating to crime, prisons, treatment of offenders, civil defence (including grants) and on fire and police services, (excluding grants and superannuation), on the provision of services under the national health service, on other health services, on research services for the disabled and certain other services including a grant in aid	1,363,137,000	131,298,000
15. For expenditure by the Scottish Education Department on schools, and certain grants to local authorities, higher and further education, libraries, miscellaneous educational services including compensation payments for redundant staff at colleges of education, research and administration, the Royal Scottish Museum, certain grants for the arts, including purchase grants in aid, sport, social work and other grants in aid	112,744,000	8,000

Vote		
16. For expenditure by the Scottish Education Department on awards to students receiving higher and further education - - - - - - - - -	107,400,000	—
17. For expenditure by the National Library of Scotland, including a purchase grant in aid	2,781,000	138,000
18. For the expenditure of the National Gallery of Scotland, the Scottish National Gallery of Modern Art, the Scottish National Portrait Gallery and the Department of Prints and Drawings, including purchase grants in aid - - - - - -	2,709,000	—
19. For the expenditure of the National Museum of Antiquities of Scotland, including a purchase grant in aid - - - - - - - - - - - -	799,000	—
20. For expenditure by the Scottish Home and Health Department on the provision of services under the National Health Service in Scotland, on welfare food and certain other services - - - - - - - - - - - - -	290,475,000	32,617,000
21. For the expenditure of the Scottish Record Office and on certain other services including a grant in aid - - - - - - - - - - -	1,445,000	315,000
22. For the expenditure of the General Register Office for Scotland - - - -	3,895,000	727,000
23. For the expenditure of the Department of the Registers of Scotland - - -	1,000	7,959,000
24. For expenditure by the Scottish Office on administration, Royal Commissions and certain other services - - - - - - - - - - -	94,430,000	3,165,000
TOTAL, CIVIL, CLASS XV - - - - - - - - - - £	3,029,267,000	216,723,000

SCHEDULE (B).—PART 20

Civil, Class XVI, 1983–84.

CIVIL.—CLASS XVI

SCHEDULE OF SUMS granted, and of the sums which may be applied as appropriations in aid in addition thereto, to defray the charges of the several Civil Services herein particularly mentioned, which will come in course of payment during the year ending on 31st March 1984, viz.:—

	Sums not exceeding	
	Supply Grants	Appropriations in Aid
Vote	£	£
1. For expenditure by the Welsh Office on tourism; roads and certain associated services including road safety; housing subsidies and administration; historic buildings and ancient monuments, other environmental services; schools, higher and further education, grants in aid of the National Library of Wales and the National Museum of Wales, miscellaneous educational services and other arts; services under the National Health Service, other health and personal social services, services for the disabled; grants in aid, other grants and certain other services including research	718,138,000	64,815,000
2. For expenditure by the Welsh Office on production grants and subsidies, grants and loans for capital and other improvements, support for agriculture in special areas, assistance to marketing and processing, animal health and support services, land drainage and certain other services	45,842,000	10,342,000
3. For expenditure by the Welsh Office on selective assistance to industry in assisted areas, and special assistance to rural areas	14,850,000	3,100,000
4. For expenditure by the Welsh Office on the Manpower Services Commission	70,895,000	—

Vote		
5. For expenditure by the Welsh Office on assistance to marketing and processing, pest control, land management and smallholdings, research, support to the fishing industry, protective and other services to the fishing industry, special assistance for rural and highland areas, on the Welsh Development Agency and some special and other services including grants in aid - - - - - - - -	56,215,000	155,000
6. For expenditure by the Welsh Office on subsidies, the option mortgage scheme, improvements, investment, grants to housing associations, and sundry other housing services - - - - - - - - - - - -	78,854,000	—
7. For expenditure by the Welsh Office on central administration and certain other services - - - - - - - - - - - -	31,244,000	1,171,000
8. For expenditure by the Welsh Office in connection with water supply, sewerage, town and country planning (including compensation), recreation, other local services including clean air grants, coast protection, urban programme, schools, student awards, miscellaneous educational services, services under the national health service, on other health and personal social services, including welfare food - -	179,819,000	19,605,000
Total, Civil, Class XVI - - - - - - - - - -£	1,195,857,000	99,188,000

SCHEDULE (B).—PART 21

Civil, Class XVII, 1983–84.

CIVIL.—CLASS XVII

SCHEDULE OF SUMS granted, and of the sums which may be applied as appropriations in aid in addition thereto, to defray the charges of the several Civil Services herein particularly mentioned, which will come in course of payment during the year ending on 31st March 1984, viz.:—

	Sums not exceeding	
	Supply Grants	Appropriations in Aid
Vote	£	£
1. For expenditure by the Northern Ireland Office on crown prosecutions and other legal services, services related to crime, compensation schemes, prisons, probation, training schools and after-care, etc., police, central and miscellaneous services, a grant in aid to the Police Complaints Board and certain other grants	390,313,000	2,739,000
2. For expenditure by the Northern Ireland Office on a grant in aid of the Northern Ireland Consolidated Fund and other transfers	780,000,000	—
TOTAL, CIVIL, CLASS XVII £	1,170,313,000	2,739,000

SCHEDULE (B).—PART 22

Civil, Class XVIII, 1983–84.

CIVIL.—CLASS XVIII

SCHEDULE OF SUMS granted, and of the sums which may be applied as appropriations in aid in addition thereto, to defray the charges of the several Civil Services herein particularly mentioned, which will come in course of payment during the year ending on 31st March 1984, viz.:—

	Sums not exceeding	
	Supply Grants	Appropriations in Aid
Vote	£	£
1. For rate support grants (in respect of 1983–84) to local authorities in England	9,416,000,000	—
2. For rate support grants (in respect of 1983–84) to local authorities in Wales	827,500,000	—
3. For national parks supplementary grants (in respect of 1983–84) to county councils	5,265,000	—
4. For national parks supplementary grants (in respect of 1983–84) to county councils in Wales	1,800,000	—
5. For rate support grants (in respect of 1983–84) in Scotland	1,744,250,000	—
6. For rate rebates and domestic rate relief grants to local authorities in England and for additional rate support grants and payments and compensation for loss of rates to local authorities in England and Wales	114,919,000	—
7. For rate rebate grants in Wales	5,685,000	—
8. For rate rebate grants to local authorities in Scotland	11,920,000	—

SCHEDULE (B).—PART 22—*continued*

Vote	Sums not exceeding	
	Supply Grants	Appropriations in Aid
	£	£
9. For expenditure by the Home Office on grants to the British Broadcasting Corporation for home broadcasting and sundry other services	772,400,000	—
10. For sums payable out of the Consolidated Fund to the National Insurance Fund	2,785,000,000	—
11. For expenditure by the Department of Education and Science on superannuation allowances and gratuities, etc., in respect of teachers, and the widows, children and dependants of deceased teachers	120,974,000	767,330,000
12. For expenditure by the Scottish Home and Health Department on superannuation allowances and gratuities, etc., in respect of teachers, and the widows and dependants of deceased teachers	26,424,000	88,196,000
13. For expenditure by the Department of Health and Social Security on pensions, allowances, gratuities, etc., to or in respect of persons engaged in health services or in other approved employment	1,000	684,000,000
14. For expenditure by the Scottish Home and Health Department on pensions, allowances, gratuities, etc., to or in respect of persons engaged in health services or in other approved employment	1,000	86,309,000
15. For the salaries and expenses of the Crown Estate Office	1,681,000	—
16. For transitional relief under the Finance Acts 1965 and 1972, for companies with an overseas source of trading income	100,000	—
17. For payment of pensions, etc., to members of the United Kingdom Atomic Energy Authority's superannuation schemes and other related expenditure	1,000	34,258,000

18. For supplementary grants (in respect of 1983–84) for transport purposes to county councils and the Greater London Council - - - - - - - -	450,000,000	—
19. For supplementary grants (in respect of 1983–84) for transport purposes to county councils - - - - - - - - - - - - -	31,000,000	—
TOTAL, CIVIL, CLASS XVIII - - - - - - - - - £	16,314,921,000	1,660,093,000

Section 3.

SCHEDULE (C)

ENACTMENTS REPEALED

Chapter	Short title
1981 c. 4	Consolidated Fund Act 1981.
1981 c. 51	Appropriation Act 1981.
1981 c. 70	Consolidated Fund (No. 2) Act 1981.

Finance Act 1983

1983 CHAPTER 28

An Act to grant certain duties, to alter other duties, and to amend the law relating to the National Debt and the Public Revenue, and to make further provision in connection with Finance. [13th May 1983]

Most Gracious Sovereign,

WE, Your Majesty's most dutiful and loyal subjects, the Commons of the United Kingdom in Parliament assembled, towards raising the necessary supplies to defray Your Majesty's public expenses, and making an addition to the public revenue, have freely and voluntarily resolved to give and grant unto Your Majesty the several duties hereinafter mentioned; and do therefore most humbly beseech Your Majesty that it may be enacted, and be it enacted by the Queen's most Excellent Majesty, by and with the advice and consent of the Lords Spiritual and Temporal, and Commons, in this present Parliament assembled, and by the authority of the same, as follows:—

PART I

Customs and Excise

Duties on spirits, beer, wine, made-wine and cider.

1979 c. 4.

1.—(1) In section 5 of the Alcoholic Liquor Duties Act 1979 (excise duty on spirits) for " £14·47 " there shall be substituted " £15·19 ".

PART I

(2) In section 36 of that Act (excise duty on beer) for " £20·40 " and " £0·68 " there shall be substituted " £21·60 " and " £0·72 " respectively.

(3) For the provisions of Schedule 1 to that Act (rates of excise duty on wine) there shall be substituted the provisions of Schedule 1 to this Act.

(4) For the provisions of Schedule 2 to that Act (rates of excise duty on made-wine) there shall be substituted the provisions of Schedule 2 to this Act.

(5) In section 62(1) of that Act (excise duty on cider) for " £8·16 " there shall be substituted " £9·69 ".

(6) This section shall be deemed to have come into force on 16th March 1983.

Tobacco products. 1979 c. 7.

2.—(1) For the Table in Schedule 1 to the Tobacco Products Duty Act 1979 there shall be substituted—

" TABLE

1. Cigarettes	An amount equal to 21 per cent. of the retail price plus £21·67 per thousand cigarettes.
2. Cigars	£40·85 per kilogram.
3. Hand-rolling tobacco	£35·40 per kilogram.
4. Other smoking tobacco and chewing tobacco	£24·95 per kilogram."

(2) This section shall be deemed to have come into force on 18th March 1983.

Hydrocarbon oil. 1979 c. 5.

3.—(1) In section 6(1) of the Hydrocarbon Oil Duties Act 1979 (rates of duty on hydrocarbon oil) for " £0·1554 " (light oil) and " £0·1325 " (heavy oil) there shall be substituted " £0·1630 " and " £0·1382 " respectively.

(2) This section shall be deemed to have come into force at 6 o'clock in the evening of 15th March 1983.

Vehicle excise duty. 1971 c. 10. 1972 c. 10. (N.I.).

4.—(1) The Vehicles (Excise) Act 1971 and the Vehicles (Excise) Act (Northern Ireland) 1972 shall be amended as follows.

(2) For the provisions of Part II of Schedules 1 to 5 to each of those Acts (annual rates of duty) there shall be substituted the provisions set out in Part I of Schedule 3 to this Act.

(3) The provisions of Part I of Schedule 4 to each of those Acts (annual rates of duty on goods vehicles: general provisions) shall have effect subject to the amendments made by Part II of Schedule 3 to this Act.

(4) In sections 2(1)(*c*) of the Act of 1971 and 2(1)(*d*) of the Act of 1972 (seven-day licences for certain vehicles), for sub-paragraphs (i) and (ii) there shall be substituted—

" (i) in respect of which duty is chargeable by reference to an annual rate applicable to haulage vehicles in accordance with the second and third categories in Part II of Schedule 3 to this Act or applicable to goods vehicles in accordance with Schedule 4 to this Act ; and

(ii) the unladen weight of which exceeds 11,176·5 kilograms ; ".

(5) In subsection (5) of section 16 of the Act of 1971 (rates of duty for trade licences), including that subsection as set out in paragraph 12 of Part I of Schedule 7 to that Act, for " £40 " and " £8 " there shall be substituted, respectively, " £42 " and " £8·50 ".

(6) In subsection (6) of section 16 of the Act of 1972 (rates of duty for trade licences), including that subsection as set out in paragraph 12 of Part I of Schedule 9 to that Act, for " £40 " and " £8 " there shall be substituted, respectively, " £42 " and " £8·50 ".

(7) The provisions set out in Schedule 3 to this Act as being substituted for provisions of Schedule 4 to the Act of 1972 shall have effect in that Act with the substitution for any reference to a plated gross weight of a reference to a relevant maximum weight and for any reference to a plated train weight of a reference to a relevant maximum train weight.

(8) This section applies in relation to licences taken out after 15th March 1983.

Bingo duty and gaming machine licence duty.

1981 c. 63.

5.—(1) In paragraph 2 of Schedule 3 to the Betting and Gaming Duties Act 1981 (exemption limits for small-scale bingo) after sub-paragraph (1) there shall be inserted the following sub-paragraph—

" (1A) Where the total value of the card money taken in the bingo in question played at any premises exceeds during, or on any day in, a relevant week the total value of the prizes won in that bingo during that week or, as the case may be, on that day, any reference in sub-paragraph (1) above to the total value of the prizes so won shall be read as a reference to the total of the card money so taken.

In this sub-paragraph " card money " means money taken by or on behalf of the promoter of the bingo as payment by players for their cards (within the meaning of section 17(3) of this Act) ".

PART I

(2) In Schedule 4 to the Act of 1981, in paragraph 1, for sub-paragraph (3) (meaning of private gain in relation to exemption from gaming machine licence duty for charitable entertainments etc.) there shall be substituted the following—

" (3) In construing sub-paragraph (2)(*a*) above, proceeds of an entertainment promoted on behalf of a society falling within this sub-paragraph which are applied for any purpose calculated to benefit the society as a whole shall not be held to be applied for purposes of private gain by reason only that their application for that purpose results in benefit to any person as an individual.

(4) A society falls within sub-paragraph (3) above if it is established and conducted either—

(*a*) wholly for purposes other than purposes of any commercial undertaking, or

(*b*) wholly or mainly for the purpose of participation in or support of athletic sports or athletic games;

and in this paragraph " society " includes any club, institution, organisation or association of persons, by whatever name called, and any separate branch or section of such a club, institution, organisation or association."

Deferred payment of excise duty on goods.

1979 c. 2.

6. The following section shall be inserted in Part X of the Customs and Excise Management Act 1979 (duties and drawbacks: general provisions), after section 127—

" *Deferred payment of excise duty on goods*

Deferred payment of excise duty on goods.

127A.—(1) The Commissioners may by regulations make provision for the payment of any excise duty on goods of a prescribed kind to be deferred, in prescribed cases, subject to such conditions or requirements as may be imposed—

(*a*) by the regulations; or

(*b*) where the regulations so provide, by the Commissioners.

(2) Any duty payment of which is deferred under the regulations shall be treated, for prescribed purposes, as if it had been paid.

(3) Where—

(*a*) any excise duty to which an application for deferment of duty made under the regulations relates is payable on goods on their removal from an excise warehouse; and

(*b*) the Commissioners are not satisfied—

(i) that the conditions imposed under section 92(1) above in relation to the warehouse have been complied with by the occupier of the warehouse ; or

(ii) that the warehousing regulations made by virtue of section 93(2)(*g*) above have been complied with by the occupier or by the proprietor of the goods ;

the Commissioners may, notwithstanding any provision of the regulations, refuse the application or refuse it in so far as it relates to those goods.

Nothing in this subsection shall be taken to prejudice the power of the Commissioners to prescribe the cases in which excise duty may be deferred.

(4) Regulations under this section may make different provision for goods of different descriptions or for goods of the same description in different circumstances.

(5) In this section " prescribed " means prescribed by regulations made under this section.".

Imports to and exports from Northern Ireland.
1979 c. 2.

7.—(1) In section 26 of the Customs and Excise Management Act 1979 (power to regulate movement of goods into and out of Northern Ireland by land),—

(*a*) in paragraph (*a*) of subsection (1) after the words " " approved routes ") " there shall be inserted the words " or at such places on the boundary " ; and

(*b*) at the end of subsection (1) there shall be added the words " and any such regulations may make different provision in relation to different classes or descriptions of goods and, in particular, in relation to different classes or descriptions of vehicles ".

(2) After subsection (1) of that section there shall be added the following subsection:—

" (1A) In such cases and subject to compliance with such conditions as appear to the Commissioners to be appropriate, the Commissioners may dispense with any requirement of a regulation made under subsection (1) above ".

(3) In subsection (2) of that section (penalties) after the words " subsection (1) above " there shall be inserted the words " or any condition of a dispensation given under subsection (1A) above ".

(4) In section 27(1) of that Act (powers to board ships and aircraft and vehicles on approved routes) for the words " on

PART I

an approved route " there shall be substituted the words " within the prescribed area ".

(5) In section 51(1) of that Act (control of importation: special provisions as to proof where goods are within the prescribed area in Northern Ireland) the words " within the prescribed area " shall be omitted.

Export from Northern Ireland of goods chargeable with agricultural levies.
1979 c. 2.

8. At the end of Part V of the Customs and Excise Management Act 1979 (control of exportation), after section 68A, there shall be inserted the following section—

" Special provisions as to proof in Northern Ireland.

68B.—(1) If goods of any class or description chargeable with agricultural levies on their exportation from the United Kingdom are found in the possession or control of any person within the prescribed area in Northern Ireland, any officer or any person having by law in Northern Ireland the powers of an officer may require that person to furnish proof either—

(*a*) that the goods are not intended for such exportation ; or

(*b*) that the goods are intended for such exportation and any entry required to be made or security required to be given in connection with that exportation has been or will be made or given.

(2) If proof of any matter is required to be furnished in relation to any goods under subsection (1) above but is not so furnished, the goods shall be liable to forfeiture.

1972 c. 68.

(3) In subsection (1) above " agricultural levy " has the same meaning as in section 6 of the European Communities Act 1972."

Miscellaneous customs and excise repeals.
1964 c. 26.
1976 c. 66.

9.—(1) Subsection (5) of section 30 of the Licensing Act 1964 (duty of clerk to licensing justices to supply to Collector of Customs and Excise a list of new licences granted and licences not renewed) and section 22 of the Licensing (Scotland) Act 1976 (which makes corresponding provision for Scotland) shall cease to have effect.

1969 c. 32.
1979 c. 4.

(2) Paragraph 1 of Schedule 7 to the Finance Act 1969 (definition of " whisky " or " whiskey " for customs and excise purposes) and section 92(7) of the Alcoholic Liquor Duties Act 1979 (saving in relation to spirits distilled before 1st August 1969) shall cease to have effect on the appointed day.

(3) In subsection (2) above, " the appointed day " means such day as the Treasury may by order made by statutory instrument

appoint; but the Treasury may not so appoint a day unless they are satisfied that on that day there will be in force as part of the law of each part of the United Kingdom a definition given by or under any enactment of the expressions "whisky" and "whiskey".

PART II

INCOME TAX, CORPORATION TAX AND CAPITAL GAINS TAX

CHAPTER I

GENERAL

Charge of income tax for 1983-84.

10.—(1) Income tax for the year 1983-84 shall be charged at the basic rate of 30 per cent.; and

(*a*) in respect of so much of an individual's total income as exceeds £12,800 at such higher rates as are specified in the Table below; and

(*b*) in respect of so much of the investment income included in an individual's total income as exceeds £6,250 at the additional rate of 15 per cent.

TABLE

Part of excess over £12,800	*Higher rate*
The first £2,300	40 per cent.
The next £4,000	45 per cent.
The next £6,200	50 per cent.
The next £6,200	55 per cent.
The remainder	60 per cent.

(2) Nothing in this section requires any change to be made in the amounts deductible or repayable under section 204 of the Taxes Act (pay as you earn) before 31st August 1983.

(3) Notwithstanding anything in the preceding provisions of this section, the amounts deductible or repayable under section 204 of the Taxes Act on and after 11th May 1983 and before 31st August 1983 may be such as would be requisite to give effect to the provisions as to higher rate tax and the investment income surcharge contained in a Resolution passed by the House of Commons on 21st March 1983.

(4) Section 24(4) of the Finance Act 1980 (increase of basic rate limit, higher rate bands and investment income threshold) shall not apply for the year 1983-84. 1980 c. 48.

PART II

Charge of corporation tax for financial year 1982.

11. Corporation tax shall be charged for the financial year 1982 at the rate of 52 per cent.

Rate of advance corporation tax for financial year 1983.

12. The rate of advance corporation tax for the financial year 1983 shall be three-sevenths.

Corporation tax: small companies.

1972 c. 41.

13. The small companies rate for the financial year 1982 shall be 38 per cent., and for that year the fraction mentioned in subsection (2) of section 95 of the Finance Act 1972 (marginal relief for small companies) shall be seven seventy-fifths.

Personal reliefs.

1980 c. 48.

14.—(1) Section 24(5) of the Finance Act 1980 (increase of personal reliefs) shall not apply for the year 1983-84.

(2) In section 8 of the Taxes Act (personal reliefs)—

(*a*) in subsection (1)(*a*) (married) for " £2,445 " there shall be substituted " £2,795 ";

(*b*) in subsections (1)(*b*) (single) and (2) (wife's earned income relief) for " £1,565 " there shall be substituted " £1,785 ";

(*c*) in subsection (1A) (age allowance) for " £3,295 " and " £2,070 " there shall be substituted " £3,755 " and " £2,360 " respectively; and

(*d*) in subsection (1B) (income limit for age allowance) for " £6,700 " there shall be substituted " £7,600 ".

Widow's bereavement allowance.

15.—(1) In section 15A of the Taxes Act (widow's bereavement allowance) for the words " for that year " there shall be substituted the following paragraphs—

" (*a*) for that year of assessment, and

(*b*) unless she marries again before the beginning of it, for the next following year of assessment ".

1976 c. 40.

(2) In section 36(8)(*b*)(i) of the Finance Act 1976 (deductions which are not transferable between husband and wife) for the words " and 14 " there shall be substituted the words " 14 and 15A ".

(3) Subsection (1) above has effect in any case where the widow's bereavement occurred or occurs in the year 1982-83 or in any subsequent year of assessment and subsection (2) above has effect for the year 1983-84 and subsequent years of assessment.

PART II

16.—(1) In sub-paragraph (1) of paragraph 5 of Schedule 1 to the Finance Act 1974 (limit on relief for interest on certain loans for the purchase or improvement of land) the references to £25,000 shall have effect for the year 1983-84. Relief for interest. 1974 c. 30.

(2) Nothing in this section requires any change to be made in the amounts deductible or repayable under section 204 of the Taxes Act (pay as you earn) before 31st August 1983.

(3) Notwithstanding anything in the preceding provisions of this section, the amounts deductible or repayable under section 204 of the Taxes Act on and after 11th May 1983 and before 31st August 1983 may be such as would be requisite to give effect to the provisions as to relief for interest contained in a Resolution passed by the House of Commons on 21st March 1983.

17.—(1) In paragraph 4 of Schedule 7 to the Finance Act 1982 (interest on home improvement loans to qualify as relevant loan interest only if certain conditions are fulfilled) at the end of paragraph (*b*) of sub-paragraph (1) there shall be added the words " or Loan interest paid under deduction of tax. 1982 c. 39.

(*c*) it is interest to which sub-paragraph (3) of paragraph 2 above applies ".

(2) In paragraph 5 of that Schedule (loans over the tax relief limit) after sub-paragraph (3) there shall be inserted the following sub-paragraph:—

" (3A) The reference in sub-paragraph (1) above to a loan only part of the interest on which would (apart from the principal section) be eligible for relief under section 75 of the Finance Act 1972 includes a reference to each of two or more loans if, by virtue of sub-paragraph (4)(*b*) of paragraph 5 of the 1974 Schedule, the interest on the loans falls to be treated for the purposes of that paragraph as payable on one loan; but, notwithstanding that each of those loans is accordingly a limited loan for the purposes of this paragraph, none of the interest on any of them is relevant loan interest unless each of the loans was made by the same qualifying lender "; 1972 c. 41.

and in sub-paragraph (4) of that paragraph after the words " sub-paragraph (3) " there shall be inserted the words " or sub-paragraph (3A) ".

(3) In paragraph 14 of that Schedule (qualifying lenders for the purposes of deduction of tax from certain loan interest) after paragraph (*n*) of sub-paragraph (1) there shall be inserted the following paragraph:—

" (*nn*) the Church of England Pensions Board ";

PART II

and at the end of paragraph (*o*) of sub-paragraph (1) there shall be added the words " and any other body whose activities and objects appear to the Treasury to qualify it for inclusion in this paragraph ".

(4) In sub-paragraph (2) of paragraph 14 of that Schedule (Treasury orders) after the words " by order " there shall be inserted the words " made by statutory instrument ".

1972 c. 41.

(5) In paragraph 1 of Schedule 9 to the Finance Act 1972 (interest eligible for relief on loans for purchase or improvement of land) at the end of sub-paragraph (*c*) (replacement loans) there shall be added the words " or would have been so eligible apart from section 26 of the Finance Act 1982 ".

1982 c. 39.

(6) This section has effect with respect to interest due on or after 6th April 1983 or, where sub-paragraph (3) or sub-paragraph (4) of paragraph 2 of Schedule 7 to the Finance Act 1982 applies, on or after 1st April 1983.

Assigned life policies and annuity contracts.

18.—(1) Subsection (4) of section 394 of the Taxes Act (no chargeable event where life policy has previously been assigned for money or money's worth) shall be amended as follows:—

(*a*) at the beginning there shall be inserted the words " Except as provided by Schedule 4 to the Finance Act 1983 ";

(*b*) after the word " policy ", where it first occurs, there shall be inserted the words " issued in respect of an insurance made before 26th June 1982 " ; and

(*c*) after the words " at any time " there shall be inserted the words " before that date and ".

(2) Subsection (2) of section 396 of the Taxes Act (which makes corresponding provision in relation to life annuity contracts) shall be amended as follows:—

(*a*) at the beginning there shall be inserted the words " Except as provided by Schedule 4 to the Finance Act 1983 ";

(*b*) after the word " contract ", where it first occurs, there shall be inserted the words " made before 26th June 1982 " ; and

(*c*) after the words " at any time " there shall be inserted the words " before that date and ".

(3) Schedule 4 to this Act shall have effect for the purposes of this section and in that Schedule " the relevant provision " means,—

(*a*) in relation to a life policy, section 394(4) of the Taxes Act ; and

PART II

(b) in relation to a contract for a life annuity, section 396(2) of that Act.

(4) Expressions used in this section and in Schedule 4 to this Act have the same meaning as in Chapter III of Part XIV of the Taxes Act.

(5) This section and Schedule 4 to this Act shall be deemed to have come into force on 26th June 1982.

Retirement annuity relief: early retirement.

19.—(1) In section 226 of the Taxes Act (approval of retirement annuity contracts and trust schemes) in subsection (3)(c) (occupations from which retirement before attaining the age of sixty is customary) the words " (but not before he attains the age of fifty) " shall cease to have effect.

(2) This section shall be deemed to have come into force on 6th April 1983.

Scholarships. 1976 c. 40.

20.—(1) In Chapter II of Part III of the Finance Act 1976 (benefits derived by company directors and others from their employment), the following section shall be inserted after section 62—

" Scholarships.

62A.—(1) Nothing in section 375 of the Taxes Act (scholarship income not to be taken into account as income for income tax purposes) shall be construed as conferring on any person other than the person holding the scholarship in question any exemption from the charge to tax under section 61 above.

(2) For the purposes of this Chapter, any scholarship provided for a member of a person's family or household shall, without prejudice to any other provision of this Chapter, be taken to have been provided by reason of that person's employment if it is provided under arrangements entered into by, or by any person connected with, his employer (whether or not those arrangements require the employer or connected person to contribute directly or indirectly to the cost of providing the scholarship).

(3) Section 61 above does not apply to a benefit consisting in a payment in respect of a scholarship—

(a) provided from a trust fund or under a scheme; and

(b) held by a person receiving full-time instruction at a university, college, school or other educational establishment;

PART II

if, in the year in which the payment is made, not more than 25 per cent. of the total amount of the payments made from that fund, or under that scheme, in respect of scholarships so held would (apart from this subsection) represent benefits chargeable to tax under section 61 above.

(4) In this section " scholarship " includes an exhibition, bursary or other similar educational endowment; and section 533 of the Taxes Act (connected persons) applies for the purposes of this section.".

(2) This section has effect in relation to payments made on or after 15th March 1983, but does not apply in relation to any payment made at a time when the conditions mentioned in subsection (3) below are satisfied.

(3) The conditions are that—

(*a*) the scholarship was awarded before 15th March 1983;

(*b*) the first payment in respect of the scholarship is made before 6th April 1984; and

(*c*) the person holding the scholarship is receiving full-time instruction at the university, college, school or other educational establishment at which he was receiving that instruction at the time when the first such payment was made.

(4) For the purpose of ascertaining, in accordance with subsection (3) of the section inserted by subsection (1) above, the percentage of the total amount of the payments made in any year of assessment beginning after 5th April 1982 in respect of scholarships from any fund or under any scheme which apart from subsection (3)) would represent benefits chargeable to tax under section 61 of the Act of 1976, this section shall be deemed to have had effect in relation to all such payments made in that year.

Living accommodation provided for employee.
1977 c. 36.

21.—(1) The following section shall be inserted in the Finance Act 1977, after section 33—

" Living " accommodation provided for employee: additional charge.

33A.—(1) This section applies where—

(*a*) living accommodation is provided for a person in any period, by reason of his employment;

(*b*) by virtue of section 33 above he is treated for Schedule E purposes as being in receipt of emoluments of an amount calculated by reference to the value to him of that accommodation, or would be so treated if there were disregarded any sum made good by him to those at whose cost the accommodation is provided ; and PART II

(*c*) the cost of providing the accommodation exceeds £75,000.

(2) Where this section applies, the employee shall be treated for Schedule E purposes as being in receipt of emoluments (in addition to those which he is treated as receiving by virtue of section 33) of an amount equal to the additional value to him of the accommodation for the period, less so much of any rent paid by the employee, in respect of the accommodation, to the person providing it as exceeds the value to the employee of the accommodation for the period (as determined under section 33).

(3) The additional value of the accommodation to the employee in any period is the rent which would have been payable for that period if the premises had been let to him at an annual rent equal to the appropriate percentage of the amount by which the cost of providing the accommodation exceeds £75,000.

(4) For the purposes of this section, the cost of providing any living accommodation shall be taken to be the aggregate of—

(*a*) the amount of any expenditure incurred in acquiring the estate or interest in the property held by any relevant person ; and

(*b*) the amount of any expenditure incurred by any relevant person before the year of assessment in question on improvements to the property.

(5) The aggregate amount mentioned in subsection (4) above shall be reduced by the amount of any payment made by the employee to any relevant person, so far as that amount represents a reimbursement of any such expenditure as is mentioned in paragraph (*a*) or (*b*) of that subsection or represents consideration for the grant to the employee of a tenancy of the property.

(6) Subject to subsection (8) below, where throughout the period of six years ending with the date when the employee first occupied the property, any estate or interest in the property was held by any relevant

PART II

person (whether or not it was the same estate, interest or person throughout), the additional value shall be calculated as if in subsection (4) above—

(*a*) the amount referred to in paragraph (*a*) were the market value of the property as at that date; and

(*b*) the amount referred to in paragraph (*b*) did not include expenditure on improvements made before that date.

(7) " Relevant person " means any of the following—

(*a*) the person providing the accommodation;

(*b*) where the person providing the accommodation is not the employee's employer, that employer; and

(*c*) any person, other than the employee, who is connected with a person falling within paragraph (*a*) or (*b*) above.

(8) Subsection (6) above does not apply where the employee first occupied the property before 31st March 1983.

(9) Any amount which is deductible, by virtue of subsection (3) of section 33, from an amount to be treated as emoluments under that section may, to the extent to which it exceeds the amount of those emoluments, be deductible from the amount to be treated as emoluments under this section.

(10) For the purposes of this section, living accommodation shall be treated as provided for a person by reason of his employment if it is so treated for the purposes of section 33; and in this section " employment " has the same meaning as in that section.

(11) In this section—

" the appropriate percentage " means the rate prescribed by the Treasury under section 66(9) of the Finance Act 1976 (beneficial loan arrangements etc.) as at the beginning of the year of assessment in question;

1976 c. 40.

" property ", in relation to any living accommodation, means the property consisting of that accommodation;

" market value ", in relation to any property, means the price which that property might reasonably be expected to fetch on a sale in

PART II

the open market with vacant possession, no reduction being made, in estimating the market value, on account of any option in respect of the property held by the employee, or a person connected with him, or by any of the persons mentioned in subsection (7) above; and

" tenancy " includes a sub-tenancy.

(12) Section 533 of the Taxes Act (connected persons) shall apply for the purposes of this section.".

(2) This section has effect for the year 1984-85 and for subsequent years of assessment.

Benefits derived by directors: Schedule E payments. 1976 c. 40.

22.—(1) The following section shall be inserted in Chapter II of Part III of the Finance Act 1976 (benefits derived by company directors and others from their employment), after section 66—

" Schedule E: director's tax paid by employer.

66A.—(1) Subject to the provisions of this Chapter, where in any year a person (the " recipient ") is employed as a director of a company and—

(*a*) a payment of, or on account of, income assessable to income tax under Schedule E as emoluments of that employment is made to him in circumstances in which the person making the payment is required, by regulations made under section 204 of the Taxes Act (pay as you earn), to deduct an amount of income tax on making the payment; and

(*b*) the whole of that amount is not so deducted but is, or any part of it is, accounted for to the Board by someone other than the recipient;

the amount so accounted for to the Board, less so much (if any) as is made good by the recipient to that other person or so deducted, shall be treated as emoluments of the employment and accordingly chargeable to income tax under Schedule E.

(2) A person shall not be treated, for the purposes of subsection (1) above, as employed as a director of a company if he has no material interest in the company and either paragraph (*a*) or paragraph (*b*) of section 69(5) of this Act is satisfied.

(3) Where an amount treated as emoluments of a person's employment, by subsection (1) above, is accounted for to the Board at a time when the

PART II

employment has come to an end, those emoluments shall be treated, for the purposes of the Income Tax Acts, as having arisen in the year of assessment in which the employment ended; but that subsection shall not apply in relation to any amount accounted for to the Board after the death of the director in question."

(2) This section has effect in relation to amounts accounted for on or after 6th April 1983.

Covenanted payments to charity; increase of exemption from excess tax liability.

23.—(1) In section 457 of the Taxes Act, in subsection (1A) (covenanted payments to charity: first £3,000 exempt from excess liability) for "£3,000" there shall be substituted "£5,000".

1972 c. 41.

(2) In Schedule 16 to the Finance Act 1972 (close companies' apportionment of income) in paragraph 5, in sub-paragraph (5A) (total income reduced by amount of covenanted payments to charities, subject to the £3,000 limit) for "£3,000" there shall be substituted "£5,000".

(3) This section has effect for the year 1983-84 and subsequent years of assessment in relation to payments made after 5th April 1983.

Relief for interest: money borrowed for investment in employee-controlled company.

1974 c. 30.

24.—(1) In Part III of Schedule 1 to the Finance Act 1974 (interest eligible for relief), the following shall be inserted after paragraph 10B—

"*Loan applied in investing in employee-controlled company*

10C. Subject to the following provisions of this Part of this Schedule, interest is eligible for relief under section 75 of the Finance Act 1972 if it is interest on a loan to an individual to defray money applied—

(*a*) in acquiring any part of the ordinary share capital of an employee-controlled company; or

(*b*) in paying off another loan, interest on which would have been eligible for relief under section 75 of the Act of 1972 had the loan not been paid off (on the assumption, if the loan was free of interest, that it carried interest);

and the conditions stated in paragraph 10D below are satisfied.

10D.—(1) The conditions referred to in paragraph 10C above are that—

(*a*) the company is, throughout the period beginning with the date on which the shares are acquired and ending with the date on which the interest is paid,—

(i) an unquoted company resident in the United Kingdom and not resident elsewhere; and

(ii) a trading company or the holding company of a trading group;

(*b*) the shares are acquired before, or not later than twelve months after, the date on which the company first becomes an employee-controlled company;

(*c*) during the year of assessment in which the interest is paid the company either—

(i) first becomes an employee-controlled company; or

(ii) is such a company throughout a period of at least nine months;

(*d*) the individual or his spouse is a full-time employee of the company throughout the period beginning with the date on which the proceeds of the loan are applied and ending with the date on which the interest is paid or, if at that date he has ceased to be such an employee, ending with whichever is the later of—

(i) the date on which he ceased to be such an employee;

(ii) the date twelve months before the payment of the interest; and

(*e*) the individual shows that in the period from the application of the proceeds of the loan to the payment of the interest he has not recovered any capital from the company, apart from any amount taken into account under paragraph 13 below.

(2) For the purposes of paragraph 10C above and this paragraph, a company is employee-controlled at any time when at least 75 per cent.—

(*a*) of the issued ordinary share capital of the company; and

(*b*) of the voting power in the company;

is beneficially owned by persons who, or whose spouses, are full-time employees of the company.

(3) Where an individual owns beneficially, or he and his spouse together own beneficially, more than 5 per cent. of the issued ordinary share capital of, or voting power in, a

PART II

company, the excess shall be treated for the purposes of sub-paragraph (2) above as being owned by an individual who is neither a full-time employee of the company nor the spouse of such an employee.

(4) In this paragraph—

" full-time employee ", in relation to a company, means a person who works for the greater part of his time as an employee or director of the company or of a 51 per cent. subsidiary of the company;

" holding company " means a company whose business (disregarding any trade carried on by it) consists wholly or mainly of the holding of shares or securities of one or more companies which are its 75 per cent. subsidiaries;

" trading company " means a company whose business consists wholly or mainly of the carrying on of a trade or trades;

" trading group " means a group the business of whose members, taken together, consists wholly or mainly of the carrying on of a trade or trades, and for this purpose " group " means a company which has one or more 75 per cent. subsidiaries, together with those subsidiaries; and

" unquoted company " means a company none of whose shares are listed in the Official List of the Stock Exchange.".

(2) Paragraphs 13 to 15 of Part III of Schedule 1 to the Act of 1974 shall be amended as follows—

(*a*) in paragraphs 13 and 14, after the words " co-operative ", wherever they occur, there shall be inserted the words " employee-controlled company "; and

(*b*) in paragraph 15, after " 10B " there shall be inserted " 10D " and after " 10A(*c*) " there shall be inserted " 10C(*b*) ".

(3) This section has effect in relation to interest paid after 5th April 1983.

Profit sharing schemes.
1978 c. 42.

25.—(1) In Chapter III of Part III of the Finance Act 1978 (approved profit sharing schemes) for the sum of money specified in section 58(1), section 58(2) and paragraph 1 (4) of Schedule 9 (each of which relates to the limit on the initial market value of shares in any year) there shall be substituted the words " the relevant amount"; and in section 61(1) of that Act (interpretation) after the definition of "the release date" there shall be inserted— PART II

"'the relevant amount', in relation to a participant, means an amount which is not less than £1,250 and not more than £5,000 but which, subject to that, is 10 per cent. of his salary (determined under subsection (4) below) for the year of assessment in question or the preceding year of assessment, whichever is the greater".

(2) At the end of section 61 of the Finance Act 1978 (interpretation) there shall be inserted the following subsection:— 1978 c. 42.

"(4) For the purposes of subsection (1) above, a participant's salary for a year of assessment means such of the emoluments of the office or employment by virtue of which he is entitled to participate in the scheme as are liable to be paid in that year under deduction of tax pursuant to section 204 of the Taxes Act (pay as you earn) after deducting therefrom amounts included by virtue of Chapter II of Part III of the Finance Act 1976 (benefits derived by directors and others from their employment)." 1976 c. 40.

(3) As respects subsections (1) and (2) of section 58 of the Finance Act 1978, the amendments effected by subsections (1) and (2) above apply in relation to shares appropriated on or after 6th April 1983 and, as respects paragraph 1(4) of Schedule 9 to that Act, those amendments shall be deemed to have come into force on that date.

(4) In paragraph 2 of Schedule 9 to the Finance Act 1978 (matters as to which the Board must be satisfied for approval of schemes)—

(*a*) at the end of sub-paragraph (1) there shall be added the words "and that those who do participate in the scheme actually do so on similar terms"; and

(*b*) at the end of sub-paragraph (2) there shall be added the words "or do not actually do so".

(5) At the end of the said paragraph 2 there shall be inserted the following sub-paragraphs:—

"(3) The Board must also be satisfied—

(*a*) that there are no features of the scheme which have or would have the effect of discouraging any description of employees or former employees who fulfil the conditions in sub-paragraph (1) above from actually participating in the scheme (subject to Part III below); and

PART II

(*b*) where the company concerned is a member of a group of companies, that the scheme does not and would not have the effect of conferring benefits wholly or mainly on directors of companies in the group or on those employees of companies in the group who are in receipt of the higher or highest levels of remuneration.

(4) For the purposes of sub-paragraph (3) above a group of companies means a company and any other companies of which it has control."

1978 c. 42.

(6) In paragraph 3(1) of Schedule 9 to the Finance Act 1978 (grounds for withdrawing approval) at the end of paragraph (*d*) there shall be added " or

(*e*) the trustees, the company concerned or, in the case of a group scheme, a company which is or has been a participating company fail or fails to furnish any information which they are or it is required to furnish pursuant to section 53(7) of this Act ".

Relief for investment in corporate trades.

26.—(1) Part I of Schedule 5 to this Act shall have effect, in relation to shares issued in the year of assessment 1983-84 or in any of the next three years of assessment, for the purpose of making provision with respect to relief from income tax for investment in corporate trades, in place of that made by Chapter II of Part IV of the Finance Act 1981.

1981 c. 35.

(2) The provisions of Chapter II of Part IV of the Act of 1981 (relief for investment in new corporate trades) shall continue to have effect in relation to shares issued in the years of assessment 1981-82 and 1982-83, but subject to the amendments set out in Part II of Schedule 5 to this Act.

1970 c. 9.

(3) The Table in section 98 of the Taxes Management Act 1970 (penalties) shall be amended as follows—

(*a*) at the end of the first column there shall be inserted—

" Paragraph 15(3) and (4) of Schedule 5 to the Finance Act 1983." ; and

(*b*) at the end of the second column there shall be inserted—

" Paragraph 15(1) and (2) of Schedule 5 to the Finance Act 1983."

Public lending right.

27. The following enactments shall have effect in relation to public lending right as they have effect in relation to copyright—

(*a*) section 16 of the Taxes Management Act 1970 (returns of periodical or lump sum payments) ;

(*b*) sections 143(3)(*b*) (charge on receipts after discontinuance of trade, etc. not to apply to lump sum paid to personal representatives for assignment), 389 and 390 (reliefs), 391 (taxation of royalties where owner's usual place of abode is abroad), and 521 (under-deductions from payments) of the Taxes Act. PART II

Employees seconded to charities.

28.—(1) If a company makes available to a charity, on a basis which is expressed and intended to be of a temporary nature, the services of a person in the employment of the company then, notwithstanding anything in—

(*a*) section 130 of the Taxes Act (general rules as to deductions not allowable in computing profits or gains), or

(*b*) section 304 of that Act (expenses of management of investment companies etc.),

any expenditure incurred (or disbursed) by the company which is attributable to the employment of that person shall continue to be deductible in the manner and to the like extent as if, during the time that his services are so made available to the charity, they continued to be available for the purpose of the company's trade or business.

(2) In subsection (1) above—

" charity " has the same meaning as in section 360 of the Taxes Act ; and

" deductible " means deductible as an expense in computing the profits or gains of the company concerned to be charged under Case I of Schedule D or, as the case may be, deductible as expenses of management for the purposes of section 304 of the Taxes Act.

(3) This section applies to expenditure attributable to the employment of a person on or after 1st April 1983.

Building societies: interest to be payable gross on certificates of deposit.

29.—(1) In paragraph (iii) of the proviso to subsection (3) of section 343 of the Taxes Act (arrangements for payment of income tax on interest etc. paid by building societies) after the word " loan " there shall be inserted the words " or under a qualifying certificate of deposit ".

(2) After subsection (8) of that section there shall be inserted the following subsection—

" (8A) In subsection (3) above " qualifying certificate of deposit " means a certificate of deposit, as defined in section 55(3) of the Finance Act 1968, which is issued by a building society and under which— 1968 c. 44.

(*a*) the amount payable by the society, exclusive of interest, is not less than £50,000 ; and

PART II

(*b*) the obligation of the society to pay that amount arises before the expiry of the period of twelve months beginning on the date of issue of the certificate."

(3) This section has effect in relation to documents issued after 5th April 1983.

CHAPTER II

CAPITAL ALLOWANCES

Industrial building or structure.
1968 c. 3.

30.—(1) In section 7 of the Capital Allowances Act 1968 (definition of industrial building or structure) in subsection (4) (disregard of non-industrial part representing not more than one-tenth of total expenditure) for the words " one-tenth " there shall be substituted the words " one quarter ".

(2) Subsection (1) above has effect in relation to expenditure incurred after 15th March 1983 and to expenditure which, by virtue of section 5(1) of the Capital Allowances Act 1968 (purchase of unused buildings or structures), is deemed to have been incurred after that date; but expenditure shall not be treated for the purposes of this section as having been incurred after the date on which it was in fact incurred by reason only of section 1(6) of that Act (expenditure incurred before trade begins).

Buildings converted into very small workshops.
1982 c. 39.

31.—(1) Where the conditions mentioned in subsection (2) below are satisfied in relation to an industrial building, section 73 of the Finance Act 1982 (industrial buildings allowance: very small workshops) shall apply in relation to capital expenditure on the construction of that building notwithstanding that the gross internal floor space of the whole building will exceed 1,250 square feet.

(2) The conditions referred to in subsection (1) above are that—

(*a*) the industrial building has been constructed by means of the conversion of a building (the " existing building ") into two or more industrial buildings;

(*b*) each of those industrial buildings is—

(i) permanently separated from the remainder of the existing building;

(ii) intended for occupation separately from the remainder of the existing building; and

(iii) suitable for being so occupied; and

(*c*) the average gross internal floor space does not exceed 1,250 square feet.

(3) For the purposes of subsection (2)(*c*) above, the average gross internal floor space shall be calculated—

(*a*) as at the date at which the following condition is first satisfied, namely that all the buildings which have been constructed by means of the conversion have come into use; or

(*b*) if that condition is not satisfied before 27th March 1986, as at that date;

and shall be taken to be the average of the gross internal floor space of all those parts of the existing building which are industrial buildings at that date.

(4) This section does not apply where the existing building, or any part of it, remained unused throughout the period before the conversion.

(5) Where—

(*a*) in anticipation of the conditions mentioned in subsection (2) above being complied with in relation to an industrial building, section 73 of the Act of 1982 has been taken to apply in relation to capital expenditure on the construction of that building; and

(*b*) those conditions have not been complied with in relation to that industrial building;

all such assessments shall be made as are necessary to secure that the Capital Allowances Act 1968 shall have effect in relation to that expenditure as if it had never been expenditure to which section 73 applies. 1968 c. 3.

(6) The Tax Acts shall have effect as if this section were contained in Chapter I of Part I of the Act of 1968.

Capital allowances for expenditure on production or acquisition of certain films etc.

32.—(1) In section 72 of the Finance Act 1982 (expenditure on production and acquisition of films etc.) in subsection (7) (transitional relief for expenditure incurred on or before 31st March 1984 either pursuant to a contract entered into before 10th March 1982 or on the production or acquisition of certain qualifying films, tapes or discs) for the words "or it is incurred" there shall be substituted the words "nor to expenditure which is incurred by any person on or before 31st March 1987 if it is incurred". 1982 c. 39.

(2) At the end of that section there shall be added the following subsection:—

"(10) Section 50(4) of the Finance Act 1971 (construction of references to the date on which expenditure is incurred for the purposes of Chapter I of Part III of that Act) applies in relation to the preceding provisions of this section as though they were comprised in that Chapter." 1971 c. 68.

PART II

Extended transitional period for teletext receivers etc.

1980 c. 48.

33. In paragraph 7 of Schedule 12 to the Finance Act 1980 (transitional period for 100 per cent. first year allowances for television sets) sub-paragraph (2) (definition of " the transitional period ") shall be amended as follows:—

(*a*) paragraph (*aa*) (which provides for a five year period for teletext receivers and adaptors) shall be omitted; and

(*b*) in paragraph (*b*) (which provides for a six year period for viewdata receivers and adaptors) after the words " the provision of " there shall be inserted the words " a teletext receiver or ";

and sub-paragraph (5) of paragraph 7 (which, among other matters, extends, in relation to certain expenditure, references in sub-paragraph (2) to teletext receivers to include references to teletext adaptors) shall apply accordingly.

CHAPTER III

CAPITAL GAINS

Election for pooling: indexation.

34.—(1) The provisions of Schedule 6 to this Act shall have effect for the purposes of, and in connection with,—

(*a*) enabling a company to elect that, with respect to disposals after 31st March 1982, each of its holdings of certain securities of the same class which are held by it solely and beneficially and which have been so held for the length of time referred to in that Schedule shall be regarded for the purposes of the Capital Gains Tax Act 1979 as constituting a single asset; and

1979 c. 14.

(*b*) computing the indexation allowance applicable on a disposal of such a single asset.

1982 c. 39.

(2) In section 88 of the Finance Act 1982 (identification of securities etc. disposed of: general rules) after subsection (5) there shall be inserted the following subsection—

" (5A) If an election has been made under Schedule 6 to the Finance Act 1983, securities disposed of shall be identified with securities comprised in a holding, within the meaning of paragraph 3 of that Schedule, rather than with securities of a description specified in paragraph 1(2)(*b*) thereof."

PART III

OIL TAXATION

35.—(1) In section 139 of the Finance Act 1982 (liability for APRT etc.) in subsection (1) (the periods for which the liability arises)— Phasing out of APRT. 1982 c. 39.

(*a*) in paragraph (*a*) after the words " after 31st December 1982 " there shall be inserted the words " and before 1st January 1987 " ; and

(*b*) in paragraph (*b*) for the words " nine immediately succeeding chargeable periods " there shall be substituted the words " immediately succeeding chargeable periods (if any) which ends before 1st January 1987 and ".

(2) In subsection (2) of that section (the rate of APRT) for the words " at the rate of 20 per cent." there shall be substituted the following paragraphs:—

" (*a*) for the chargeable period ending on 30th June 1983, at the rate of 20 per cent. ;

(*b*) for subsequent chargeable periods ending on or before 31st December 1984, at the rate of 15 per cent. ;

(*c*) for chargeable periods ending in 1985, at the rate of 10 per cent. ; and

(*d*) for chargeable periods ending in 1986, at the rate of 5 per cent."

(3) In consequence of subsections (1) and (2) above—

(*a*) in each of subsections (3)(*a*) and (4)(*a*) of section 139 of the Finance Act 1982, for the words " the APRT which is paid " there shall be substituted the words " any APRT which is payable and paid " ;

(*b*) in subsection (4) of that section for the words " the APRT paid ", in each place where they occur, there shall be substituted the words " any APRT paid " ; and

(*c*) Schedule 19 to that Act shall have effect subject to the modifications set out in Schedule 7 to this Act.

36.—(1) For all relevant new fields, as defined in subsection (2) below, section 8 of the principal Act (the oil allowance) shall have effect subject to the following modifications:— Increased oil allowance for certain new fields.

(*a*) in subsection (2) (the amount of the allowance for each chargeable period) for " 250,000 metric tonnes " there shall be substituted " 500,000 metric tonnes " ; and

PART III

(*b*) in subsection (6) (the total allowance for a field) for " 5 million metric tonnes " there shall be substituted " 10 million metric tonnes ".

(2) Subject to subsection (3) below, in this section " relevant new field " means an oil field—

S.I. 1982/1000.

(*a*) no part of which lies in a landward area, within the meaning of the Petroleum (Production) Regulations 1982 or in an area to the East of the United Kingdom and between latitudes 52° and 55° North ; and

(*b*) for no part of which consent for development has been granted to the licensee by the Secretary of State before 1st April 1982 ; and

(*c*) for no part of which a programme of development had been served on the licensee or approved by the Secretary of State before that date.

(3) In determining, in accordance with subsection (2) above, whether an oil field (in this subsection referred to as " the new field ") is a relevant new field, no account shall be taken of a consent for development granted before 1st April 1982 or a programme of development served on the licensee or approved by the Secretary of State before that date if—

(*a*) in whole or in part that consent or programme related to another oil field for which a determination under Schedule 1 to the principal Act was made before the determination under that Schedule for the new field ; and

(*b*) on or after 1st April 1982, a consent for development is or was granted or a programme of development is or was served on the licensee or approved by the Secretary of State and that consent or programme relates, in whole or in part, to the new field.

(4) In subsections (2) and (3) above " development " means—

(*a*) the erection or carrying out of permanent works for the purpose of getting oil from the field or for the purpose of conveying oil won from the field to a place on land ; or

(*b*) winning oil from the field otherwise than in the course of searching for oil or drilling wells ;

and consent for development does not include consent which is limited to the purpose of testing the characteristics of an oil-bearing area and does not relate to the erection or carrying out of permanent works.

(5) In subsection (4) above " permanent works " means any structures or other works whatsoever which are intended by the licensee to be permanent and are neither designed to be

moved from place to place without major dismantling nor intended by the licensee to be used only for searching for oil.

PART III

Reliefs for exploration and appraisal expenditure etc.

37.—(1) The section set out in Part I of Schedule 8 to this Act shall be inserted in the principal Act after section 5 for the purpose of setting up a new allowance by virtue of which a participator in an oil field may obtain relief for certain expenditure which is incurred otherwise than in connection with that field.

(2) For the purpose of giving effect to, and in consequence of, the new allowance, the enactments specified in Part II of Schedule 8 to this Act shall have effect subject to the amendments there specified.

(3) Part III of Schedule 8 to this Act shall have effect with respect to sums received after 15th March 1983 and falling to be set off against expenditure which would otherwise be allowable under section 5 of the principal Act or under the new section set out in Part I of that Schedule.

(4) In paragraph 1 of Schedule 7 to the principal Act (claims for certain allowances)—

(*a*) in sub-paragraph (1) the words from " but may not " to the end of the sub-paragraph (which impose a time limit on claims) shall be, and shall be deemed always to have been, omitted ; and

(*b*) in sub-paragraph (2) the words " within the time allowed for making the original claim " shall be, and shall be deemed always to have been, omitted ;

and, accordingly, any claim which, immediately before the passing of this Act, could not have been made by virtue of the time bar may be made thereafter.

Terms of payment to be implied in determining market value.

38. In paragraph 2 of Schedule 3 to the principal Act (definition of market value of oil) at the end of sub-paragraph (2) (the price under a contract of sale at arm's length) there shall be added the words—

" and, for the avoidance of doubt, it is hereby declared that the terms as to payment which are to be implied in the contract shall be those which are customarily contained in contracts for the sale at arm's length of oil of the kind in question ".

Exclusion of oil appropriated for production purposes in other fields.

39.—(1) In section 12(1) of the principal Act (interpretation of Part I) in the definition of " relevantly appropriated " (which, among other matters, excludes oil appropriated for production purposes) after the word " purposes " there shall be added the words " in relation to that or any other oil field ".

PART III

(2) This section has effect, and shall be deemed to have had effect, for chargeable periods ending after 31st December 1977.

Variation of decisions on claims for allowable expenditure.

40.—(1) At the end of Schedule 5 to the principal Act (allowance of expenditure under section 3 or 4 of that Act) there shall be inserted the following paragraph—

" 9.—(1) If, within the period of three years commencing with the date on which notice of a decision of the Board under paragraph 3 above was given to the responsible person for an oil field, it appears to the Board that the relevant amount was incorrectly stated in the notice, the Board may before the expiry of that period serve on the responsible person a notice stating what appears to the Board to be the correct amount (referred to below as " the notice of variation ").

(2) In this paragraph " the relevant amount ", in relation to a notice of a decision on a claim under paragraph 3 above, means any one or more of the following—

(*a*) the amount of expenditure allowed on the claim ;

(*b*) the amount of that expenditure allowed as qualifying for supplement under section 2(9)(*b*)(ii) of this Act ;

(*c*) where different percentages were stated in that notice to apply to different parts of that expenditure for the purpose of calculating the supplement, each of those parts of that expenditure.

(3) The responsible person may, by notice in writing given to the Board not more than thirty days after the notice of variation was served on him, appeal to the Special Commissioners against the notice of variation.

(4) A notice of appeal under sub-paragraph (3) shall state the grounds on which the appeal is brought.

(5) An appeal under this paragraph may at any time be abandoned by notice in writing given to the Board by the responsible person.

(6) A notice of variation may be withdrawn at any time before it becomes effective.

(7) In any case where—

(*a*) the responsible person gives notice of appeal against a notice of variation, and

(*b*) before the appeal is determined by the Special Commissioners, the Board and the responsible person agree as to what the relevant amount ought to be, the notice of variation shall have effect subject to such modifications as may be necessary to give effect to that agreement; and thereupon the appeal shall be treated as having been abandoned.

(8) On an appeal against a notice of variation the Special Commissioners may vary the notice, quash the notice or dismiss the appeal; and the notice may be varied whether or not the variation is to the advantage of all or any of the participators in the oil field in question.

(9) Where a notice of variation relating to a decision on a claim becomes effective, the relevant amount shall be taken for the purposes of this Part of this Act as having been reduced or increased, as the case may require, on the date on which notice of the decision was given, by such amount as may be necessary to give effect to that notice, and the Board may make such computations under section 2 of this Act and such assessments or determinations or such amendments of assessments or determinations as may be necessary in consequence of that reduction or increase.

(10) A notice of variation becomes effective for the purposes of this paragraph either—

(*a*) on the expiry of the period during which notice of appeal against the notice of variation may be given to the Special Commissioners under sub-paragraph (3) above without such notice of appeal being given; or

(*b*) where such notice of appeal is given, when the notice of variation can no longer be varied or quashed by the Special Commissioners or by the order of any court.

(11) This paragraph has effect in relation to notices of decisions of the Board under paragraph 3 above given after 15th March 1983."

(2) In Schedule 6 to the principal Act (allowance of expenditure on claim by participator) at the end of the first column of the Table set out in paragraph 2 (application of provisions of Schedule 5) there shall be added " 9 ".

Transfers of interests in oil fields.
1980 c. 48.

41.—(1) In sub-paragraph (1) of paragraph 7 of Schedule 17 to the Finance Act 1980 (transfers of unused losses from old participator to new in cases of transfers of interests in fields) for the words " in any chargeable period before the transfer period " there shall be substituted the words " in the transfer period or any earlier chargeable period ".

PART III

(2) In sub-paragraph (2) of that paragraph at the end there shall be added the words " and, for the purposes of effecting such relief, subsection (1) of section 7 shall have effect as if the word " succeeding " were omitted ".

1980 c. 48.

(3) This section has effect in relation to transfer periods (within the meaning of paragraph 1 of Schedule 17 to the Finance Act 1980) ending after 31st December 1982.

PART IV

MISCELLANEOUS AND SUPPLEMENTARY

National insurance surcharge

Reduction of national insurance surcharge.
1976 c. 85.

42.—(1) In section 1(1) of the National Insurance Surcharge Act 1976 (surcharge on earnings in respect of which secondary Class 1 contributions are payable), for the words " 1½ per cent." there shall be substituted the words " 1 per cent.".

1982 c. 55.

(2) Subject to section 1(2) of the National Insurance Surcharge Act 1982, this section applies with respect to earnings paid on or after 1st August 1983.

Miscellaneous

National savings: supplements.

43.—(1) Where any sum has been borrowed by the Treasury on terms set out—

(*a*) in the prospectus for Save As You Earn Savings Contracts (Third Issue) ; or

(*b*) in the prospectus for Index-Linked National Savings Certificates Retirement Issue ;

that prospectus shall (whether the sum was borrowed before or after the passing of this Act) be taken to have included a provision empowering the Treasury to supplement, from time to time, the due amount and requiring any such supplement to be paid on such terms as may be notified by the Treasury in the London, Edinburgh and Belfast Gazettes.

(2) " The due amount " means—

(*a*) in the case of the prospectus mentioned in subsection (1)(*a*) above, the amount due under paragraph 7, 8, 9 or 10 ; and

(*b*) in the case of the other prospectus, the amount due under paragraph 4.

Rates of interest for government lending.
1968 c. 13.
1982 c. 39.

44.—(1) Section 5 of the National Loans Act 1968 (which, as set out in section 153 of the Finance Act 1982, provides for the determination of rates of interest for government lending) shall be amended in accordance with this section.

(2) In subsection (5) (withdrawal of determination or approval of rate of interest which no longer fulfils the requirements of the section)—

(*a*) for the words from " approved for " to " not yet made " there shall be substituted the words " approved for a class of loans "; and

(*b*) for the words from " withdrawn " to the end of the subsection there shall be substituted the words " withdrawn at the earliest convenient time, and, subject to subsection (5A) below, from that or such later time as may be convenient another rate determined or approved in accordance with subsection (3) or, as the case may be, subsection (4) above shall come into force for further loans of that class ".

(3) After subsection (5) there shall be inserted the following subsections:—

" (5A) If, in the case of a loan of any class,—

(*a*) an undertaking was given to the person to whom the loan was to be made that the rate of interest which would apply to that loan would be that which, at a time specified in or determined in accordance with the undertaking, was or would be in force for loans of that class, and

(*b*) before the loan was in fact made, the determination or approval of that rate of interest was withdrawn by virtue of subsection (5) above or otherwise ceased to be effective,

the rate of interest which applies to that loan shall be that which was in force for loans of that class at the time specified in, or as the case may be determined in accordance with, the undertaking.

(5B) In subsection (5A) above " undertaking " means an undertaking given by the person by whom the loan in question was to be made and, where that person is not the Treasury, given by that person with the consent of the Treasury."

Suspension of certain payments into National Loans Fund in respect of new towns.

45.—(1) Subject to subsection (4) below, the Treasury may, on the recommendation of the Secretary of State, by order specify any new town development loan as a loan the repayment of which to the Secretary of State (and subsequently into the National Loans Fund) is to be suspended by virtue of this section.

(2) Where a loan is specified by an order under subsection (1) above—

(*a*) the terms of the loan shall have effect as if any payment by way of repayment of or interest on the loan

PART IV

which (apart from this section) would fall due at any time within the unexpired period for repayment of the loan fell due instead at the corresponding time within the period of the same duration beginning with 1st October 1986; and

(*b*) no interest shall accrue in respect of the loan during the period beginning with the coming into force of the order and ending with 30th September 1986.

(3) In this section, " new town development loan " means any sum—

1981 c. 64.

(*a*) falling within section 60(*a*) of the New Towns Act 1981 (sums advanced by Secretary of State to development corporations in England and Wales for the purpose of enabling them to meet expenditure properly chargeable to capital account or to make good to revenue account sums applied in meeting liabilities so chargeable); or

1976 c. 75.

(*b*) borrowed by the Development Board for Rural Wales under section 9(2)(*a*) of the Development of Rural Wales Act 1976 (loans by Secretary of State, other than temporary loans) for the purposes of the Board's function in respect of the development of new towns;

and " the unexpired period for repayment of the loan ", in relation to any loan specified by an order under subsection (1) above, means the period beginning with the coming into force of the order and ending with the date which (apart from this section) would be the last date on which any payment by way of repayment of or interest on the loan would fall due under the terms of the loan.

(4) The aggregate amount of new town development loans specified by order under subsection (1) above shall not exceed £1,250 million.

(5) The power to make an order under subsection (1) above shall be exercisable by statutory instrument.

Historic Buildings and Monuments Commission for England.

46.—(1) On a claim in that behalf to the Board there shall be allowed in the case of the Historic Buildings and Monuments Commission for England (in this section referred to as " the Commission ") such exemption from tax as falls to be allowed under section 360 of the Taxes Act in the case of a charity the whole income of which is applied to charitable purposes.

(2) The Commission shall be exempt from tax in respect of all chargeable gains.

(3) For the purposes of the enactments set out below, the Commission shall be treated as a body of persons established for charitable purposes only:—

(*a*) sections 248(9) and 434(2) of the Taxes Act (covenanted donations to charities);

(*b*) section 54 of the Finance Act 1980 (charitable donations by traders); and 1980 c. 48.

(*c*) section 99 of the Finance Act 1980 and section 129 of the Finance Act 1982 (reliefs from stamp duty). 1982 c. 39.

(4) Section 24 of the Development Land Tax Act 1976 (exemption of charities) and section 57 of the Finance Act 1977 (exemption of charities from national insurance surcharge) shall have effect as if the Commission were a charity within the meaning of section 360 of the Taxes Act. 1976 c. 24. 1977 c. 36.

(5) In paragraph 12(1) of Schedule 6 to the Finance Act 1975 (capital transfer tax exemptions) immediately before the entry relating to the National Trust for Places of Historic Interest or Natural Beauty there shall be inserted— 1975 c. 7.

" The Historic Buildings and Monuments Commission for England ".

Pre-consolidation amendments.

47. Schedule 9 to this Act (which contains amendments designed to facilitate, or otherwise desirable in connection with, the consolidations of the law relating to value added tax, the law relating to car tax and the law relating to capital transfer tax) shall have effect.

Short title, interpretation, construction and repeals.

48.—(1) This Act may be cited as the Finance Act 1983.

(2) In this Act " the Taxes Act " means the Income and Corporation Taxes Act 1970. 1970 c. 10.

(3) Part II of this Act, so far as it relates to income tax, shall be construed as one with the Income Tax Acts, so far as it relates to corporation tax, shall be construed as one with the Corporation Tax Acts and, so far as it relates to capital gains tax, shall be construed as one with the Capital Gains Tax Act 1979. 1979 c. 14.

(4) Part III of this Act shall be construed as one with Part I of the Oil Taxation Act 1975 and references in Part III to the principal Act are references to that Act. 1975 c. 22.

(5) The enactments specified in Schedule 10 to this Act are hereby repealed to the extent specified in the third column of that Schedule, but subject to any provision at the end of any Part of that Schedule.

SCHEDULES

Section 1(3).

SCHEDULE 1

WINE: RATES OF DUTY

Description of wine	Rates of duty per hectolitre
	£
Wine of a strength—	
not exceeding 15 per cent. ...	113·00
exceeding 15 but not exceeding 18 per cent.	145·90
exceeding 18 but not exceeding 22 per cent.	171·70
exceeding 22 per cent. ...	171·70 plus £15·19 for every 1 per cent. or part of 1 per cent. in excess of 22 per cent.; each of the above rates of duty being, in the case of sparkling wine, increased by £24·80 per hectolitre.

Section 1(4).

SCHEDULE 2

MADE-WINE: RATES OF DUTY

Description of made-wine	Rates of duty per hectolitre
	£
Made-wine of a strength—	
not exceeding 10 per cent. ...	79·30
exceeding 10 but not exceeding 15 per cent.	109·80
exceeding 15 but not exceeding 18 per cent.	135·20
exceeding 18 per cent. ...	135·20 plus £15·19 for every 1 per cent. or part of 1 per cent. in excess of 18 per cent.; each of the above rates of duty being, in the case of sparkling made-wine, increased by £11·35 per hectolitre.

SCHEDULE 3

Section 4.

Vehicles Excise Duty

Part I

Provisions Substituted in Part II of Schedules 1 to 5 to the Vehicles (Excise) Act 1971 and the Vehicles (Excise) Act (Northern Ireland) 1972

1971 c. 10.
1972 c. 10 (N.I.).

1. The following are the provisions substituted in the Act of 1971 and the Act of 1972 for Part II of Schedule 1—

Description of vehicle	Rate of duty
	£
1. Bicycles and tricycles of which the cylinder capacity of the engine does not exceed 150 cubic centimetres	8·50
2. Bicycles of which the cylinder capacity of the engine exceeds 150 cubic centimetres but does not exceed 250 cubic centimetres; tricycles (other than those in the foregoing paragraph) and vehicles (other than mowing machines) with more than three wheels, being tricycles and vehicles neither constructed nor adapted for use nor used for the carriage of a driver or passenger	17·00
3. Bicycles and tricycles not in the foregoing paragraphs ...	34·00

2. The following are the provisions substituted in the Act of 1971 and the Act of 1972 for Part II of Schedule 2—

Description of vehicle	Rate of duty
	£
Hackney carriages	42·00 with an additional 85p for each person above 20 (excluding the driver) for which the vehicle has seating capacity.

SCH. 3

3. The following are the provisions substituted in the Act of 1971 for Part II of Schedule 3—

1.	Weight unladen of vehicle		Rate of duty	
	2.	3.	4.	5.
Description of vehicle	Exceeding	Not exceeding	Initial	Additional for each ton or part of a ton in excess of the weight in column 2
			£	£
1. Agricultural machines; digging machines; mobile cranes; works trucks; mowing machines; fishermen's tractors.	—	—	14·00	—
2. Haulage vehicles, being showmen's vehicles.	—	7¼ tons	137·00	—
	7¼ tons	8 tons	164·00	—
	8 tons	10 tons	193·00	—
	10 tons	—	193·00	30·00
3. Haulage vehicles, not being showmen's vehicles.	—	2 tons	163·00	—
	2 tons	4 tons	293·00	—
	4 tons	6 tons	424·00	—
	6 tons	7¼ tons	553·00	—
	7¼ tons	8 tons	676·00	—
	8 tons	10 tons	676·00	115·00
	10 tons	—	906·00	130·00

4. The following are the provisions substituted in the Act of 1972 for Part II of Schedule 3— SCH. 3

1. Description of vehicle	Weight unladen of vehicle 2. Exceeding	3. Not exceeding	Rate of duty 4. Initial	5. Additional for each ton or part of a ton in excess of the weight in column 2
			£	£
1. Agricultural machines; digging machines; mobile cranes; works trucks; mowing machines; fishermen's tractors.	—	—	14·00	—
2. Haulage vehicles, being showmen's vehicles.	—	7¼ tons	137·00	—
	7¼ tons	8 tons	164·00	—
	8 tons	10 tons	193·00	—
	10 tons	—	193·00	30·00
3. Haulage vehicles, not being showmen's vehicles.	—	2 tons	147·00	—
	2 tons	4 tons	262·00	—
	4 tons	6 tons	374·00	—
	6 tons	7¼ tons	489·00	—
	7¼ tons	8 tons	603·00	—
	8 tons	—	603·00	130·00

SCH. 3

5. The following are the provisions substituted in the Act of 1971 and the Act of 1972 for Part II of Schedule 4—

TABLE A

RATES OF DUTY ON RIGID GOODS VEHICLES EXCEEDING 12 TONNES PLATED GROSS WEIGHT

GENERAL RATES

Plated gross weight of vehicle		Rate of duty		
1 Exceeding	2 Not exceeding	3 Two axle vehicle	4 Three axle vehicle	5 Four or more axle vehicle
tonnes	tonnes	£	£	£
12	13	410	320	320
13	14	500	320	320
14	15	610	320	320
15	16	670	320	320
16	17	780	320	320
17	18	—	380	320
18	19	—	440	320
19	20	—	500	320
20	21	—	580	320
21	22	—	660	390
22	23	—	740	470
23	24	—	920	560
24	25	—	1,150	660
25	26	—	—	770
26	27	—	—	880
27	28	—	—	1,010
28	29	—	—	1,140
29	30	—	—	1,500
30	30·49	—	—	1,990

Table A(1)

Rates of Duty on Rigid Goods Vehicles Exceeding 12 Tonnes Plated Gross Weight

Rates for Farmers' Goods Vehicles

Plated gross weight of vehicle		Rate of duty		
1 Exceeding	2 Not exceeding	3 Two axle vehicle	4 Three axle vehicle	5 Four or more axle vehicle
tonnes	tonnes	£	£	£
12	13	135	120	120
13	14	140	120	120
14	15	145	120	120
15	16	165	125	120
16	17	180	130	120
17	18	—	135	120
18	19	—	140	120
19	20	—	145	125
20	21	—	150	130
21	22	—	155	135
22	23	—	160	140
23	24	—	180	145
24	25	—	210	150
25	26	—	—	160
26	27	—	—	180
27	28	—	—	200
28	29	—	—	215
29	30	—	—	275
30	30·49	—	—	340

SCH. 3

TABLE A(2)

RATES OF DUTY ON RIGID GOODS VEHICLES EXCEEDING 12 TONNES PLATED GROSS WEIGHT

RATES FOR SHOWMEN'S GOODS VEHICLES

Plated gross weight of vehicle		Rate of duty		
1 Exceeding	2 Not exceeding	3 Two axle vehicle	4 Three axle vehicle	5 Four or more axle vehicle
tonnes	tonnes	£	£	£
12	13	135	120	120
13	14	140	120	120
14	15	145	120	120
15	16	165	125	120
16	17	180	130	120
17	18	—	135	120
18	19	—	140	125
19	20	—	150	130
20	21	—	160	140
21	22	—	165	150
22	23	—	175	160
23	24	—	210	165
24	25	—	250	180
25	26	—	—	200
26	27	—	—	220
27	28	—	—	245
28	29	—	—	265
29	30	—	—	340
30	30·49	—	—	430

TABLE B

SUPPLEMENTARY RATES OF DUTY ON RIGID GOODS VEHICLES OVER 12 TONNES USED FOR DRAWING TRAILERS EXCEEDING 4 TONNES PLATED GROSS WEIGHT

GENERAL RATES

Gross weight of trailer		Duty supplement
Exceeding	Not exceeding	
tonnes	tonnes	£
4	8	70
8	10	90
10	12	115
12	14	160
14	—	300

TABLE B(1)

SUPPLEMENTARY RATES OF DUTY ON RIGID GOODS VEHICLES OVER 12 TONNES USED FOR DRAWING TRAILERS EXCEEDING 4 TONNES PLATED GROSS WEIGHT

RATES FOR FARMERS' GOODS VEHICLES

Gross weight of trailer		Duty supplement
Exceeding	Not exceeding	
tonnes	tonnes	£
4	8	70
8	10	90
10	12	115
12	14	160
14	—	300

TABLE B(2)

SUPPLEMENTARY RATES OF DUTY ON RIGID GOODS VEHICLES OVER 12 TONNES USED FOR DRAWING TRAILERS EXCEEDING 4 TONNES PLATED GROSS WEIGHT

RATES FOR SHOWMEN'S GOODS VEHICLES

Gross weight of trailer		Duty supplement
Exceeding	Not exceeding	
		£
—	—	70

SCH. 3

TABLE C

RATES OF DUTY ON TRACTOR UNITS EXCEEDING 12 TONNES PLATED TRAIN WEIGHT AND HAVING ONLY 2 AXLES

GENERAL RATES

Plated train weight of tractor unit		Rate of duty		
1. Exceeding	2. Not exceeding	3. For a tractor unit to be used with semi-trailers with any number of axles	4. For a tractor unit to be used only with semi-trailers with not less than two axles	5. For a tractor unit to be used only with semi-trailers with not less than three axles
tonnes	tonnes	£	£	£
12	13	420	420	420
13	14	470	420	420
14	15	510	420	420
15	16	560	420	420
16	17	610	420	420
17	18	660	420	420
18	19	710	420	420
19	20	770	420	420
20	21	830	470	420
21	22	890	520	420
22	23	950	590	420
23	24	1,020	660	420
24	25	1,090	740	420
25	26	1,090	830	500
26	27	1,090	940	590
27	28	1,090	1,040	680
28	29	1,150	1,150	780
29	30	1,390	1,390	890
30	31	1,600	1,600	1,000
31	32	1,820	1,820	1,110
32	32·52	2,290	2,290	1,600
32·52	33	2,290	2,290	1,840
33	34	2,290	2,290	2,140
34	35	2,450	2,450	2,450
35	36	2,610	2,610	2,610
36	37	2,730	2,730	2,730
37	38	2,940	2,940	2,940

SCH. 3

TABLE C(1)

RATES OF DUTY ON TRACTOR UNITS EXCEEDING 12 TONNES PLATED TRAIN WEIGHT AND HAVING ONLY 2 AXLES

RATES FOR FARMERS' GOODS VEHICLES

Plated train weight of tractor unit		Rate of duty		
1. Exceeding	2. Not exceeding	3. For a tractor unit to be used with semi-trailers with any number of axles	4. For a tractor unit to be used only with semi-trailers with not less than two axles	5. For a tractor unit to be used only with semi-trailers with not less than three axles
tonnes	tonnes	£	£	£
12	13	135	135	135
13	14	140	135	135
14	15	145	135	135
15	16	150	135	135
16	17	155	135	135
17	18	160	135	135
18	19	160	135	135
19	20	165	135	135
20	21	170	135	135
21	22	175	140	135
22	23	180	145	135
23	24	190	150	135
24	25	200	155	140
25	26	200	160	145
26	27	200	170	150
27	28	200	180	165
28	29	200	195	175
29	30	235	235	195
30	31	265	265	210
31	32	300	300	230
32	32·52	370	370	305
32·52	33	610	610	610
33	34	710	710	710
34	35	810	810	810
35	36	860	860	860
36	37	900	900	900
37	38	970	970	970

SCH. 3

TABLE C(2)

RATES OF DUTY ON TRACTOR UNITS EXCEEDING 12 TONNES PLATED TRAIN WEIGHT AND HAVING ONLY 2 AXLES

RATES FOR SHOWMEN'S GOODS VEHICLES

Plated train weight of tractor unit		Rate of duty		
1. Exceeding	2. Not exceeding	3. For a tractor unit to be used with semi-trailers with any number of axles	4. For a tractor unit to be used only with semi-trailers with not less than two axles	5. For a tractor unit to be used only with semi-trailers with not less than three axles
tonnes	tonnes	£	£	£
12	13	135	135	135
13	14	140	135	135
14	15	145	135	135
15	16	150	135	135
16	17	155	135	135
17	18	160	135	135
18	19	160	135	135
19	20	170	145	145
20	21	180	150	150
21	22	195	155	155
22	23	210	160	160
23	24	220	170	165
24	25	235	180	165
25	26	235	195	175
26	27	235	215	185
27	28	235	230	205
28	29	245	245	220
29	30	295	295	240
30	31	335	335	260
31	32	375	375	285
32	32·52	465	465	385
32·52	33	750	750	750
33	34	880	880	880
34	35	1,000	1,000	1,000
35	36	1,070	1,070	1,070
36	37	1,120	1,120	1,120
37	38	1,200	1,200	1,200

TABLE D

Sch. 3

Rates of Duty on Tractor Units Exceeding 12 Tonnes Plated Train Weight and Having 3 or More Axles

General Rates

Plated train weight of tractor unit		Rate of duty		
1. Exceeding	2. Not exceeding	3. For a tractor unit to be used with semi-trailers with any number of axles	4. For a tractor unit to be used only with semi-trailers with not less than two axles	5. For a tractor unit to be used only with semi-trailers with not less than three axles
tonnes	tonnes	£	£	£
12	20	420	420	420
20	21	470	420	420
21	22	520	420	420
22	23	590	420	420
23	24	660	420	420
24	25	740	420	420
25	26	830	420	420
26	27	940	420	420
27	28	1,040	420	420
28	29	1,150	490	420
29	30	1,390	550	420
30	31	1,600	610	420
31	32	1,820	680	420
32	32·52	2,290	920	420
32·52	33	2,290	1,080	420
33	34	2,290	1,350	520
34	35	2,290	1,630	670
35	36	2,290	1,930	790
36	37	2,290	2,240	980
37	38	2,590	2,590	1,180

SCH. 3

TABLE D(1)

RATES OF DUTY ON TRACTOR UNITS EXCEEDING 12 TONNES PLATED TRAIN WEIGHT AND HAVING 3 OR MORE AXLES

RATES FOR FARMERS' GOODS VEHICLES

Plated train weight of tractor unit		Rate of duty		
1. Exceeding	2. Not exceeding	3. For a tractor unit to be used with semi-trailers with any number of axles	4. For a tractor unit to be used only with semi-trailers with not less than two axles	5. For a tractor unit to be used only with semi-trailers with not less than three axles
tonnes	tonnes	£	£	£
12	20	135	135	135
20	21	135	135	135
21	22	140	135	135
22	23	145	135	135
23	24	150	135	135
24	25	155	135	135
25	26	160	140	135
26	27	170	150	135
27	28	180	160	145
28	29	195	170	155
29	30	235	190	165
30	31	265	205	185
31	32	300	225	205
32	32·52	370	300	220
32·52	33	370	355	220
33	34	445	445	270
34	35	535	535	350
35	36	635	635	410
36	37	740	740	510
37	38	855	855	615

TABLE D(2)

RATES OF DUTY ON TRACTOR UNITS EXCEEDING 12 TONNES PLATED TRAIN WEIGHT AND HAVING 3 OR MORE AXLES

RATES FOR SHOWMEN'S GOODS VEHICLES

Plated train weight of tractor unit		Rate of duty		
1. Exceeding	2. Not exceeding	3. For a tractor unit to be used with semi-trailers with any number of axles	4. For a tractor unit to be used only with semi-trailers with not less than two axles	5. For a tractor unit to be used only with semi-trailers with not less than three axles
tonnes	tonnes	£	£	£
12	18	135	135	135
18	19	135	135	135
19	20	140	140	135
20	21	145	145	135
21	22	155	150	135
22	23	160	155	135
23	24	170	160	135
24	25	180	160	145
25	26	195	170	155
26	27	210	180	160
27	28	230	200	170
28	29	245	215	190
29	30	295	235	205
30	31	335	255	230
31	32	375	280	250
32	32·52	465	375	275
32·52	33	465	440	275
33	34	550	550	335
34	35	665	665	435
35	36	790	790	515
36	37	915	915	635
37	38	1,060	1,060	765

SCH. 3

6. The following are the provisions substituted in the Act of 1971 for Part II of Schedule 5—

Description of vehicle	Rate of duty
	£
1. Vehicles not exceeding seven horse-power, if registered under the Roads Act 1920 for the first time before 1st January 1947	60·00
2. Vehicles not included above	85·00

7. The following are the provisions substituted in the Act of 1972 for Part II of Schedule 5—

Description of vehicle	Rate of duty
	£
1. Vehicles first registered under the Roads Act 1920 before 1st January 1947, or which, if its first registration for taxation purposes had been effected in Northern Ireland would have been so first registered as aforesaid under the Act as in force in Northern Ireland:	
(i) not exceeding 6 horse-power	51·00
(ii) exceeding 6 horse-power but not exceeding 9 horse-power—for each unit or part of a unit of horse-power	8·50
2. Other vehicles	85·00

PART II

1971 c. 10.
1972 c. 10 (N.I.).

AMENDMENT OF PART I OF SCHEDULE 4 TO THE VEHICLES (EXCISE) ACT 1971 AND THE VEHICLES (EXCISE) ACT (NORTHERN IRELAND) 1972

Amendments made in both Acts

8.—(1) Part I of Schedule 4 to the Act of 1971 and the Act of 1972 (annual rates of duty on goods vehicles) shall be amended as follows.

(2) In paragraph 1(1), for "£170" there shall be substituted "£150".

(3) In paragraph 2, for "£360" there shall be substituted "£320".

(4) In paragraph 5(3)(*b*), for "32 tonnes" and "32.52 tonnes" there shall be substituted, respectively, "37 tonnes" and "38 tonnes".

(5) In paragraph 6— Sch. 3

(a) in sub-paragraph (1), for " £60 " there shall be substituted " £63 ";

(b) in sub-paragraphs (2)(a) and (4), for " £100 " there shall, in each case, be substituted " £90 "; and

(c) in sub-paragraph (2)(b), for " £130 " there shall be substituted " £115 ".

(6) In paragraph 7, for " £80 " there shall be substituted " £85 ".

(7) After paragraph 14 there shall be inserted the following paragraphs—

" *Tractor units having two axles used with semi-trailers having two axles when duty paid by reference to use with semi-trailers having not less than three axles*

14A.—(1) This paragraph applies in any case where—

(a) a vehicle licence has been taken out for a tractor unit having two axles which is to be used only with semi-trailers with not less than three axles; and

(b) the rate of duty paid on taking out the licence is equal to or exceeds the rate of duty applicable to a tractor unit having two axles—

(i) which has a plated train weight equal to the maximum laden weight at which a tractor unit having two axles may lawfully be used in Great Britain with a semi-trailer with two axles; and

(ii) which is to be used with semi-trailers with not less than two axles.

(2) If, in a case to which this paragraph applies, the tractor unit is used with a semi-trailer with two axles and, when so used, the laden weight of the tractor unit and semi-trailer taken together does not exceed the maximum laden weight mentioned in sub-paragraph (1)(b)(i) above, the tractor unit shall, when so used, be taken to be licensed in accordance with the requirements of this Act.

Tractor units having three or more axles used with semi-trailers having only one axle when duty paid by reference to use with semi-trailers having more than one axle

14B.—(1) This paragraph applies in any case where—

(a) a vehicle licence has been taken out for a tractor unit having three or more axles which is to be used only with semi-trailers with not less than two axles; and

(b) the rate of duty paid on taking out the licence is equal to or exceeds the rate of duty applicable to a tractor unit having three or more axles—

(i) which has a plated train weight equal to the maximum laden weight at which a tractor unit having three or more axles may lawfully be used in Great Britain with a semi-trailer with a single axle; and

Sch. 3

(ii) which is to be used with semi-trailers with any number of axles.

(2) If, in a case to which this paragraph applies, the tractor unit is used with a semi-trailer with a single axle and, when so used, the laden weight of the tractor unit and semi-trailer taken together does not exceed the maximum laden weight mentioned in sub-paragraph (1)(*b*)(i) above, the tractor unit shall, when so used, be taken to be licensed in accordance with the requirements of this Act."

Amendments made only in the Act of 1971

9. In paragraph 5(1) of Part I of Schedule 4 to the Act of 1971 (special types of vehicles) for the words from " vehicle — " to " (*c*) " there shall be substituted " vehicle (other than, in the case of a vehicle falling within paragraph (*a*) below, one of a prescribed class) which has an unladen weight exceeding 1,525 kilograms ; and

(*a*) which has, for the purpose of this Schedule a plated gross weight or plated train weight by virtue only of paragraph 9(2A)(*c*) below ; or

(*b*) ".

10. In paragraph 9 of Part I of Schedule 4 to the Act of 1971 (plated and unladen weights)—

(*a*) in sub-paragraph (1)(*a*), for the words from " plated weight " to " Act 1972 " there shall be substituted the word " weight " and at the end there shall be inserted the words " as indicated on the appropriate plate " ;

(*b*) in sub-paragraph (1)(*b*) for the words " a plated gross weight " there shall be substituted the words " such a plate " ; and

(*c*) in sub-paragraph (2), for the words from " plated weight " to " Part II " there shall be substituted the word " weight " and at the end there shall be inserted the words " as indicated on the appropriate plate ".

11. In the said paragraph 9 there shall be inserted, after sub-paragraph (2), the following sub-paragraph—

" (2A) In this paragraph " appropriate plate ", in relation to a vehicle or trailer, means—

(*a*) where a Ministry plate (within the meaning of regulations made under section 40 or 45 of the Road Traffic Act 1972) has been issued, or has effect as if issued, for the vehicle or trailer following the issue or amendment of a plating certificate (within the meaning of Part II of that Act), that plate ;

1972 c. 10.

(*b*) where paragraph (*a*) does not apply, but such a certificate is in force for the vehicle or trailer, that certificate ; and (*c*) where neither paragraph (*a*) nor paragraph (*b*) above applies but the vehicle or trailer has been equipped with a plate in accordance with regulations made under section 40 of the Act of 1972, that plate."

Amendments made only in the Act of 1972

12. For paragraph 5(1) of Part I of Schedule 4 to the Act of 1972 (special types of vehicles) there shall be substituted the following paragraph—

"(1) This paragraph applies to a goods vehicle—

(*a*) which has an unladen weight exceeding 1,525 kilograms; and

(*b*) which is for the time being authorised for use on roads by virtue of an order under Article 29(3) of the Road Traffic (Northern Ireland) Order 1981 (authorisation of special vehicles)."

SCHEDULE 4

Section 18.

EVENTS RESTORING THE INCOME TAX CHARGE IN CONNECTION WITH ASSIGNED LIFE POLICIES AND ANNUITY CONTRACTS

1.—(1) In this Schedule " assigned policy " means a policy of life assurance—

(*a*) which was issued in respect of an insurance made before 26th June 1982; and

(*b*) the rights conferred by which have been assigned for money or money's worth before that date; and

(*c*) in relation to which an event occurring on or after that date would not, apart from the provisions of this Schedule, be a chargeable event.

(2) In this Schedule " assigned contract " means a contract for a life annuity—

(*a*) which was made before 26th June 1982; and

(*b*) the rights conferred by which have been assigned for money or money's worth before that date; and

(*c*) in relation to which an event occurring on or after that date would not, apart from the provisions of this Schedule, be a chargeable event.

2.—(1) The relevant provision shall cease to apply to an assigned policy or assigned contract if, after 23rd August 1982,—

(*a*) the rights conferred by the policy or contract are again assigned for money or money's worth; or

(*b*) a payment is made by way of premium or as lump sum consideration under the policy or contract; or

(*c*) subject to paragraph 3 below, a sum is lent by or by arrangement with the body issuing the policy or, as the case may be, the body with which the contract was made.

SCH. 4

(2) No account shall be taken for the purposes of sub-paragraph (1)(*a*) above of any assignment effected by way of security for a debt, or on the discharge of a debt secured by the rights concerned, or of an assignment between spouses living together.

3.—(1) Paragraph 2(1)(*c*) above does not apply unless—

(*a*) the policy was issued in respect of an insurance made after 26th March 1974 or, as the case may be, the contract was made after that date ; and

(*b*) the sum concerned is lent to or at the direction of the individual who, in accordance with sub-paragraph (2) below, is at the time of the loan the chargeable individual.

(2) The individual who is at any time the chargeable individual for the purposes of sub-paragraph (1)(*b*) above shall be determined as follows,—

(*a*) if at the time the rights conferred by the policy or contract are vested in an individual as beneficial owner or are held on trusts created by an individual (including such trusts as are referred to in section 399(1)(*a*) of the Taxes Act), that individual is the chargeable individual ; and

(*b*) if at the time those rights are held as security for a debt owed by an individual, that individual is the chargeable individual.

(3) Paragraph 2(1)(*c*) above does not apply in relation to a policy if—

(*a*) it is a qualifying policy within the meaning of Schedule 1 to the Taxes Act ; and

(*b*) either interest at a commercial rate is payable on the sum lent or the sum is lent to a full-time employee of the body issuing the policy for the purpose of assisting him in the purchase or improvement of a dwelling-house to be used as his only or main residence.

4. Where the relevant provision ceases to apply to an assigned policy or assigned contract by virtue of paragraph 2(1)(*c*) above, the lending of the sum concerned shall be regarded for the purposes of the Income Tax Acts (other than that paragraph) as taking place immediately after the time at which the relevant provision ceases so to apply.

Section 26.

SCHEDULE 5

RELIEF FOR INVESTMENT IN CORPORATE TRADES

PART I

INVESTMENT AFTER 5th APRIL 1983 IN UNQUOTED TRADING COMPANIES

1981 c. 35.

1.—(1) In this Part of this Schedule " Chapter II " means Chapter II of Part IV of the Finance Act 1981 (relief for investment in new corporate trades).

(2) Any provision of this Part which applies provisions of Chapter II shall be construed as applying those provisions for the purposes of this Part as they apply for the purposes of Chapter II; and references in any provision so applied to any other provision of Chapter II shall, except where this Part otherwise requires, be construed as references to that other provision as so applied.

The relief

2.—(1) This Part of this Schedule has effect for affording relief from income tax where—

(*a*) an individual who qualifies for the relief subscribes for eligible shares in a qualifying company; and

(*b*) those shares are issued to him for the purpose of raising money for a qualifying trade which is being carried on by the company or which it intends to carry on.

(2) In this Part "eligible shares" means new ordinary shares which, throughout the period of five years beginning with the date on which they are issued, carry no present or future preferential right to dividends or to a company's assets on its winding up and no present or future preferential right to be redeemed.

(3) The relief in respect of the amount subscribed by an individual for any eligible shares shall be given as a deduction of that amount from his total income for the year of assessment in which the shares are issued, and references in this Part to the amount of the relief are references to the amount of that deduction.

(4) The relief shall be given on a claim and shall not be allowed—

(*a*) unless and until the company has carried on the trade for four months; and

(*b*) if the company is not carrying on that trade at the time when the shares are issued, unless the company begins to carry it on within two years after that time.

(5) A claim for the relief may be allowed at any time after the trade has been carried on by the company for four months if the conditions for the relief are then satisfied; but no claim shall be allowed before 1st January 1984.

(6) In the case of a claim allowed before the end of the relevant period, the relief shall be withdrawn if by reason of any subsequent event it appears that the claimant was not entitled to the relief allowed.

(7) In this Part, "the relevant period", in relation to relief in respect of any eligible shares issued by a company, means—

(*a*) as respects paragraphs 4, 7, 8, 9 and 10 below, the period beginning with the incorporation of the company (or, if the company was incorporated more than two years before the date on which the shares were issued, beginning two years before that date) and ending five years after the issue of the shares; and

SCH. 5

(b) as respects paragraphs 5, 6 and 17 below, the period beginning with the date on which the shares were issued and ending either three years after that date or, where the company was not at that date carrying on a qualifying trade, three years after the date on which it subsequently began to carry on such a trade.

(8) Where by reason of its being wound up, or dissolved without winding up, the company carries on the qualifying trade for a period shorter than four months, sub-paragraph (4)(a) above shall have effect as if it referred to that shorter period but only if it is shown that the winding up or dissolution was for bona fide commercial reasons and not as part of a scheme or arrangement the main purpose or one of the main purposes of which was the avoidance of tax.

(9) Section 52(7) to (8A) of Chapter II shall apply, but in the case of subsection (7) with the deletion of the reference to section 204(3) of the Taxes Act (pay as you earn) and, in the case of subsection (8), with the substitution for the reference to subsection (3)(a) of section 52 of a reference to sub-paragraph (4)(a) above.

Limits on relief

3.—(1) Subject to paragraph 19 below, the relief shall not be given in respect of any amount subscribed by an individual for eligible shares issued to him by any company in any year of assessment unless the amount or total amount subscribed by him for the eligible shares issued to him by the company in that year is £500 or more.

(2) The relief shall not be given to the extent to which the amount or total amount subscribed by an individual for eligible shares issued to him in any year of assessment (whether or not by the same company) exceeds £40,000.

Individuals qualifying for relief

4.—(1) An individual qualifies for the relief if he subscribes for the eligible shares on his own behalf, is resident and ordinarily resident in the United Kingdom throughout the year of assessment in which they are issued and is not at any time in the relevant period connected with the company.

(2) Section 54(2) to (8) of Chapter II shall apply.

(3) In determining, for the purposes of this paragraph, whether an individual is connected with a company, no debt incurred by the company by overdrawing an account with a person carrying on a business of banking shall be treated as loan capital of the company if the debt arose in the ordinary course of that business.

(4) Where an individual subscribes for shares in a company with which he is not connected (either within the meaning of this paragraph or by virtue of paragraph 2(1B)(b) of Schedule 12, as applied by paragraph 18(5) below) he shall nevertheless be treated as connected with it if he subscribes for the shares as part of any arrangement which provides for another person to subscribe for shares in

another company with which that or any other individual who is a party to the arrangement is connected (within the meaning of this paragraph or by virtue of that paragraph). SCH. 5

Qualifying companies

5.—(1) A company is a qualifying company if it is incorporated in the United Kingdom and complies with the requirements of this paragraph.

(2) The company must, throughout the relevant period, be an unquoted company which is resident in the United Kingdom and not resident elsewhere, and be—

(*a*) a company which exists wholly, or substantially wholly, for the purpose of carrying on wholly or mainly in the United Kingdom one or more qualifying trades ; or

(*b*) a company whose business consists wholly of—

(i) the holding of shares or securities of, or the making of loans to, one or more qualifying subsidiaries of the company ; or

(ii) both the holding of such shares or securities, or the making of such loans and the carrying on of one or more qualifying trades.

(3) In this paragraph " qualifying subsidiary ", in relation to a company, means a subsidiary of that company of a kind which may be held by virtue of paragraph 17 below.

(4) Without prejudice to the generality of sub-paragraph (2) above, but subject to sub-paragraph (5) below, a company ceases to comply with that sub-paragraph if before the end of the relevant period a resolution is passed, or an order is made, for the winding up of the company (or, in the case of a winding up otherwise than under the Companies Act 1948 or the Companies Act (Northern Ireland) 1960, any other act is done for the like purpose) or the company is dissolved without winding up. 1948 c. 38. 1960 c. 22 (N.I.).

(5) A company shall not be regarded as ceasing to comply with sub-paragraph (2) above if it does so by reason of being wound up or dissolved without winding up and—

(*a*) it is shown that the winding up or dissolution is for bona fide commercial reasons and not part of a scheme or arrangement the main purpose or one of the main purposes of which is the avoidance of tax ; and

(*b*) the company's net assets, if any, are distributed to its members or dealt with as bona vacantia before the end of the relevant period or, in the case of a winding up, the end (if later) of three years from the commencement of the winding up.

(6) The company's share capital must not, at any time in the relevant period, include any issued shares that are not fully paid up.

SCH. 5

(7) Subject to paragraph 17 below, the company must not at any time in the relevant period—

(*a*) control (or together with any person connected with it control) another company or be under the control of another company (or of another company and any person connected with that other company) ; or

(*b*) be a 51 per cent. subsidiary of another company or itself have a 51 per cent. subsidiary ;

and no arrangements must be in existence at any time in that period by virtue of which the company could fall within paragraph (*a*) or (*b*) above.

(8) A company is not a qualifying company if—

(*a*) an individual has acquired a controlling interest in the company's trade after 5th April 1983 ; and

(*b*) at any time in the period mentioned in sub-paragraph (10) below he has, or has had, a controlling interest in another trade ; and

(*c*) the trade carried on by the company, or a substantial part of it—

(i) is concerned with the same or similar types of property or parts thereof or provides the same or similar services or facilities as the other trade ; or

(ii) serves substantially the same or similar outlets or markets as the other trade.

(9) Section 56(8) and (9) of Chapter II shall apply for the purposes of sub-paragraph (8) above.

(10) The period referred to in sub-paragraph (8) above is the period beginning two years before and ending three years after—

(*a*) the date on which the shares were issued ; or

(*b*) if later, the date on which the company began to carry on the trade.

Qualifying trades

6.—(1) A trade is a qualifying trade if it complies with the requirements of this paragraph.

(2) The trade must not at any time in the relevant period consist to any substantial extent of any of the activities mentioned in section 56(2) of Chapter II (as read with section 56(3) and Schedule 11).

(3) The trade must, during the relevant period, be conducted on a commercial basis and with a view to the realisation of profits.

(4) Section 56(10) of Chapter II shall apply.

Disposal of shares

7.—(1) Where an individual disposes of any eligible shares before the end of the relevant period, then—

(*a*) if the disposal is otherwise than by way of a bargain made at arm's length, he shall not be entitled to any relief in respect of those shares ; and (*b*) in any other case, the amount of relief to which he is entitled in respect of those shares shall be reduced by the amount or value of the consideration which he receives for them.

(2) Where an individual holds ordinary shares in a company and the relief has been given in respect of some but not others, any dispostal by him of ordinary shares in the company shall be treated for the purposes of this paragraph as relating—

(*a*) first, to those (if any) in respect of which relief has been given under Chapter II rather than to others; and

(*b*) then, to those in respect of which relief has been given under this Part rather than to others.

(3) Section 57(3) and (4) of Chapter II shall apply but, in the case of subsection (4), with the substitution for the reference to subsection (2) of a reference to sub-paragraph (2) above.

Value received from company

8.—(1) Where an individual who subscribes for eligible shares in a company—

(*a*) has, before the issue of the shares but within the relevant period, received any value from the company; or

(*b*) after their issue but before the end of the relevant period, receives any such value;

the amount of the relief to which he is entitled in respect of the shares shall be reduced by the value received; but the value received shall be disregarded to the extent to which relief under Chapter II has, by virtue of section 58(1) of that Chapter, been reduced on its account.

(2) Subject to sub-paragraph (3) below, section 58(2) to (9) of Chapter II shall apply but, in the case of subsection (3), with the substitution for the reference to section 55(5) of a reference to paragraph 5(5) above.

(3) For the purposes of this paragraph an individual also receives value from the company if any person connected with the company (within the meaning of section 54 of Chapter II)—

(*a*) purchases any of its share capital or securities which belong to the individual; or

(*b*) makes any payment to him for giving up any right in relation to any of the company's share capital or securities,

and the value received by the individual is the amount receivable by the individual or, if greater, the market value of the shares or securities in question.

Replacement capital

9.—(1) An individual is not entitled to relief in respect of any shares in a company where—

(*a*) at any time in the relevant period, the company or any of its subsidiaries—

(i) begins to carry on a trade which was previously carried on at any time in that period by a person other than the company or any of its subsidiaries; or

SCH. 5

(ii) acquires the whole, or greater part, of the assets used for the purposes of a trade previously so carried on ; and

(*b*) sub-paragraph (2) below applies in relation to that individual.

(2) This sub-paragraph applies in relation to an individual where—

(*a*) the person or persons to whom an interest amounting in the aggregate to more than a half share in the trade (as previously carried on) belonged, at any time in the relevant period, is or are the person or persons to whom such an interest in the trade (as transferred) belongs or has, at any such time, belonged ; or

(*b*) the person or persons who control or, at any such time, have controlled the company are the person or persons who, at any such time, controlled another company which previously carried on the trade ;

and the individual is that person or one of those persons.

(3) An individual is not entitled to relief in respect of any shares in a company where—

(*a*) the company comes to acquire all of the issued share capital of another company, at any time in the relevant period ; and

(*b*) the person or persons who control or have, at any such time, controlled the company are the person or persons who, at any such time, controlled that other company ;

and the individual is that person, or one of those persons.

(4) For the purposes of sub-paragraph (2) above—

(*a*) the persons to whom a trade belongs and, where a trade belongs to two or more persons, their respective shares in that trade shall be determined in accordance with subsections (1)(*a*) and (*b*), (2) and (3) of section 253 of the Taxes Act ; and

(*b*) any interest, rights or powers of a person who is an associate (as defined by section 67(1) of Chapter II) of another person shall be treated as those of that other person.

(5) In this paragraph—

" subsidiary " means a subsidiary of a kind which a qualifying company may have by virtue of paragraph 17 below ; and

" trade " includes any business, profession or vocation and any part of a trade.

Value received by persons other than claimants

10.—(1) The relief to which an individual is entitled in respect of any shares in a company shall be reduced in accordance with section 59(3) of Chapter II, as applied by sub-paragraph (2) below, if at any time in the relevant period the company repays, redeems or repurchases any of its share capital which belongs to any member other than—

(*a*) that individual ; or

(*b*) another individual whose relief is thereby reduced by virtue of section 58(2)(*a*) of Chapter II as applied by paragraph 8 above, Sch. 5

or makes any payment to any such member for giving up his right to any of the company's share capital on its cancellation or extinguishment.

(2) Section 59(3) to (8) of Chapter II shall apply, but with the deletion, in subsection (4), of the reference to section 53(3) and (7) and, in subsection (6), of paragraphs (*a*) and (*b*).

(3) Sub-paragraph (1) above does not apply in relation to the redemption of any share capital for which the redemption date was fixed before 15th March 1983.

(4) Where—

(*a*) after 5th April 1983 a company issues share capital (" the original shares ") of nominal value equal to the authorised minimum (within the meaning of the Companies Act 1980) 1980 c. 22. for the purposes of complying with the requirements of section 4 of that Act (public company not to do business unless requirements as to share capital complied with) ; and

(*b*) after the registrar of companies has issued the company with a certificate under section 4 it issues eligible shares,

sub-paragraph (1) above shall not apply in relation to any redemption of any of the original shares within 12 months of the date on which those shares were issued.

(5) Where—

(*a*) a company has issued shares in respect of which one or more individuals are entitled to relief under this Part and has also issued shares in respect of which one or more individuals are entitled to relief under Chapter II ; and

(*b*) sub-paragraph (1) above applies ;

then, for the purposes of section 59(3) of Chapter II (as it applies both to this Part and to Chapter II), the relief given under Chapter II shall be treated as if it were relief given under this Part.

Prevention of misuse

11. An individual is not entitled to relief in respect of any shares unless the shares are subscribed for and issued for bona fide commercial purposes and not as part of a scheme or arrangement the main purpose or one of the main purposes of which is the avoidance of tax.

Husband and wife

12.—(1) In the case of any amount subscribed by a married woman for eligible shares issued to her at a time—

(*a*) when she is living with her husband ; and

(*b*) which falls in a year of assessment for which his income includes (or, if there were any, would include) any of hers,

SCH. 5 the deduction under paragraph 2(3) above shall, subject to sub-paragraph (2) below, be made from his total income, and references in this Part to the relief to which an individual is entitled in respect of any shares shall be construed accordingly.

(2) Section 60(2) to (7) of Chapter II shall apply, with the substitution, for references to sections 52(2), 53(1) and (2) and 57(1) of references to, respectively, paragraphs 2(3), 3(1) and (2) and 7(1) above.

Claims

13.—(1) A claim for the relief in respect of eligible shares issued by a company in any year of assessment shall be made—

(*a*) not earlier than 1st January 1984 or, if later, the end of the period of four months mentioned in paragraph 2(4)(*a*) above ; and

(*b*) not later than two years after the end of that year of assessment or, if that period of four months ended after the end of that year, not later than two years after the end of that period.

(2) A claim for relief in respect of eligible shares in a company shall not be allowed unless it is accompanied by a certificate issued by the company in such form as the Board may direct and certifying that the conditions for the relief, so far as applying to the company and the trade, are satisfied in relation to those shares.

(3) Before issuing a certificate for the purposes of sub-paragraph (2) above a company shall furnish the inspector with a statement to the effect that it satisfies the conditions for the relief, so far as they apply in relation to the company and the trade, and has done so at all times since the beginning of the relevant period.

(4) No such certificate shall be issued without the authority of the inspector or where the company, or a person connected with the company, has given notice to the inspector under paragraph 15(2) below.

(5) Any statement under sub-paragraph (3) above shall contain such information as the Board may reasonably require, shall be in such form as the Board may direct and shall contain a declaration that it is correct to the best of the company's knowledge and belief.

(6) Where a company has issued a certificate for the purposes of sub-paragraph (2) above, or furnished a statement under sub-paragraph (3) above and—

(*a*) the certificate or statement is made fraudulently or negligently ; or

(*b*) the certificate was issued in contravention of sub-paragraph (4) above ;

the company shall be liable to a penalty not exceeding £250 or, in the case of fraud, £500.

(7) For the purpose of regulations made under section 204 of the Taxes Act (pay as you earn), no regard shall be had to the relief unless a claim for it has been duly made and admitted. Sch. 5

(8) Section 61(6) of Chapter II shall apply.

(9) For the purposes of section 86 of the Taxes Management Act 1970 (interest on overdue tax), tax charged by an assessment— 1970 c. 9.

(*a*) shall be regarded as due and payable notwithstanding that relief from the tax (whether by discharge or repayment) is subsequently given on a claim for the relief; but

(*b*) shall, unless paid earlier or due and payable later, be regarded as paid on the date of the making of the claim on which the relief is given;

and section 91 of that Act (effect on interest of reliefs) shall not apply in consequence of any discharge or repayment for giving effect to the relief.

Assessments for withdrawing relief

14.—(1) Where any relief has been given which is subsequently found not to have been due, it shall be withdrawn by the making of an assessment to tax under Case VI of Schedule D for the year of assessment for which the relief was given.

(2) Section 62(2) to (7) of Chapter II shall apply but, in the case of subsection (4), with the substitution for the reference to section 57(1)(*b*) of a reference to paragraph 7(1)(*b*) above and, in the case of subsection (6), with the substitution for paragraphs (*a*) to (*d*) of the following paragraphs—

"(*a*) in the case of relief withdrawn by virtue of paragraphs 4, 5, 6 or 10(1) of Schedule 5 to the Finance Act 1983 in consequence of any event after the grant of the relief, the date of that event;

(*b*) in the case of relief withdrawn by virtue of paragraph 7(1) of that Schedule in consequence of a disposal after the grant of the relief, the date of the disposal;

(*c*) in the case of relief withdrawn by virtue of paragraph 8 of that Schedule in consequence of a receipt of value after the grant of the relief, the date of the receipt;

(*d*) in the case of relief withdrawn by virtue of paragraph 11 of that Schedule—

(i) so far as effect has been given to the relief in accordance with regulations under section 204 of the Taxes Act (pay as you earn), 5th April in the year of assessment in which effect was so given; and

(ii) so far as effect has not been so given, the date on which the relief was granted."

Information

15.—(1) Where an event occurs by reason of which any relief given to an individual falls to be withdrawn by virtue of paragraph 4, 7, 8 or 12(2) above the individual shall within sixty days of his

Sch. 5 coming to know of the event give a notice in writing to the inspector containing particulars of the event.

(2) Where an event occurs by reason of which any relief in respect of any shares in a company falls to be withdrawn by virtue of paragraph 5, 6, 8, 9, 10 or 11 above—

(*a*) the company ; and

(*b*) any person connected with the company who has knowledge of that matter ;

shall within sixty days of the event or, in the case of a person within paragraph (*b*) above, of his coming to know of it, give a notice in writing to the inspector containing particulars of the event or payment.

(3) If the inspector has reason to believe that a person has not given a notice which he is required to give under sub-paragraph (1) or (2) above in respect of any event, the inspector may by notice in writing require that person to furnish him within such time (not being less than sixty days) as may be specified in the notice with such information relating to the event as the inspector may reasonably require for the purposes of this Part.

(4) Where relief is claimed in respect of shares in a company and the inspector has reason to believe that it may not be due by reason of any such arrangement or scheme as is mentioned in paragraph 4(4), 5(7) or 11 above, he may by notice in writing require any person concerned to furnish him within such time (not being less than sixty days) as may be specified in the notice with—

(*a*) a declaration in writing stating whether or not, according to the information which that person has or can reasonably obtain, any such arrangement or scheme exists or has existed;

(*b*) such other information as the inspector may reasonably require for the purposes of the provision in question and as that person has or can reasonably obtain.

(5) References in sub-paragraph (4) above to the person concerned are, in relation to paragraphs 4(4) and 11, the claimant and, in relation to paragraphs 5(7) and 11, the company and any person controlling the company.

(6) Section 63(7) to (9) of Chapter II shall apply but with the substitution, for the reference to section 58, of a reference to paragraph 8 above.

Capital gains tax

16.—(1) The sums allowable as deductions from the consideration in the computation for the purposes of capital gains tax of the gain or loss accruing to an individual on the disposal of shares in respect of which any relief has been given and not withdrawn shall be determined without regard to that relief, except that where those sums exceed the consideration they shall be reduced by an amount equal to— Sch. 5

(a) the amount of that relief, or

(b) the excess,

whichever is the less, but the foregoing provisions of this sub-paragraph shall not apply to a disposal falling within section 44(1) of the Capital Gains Tax Act 1979 (disposals between husband and wife). 1979 c. 14.

(2) Sections 88 and 89 of the Finance Act 1982 (identification of securities disposed of) shall not apply to shares in respect of which any relief has been given and not withdrawn; and any question— 1982 c. 39.

(a) as to which of any such shares issued to a person at different times a disposal relates; or

(b) whether a disposal relates to such shares or to other shares;

shall for the purposes of capital gains tax be determined as for the purposes of paragraph 7 above.

(3) Where an individual holds ordinary shares in a company and the relief has been given in respect of some but not others, then, if there is within the meaning of section 77 of the Act of 1979 a reorganisation affecting those shares, section 78 of that Act shall apply separately to the shares in respect of which the relief has been given and to the other shares (so that the shares of each kind are treated as a separate holding of original shares and identified with a separate new holding).

(4) There shall be made all such adjustments of capital gains tax, whether by way of assessment or by way of discharge or repayment of tax, as may be required in consequence of the relief being given or withdrawn.

Application to subsidiaries

17.—(1) A qualifying company may, in the relevant period, have one or more subsidiaries if—

(a) the conditions mentioned in section 65(2) of Chapter II are satisfied in respect of the subsidiary or each subsidiary and, except as provided in section 65(3), continue to be so satisfied until the end of the relevant period; and

(b) the subsidiary or each subsidiary was incorporated in the United Kingdom and is a company falling within sub-paragraph (2)(a) of paragraph 5 above; and

(c) the subsidiary or each subsidiary complies with paragraph 5(2) above.

(2) Where a qualifying company has one or more subsidiaries in the relevant period this Part shall have effect subject to paragraph 18 below.

18.—(1) The shares issued by the qualifying company may, instead of or as well as being issued for the purpose mentioned in

SCH. 5 sub-paragraph (1)(*b*) of paragraph 2 above, be issued for the purpose of raising money for a qualifying trade which is being carried on by a subsidiary or which a subsidiary intends to carry on within the next four months; and where shares are so issued sub-paragraphs (4), (5) (7)(*b*) and (8) of that paragraph shall have effect as if references to the company were or, as the case may be, included references to the subsidiary.

(2) In relation to a qualifying trade carried on by a subsidiary the reference in section 56(2)(*f*) of Chapter II (as applied for the purposes of this Part) to another person shall not include a reference to the company of which it is a subsidiary.

(3) In sub-paragraph (1) of paragraph 10 above references to the company (except the first) shall include references to a company which during the relevant period is a subsidiary of the company, whether it becomes a subsidiary before or after the redemption, repayment, repurchase or payment referred to in that sub-paragraph.

(4) Sub-paragraphs (4) and (5) of paragraph 15 above shall have effect in relation to any such arrangements as are mentioned in section 65(2)(*c*) of Chapter II as they have effect in relation to any such arrangement as is mentioned in paragraph 11 above.

(5) The following provisions of Chapter II shall apply: paragraphs 2 and 4 of Schedule 12; but paragraph 4 shall apply with the substitution of a reference to paragraph 8(1) above for the reference to section 58(1).

Nominees and approved investment funds

19.—(1) Shares subscribed for, issued to, held by or disposed of for an individual by a nominee shall be treated for the purposes of this Part as subscribed for, issued to, held by or disposed of by that individual.

(2) Paragraph 3(1) above shall not apply where the amount is subscribed as nominee for an individual by the person or persons having the management of an investment fund approved for the purposes of this paragraph by the Board ("the managers of an approved fund").

(3) Where an individual claims relief in respect of eligible shares in a company which have been issued to the managers of an approved fund as nominee for that individual, paragraph 13(2) above shall apply as if it required—

(*a*) the certificate referred to in that paragraph to be issued by the company to the managers; and

(*b*) the claim for relief to be accompanied by a certificate issued by the managers, in such form as the Board may authorise, certifying that the managers hold certificates issued to them by the companies concerned, for the purposes of paragraph 13(2) above, in respect of the holdings of eligible shares shown on the managers' certificate.

(4) The managers of an approved fund may be required by a notice given to them by an inspector or other officer of the Board to deliver to the officer, within the time limited by the notice, a return of the holdings of eligible shares shown on certificates issued by them in accordance with sub-paragraph (3) above in the year of assessment to which the return relates. SCH. 5

(5) Paragraph 13(6) above shall not apply in relation to any certificate issued by the managers of an approved fund for the purposes of sub-paragraph (3) above.

Interpretation

20.—(1) Subject to sub-paragraph (2) below, section 67 of Chapter II shall apply.

(2) In this Part, including provisions of Chapter II as applied by this Part—

" debenture " has the meaning given by section 455 of the Companies Act 1948 ; 1948 c. 38.

" the relevant period " has the meaning given in paragraph 2(7) above ;

" the relief " and " relief ", except in references to relief under Chapter II, means relief under paragraph 2 above and references to the amount of the relief shall be construed in accordance with sub-paragraph (3) of that paragraph ; and

" unquoted company " means a company none of whose shares, stocks or debentures are listed in the Official List of the Stock Exchange or dealt in on the Unlisted Securities Market.

PART II

AMENDMENTS OF CHAPTER II OF PART IV OF THE FINANCE ACT 1981

21. In section 52(9) of the Finance Act 1981 (relief available only where shares issued in 1981-82 or the next two years) for the words " or either of the next two years of assessment " there shall be substituted the words " or the year 1982-83 ". 1981 c. 35.

22. Section 53(7) of the Act of 1981 (withdrawal of relief where more than 50 per cent. of the company's share capital consists of shares in respect of which relief has been given) shall cease to have effect in relation to events occurring on or after 6th April 1983.

23. Where, at any time after 5th April 1983, a company has any share capital of a kind falling within paragraph (*a*) or (*b*) of section 55(7) of the Act of 1981 (restrictions on types of share capital) that section shall apply as if paragraphs (*a*) and (*b*) were omitted.

Section 34.

SCHEDULE 6

Capital Gains: Election for Pooling

Interpretation

1.—(1) In this Schedule—

1979 c. 14. (*a*) "the principal Act" means the Capital Gains Tax Act 1979;

1982 c. 39. (*b*) "the 1982 Act" means the Finance Act 1982;

(*c*) "the qualifying period" has the meaning assigned to it by section 86(1)(*b*) of the 1982 Act; and

(*d*) "relevant allowable expenditure" has the meaning assigned to it by subsections (2)(*b*) and (3) of section 86 of the 1982 Act.

(2) For the purposes of this Schedule, "qualifying securities" are securities, as defined in section 88(9) of the 1982 Act, which are neither—

(*a*) gilt-edged securities, as defined in Schedule 2 to the principal Act; nor

(*b*) securities which on 6th April 1965 were held by the company making the election concerned and which, disregarding the effect of sections 88 and 89 of the 1982 Act, would for the time being be excluded from the effect of section 65 of the principal Act by virtue of subsection (1)(*b*) of that section.

Election for pooling

2.—(1) An election under this Schedule shall be made by notice in writing to the inspector not later than the expiry of two years from the end of the accounting period in which the first relevant disposal is made or such further time as the Board may allow.

(2) For the avoidance of doubt it is hereby declared—

(*a*) that where a company makes an election under this Schedule with respect to qualifying securities which it holds solely and beneficially, that election does not apply to qualifying securities which it holds in another capacity; and

(*b*) that an election under this Schedule is irrevocable.

(3) In this paragraph the "first relevant disposal", in relation to an election, means the first disposal after 31st March 1982 by the company making the election of qualifying securities which are held by it solely and beneficially.

Effect of election

3.—(1) The provisions of this paragraph have effect where an election is made under this Schedule.

(2) The election shall have effect with respect to all disposals after 31st March 1982 of qualifying securities held solely and beneficially by the company making the election.

(3) For the purposes of the principal Act, qualifying securities— Sch. 6

(a) which are of the same class, and

(b) which have been held by the company making the election for such a length of time that, on a disposal of them, the disposal would not be regarded as occurring within the qualifying period,

shall be regarded as indistinguishable parts of a single asset (in this paragraph referred to as a holding) diminishing or growing on the occasions on which some of the securities of the class in question are disposed of or additional securities of the class in question which have been previously acquired become held as mentioned in paragraph (b) above.

(4) Without prejudice to the generality of sub-paragraph (3) above, a disposal of securities in a holding, other than the disposal outright of the entire holding, is a disposal of part of an asset and the provisions of the principal Act relating to the computation of a gain accruing on a disposal of part of an asset shall apply accordingly.

(5) In accordance with the preceding provisions of this paragraph, where an election is made under this Schedule, the holding shall come (or, as the case may be, shall be treated as having come) into being—

(a) on the first anniversary of the first acquisition of qualifying securities of a particular description ; or

(b) if Part II of Schedule 13 to the 1982 Act applies so that " the holding " for the purposes of this paragraph consists of or includes what is " the holding " or " the reduced holding " referred to in paragraph 8 or paragraph 9 of that Schedule, on 1st April 1982.

(6) In its application to a holding, subsection (1) of section 86 of the 1982 Act (conditions for the existence of the indexation allowance) shall have effect as if the condition in paragraph (b) (the qualifying period) were always fulfilled.

(7) Shares or securities of a company shall not be treated for the purposes of this Schedule as being of the same class unless they are so treated by the practice of The Stock Exchange or would be so treated if dealt with on The Stock Exchange.

The 1982 identification rules

4.—(1) The provisions of sections 88 and 89 of, and Part II of Schedule 13 to, the 1982 Act shall have effect for determining whether qualifying securities have been held as mentioned in paragraph (b) of sub-paragraph (3) of paragraph 3 above but, subject to that, those provisions shall not apply to securities forming part of the single asset referred to in that sub-paragraph.

(2) Any reference in sub-paragraph (1) above to qualifying securities includes a reference to a single asset consisting of qualifying securities which continued in existence on and after 1st April 1982

SCH. 6 by virtue of paragraph 8 or paragraph 9(3)(*a*) of Schedule 13 to the 1982 Act.

The indexation allowance

5.—(1) Where an election has been made under this Schedule, the following provisions of this Schedule have effect in place of the provisions of section 87 of the 1982 Act for the purpose of computing the indexation allowance on a disposal to which section 86 of that Act applies of the single asset (in the following provisions of this Schedule referred to as " the holding ") which by virtue of paragraph 3(3) above results from the election.

(2) On any disposal of the holding falling within sub-paragraph (1) above, other than a disposal of the whole of it,—

(*a*) the unindexed and indexed pools of expenditure shall each be apportioned between the part disposed of and the remainder in the same proportions as, under the principal Act, the relevant allowable expenditure is apportioned ; and

(*b*) the indexation allowance is the amount by which the portion of the indexed pool which is attributed to the part disposed of exceeds the portion of the unindexed pool which is attributed to that part.

(3) On a disposal falling within sub-paragraph (1) above of the whole of the holding, the indexation allowance is the amount by which the indexed pool of expenditure at the time of the disposal exceeds the unindexed pool of expenditure at that time.

6.—(1) Subject to sub-paragraph (2) below, in relation to the holding, the unindexed pool of expenditure is at any time the amount which would be the aggregate of the relevant allowable expenditure in relation to a disposal of the whole of the holding occurring at that time.

(2) Where any item of the relevant allowable expenditure referred to in sub-paragraph (1) above was incurred after the time at which the securities to which it relates were acquired, it shall not be taken into account for the purpose of determining the unindexed pool of expenditure at any time before the expiry of the period of twelve months beginning on the date on which it was incurred ; but at the expiry of that period the unindexed pool of expenditure shall be increased, subject to sub-paragraph (3) below, by the addition of a sum equal to it.

(3) If, before the expiry of the period of twelve months referred to in sub-paragraph (2) above, there is a disposal of any of the securities to which the item of relevant expenditure referred to in that sub-paragraph relates, only the portion of that expenditure which is attributable to the securities which are not so disposed of shall be added to the unindexed pool of expenditure by virtue of sub-paragraph (2) above.

(4) If, by virtue of any enactment, any item of the relevant allowable expenditure referred to in sub-paragraph (1) above falls to be

reduced by reference to a relevant event, within the meaning of paragraph 4 of Schedule 13 to the 1982 Act, occurring after the time at which the securities to which it relates were acquired, that reduction shall not be taken into account for the purpose of determining the unindexed pool of expenditure until the expiry of the period of twelve months beginning on the date of the relevant event in question.

(5) If, before the expiry of the period of twelve months referred to in sub-paragraph (4) above, there is a disposal of any of the securities to which the item of relevant expenditure referred to in that sub-paragraph relates, the amount by which the unindexed pool of expenditure falls to be reduced at the expiry of that period shall itself be reduced so that only that portion of the reduction which is attributable to the securities which are not so disposed of shall then be made in the unindexed pool of expenditure.

(6) Subsection (5) of section 87 of the 1982 Act (date on which expenditure was incurred) and any provision of Schedule 13 to that Act which, in particular circumstances, displaces that subsection shall apply for the purposes of sub-paragraph (2) above as they apply for the purpose of computing the indexation allowance in accordance with that section.

7.—(1) The provisions of this paragraph have effect, subject to paragraphs 9 and 10 below, for determining, in relation to the holding, the indexed pool of expenditure at any time.

(2) The indexed pool of expenditure shall come into being at the time that the holding comes into being and shall at that time consist of the aggregate of—

(*a*) the unindexed pool of expenditure at that time; and

(*b*) any indexation allowance which, by virtue of paragraph 7(3) of Schedule 13 to the 1982 Act (options), would have applied to a disposal of the whole of the holding at that time.

(3) Any reference in the following provisions of this Schedule to an operative event is a reference to any event (whether a disposal, the expiry of a period of twelve months from an acquisition or otherwise) which has the effect of reducing or increasing the unindexed pool of expenditure attributable to the holding.

(4) Whenever an operative event occurs,—

(*a*) there shall be added to the indexed pool of expenditure the indexed rise, as calculated under paragraph 8 below, in the value of that pool since the last operative event or, if there has been no previous operative event, since the pool came into being; and

(*b*) if the operative event results in an increase in the unindexed pool of expenditure then, in addition to any increase under paragraph (*a*) above, the same increase shall be made to the indexed pool of expenditure;

(*c*) if the operative event is a disposal resulting in a reduction in the unindexed pool of expenditure, then, whether or not it

SCH. 6

is a disposal to which section 86 of the 1982 Act applies, the indexed pool of expenditure shall be reduced in the same proportion as the unindexed pool is reduced ; and

(*d*) if the operative event results in a reduction in the unindexed pool of expenditure but is not a disposal, the same reduction shall be made to the indexed pool of expenditure.

(5) Where the operative event is a disposal to which section 86 of the 1982 Act applies,—

(*a*) any addition under paragraph (*a*) of sub-paragraph (4) above shall be made before the calculation of the indexation allowance under paragraph 5 above ; and

(*b*) the reduction under paragraph (*c*) of that sub-paragraph shall be made after that calculation.

8.—(1) At the time of any operative event, the indexed rise in the indexed pool of expenditure is a sum produced by multiplying the value of that pool immediately before the event by a figure expressed as a decimal and determined, subject to sub-paragraphs (2) and (3) below, by the formula—

$$\frac{RE-RL}{RL}$$

where—

RE is the retail prices index for the month in which the operative event occurs ; and

RL is the retail prices index for the month in which occurred the immediately preceding operative event or, if there has been no such event, in which the indexed pool of expenditure came into being.

(2) If RE, as defined in sub-paragraph (1) above, is equal to or less than RL, as so defined, the indexed rise is nil.

(3) If the figure determined in accordance with the formula in sub-paragraph (1) above would, apart from this sub-paragraph, be a figure having more than three decimal places, it shall be rounded to the nearest third decimal place.

Transfers on a no gain/no loss basis

9.—(1) This paragraph applies in any case where—

(*a*) a company (in this paragraph referred to as " the first company ") disposes of securities to another company, (in this paragraph referred to as " the second company ") which has made an election under this Schedule, and

(*b*) the disposal is one to which section 267 or section 273 of the Taxes Act applies (transfers on a company reconstruction etc. and within a group of companies to be on a no gain/no loss basis), and

(*c*) the disposal by the first company takes place outside the qualifying period.

(2) Nothing in this paragraph affects the operation of paragraph 2 of Schedule 13 to the 1982 Act, but paragraph 3 of that Schedule shall have effect subject to the provisions of this Schedule. SCH. 6

(3) On the disposal referred to in sub-paragraph (1) above (which is the initial disposal within the meaning of the said paragraph 3)—

(*a*) the consideration for the disposal shall become part of the second company's indexed pool of expenditure ; and

(*b*) so much of that consideration as does not consist of the indexation allowance on the disposal shall become part of the second company's unindexed pool of expenditure.

Consideration for options

10.—(1) If, in a case where sub-paragraph (4)(*b*) of paragraph 7 above applies, the increase in the unindexed pool of expenditure is, in whole or in part, attributable to the cost of acquiring an option binding the grantor to sell (in this paragraph referred to as " the option consideration "), then, in addition to any increase under paragraph (*a*) or paragraph (*b*) of sub-paragraph (4) of paragraph 7 above, the indexed pool of expenditure shall be increased by an amount equal to the indexed rise in the option consideration, as determined under sub-paragraph (2) below.

(2) The indexed rise in the option consideration is a sum produced by multiplying the consideration by a figure expressed as a decimal and determined, subject to sub-paragraphs (3) and (4) below, by the formula—

$$\frac{RO - RA}{RA}$$

where—

RO is the retail prices index for the month in which falls the first anniversary of the date on which the option is exercised ; and

RA is the retail prices index for the month in which falls the first anniversary of the date on which the option was acquired or, if it is later, March 1982.

(3) If RO, as defined in sub-paragraph (2) above, is equal to or less than RA, as so defined, the indexed rise is nil.

(4) If the figure determined in accordance with the formula in sub-paragraph (2) above would, apart from this sub-paragraph, be a figure having more than three decimal places, it shall be rounded to the nearest third decimal place.

Supplementary

11. All such adjustments shall be made, whether by way of discharge or repayment of tax, or the making of assessments or otherwise, as are required to give effect to an election under this Schedule.

Section 35.

SCHEDULE 7

1982 c. 39.

APRT: Modifications of Finance Act 1982, Schedule 19

1. In paragraph 1(3) (returns for periods after liability for APRT has ceased) the word " nine " shall be omitted.

2. In paragraph 2(2) (instalment payments where liability for APRT expires) for the words from " the chargeable period " to " for that field " there shall be substituted the words " any chargeable period ending on or after 31st December 1984."

3.—(1) In paragraph 14 (repayment of APRT) in sub-paragraph (1) for the words from " for the last " to " section 139(1)(*b*) " there shall be substituted the words " for the ninth chargeable period following the first chargeable period referred to in section 139(1)(*a*) ".

(2) In sub-paragraph (2) of that paragraph for the words from " the last " to " this Act " there shall be substituted the words " the ninth chargeable period referred to in sub-paragraph (1) above " and for the words " subsection (4) of that section " there shall be substituted the words " section 139(4) of this Act ".

(3) In sub-paragraph (3) of that paragraph for the words " the last chargeable period " and in sub-paragraph (4)(*a*) of that paragraph for the words " the chargeable period " there shall be substituted the words " the ninth chargeable period ".

4. In paragraph 17 (abandoned fields) in sub-paragraph (1)(*c*) for the words from " last " to " section 139(1)(*b*) " there shall be substituted the words " ninth chargeable period following the first chargeable period referred to in section 139(1)(*a*) ".

Section 37.

SCHEDULE 8

Reliefs for Exploration and Appraisal Expenditure etc

Part I

Section to be inserted after Section 5 of the Principal Act

"Allowance of exploration and appraisal expenditure.

5A.—(1) The exploration and appraisal expenditure which, subject to the provisions of this section and Schedule 7 to this Act, is allowable in the case of a person who is a participator in an oil field is any expenditure (whether or not of a capital nature) which—

(*a*) is incurred after 15th March 1983 by that person or, if that person is a company, by that company or a company associated with it in respect of the expenditure ; and

(*b*) is so incurred wholly and exclusively for one or more of the purposes specified in subsection (2) below ; and

(*c*) at the time it is so incurred, does not relate to a field for which a development decision has previously been made.

(2) The purposes referred to in subsection (1) above are—

(*a*) the purpose of searching for oil in the United Kingdom, the territorial sea thereof or a designated area ;

(*b*) the purpose of ascertaining the extent or characteristics of any oil-bearing area in the United Kingdom, the territorial sea thereof or a designated area ; Sch. 8

(*c*) the purpose of ascertaining what are the reserves of oil of any such oil-bearing area ; and

(*d*) subject to subsection (3) below, the purpose of making to the Secretary of State any payment under or for the purpose of obtaining a licence (not being a payment by way of royalty or other periodic payment).

(3) Expenditure incurred for the purpose mentioned in subsection (2)(*d*) above is not allowable under this section unless, at the time the allowance is claimed,—

(*a*) the licence to which the expenditure related has expired or has been determined or revoked ; or

(*b*) part of the licensed area has been surrendered ;

and where paragraph (*b*) above applies only that proportion of the expenditure which corresponds to the proportion of the licensed area which has been surrendered is expenditure falling within subsection (1) above.

(4) Subject to subsection (5) below, subsections (2) and (4) to (8) of section 5 of this Act apply for the purposes of this section as they apply for the purposes of that section.

(5) In the application for the purposes of this section of the provisions of section 5 of this Act referred to in subsection (4) above,—

(*a*) any reference in subsection (2) of section 5 to the purpose mentioned in subsection (1)(*b*) of that section shall be construed as a reference to any of the purposes specified in subsection (2) of this section ;

(*b*) the reference in subsection (2)(*a*) of section 5 to subsection (1) of that section shall be construed as a reference to subsection (1) of this section ; and

(*c*) the reference in subsection (6) of section 5 to a sum received does not include a reference—

(i) to a sum received from the disposal of oil won in the course of operations carried out for any of the purposes in paragraphs (*a*) to (*c*) of subsection (2) of this section ; or

(ii) to a sum received for the assignment of any of the rights conferred by a licence or of any interest in a licensed area.

(6) Expenditure is not allowable under this section in connection with an oil field if, or to the extent that, it has been allowed under Schedule 5, Schedule 6 or Schedule 7 to this Act in connection with any oil field.

(7) For the purposes of subsection (1)(*c*) above, a development decision is made when—

(*a*) consent for development is granted to a licensee by the Secretary of State in respect of the whole or part of an oil field ; or

SCH. 8

(*b*) a programme of development is served on a licensee or approved by the Secretary of State for the whole or part of an oil field ;

and subsections (4) and (5) of section 36 of the Finance Act 1983 (meaning of development etc.) apply in relation to this subsection as they apply in relation to subsections (2) and (3) of that section.

(8) If, at the time when it is incurred, expenditure relates to an area—

(*a*) which is not then an oil field, but

(*b*) in respect of which notice of a proposed determination has previously been given under paragraph 2(*a*) of Schedule 1 to this Act,

that area shall be treated for the purposes of this section as having become an oil field at the time the notice was given unless, when the actual determination is made, the area is not included in an oil field."

PART II

AMENDMENTS RELATING TO THE NEW ALLOWANCE

The principal Act

1. In section 2(9) of the principal Act (amounts to be taken into account in respect of expenditure) at the end of paragraph (*e*) there shall be added " and

(*f*) any exploration and appraisal expenditure allowable in the case of the participator under section 5A of this Act which, on a claim made by him under Schedule 7 to this Act, has been allowed under that Schedule before the Board have made an assessment to tax or a determination on or in relation to him for the period in respect of the field, so far as that expenditure has not been taken into account in any previous assessment to tax or determination."

2. At the end of subsection (3) of section 3 of the principal Act (expenditure not allowable under that section if already allowed under other provisions) there shall be added the words " but where expenditure allowable under section 5A of this Act has been allowed on a claim under Schedule 7 to this Act, nothing in this subsection shall prevent a claim being made for an allowance under this section in respect of the same expenditure unless the person making the claim is the participator who made the claim under that Schedule ".

3. In section 5 of the principal Act (allowance of abortive exploration expenditure) in subsection (1) after the words " 1st January 1960 " there shall be inserted the words " and before 16th March 1983 ".

4. In section 9 of the principal Act (limit on amount of tax payable) in subsection (2)(*a*)(ii) for the words " and (*e*) " there shall be substituted the words " (*e*) and (*f*) ".

5. In paragraph 2 of Schedule 2 to the principal Act (returns by participators) at the end of sub-paragraph (2) there shall be inserted the following sub-paragraph:— Sch. 8

"(2A) Every participator in an oil field shall, in the first return under this paragraph which he makes for that field, state whether any and, if any, how much exploration and appraisal expenditure to which section 5A of this Act applies and which relates to, or to a licence for, any part of the field has been claimed under Schedule 7 to this Act—

(*a*) by him, or

(*b*) by a company associated with him in respect of that expenditure, or

(*c*) if he or such a company is the new participator, within the meaning of Schedule 17 to the Finance Act 1980, by the old participator, within the meaning of that Schedule, or by a company associated with him in respect of that expenditure, 1980 c. 48.

and subsection (7) of section 5 of this Act applies for the purposes of this sub-paragraph as it applies for the purposes of that section."

6.—(1) In Schedule 7 to the principal Act (claims for allowance of abortive exploration expenditure) in paragraph 1(1), for the words from " of any " to " of this Act " there shall be substituted:—

" (*a*) of any abortive exploration expenditure allowable under section 5 of this Act, or

(*b*) of any exploration and appraisal expenditure allowable under section 5A of this Act ".

(2) In paragraph 1(3) of that Schedule, after the words " section 5 " there shall be added the words " or, as the case may be, section 5A."

The Petroleum Revenue Tax Act 1980

7. In the Schedule to the Petroleum Revenue Tax Act 1980 (computation of payment on account) in paragraph 2(4) for the words " or (*d*) " there shall be substituted the words " (*d*) or (*f*) ". 1980 c. 1.

The Finance Act 1980

8. In Schedule 17 to the Finance Act 1980 (transfers of interests in oil fields) after paragraph 16 (abortive exploration expenditure) there shall be inserted—

" *Exploration and appraisal expenditure*

16A. In relation to exploration and appraisal expenditure to which section 5A applies, paragraph 16 above has effect as if any reference therein to section 5 were a reference to section 5A."

The Finance Act 1981

9. In section 111 of the Finance Act 1981 (restriction of expenditure supplement) in subsection (3)(*a*) after the words " abortive 1981 c. 35.

SCH. 8 exploration expenditure " there shall be added the words " exploration and appraisal expenditure."

PART III

RECEIPTS TO BE SET AGAINST ALLOWABLE EXPENDITURE

10. In this Part of this Schedule—

" allowable expenditure " means expenditure which, in accordance with section 5 or section 5A of the principal Act, is allowable on a claim made by a participator under Schedule 7 to that Act ; and

" qualifying receipt " means a sum the amount of which falls, by virtue of subsection (6) of section 5 of the principal Act, to be applied by way of reduction in the amount of expenditure which would otherwise be allowable expenditure.

11.—(1) A return made by a participator for a chargeable period under paragraph 2 of Schedule 2 to the principal Act shall give details of any qualifying receipt (whether received by him or by a person connected with him) of which details have not been given in a return made by him for an earlier chargeable period.

(2) Section 533 of the Taxes Act (connected persons) applies for the purposes of this paragraph.

12.—(1) This paragraph applies where—

(*a*) a claim for allowable expenditure has been made by a participator under Schedule 7 to the principal Act ; and

(*b*) as a result of the receipt (whether before or after the making of the claim) of a qualifying receipt, the amount allowed by way of allowable expenditure on the claim exceeds what it should have been.

(2) In determining, in a case where this paragraph applies, the assessable profit or allowable loss accruing to the participator in the chargeable period in which the qualifying receipt is received, the amount of the excess referred to in sub-paragraph (1)(*b*) above shall be taken into account under section 2 of the principal Act as an amount which is to be included among the positive amounts referred to in subsection (3)(*a*) of that section.

(3) In the application of section 9 of the principal Act (limit on amount of tax payable) to a chargeable period in respect of which sub-paragraph (2) above applies, the amount of the excess referred to in sub-paragraph (1)(*b*) above shall be deducted from the amount which would otherwise be the total ascertained under subsection (2)(*a*)(ii) of that section and, if the amount of that excess is greater than the amount which would otherwise be that total, that total shall be a negative amount equal to the difference.

SCHEDULE 9

Section 47.

VALUE ADDED TAX, CAR TAX AND CAPITAL TRANSFER TAX CONSOLIDATION AMENDMENTS

Value added tax and car tax

1.—(1) Sections 32(1), 64(1) and 65(2) of and paragraph 1 of Schedule 14 to the Criminal Law Act 1977, sections 31, 32 and 143 of the Magistrates' Courts Act 1980, sections 37, 38, 46, 47, 74 and 75 of the Criminal Justice Act 1982 and any order under section 143 of the said Act of 1980 which alters the sums specified in the definition of "the prescribed sum" in section 32(9) of that Act or section 37(2) of the said Act of 1982 shall extend to Northern Ireland for the purposes of any pecuniary or other penalties which may be imposed under any of the following provisions, namely— 1977 c. 45. 1980 c. 43. 1982 c. 48.

section 38 of the Finance Act 1972 1972 c. 41.

paragraph 22 of Schedule 7 to the Finance Act 1972

section 55 of the Finance Act 1973 1973 c. 51.

section 16 of the Finance Act 1980. 1980 c. 48.

(2) In the application of section 31 of the Magistrates' Courts Act 1980 to Northern Ireland—

(*a*) the reference in subsection (1) of that section to section 133 of that Act shall be construed as a reference to Article 56 of the Magistrates' Courts (Northern Ireland) Order 1981; and

(*b*) the references in subsections (1) and (3) of that section to a magistrates' court shall be construed as references to a court of summary jurisdiction.

2. For section 44 of the Finance Act 1972 (service of notices) there shall be substituted—

"44. Any notice, notification, requirement or demand to be served on, given to or made of any person for the purposes of this Act may be served, given or made by sending it by post in a letter addressed to that person at his last or usual residence or place of business."

Capital transfer tax

3. In section 37(1)(*b*) of the Finance Act 1975, after the words "transferred by" there shall be inserted the word "previous". 1975 c. 7.

4. In paragraph 2(2A) of Schedule 4 to that Act, for the words "relevant property" there shall be substituted the words "appropriate property".

5. In paragraph 4(10) of Schedule 5 to that Act, after the words "in this paragraph" there shall be inserted the words "and in section 46(5) of this Act".

6. In section 78(4)(*b*) of the Finance Act 1976, the words "to the Board" and the words from "or" to "tax)" shall cease to have effect. 1976 c. 40.

SCH. 9

7. In section 114(6) of that Act, for the words "the said section 37" there shall be substituted the words "section 37 of the said Act of 1975".

Section 48.

SCHEDULE 10

REPEALS

PART I

MISCELLANEOUS CUSTOMS AND EXCISE

Chapter	Short title	Extent of repeal
1964 c. 26.	The Licensing Act 1964.	Section 30(5).
1967 c. 54.	The Finance Act 1967.	In Schedule 7, paragraph 4.
1969 c. 32.	The Finance Act 1969.	Section 1(5). Schedule 7.
1976 c. 66.	The Licensing (Scotland) Act 1976.	Section 22.
1977 c. 45.	The Criminal Law Act 1977.	In Schedule 12, in the entry relating to the Licensing Act 1964, paragraph 1.
1979 c. 2.	The Customs and Excise Management Act 1979.	In section 51(1), the words "within the prescribed area".
1979 c. 4.	The Alcoholic Liquor Duties Act 1979.	Section 92(7).
1980 c. 48.	The Finance Act 1980.	Section 9.
1982 c. 39.	The Finance Act 1982.	In Schedule 5, in part B, paragraph 16(3).

The repeals in the Finance Act 1969, the Alcoholic Liquor Duties Act 1979 and the Finance Act 1980 have effect on the appointed day within the meaning of section 9(2) of this Act.

Part II

Sch. 10

Income Tax, Corporation Tax and Capital Gains Tax

Chapter	Short title	Extent of repeal
1970 c. 10.	The Income and Corporation Taxes Act 1970.	In section 226(3)(*c*) the words " (but not before he attains the age of fifty) ".
1980 c. 48.	The Finance Act 1980.	In Schedule 12, paragraph 7(2)(*aa*).
1981 c. 35.	The Finance Act 1981.	Section 53(7). In section 59, in subsection (4) the words " and (7) " and in subsection (6), paragraph (*b*). In section 62(6)(*a*) the words " 53(7),". In section 63(2) the words " 53(7),".
1982 c. 39.	The Finance Act 1982.	In section 77, in subsection (2), the words from " and at the end " onwards.

1. The repeal in section 226(3)(*c*) of the Income and Corporation Taxes Act 1970 shall be deemed to have come into force on 6th April 1983.

2. The repeals in sections 53, 59, 62 and 63 of the Finance Act 1981 have effect in relation to events occurring on or after 6th April 1983.

Part III

Oil Taxation

Chapter	Short title	Extent of repeal
1975 c. 22.	The Oil Taxation Act 1975.	In Schedule 7, in paragraph 1, in sub-paragraph (1) the words from " but may not " to the end, and, in sub-paragraph (2) the words " within the time allowed for making the original claim ".
1982 c. 39.	The Finance Act 1982.	In Schedule 19, in paragraph 1(3) the word " nine ".

Miscellaneous Financial Provisions Act 1983

1983 CHAPTER 29

An Act to establish a Development Commission in place of the Commissioners appointed under the Development and Road Improvement Funds Act 1909; to authorise the making of grants by the Secretary of State to bodies promoting industrial or commercial development in areas in England; to extinguish liability in respect of certain guarantees given under the Colonial Loans Act 1949; to amend certain enactments authorising the Treasury to give guarantees; to extend the power of the Crown Estate Commissioners to grant leases; to make provision for the redemption of certain annuities and allowances which have been payable out of public funds since before 1874; to amend section 173A of the Local Government Act 1972; and for connected purposes. [13th May 1983]

BE IT ENACTED by the Queen's most Excellent Majesty, by and with the advice and consent of the Lords Spiritual and Temporal, and Commons, in this present Parliament assembled, and by the authority of the same, as follows:—

The Development Commission.

1.—(1) There shall be a body corporate called the Development Commission.

(2) The first members of the Commission shall be the persons who, immediately before the commencement of this section, are the Development Commissioners under the Development and Road Improvement Funds Act 1909; and Part I of that Act shall cease to have effect. 1909 c. 47.

(3) The Development Commission shall keep under review and advise the Secretary of State upon all matters relating to the economic and social development of rural areas in England and may carry out or assist others to carry out measures likely to further such development.

(4) Subject to subsections (7) and (8) below, the Commission may do anything which is conducive or incidental to the discharge of its functions and in particular (but without prejudice to the generality of the foregoing) may—

(*a*) make grants and loans and give guarantees and any other form of financial assistance;

(*b*) acquire land and other property;

(*c*) provide or facilitate the provision of premises for occupation by industrial or commercial undertakings;

(*d*) form, and hold controlling or other interests in, bodies corporate;

(*e*) act alone or with other persons, either in partnership or otherwise.

(5) The power of the Commission to acquire land includes power, if authorised by the Secretary of State, to purchase land compulsorily; and the Acquisition of Land Act 1981 shall apply to any compulsory purchase by the Commission.

1981 c. 67.

(6) The Secretary of State may make to the Commission out of money provided by Parliament grants of such amount and subject to such conditions as he may, with the approval of the Treasury, think fit.

(7) The Commission shall not give financial assistance to any person except in accordance with arrangements approved by the Secretary of State and the Treasury.

(8) The Secretary of State may give the Commission general directions as to the exercise of its functions, and the Commission shall comply with any such directions.

(9) Schedule 1 to this Act shall have effect.

Grants to regional development organisations.

2.—(1) The Secretary of State may out of money provided by Parliament make grants to any body within subsection (2) below for the purpose of assisting it to promote industrial or commercial development in the area with which it is concerned.

(2) The bodies referred to in subsection (1) above are—

(*a*) the Devon and Cornwall Development Bureau;

(*b*) the North of England Development Council;

(*c*) the North West Industrial Development Association ;

(*d*) the Yorkshire and Humberside Development Association ;

(*e*) any other body, whether corporate or unincorporate, whose principal object appears to the Secretary of State to be the promotion of industrial or commercial development in an area in England.

(3) The Secretary of State shall obtain the consent of the Treasury before making a grant under this section to any body other than one named in subsection (2)(*a*) to (*d*) above.

(4) In making a grant under this section the Secretary of State may impose such conditions as he thinks fit, including in particular—

(*a*) a condition requiring the recipient to keep proper accounts and records in respect of the application of the grant ;

(*b*) a condition requiring the recipient to submit to the Secretary of State such periodic statements of accounts and reports relating to the application of the grant as the Secretary of State may direct ; and

(*c*) a condition requiring the recipient to repay the whole or any part of the grant if any condition of the grant is not complied with.

(5) The Secretary of State shall lay before each House of Parliament a copy of every statement and report submitted to him in compliance with a condition of the kind described in subsection (4)(*b*) above.

Extinguishment of certain Zimbabwean debts.

1949 c. 50.

3. There is hereby extinguished any liability to make payments in consequence of the fulfilment of the guarantees specified in the table below (which were given by the Treasury under the Colonial Loans Act 1949 in respect of loans by the International Bank for Reconstruction and Development).

TABLE

Date of guarantee	*Particulars of loan guaranteed*
27th February 1952	Loan of an amount equivalent to $28,000,000 to the Colony of Southern Rhodesia.
16th June 1958	Loan of an amount equivalent to $19,000,000 to the Federation of Rhodesia and Nyasaland.
1st April 1960	Loan of an amount equivalent to $5,600,000 to the Federation of Rhodesia and Nyasaland.

Treasury guarantees.

4.—(1) In the enactments mentioned in Schedule 2 to this Act (which enable the Treasury to guarantee the repayment of the principal of, and the payment of interest on, sums borrowed by the bodies mentioned in the third column of that Schedule) for the words " and the payment of interest on " or " and the payment of any interest on " there shall be substituted the words " the payment of interest on and the discharge of any other financial obligation in connection with ".

1978 c. 2.

(2) In section 11(1) of the Commonwealth Development Corporation Act 1978 (Treasury guarantees in respect of sums borrowed by the Commonwealth Development Corporation) for the words " and the payment of interest and other charges on " there shall be substituted the words " the payment of interest on and the discharge of any other financial obligation in connection with ".

1979 c. 11.

(3) In section 25 of the Electricity (Scotland) Act 1979 (Treasury guarantees in respect of sums borrowed by Electricity Boards)—

(*a*) in subsection (1), for the words from " payment of " to the end there shall be substituted the words " repayment of the principal of, the payment of interest on and the discharge of any other financial obligation in connection with any loan proposed to be raised by either Board " ; and

(*b*) in subsection (3), after the word " of " in the fourth place where it occurs there shall be inserted the words ", and any other financial obligation in connection with,".

1980 c. 63.

(4) In section 8 of the Overseas Development and Co-operation Act 1980 (Treasury guarantees in respect of certain loans made by the International Bank)—

(*a*) in subsection (1), for the words " and the payment of the interest on and other charges in respect of " there shall be substituted the words " the payment of interest on and the discharge of any other financial obligation in connection with " ;

(*b*) in subsection (5)(*d*)(i), for the words " charges in respect of " there shall be substituted the words " payments in discharge of financial obligations in connection with " ;

(*c*) in subsection (6), for the words " other charges in respect of " there shall be substituted the words " the discharge of any other financial obligation in connection with ".

1981 c. 64.

(5) In section 62(1) of the New Towns Act 1981 (Treasury guarantees in respect of sums borrowed by a development corporation or the Commission for the New Towns) for paragraphs (*a*) and (*b*) there shall be substituted the words " the

repayment of the principal of, the payment of interest on and the discharge of any other financial obligation in connection with ".

5. In section 3(2) of the Crown Estate Act 1961 (restriction on term for which a lease may be granted by Crown Estate Commissioners) for the words " one hundred years " there shall be substituted the words " one hundred and fifty years ".

Power of Crown Estate Commissioners to grant leases.

1961 c. 55.

6.—(1) If the Treasury, in respect of an annuity to which this subsection applies—

Redemption of certain annuities.

- (*a*) by notice in writing inform the person appearing to them to be entitled for the time being to receive the annuity that they propose to redeem it on a date specified in the notice (" the redemption date "), and
- (*b*) tender to that person, not later than the redemption date, a payment calculated in accordance with subsection (7) below,

the annuity shall cease to be payable on the redemption date.

(2) Subsection (1) above applies to any annuity not exceeding £2,000 a year for the redemption of which the Treasury may contract under section 2 of the Consolidated Fund (Permanent Charges Redemption) Act 1873 (and does not apply to an annuity first payable after the passing of that Act).

1873 c. 57.

(3) Where a person entitled by virtue of any hereditary office to receive an annuity to which subsection (1) above applies has the right, as holder of the office, to nominate another person to an office which carries an allowance charged on the Consolidated Fund, the amount of the annuity shall, for the purpose of calculating the payment referred to in that subsection, be taken to be increased by the amount of the allowance; and the allowance shall cease to be payable when the annuity ceases to be payable.

(4) The redemption date specified in a notice given under subsection (1) above shall not be later than fourteen days after the date on which the notice is served; and the notice may be served by post or in any other way.

(5) If, in respect of an annuity payable by virtue of any of the enactments specified in the first column of the table below, the Treasury pay and the person specified (in relation to that enactment) in the second column of the table accepts a sum calculated in accordance with subsection (7) below, the annuity shall cease to be payable.

TABLE

Enactment by virtue of which annuity is payable	*Person to whom payment is to be made*
Section 1 of the Prisage and Butlerage Act 1803 (c.156).	The Receiver General of the Duchy of Lancaster.
Section 3 of the Tin Duties Act 1838 (c.120).	The Receiver General of the Duchy of Cornwall.
Section 9 of the Greenwich Hospital Act 1869 (c.44).	The Secretary of State.

(6) Any payment accepted by the Secretary of State under subsection (5) above shall be credited to the Greenwich Hospital capital account with the Paymaster General.

(7) The sum to be paid in respect of an annuity under subsection (1) or (5) above shall be such as would, according to the average price of undated government stock at the end of the relevant day, purchase an amount of such stock yielding annual dividends equal to the amount of the annuity ; and in this subsection—

" the relevant day ", in relation to subsection (1) above, means a day specified in the notice given under that subsection, being a day not more than seven days earlier than that on which the notice is served ; and in relation to subsection (5) above, means a day agreed between the Treasury and the person to whom the payment is to be made ; and

1972 c. 65. " undated government stock " means government stock, within the meaning of section 15(1) of the National Debt Act 1972, issued on terms which do not specify a date on or before which the stock is to be redeemed.

(8) Payments under this section shall be charged on and paid out of the Consolidated Fund.

Local government allowances. 1972 c. 70.

7.—(1) Section 173A of the Local Government Act 1972 (which enables councillors to give notices opting for financial loss allowance instead of attendance allowance) shall be amended as follows.

(2) In subsection (3) (notices given within four weeks from election)—

(*a*) for the words " four weeks from " there shall be substituted the words " one month beginning with the day of " ; and

(*b*) after the words " of the authority " there shall be inserted the words " then, subject to subsection (4A) below ".

(3) For subsections (4) to (6) (later notices, and notices of withdrawal) there shall be substituted—

" (4) If a councillor gives a financial loss allowance notice to the local authority otherwise than in accordance with subsection (3) above, then, subject to subsection (4A) below, he shall be entitled to receive financial loss allowance for the performance of any approved duty after the end of the period of one month beginning with the day on which the notice is given.

(4A) If a councillor who has given a local authority a financial loss allowance notice gives them notice in writing that he withdraws that notice, it shall not have effect in relation to any duty performed after the day on which the notice of withdrawal is given.".

8. The enactments mentioned in Schedule 3 to this Act are hereby repealed to the extent specified in the third column of that Schedule. Repeals.

9.—(1) Sections 1 and 8 above (and Schedules 1 and 3) shall come into force on such day as the Secretary of State may appoint by order made by statutory instrument; and an order under this subsection may appoint different days for different purposes. Commencement.

(2) Except as provided in subsection (1) above this Act shall come into force at the end of the period of two months beginning with the day on which it is passed.

10.—(1) Sections 1 and 2 above, and Schedule 1 to this Act (except paragraph 12), shall not extend to Northern Ireland. Extent.

(2) Any amendment or repeal by section 4, 7 or 8 above of an enactment which does not extend throughout the United Kingdom shall extend only to the part of the United Kingdom to which the enactment amended or repealed extends.

(3) Subject to subsections (1) and (2) above, this Act extends to Northern Ireland.

(4) Section 5 of this Act extends to the Isle of Man so far as is material to any powers or duties of the Crown Estate Commissioners in the Isle of Man.

11. This Act may be cited as the Miscellaneous Financial Provisions Act 1983. Short title.

SCHEDULES

Section 1.

SCHEDULE 1

The Development Commission

Status

1.—(1) The Commission shall not be regarded as the servant or agent of the Crown or as enjoying any status, immunity or privilege of the Crown; and, subject to sub-paragraph (2) below, the Commission's property shall not be regarded as property of, or property held on behalf of, the Crown.

(2) Any land occupied by the Commission shall, for the purpose of any rate on property, be treated as if it were property occupied by or on behalf of the Crown for public purposes.

Membership

2.—(1) The Commission shall consist of not more than eight members appointed by Her Majesty by warrant under the sign manual, and one of those members shall be appointed as chairman.

(2) Subject to the following provisions of this Schedule, a person shall hold and vacate office as a member or as chairman of the Commission in accordance with the terms of his appointment.

(3) A person shall not hold office as a member of the Commission for more than five years under any one appointment, but a person who ceases or has ceased to be a member shall be eligible for reappointment.

(4) A person may at any time resign his office as a member or as chairman of the Commission.

(5) Sub-paragraph (1) above has effect subject to section 1(2) of this Act; and

- (*a*) notwithstanding the provisions of that sub-paragraph, a member of the Commission who is immediately before the commencement of this Schedule the chairman of the Commissioners appointed under section 3 of the Development and Road Improvement Funds Act 1909 shall be the first chairman of the Commission; and

1909 c. 47.

- (*b*) a person who is a member by virtue of section 1(2) of this Act may, notwithstanding the restriction imposed by sub-paragraph (3) above, continue to hold office for the unexpired term of his appointment under the said section 3.

3.—(1) The Commission shall pay to its members such remuneration and allowances as the Secretary of State may, with the approval of the Treasury, determine.

(2) In the case of any such member or past member of the Commission as the Secretary of State may with the approval of the

Treasury determine, the Commission shall pay such pension, allowance or gratuity to or in respect of him, or make such payment towards the provision of such a pension, allowance and gratuity as the Secretary of State may so determine. SCH. 1

(3) Where a person ceases to be a member of the Commission, and it appears to the Secretary of State that there are special circumstances which make it right for that person to receive compensation, the Secretary of State may with the approval of the Treasury direct the Commission to make to that person a payment of such amount as the Secretary of State may with that approval determine.

Staff

4.—(1) There shall be a chief officer of the Commission who shall be appointed by the Commission with the approval of the Secretary of State.

(2) The number of the Commission's employees, and the terms and conditions of their employment, shall be such as the Commission may, with the approval of the Secretary of State given with the consent of the Treasury, determine.

(3) The Commission may in the case of such of its employees as it may, with the approval of the Secretary of State given with the consent of the Treasury, determine—

(*a*) pay such pensions, allowances or gratuities to or in respect of them as may be so determined ;

(*b*) make such payments towards the provision of pensions, allowances or gratuities to or in respect of any of them as may be so determined ; or

(*c*) provide and maintain such schemes (whether contributory or not) for the payment of pensions, allowances or gratuities to or in respect of them as may be so determined ;

and any scheme under this paragraph shall be so framed as to correspond, so far as is appropriate, with the principal civil service pension scheme within the meaning of section 2 of the Superannuation Act 1972 and for the time being in force. 1972 c. 11.

Proceedings and instruments

5.—(1) The Commission shall make rules of procedure requiring its members to disclose any interests that they may have in transactions effected or proposed by the Commission.

(2) The quorum of the Commission and, subject to sub-paragraph (1) above, its procedure shall be such as the Commission may determine.

6. The validity of any proceedings of the Commission shall not be affected by any defect in the appointment of a member or by a vacancy in the office of chairman.

7. A document purporting to be duly executed under the seal of the Commission or to be signed on behalf of the Commission shall, until the contrary is proved, be deemed to be a document so executed or issued.

SCH. 1

Committees

8. If the Commission appoints committees for the purpose of advising it on the discharge of its functions, any payments made by the Commission in respect of expenses or allowances to members of the committees who are not members of the Commission shall be such as the Commission may, with the approval of the Secretary of State given with the consent of the Treasury, determine.

Accounts and information

9.—(1) The Commission shall—

(*a*) keep proper accounts and proper records in relation to the accounts;

(*b*) prepare in respect of each financial year a statement of accounts in such form as the Secretary of State may, with the approval of the Treasury, direct.

(2) The statement of accounts prepared by the Commission for each financial year shall be submitted to the Secretary of State at such time as he shall with the approval of the Treasury direct.

(3) The Secretary of State shall, on or before 30th November in any year, send to the Comptroller and Auditor General the statement of accounts prepared by the Commission under sub-paragraph (1) above for the financial year last ended.

(4) The Comptroller and Auditor General shall examine, certify and report on the statement of accounts sent to him under sub-paragraph (3) above and shall lay copies of the statement and of his report before each House of Parliament.

(5) In this paragraph " financial year " means the period beginning with the day on which this Schedule comes into force and ending with 31st March following that day and each successive period of twelve months.

10. The Commission shall provide the Secretary of State with such information relating to its activities or proposed activities as he may from time to time require, and shall permit any person authorised by the Secretary of State to inspect and make copies of its accounts, books, documents or papers.

11.—(1) As soon as possible after the end of each financial year (within the meaning of paragraph 9 above) the Commission shall make to the Secretary of State a report on the exercise of its functions during that year.

(2) The report for any financial year shall set out any direction given to the Commission by the Secretary of State under section 1(8) of this Act during that year.

(3) The Secretary of State shall lay before each House of Parliament a copy of every report made by the Commission under this paragraph.

House of Commons disqualification

SCH. 1

12. In Part II of Schedule 1 to the House of Commons Disqualification Act 1975 (bodies of which all members are disqualified under that Act), in the entry relating to the Development Commission, the words " established under the Development and Road Improvement Funds Act 1909 " shall cease to have effect. 1975 c. 24.

Transfer of property etc.

13.—(1) On the day on which this Schedule comes into force all the property, rights and liabilities to which the Development Commissioners appointed under the Development and Road Improvement Funds Act 1909 (" the unincorporated Commission ") were entitled or subject immediately before that day shall by virtue of this paragraph become property, rights and liabilities of the Commission. 1909 c. 47.

(2) This paragraph shall have effect to transfer to the Commission any rights and liabilities of the unincorporated Commission under contracts of employment.

(3) For the purpose of determining the length of service as an employee of the Commission of any person who becomes its employee by virtue of this paragraph, any service with the unincorporated Commission shall be treated as service with the Commission.

14. Every document referring to the unincorporated Commission shall be construed as if for that reference there were substituted, in relation to anything falling to be done or occurring on or after the day on which this Schedule comes into force, a reference to the Commission.

15. Anything done by or in relation to the unincorporated Commission and having effect immediately before the day on which this Schedule comes into force shall so far as is required for continuing its effect thereafter be treated as if it had been done by or in relation to the Commission; and in particular any legal proceedings then pending to which the unincorporated Commission is a party may be continued by or in relation to the Commission.

16. The Commission shall as soon as possible after the day on which this Schedule comes into force make to the Secretary of State a report on the proceedings of the unincorporated Commission since the end of the period for which the last report under section 4(6) of the Development and Road Improvement Funds Act 1909 was made; and the Secretary of State shall lay a copy of the report before each House of Parliament.

The development fund

17.—(1) The assets and liabilities, immediately before the day on which this Schedule comes into force, of the development fund established under section 2 of the Development and Road Improvement Funds Act 1909 shall on that day become assets and liabilities of the Commission.

Sch. 1

(2) The reference in sub-paragraph (1) above to the assets of the development fund includes a reference to any right of the Secretary of State under the terms of an advance made under Part I of the Development and Road Improvement Funds Act 1909; and accordingly, so far as may be necessary for giving effect to this paragraph, any reference in those terms to the Secretary of State shall be construed as a reference to the Commission.

1909 c. 47.

(3) The reference in sub-paragraph (1) above to the liabilities of the development fund is a reference to liabilities falling to be discharged by payments out of the development fund.

(4) The Secretary of State may with the approval of the Treasury give the Commission directions as to the application of any sums received by the Commission by virtue of this paragraph, and the Commission shall comply with any such directions.

18.—(1) The Secretary of State shall, not later than eight months after the day on which this Schedule comes into force, prepare and send to the Comptroller and Auditor General an account showing the receipts into and payments out of the development fund in the period between the end of the financial year for which the last account under section 2(4) of the Development and Road Improvement Funds Act 1909 was prepared and the day on which this Schedule comes into force.

(2) The Comptroller and Auditor General shall examine, certify and report on the account sent to him under sub-paragraph (1) above and shall lay copies of the statement and of his report before each House of Parliament.

SCHEDULE 2

Section 4.

Treasury Guarantees

Act	Provision amended	Borrowers
The Coal Industry Nationalisation Act 1946 (c. 59).	Section 27(4).	The National Coal Board.
The Electricity Act 1957 (c. 48).	Section 17(1).	The Electricity Council, the Central Electricity Generating Board and Area Boards.
The Transport Act 1962 (c. 46).	Section 21(1).	The British Railways Board, the British Transport Docks Board, the British Waterways Board, the National Bus Company and the Scottish Transport Group.
The New Towns (Scotland) Act 1968 (c. 16).	Section 38A(1).	New town development corporations.
The Post Office Act 1969 (c. 48).	Section 38(1).	The Post Office.
The Gas Act 1972 (c. 60).	Section 22(1).	The British Gas Corporation.
The Water Act 1973 (c. 37).	Schedule 3, paragraph 36(1).	Water authorities and the National Water Council.
The Housing Act 1974 (c. 44).	Section 8(1).	The Housing Corporation.
The Industry Act 1975 (c. 68).	Schedule 2, paragraph 4(1).	The National Enterprise Board.
The Scottish Development Agency Act 1975 (c. 69).	Schedule 2, paragraph 6(1).	The Scottish Development Agency.
The Welsh Development Agency Act 1975 (c. 70).	Schedule 3, paragraph 6(1).	The Welsh Development Agency.
The Petroleum and Submarine Pipe-lines Act 1975 (c. 74).	Section 8(1).	The British National Oil Corporation.
The Airports Authority Act 1975 (c. 78).	Section 7(1).	The British Airports Authority.
The Development of Rural Wales Act 1976 (c. 75).	Section 10(1).	The Development Board for Rural Wales.
The Aircraft and Shipbuilding Industries Act 1977 (c. 3).	Section 13(1).	British Shipbuilders.
The British Airways Board Act 1977 (c. 13).	Section 11(1).	The British Airways Board.
The Local Government, Planning and Land Act 1980 (c. 65).	Schedule 21, paragraph 2(1).	The Land Authority for Wales.
The Local Government, Planning and Land Act 1980 (c. 65).	Schedule 31, paragraph 5(1).	Urban development corporations.

SCH. 2

Act	Provision amended	Borrowers
The English Industrial Estates Corporation Act 1981 (c. 13).	Section 5(1).	The English Industrial Estates Corporation.
The British Telecommunications Act 1981 (c. 38).	Section 29(1).	British Telecommunications.
The Civil Aviation Act 1982 (c. 16).	Section 14(1).	The Civil Aviation Authority.
The Iron and Steel Act 1982 (c. 25).	Section 21(1).	The British Steel Corporation.
The Local Government Finance Act 1982 (c. 32).	Schedule 3, paragraph 11(1).	The Audit Commission for Local Authorities in England and Wales.

SCHEDULE 3

Section 8.

Enactments Repealed

Chapter	Short title	Extent of repeal
1 & 2 Vict. c. 120.	The Tin Duties Act 1838.	The whole Act.
32 & 33 Vict. c. 44.	The Greenwich Hospital Act 1869.	Section 9.
9 Edw. 7. c. 47.	The Development and Road Improvement Funds Act 1909.	Part I. Section 19. The Schedule.
10 Edw. 7 & 1 Geo. 5. c. 7.	The Development and Road Improvement Funds Act 1910.	The whole Act.
1 & 2 Geo. 5. c. 49.	The Small Landholders (Scotland) Act 1911.	In Schedule 1, the reference to the Development and Road Improvement Funds Acts 1909 and 1910.
6 & 7 Geo. 5. c. 38.	The Small Holding Colonies Act 1916.	In section 3, the words " or the Development and Road Improvement Funds Act, 1909,". In section 5(1), the words " or to be acquired ".
9 & 10 Geo. 6. c. 49.	The Acquisition of Land (Authorisation Procedure) Act 1946.	In Schedule 4, the entries relating to the Development and Road Improvement Funds Act 1909.
9 & 10 Eliz. 2. c. 33.	The Land Compensation Act 1961.	Section 8(7)(*b*).
1963 c. 51.	The Land Compensation (Scotland) Act 1963.	Section 15(7)(*b*).
1972 c. 11.	The Superannuation Act 1972.	In Schedule 6, paragraph 4.
1975 c. 24.	The House of Commons Disqualification Act 1975.	In Part II of Schedule 1, in the entry relating to the Development Commission, the words " established under the Development and Road Improvement Funds Act 1909 ".
1981 c. 13.	The English Industrial Estates Corporation Act 1981.	Section 3(*a*).

Diseases of Fish Act 1983

1983 CHAPTER 30

An Act to make further provision for preventing the spread of disease among fish, including shellfish and fish bred or reared in the course of fish farming. [13th May 1983]

BE IT ENACTED by the Queen's most Excellent Majesty, by and with the advice and consent of the Lords Spiritual and Temporal, and Commons, in this present Parliament assembled, and by the authority of the same, as follows:—

Amendments of 1937 *Act*

1.—(1) In the Diseases of Fish Act 1937 (" the 1937 Act ") section 1 (restriction on importation of live fish and eggs of fish) shall be amended as follows. Importation of live salmon. 1937 c. 33.

(2) In subsection (1) (unlawful to import or bring into Great Britain any live fish of the salmon family) there shall be inserted at the beginning " Subject to subsection (6) of this section ".

(3) At the end of the section there shall be inserted—

" (6) Subsection (1) of this section shall not apply to any fish of a description specified in an order made by the Minister under this subsection.

(7) The description may be made by reference to species, place of origin or any other factor.

(8) Where an order under subsection (6) of this section has effect in relation to any fish, subsections (2) to (5) of this section shall have effect as if it were a freshwater fish.

(9) The power to make an order under subsection (6) of this section shall be exercisable by statutory instrument, and no such order shall be made unless a draft of the order has been laid before and approved by resolution of each House of Parliament.

(10) An order under subsection (6) of this section may be varied or revoked by a subsequent order made under that subsection."

Infected waters.

2. The following shall be substituted for section 2 of the 1937 Act (provisions as to infected areas)—

" Power to designate areas.

2.—(1) If, at any time, the Minister has reasonable grounds for suspecting that any inland or marine waters are or may become infected waters, he may by order designate the waters and such land adjacent to them as he considers appropriate in the circumstances; and in the following provisions of this section 'designated area' means anything designated by an order under this section.

(2) The Minister may, to such extent as he considers practicable and desirable for the purpose of preventing the spread of infection among fish, by the same or a subsequent order—

(*a*) prohibit or regulate the taking into or out of the designated area of such of the following (or of such description of them) as may be specified in the order, namely, live fish, live eggs of fish and foodstuff for fish;

(*b*) regulate the movement within the area of such of those things (or of such description of them) as may be specified in the order.

(3) Any person who is the occupier of any inland waters in a designated area, or carries on the business of fish farming in any marine waters in such an area, shall be entitled, on application, to be supplied by the Minister free of charge with a report of the evidence on which the order was made.

This subsection does not apply to Scotland.

(4) In Scotland any person who—

(*a*) is the occupier of any inland waters;

(*b*) carries on the business of fish farming in any marine waters;

(*c*) has a right to fish for salmon in any marine waters; or (*d*) has a right of fishing in any private non-navigable marine waters,

which are in a designated area, shall be entitled, on application, to be supplied by the Secretary of State free of charge with a report of the evidence on which the order was made.

(5) Any order under this section shall be published in the prescribed manner and may be varied or revoked by a subsequent order made under this section.

(6) If any person intentionally contravenes any provision of an order under this section he shall be guilty of an offence.

Designated areas: direction to remove fish.

2A.—(1) Where an order is in force under section 2 of this Act, the Minister may serve a notice in writing on—

(*a*) any occupier of inland waters situated in the designated area (that is, the area designated by the order);

(*b*) any person carrying on the business of fish farming in marine waters situated in the designated area.

(2) A notice served on a person under subsection (1)(*a*) of this section may direct him to take such practicable steps as are specified in the notice to secure the removal of dead or dying fish from the waters concerned, and may regulate the manner in which any fish removed from the waters, and any parts of such fish, are to be disposed of.

(3) A notice served on a person under subsection (1)(*b*) of this section may direct him to take such practicable steps as are specified in the notice to secure the removal of dead or dying fish from any cage which is owned or possessed by him, is used for the purposes of the business and is situated in the waters concerned, and may regulate the manner in which any fish removed from such a cage, and any parts of such fish, are to be disposed of.

(4) No notice may be served under subsection (1)(*a*) of this section in respect of waters in the area of a water authority, not being a fish farm.

(5) If the Minister is satisfied that a direction contained in a notice served under this section has not been complied with within the time specified in the

notice, he may authorise an inspector to carry out the direction, and any expenses reasonably incurred by the inspector in so doing shall be recoverable by the Minister from the person upon whom the notice was served; and if any person intentionally does any act which is prohibited by such a notice, he shall be guilty of an offence unless he shows that he did not know that the act was so prohibited.

Designated areas: authority to remove fish.

2B.—(1) Where an order is in force under section 2 of this Act, the Minister, if he is satisfied that for the protection against disease of the stock of fish in any waters it is necessary to do so, may by a notice served under section 2A of this Act or otherwise in writing give authority falling within subsection (2) or (3) of this section; and in those subsections 'the designated area' means the area designated by the order.

(2) Authority falling within this subsection is authority to any occupier of inland waters situated in the designated area to remove, notwithstanding anything in any agreement to the contrary, any fish (or any fish of a description specified in the authorisation) from the waters, and to do so by such agents and by such methods (including methods otherwise illegal) as the Minister considers to be most expedient for the purpose.

(3) Authority falling within this subsection is authority to any person carrying on the business of fish farming in marine waters situated in the designated area to remove, notwithstanding anything in any agreement to the contrary, any fish (or any fish of a description specified in the authorisation) from any cage which is owned or possessed by him, is used for the purposes of the business and is situated in the waters, and to do so by such agents and by such methods (including methods otherwise illegal) as the Minister considers to be most expedient for the purpose.

(4) No authority may be given as mentioned in subsection (2) of this section in respect of waters in the area of a water authority, not being a fish farm.

(5) Where a person has in pursuance of an authority under this section removed any fish, he shall comply with any directions given to him by the Minister as to the manner in which the fish, and any parts of such fish, are to be disposed of; and, if he

intentionally fails to comply with any such directions, he shall be guilty of an offence."

Infected waters: preliminary precautions.

3. The following shall be substituted for section 4 of the 1937 Act (preliminary precautions where waters of fish farm are suspected to be infected)—

" Preliminary precautions: inland waters.

4.—(1) If an inspector has reasonable grounds for suspecting that any inland waters which are the waters of any fish farm are infected waters, he may serve the prescribed notice upon the occupier of the fish farm and (if the inspector serves such a notice) he shall report the facts to the Minister.

(2) Where a notice has been served under subsection (1) of this section—

(*a*) no live fish and no live eggs of fish shall, without the permission of the Minister, be taken into or out of the fish farm, and

(*b*) no foodstuff for fish shall, without the permission of the Minister, be taken out of the fish farm,

until after the expiration of thirty days from the service of the notice, unless before the expiration of that period the occupier receives from the Minister a written intimation that such permission is no longer required.

(3) Where a notice has been served upon an occupier under subsection (1) of this section, the Minister may if he thinks it desirable authorise an inspector to serve a further prescribed notice upon the occupier so long as no written intimation under subsection (2) above has been given to the occupier; and if the inspector does so before the expiration of thirty days from the service of the first notice, that subsection shall have effect in relation to the fish farm concerned as if for ' thirty ' there were substituted ' sixty '.

(4) A person who intentionally takes any fish, eggs or foodstuff into or out of a fish farm while the taking is prohibited by this section shall be guilty of an offence, unless he shows that he did not know that the taking was prohibited.

(5) If any person entitled to take fish from any inland waters, or employed for the purpose of having the care of any inland waters, has reasonable grounds for suspecting that the waters are infected waters,

it shall be his duty forthwith to report the facts in writing to the Minister or, if the waters are not a fish farm, to the water authority in whose area the waters are situated; and if without reasonable excuse he fails to do so, he shall be guilty of an offence.

This subsection does not apply to Scotland.

(6) In Scotland if any person entitled to take fish from any inland waters, or employed for the purpose of having the care of any inland waters, has reasonable grounds for suspecting that the waters are infected waters, it shall be his duty forthwith to report the facts in writing to the Secretary of State, or, if the waters are situated in the area of a district board and are not a fish farm, to the board; and if without reasonable excuse he fails to do so, he shall be guilty of an offence.

Preliminary precautions: marine waters.

4A.—(1) If an inspector has reasonable grounds for suspecting that any marine waters are infected waters—

(*a*) he may serve, upon any person who owns or possesses a cage which is situated in the waters and is used by him for the purposes of a business of fish farming carried on by him, the prescribed notice specifying the waters suspected to be infected waters, and

(*b*) if the inspector serves such a notice, he shall report the facts to the Minister,

and in the following provisions of this section 'the farmer' means the person so served.

(2) Where a notice has been served under subsection (1) of this section—

(*a*) no live fish and no live eggs of fish shall, without the permission of the Minister, be taken into or out of any cage which is situated in the waters specified in the notice and is used by the farmer for the purposes of a business of fish farming carried on by him, and

(*b*) no foodstuff for fish shall, without the permission of the Minister, be taken out of any such cage,

until after the expiration of thirty days from the service of the notice, unless before the expiration of that period the farmer receives from the Minister a written intimation that such permission is no longer required.

(3) Where a notice has been served upon a farmer under subsection (1) of this section, the Minister may if he thinks it desirable authorise an inspector to serve a further prescribed notice upon the farmer so long as no written intimation under subsection (2) above has been given to the farmer; and if the inspector does so before the expiration of thirty days from the service of the first notice, that subsection shall have effect in relation to any cage concerned as if for ' thirty ' there were substituted ' sixty '.

(4) A person who intentionally takes any fish, eggs or foodstuff into or out of a cage while the taking is prohibited by this section shall be guilty of an offence, unless he shows that he did not know that the taking was prohibited.

(5) If any person who—

(*a*) owns or possesses a cage which is situated in marine waters and is used by him for the purposes of a business of fish farming carried on by him, or

(*b*) is employed for the purpose of having the care of a cage so situated and used for the purposes of a business of fish farming,

has reasonable grounds for suspecting that the waters in which the cage is situated are infected waters, it shall be his duty forthwith to report the facts in writing to the Minister; and if without reasonable excuse he fails to do so, he shall be guilty of an offence.

(6) In Scotland if any person who—

(*a*) has a right to fish for salmon in any marine waters; or

(*b*) has a right of fishing in any private non-navigable marine waters; or

(*c*) is employed for the purpose of having the care of any waters mentioned in paragraph (*a*) or (*b*) above,

has reasonable grounds for suspecting that the waters (excluding any marine waters in which a cage used for the purposes of a business of fish farming is situated) are infected waters, it shall be his duty forthwith to report the facts in writing to the Secretary of State; and if without reasonable excuse he fails to do so, he shall be guilty of an offence."

Definitions.

4.—(1) Section 10(1) of the 1937 Act (interpretation) shall be amended as mentioned in subsections (2) to (4) below.

(2) The following shall be inserted at the appropriate places—

" 'business of fish farming' means business of keeping live fish (whether or not for profit) with a view to their sale or to their transfer to other waters ;"

" 'cage' means any structure for containing live fish ;"

" 'district board' has the same meaning as in the Salmon Fisheries (Scotland) Acts 1828 to 1868 ;"

" 'fish' does not include shellfish but otherwise means fish of any kind ;"

" 'inland waters' means waters within Great Britain which do not form part of the sea or of any creek, bay or estuary or of any river as far as the tide flows ;"

" 'marine waters' means waters (other than inland waters) within the seaward limits of the territorial sea adjacent to Great Britain ;"

" 'shellfish' includes crustaceans and molluscs of any kind ;".

(3) In the definition of " fish farm " the words " of the salmon family, live freshwater fish " shall be omitted and in the definition of " waters " the words " of the salmon family or live freshwater fish " shall be omitted.

(4) In the definition of " land " for " water " there shall be substituted " inland waters ", and in the definition of " occupier " for " any waters " there shall be substituted " any inland waters ".

(5) In section 10(2) of the 1937 Act (" occupier ") for " any waters " (in both places) there shall be substituted " any inland waters ".

(6) For section 13 of the 1937 Act (power to extend Act by Order in Council to other diseases) there shall be substituted—

" Power to amend definition of 'infected'.

13.—(1) The Minister may by order add to or remove any disease for the time being set out in the definition of 'infected' in section 10(1) of this Act.

(2) The power to make an order under this section shall be exercisable by statutory instrument subject to annulment in pursuance of a resolution of either House of Parliament."

Further amendments of 1937 Act.

5. The Schedule to this Act (which contains further amendments of the 1937 Act, including amendments consequential on the preceding provisions of this Act) shall have effect.

Shellfish

Taking of shellfish from certain areas. 1967 c. 83.

6.—(1) In the Sea Fisheries (Shellfish) Act 1967 (" the 1967 Act ") in section 12 (power to prohibit deposit of shellfish) there shall be inserted after subsection (3)—

" (3A) Where the appropriate Minister considers it desirable for the purpose of preventing the spread of diseases or pests carried by shellfish, an order under this section may also prohibit the taking from any waters or land designated by the order of shellfish of any description or of shellfish of a description specified in the order."

(2) In subsection (4) of that section (deposit under licence) for " the prohibition " there shall be substituted " any prohibition " and after "deposited " there shall be inserted " or (as the case may be) taken ".

(3) In section 14(3)(*a*) of the 1967 Act (power of entry) after " order " there shall be inserted " in pursuance of subsection (1) of that section ".

Information about fish farming

Power to require information.

7.—(1) If it appears to the Minister necessary to do so for the purpose of obtaining information with a view to preventing the spread of disease among fish, he may make an order under this section.

(2) An order under this section may require any person who occupies an inland fish farm for the purposes of a business of fish farming carried on by him (whether or not for profit)—

(*a*) to register the business in a register kept for the purpose by the Minister,

(*b*) to furnish in writing to the Minister such information as may be specified in the order in relation to the farm and to fish, eggs of fish and foodstuff for fish,

(*c*) to compile such records as may be so specified in relation to the matters mentioned in paragraph (*b*) above, and

(*d*) to retain for such period (not exceeding 3 years) as may be so specified any records compiled in accordance with paragraph (*c*) above.

In this subsection " fish " does not include shellfish.

(3) An order under this section may require any person who owns or possesses any cage, pontoon or other structure which is anchored or moored in marine waters and is used by him for the

purposes of a business of fish farming carried on by him (whether or not for profit)—

(*a*) to register the business in a register kept for the purpose by the Minister,

(*b*) to furnish in writing to the Minister such information as may be specified in the order in relation to any such cage, pontoon or other structure and to fish, eggs of fish and foodstuff for fish,

(*c*) to compile such records as may be so specified in relation to the matters mentioned in paragraph (*b*) above, and

(*d*) to retain for such period (not exceeding 3 years) as may be so specified any records compiled in accordance with paragraph (*c*) above.

In this subsection " fish " does not include shellfish.

(4) An order under this section may require any person who carries on a business of shellfish farming (whether or not for profit)—

(*a*) to register the business in a register kept for the purpose by the Minister,

(*b*) to furnish in writing to the Minister such information as may be specified in the order in relation to any activity carried on (whether in marine or inland waters or on land) for the purpose of cultivating or propagating shellfish in the course of the business, and in relation to shellfish deposited in or on or taken from such waters or land in the course of the business,

(*c*) to compile such records as may be so specified in relation to the matters mentioned in paragraph (*b*) above, and

(*d*) to retain for such period (not exceeding 3 years) as may be so specified any records compiled in accordance with paragraph (*c*) above.

(5) An order under this section may require any person registering a business as mentioned in subsection (2)(*a*), (3)(*a*) or (4)(*a*) above to pay to the Minister in respect of each registration such fee (complying with subsection (6) below) as may be specified in the order.

(6) The fee shall be such as the Minister may determine with the Treasury's approval but shall not exceed the cost to the Minister of effecting the registration.

(7) Any person authorised by the Minister may, on producing on demand evidence of his authority, require the production of, and inspect and take copies of, any records which a

person is required to retain by virtue of an order under this section.

(8) In this section—

"fish farming" means the keeping of live fish with a view to their sale or to their transfer to other waters;

"inland fish farm" means any place where inland waters are used for the keeping of live fish with a view to their sale or to their transfer to other waters (whether inland or not);

"inland waters" means waters within Great Britain which do not form part of the sea or of any creek, bay or estuary or of any river as far as the tide flows;

"marine waters" means waters (other than inland waters) within the seaward limits of the territorial sea adjacent to Great Britain;

"the Minister" means—

(*a*) in relation to England, and any marine waters adjacent to England, the Minister of Agriculture, Fisheries and Food;

(*b*) in relation to Wales, and any marine waters adjacent to Wales, the Secretary of State;

(*c*) in relation to Scotland (including the marine waters thereof), the Secretary of State;

"shellfish" includes crustaceans and molluscs of any kind, and includes any brood, ware, half-ware, spat or spawn of shellfish;

"shellfish farming" means the cultivation or propagation of shellfish (whether in marine or inland waters or on land) with a view to their sale or to their transfer to other waters or land.

(9) The power to make an order under this section shall be exercisable by statutory instrument subject to annulment in pursuance of a resolution of either House of Parliament.

Information: enforcement.

8.—(1) Any person who—

(*a*) fails without reasonable excuse to comply with a requirement of an order under section 7 above (other than a requirement mentioned in subsection (5) of that section), or

(*b*) in purported compliance with a requirement of an order under section 7 above knowingly furnishes any information or compiles a record which is false in a material particular, or (*c*) knowingly alters a record compiled in compliance with a requirement of an order under section 7 above so that the record becomes false in a material particular, or

(*d*) fails without reasonable excuse to comply with a requirement imposed by virtue of section 7(7) above, or

(*e*) intentionally obstructs a person in the exercise of his powers under section 7(7) above,

shall be guilty of an offence and liable on summary conviction to a fine not exceeding level 4 on the standard scale (as defined in section 75 of the Criminal Justice Act 1982). 1982 c. 48.

(2) Where an offence under this section which has been committed by a body corporate is proved to have been committed with the consent or connivance of, or to be attributable to any neglect on the part of, a director, manager, secretary or other similar officer of the body corporate, or any person who was purporting to act in any such capacity, he, as well as the body corporate, shall be guilty of that offence and shall be liable to be proceeded against and punished accordingly.

(3) For the purposes of and incidental to the jurisdiction of any magistrates' court or, in Scotland, of the sheriff, any offence under this section committed in, or in relation to anything in, the territorial sea adjacent to Great Britain shall be taken to have been committed in any place in which the offender may for the time being be found.

Disclosure of information.

9.—(1) Information (including information in records) obtained by any person in pursuance of section 7 above or an order under that section shall not be disclosed except—

(*a*) with the written consent of the person by whom the information was provided, or

(*b*) in the form of a summary of similar information obtained from a number of persons, where the summary is so framed as not to enable particulars relating to any one person or business to be ascertained from it, or

(*c*) for the purpose of any criminal proceedings or for the purpose of a report of any such proceedings.

(2) Any person who discloses any information in contravention of subsection (1) above shall be guilty of an offence and liable on summary conviction to a fine not exceeding level 4 on the standard scale (as defined in section 75 of the Criminal Justice Act 1982).

(3) In this section " the Minister " has the same meaning as in section 7 above.

General

10. There shall be paid out of money provided by Parliament— Finance.

(*a*) the expenses of any Minister of the Crown incurred in consequence of this Act;

(*b*) any increase attributable to this Act in the sums so payable under any other Act.

11.—(1) This Act may be cited as the Diseases of Fish Act 1983. Short title, etc.

(2) This Act (except this section) shall come into force on such day as the Minister of Agriculture, Fisheries and Food and the Secretary of State acting jointly may by order made by statutory instrument appoint, and an order under this subsection may appoint different days for different provisions or different purposes.

(3) An order under subsection (2) above may include such transitionals or savings as appear to that Minister and the Secretary of State to be necessary or expedient in connection with the provisions brought into force by the order, but nothing shall be so included if it would conflict with subsection (4) or (5) below.

(4) The definitions of " infected " and " infected waters " contained in section 10(1) of the 1937 Act immediately before the coming into force of section 4(6) above shall continue to have effect on and after its coming into force (subject to any order made, after its coming into force, under section 13 of the 1937 Act).

(5) The coming into force of sub-paragraph (2) of paragraph 6 of the Schedule to this Act shall not affect the punishment for an offence committed before its coming into force.

(6) This Act does not extend to Northern Ireland.

Section 5.

SCHEDULE

FURTHER AMENDMENTS OF 1937 ACT

1. In section 1(3) of the 1937 Act (Minister may grant licences as to certain imported fish) for the words from " Minister " (in the first place) to " Minister ") " (in the second place) there shall be substituted " Minister ".

2.—(1) Section 3 of the 1937 Act (functions of water authorities as to infected waters) shall be amended as follows.

(2) In subsection (1) (water authority to report to Minister if waters suspected to be infected) for "any waters " (in both places) there shall be substituted " any inland waters ".

(3) For subsection (2) (Minister may authorise water authority to remove fish) there shall be substituted—

> " (2) Where an order is in force in relation to an area under section 2 of this Act, the Minister may authorise any water authority to remove any fish (or any fish of a description specified in the authorisation) from any inland waters in that area (not being a fish farm) and to do so by such agents and by such methods (including methods otherwise illegal) as he considers to be most expedient for the purpose."

(4) In subsection (3)(*b*) (returns to Minister) the words from " and " to the end shall be omitted.

3. In section 5 of the 1937 Act (Minister's duty to examine waters on demand of water authority or occupier to discover whether waters are infected) for " occupier of any waters " there shall be substituted " occupier of any inland waters ".

4.—(1) Section 6 of the 1937 Act (powers of entry and inspection) shall be amended as follows.

(2) At the end of subsection (1) (power to authorise entry on land) there shall be inserted—

> " The preceding provisions of this subsection shall have effect for the purpose of authorising the boarding of and entry into a cage situated in marine waters and used for the purposes of a business of fish farming as they have effect for the purpose of authorising entry on land."

(3) In subsection (2) (power of inspector to inspect waters, take samples and enter land) after " power " there shall be inserted " (to the extent that he does not have it apart from this subsection) ".

(4) For paragraph (*a*) of subsection (2) there shall be substituted—

> " (*a*) to inspect any inland waters in which fish or the eggs of fish or foodstuff for fish are likely to be found, and to take therefrom samples of any fish or of any such eggs or foodstuff or of water, mud, vegetation or other matter ;

(*aa*) to inspect any cage situated in marine waters and used for the purposes of a business of fish farming, and to take therefrom samples of any fish or of any eggs of fish or of foodstuff for fish or of water or other matter;

(*ab*) to inspect any marine waters in which fish of the salmon family or freshwater fish or the eggs of such fish or foodstuff for fish are likely to be found, and to take therefrom samples of any such fish, eggs or foodstuff or of water, mud, vegetation or other matter; ".

(5) After paragraph (*b*) of subsection (2) there shall be inserted—

" (*c*) for the purpose of exercising any powers or performing any duties under this Act, to board and enter, upon production on demand of his authority, any cage situated in marine waters and used for the purposes of a business of fish farming."

(6) In subsection (2) for " obstructs " there shall be substituted " intentionally obstructs ".

(7) In subsection (3) (compensation to occupier where non-infected fish taken from waters by inspector) for " any waters " there shall be substituted " any inland waters ".

(8) After subsection (3) there shall be inserted—

" (3A) If in any sample of fish taken from a cage by an inspector under the powers conferred by subsection (2)(*aa*) of this section none is found to be infected, the Minister shall pay to the person who owns or possesses the cage and uses it for the purposes of a business of fish farming carried on by him a sum equal to the market value of the fish taken in that sample."

(9) In subsection (4) for " obstructs " there shall be substituted " intentionally obstructs ".

5.—(1) Section 7 of the 1937 Act (service of notices etc.) shall be amended as follows.

(2) In subsection (1) (service of notice on occupier of waters) for " occupier of any waters " there shall be substituted " occupier of any inland waters ".

(3) After subsection (1) there shall be inserted—

" (1A) Any notice required or authorised to be served for the purposes of this Act upon a person carrying on the business of fish farming in marine waters may be served by delivering it to him or by sending it by registered post to his usual or last-known address."

(4) In subsection (2) (servant's or agent's authority) for " occupier of any waters " there shall be substituted " occupier of any inland waters ".

6.—(1) Section 8 of the 1937 Act (penalties and legal proceedings) shall be amended as follows.

(2) In subsection (1) (amount of fine) for the words from the beginning to " ; and " there shall be substituted " Any person guilty of an offence under this Act shall be liable on summary conviction to a fine not exceeding level 4 on the standard scale (as defined in section 75 of the Criminal Justice Act 1982) ; and ".

1982 c. 48.

(3) In subsection (2) (water authorities' power to enforce Act as respects waters in their areas) for " waters " there shall be substituted " inland waters ".

(4) In subsection (3) (prosecution of offences in Scotland etc.) for " Scotland " there shall be substituted " inland waters in Scotland " and for " waters " there shall be substituted " inland waters ".

(5) After subsection (3) there shall be inserted—

> " (4) For the purposes of and incidental to the jurisdiction of any magistrates' court or, in Scotland, of the sheriff, any offence under this Act committed in the territorial sea adjacent to Great Britain shall be taken to have been committed in any place in which the offender may for the time being be found."

7. In section 9(*b*) of the 1937 Act (regulations may prescribe manner of publishing orders made under the Act) after " Act " there shall be inserted "(other than those made under section 1(6) or 13) ".

8. In section 10(1) of the 1937 Act (interpretation) after the definition of " marine waters " there shall be inserted—

> " ' the Minister ' means—
>
> (*a*) in relation to England, and any marine waters adjacent to England, the Minister of Agriculture, Fisheries and Food ;
>
> (*b*) in relation to Wales, and any marine waters adjacent to Wales, the Secretary of State ;
>
> (*c*) in relation to Scotland (including the marine waters thereof), the Secretary of State ; ".

9. For section 11 of the 1937 Act (application to Scotland) there shall be substituted—

> " 11. In the application of this Act to Scotland, for references to a water authority there shall be substituted references to a district board.".

Coroners' Juries Act 1983

1983 CHAPTER 31

An Act to make fresh provision with respect to the qualifications of persons eligible to serve on coroners' juries; to provide criminal penalties for evasion of service on a coroner's jury; to amend section 26 of the Coroners (Amendment) Act 1926; and for connected purposes.

[13th May 1983]

BE IT ENACTED by the Queen's most Excellent Majesty, by and with the advice and consent of the Lords Spiritual and Temporal, and Commons, in this present Parliament assembled, and by the authority of the same, as follows:—

Qualifications of jurors. 1887 c. 71.

1. The following section shall be inserted in the Coroners Act 1887 after section 3—

" Qualifications of jurors.

3A.—(1) A person shall not be qualified to serve as a juror at an inquest held by a coroner unless he is for the time being qualified to serve as a juror in the Crown Court, the High Court and county courts in accordance with section 1 of the Juries Act 1974. 1974 c. 23.

(2) If a person serves on a jury knowing that he is ineligible for such service under Group A, B or C in Part I of Schedule 1 to that Act he shall be guilty of an offence and liable on summary conviction to a fine not exceeding level 3 on the standard scale.

(3) If a person serves on a jury knowing that he is disqualified for such service under Part II of that Schedule he shall be guilty of an offence and liable on summary conviction to a fine not exceeding level 5 on the standard scale.

(4) The appropriate officer may at any time put or cause to be put to any person who is summoned under section 3 of this Act such questions as he thinks fit in order to establish whether or not the person is qualified to serve as a juror at an inquest.

(5) Where a question is put to any person under subsection (4) of this section, if that person refuses without reasonable excuse to answer, or gives an answer which he knows to be false in a material particular, or recklessly gives an answer which is false in a material particular, he shall be guilty of an offence and liable on summary conviction to a fine not exceeding level 3 on the standard scale.

(6) If any person—

(*a*) duly summoned as a juror at an inquest makes, or causes or permits to be made on his behalf, any false representation to the coroner or the appropriate officer with the intention of evading service as such juror; or

(*b*) makes or causes to be made on behalf of another person who has been so summoned any false representation to the coroner or the appropriate officer with the intention of enabling that other person to evade such service;

he shall be guilty of an offence and liable on summary conviction to a fine not exceeding level 3 on the standard scale.

(7) A coroner may authorise a person to perform the functions conferred on the appropriate officer by subsection (4) of this section and references in this section to the appropriate officer shall be construed as references to the person so authorised.

1982 c. 48.

(8) In this section " the standard scale " has the meaning given by section 75 of the Criminal Justice Act 1982. "

Extension of rule-making power under section 26 of the Act of 1926.

1926 c. 59.

2. In section 26 of the Coroners (Amendment) Act 1926 (power of Lord Chancellor to make procedural rules) the following subsection shall be inserted as subsection (2)—

" (2) Without prejudice to the generality of the preceding provisions of this section, rules under this section may make provision for persons to be excused service as jurors at inquests in such circumstances as the rules may specify. "

3.—(1) This Act may be cited as the Coroners' Juries Act 1983. Citation, commencement etc.

(2) This Act shall come into force on such day as the Secretary of State may by order made by statutory instrument appoint.

(3) In section 3(2) of the Coroners Act 1887 (restriction on eligibility of certain persons to serve on coroners' juries) the words " an officer of the prison or " shall cease to have effect.

(4) Nothing in this Act shall have effect in relation to any inquest begun before the commencement of this Act or held by the coroner of the Queen's household.

(5) This Act shall not extend to Scotland or Northern Ireland.

Marriage Act 1983

1983 CHAPTER 32

An Act to enable marriages of house-bound and detained persons to be solemnized at the place where they reside; and for connected purposes. [13th May 1983]

BE IT ENACTED by the Queen's most Excellent Majesty, by and with the advice and consent of the Lords Spiritual and Temporal, and Commons, in this present Parliament assembled, and by the authority of the same, as follows:—

Marriages in England and Wales

Marriages of house-bound and detained persons in England and Wales.

1949 c. 76.

1.—(1) Subject to the provisions of this Act and the Marriage Act 1949, the marriage of a person who is house-bound or is a detained person may be solemnized in England and Wales, on the authority of a superintendent registrar's certificate issued under Part III of the Marriage Act 1949, at the place where that person usually resides.

(2) For the purposes of this section a person is house-bound if—

(*a*) the notice of his or her marriage given in accordance with section 27 of the Marriage Act 1949 is accompanied by a statement, made in a form prescribed under that Act by a registered medical practitioner not more than fourteen days before that notice is given, that, in his opinion—

(i) by reason of illness or disability, he or she ought not to move or be moved from his or her home or the other place where he or she is at that time, and

(ii) it is likely that it will be the case for at least the three months following the date on which the statement is made that by reason of the illness or disability he or she ought not to move or be moved from that place; and

(*b*) he or she is not a detained person.

(3) For the purposes of this section, a person is a detained person if he or she is for the time being detained—

1983 c. 20. (*a*) otherwise than by virtue of section 2, 4, 5, 35, 36 or 136 of the Mental Health Act 1983 (short term detentions), as a patient in a hospital; or

1952 c. 52. (*b*) in a prison or other place to which the Prison Act 1952 applies.

(4) In subsection (3) above " hospital " and " patient " have the same meanings as in Part II of the Mental Health Act 1983.

(5) For the purposes of this section, a person who is housebound or is a detained person shall be taken, if he or she would not otherwise be, to be usually resident at the place where he or she is for the time being.

(6) Nothing in the preceding provisions of this section shall be taken to relate or have any reference to any marriage according to the usages of the Society of Friends or any marriage between two persons professing the Jewish religion according to the usages of the Jews.

1949 c. 76. (7) Schedule 1 to this Act (amendment of the Marriage Act 1949 in consequence of this section) shall have effect.

Consequential amendments of enactments.

2.—(1) Any reference in the Registration Service Act 1953 to the Marriage Act 1949 includes a reference to that Act as amended by this Act.

1953 c. 37.
1968 c. 14. (2) In Schedule 3 to the Public Expenditure and Receipts Act 1968 (variation of fees payable under certain enactments) the reference to the Marriage Act 1949 includes a reference to that Act as amended by this Act.

1970 c. 34. (3) At the end of subsection (2) of section 1 of the Marriage (Registrar General's Licence) Act 1970 (restrictions on Registrar General's power to issue licences under subsection (1) of that section) there shall be added the words " (disregarding for this purpose the provisions of that Act relating to marriages in pursuance of section 26(1)(*dd*) of that Act) ".

1973 c. 18. (4) In section 11 of the Matrimonial Causes Act 1973 (void marriages) for the words in paragraph (*a*) " the Marriages Acts 1949 to 1970 " there shall be substituted the words " the Marriage Acts 1949 to 1983 ".

Marriages in Northern Ireland

Marriages of house-bound and detained persons in Northern Ireland.

3.—(1) Subject to the provisions of this Act and the enactments relating to marriage in Northern Ireland, the marriage of a person who is house-bound or is a detained person may be solemnized in Northern Ireland on the authority of a licence issued by the Registrar General under section 4 below at the place where that person resides.

(2) Where a marriage is intended to be solemnized on the authority of the Registrar General's licence, notice of the intended marriage must be given in the prescribed form to the registrar of the district in which each party to the intended marriage has resided for at least seven days immediately before the notice is given.

(3) Where a person other than a detained person is to be married at his or her residence in pursuance of subsection (1) above, the notice of marriage required by subsection (2) above shall, where it is given to the registrar of the district in which the person resides, be accompanied by a medical statement relating to him or her made not more than fourteen days before the date on which the notice is given.

(4) In the case of the marriage of a detained person, the notice of marriage required by subsection (2) above shall, where it is given to the registrar of the district in which the detained person resides, be accompanied by a statement made in the prescribed form by the responsible authority not more than twenty-one days before the date on which notice of the marriage is given under that subsection—

(*a*) identifying the establishment where the person is detained; and

(*b*) stating that the responsible authority has no objection to that establishment being specified in the notice of marriage as the place where that marriage is to be solemnized.

(5) Where notice is given under subsection (2) above, the person giving the notice shall give the registrar the prescribed particulars, in the prescribed form, of the person by or before whom the marriage is intended to be solemnized.

(6) The registrar shall not enter the particulars given in the notice of the marriage in the marriage notice book until he has received the statement required by subsection (3) or (4) above and the particulars required by subsection (5) above.

(7) The fact that a registrar has received a statement under subsection (3) or (4) above shall be entered in the marriage notice book.

(8) In subsection (4) above " responsible authority " means—

(*a*) if the person named in the statement is detained in a prison, the governor or other officer for the time being in charge of that prison;

(*b*) if the person named in the statement is detained in a hospital or special accommodation, the Health and Social Services Board administering that hospital or the Department, respectively;

(*c*) if the person named in the statement is detained in a private hospital, the person in charge of that hospital.

(9) For the purposes of this section—

(*a*) a person is house-bound if—

(i) the notice of his or her marriage given in accordance with subsection (2) above to the registrar of the district in which he or she resides is accompanied by a medical statement relating to him or her; and

(ii) he or she is not a detained person; and

(*b*) a person is a detained person if he or she is for the time being detained—

1961 c. 15 (N.I.).

(i) otherwise than by virtue of section 15, 16 or 106 of the Mental Health Act (Northern Ireland) 1961 (short term detentions), as a patient in a hospital; or

(ii) in a prison.

(10) For the purposes of this section, a person who is house-bound or is a detained person shall be taken, if he or she would not otherwise be, to be resident at the place where he or she is for the time being and, in relation to such a person, references in the Marriage Acts, as applied by Schedule 2 to this Act, to his or her dwelling place or usual place of abode shall be construed accordingly.

(11) In this section—

" hospital " has the same meaning as in the Mental Health Act (Northern Ireland) 1961;

" medical statement ", in relation to any person, means a statement made in the prescribed form by a registered medical practitioner that in his opinion, at the time the statement is made—

(*a*) by reason of illness or disability, he or she ought not to move or be moved from the place where he or she is at that time, and

(*b*) it is likely that it will be the case for at least the following three months that by reason of the illness or disability he or she ought not to move or be moved from that place;

"patient" has the same meaning as in the Mental Health Act (Northern Ireland) 1961; 1961 c. 15 (N.I.).

"prison" includes a remand centre and a young offenders centre;

"private hospital" has the same meaning as in the Mental Health Act (Northern Ireland) 1961;

"special accommodation" has the same meaning as in the Mental Health Act (Northern Ireland)1961.

Issue of licence by Registrar General.

4.—(1) Where notice of an intended marriage is given to a registrar under section 3(2) above, the registrar shall—

(*a*) inform the Registrar General; and

(*b*) comply with any directions relating to the notice or the statement or particulars required by section 3(3), (4) or (5) which may be given to him by the Registrar General.

(2) Where the Registrar General—

(*a*) is informed under subsection (1) above of an intended marriage; and

(*b*) is satisfied that a licence should be granted,

he shall issue a licence in the prescribed form authorising the solemnization of the marriage unless—

(i) any lawful impediment to the issue of the licence has been shown to his satisfaction to exist; or

(ii) the issue of the licence has been forbidden under section 18 of the Marriages Act, as applied by Schedule 2 to this Act.

(3) The Registrar General shall send any licence issued by him under subsection (2) above authorising the solemnization of a marriage—

(*a*) subject to paragraph (*b*) below, to the registrar of the district in which the marriage is to be solemnized;

(*b*) where the marriage is to be solemnized in accordance with the rites of the Roman Catholic Church, to the priest who is to solemnize the marriage.

(4) The Registrar General shall not issue a licence under subsection (2) above before the expiration of seven days after the day on which notice of the marriage is entered in the marriage notice book under section 14 of the Marriage Act, as applied by Schedule 2 to this Act.

Solemnization of marriage pursuant to Registrar General's licence.

5.—(1) A marriage to be solemnized on the authority of the Registrar General's licence shall be solemnized, at the wish of the persons to be married—

(*a*) according to such religious form or ceremony as the persons to be married see fit to adopt; or

(*b*) by a ceremony performed by the registrar of the district in which it is solemnized.

(2) A marriage to be solemnized on the authority of the Registrar General's licence shall be solemnized in the presence of—

(*a*) subject to subsection (4) below, the registrar of the district in which it is solemnized; and

(*b*) two witnesses in addition to the person solemnizing the marriage.

(3) Where a marriage is to be solemnized on the authority of the Registrar General's licence the persons to be married shall, subject to subsection (5) below, in some part of the ceremony in the presence of the witnesses and of the registrar of the district in which it is solemnized, make the declaration and say to each other the words set out in section 29 of the Marriages Act.

(4) Subsection (2)(*a*) does not apply to a marriage which is solemnized according to the rites of the Roman Catholic Church.

(5) Subsection (3) does not apply to a marriage solemnized—

(*a*) according to the rites of the Church of Ireland or the Roman Catholic Church; or

(*b*) by the ceremony used by Presbyterians in Northern Ireland; or

(*c*) by the ceremony of any church, denomination or body of Protestant Christians who use a building registered under section 12 of the Marriage Law (Ireland) Amendment Act 1863.

1863 c. 27.

(6) A marriage on the authority of the Registrar General's licence may be solemnized at any time between 8 a.m. and 6 p.m.

Void marriages.

6. If any persons knowingly purport to intermarry in pursuance of section 3 above—

(*a*) in any place other than that specified in the Registrar General's licence; or

(*b*) in the absence of the registrar of the district in which it is solemnized, unless the marriage is solemnized in accordance with the rites of the Roman Catholic Church; or

(*c*) without the Registrar General's licence,

the marriage shall be void.

7.—(1) Any person who knowingly— Offences.

(*a*) purports to solemnize a marriage on the authority of the Registrar General's licence in any place other than that specified in the licence ; or

(*b*) purports to solemnize a marriage on the authority of that licence without the presence of the registrar of the district in which it is solemnized, unless the marriage is solemnized in accordance with the rites of the Roman Catholic Church ; or

(*c*) solemnizes a marriage on the authority of that licence at any other time than between 8 a.m. and 6 p.m. ; or

(*d*) purports to solemnize a marriage on the authority of that licence after the expiration of three months beginning on the day on which notice of the marriage is entered in the marriage notice book under section 14 of the Marriages Act, as applied by Schedule 2 to this Act,

shall be guilty of an offence and liable—

(i) on summary conviction, to a fine not exceeding £1,000 or to imprisonment for a term not exceeding six months, or to both ;

(ii) on conviction on indictment, to a fine or to imprisonment for a term not exceeding three years, or to both.

(2) No prosecution under this section shall be commenced after the expiration of three years from the commission of the offence.

8. Schedule 2 to this Act (application and amendment of Marriage Acts) shall have effect. Application of Marriage Acts.

9. An order under section 1 of the Registration of Births, Deaths and Marriages (Fees, etc.) Act (Northern Ireland) 1955 may make provision with respect to— Fees. 1955 c. 29 (N.I.).

(*a*) the fees payable for licences of the Registrar General under section 4 above and for the performance by registrars of any functions for the purposes of this Act ; and

(*b*) the persons by and to whom such fees are to be paid.

10.—(1) The Department may make regulations prescribing— Regulations.

(*a*) the form of notice of a marriage which is intended to be solemnized on the authority of the Registrar General's licence ;

(*b*) anything which is authorised or required to be prescribed under sections 3 to 9 above, Schedule 2 to this Act or any provision applied by that Schedule.

(2) Regulations under subsection (1) above—

S.I. 1979/1573 (N.I. 12).

(*a*) shall be a statutory rule for the purposes of the Statutory Rules (Northern Ireland) Order 1979;

1954 c. 33 (N.I.).

(*b*) shall be subject to negative resolution (as defined in section 41(6) of the Interpretation Act (Northern Ireland) 1954).

Interpretation and savings (Northern Ireland).

11.—(1) In sections 3 to 10 above and Schedule 2 to this Act—

"the Department" means the Department of Health and Social Services for Northern Ireland;

"the Marriage Acts" means the Acts applied or amended by Schedule 2 to this Act;

1844 c. 81.

"the Marriages Act" means the Marriages (Ireland) Act 1844;

"the Registrar General" means the Registrar General in Northern Ireland or any officer of the Department authorised by it to exercise the functions of the Registrar General for the purposes of this Act;

"the Registrar General's licence" means a licence issued by the Registrar General under section 4 above.

(2) Nothing in sections 3 to 10 above or Schedule 2 to this Act shall be taken to relate or have any reference to—

(*a*) any marriage between two persons professing the Roman Catholic religion according to the rites of the Roman Catholic Church;

(*b*) any marriage according to the usages of the Society of Friends or any marriage between two persons professing the Jewish religion according to the usages of the Jews.

1870 c. 110.

(3) Nothing in sections 3 to 10 above or Schedule 2 to this Act shall affect the right of any person by virtue of section 36 or 37 of the Matrimonial Causes and Marriage Law (Ireland) Amendment Act 1870 to grant special licences to marry at any convenient time at any place or affect the validity of any marriage solemnized on the authority of such a licence.

General

Citation, commencement, etc.

12.—(1) This Act may be cited as the Marriage Act 1983 and this Act as it extends to England and Wales and the Marriages Acts 1949 to 1970 may be cited as the Marriage Acts 1949 to 1983.

(2) Sections 3 to 11 above shall be construed as one with the Acts relating to marriage in Northern Ireland.

(3) Nothing in this Act shall affect any law or custom relating to the marriage of members of the Royal Family.

(4) Nothing in this Act shall affect the right of the Archbishop of Canterbury or any other person by virtue of the Ecclesiastical Licences Act 1533 to grant special licences to marry at any convenient time or place or affect the validity of any marriage solemnized on the authority of such a licence. 1533 c. 21.

(5) This Act shall come into force on such day as the Secretary of State may by order made by statutory instrument appoint, and different days may be appointed for different purposes.

(6) This Act shall not extend to Scotland.

(7) Sections 1 and 2 above and Schedule 1 to this Act, except paragraph 9, shall not extend to Northern Ireland and sections 3 to 11 above and Schedule 2 to this Act, except paragraph 11, shall not extend to England and Wales.

SCHEDULES

Section 1(7).

SCHEDULE 1

AMENDMENT OF MARRIAGE ACT 1949

1949 c. 76.

1. The Marriage Act 1949 shall have effect subject to the following amendments.

2. In section 17 (place of Church of England marriage)—

(*a*) after the words " may be published " there shall be inserted the words " or in the case of a marriage in pursuance of section 26(1)(*dd*) of this Act the place specified in the notice of marriage and certificate as the place where the marriage is to be solemnized " ; and

(*b*) after the words " thereof or " there shall be inserted the words " (wherever the marriage is solemnized) ".

3. In section 25 (void marriages)—

(*a*) at the beginning of paragraph (*a*) there shall be inserted the words " except in the case of a marriage in pursuance of section 26(1)(*dd*) of this Act, " ; and

(*b*) in paragraph (*d*) for the words " or other building specified in the notice of marriage and certificate " there shall be substituted the words " building or other place specified in the notice of marriage and certificate as the place where the marriage is to be solemnized ".

4. In section 26 (marriages which may be solemnized by superintendent registrar's certificate)—

(*a*) in subsection (1) the following paragraph shall be inserted after paragraph (*d*)—

" (*dd*) the marriage (other than a marriage in pursuance of paragraph (*c*) or (*d*) above) of a person who is house-bound or is a detained person at the place where he or she usually resides ; "

and in paragraph (*e*) after the words " Church of England " there shall be inserted the words " in any church or chapel in which banns of matrimony may be published." ; and

(*b*) in subsection (2) after the words " shall not issue a licence " there shall be inserted the words " for a marriage intended to be solemnized at a person's residence in pursuance of subsection (1)(*dd*) of this section or ".

5. In section 27 (notice of marriage)—

(*a*) in subsection (3) after the words " to be married and " there shall be inserted the words " in the case of a marriage intended to be solemnized at a person's residence in pursuance of section 26(1)(*dd*) of this Act, which residence is to be the place of solemnization of the marriage and, in any other case, " ;

(*b*) in subsection (4) after the words " and shall " there shall be inserted the words " subject to section 27A of this Act " ; and (*c*) the following subsection shall be inserted after subsection (6)— SCH. 1

" (7) The superintendent registrar shall be entitled to receive from any person intending to be married in pursuance of section 26(1)(*dd*) of this Act upon whom he attends at a place other than his office in order to be given notice of marriage under this section the sum of £20.".

6. After section 27 there shall be inserted the following section—

" Additional information required in certain cases.

27A.—(1) This section applies in relation to any marriage intended to be solemnized at a person's residence in pursuance of section 26(1)(*dd*) of this Act, and in the following provisions of this section that person is referred to as " the relevant person ".

(2) Where the relevant person is not a detained person, the notice of marriage required by section 27 of this Act shall be accompanied by a medical statement relating to that person made not more than fourteen days before the date on which the notice is given.

(3) Where the relevant person is a detained person, the notice of marriage required by section 27 of this Act shall be accompanied by a statement made in the prescribed form by the responsible authority not more than twenty-one days before the date on which notice of the marriage is given under section 27—

(*a*) identifying the establishment where the person is detained ; and

(*b*) stating that the responsible authority has no objection to that establishment being specified in the notice of marriage as the place where that marriage is to be solemnized.

(4) The person who gives notice of the marriage to the superintendent registrar in accordance with section 27 of this Act shall give the superintendent registrar the prescribed particulars, in the prescribed form, of the person by or before whom the marriage is intended to be solemnized.

(5) The superintendent registrar shall not enter the particulars given in the notice of the marriage in the marriage notice book until he has received the statement and the particulars required by subsections (2) or (3) and (4) of this section.

(6) The fact that a superintendent registrar has received a statement under subsection (2) or (as the case may be) (3) of this section shall be entered in the marriage notice book together with the particulars given in the notice of marriage and any such statement together with the form received under subsection (4) of this section shall be filed and kept with the records of the office of the superintendent registrar or, where notice of marriage is required

SCH. 1

to be given to two superintendent registrars, of either of them.

(7) In this section—

" medical statement ", in relation to any person, means a statement made in the prescribed form by a registered medical practitioner that in his opinion at the time the statement is made—

(*a*) by reason of illness or disability, he or she ought not to move or be moved from the place where he or she is at that time, and

(*b*) it is likely that it will be the case for at least the following three months that by reason of the illness or disability he or she ought not to move or be moved from that place ; and

" registered medical practitioner " has the meaning given by Schedule 1 to the Interpretation Act 1978 ; and

1978 c. 30.

" responsible authority " means—

(*a*) if the person is detained in a hospital (within the meaning of Part II of the Mental Health Act 1983), the managers of that hospital (within the meaning of section 145(1) of that Act) ; or

1983 c. 20.

(*b*) if the person is detained in a prison or other place to which the Prison Act 1952 applies, the governor or other officer for the time being in charge of that prison or other place.".

1952 c. 52.

7. In section 34 (solemnization of marriages in registration district in which one of the parties resides) for the words " in a building which is not " there shall be substituted the words " elsewhere than ".

8. In section 37 (notice of marriage given in Scotland) in subsection (1)(*b*) after " twenty-seven " there shall be inserted " 27A ".

9. In section 38(2) (notice of marriage given in Northern Ireland) for the words " church or other building in which " there shall be substituted the words " place where ".

10. In section 39 (notice of marriage given on board Her Majesty's ships)—

(*a*) in subsection (2) after the words " including penal provisions " there shall be inserted the words " but excluding section 27A " ; and

(*b*) in subsection (3) after " twenty-seven " there shall be inserted " 27A ".

11. The following section shall be inserted after section 45—

" Solemnization of certain marriages.

45A.—(1) This section applies to marriages solemnized, otherwise than according to the rites of the Church of England, in pursuance of section 26(1)(*dd*) of this Act at the place where a person usually resides.

(2) The marriage may be solemnized according to a relevant form, rite or ceremony in the presence of a registrar of the registration district in which the place where the marriage is solemnized is situated and of two witnesses and each of the persons contracting the marriage shall make the declaration and use the form of words set out in subsection (3) of section 44 of this Act in the case of marriages in registered buildings in the presence of a registrar. SCH. 1

(3) Where the marriage is not solemnized in pursuance of subsection (2) of this section it shall be solemnized in the presence of the superintendent registrar and a registrar of the registration district in which the place where the marriage is solemnized is situated and in the presence of two witnesses, and the persons to be married shall make the declarations and use the form of words set out in subsection (3) of section 44 of this Act in the case of marriages in registered buildings in the presence of a registrar.

(4) No religious service shall be used at any marriage solemnized in the presence of a superintendent registrar.

(5) In subsection (2) of this section a " relevant form, rite or ceremony " means a form, rite or ceremony of a body of persons who meet for religious worship in any registered building being a form, rite or ceremony in accordance with which members of that body are married in any such registered building.".

12. In section 46 (civil marriage followed by religious ceremony) for the words " solemnized in the office of a superintendent registrar " in each place where they occur, there shall be substituted the words " solemnized in the presence of a superintendent registrar ".

13. In section 49 (void marriages) the following shall be inserted after paragraph (*g*)—

" or

(*h*) in the case of a marriage to which section 45A of this Act applies, in the absence of any superintendent registrar or registrar whose presence at that marriage is required by that section ; "

14. In section 50 (delivery of certificate to registrar) in subsection (1)(*a*) after the words " registered building " there shall be inserted the words " or at a person's residence ".

15. In section 51 (fees) at the beginning there shall be inserted " (1) " and at the end there shall be added the following subsection—

" (2) A superintendent registrar shall be entitled to receive from persons married in his presence in pursuance of section 26(1)(*dd*) of this Act the sum of £20.".

16. In section 53 (persons by whom marriages are to be registered) in paragraph (*d*) after the words " registered building " there shall be inserted the words " or at a person's residence ".

Sch. 1

17. In section 55 (manner of registration of marriages) the following subsections shall be added after subsection (3)—

"(4) Where a marriage is solemnized according to the rites of the Church of England in pursuance of section 26(1)(*dd*) of this Act, the marriage shall be registered in accordance with the provisions of this section in the marriage register books of any church or chapel which is in the same parish or extra-parochial place as is the place where the marriage is solemnized or, if there is no such church or chapel, of any church or chapel in any adjoining parish.

(5) Where by virtue of subsection (4) of this section a clergyman is required to register a marriage in the marriage register books of a church or chapel of which he is not the incumbent, the incumbent may give the books into his custody at a convenient time before the marriage is solemnized and he shall keep them safely and return them to the custody of the incumbent as soon as is reasonably practicable.".

18. In section 59 (custody of register books) at the beginning there shall be inserted the words "Subject to section 55(5) of this Act".

19. In section 67 in paragraph (*a*) of the definition of "superintendent registrar" for the words from "the church" to the end there shall be substituted the words "is situated the church or chapel of which the incumbent keeps the marriage register book in which that marriage is registered;".

20. In section 75 (criminal offences)—

(*a*) in paragraph (*c*) of subsection (1) after the words "special licence" there shall be inserted the words "or a marriage in pursuance of section 26(1)(*dd*) of this Act";

(*b*) in subsection (2)(*a*)(ii) for the words "or office specified" there shall be substituted the words "office or person's residence specified as the place where the marriage was to be solemnized";

(*c*) after subsection (2)(*b*) there shall be inserted the following paragraph—

"(*bb*) solemnizes a marriage in pursuance of section 26(1)(*dd*) of this Act, otherwise than according to the rites of the Church of England, in the absence of a registrar of the registration district in which the place where the marriage is solemnized is situated;";

(*d*) in subsection (3)(*d*) after the words "in his office" there shall be inserted the words "or, in the case of a marriage in pursuance of section 26(1)(*dd*) of this Act, in any other place".

21. In section 78 (interpretation) the following subsections shall be inserted after subsection (2)—

"(3) For the purposes of this Act a person is house-bound if—

(*a*) the notice of his or her marriage given in accordance with section 27 of this Act is accompanied by a medical statement (within the meaning of section 27A(7) of this Act) made, not more than fourteen days before the date on which that notice was given, in relation to that person ; and Sch. 1

(*b*) he or she is not a detained person.

(4) For the purposes of this Act a person is a detained person if he or she is for the time being detained—

(*a*) otherwise than by virtue of section 2, 4, 5, 35, 36 or 136 of the Mental Health Act 1983 (short term detentions), as a patient in a hospital ; or 1983 c. 20.

(*b*) in a prison or other place to which the Prison Act 1952 applies, 1952 c. 52.

and in paragraph (*a*) above " patient " and " hospital " have the same meanings as in Part II of the Mental Health Act 1983.

(5) For the purposes of this Act a person who is house-bound or is a detained person shall be taken, if he or she would not otherwise be, to be resident and usually resident at the place where he or she is for the time being.".

SCHEDULE 2

Section 8.

Application etc. of Marriage Acts in Northern Ireland

THE MARRIAGES (IRELAND) ACT 1844 (c.81)

1. Section 14 (marriage notice book) shall apply to a notice under section 3(2) of this Act as it applies to a notice under section 13 of that Act.

2. Section 16 (certificate of entry in marriage notice book of notice under section 13) shall not apply to a notice entered in the marriage notice book under section 14 as applied by paragraph 1 above.

3. Section 18 (forbidding the issue of a registrar's certificate) shall apply to the issue of a licence by the Registrar General under section 4 of this Act as it applies to the issue of a registrar's certificate under that Act.

4. Section 23 (caveat against issue of certificate or licence by registrar) shall apply to the issue of a licence by the Registrar General under section 4 of this Act as it applies to the grant of a certificate or licence under that Act, but as if—

(*a*) for the word " registrar " (wherever it occurs) there were substituted the words " Registrar General " ;

(*b*) for the words from " provided that " onwards there were substituted the following subsection—

" (2) The decision of the Registrar General under this section, as applied by Schedule 2 to the Marriage Act 1983, shall be final.".

5. Section 25 (new notice required if marriage not solemnized within three months) shall apply to a notice under section 3(2) of this Act and to the Registrar General's licence as it applies to a notice, certificate and licence under that Act.

SCH. 2

6. Section 31 (fee payable to registrar) shall apply to a marriage solemnized in pursuance of section 3 of this Act and to the Registrar General's licence as it applies to a marriage solemnized under that Act and to a licence under that Act.

7. Section 32 (proof of certain matters not necessary to establish a marriage) shall apply to a marriage solemnized in pursuance of section 3 of this Act as it applies to a marriage solemnized under that Act, but as if the words from " and where a marriage shall have been solemnized " to " where such production is required by this Act " were omitted.

8. Section 43 (civil liability of persons vexatiously entering caveats) shall apply to a caveat against the grant of a licence by the Registrar General under section 4 of this Act as it applies to a caveat against the grant of a licence under that Act.

9. Sections 45, 46 and 49 (offences and void marriages) shall not apply to a marriage solemnized on the authority of the Registrar General's licence.

10.—(1) Section 66 (registration of marriages) shall, subject to sub-paragraph (2), apply to a marriage solemnized in pursuance of section 3 of this Act as it applies to a marriage solemnized in the office of a registrar but as if for the words " form in schedule (G.) " there were substituted the words " prescribed form ".

(2) Section 66 shall not apply to a marriage solemnized in accordance with the rites of the Roman Catholic Church.

THE MARRIAGES (IRELAND) ACT 1846 (c.72)

11. In section 1 (notice of marriage given in England) for the words " church or other building in which " there shall be substituted the words " place where ".

THE MARRIAGE LAW (IRELAND) AMENDMENT ACT 1863 (c.27)

12. Section 2 and Schedule (A) (form of notice of intended marriage given to registrar under that Act) shall, subject to such modifications as the Department may prescribe, apply to a notice under section 3(2) of this Act as they apply to a notice under that Act.

13. Section 3 (procedure after notice of intended marriage is given to the registrar) shall apply to a notice under section 3(2) of this Act as it applies to a notice under that Act—

(*a*) but as if the amendment of section 3 set out in section 41 of the Matrimonial Causes and Marriage Law (Ireland) Amendment Act 1870 were omitted ; and

1870 c. 110.

(*b*) subject to such other modifications as the Department may prescribe.

14. Section 4 (declaration by party intending marriage under that Act) shall apply to a party intending marriage in pursuance of

section 3 of this Act as it applies to a party intending marriage under that Act, but as if— Sch. 2

(*a*) for any reference to the notice required by that Act there were substituted a reference to the notice required by section 3(2) of this Act;

(*b*) the words from " and that the parties to the said marriage have " to " meeting-house named in such notice " were omitted;

(*c*) the words " in case the marriage is intended to be had without licence " were omitted;

(*d*) the words from " or in case such marriage " to " such notice shall be so given " were omitted;

(*e*) for the words " certificate or licence for marriage shall be issued or granted " there shall be substituted the words " licence shall be issued by the Registrar General under the Marriage Act 1983 ".

15. Schedule (B) (form of declaration by party to intended marriage under that Act) shall apply to an intended marriage in pursuance of section 3 of this Act as it applies to an intended marriage under that Act, but as if the words from " and that we the above named " to " County of " (where first occurring) were omitted.

THE REGISTRATION OF MARRIAGES (IRELAND) ACT 1863 (c.90)

16. Section 11 shall apply to a marriage solemnized in pursuance of section 3 of this Act, but only if it is solemnized according to the rites of the Roman Catholic Church and, in its application to such a marriage, shall have effect as if for the words " according to the form A in the schedule hereunto annexed " there were substituted the words " in the prescribed form " and for the words " the said schedule " there were substituted the words " the said form ".

Solvent Abuse (Scotland) Act 1983

1983 CHAPTER 33

An act to amend the Social Work (Scotland) Act 1968 to add solvent abuse to the conditions indicating the need for compulsory measures of care. [13th May 1983]

BE IT ENACTED by the Queen's most Excellent Majesty, by and with the advice and consent of the Lords Spiritual and Temporal, and Commons, in this present Parliament assembled, and by the authority of the same, as follows:—

Solvent abuse may indicate child in need of compulsory measures of care. 1968 c. 49.

1. In section 32(2) of the Social Work (Scotland) Act 1968 (conditions which if satisfied indicate that a child may be in need of compulsory measures of care within the meaning of Part III of that Act), the following paragraph shall be inserted after paragraph (*g*):

" (*gg*) he has misused a volatile substance by deliberately inhaling, other than for medicinal purposes, that substance's vapour; or "

Expenses.

2. There shall be paid out of money provided by Parliament any increase attributable to this Act in the sums so payable under any other Act.

Short title.

3.—(1) This Act may be cited as the Solvent Abuse (Scotland) Act 1983.

(2) This Act shall come into force at the end of the period of two months beginning with the day on which it is passed.

Mobile Homes Act 1983

1983 CHAPTER 34

An Act to make new provision in place of sections 1 to 6 of the Mobile Homes Act 1975. [13th May 1983]

BE IT ENACTED by the Queen's most Excellent Majesty, by and with the advice and consent of the Lords Spiritual and Temporal, and Commons, in this present Parliament assembled, and by the authority of the same, as follows:—

1.—(1) This Act applies to any agreement under which a person (" the occupier ") is entitled— Particulars of agreements.

(*a*) to station a mobile home on land forming part of a protected site ; and

(*b*) to occupy the mobile home as his only or main residence.

(2) Within three months of the making of an agreement to which this Act applies, the owner of the protected site (" the owner ") shall give to the occupier a written statement which—

(*a*) specifies the names and addresses of the parties and the date of commencement of the agreement ;

(*b*) includes particulars of the land on which the occupier is entitled to station the mobile home sufficient to identify it ;

(*c*) sets out the express terms of the agreement ;

(*d*) sets out the terms implied by section 2(1) below ; and

(*e*) complies with such other requirements as may be prescribed by regulations made by the Secretary of State.

(3) If the agreement was made before the day on which this Act comes into force, the written statement shall be given within six months of that day.

(4) Any reference in subsection (2) or (3) above to the making of an agreement to which this Act applies includes a reference to any variation of an agreement by virtue of which the agreement becomes one to which this Act applies.

(5) If the owner fails to comply with this section, the occupier may apply to the court for an order requiring the owner so to comply.

(6) Regulations under this section—

(*a*) shall be made by statutory instrument; and

(*b*) may make different provision with respect to different cases or descriptions of case, including different provision for different areas.

Terms of agreements.

2.—(1) In any agreement to which this Act applies there shall be implied the terms set out in Part I of Schedule 1 to this Act; and this subsection shall have effect notwithstanding any express term of the agreement.

(2) The court may, on the application of either party made within six months of the giving of the statement under section 1(2) above, order that there shall be implied in the agreement terms concerning the matters mentioned in Part II of Schedule 1 to this Act.

(3) The court may, on the application of either party made within the said period of six months, by order vary or delete any express term of the agreement.

(4) On an application under this section, the court shall make such provision as the court considers just and equitable in the circumstances.

Successors in title.

3.—(1) An agreement to which this Act applies shall be binding on and enure for the benefit of any successor in title of the owner and any person claiming through or under the owner or any such successor.

(2) Where an agreement to which this Act applies is lawfully assigned to any person, the agreement shall enure for the benefit of and be binding on that person.

(3) Where a person entitled to the benefit of and bound by an agreement to which this Act applies dies at a time when he is occupying the mobile home as his only or main residence, the agreement shall enure for the benefit of and be binding on—

(*a*) any person residing with that person (" the deceased ") at that time being—

(i) the widow or widower of the deceased; or

(ii) in default of a widow or widower so residing, any member of the deceased's family; or

(*b*) in default of any such person so residing, the person entitled to the mobile home by virtue of the deceased's will or under the law relating to intestacy but subject to subsection (4) below.

(4) An agreement to which this Act applies shall not enure for the benefit of or be binding on a person by virtue of subsection (3)(*b*) above in so far as—

(*a*) it would, but for this subsection, enable or require that person to occupy the mobile home; or

(*b*) it includes terms implied by virtue of paragraph 5 or 9 of Part I of Schedule 1 to this Act.

Jurisdiction of the court.

4. The court shall have jurisdiction to determine any question arising under this Act or any agreement to which it applies, and to entertain any proceedings brought under this Act or any such agreement.

Interpretation.

5.—(1) In this Act, unless the context otherwise requires—

"the court" means—

(*a*) in relation to England and Wales, the county court for the district in which the protected site is situated or, where the parties have agreed in writing to submit any question arising under this Act or, as the case may be, any agreement to which it applies to arbitration, the arbitrator;

(*b*) in relation to Scotland, the sheriff having jurisdiction where the protected site is situated or, where the parties have so agreed, the arbiter;

"local authority" has the same meaning as in Part I of the Caravan Sites and Control of Development Act 1960; 1960 c. 62.

"mobile home" has the same meaning as "caravan" has in that Part of that Act;

"owner", in relation to a protected site, means the person who, by virtue of an estate or interest held by him, is entitled to possession of the site or would be so entitled but for the rights of any persons to station mobile homes on land forming part of the site;

"planning permission" means permission under Part III of the Town and Country Planning Act 1971 or Part III of the Town and Country Planning (Scotland) Act 1972; 1971 c. 78. 1972 c. 52.

"protected site" does not include any land occupied by a local authority as a caravan site providing accommodation for gipsies or, in Scotland, for persons to whom section 24(8A) of the Caravan Sites and Control of Development Act 1960 applies but, subject to that, has the same meaning as in Part I of the Caravan Sites Act 1968.

1968 c. 52.

(2) In relation to an agreement to which this Act applies—

(*a*) any reference in this Act to the owner includes a reference to any person who is bound by and entitled to the benefit of the agreement by virtue of subsection (1) of section 3 above; and

(*b*) subject to subsection (4) of that section, any reference in this Act to the occupier includes a reference to any person who is entitled to the benefit of and bound by the agreement by virtue of subsection (2) or (3) of that section.

(3) A person is a member of another's family within the meaning of this Act if he is his spouse, parent, grandparent, child, grandchild, brother, sister, uncle, aunt, nephew or niece; treating—

(*a*) any relationship by marriage as a relationship by blood, any relationship of the half blood as a relationship of the whole blood and the stepchild of any person as his child; and

(*b*) an illegitimate person as the legitimate child of his mother and reputed father;

or if they live together as husband and wife.

Short title, repeals, commencement and extent.

6.—(1) This Act may be cited as the Mobile Homes Act 1983.

(2) The enactments mentioned in Schedule 2 to this Act are hereby repealed to the extent specified in the third column of that Schedule.

(3) This Act shall come into force on the expiry of the period of one week beginning with the day on which it is passed.

(4) This Act does not extend to Northern Ireland.

SCHEDULES

SCHEDULE 1

Section 2.

AGREEMENTS UNDER ACT

PART I

TERMS IMPLIED BY ACT

Duration of agreement

1. Subject to paragraph 2 below, the right to station the mobile home on land forming part of the protected site shall subsist until the agreement is determined under paragraph 3, 4, 5 or 6 below.

2.—(1) If the owner's estate or interest is insufficient to enable him to grant the right for an indefinite period, the period for which the right subsists shall not extend beyond the date when the owner's estate or interest determines.

(2) If planning permission for the use of the protected site as a site for mobile homes has been granted in terms such that it will expire at the end of a specified period, the period for which the right subsists shall not extend beyond the date when the planning permission expires.

(3) If before the end of a period determined by this paragraph there is a change in circumstances which allows a longer period, account shall be taken of that change.

Termination by occupier

3. The occupier shall be entitled to terminate the agreement by notice in writing given to the owner not less than four weeks before the date on which it is to take effect.

Termination by owner

4. The owner shall be entitled to terminate the agreement forthwith if, on the application of the owner, the court—

(*a*) is satisfied that the occupier has breached a term of the agreement and, after service of a notice to remedy the breach, has not complied with the notice within a reasonable time; and

(*b*) considers it reasonable for the agreement to be terminated.

5. The owner shall be entitled to terminate the agreement forthwith if, on the application of the owner, the court is satisfied that the occupier is not occupying the mobile home as his only or main residence.

6.—(1) The owner shall be entitled to terminate the agreement at the end of a relevant period if, on the application of the owner, the court is satisfied that, having regard to its age and condition, the mobile home—

SCH. 1

(*a*) is having a detrimental effect on the amenity of the site; or

(*b*) is likely to have such an effect before the end of the next relevant period.

(2) In sub-paragraph (1) above " relevant period " means the period of five years beginning with the commencement of the agreement and each succeeding period of five years.

Recovery of overpayments by occupier

7. Where the agreement is terminated as mentioned in paragraph 3, 4, 5 or 6 above, the occupier shall be entitled to recover from the owner so much of any payment made by him in pursuance of the agreement as is attributable to a period beginning after the termination.

Sale of mobile home

8.—(1) The occupier shall be entitled to sell the mobile home, and to assign the agreement, to a person approved of by the owner, whose approval shall not be unreasonably withheld.

(2) Where the occupier sells the mobile home, and assigns the agreement, as mentioned in sub-paragraph (1) above, the owner shall be entitled to receive a commission on the sale at a rate not exceeding such rate as may be specified by an order made by the Secretary of State.

(3) An order under this paragraph—

(*a*) shall be made by statutory instrument which shall be subject to annulment in pursuance of a resolution of either House of Parliament; and

(*b*) may make different provision for different areas or for sales at different prices.

Gift of mobile home

9. The occupier shall be entitled to give the mobile home, and to assign the agreement, to a member of his family approved by the owner, whose approval shall not be unreasonably withheld.

Re-siting of mobile home

10. If the owner is entitled to require that the occupier's right to station the mobile home shall be exercisable for any period in relation to other land forming part of the protected site—

(*a*) that other land shall be broadly comparable to the land on which the occupier was originally entitled to station the mobile home; and

(*b*) all costs and expenses incurred in consequence of the requirement shall be paid by the owner.

PART II

MATTERS CONCERNING WHICH TERMS MAY BE IMPLIED BY COURT

1. The right of the occupier to quiet enjoyment or, in Scotland, undisturbed possession of the mobile home.

2. The sums payable by the occupier in pursuance of the agreement and the times at which they are to be paid. Sch. 1

3. The review at yearly intervals of the sums so payable.

4. The provision or improvement of services available on the protected site, and the use by the occupier of such services.

5. The preservation of the amenity of the protected site.

6. The maintenance and repair of the protected site by the owner, and the maintenance and repair of the mobile home by the occupier.

7. Access by the owner to the land on which the occupier is entitled to station the mobile home.

SCHEDULE 2

Section 6.

Repeals

Chapter	Short title	Extent of repeal
1975 c. 49.	The Mobile Homes Act 1975.	Sections 1 to 6. In section 9, in subsection (1), all definitions except those of " the Act of 1960 ", " the Act of 1968 " and " mobile home ", and subsection (2).

Litter Act 1983

1983 CHAPTER 35

An Act to consolidate the Litter Acts 1958 and 1971, together with section 51 of the Public Health Act 1961, section 4 of the Local Government (Development and Finance) (Scotland) Act 1964 and section 24 of the Control of Pollution Act 1974 and related provisions of those Acts. [13th May 1983]

BE IT ENACTED by the Queen's most Excellent Majesty, by and with the advice and consent of the Lords Spiritual and Temporal, and Commons, in this present Parliament assembled, and by the authority of the same, as follows:—

Penalty for leaving litter.

1.—(1) If any person throws down, drops or otherwise deposits in, into or from any place in the open air to which the public are entitled or permitted to have access without payment, and leaves, any thing whatsoever in such circumstances as to cause, or contribute to, or tend to lead to, the defacement by litter of any place in the open air, he shall be guilty of an offence, unless that depositing and leaving was authorised by law or was done with the consent of the owner, occupier or other person or authority having control of the place in or into which that thing was deposited.

(2) For the purposes of subsection (1) above, any covered place open to the air on at least one side and available for public use shall be treated as being a place in the open air.

(3) A person guilty of an offence under this section shall be liable on summary conviction to a fine not exceeding level 3 on the standard scale.

(4) In sentencing a person convicted of an offence under this section, the court shall have regard not only to the purpose of the section in preventing the defacement by litter of places in the open air, but also to the nature of the litter and any resulting risk (in the circumstances of the offence) of injury to persons or animals or of damage to property.

(5) In England and Wales, without prejudice to the powers of any other person, a litter authority shall have power to institute proceedings for an offence under this section committed within their area or on land controlled or managed by them.

(6) In subsection (5) above, " litter authority " includes the Greater London Council.

(7) In Scotland, an offence under this section may be prosecuted in any court of summary jurisdiction within the meaning of the Criminal Procedure (Scotland) Act 1975 having jurisdiction in the place where the offence was committed.

1975 c. 21.

Publicity regarding penalty for leaving litter.

2. A local authority, with a view to promoting the abatement of litter, may take such steps as the authority think appropriate for making the effect of section 1(3) and (4) above known to the public in their area.

Grants for publicity discouraging litter.

3. The Secretary of State may with the consent of the Treasury make grants to any body for the purpose of assisting the body to encourage the public not to deface places by litter.

Consultations and proposals for abatement of litter.

4.—(1) In England and Wales, it shall be the duty of—

(*a*) the council of each county and the other litter authorities whose areas are included in the county, and

(*b*) where the county includes land in a National Park without a Park board, the National Park Committee for that Park,

to consult from time to time together, and with such voluntary bodies as they consider appropriate and as agree to participate in the consultations, about the steps which the county council, each of the other litter authorities, the National Park Committee (if any) and each of the bodies are to take for the purpose of abating litter in the county; and it shall be the duty of the county council—

(i) to prepare and from time to time revise a statement of the steps which the council, each of the other litter authorities, the National Park Committee (if any) and each of the bodies agree to take for that purpose, and

(ii) to take such steps as in their opinion will give adequate publicity in the county to the statement, and

(iii) to keep a copy of the statement available at their principal office for inspection by the public free of charge at all reasonable hours.

(2) Subsection (1) above applies to Greater London and the Greater London Council as it applies to a county and the council of a county.

(3) In subsection (1) above, " litter authority " includes a parish meeting but not a joint body.

(4) In Scotland, it shall be the duty of—

(*a*) the council of each region, and the district councils of which the districts are included in the region, to consult from time to time together, and with such voluntary bodies as the regional council and the district councils consider appropriate and as agree to participate in the consultations, and

(*b*) the council of each islands area to consult with such voluntary bodies as the council consider appropriate and as agree to participate in the consultations,

about the steps which the regional or islands council and each of the bodies with which they consulted (including, in the case of a regional council, each district council) are to take for the purpose of abating litter in the region or, as the case may be, islands area ; and it shall be the duty of the regional or islands council—

(i) to prepare and from time to time revise a statement of the steps which the regional or islands council and each of the bodies agree to take for the purpose,

(ii) to take such steps as in their opinion will give adequate publicity in their area to the statement, and

(iii) to keep a copy of the statement available at their principal office for inspection by the public free of charge at all reasonable hours.

(5) The Secretary of State may by order repeal or amend any provision of—

(*a*) any local Act (including an Act confirming a provisional order) passed before 31st July 1974 (the date on which the Control of Pollution Act 1974 was passed), or 1974 c. 40.

(*b*) any order or other instrument made under an Act so passed, if it appears to him that the provision is inconsistent with, or has become unnecessary or requires alteration in consequence of, any provision of this section.

Litter bins in England and Wales.

5.—(1) A litter authority in England and Wales may provide and maintain in any street or public place receptacles for refuse or litter (in this section referred to as " litter bins ").

(2) It shall be the duty of a litter authority in England and Wales to make arrangements for the regular emptying and cleansing of any litter bins provided or maintained by them
1980 c. 66 under this section or under section 185 of the Highways Act 1980; and such an authority shall have power to cleanse and empty litter bins provided in any street or public place by them or any other person.

(3) The regular emptying mentioned in subsection (2) above shall be sufficiently frequent to ensure that no such litter bin or its contents shall become a nuisance or give reasonable ground for complaint.

(4) In any place where a litter bin may be provided or maintained under this section or under section 185 of the Highways Act 1980, a litter authority may put up notices about the leaving of refuse and litter, and for that purpose may, subject to the provisions of this section, erect and maintain notice boards.

1971 c. lxi. (5) Subject to section 13 of the City of London (Various Powers) Act 1971 (which empowers the Common Council of the City of London to affix litter bins), a litter authority shall not have power under this section to place any litter bin or any notice board—

(*a*) on any land forming part of an open space as defined
1906 c. 25. in the Open Spaces Act 1906 which is provided by or under the management and control of some other litter authority or a parish meeting, without the consent of that authority or meeting, or

(*b*) on any other land not forming part of a street, without the consent of the owner and of the occupier of that land.

(6) The powers conferred by this section shall only be exercisable with the consent of the persons mentioned in the Table in paragraph 1 of Schedule 1 to this Act, and paragraphs 2 and 3 of that Schedule shall have effect in relation to those consents.

(7) A litter authority may sell refuse or litter removed by them from any litter bins.

(8) A litter authority may not, under this section, do anything that is unlawful under the law relating to ancient monuments or to town and country planning.

(9) Any person who wilfully removes or otherwise interferes with any litter bin or notice board provided or erected under this section or section 185 of the Highways Act 1980 shall be liable on summary conviction to a fine not exceeding level 1 on the standard scale. 1980 c. 66.

(10) The court by which a person is convicted under subsection (9) above may order him to pay a sum not exceeding £20 as compensation to the litter authority concerned, and any such order shall be enforceable in the same way as an order for costs to be paid by the offender.

(11) This section applies to a receptacle provided under section 76 of the Public Health Act 1936 or section 51 of the Public Health Act 1961 as if it had been provided under this section. 1936 c. 49. 1961 c. 64.

Provisions supplementary to s. 5.

6.—(1) A county council may if they think fit make a contribution to any expenditure incurred by a parish council or a community council under section 5 above.

(2) A parish council or community council may contribute towards—

(*a*) the reasonable expenses incurred by any person in doing anything which the council have power to do under section 5 above, and

(*b*) the expenses incurred by any other parish council or community council in exercising their powers under that section.

(3) Two or more parish councils or community councils may by agreement combine for the purpose of exercising their powers under section 5 above.

(4) The Secretary of State may, subject to subsection (5) below, by order repeal or amend any provision—

(*a*) in any local Act passed before 3rd August 1961 (the date on which the Public Health Act 1961 was passed),

(*b*) in any Act passed before that date and confirming a provisional order, or

(*c*) in any order or other instrument made under an Act before that date,

where it appears to him that that provision is inconsistent with, or has become unnecessary in consequence of, section 5 above or this section.

(5) The Secretary of State shall not make an order under subsection (4) above repealing or amending a provision in a local Act the Bill for which was promoted by—

(*a*) a county council, a district council, a London borough council, the Common Council of the City of London, the Sub-Treasurer of the Inner Temple, the Under Treasurer of the Middle Temple or the Council of the Isles of Scilly, or

(*b*) any authority, board, commissioners, trustees or other body whose functions under the local Act have become exercisable by such a council, Sub-Treasurer or Under Treasurer as aforesaid,

except on the application of that council, Sub-Treasurer or Under Treasurer.

(6) Where—

1972 c. 70. (*a*) a resolution under subsection (3) of section 147 of the Local Government Act 1972 (resolution declaring expenses to be special expenses chargeable only on part of a district council's area), or

1933 c. 51. (*b*) an order under section 190(3) of the Local Government Act 1933 that, by virtue of subsection (6) of the said section 147, continues to have effect as if it were such a resolution,

1961 c. 64. contains, or has effect as if it included, a reference to section 51 of the Public Health Act 1961 (litter bins), that reference shall have effect as if it were a reference to the said section 51 or section 5 above.

(7) Sections 283 to 285, 288, 304, 305, 341 and 343 of the Public Health Act 1936 apply in relation to section 5 above, this section and Schedule 1 to this Act as if section 5, this section and that Schedule were contained in the said Act of 1936.

(8) In section 5 above, " litter authority " includes the Council of the Isles of Scilly but not a joint body or a Park board.

Litter bins in Scotland.

7.—(1) A litter authority in Scotland may provide and maintain receptacles for the deposit of litter (in this section referred to as " litter bins "), and may within their area set up litter bins in any place situated—

(*a*) in or adjacent to any road maintainable, or public way maintained, by any local authority or general, regional or district planning authority within the meaning of Part IX of the Local Government (Scotland) Act 1973, or (1973 c. 65.)

(*b*) on any land owned or occupied by the litter authority.

(2) A litter authority in Scotland—

(*a*) shall from time to time empty and cleanse any litter bins set up by them under subsection (1) above,

(*b*) may so deal with any other litter bins set up in any place in their area, being a place situated as mentioned in subsection (1) above,

(*c*) may in such manner as they think fit remove and dispose of litter taken from such litter bins or any litter found lying in any such place.

(3) For the purpose of the exercise of their powers under subsection (2) above, a litter authority may provide and use such plant or apparatus for treating or disposing of litter as they may think necessary.

(4) The powers conferred on a litter authority by this section shall be exercisable in relation to any place in their area which is not situated as mentioned in subsection (1) above, but in relation to such a place the powers shall be so exercisable—

(*a*) only with the consent of all persons having an interest in the land on which the place is situated,

(*b*) on such terms as may be arranged between the litter authority and those persons.

(5) A litter authority may arrange by agreement for any power conferred or duty imposed on them by this section to be exercised or performed on their behalf by some other person on such terms as may be specified in the agreement.

(6) This section has effect in substitution for the corresponding provisions of any local Act regarding the provision of litter bins and the removal and disposal of litter by a litter authority in Scotland, and every such corresponding provision shall cease to have effect.

Provisions supplementary to s. 7.

8.—(1) A litter authority may make contributions towards expenditure incurred or to be incurred by any other local authority or by any voluntary organisation in the doing of anything which could have been done under section 7 above by the litter authority; and a litter authority may receive from any other person contributions towards expenditure incurred or to be incurred by them under that section.

(2) In subsection (1) above, " voluntary organisation " means any body of persons, whether corporate or unincorporate, carrying on or proposing to carry on an undertaking otherwise than for profit, and includes a community council within the meaning of the Local Government (Scotland) Act 1973. 1973 c. 65.

(3) Subject to subsection (4) below, where any person having such an interest in any land as enables him to bind the land enters into any agreement relating to the land with a litter

authority acting in exercise of powers conferred on them by section 7 above, the agreement may be registered in the Land Register of Scotland, and if so registered shall, subject to subsection (5) below, be enforceable at the instance of the litter authority against persons deriving title to the land from the person who entered into the agreement.

(4) Where the land is wholly in an area in respect of which
1979 c. 33. the provisions of the Land Registration (Scotland) Act 1979 relating to registration have not come into operation, subsection (3) above shall apply as if for the words " registered in the Land Register of Scotland, and if so registered " there were substituted the words " recorded in the Register of Sasines, and if so recorded ".

(5) An agreement under subsection (3) above shall not be enforceable against a third party who has in good faith and for value acquired right (whether completed by infeftment or not) to the land before the agreement was registered or recorded as aforesaid, or against any person deriving title from such third party.

(6) On the application of any local authority directly concerned, the Secretary of State may by order repeal or amend any provision—

(*a*) in any local Act passed before the 31st July 1964 (the
1964 c. 67. date on which the Local Government (Development and Finance) (Scotland) Act 1964 was passed), or

(*b*) in any Act passed before that date and confirming a provisional order,

where it appears to him that the provision is inconsistent with, or has become unnecessary in consequence of, section 7 above or this section.

(7) In section 7 above and this section—

" land " includes any structure or erection on land, land covered with water and any interest or right in or over land;

" litter " includes derelict vehicles, vessels and scrap metal and rubbish of any description;

" litter authority " means an islands or district council;

" local authority " means a regional, islands or district council.

Orders. **9.**—(1) An order under this Act shall be made by statutory instrument.

(2) Any such statutory instrument, other than one made under section 13(2) below, shall be subject to annulment in pursuance of a resolution of either House of Parliament.

(3) An order under section 4 above may make different provision for different circumstances.

(4) Before making an order under section 6 or 8 above, the Secretary of State shall consult—

(*a*) as to an order under section 6, with any of the authorities mentioned in section 6(5)(*a*),

(*b*) as to an order under section 8, with any local authority (as defined in that section),

who appear to him to be concerned, not being an authority on whose application the order is made.

(5) An order under this Act, other than one made under section 13(2) below, may contain such transitional, supplemental or incidental provisions as appear to the Secretary of State to be appropriate.

10. In this Act— Interpretation.

" joint body " means a joint body constituted solely of two or more such councils as are mentioned in paragraphs (*a*) to (*f*) of the definition of " litter authority " below ;

" litter authority ", in relation to England and Wales, means, except so far as is otherwise provided—

(*a*) a county council,

(*b*) a district council,

(*c*) a London borough council,

(*d*) the Common Council of the City of London,

(*e*) a parish council,

(*f*) a community council,

(*g*) a joint body,

(*h*) a Park board,

(*i*) the Sub-Treasurer of the Inner Temple, or

(*j*) the Under Treasurer of the Middle Temple ;

" National Park Committee " means a committee appointed to perform functions under paragraph 5 of Schedule 17 to the Local Government Act 1972 ; 1972 c. 70.

" Park board ", in relation to a National Park, means—

(*a*) a joint planning board reconstituted under paragraph 1 of Schedule 17 to the Local Government Act 1972 ; or

(*b*) a board reconstituted as a special planning board under paragraph 3 of that Schedule ;

" standard scale " has the meaning given to it by section 75 of the Criminal Justice Act 1982. 1982 c. 48.

Isles of Scilly.

11. Sections 3 and 4 above shall have effect in their application to the Isles of Scilly with such modifications, additions, omissions and amendments as the Secretary of State may by order specify.

Consequential amendments and repeals.

1968 c. 41.

1971 c. lxi.

12.—(1) Section 42(4)(*a*) of the Countryside Act 1968 is amended by substituting for the words " the provisions of the Litter Act 1958 " the words " section 1 of the Litter Act 1983 ".

(2) Section 13(1) of the City of London (Various Powers) Act 1971 is amended by substituting for the words " section 51 of the Public Health Act 1961 " the words " sections 5 and 6 of the Litter Act 1983 ".

(3) The enactments specified in Schedule 2 to this Act are repealed to the extent specified in the third column of that Schedule.

Short title, commencement and extent.

1974 c. 40.

13.—(1) This Act may be cited as the Litter Act 1983.

(2) Section 4 of this Act, and sections 12(3) and Schedule 2 so far as they repeal section 24(1) to (3) of the Control of Pollution Act 1974, shall come into force on such day as the Secretary of State may by order appoint, and different days may be appointed for different provisions or for different purposes thereof.

(3) The rest of this Act shall come into force at the end of the period of three months beginning with the day on which this Act is passed.

(4) Sections 1(5) and (6), 4(1) to (3), 5 and 6 above and Schedule 1 to this Act extend only to England and Wales, and sections 1(7), 4(4), 7 and 8 above extend only to Scotland.

(5) This Act does not extend to Northern Ireland.

SCHEDULES

SCHEDULE 1

Section 5.

CONSENTS REQUIRED UNDER SECTION 5

1. A litter authority shall not carry out works under section 5 above in any such situation or position as is described in an entry in column 1 of the following Table except with the consent of the person described in the corresponding entry in column 2.

TABLE

1.	2.
1. In a street which is a highway for which the litter authority are not the highway authority.	1. The highway authority for the street.
2. In a street belonging to and repairable by any railway, dock, harbour, canal, inland navigation or passenger road transport undertakers and forming the approach to a station, dock, wharf or depot of those undertakers.	2. The undertakers.
3. On a bridge not vested in the litter authority or on the approaches to such a bridge.	3. The authority or other person in whom the bridge is vested.
4. On a bridge carrying a street over a railway, canal or inland navigation, or on the approaches to such a bridge, or under a bridge carrying a railway, canal or inland navigation over a street.	4. The railway, canal or inland navigation undertakers concerned.
5. In a position obstructing or interfering with any existing access to land or premises abutting upon a street.	5. The owner and the occupier of the land or premises.

2. A consent required by this Schedule shall not unreasonably be withheld but may be given subject to any reasonable conditions, including a condition that the authority shall remove a litter bin or notice board either at any time or after the expiration of a period if reasonably required so to do by the person giving the consent.

3. Where the consent of the Secretary of State is required under this Schedule, any dispute between him and the authority as to—

(*a*) whether the consent is unreasonably withheld or is given subject to reasonable conditions, or

SCH. 1

(*b*) whether the removal of anything to the provision of which the consent relates in accordance with any condition of the consent is reasonably required,

shall be referred to and determined by an arbitrator to be appointed in default of agreement by the President of the Institution of Civil Engineers.

Section 12(3).

SCHEDULE 2

REPEALS

Chapter	Short title	Extent of repeal
6 & 7 Eliz. 2. c. 34.	Litter Act 1958.	The whole Act.
9 & 10 Eliz. 2. c. 64.	Public Health Act 1961.	Section 51.
1963 c. 33.	London Government Act 1963.	In Schedule 2, in paragraph 31, sub-paragraph (iv).
1964 c. 67.	Local Government (Development and Finance) (Scotland) Act 1964.	Section 4.
1971 c. 35.	Dangerous Litter Act 1971.	The whole Act.
1971 c. lxi.	City of London (Various Powers) Act 1971.	In section 13(1), the words ", notwithstanding the provisions of subsection (5) of the said section 51,".
1972 c. 70.	Local Government Act 1972.	In Schedule 14, paragraph 41.
1973 c. 65.	Local Government (Scotland) Act 1973.	In Schedule 27, in Part II, paragraph 153.
1974 c. 40.	Control of Pollution Act 1974.	Section 24.
1980 c. 65.	Local Government, Planning and Land Act 1980.	In Schedule 7, paragraph 6(5).
1980 c. 66.	Highways Act 1980.	In Schedule 24, paragraph 9.

INDEX
TO THE
PUBLIC GENERAL ACTS
AND
GENERAL SYNOD MEASURE 1983

A

B

C

D

PART III

REGISTRATION OF PERSONS QUALIFYING OVERSEAS

PART IV

GENERAL PROVISIONS CONCERNING REGISTRATION

PART V

PROFESSIONAL CONDUCT AND FITNESS TO PRACTISE

PART VI

PRIVILEGES OF REGISTERED PRACTITIONERS

PART VII

MISCELLANEOUS AND GENERAL

PART I

APPLICATION OF ACT

PART II

COMPULSORY ADMISSION TO HOSPITAL AND GUARDIANSHIP

Procedure for hospital admission

Guardianship

General provisions as to applications and recommendations

Position of patients subject to detention or guardianship

Duration of detention or guardianship and discharge

N

O

P

PART I

PROCEDURE FOR MAKING PASTORAL SCHEMES AND ORDERS

Pastoral committees

Procedure for schemes and orders affecting a single diocese

Part II

Principal Pilotage Provisions

Compulsory Pilotage

Provisions with respect to Licensed Pilots

Pilot Boats and Pilot Signals

Offences by Pilots

Part III

Liability of Pilotage Authorities for Loss or Damage to Vessels or Goods, etc.

Limitation of liability

Interpretation

Part IV

Miscellaneous and General

Recovery, etc. of Pilotage Charges

T

W